Handbook of
FINANCIAL ECONOMETRICS

VOLUME 2

HANDBOOKS IN FINANCE

Series Editor

WILLIAM T. ZIEMBA

Advisory Editors

KENNETH J. ARROW
GEORGE C. CONSTANTINIDES
B. ESPEN ECKBO
HARRY M. MARKOWITZ
ROBERT C. MERTON
STEWART C. MYERS
PAUL A. SAMUELSON
WILLIAM F. SHARPE

Handbook of
FINANCIAL ECONOMETRICS
Applications

VOLUME 2

Edited by

YACINE AÏT-SAHALIA
Bendheim Center for Finance
Princeton University
Princeton, NJ

LARS PETER HANSEN
Department of Economics
The University of Chicago
Chicago, IL

Amsterdam • Boston • Heidelberg • London
New York • Oxford • Paris • San Diego
San Francisco • Singapore • Sydney • Tokyo

North-Holland is an imprint of Elsevier

ELSEVIER

North-Holland is an imprint of Elsevier
The Boulevard, Langford Lane, Kidlington, Oxford OX5 1GB, UK
Radarweg 29, PO Box 211, 1000 AE Amsterdam, The Netherlands

Notices
Knowledge and best practice in this field are constantly changing. As new research and experience broaden our understanding,
changes in research methods, professional practices, or medical treatment may become necessary.

Practitioners and researchers must always rely on their own experience and knowledge in evaluating and using any information,
methods, compounds, or experiments described herein. In using such information or methods they should be mindful of their
own safety and the safety of others, including parties for whom they have a professional responsibility.

To the fullest extent of the law, neither the Publisher nor the authors, contributors, or editors, assume any liability for any injury
and/or damage to persons or property as a matter of products liability, negligence or otherwise, or from any use or operation of
any methods, products, instructions, or ideas contained in the material herein.

British Library Cataloguing in Publication Data
A catalogue record for this book is available from the British Library

Library of Congress Cataloging-in-Publication Data
Application submitted

ISBN: 978-0-444-53548-1

For information on all North-Holland publications
visit our website at *www.elsevierdirect.com*

Typeset by: diacriTech, India

Printed and bound by CPI Group (UK) Ltd, Croydon, CR0 4YY
Transferred to Digital Print 2012

INTRODUCTION TO THE SERIES

Advisory Editors

Kenneth J. Arrow, Stanford University; George C. Constantinides, University of Chicago; B. Espen Eckbo, Dartmouth College; Harry M. Markowitz, University of California, San Diego; Robert C. Merton, Harvard University; Stewart C. Myers, Massachusetts Institute of Technology; Paul A. Samuelson, Massachusetts Institute of Technology; and William F. Sharpe, Stanford University.

The *Handbooks in Finance* are intended to be a definitive source for comprehensive and accessible information. Each volume in the series presents an accurate, self-contained survey of a subfield of finance, suitable for use by finance and economics professors and lecturers, professional researchers, and graduate students and as a teaching supplement. The goal is to have a broad group of outstanding volumes in various areas of finance.

William T. Ziemba
University of British Columbia

CONTENTS

14 The Analysis of the Cross-Section of Security Returns   73

Ravi Jagannathan, Georgios Skoulakis, *and* Zhenyu Wang

16 Inference for Stochastic Processes   **197**

Jean Jacod

17 Stock Market Trading Volume   **241**

Andrew W. Lo *and* Jiang Wang

CONTENTS

3 Nonstationary Continuous-Time Processes   **139**

Federico M. Bandi *and* Peter C. B. Phillips

4 Estimating Functions for Discretely Sampled Diffusion-Type Models   **203**

Bo Martin Bibby, Martin Jacobsen, *and* Michael Sørensen

5. Reprojection: Analysis of Postestimation Simulations   453
     5.1. Simple Illustration of Volatility Extraction   453
     5.2. General Theory of Reprojection   455
6. Applications   459
     6.1. Multifactor Stochastic Volatility Models for Stock Returns   460
       6.1.1. Jump Diffusions   460
       6.1.2. Alternative Models   461
       6.1.3. Volatility Index Models   461
     6.2. Term Structure of Interest Rates   462
       6.2.1. Affine Term Structure Models   462
       6.2.2. Regime-Switching Affine Term Structure Models   463
       6.2.3. Nonaffine Models   464
     6.3. Exchange Rates   464
     6.4. General Equilibrium Models   465
     6.5. Additional Applications   465
7. Software and Practical Issues   466
     7.1. Code   466
     7.2. Troubleshooting, Numerical Stability, and Convergence Problems 467
       7.2.1. Start Value Problems and Scaling   467
       7.2.2. Enforcing Dynamic Stability   468
       7.2.3. Bulletproofing the Data Generating Process   468
     7.3. The Chernozukov–Hong Method   469
8. Conclusion   472
References   473

9 The Econometrics of Option Pricing   **479**
René Garcia, Eric Ghysels, *and* Eric Renault

1. Introduction and Overview   480
2. Pricing Kernels, Risk-Neutral Probabilities, and Option Pricing   483
     2.1. Equivalent Martingale Measure and Volatility Smile   484
     2.2. How to Graph the Smile?   486
     2.3. Stochastic Discount Factors and Pricing Kernels   488
     2.4. Black–Scholes-Implied Volatility as a Calibrated Parameter   491
     2.5. Black–Scholes-Implied Volatility as an Expected Average Volatility 492
     2.6. Generalized Black–Scholes Option Pricing Formula   494
3. Modeling Asset Price Dynamics via Diffusions for the Purpose of Option Pricing 496
     3.1. The Affine Jump-Diffusion Class of Models   497
       3.1.1. Models with a Single Volatility Factor   497
       3.1.2. Multiple Volatility Factors   500
     3.2. Other Continuous-Time Processes   501
       3.2.1. Nonaffine Index Models   501

LIST OF CONTRIBUTORS

Yacine Aït-Sahalia
Department of Economics, Princeton University, Princeton, NJ

Torben G. Andersen
Department of Finance, Kellogg School of Management, Northwestern University, Evanston, IL; NBER, Cambridge, MA; and CREATES, Aarhus, Denmark

Federico M. Bandi
Carey Business School, Johns Hopkins University, Baltimore, MD

Bo M. Bibby
Institute of Mathematics and Physics, the Royal Veterinary and Agricultural University, Frederiksberg, Denmark

Tim Bollersley
Department of Economics, Duke University, Durham, NC; NBER, Cambridge, MA; and CREATES, Aarhus, Denmark

Michael W. Brandt
The Fuqua School of Business, Duke University, Durham, NC

Stephanie E. Curcuru
Board of Governors of the Federal Reserve System, Washington, DC

Francis X. Diebold
Department of Economics, University of Pennsylvania, Philadelphia, PA; and NBER, Cambridge, MA

Robert F. Engle
Stern School of Business, New York University, New York, NY

A. Ronald Gallant
The Fuqua School of Business, Duke University, Durham, NC

Rene Garcia
Département de Sciences Économiques, Université de Montréal CIREQ, Montréal, QC, Canada

Eric Ghysels
Department of Economics, University of North Carolina, Chapel Hill, NC

Christian Gourieroux
Department of Economics, University of Toronto, Toronto, ON, Canada

Lars Peter Hansen
Department of Economics, University of Chicago, Chicago, IL

John Heaton
Booth School of Business, University of Chicago, Chicago, IL

Martin Jacobsen
Department of Mathematical Sciences, University of Copenhagen, Denmark

Jean Jacod
Institut de Mathématiques de Jussieu, Université P. et M. Curie (Paris-6), Paris, France

Ravi Jagannathan
Department of Finance, Kellogg School of Management, Northwestern University, Evanston, IL

Joann Jasiak
Department of Economics, York University, Toronto, ON, Canada

Michael Johannes
Graduate School of Business, Columbia University, New York, NY

Martin Lettau
Haas School of Business, University of California at Berkeley, Berkeley, CA

Andrew Lo
Sloan School of Management, Massachusetts Institute of Technology, Cambridge, MA; and NBER, Cambridge, MA

Sidney C. Ludvigson
Department of Economics, New York University, New York, NY

Deborah Lucas
Kellogg School of Management, Northwestern University, Evanston, IL

Damien Moore
Congressional Budget Office, Washington, DC

Per A. Mykland
Department of Statistics, University of Chicago, Chicago, IL

Peter C. B. Phillips
Cowles Foundation for Research in Economics, Yale University, New Haven, CT

Monika Piazzesi
Department of Economics, Stanford University, Stanford, CA

Nicholas Polson
Booth School of Business, University of Chicago, Chicago, IL

Eric Renault
Department of Economics, University of North Carolina, Chapel Hill, NC

Jeffrey R. Russell
Booth School of Business, University of Chicago, Chicago, IL

Jose A. Scheinkman
Department of Economics, Princeton University, Princeton, NJ

Georgios Skoulakis
Department of Finance, R. H. Smith School of Business, University of Maryland, College Park, MD

Michael Sørensen
Department of Mathematical Sciences, University of Copenhagen, Denmark

George Tauchen
Department of Economics, Duke University, Durham, NC

Jiang Wang
Sloan School of Management, Massachusetts Institute of Technology, Cambridge, MA; NBER, Cambridge, MA

Zhenyu Wang
Federal Reserve Bank of New York, New York, NY

CHAPTER 13

MCMC Methods for Continuous-Time Financial Econometrics

Michael Johannes* *and* **Nicholas Polson****

*Graduate School of Business, Columbia University, New York, NY
**Booth School of Business, University of Chicago, Chicago, IL

Contents

Abstract

This chapter develops Markov Chain Monte Carlo (MCMC) methods for Bayesian inference in continuous-time asset pricing models. The Bayesian solution to the inference problem is the distribution of parameters and latent variables conditional on observed data, and MCMC methods provide a tool for exploring these high-dimensional, complex distributions. We first provide a description of the foundations and mechanics of MCMC algorithms. This includes a discussion of the Clifford–Hammersley theorem, the Gibbs sampler, the Metropolis–Hastings algorithm, and theoretical convergence properties of MCMC algorithms. We next provide a tutorial on building MCMC algorithms for a range of continuous-time asset pricing models. We include detailed examples for equity price models, option pricing models, term structure models, and regime-switching models.

Keywords: continuous-time; Markov Chain Monte Carlo; financial econometrics; Bayesian inference; derivative pricing; volatility; jump diffusions; stochastic volatility; option pricing

1. INTRODUCTION

Dynamic asset pricing theory uses arbitrage and equilibrium arguments to derive the functional relationship between asset prices and the fundamentals of the economy: state variables, structural parameters, and market prices of risk. Continuous–time models are the centerpiece of this approach because of their analytical tractability. In many cases, these models lead to closed form solutions or easy to solve differential equations for objects of interest such as prices or optimal portfolio weights. The models are also appealing from an empirical perspective: through a judicious choice of the drift, diffusion, jump intensity, and jump distribution, these models accommodate a wide range of dynamics for state variables and prices.

Empirical analysis of dynamic asset pricing models tackles the *inverse problem:* extracting information about latent state variables, structural parameters, and market prices of risk from observed prices. The Bayesian solution to the inference problem is the distribution of the parameters, Θ, and state variables, X, conditional on observed prices, Y. This posterior distribution, $p(\Theta, X|Y)$, combines the information in the model and the observed prices and is the key to inference on parameters and state variables.

This chapter describes Markov Chain Monte Carlo (MCMC) methods for exploring the posterior distributions generated by continuous–time asset pricing models. MCMC samples from these high-dimensional, complex distributions by generating a Markov Chain over (Θ, X), $\left\{ \Theta^{(g)}, X^{(g)} \right\}_{g=1}^{G}$, whose equilibrium distribution is $p(\Theta, X|Y)$. The Monte Carlo method uses these samples for numerical integration for parameter estimation, state estimation, and model comparison.

Characterizing $p(\Theta, X|Y)$ in continuous–time asset pricing models is difficult for a variety of reasons. First, prices are observed discretely while the theoretical models specify that prices and state variables evolve continuously in time. Second, in many cases, the state variables are latent from the researcher's perspective. Third, $p(\Theta, X|Y)$ is typically of very high dimension and thus standard sampling methods commonly fail. Fourth, many continuous-time models of interest generate transition distributions for prices and state variables that are nonnormal and nonstandard, complicating standard estimation methods such as MLE. Finally, in term structure and option pricing models, parameters enter nonlinearly or even in a nonanalytic form as the implicit solution to ordinary or partial differential equations. We show that MCMC methods tackle all of these issues.

To frame the issues involved, it is useful to consider the following example: Suppose an asset price, S_t, and its stochastic variance, V_t, jointly solve:

$$dS_t = S_t(r_t + \mu_t)\,dt + S_t\sqrt{V_t}dW_t^s(\mathbb{P}) + d\left(\sum_{j=1}^{N_t(\mathbb{P})} S_{\tau_j-}\left(e^{Z_j(\mathbb{P})} - 1\right)\right) - \mu_t^{\mathbb{P}} S_t dt \qquad (1.1)$$

$$dV_t = \kappa_v(\theta_v - V_t)\,dt + \sigma_v\sqrt{V_t}dW_t^v(\mathbb{P}) \qquad (1.2)$$

where $W_t^s(\mathbb{P})$ and $W_t^v(\mathbb{P})$ are Brownian motions under $\mathbb{P}$, $N_t(\mathbb{P})$ counts the observed number of jump times, τ_j, prior to time t realized under $\mathbb{P}$, μ_t is the equity risk premium, $Z_j(\mathbb{P})$ are the jump sizes with a given predictable distribution $\pi\left(Z_j|\mathcal{F}_{\tau_j-}\right)$ under $\mathbb{P}$, r_t is the spot interest rate, and $\mu_t^{\mathbb{P}}$ is the expected jump size conditional on information available at time t. For simplicity, assume both the spot interest rate and equity premium are constants, although this is easily relaxed. Researchers also often observe derivative prices, such as options. To price these derivatives, it is common to assert that in the absence of arbitrage, there exists a probability measure, $\mathbb{Q}$, such that

$$dS_t = r_t S_t dt + S_t\sqrt{V_t}dW_t^s(\mathbb{Q}) + d\left(\sum_{j=1}^{N_t(\mathbb{Q})} S_{\tau_j-}\left(e^{Z_j(\mathbb{Q})} - 1\right)\right) - \mu_t^{\mathbb{Q}} S_t dt$$

$$dV_t = \left[\kappa_v^{\mathbb{Q}}\left(\theta_v^{\mathbb{Q}} - V_t\right)\right]dt + \sigma_v\sqrt{V_t}dW_t^v(\mathbb{Q}),$$

where $W_t^s(\mathbb{Q})$, $N_t(\mathbb{Q})$, and $W_t^v(\mathbb{Q})$ are defined under $\mathbb{Q}$. The parameters $\kappa_v^{\mathbb{Q}}$ and $\theta_v^{\mathbb{Q}}$ capture the diffusive "price of volatility risk," and $\mu_t^{\mathbb{Q}}$ is expected jump sizes under $\mathbb{Q}$. Under $\mathbb{Q}$, the price of a call option on S_t maturing at time T, struck at K, is

$$C_t = C(S_t, V_t, \Theta) = E^{\mathbb{Q}}\left[e^{-\int_t^T r_s ds}(S_T - K)_+ |V_t, S_t, \Theta\right] \qquad (1.3)$$

where $\Theta = \left(\Theta^{\mathbb{P}}, \Theta^{\mathbb{Q}}\right)$ are the structural and risk neutral parameters. The state variables, X, consist of the volatilities, the jump times, and jump sizes.

The goal of empirical asset pricing is to learn about the risk neutral and objective parameters, the state variables, namely, volatility, jump times, and jump sizes, and the model specification from the observed equity returns and option prices. In the case of the parameters, the marginal posterior distribution $p(\Theta|Y)$ characterizes the sample information about the objective and risk-neutral parameters and quantifies the estimation risk: the uncertainty inherent in estimating parameters. For the state variables, the marginal distribution, $p(X|Y)$, combines the model and data to provide a consistent approach for separating out the effects of jumps from stochastic volatility. This is important for empirical problems such as option pricing or portfolio applications that require volatility estimates. Classical methods are difficult to apply in this model as the parameters and volatility enter in a nonanalytic manner in the option pricing formula, volatility, jump times, and jump sizes are latent, and the transition density for observed prices is not known.

To design MCMC algorithms for exploring $p(\Theta, X|Y)$, we first follow Duffie (1996) and interpret asset pricing models as state space models. This interpretation is convenient for constructing MCMC algorithms as it highlights the modular nature of asset pricing models. The observation equation is the distribution of the observed asset prices conditional on the state variables and parameters, while the evolution equation consists of the dynamics of state variables conditional on the parameters. In the example mentioned earlier, (1.1) and (1.3) form the observation equations and (1.2) is the evolution equation. Viewed in this manner, all asset pricing models take the general form of nonlinear, non-Gaussian state space models.

MCMC methods are particularly well suited for continuous-time finance applications for several reasons.

1. Continuous-time asset models specify that prices and state variables solve parameterized stochastic differential equations (SDEs), which are built from Brownian motions, Poisson processes, and other i.i.d. shocks whose distributions are easy to characterize. When discretized at any finite time-interval, the models take the form of familiar time series models with normal, discrete mixtures of normals or scale mixtures of normals error distributions. This implies that the standard tools of Bayesian inference directly apply to these models. We will also later discuss the accuracy of discrete-time variants of continuous-time models.

2. MCMC is a unified estimation procedure, simultaneously estimating both parameters and latent variables. MCMC directly computes the distribution of the latent variables and parameters given the observed data. This is a stark alternative, the usual approach in the literature of applying approximate filters or noisy latent variable proxies. This allows the researcher, for example, to separate out the effects of jumps and stochastic volatility in models of interest rates or equity prices using discretely observed data.[1]

3. MCMC methods allow the researcher to quantify estimation and model risk. Estimation risk is the inherent uncertainty present in estimating parameters or state variables, while model risk is the uncertainty over model specification. Increasingly in practical problems, estimation risk is a serious issue whose impact must be quantified. In the case of option pricing and optimal portfolio problems, Merton (1980) argues that the "most important direction is to develop accurate variance estimation models which take into account of the errors in variance estimates" (p. 355).

4. MCMC is based on conditional simulation, therefore avoiding any optimization or unconditional simulation. From a practical perspective, MCMC estimation is typically

---

[1] Alternative approaches to separating out jumps and stochastic volatility rely on decreasing interval estimators. See, for example, Aït-Sahalia (2003), Barndorff-Nielson and Shephard (2002), and Andersen et al. (2002).

extremely fast in terms of computing time. This has many advantages, one of which is that it allows the researcher to perform simulation studies to study the algorithms accuracy for estimating parameters or state variables, a feature not shared by many other methods.

The rest of the chapter is outlined as follows. Section 2 provides a brief, nontechnical overview of Bayesian inference and MCMC methods. Section 3 describes the mechanics of MCMC algorithms, provides an overview of the limiting properties of MCMC algorithms, and provides practical recommendations for implementing MCMC algorithms. Section 4 discusses the generic problem of Bayesian inference in continuous-time models. Section 5 provides a tutorial on MCMC methods, building algorithms for equity price, option price, term structure, and regime switching models. Section 6 concludes and provides directions for future research.

2. OVERVIEW OF BAYESIAN INFERENCE AND MCMC

This section provides a brief, nontechnical overview of MCMC and Bayesian methods. We first describe the mechanics of MCMC simulation, and then we show how to use MCMC methods to compute objects of interest in Bayesian inference.

2.1. MCMC Simulation and Estimation

MCMC generates random samples from a given target distribution, in our case, the distribution of parameters and state variables given the observed prices, $p(\Theta, X|Y)$. One way to motivate the construction of MCMC algorithms is via a result commonly known as the Clifford–Hammersley theorem. The theorem states that a joint distribution can be characterized by its so-called complete conditional distributions. Specifically, the theorem implies that $p(X|\Theta, Y)$ and $p(\Theta|X, Y)$ completely characterize the joint distribution $p(\Theta, X|Y)$.

MCMC provides the recipe for combining the information in these distributions to generate samples from $p(\Theta, X|Y)$. Consider the following algorithm. Given two initial values, $\Theta^{(0)}$ and $X^{(0)}$, draw $X^{(1)} \sim p(X|\Theta^{(0)}, Y)$ and then $\Theta^{(1)} \sim p(\Theta|X^{(1)}, Y)$. Continuing in this fashion, the algorithm generates a sequence of random variables, $\{X^{(g)}, \Theta^{(g)}\}_{g=1}^{G}$. This sequence is not i.i.d., but instead forms a *Markov Chain* with attractive properties: under a number of metrics and mild conditions, the distribution of the chain converges to $p(\Theta, X|Y)$, the target distribution.

The key to MCMC is that it is typically easier to characterize the complete conditional distributions, $p(\Theta|X, Y)$ and $p(X|\Theta, Y)$, then to directly analyze the higher-dimensional joint distribution, $p(\Theta, X|Y)$. In many models, the distribution of the state variables conditional on parameters and data, $p(X|\Theta, Y)$, can be computed using standard filtering and smoothing techniques. For example, in linear and Gaussian models, the Kalman filter generates samples from $p(X|\Theta, Y)$. Moreover, the distribution of the parameters given observed data and state variables, $p(\Theta|X, Y)$, is typically easy to simulate as it conditions on the latent states.

MCMC algorithms generically consist of two different steps. If the complete conditional distribution is known in closed form and can be directly sampled, the step in the MCMC algorithm is known as a "Gibbs" step. If all the conditionals can be directly sampled, the algorithm is referred to as a "Gibbs sampler." In many situations, one or more of the conditionals cannot be directly sampled and methods known as "Metropolis-Hastings algorithms" apply. These algorithms sample a candidate draw from a proposal density and then accept or reject the candidate draw based on an acceptance criterion. These algorithms generate random samples that form a Markov Chain with the appropriate equilibrium distribution. An algorithm can include only Gibbs steps, only Metropolis-Hastings steps, or any combination of the two. This latter case, usually encountered in practice, generates a "hybrid" MCMC algorithm.

The samples $\left\{\Theta^{(g)}, X^{(g)}\right\}_{g=1}^{G}$ from the joint posterior can be used for parameter and state variable estimation using the *Monte Carlo* method. For a function $f(\Theta, X)$ satisfying technical regularity conditions, the Monte Carlo estimate of

$$E[f(\Theta, X)|Y] = \int f(\Theta, X) p(\Theta, X|Y) \, dX d\Theta$$

is given by $\frac{1}{G}\sum_{g=1}^{G} f\left(\Theta^{(g)}, X^{(g)}\right)$.

MCMC algorithms have attractive limiting behavior as $G \to \infty$. There are two types of convergence operating simultaneously. First, there is the convergence of the distribution of the Markov Chain to $p(\Theta, X|Y)$. Second, there is the convergence of the partial sums, $\frac{1}{G}\sum_{g=1}^{G} f\left(\Theta^{(g)}, X^{(g)}\right)$ to the conditional expectation $E[f(\Theta, X)|Y]$. The Ergodic Theorem for Markov Chains guarantees both types of convergence, and the conditions under which it holds can be generically verified for MCMC algorithms. In many cases, these limiting results can often be sharpened by deriving the rate of convergence of the Markov chain and geometric convergence rates are common. We discuss these issues in detail in Section 3.4.

2.2. Bayesian Inference

We now provide a brief, nontechnical overview of Bayesian inference. We refer the reader to Lindley (1972) or Bernardo and Smith (1995) for textbook treatments of Bayesian methods. The main advantage of Bayesian methods are the strong theoretical foundations of the Bayesian approach to inference and decision making. Bayesian inference provides a coherent approach for inference and is merely an implication of the laws of probability applied to the parameters and state variables. This approach is consistent with axiomatic decision theory. See, for example, the seminal work of Ramsey (1931), de Finetti (1931), and Savage (1954). We now discuss the key elements of Bayesian inference and decision-making problems.

2.2.1. The Posterior Distribution

The posterior distribution summarizes the information embedded in prices regarding latent state variables and parameters. Bayes rule factors the posterior distribution into is constituent components:

$$p(\Theta, X|Y) \propto p(Y|X, \Theta) \, p(X|\Theta) \, p(\Theta), \tag{2.1}$$

where $Y = \{Y_t\}_{t=1}^{T}$ is the observed prices, $X = \{X_t\}_{t=1}^{T}$ is the unobserved state variables, Θ is the parameters, $p(Y|X, \Theta)$ is the likelihood function, $p(X|\Theta)$ is the distribution of the state variables, and $p(\Theta)$ is the distribution of the parameters, commonly called the prior. The parametric asset pricing model generates $p(Y|X, \Theta)$ and $p(X|\Theta)$ and $p(\Theta)$ summarizes any nonsample information about the parameters.

2.2.2. The Likelihood

There are two types of likelihood functions of interest. The distribution $p(Y|X, \Theta)$ is the full-information (or data-augmented) likelihood and conditions on the state variables and parameters. This is related to marginal likelihood function, $p(Y|\Theta)$, which integrates the latent variables from the augmented likelihood:

$$p(Y|\Theta) = \int p(Y, X|\Theta) \, dX = \int p(Y|X, \Theta) \, p(X|\Theta) \, dX.$$

In most continuous-time asset pricing models, $p(Y|\Theta)$ is not available in closed form and simulation methods are required to perform likelihood-based inference. On the other hand, the full-information likelihood is usually known in closed form that is a key to MCMC estimation.

2.2.3. The Prior Distribution

The prior distribution, as an implication of Bayes rule, enters in the posterior distribution in (2.1). It is important to recognize that the importance of $p(\Theta)$ cannot be ignored: its presence in the posterior, like the presence of the likelihood, is merely an implication of the laws of probability. In addition, this distribution serves important economic and statistical roles. The prior allows the researcher to incorporate nonsample information in a consistent manner. For example, the prior provides a consistent mechanism to impose important economic information such as positivity of certain parameters or beliefs over the degree of mispricing in a model. Statistically, the prior can impose stationarity, rule out near unit-root behavior, or separate mixture components, to name a few applications.

2.2.4. Marginal Parameter Posterior

The information contained in the observed data regarding an individual parameter is summarized via the marginal posterior distribution

$$p(\Theta_i|Y) = \int p(\Theta_i, \Theta_{(-i)}, X|Y) \, dX d\Theta_{(-i)}, \tag{2.2}$$

where Θ_i is the ith element of the parameter vector and $\Theta_{(-i)}$ denotes the remaining parameters. The marginal posterior provides estimates (posterior means or medians) and characterizes estimation risk (posterior standard deviations, quantiles, or credible sets).

2.2.5. State Estimation

State estimation is similar to parameter inference, but it is now important to focus on a number of different posteriors, depending on how much conditioning information is used. The following posterior distributions are all of interest:

$$
\begin{aligned}
\text{Filtering} &: \quad p(X_t|Y^t) \; t = 1, \ldots, T \\
\text{Forecasting} &: \quad p(X_{t+1}|Y^t) \; t = 1, \ldots, T \\
\text{Smoothing} &: \quad p(X_t|Y^T) \; t = 1, \ldots, T.
\end{aligned}
$$

Here Y^t denotes the observed prices up to time t. The smoothing problem is a static problem, solved once using all of the data, the filtering and forecasting problems are inherently sequential.

2.2.6. Model Specification

The posterior distribution provides both formal and informal methods to evaluate model specification and to compare different models. Informally, the posterior can be used to analyze the in-sample fit. For example, the posterior can be used to test the normality of residuals or the independence of random variables, taking into account estimation risk. When there are a finite set of models under consideration, $\{\mathcal{M}_i\}_{i=1}^M$, we can compute the posterior odds of model i versus j. Formally, the posterior odds of $\mathcal{M}_i$ versus $\mathcal{M}_j$ is

$$\frac{p(\mathcal{M}_i|Y)}{p(\mathcal{M}_j|Y)} = \frac{p(Y|\mathcal{M}_i)}{p(Y|\mathcal{M}_j)} \frac{p(\mathcal{M}_i)}{p(\mathcal{M}_j)}.$$

Here, the ratio, $p(Y|\mathcal{M}_i)/p(Y|\mathcal{M}_j)$, is commonly referred to as the Bayes factor. If it is greater than one, the data favors model i over model j and vice versa. Formal Bayesian diagnostic tools such as Odds ratios or Bayes Factors can be computed using the output of MCMC algorithms, see, e.g., Kass and Raftery (1995) or Han and Carlin (2000) for reviews of the large literature analyzing this issue.

3. MCMC: METHODS AND THEORY

In this section, we describe the mechanics of MCMC algorithms, their theoretical under-pinnings and convergence properties. For a full textbook discussion, we recommend the books by Robert and Casella (2005) and Gamerman and Lopes (2006) that contain numerous illustrations and a historical perspective.

3.1. Clifford–Hammersley Theorem

In many continuous-time asset pricing models, $p(\Theta, X|Y)$ is an extremely complicated, high-dimensional distribution and it is prohibitive to directly generate samples from this distribution. However, MCMC solves this problem by first breaking the joint distribution into its complete set of conditionals, which are of lower dimension and are easier to sample. It is in this manner that MCMC algorithms attacks the curse of dimensionality that plagues other methods.

The theoretical justification for breaking $p(\Theta, X|Y)$ into its complete conditional distributions is a remarkable theorem by Clifford and Hammersley.[2] The general version of the Clifford–Hammersley theorem (Besag, 1974; Hammersley and Clifford, 1970) provides conditions for when a set of conditional distributions characterizes a unique joint distribution. For example, in our setting, the theorem indicates that $p(\Theta|X, Y)$ and $p(X|\Theta, Y)$ uniquely determine $p(\Theta, X|Y)$.

This characterization of the joint posterior into two conditional posteriors may not be sufficient to break the curse of dimensionality, as may not be possible to directly sample from $p(\Theta|X, Y)$ and $p(X|\Theta, Y)$. If this case, another application of the Clifford–Hammersley theorem can be used to further simplify the problem. Consider $p(\Theta|X, Y)$ and assume that the K-dimensional vector Θ can be partitioned into $k \leq K$ components $\Theta = (\Theta_1, \ldots, \Theta_k)$, where each component could be uni- or multidimensional. Given the partition, the Clifford–Hammersley theorem implies that the following set of conditional distributions

$$p(\Theta_1|\Theta_2, \Theta_3, \ldots, \Theta_k, X, Y)$$
$$p(\Theta_2|\Theta_1, \Theta_3, \ldots, \Theta_k, X, Y)$$
$$\vdots$$
$$p(\Theta_k|\Theta_2, \Theta_3, \ldots, \Theta_{k-1}, X, Y)$$

uniquely determines $p(\Theta|X, Y)$. In the case of the state vector, the joint distribution $p(X|\Theta, Y)$ can be characterized by its own complete set of conditionals:

---

[2]Somewhat surprisingly, Clifford and Hammersley never published their results as they could not relax the positivity condition. For a discussion of the circumstances surrounding this, see the interesting discussion by Hammersley (1974) after the paper by Besag (1974).

$p(X_t|\Theta, X_{(-t)}, Y)$ for $t = 1, \ldots, T$, where $X_{(-t)}$ denotes the elements of X excluding X_t. In the extreme, the Clifford–Hammersley theorem implies that instead of drawing from a $T + K$ dimensional posterior, the same information is contained in $T + K$ *one*-dimensional distributions.

The fact that complete conditionals fully characterize a joint distribution is not at all intuitively obvious. It is something unique to the problem of sampling from a joint distribution. A proof of the Clifford–Hammersley theorem based on the Besag formula (Besag, 1974) uses the insight that for any pair (Θ^0, X^0) of points, the joint density $p(\Theta, X|Y)$ is determined as

$$\frac{p(\Theta, X|Y)}{p(\Theta^0, X^0|Y)} = \frac{p(\Theta|X^0, Y) p(X|\Theta, Y)}{p(\Theta^0|X^0, Y) p(X^0|\Theta, Y)}$$

as long as a *positivity* condition is satisfied. The formula is derived using the identities

$$p(\Theta^0, X^0|Y) = p(\Theta^0|X^0, Y) p(X^0|Y) \quad \text{and} \quad p(X^0|Y) = \frac{p(X^0|\Theta, Y) p(\Theta|Y)}{p(\Theta|X^0, Y)},$$

which in turn follows from Bayes rule. Thus, knowledge of $p(\Theta|X, Y)$ and $p(X|\Theta, Y)$, up to a constant of proportionality, is equivalent to knowledge of the joint distribution. The positivity condition in our case requires that for each point in the sample space, $p(\Theta, X|Y)$ and the marginal densities are positive, assuming the support is continuous. Under very mild regularity conditions the positivity condition is always satisfied.

3.2. Gibbs Sampling

The simplest MCMC algorithm is called the Gibbs sampler, a label often attributed to the paper of Geman and Geman (1984), although there are clearly some logical predecessors (see Robert and Casella, 2005; Chapter 7). When it is possible to directly sample iteratively from all of the complete conditionals, the resulting MCMC algorithm is a Gibbs sampler. For example, the following defines a Gibbs sampler: given $(\Theta^{(0)}, X^{(0)})$

$$1. \text{ Draw } \Theta^{(1)} \sim p\left(\Theta|X^{(0)}, Y\right)$$

$$2. \text{ Draw } X^{(1)} \sim p\left(X|\Theta^{(1)}, Y\right).$$

Continuing in this fashion, the Gibbs sampler generates a sequence of random variables, $\left\{\Theta^{(g)}, X^{(g)}\right\}_{g=1}^{G}$, which, as we discuss later, converges to $p(\Theta, X|Y)$. Because the researcher controls G, the algorithm is run until it has converged, and then a sample is drawn from the limiting distribution.

If it is not possible generate direct draws from $p(\Theta|X, Y)$ and $p(X|\Theta, Y)$, these distributions can be further simplified via Clifford–Hammersley. For example, consider following Gibbs sampler: given $\left(\Theta^{(0)}, X^{(0)}\right)$

$$1.\ \text{Draw}\ \Theta_1^{(1)} \sim p\left(\Theta_1|\Theta_2^{(0)}, \Theta_3^{(0)}, \Theta_r^{(0)}, X^{(0)}, Y\right)$$

$$2.\ \text{Draw}\ \Theta_2^{(1)} \sim p\left(\Theta_2|\Theta_1^{(1)}, \Theta_3^{(0)}, \Theta_r^{(0)}, X^{(0)}, Y\right)$$

$$\vdots$$

$$r.\ \text{Draw}\ \Theta_r^{(1)} \sim p\left(\Theta_r|\Theta_1^{(1)}, \Theta_2^{(1)}, \dots, \Theta_{r-1}^{(1)}, X^{(0)}, Y\right)$$

and then draw the states $p(X|\Theta, Y)$. If the states cannot be drawn in a block, then a similar argument implies that we can factor $p(X|\Theta, Y)$ into a set of lower dimensional distributions.

The Gibbs sampler requires that one can conveniently draw from the complete set of conditional distributions. In many cases, implementing the Gibbs sampler requires drawing random variables from standard continuous distributions such as normal, t, beta, or gamma or discrete distributions such as binomial, multinomial, or Dirichlet. The reference books by Devroye (1986) or Ripley (1992) provide algorithms for generating random variables from a wide class of recognizable distributions.

3.2.1. The Griddy Gibbs Sampler

The Griddy Gibbs sampler is an approximation that can be applied to approximate the conditional distribution by a discrete set of points. Suppose that Θ is continuously distributed and univariate and that $p(\Theta|X, Y)$ can be evaluated on a point-by-point basis, but that the distribution $p(\Theta|X, Y)$ is nonstandard and direct draws are not possible. The Griddy Gibbs sample approximates the continuously distributed Θ with a discrete mass of N-points, $\{\Theta_j\}_{j=1}^{N}$. Given this approximation, Ritter and Tanner (1992) suggest the following algorithm:

Step 1 : Compute $p\left(\Theta_j|X, Y\right)$ and set $w_j = p(\Theta_j|X, Y)\,/\sum_{j=1}^{N} p\left(\Theta_j|X, Y\right);$ (3.1)

Step 2 : Approximate the inverse CDF of $p(\Theta|X, Y);$ (3.2)

Step 3 : Generate a uniform on $[0, 1]$ and invert the approximate CDF.   (3.3)

Ritter and Tanner (1991) discuss issues involved with the choice of grid of points and show that this algorithm can provide accurate characterization of the conditional distribution in certain cases. In general, the algorithm performs well when the discretization is performed on a small number of parameters. In high-dimensional systems, the algorithm is not likely to perform extremely well.

3.3. Metropolis–Hastings

In some cases, one or more of the conditional distribution cannot be conveniently sampled, and thus the Gibbs sampler does not apply. For example, in models that are nonlinear in the parameters, parameter conditional distribution may be unrecognizable. In other cases, the distribution might be known, but there are not efficient algorithms for sampling from it. In these cases, a very general approach known as the Metropolis–Hastings algorithms will often apply.

Consider the case where one of the parameter posterior conditionals, generically, $\pi(\Theta_i) \triangleq p(\Theta_i | \Theta_{(-i)}, X, Y)$, can be evaluated (as a function of Θ_i), but it is not possible to generate a sample from the distribution. For simplicity, consider the case of a single parameter and suppose we are trying to sample from a one-dimensional distribution, $\pi(\Theta)$. This is equivalent to suppressing the dependence of the other parameters and states in the conditional posterior, $p(\Theta_i | \Theta_{(-i)}, X, Y)$, and significantly reduces the notational demands.

To generate samples from $\pi(\Theta)$, a Metropolis–Hastings algorithm requires the researcher to specify a recognizable proposal or candidate density $q\left(\Theta^{(g+1)} | \Theta^{(g)}\right)$. In most cases this distribution will depend critically on the other parameters, the state variables and the previous draws for the parameter being drawn. As in Metropolis et al. (1953), we only require that we can evaluate density ratio $\pi\left(\Theta^{(g+1)}\right) / \pi\left(\Theta^{(g)}\right)$ easily. This is a mild assumption, which is satisfied in all of the continuous–time models that we consider.

The Metropolis–Hastings algorithm then samples iteratively similar to the Gibbs sampler method, but it first draws a candidate point that will be accepted or rejected based on the acceptance probability. The Metropolis–Hastings algorithm replaces a Gibbs sampler step with the following two-stage procedure:

$$\text{Step 1} \quad : \quad \text{Draw } \Theta^{(g+1)} \text{ from the proposal density } q\left(\Theta^{(g+1)} | \Theta^{(g)}\right) \tag{3.4}$$

$$\text{Step 2} \quad : \quad \text{Accept } \Theta^{(g+1)} \text{ with probability } \alpha\left(\Theta^{(g)}, \Theta^{(g+1)}\right) \tag{3.5}$$

where

$$\alpha\left(\Theta^{(g)}, \Theta^{(g+1)}\right) = \min\left(\frac{\pi\left(\Theta^{(g+1)}\right) / q\left(\Theta^{(g+1)} | \Theta^{(g)}\right)}{\pi\left(\Theta^{(g)}\right) / q\left(\Theta^{(g)} | \Theta^{(g+1)}\right)}, 1\right). \tag{3.6}$$

Implementing Metropolis–Hastings requires only drawing from the proposal, drawing a uniform random variable, and evaluating the acceptance criterion.[3] Intuitively, this algorithm "decomposes" the unrecognizable conditional distribution into two parts:

---

[3] Mechanically, the Metropolis–Hastings algorithm consists of the following steps: (1) draw a candidate $\widehat{\Theta}$ from $q(\Theta | \Theta^{(g)})$, (2) draw $u \sim$ Uniform$[0, 1]$, (3) accept the draw, that is set $\Theta^{(g+1)} = \widehat{\Theta}$ if $u < \alpha(\Theta^{(g)}, \Theta^{(g+1)})$, and (4) otherwise reject the draw, that is, set $\Theta^{(g+1)} = \Theta^{(g)}$.

a recognizable distribution to generate candidate points and an unrecognizable part from which the acceptance criteria arises. The acceptance criterion insures that the algorithm has the correct equilibrium distribution. Continuing in this manner, the algorithm generates samples $\left\{\Theta^{(g)}\right\}_{g=1}^{G}$ whose limiting distribution is $\pi(\Theta)$.

The Metropolis–Hastings algorithm significantly extends the number of applications that can be analyzed as the complete conditionals conditional density need not be known in closed form. A number of points immediately emerge:

1. Gibbs sampling is a special case of Metropolis–Hastings, where $q\left(\Theta^{(g+1)}|\Theta^{(g)}\right) \propto \pi\left(\Theta^{(g+1)}\right)$ and from (3.6) this implies that the acceptance probability is always one and the algorithm always moves. As Gibbs sampling is a special case of Metropolis, one can design algorithms consisting of Metropolis–Hastings or Gibbs steps as it is really only Metropolis. The case with both Metropolis and Gibbs steps is generally called a hybrid algorithm;

2. The Metropolis–Hastings algorithm allows the functional form of the density to be nonanalytic, for example, which occurs when pricing functions require the solution of partial or ordinary differential equations. One only has to evaluate the true density at two given points;

3. There is an added advantage when there are constraints in the parameter space – one can just reject these draws. Alternatively, sampling can be done conditional on specific region, see, e.g. Gelfand et al. (1992). This provides a convenient approach for analyzing parameter restrictions imposed by economic models.

Although theory places no restrictions on the proposal density, it is important to note that the choice of proposal density will greatly effect the performance of the algorithm. For example, if the proposal density has tails that are too thin relative to the target, the algorithm may converge slowly. In extreme case, the algorithm can get stuck in a region of the parameter space and may never converge. Later, we provide some practical recommendations based on the convergence rates of the algorithm.

There are two important special cases of the general Metropolis–Hastings algorithm that deserve special attention.

3.3.1. Independence Metropolis–Hastings

The general Metropolis–Hastings algorithm draws $\Theta^{(g+1)}$ from proposal density, $q\left(\Theta^{(g+1)}|\Theta^{(g)}\right)$, which depends on the previous Markov state $\Theta^{(g)}$ (and, in general, other parameters and states also). An alternative is to draw the candidate $\Theta^{(g+1)}$ from a distribution independent of the previous state, $q\left(\Theta^{(g+1)}|\Theta^{(g)}\right) = q\left(\Theta^{(g+1)}\right)$. This is known as an independence Metropolis–Hastings algorithm:

$$\text{Step 1} \quad : \quad \text{Draw } \Theta^{(g+1)} \text{ from the proposal density } q\left(\Theta^{(g+1)}\right) \tag{3.7}$$

$$\text{Step 2} \quad : \quad \text{Accept } \Theta^{(g+1)} \text{ with probability } \alpha\left(\Theta^{(g)}, \Theta^{(g+1)}\right) \tag{3.8}$$

where

$$\alpha\big(\Theta^{(g)}, \Theta^{(g+1)}\big) = \min\left(\frac{\pi\big(\Theta^{(g+1)}\big)q\big(\Theta^{(g)}\big)}{\pi\big(\Theta^{(g)}\big)q\big(\Theta^{(g+1)}\big)}, 1\right).$$

Even though the candidate draws, $\Theta^{(g+1)}$, are drawn independently of the previous state, the sequence $\{\Theta^{(g)}\}_{g=1}^{G}$ will be not be independent because the acceptance probability depends on previous draws. When using independence Metropolis, it is common to pick the proposal density to closely match certain properties of the target distribution.

3.3.2. Random-Walk Metropolis

Random-walk Metropolis is the original algorithm considered by Metropolis et al. (1953), and it is the mirror image of the independence Metropolis–Hastings algorithm. It draws a candidate from the following random-walk model, $\Theta^{(g+1)} = \Theta^{(g)} + \varepsilon_t$, where ε_t is an independent mean zero error term, typically taken to be a symmetric density function with fat tails, like a t-distribution. Note that the choice of the proposal density is generic, in the sense that it ignores the structural features of the target density.

Because of the symmetry in the proposal density, $q\big(\Theta^{(g+1)}|\Theta^{(g)}\big) = q\big(\Theta^{(g)}|\Theta^{(g+1)}\big)$, the algorithm simplifies to

Step 1   :   Draw $\Theta^{(g+1)}$ from the proposal density $q\big(\Theta^{(g+1)}|\Theta^{(g)}\big)$ (3.9)

Step 2   :   Accept $\Theta^{(g+1)}$ with probability $\alpha\big(\Theta^{(g)}, \Theta^{(g+1)}\big)$ (3.10)

where

$$\alpha\big(\Theta^{(g)}, \Theta^{(g+1)}\big) = \min\left(\frac{\pi\big(\Theta^{(g+1)}\big)}{\pi\big(\Theta^{(g)}\big)}, 1\right).$$

In random-walk Metropolis–Hastings algorithms, the researcher controls the variance of the error term and the algorithm must be tuned, by adjusting the variance of the error term, to obtain an acceptable level of accepted draws, generally in the range of 20–40%. We discuss this issue later.

We now turn to the strong convergence theory underpinning MCMC.

3.4. Convergence Theory

Our MCMC algorithm generates sequence of draws for parameters, $\Theta^{(g)}$, and state variables, $X^{(g)}$. By construction, this sequence is Markov and the chain is characterized by its starting value, $\Theta^{(0)}$ and its conditional distribution or transition kernel $P\big(\Theta^{(g+1)}, \Theta^{(g)}\big)$, where, without any loss of generality, we abstract from the latent variables. One of the main advantages of MCMC is the attractive convergence properties that this sequence of random variables inherits from the general theory of Markov Chains.

3.4.1. Convergence of Markov Chains

Convergence properties of this sequence are based on the ergodic theory for Markov Chains. A useful reference text for Markov Chain theory is Meyn and Tweedie (1995) or Nummelin (1984). Tierney (1994) provides the general theory as applied to MCMC methods, and Robert and Casella (1999) provide many additional references. We are interested in verifying that the chain produced by the MCMC algorithm converges and then identifying the unique equilibrium distribution of the chain as the correct joint distribution, the posterior. We now briefly review the basic theory of the convergence of Markov Chains.

A Markov chain is generally characterized by its *g-step* transition probability,

$$P^{(g)}(x, A) = \text{Prob}\left[\Theta^{(g)} \in A | \Theta^{(0)} = x\right].$$

For a chain to have a unique equilibrium or stationary distribution, π, it must be irreducible and aperiodic. A Markov chain with invariant distribution π is irreducible if, for any initial state, it has positive probability of eventually entering any set that has π-positive probability. A chain is aperiodic if there are no portions of the state space that the chain visits at regularly spaced time intervals. If an irreducible and aperiodic chain has a proper invariant distribution, then π is unique and is also the equilibrium distribution of the chain, that is

$$\lim_{g \to \infty} \text{Prob}\left[\Theta^{(g)} \in A | \Theta^{(0)}\right] = \pi(A).$$

Given convergence, the obvious question is how fast does the chain converge? Here, the general theory of Markov chains also provides explicit convergence rates, see, e.g., Nummelin (1984) or Chapters 15 and 16 of Meyn and Tweedie (1995). The key condition to verify is a minorization condition for the transition kernel that leads in many cases to a convergence rate that is geometric.

While verifying geometric convergence is reassuring, there are well-known examples of geometrically ergodic Markov chains that do not converge in a realistic amount of computing time (see the witches hat example in Polson, 1991). A stronger notion of convergence, polynomial time convergence, provides explicitly bounds on the actual convergence rate of the chain. Diaconis and Stroock (1991) show how the time-reversibility property can be used to characterize a bound known as the Poincare inequality for the convergence rate.

We now discuss the application of these general results to MCMC algorithms.

3.4.2. Convergence of MCMC algorithms

As the Gibbs sampler is a special case of the Metropolis–Hastings algorithm when the acceptance probability is unity, we can focus exclusively on the convergence of

Metropolis–Hastings algorithms. In general, verifying the convergence of Markov chains is a difficult problem. Chains generated by Metropolis–Hastings algorithms, on the other hand, have special properties that allow convergence conditions to be verified in general, without reference to the specifics of a particular algorithm. We now review these conditions.

The easiest way to verify and find an invariant distribution is to check time-reversibility. Recall that for a Metropolis–Hastings algorithm, that the target distribution, π, is given and is proper being the posterior distribution. The easiest way of checking that π is an invariant distribution of the chain is to verify the detailed balance (time-reversibility) condition: a transition function P satisfies the detailed balance condition if there exists a function π such that

$$P(x, y)\pi(x) = P(y, x)\pi(y)$$

for any points x and y in the state space. Intuitively, this means that if the chain is stationary, it has the same probability of reaching x from y if started at y as it does of reaching y from x if started at x. This also implies that π is the invariant distribution since $\pi(y) = \int P(x, y)\pi(dx)$.

Checking time reversibility for Metropolis–Hastings algorithms is straightforward. The transition function in the Metropolis–Hastings algorithm is

$$P(x, y) = \alpha(x, y)Q(x, y) + (1 - r(x))\delta_x(y), \tag{3.11}$$

where $r(x) = \int \alpha(x, y)Q(x, y)dy$ and $Q(x, y) = q(y|x)$. For the first term, the detailed balance condition holds because

$$\alpha(x, y)Q(x, y)\pi(x) = \min\left\{\frac{\pi(y)Q(y, x)}{\pi(x)Q(x, y)}, 1\right\}Q(x, y)\pi(x)$$

$$= \min\{\pi(y)Q(y, x), Q(x, y)\pi(x)\}$$

$$= \min\left\{1, \frac{Q(x, y)\pi(x)}{\pi(y)Q(y, x)}\right\}\pi(y)Q(y, x)$$

$$= \alpha(y, x)Q(y, x)\pi(y)$$

and the derivation for the second term in 3.11 is similar. Thus, Gibbs samplers and Metropolis–Hastings algorithms generate Markov Chains that are time-reversible and have the target distribution as an invariant distribution. Of course, the Gibbs sampler can also be viewed as a special case of Metropolis.

It is also straightforward to verify π-*irreducibility*, see Roberts and Polson (1994) for the Gibbs samplers and Smith and Roberts (1993) and Robert and Casella (1999) for

Metropolis–Hastings algorithms. One sufficient condition is that $\pi(y) > 0$ implies that $Q(x, y) > 0$ (e.g., Mengersen and Tweedie, 1996). In the case of the Gibbs sampler, these conditions can be significantly relaxed to the assumption that x and y communicate, which effectively means that starting from x one can eventually reach state y. To verify aperiodicity, one can appeal to a theorem in Tierney (1994) which states that all π-irreducible Metropolis algorithms are Harris recurrent. Hence, there exists a unique stationary distribution to which the Markov chain generated by Metropolis–Hastings algorithms converges and hence the chain is ergodic.

Having discussed these results, it is important to note that we are rarely purely interested in convergence of the Markov chain. In practice, we are typically interested in sample averages of functionals along the chain. For example, to estimate the posterior mean for a given parameter, we are interested in the convergence of $\frac{1}{G} \sum_{g=1}^{G} f(\Theta^{(g)})$. There are two subtle forms of convergence operating: first the distributional convergence of the chain, and second the convergence of the sample average. The following result provides both:

Proposition 1 (Ergodic Averaging): *Suppose $\Theta^{(g)}$ is an ergodic chain with stationary distribution π and suppose f is a real-valued function with $\int |f| \, d\pi < \infty$. Then for all $\Theta^{(g)}$ for any initial starting value $\Theta^{(g)}$*

$$\lim_{G \to \infty} \frac{1}{G} \sum_{g=1}^{G} f\left(\Theta^{(g)}\right) = \int f(\Theta) \, \pi(\Theta) \, d\Theta$$

almost surely.

In many cases, we go further with an ergodic central limit theorem:

Proposition 2 (Central Limit Theorem): *Suppose $\Theta^{(g)}$ is an ergodic chain with stationary distribution π and suppose that f is real-valued and $\int |f| \, d\pi < \infty$. Then there exists a real number $\sigma(f)$ such that*

$$\sqrt{G} \left(\frac{1}{G} \sum_{g=1}^{G} f\left(\Theta^{(g)}\right) - \int f(\Theta) \, d\pi \right)$$

converges in distribution to a mean zero normal distribution with variance $\sigma^2(f)$ for any starting value.

While reassuring, these limiting theorems should be taken with a grain of salt. A warning regarding the use asymptotics of this type is given in Aldous (1989, p. vii),

The proper business of probabilists is calculating probabilities. Often exact calculations are tedious or impossible, so we resort to approximations. A limit theorem is an assertion of the form: the error in a certain approximation tends to 0 as (say) G → ∞. Call such limit theorems naive if there is no explicit error bound in terms of G and the parameters of the underlying process. Such theorems are so prevalent in theoretical and applied probability that people seldom stop to ask their purpose.... It is hard to give any argument for the relevance of a proof of a naive limit theorem, except as a vague reassurance that your approximation is sensible, and a good heuristic argument seems equally reassuring.

One measure of speed of convergence, geometric convergence, implies that there exists a $\lambda < 1$ and a constant K such that

$$\left\| P^g\left(\cdot, \Theta^{(0)}\right) - \pi\left(\cdot\right) \right\| \leq K\lambda^{-G}$$

where $\|\|$ could denote any number of norms. In particular, it is possible that a bound is satisfied for certain moments, or test functions, and not others. Roberts and Polson (1994) prove that all Gibbs samplers are geometrically convergent under a minorization condition. For the Metropolis–Hastings algorithm, there are a number of results on the geometric convergence and the results rely on the tail behavior of the target and proposal density. Mengersen and Tweedie (1996) show that a sufficient condition for the geometric ergodicity of *independence* Metropolis–Hastings algorithms is that the tails of the proposal density dominate the tails of the target, which requires that the proposal density q is such that q/π is bounded over the entire support. Mengersen and Tweedie (1996) show that random-walk algorithms converge at a geometric rate if the target density has geometric tails.

Although geometric convergence is an improvement on the central limit theorem, it can still give a false sense of security. A popular example of this is the witch's hat distribution (see Polson, 1992; Geyer, 1992). This distribution looks like a witch's hat: a broad flat brim with a sharp peak in the center. In this case, the Gibbs sampler is geometrically convergent, however, λ is so close to 1, that practically speaking, the algorithm never converges. The chance of moving from brim to peak is exponentially small and therefore in finite computing, one may never visit this region of the space. Another example of this sort of potentially degenerate behavior is given by an example from Elekes (1986).[4]

A stronger notion of convergence, polynomial convergence, is faster than geometric. Diaconis and Stroock (1991), Frieze et al. (1994), Polson (1996), and Rosenthal (1995a,b) provide polynomial convergence in a number of different cases. For example,

[4]Suppose that the state space is the unit ball in k-dimensions and consider any G points in this space. These G-points are the draws from the MCMC algorithm. The volume of the convex hull of these points is bounded by $G/2^k$. For example, suppose that $k = 50$ and one runs the MCMC algorithm for one billion draws, $G = 10^9$. The volume of the convex hull is $10^9/2^{50}$, which implies that any run of the Gibbs sampler will cover only an exponentially small portion of the state space.

Frieze et al. (1994) show that MCMC algorithms that draw from log-concave distributions generate polynomial convergent algorithms. Although this assumption may seem restrictive, Polson (1996) shows that data augmentation can be used to convert a non-log-concave sampling problem into a log-concave problem. An example is representing a t-distribution as a scale mixture of normals with a latent variable indexing the scaling parameters. Thus, careful data augmentation can significantly improve the convergence of the MCMC algorithm.

Second, in addition to the formal convergence theory, there is a large literature that studies the information content of sequence $\{\Theta^{(g)}\}_{g=1}^{G}$. Unlike importance sampling, MCMC algorithms generate dependent Monte Carlo simulation methodology and because of this, it is important to understand the nature of this dependency. On the one hand, while theory is clear that the chains converge, it is impossible to formally diagnose convergence from the realized output of the chain.[5] On the other hand, the output of the chain clearly has some informational content. Popular observed chain-based diagnostics include calculating parameter trace plots. The trace plots, plots of $\Theta_i^{(g)}$ versus g, show the history of the chain and are useful for diagnosing chains that get stuck in a region of the state space. It is also common to analyze the correlation structure of draws by computing the autocorrelation function (ACF). Again, one needs to take care when interpreting these ACF's, as algorithms that have low autocorrelation may never converge (the witch's hat distribution mentioned earlier). It is also easy to calculate Monte Carlo estimates for the standard errors of $\frac{1}{G}\sum_{g=1}^{G}f(\Theta^{(g)})$. The informational content of the chain regarding estimation of $E_{\pi}(f(\Theta))$ is clearly summarized $\sigma^2(f)$. Geyer (1993), among others, show how to estimate the information using realizations of a provable convergent chain. This, in turn, allows the researcher to apply the Central Limit Theorem to assess the Monte Carlo errors inherent in MCMC estimation.

The following implementation procedure is typically used. Starting from a point $\Theta^{(0)}$, possibly at random, the general methodology is to discard a *burn-in* period of h initial iterations to reduce the influence of the choice of starting point. After the burn-in period the researcher makes an additional *estimation* period of G simulations, which results in one long chain of length G. When forming Monte Carlo averages every simulated point in the chain after the burn-in period should be used. The estimation period G is chosen so as to make the Monte Carlo sampling error as small as desired. Standard errors are also easily computed. See Aldous (1987), Tierney (1994), and Polson (1996) for a theoretical discussion of the choice of (h, G) and the relationship between the estimation period G and Monte Carlo standard errors.

---

[5] Peter Clifford had the following comments on detecting convergence of a chain purely from a simulated run of the chain in his discussion to Smith and Roberts (1993): "Can we really tell when a complicated Markov chain has reached equilibrium? Frankly, I doubt it" (p. 53).

3.5. MCMC Algorithms: Issues and Practical Recommendations

This section provides a number of practical recommendations for building, testing, and applying MCMC algorithms.

3.5.1. Building MCMC Algorithms

Because of the modular nature of MCMC algorithms, we recommend building the algorithms in a "bottom-up" fashion. That is, first program a simple version of the model and, after verifying that it works, add additional factors. For example, when estimating a stochastic volatility model with jumps, first implement a pure stochastic volatility model and a pure jump model, and then after both are working, combine them.

Moreover, there are always multiple ways of implementing a given model. For example, Robert and Casella (1999) provide examples where a Metropolis step may be preferred to Gibbs even when the conditional can directly be sampled. Therefore, we recommend trying multiple algorithms, assessing their accuracy and computational efficiency and then carefully choosing an algorithm along these two dimensions. Algorithms that appear to be "fast" in terms of computational properties may be very slow in terms of their theoretical convergence rates.

Polson (1996) shows that the introduction of additional latent state variables, known as data augmentation, can dramatically increase the rate of convergence. One must be careful, however, as the introduction of state variables can also degrade the provable convergence rate of algorithms.

3.5.2. Blocking

When building algorithms, parameters or state variables that are correlated should, if possible, be drawn in blocks. As shown by Kong et al. (1994), drawing correlated parameters in blocks can improve the speed of convergence. Blocking plays a central role in models with latent states. States can be updated individually, commonly referred to as single-state updating, or in blocks. In many models, state variables are persistent which implies that the correlation between neighbor states is typically high and the gains from drawing these states together in a block can be significant.

For example, in conditionally Gaussian models, the Kalman filtering recursions allow a block update of all states in one step, a highly efficient approach for updating states. As discussed by Carter and Kohn (1994) and Kim and Shephard (1994), models that involve discrete mixture of normal distributions have a structure that is amenable to updating the states in blocks. Unfortunately, it is difficult to generate generic algorithms for block-updating, as blocking schemes must use the specific stochastic structure of the model specification. We provide examples of these algorithms later.

3.5.3. Simulation Studies

Simulation studies, whereby artificial data sets are simulated and the efficiency and convergence of the algorithm can be checked, are always recommended. These studies provide a number of useful diagnostics. First, among other things, they provide insurance against programming errors, incorrect conditionals, poorly mixing Markov chains, and improper priors. Second, they can also be used to compare MCMC against alternative estimation methodologies. For example, Andersen et al. (1998) show that in a simple stochastic volatility, MCMC outperforms GMM, EMM, QMLE, and simulated maximum likelihood in terms of root mean squared error.

Third, they characterize the impact of discretization error on the parameter estimates. Eraker et al. (2003) show that time-discretization of the double-jump model at a daily frequency does not induce any biases in the parameter estimates. Fourth, the simulation studies provide a guide for how long to run algorithms. Finally, simulation studies also allow researchers to study the role of prior distributions. Because state space models often have subtle identification issues, simulating data sets from alternative parameter values and for different priors provide a means to quantify what role, if any, the prior distributions play.

3.5.4. Provable Convergence

Provable convergence rates are always important. Algorithms that are provably geometric convergent are preferred to those that are not. For example, care must be taken in using normal proposal densities when the target has fat tails, as the results in Mengersen and Tweedie (1996) imply that this algorithm will be "slow." When using independence or random-walk Metropolis, one should use fat-tailed distributions such as a t-distribution.

3.5.5. Choosing Proposal Densities and Tuning Metropolis Algorithms

In both independence and random-walk Metropolis algorithms, the is quite a bit of latitude that is available when choosing the proposal density. In the case of independence Metropolis, the functional form of the proposal density can be specified and in random walk and Langevin Metropolis, the standard deviation of the shock distribution, also known as the scaling or tuning parameter, needs to be specified by the researcher. Theory only provides broad guidelines for how to specify these algorithms. For both independence and random-walk Metropolis, theory requires that the support of the distributions coincide and that, for "fast" convergence, the tails of the proposal density should dominate the tails of the target density.

Figure 13.1 provides three common pitfalls encountered when using Metropolis–Hastings algorithms. In each panel, the target density is shown in solid lines and the proposal density is shown as a dashed line. In each case, the proposal density is not properly chosen, scaled, or tuned and the impact on the algorithm can be different depending on the case.

In the first case, the target density is $N(5, 1)$ and the proposal density is $N(-5, 1)$. In this case, it is clear that the algorithm, while converging nicely in theory as the normal distributions have the same tail behavior, will converge very slowly in computing time.

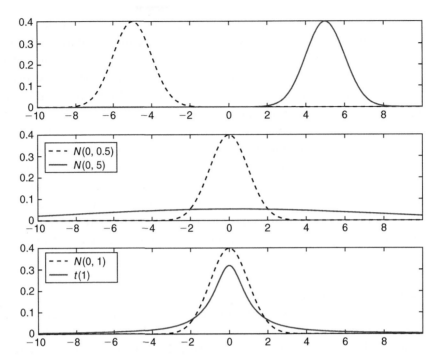

Figure 13.1 Examples of poorly chosen proposal densities. In each panel, the target density is shown as a solid line and the proposal as a dotted line.

Suppose that the current state is near the mode of the target. If a draw near the mode of the proposal is proposed, the algorithm will rarely accept this draw and the algorithm will not move. On the other hand, if the current state ever approaches, for example, the mode of the proposal density, it will continue to propose moves nearby which rarely will increase the acceptance probability. The case in the second panel is similar, except now the target has a much higher variance. In this case, the proposal will very often be accepted, however, the target distribution will not be efficiently explored because all of the proposals will be in a small range centered around zero.

The third case is maybe most insidious. In this case, the two distributions have same mean and variance, but the target distribution is $t(1)$ and has extremely fat tails while the proposal is normal. This algorithm will likely have a high acceptance probability but the algorithm will never explore the tails of the target distribution. The algorithm appears to move around nicely, but theory indicates that convergence, in a formal sense, will be slow. Thus, the researcher will receive a false sense of security as the algorithm appears to be behaving well.

How then should Metropolis proposals be chosen and tuned? We have a number of recommendations. First, as mentioned earlier, the researcher should be careful to insure that the Metropolis step is properly centered, scaled and has sufficiently fat tails. In most cases, a conditional posterior can be analytically or graphically explored and one should insure that the proposal has good properties. second, we recommend simulation studies to insure that the algorithm is properly estimating parameters and states. This typically uncovers large errors when, for example, certain parameters easily get stuck either at the true value or far away from the true value. Third, there are some asymptotic results for scaling random-walk and Langevin-diffusion Metropolis algorithms that provide the "optimal" asymptotic acceptance probability of random-walk algorithms. Of course, optimal is relative to a specific criterion, but the results indicate that the acceptance probabilities should be in the range of 0.2–0.5. In our experience, these guidelines are reasonable in most cases.

3.5.6. Noninformative Priors
One must be careful when using noninformative priors. Without care, conditional or joint posteriors can be improper, a violation of the Clifford–Hammersley Theorem. Hobert and Casella (1996) provide a number of general examples. For example, in a log-stochastic volatility, a "noninformative" prior on σ_v of $p(\sigma_v) \propto \sigma_v^{-1}$ results in a proper conditional posterior for σ_v but an improper joint posterior that leads to a degenerate MCMC algorithm. In some cases, the propriety of the joint posterior cannot be checked analytically, and in this case, simulation studies can be reassuring. We recommend using proper priors always be used unless there is a very strong justification for doing otherwise.

3.5.7. Convergence Diagnostics and Starting Values
We recommend carefully examining the parameter and state variable draws for a wide-range of starting values. For a given set of starting values, trace plots of a given parameter or state as a function of G provide important information. Trace plots are very useful for detecting poorly specified Markov chains: chains that have difficultly moving from the initial condition, chains that get trapped in certain region of the state space, or chains that move slowly. We provide examples of trace plots later. Whenever the convergence of the MCMC algorithm is in question, careful simulation studies can provide reassurance that the MCMC algorithm is providing reliable inference.

3.5.8. Rao-Blackwellization
In many cases, naive Monte Carlo estimates of the integrals can be improved using a technique known as Rao–Blackwellization. If there is an analytical form for the conditional density $p(\Theta_i | \Theta_{(-i)}, X, Y)$, then we can take advantage of the conditioning information to estimate the marginal posterior mean as

$$E(\Theta_i | Y) = E\big[E[\Theta_i | \Theta_{(-i)}, X, Y] | Y\big] \approx \frac{1}{G} \sum_{g=1}^{G} E\Big[\Theta_i | \Theta_{(-i)}^{(g)}, X^{(g)}, Y\Big].$$

Gelfand and Smith (1992) show that this estimator has a lower variance than the simple Monte Carlo estimate.

4. BAYESIAN INFERENCE AND ASSET PRICING MODELS

The key to Bayesian inference is the posterior distribution that consists of three components, the likelihood function, $p(Y|X, \Theta)$, the state variable specification, $p(X|\Theta)$, and the prior distribution $p(\Theta)$. In this section, we discuss the connections between these components and the asset pricing models. Section 4.1 discusses the continuous–time specification for the state variables, or factors, and then how the asset pricing model generates the likelihood function. These distributions are abstractly given via the solution of SDEs, and we use time-discretization methods that we discuss in Section 4.2 to characterize the likelihood and state dynamics. Finally, Section 4.3 discusses the important role of the parameter distribution, commonly called the prior.

4.1. States Variables and Prices

Classical continuous–time asset pricing models, such as the Cox et al. (1985) model, begin with an exogenous specification of the underlying factors of the economy. In all of our examples, we assume that the underlying factors, labeled as F_t, arise as the exogenous solution to parameterized SDEs with jumps:

$$dF_t = \mu_f\left(F_t, \Theta^{\mathbb{P}}\right)dt + \sigma_f\left(F_t, \Theta^{\mathbb{P}}\right)dW_t^f(\mathbb{P}) + d\left(\sum_{j=1}^{N_t^f(\mathbb{P})} Z_j^f(\mathbb{P})\right). \tag{4.1}$$

Here, $W_t^f(\mathbb{P})$ is a vector of Brownian motions, $N_t^f(\mathbb{P})$ is a counting process with stochastic intensity $\lambda_f\left(F_{t-}, \Theta^{\mathbb{P}}\right)$, $\Delta F_{\tau_j} = F_{\tau_j} - F_{\tau_j-} = Z_j^f(\mathbb{P})$, $Z_j^f(\mathbb{P}) \sim \Pi_f\left(F_{\tau_j-}, \Theta^{\mathbb{P}}\right)$, and we assume the drift and diffusion are known parametric functions. For clarity, we are careful to denote the parameters that drive the objective dynamics of F_t by $\Theta^{\mathbb{P}}$. Throughout, we assume that characteristics have sufficient regularity for a well–defined solution to exist. Although the factors are labeled F_t, we define the states as the variables that are latent from the perspective of the econometrician. Thus, the "states" include jump times and jump sizes, in addition to F_t.

Common factors, or state variables, include stochastic volatility or a time-varying equity premium. This specification nests diffusions, jump–diffusions, finite–activity jump processes, and regime-switching diffusions, where the drift and diffusion coefficients are functions of a continuous-time Markov chain. For many applications, the state variable specification is chosen for analytic tractability. For example, in many pure-diffusion models, the conditional density $p\left(F_t|F_{t-1}, \Theta^{\mathbb{P}}\right)$ can be computed in closed form or easily by numerical methods. Examples include Gaussian processes

$\left(\mu_f\left(f, \Theta^{\mathbb{P}}\right) = \alpha_f + \beta_f f, \quad \sigma_f\left(f, \Theta^{\mathbb{P}}\right) = \sigma_f \right)$, the Feller "square-root" processes $\left(\mu_f\left(f, \Theta^{\mathbb{P}}\right) = \alpha_f^{\mathbb{P}} + \beta_f^{\mathbb{P}} f, \sigma_f\left(f, \Theta^{\mathbb{P}}\right) = \sigma_f^{\mathbb{P}} \sqrt{f} \right)$, and more general affine processes (see Duffie et al., 2001, Duffie et al., 2003). In these cases, the conditional density is either known in closed form or can be computed numerically using simple integration routines. In general, the transition densities are not known in closed form and our MCMC approach relies on a time–discretization and data augmentation.

Given the state variables, arbitrage and equilibrium arguments provide the prices of other assets. We assume there are two types of prices. The first, denoted by a vector S_t are the prices whose dynamics we model. Common examples include equity prices, equity index values, or exchange rates. The second case are derivatives such as option or bond prices, which can be viewed as derivatives on the short rate.

In the first case, we assume that S_t solves a parameterized SDE

$$dS_t = \mu_s\left(S_t, F_t, \Theta^{\mathbb{P}}\right)dt + \sigma_s\left(S_t, F_t, \Theta^{\mathbb{P}}\right)dW_t^s(\mathbb{P}) + d\left(\sum_{j=1}^{N_t^s(\mathbb{P})} Z_j^s(\mathbb{P})\right), \qquad (4.2)$$

where the objective measure dynamics are driven by the state variables, a vector of Brownian motion, $W_t^s(\mathbb{P})$, a point process $N_t^s(\mathbb{P})$ with stochastic intensity $\lambda^s\left(F_{t-}, \Theta^{\mathbb{P}}\right)$, and $S_{\tau_j} - S_{\tau_{j-}} = Z_j^s$ is a jump with $\mathcal{F}_{t-}$ distribution $\Pi^s\left(F_{t-}, \Theta^{\mathbb{P}}\right)$.

In the second case, the derivative prices, D_t are a function of the state variables and parameters, $D_t = D(S_t, F_t, \Theta)$ where $\Theta = \left(\Theta^{\mathbb{P}}, \Theta^{\mathbb{Q}}\right)$ contains risk-premium parameters, $\Theta^{\mathbb{Q}}$. To price the derivatives, we assert the existence of an equivalent martingale measure, $\mathbb{Q}$,

$$dS_t = \mu_s(S_t, F_t, \Theta)dt + \sigma_s\left(S_t, F_t, \Theta^{\mathbb{P}}\right)dW_t^s(\mathbb{Q}) + d\left(\sum_{j=1}^{N_t^s(\mathbb{Q})} Z_j^s(\mathbb{Q})\right) \qquad (4.3)$$

$$dF_t = \mu_f(F_t, \Theta)dt + \sigma_f\left(F_t, \Theta^{\mathbb{P}}\right)dW_t^f(\mathbb{Q}) + d\left(\sum_{j=1}^{N_t^f(\mathbb{Q})} Z_j^f(\mathbb{Q})\right). \qquad (4.4)$$

where, it is important to note that the drift now depends potentially on both $\Theta^{\mathbb{P}}$ and $\Theta^{\mathbb{Q}}$ (we assume for simplicity that the functional form of the drift does not change under $\mathbb{Q}$), $W_t^s(\mathbb{Q})$ and $W_t^f(\mathbb{Q})$ are Brownian motions under $\mathbb{Q}$, $N_t^f(\mathbb{Q})$ and $N_t^s(\mathbb{Q})$ are point process with stochastic intensities $\left\{\lambda^i\left(F_{t-}, S_{t-}, \Theta^{\mathbb{Q}}\right)\right\}_{i=s,f}$ and $\left(Z_j^f, Z_j^s\right)$ have joint distribution $\Pi\left(F_{t-}, S_{t-}, \Theta^{\mathbb{Q}}\right)$. Because of the absolute continuity of the changes in measure, the diffusion coefficients depend only on $\Theta^{\mathbb{P}}$. The likelihood ratio generating the change of measure for jump-diffusions is given by Aase (1988) or the review paper by Runggaldier (2003).

We only assume that this pricing function, $D(s, x, \Theta)$, can be computed numerically and do not require it to be analytically known. This implies that our methodology covers the important cases of multifactor term structure and option pricing models. In multifactor term structure models, the short rate process, r_t, is assumed to be a function of a set of state variables, $r_t = r(F_t)$, and bond prices are given by

$$D_t = D(F_t, \Theta) = E_t^{\mathbb{Q}}\left[e^{-\int_t^T r(F_s)ds}\right],$$

where $\mathbb{Q}$ is an equivalent martingale measure f can be computed either analytically or as the solution to ordinary or partial differential equation. In models of option prices, the mapping is given via

$$D_t = f(S_t, F_t, \Theta) = E_t^{\mathbb{Q}}\left[e^{-\int_t^T r(F_s)ds}(S_T - K)_+ | F_t, \Theta\right]$$

and F_t could be, for example, stochastic volatility.

Derivative prices raise an important issue: the observation equation is technically a degenerate distribution as the prices are known conditional on state variables and parameters. In this case, if the parameters are known, certain state variables can often be inverted from observed prices, if the parameters were known. An common example of this is Black–Scholes implied volatility. In practice, there are typically more prices observed than parameters which introduces a stochastic singularity: the model is incapable of simultaneously fitting all of the prices. This over-identification provides a rich source of information for testing. To circumvent the stochastic singularities, researchers commonly assume there exists a pricing error, ε_t. In the case of an additive pricing error,[6]

$$D_t = D(S_t, F_t, \Theta) + \varepsilon_t,$$

where $\varepsilon_t \sim N(0, \Sigma_\varepsilon)$. Once a pricing error is assumed, it implies that prices are not fully revealing of state variables or parameters. Alternatively, in many settings it may be more sensible to use a proportional pricing error:

$$\log(D_t) = \log D(S_t, F_t, \Theta) + \varepsilon_t.$$

This is useful in option pricing settings because option prices must be positive and out-of-the money option prices are quite small. Jacquier and Jarrow (2000) provide a detailed analysis of estimation with option price errors. In particular, they discuss the sensitivity of inference to different error assumptions.

There are a number of motivations for introducing pricing errors. First, there is often a genuine concern with noisy price observations generated by bid-ask spreads. For

---

[6] In some cases, it might be more appropriate to use a multiplicative pricing error $Y_t = f(X_t, \Theta)\, e^{\varepsilon t}$, which can, for example, guarantee positive prices.

example, consider an at-the-money equity index option. For the S&P 100 or 500 the contract typically has a bid-ask spread of around 5–10% of the value of the option. In fixed income, zero yields are often measured with error as they are obtained by interpolation par bond yields. The pricing error breaks the stochastic singularity that arises when there are more observed asset prices than state variables. Second, even if the econometrician does not believe the prices are observed with error, the addition of an extremely small pricing error can be viewed as a tool to simplify econometric analysis. Third, our models are clearly abstractions from reality and will never hold perfectly. Pricing errors accommodate this misspecification in a tractable manner. These pricing errors provide a useful model diagnostic, and MCMC are useful for investigating the small sample behavior of the pricing errors.

4.2. Time-Discretization: Computing $p(Y|X, \Theta)$ and $p(X|\Theta)$

In this subsection, we describe how the time-discretization of the SDEs can be used to compute the likelihood function and state dynamics. The researcher typically observed a panel of prices, Y, where $Y = (S, D)$ and $S = (S_1, \ldots, S_T)$ and $D = (D_1, \ldots, D_T)$. We assume the prices are observed at equally spaced, discrete intervals. For simplicity, we normalize the observation interval to unity. This generates the following continuous-time state space model for the derivative prices,

$$D_t = D(S_t, F_t, \Theta) + \varepsilon_t, \tag{4.5}$$

and the prices and factors

$$S_{t+1} = S_t + \int_t^{t+1} \mu_s\left(S_u, F_u, \Theta^{\mathbb{P}}\right) du + \int_t^{t+1} \sigma_s\left(S_u, F_u, \Theta^{\mathbb{P}}\right) dW_u^s(\mathbb{P}) + \sum_{j=N_t^s(\mathbb{P})+1}^{N_{t+1}^s(\mathbb{P})} Z_j^s(\mathbb{P}) \tag{4.6}$$

$$\Gamma_{t+1} - \Gamma_t + \int_t^{t+1} \mu_f\left(F_u, \Theta^{\mathbb{P}}\right) du + \int_t^{t+1} \sigma_f\left(F_u, \Theta^{\mathbb{P}}\right) dW_u^f(\mathbb{P}) + \sum_{j=N_t^f(\mathbb{P})+1}^{N_{t+1}^f(\mathbb{P})} Z_j^f(\mathbb{P}). \tag{4.7}$$

Equations (4.5) and (4.6) are the observation equations and (4.7) is the evolution equation.

In continuous time, these models take the form of a very complicated state space model. Even if ε_t is normally distributed, $D(S_t, X_t, \Theta)$ is often nonanalytic that generates Gaussian, but nonlinear and nonanalytic observation equation. Similarly, in (4.6) the error distribution is generated by

$$\int_t^{t+1} \sigma_s\left(S_u, F_u, \Theta^{\mathbb{P}}\right) dW_u^s(\mathbb{P}) + \sum_{j=N_t^s(\mathbb{P})+1}^{N_{t+1}^s(\mathbb{P})} Z_j^s(\mathbb{P}).$$

Together, the model is clearly a nonlinear, non-Gaussian state space model.

At this stage, it is important to recognize the objects of interest. From the perspective of the econometrician, the jump times, jump sizes, and F_t are latent, although it is typically assumed that the agents in the economy pricing the assets observe these variables. Although the variables F_t solve the SDE, and thus, would commonly be referred to as the states, we include in our state vector the jump times, jump sizes, and spot factors, F_t, as these are all objects of interest in asset pricing models. Pricing models commonly integrate out of the the jump times and sizes, and condition solely on F_t and other prices.

At this level, it is clearly not possible to compute either the likelihood, $p(Y|X, \Theta)$, or the latent state distribution, $p(X|\Theta)$. To compute these quantities, we time-discretize the SDEs which then allows us to compute the likelihood and state variable evolution. To start, assume that the time-discretization interval matches the observed frequency. This generates the following time-discretized state space model:

$$D_{t+1} = D(S_{t+1}, F_{t+1}, \Theta) + \varepsilon_{t+1} \tag{4.8}$$

$$S_{t+1} = S_t + \mu_s\left(S_t, F_t, \Theta^{\mathbb{P}}\right) + \sigma_s\left(S_t, F_t, \Theta^{\mathbb{P}}\right)\varepsilon_{t+1}^s + Z_{t+1}^s J_{t+1}^s \tag{4.9}$$

$$F_{t+1} = F_t + \mu_f\left(F_t, \Theta^{\mathbb{P}}\right) + \sigma_f\left(F_t, \Theta^{\mathbb{P}}\right)\varepsilon_{t+1}^f + Z_{t+1}^f J_{t+1}^f, \tag{4.10}$$

where $\varepsilon_t \sim N\left(0, \sigma_D^2\right), \varepsilon_{t+1}^f, \varepsilon_{t+1}^s \sim \mathcal{N}(0, I), Z_{t+1}^f \sim \Pi^f\left(F_t, \Theta^{\mathbb{P}}\right), Z_{t+1}^s \sim \Pi^s\left(F_t, \Theta^{\mathbb{P}}\right),$ $J_{t+1}^f \sim \text{Ber}\left[\lambda^f\left(X_t, \Theta^{\mathbb{P}}\right)\right],$ and $J_{t+1}^f \sim \text{Ber}\left[\lambda^s\left(F_t, \Theta^{\mathbb{P}}\right)\right].$

Because the shocks, the Brownian increments, jump times and jump sizes, are conditionally independent, once the model is discretized, it is easy to characterize the likelihood and the state dynamics. We define the latent state vector as $X_t = \left(F_{t-1}, Z_t^s, Z_t^f, J_t^s, J_t^f\right),$ which implies that

$$p(Y|X, \Theta) = \prod_{t=1}^{T} p\left(S_t|S_{t-1}, X_t, \Theta^{\mathbb{P}}\right) p(D_t|S_t, F_t, \Theta),$$

where $p\left(S_t|S_{t-1}, X_t, \Theta^{\mathbb{P}}\right)$ and $p(D_t|S_t, F_t, \Theta)$ are multivariate normal distribution. This shows the simple structural form of the model given the time-discretization. It is important to note that $\Theta^{\mathbb{Q}}$ will only appear in the second term, $p(D_t|S_t, X_t, \Theta)$. For example, in the option pricing or term structure examples, the parameters determining the risk neutral behavior of stock prices, stochastic volatility, or interest rates, only appear in the option price or bond yields. The price and state evolutions, as they are observed under $\mathbb{P}$, provide no information regarding the risk-neutral behavior.

The state dynamics are given by $p(X|\Theta)$ that is given by: similarly straightforward.

$$p(X|\Theta) = \prod_{t=1}^{T} p\left(X_t|X_{t-1}, \Theta^{\mathbb{P}}\right),$$

where

$$p\left(X_{t+1}|X_t, \Theta^{\mathbb{P}}\right) = p\left(F_t|F_{t-1}, Z_t^f, J_t^f\right) p\left(Z_{t+1}^f|F_t\right) p\left(J_{t+1}^f|F_t\right) p\left(Z_{t+1}^s|F_t\right) p\left(J_{t+1}^s|F_t\right).$$

The time discretization plays an integral part: it provides a method to analytically compute the likelihood and the state variable evolution.

The previous approximation normalized the discretization interval to unity, but the accuracy of this approximation depends on the length of the interval between observations and the characteristics of the process. In the diffusion case, if the drift and diffusion are constant, the time-discretization is exact. If the time interval between observations is small (e.g., daily) and the drift and diffusion coefficients are smooth functions of the states, the approximation error via the time discretization is also likely small. For example, in a term structure model, Stanton (1997) finds that approximation errors in the conditional moments of the process of certain diffusions is negligible for time intervals up to a month, whereas Eraker et al. (2003) find that time-discretizations of equity prices models with jumps do not introduce any biases in the parameter estimates. As noted by Pritsker (1997, 1998) and Johannes (2004), the sampling variation (due to finite samples) typically dwarfs any discretization bias when data is sampled at reasonably high frequencies such as daily.

In other cases, the simple time discretization may not be accurate. This can occur when the sampling interval is long (weeks or months), or the drift and diffusion coefficients are highly variable functions of the states. In this case, the solution to the difference equation in the time discretization is substantively different than the true solution to SDE in (4.7). When this occurs, it is straightforward to use the Euler scheme to obtain a more accurate characterization of the solution. The idea is to simulate additional states between times t and $t + 1$ at intervals $1/M$ for $M > 1$:

$$S_{t_{j+1}} = S_{t_j} + \mu_s\left(S_{t_j}, F_{t_j}, \Theta^{\mathbb{P}}\right)/M + \sigma_s\left(S_{t_j}, F_{t_j}, \Theta^{\mathbb{P}}\right)\varepsilon_{t_{j+1}}^s + Z_{t_{j+1}}^s J_{t_{j+1}}^s \qquad (4.11)$$

$$F_{t_{j+1}} = F_{t_j} + \mu_f\left(F_{t_j}, \Theta^{\mathbb{P}}\right)/M + \sigma_f\left(F_{t_j}, \Theta^{\mathbb{P}}\right)\varepsilon_{t_{j+1}}^f + Z_{t_{j+1}}^f J_{t_{j+1}}^f, \qquad (4.12)$$

where $t_j = t + \frac{j}{M}$, $\varepsilon_{t_{j+1}}^f, \varepsilon_{t_{j+1}}^s \sim \mathcal{N}(0, M^{-1})$, $Z_{t_{j+1}}^f \sim \Pi^f\left(f_{t_j}, \Theta^{\mathbb{P}}\right)$, $Z_{t_{j+1}}^s \sim \Pi^s\left(F_{t_j}, \Theta^{\mathbb{P}}\right)$, $J_{t_{j+1}}^s \sim \mathrm{Ber}\left[\lambda^s\left(F_{t_j}, \Theta^{\mathbb{P}}\right) M^{-1}\right]$, and $J_{t_{j+1}}^f \sim \mathrm{Ber}\left[\lambda^f\left(F_{t_j}, \Theta^{\mathbb{P}}\right) M^{-1}\right]$.

With the additional simulations, we can augment the original state vector with the intermediate jump times, jump sizes, and f_{t_j}'s to obtain a conditionally normal distribution. Jones (1998), Eraker (2001), Elerian et al. (2001), and Chib et al. (2003) examine various approaches for using time discretizations to estimate continuous-time models using MCMC methods. We refer the interested reader to these papers for further details and examples.

4.3. Parameter Distribution

The final component of the joint posterior distribution is the prior distribution of the parameters, $p(\Theta)$. This represent nonsample information regarding the parameters and one typically chooses a parameterized distribution. This implies that the researcher must choose both a distribution for the prior and the so-called hyperparameters that index the distribution. Through both the choice of distribution and hyperparameters, the researcher can introduce nonsample information or, alternatively, choose to impose little information. In the latter case, an "uninformative" or diffuse prior is one that provides little or no information regarding the location of the parameters.

When possible we recommend using standard conjugate prior distributions, see, for example Raiffa and Schlaifer (1961) or DeGroot (1970). They provide a convenient way of finding closed-form, easy to simulate, conditional posteriors. A conjugate prior is a distribution for which the conditional posterior is the same distribution with different parameters. For example, suppose and random variable Y is normally distributed, $Y_t|\mu, \sigma^2 \sim N(\mu, \sigma^2)$. Assuming a normal prior on μ, $\mu \sim N(a, A)$, the conditional posterior distribution for the mean, $p(\mu|\sigma^2, Y)$, is also normally distributed, $N(a^*, A^*)$, where the starred parameters depend on the data, sample size, and the hyperparameters a and A. In this case, the posterior mean is a weighted combination of the prior mean and the sample information with the weights determined by the relative variances. Choosing A to be very large generates what is commonly referred to as an uninformative prior. Of course, depending on the parameter of interest, no prior can be truly uninformative (Poincare, 1901). For the variance parameter, the inverted gamma distribution is also conjugate. Bernardo and Smith (1995) provide a detailed discussion and list of conjugate priors.

In some cases, researchers may specify a flat prior, which is completely uninformative. For example, in a geometric Brownian motion model of returns, $Y_t \sim N(\mu, \sigma^2)$, it is common to assume a flat prior distribution for the mean by setting $p(\mu, \sigma^2) \propto \sigma^{-1}$. Although a flat prior distribution may represent lack of knowledge, it may also lead to serious computational problems as a flat prior does not integrate to one. For inference, the posterior distribution must be proper, that is $\int_\Theta p(\Theta|Y)\, d\Theta = 1$. In many cases, flat priors can lead to an improper posterior. This is more problematic in state space models where the marginal likelihood, $p(Y|\Theta)$, is unavailable in closed form and where one cannot always check that the propriety of the posterior. In addition, joint posterior propriety is a necessary condition for MCMC algorithms to converge as we discuss later. This implies that another motivation for using diffuse proper priors is a computational tool for implementation via MCMC.

There are often statistical and economic motivations for using informative priors. For example, in many mixture models, priors must at least partially informative to overcome degeneracies in the likelihood. Take, for example, Merton's (1976) jump diffusion model for log-returns $Y_t = \log(S_{t+\Delta}/S_t)$. In this case, returns are given by

$$Y_t = \mu + \sigma(W_{t+\Delta} - W_t) + \sum_{j=N_t}^{N_{t+\Delta}} Z_j$$

and the jump sizes are normally distributed with mean μ_J and variance σ_J^2. As shown by Lindgren (1978), Kiefer (1978), and Honore (1997), the maximum likelihood estimator is not defined as the likelihood takes infinite values from some parameters. This problem does not arise when using an informative prior, as the prior will typically preclude these degeneracies.

Informative priors can also be used to impose stationarity on the state variables. Models of interest rates and stochastic volatility often indicate near-unit-root behavior. In the stochastic volatility model discussed earlier, a very small κ_v introduces near-unit root behavior. For practical applications such as option pricing or portfolio formation, one often wants to impose mean-reversion to guarantee stationarity. This enters via the prior on the speed of mean reversion that imposes that κ_v are positive and are bounded away from zero.

For regime-switching models, the prior distribution $p(\Theta)$ can be used to solve a number of identification problems. First, the labeling problem of identifying the states. The most common way of avoiding this problem is to impose a prior that orders the mean and variance parameters. One practical advantage of MCMC methods are that they can easily handle truncated and ordered parameter spaces, and hence provide a natural approach for regime switching models.

It is increasingly common in many applications to impose economically motivated priors. For example, Pastor and Stambaugh (2000) use the prior to represent an investor's degree of belief over a multifactor model of equity returns. In other cases, an economically motivated prior might impose that risk premium are positive, for example.

Researchers should also perform sensitivity analysis to gauge the impact of prior parameters on the parameter posterior. Occasionally, the posterior for certain parameters may depend critically on the prior choice. As the posterior is just the product of the likelihood and the prior, this only indicates that the likelihood does not provide any information regarding the location of these parameters. One extreme occurs when the parameters are not identified by the likelihood and the posterior is equal to the prior. Regardless, it is important to understand how sensitive the posterior is to modeling assumptions, both in the prior and likelihood.

5. ASSET PRICING APPLICATIONS

In this section, we describe a number of asset pricing models and the associated MCMC algorithms for estimating the parameters and latent states. We first consider equity models where we assume that equity returns and option prices are observed. We consider the Black–Scholes–Merton model, time-varying equity premium models, stochastic volatility models, and multivariate models with jumps. Next, we consider models of interest rates, and consider Gaussian, square-root, and multifactor models. Finally, we discuss general estimation of regime-switching models.

5.1. Equity Asset Pricing Models
5.1.1. Geometric Brownian Motion

The simplest possible asset pricing model is the geometric Brownian specification for an asset price. Here, the price, S_t, solves the familiar SDE

$$d \log(S_t) = \mu dt + \sigma dW_t^{\mathbb{P}},$$

where μ is the continuously-compounded expected return and σ is the volatility. Prices are always recorded at discrete-spaced time intervals, and, for simplicity, we assume they are equally spaced. This model has a closed-form solution for continuously-compounded returns:

$$Y_t = \log(S_t/S_{t-1}) = \mu + \sigma \varepsilon_t,$$

where $\varepsilon_t \sim \mathcal{N}(0, 1)$. The model generates a conditional likelihood for the vector of continuously-compounded returns of

$$p(Y|\mu, \sigma^2) = \left(\frac{1}{\sqrt{2\pi\sigma^2}}\right)^T \exp\left(-\frac{1}{2\sigma^2}\sum_{t=1}^{T}(Y_t - \mu)^2\right),$$

There are no latent variables in this model which implies that the posterior is $p(\Theta|Y) = p(\mu, \sigma^2|Y)$. Under standard prior assumptions, the posterior distribution, $p(\Theta|Y) = p(\mu, \sigma^2|Y)$, is known in closed form. However, to develop intuition, we describe an MCMC approach for sampling from $p(\mu, \sigma^2|Y)$.

The first step is an application of Clifford–Hammersley theorem which implies that $p(\mu|\sigma^2, Y)$ and $p(\sigma^2|\mu, Y)$ are the complete conditionals. Assuming independent priors on μ and σ^2,[7] Bayes rule implies that

$$p(\mu|\sigma^2, Y) \propto p(Y|\mu, \sigma^2) p(\mu)$$
$$p(\sigma^2|\mu, Y) \propto p(Y|\mu, \sigma^2) p(\sigma^2),$$

---

[7] Alternatively, one could use dependent conditional conjugate priors such as $p(\mu, \sigma^2) = p(\mu|\sigma^2)p(\sigma^2)$. In this model, the $p(\mu|\sigma^2)$ is normal and $p(\sigma^2)$ is inverted gamma. Later, we discuss the multivariate version of this, the normal-inverted Wishart prior that leads to a joint posterior for μ and σ^2 which can be directly sampled.

where $p(\mu)$ and $p(\sigma^2)$ are the priors. Assuming a normal prior for μ, $p(\mu) \sim \mathcal{N}$, and an inverted gamma prior for σ^2, $p(\sigma^2) \sim \mathcal{IG}$,[8] the posteriors are conjugate, which means that $p(\mu|\sigma^2, Y)$ is normal and $p(\sigma^2|\mu, Y)$ is inverse Gamma. The MCMC algorithm consists of the following steps: given $\mu^{(g)}$ and $(\sigma^2)^{(g)}$

$$\mu^{(g+1)} \sim p\left(\mu|\, (\sigma^2)^{(g)}, Y\right) \sim \mathcal{N}$$

$$(\sigma^2)^{(g+1)} \sim p\left(\sigma^2|\mu^{(g+1)}, Y\right) \sim \mathcal{IG},$$

where the arguments of the normal and inverted gamma distributions are easy to derive. Both of these distributions can be directly sampled, thus the MCMC algorithm is a Gibbs sampler. Iterating, this algorithm produces a sample $\left\{\mu^{(g)}, (\sigma^2)^{(g)}\right\}_{g=1}^{G}$ from the posterior $p(\mu, \sigma^2|Y)$.

This simple example previews the general approach to MCMC estimation:

Step 1   :   Write out the price dynamics and state evolution in state space form;

Step 2   :   Characterize the joint distribution by its complete conditionals

Step 3   :   Use random sampling to generate draws from the joint posterior

5.1.2. Black–Scholes
In many cases, option prices are also observed. If the underlying follows a geometric Brownian motion, the Black–Scholes (1973) formula implies that the price of a call option struck at K is given by

$$C_t = \mathrm{BS}(\sigma, S_t) = S_t N(d_1) - e^{r(T-t)} K N\left(d_1 - \sigma\sqrt{T-t}\right),$$

where

$$d_1 = \frac{\log(S_t/K) + \left(r + \sigma^2/2\right)(T-t)}{\sigma\sqrt{T-t}},$$

and we assume the continuously-compounded interest rate is known. The addition of option prices generates only minor alterations to the MCMC algorithm of the previous section. Our analysis follows and is a special case of Polson and Stroud (2002) and Eraker (2003) who allow for stochastic volatility, jumps in returns, and jumps in volatility.

---

[8]The inverted gamma distribution is a common prior for a variance parameter. The inverted gamma distribution, $\mathcal{IG}(\alpha, \beta)$, has support on the positive real line and the density is given by $f(x|\alpha, \beta) = \beta^\alpha x^{-\alpha-1} e^{-\beta/x}/\Gamma(\alpha)$.

Jacquier and Jarrow (2000) provide a detailed analysis in the context of the Black–Scholes model.

The first thing to notice about the model is the stochastic singularity: if a single option price is observed without error, volatility can be inverted from the price. To break this singularity, we assume that option prices are observed with a normally distributed error. This implies the following state space model is

$$\log(S_t/S_{t-1}) = \mu + \sigma\varepsilon_t$$
$$C_t = BS(\sigma, S_t) + \varepsilon_t^c,$$

where $\varepsilon_t \sim \mathcal{N}(0,1)$ and $\varepsilon_t^c \sim \mathcal{N}(0, \sigma_c^2)$. This state space model is conditionally normal, but nonlinear in the parameters as $BS(\sigma, S_t)$ is not known analytically.

When analyzing this model, it is important to recognize the importance of the pricing errors, as Jacquier and Jarrow (2000) thoroughly demonstrate. Because both returns and option prices provide information about volatility, the structure of the pricing errors strongly influences the relative weighting of these sources of information when estimating σ. In particular, important assumptions include the the functional form (absolute vs relative pricing errors), correlation structure across different option strikes and maturities, and autocorrelation. These assumptions can be viewed similar to the choice of an objective function, when calibrating option pricing models. We use this structure here for exposition, and refer the interested reader to Jacquier and Jarrow (2000) for details.

The joint likelihood function is the product of the equity return likelihood, $p(S|\mu, \sigma^2)$, and the option likelihood, $p(C|S, \mu, \sigma^2, \sigma_c^2)$:

$$p(S, C|\mu, \sigma^2, \sigma_c^2) = \prod_{t=1}^{T} p(C_t|S_t, \sigma^2, \sigma_c^2)\, p(\log(S_t/S_{t-1})\,|\mu, \sigma^2).$$

Here $S = (S_1, \ldots, S_T)$ and $C = (C_1, \ldots, C_T)$ are the vector with the underlying and option prices. The equity return portion of the likelihood is the same as in previous section. The option price component of the likelihood is given by

$$p(C_t|S_t, \sigma^2, \sigma_c^2) \propto \exp\left(-\frac{1}{2\sigma_c^2}(C_t - BS(\sigma, S_t))^2\right).$$

Notice that the distribution of the option prices conditional on S_t, σ^2, and σ_c^2 is independent of μ and the distribution of the stock returns is independent of σ_c.

The MCMC algorithm samples from the joint posterior, $p(\mu, \sigma^2, \sigma_c^2|S, C)$. The complete conditionals are $p(\mu|\sigma^2, S)$, $p(\sigma^2|\mu, \sigma_c^2, S, C)$, and $p(\sigma_c^2|\sigma^2, S, C)$. Assuming the independent priors, $p(\mu) \sim \mathcal{N}, p(\sigma^2) \sim \mathcal{IG}$ and $p(\sigma_c^2) \sim \mathcal{IG}$, the conditional posteriors for μ and σ_c^2 are conjugate. Because of the option pricing formula, $p(\sigma^2|\mu, \sigma_c^2, S, C)$ is not a known distribution and the Metropolis–Hastings algorithm will be used to update σ^2. The MCMC algorithm cycles through the conditionals:

$$\mu^{(g+1)} \sim p\left(\mu | (\sigma^2)^{(g)}, S\right) \sim \mathcal{N}$$

$$\left(\sigma_c^2\right)^{(g+1)} \sim p\left(\sigma_c^2 | (\sigma^2)^{(g)}, S, C\right) \sim \mathcal{IG}$$

$$\left(\sigma^2\right)^{(g+1)} \sim p\left(\sigma^2 | \mu^{(g+1)}, \left(\sigma_c^2\right)^{(g+1)}, S, C\right) : \text{Metropolis.}$$

There are a number of alternatives for the Metropolis step. By Bayes rule, the conditional posterior for σ is

$$\pi(\sigma^2) \triangleq p(\sigma^2 | \mu, C, S) \propto p(C | \sigma^2, S) \, p(S | \mu, \sigma^2) \, p(\sigma^2),$$

which clearly shows how both the returns and the option prices contain information about σ^2. Because $BS(\sigma, S_t)$ is given as an integral, it is not possible to sample directly from $p(\sigma^2 | \mu, \sigma_c^2, S, Y)$ since $BS(\sigma, S_t)$ is not known distribution as a function of σ. One approach is to use independence Metropolis. In this case, the algorithm proposes using the data from the returns, $p(\sigma^2 | S, \mu)$, and then accepts/rejects based on the information contained in the option prices. Specifically, consider a proposal of the form

$$q(\sigma^2) = p(\sigma^2 | \mu, S) \propto p(S | \mu, \sigma^2) \, p(\sigma^2) \sim \mathcal{IG}.$$

The Metropolis algorithm is

$$\text{Step 1 : Draw } (\sigma^2)^{(g+1)} \text{ from } q(\sigma^2) \sim \mathcal{IG} \tag{5.1}$$

$$\text{Step 2 : Accept } (\sigma^2)^{(g+1)} \text{ with probability } \alpha\left((\sigma^2)^{(g+1)}, (\sigma^2)^{(g)}\right) \tag{5.2}$$

where

$$\alpha\left((\sigma^2)^{(g)}, (\sigma^2)^{(g+1)}\right) = \min\left(\frac{p\left(C | (\sigma^2)^{(g+1)}, S\right)}{p\left(C | (\sigma^2)^{(g)}, S\right)}, 1\right).$$

As the Black–Scholes price is always bounded by the underlying price, $BS(\sigma, S_t) \leq S_t$, so the tail behavior of $\pi(\sigma^2)$ is determined by the likelihood component.

In practice, this algorithm is susceptible to two common problems mentioned earlier. First, option prices often embed volatility or jump risk premiums that implies that Black–Scholes implied volatility is generally higher than historical volatility. In fact, for the period from 1997 to 2002, Black–Scholes implied volatility as measured by the VIX index has averaged about 30%, while the underlying volatility is about 18%. In this case, the target may be located to the right of the proposal, as historical volatility is lower than implied volatility. This would result in very low acceptance probabilities. Of course, this is not a problem with MCMC per se but is due to a misspecified model. Second, option prices are likely to be more informative about volatility than historical returns. This implies that the target will have lower variance than the proposal. The proposal will generate large moves that will often be rejected by the Metropolis algorithm, again, potentially generating a slowly moving chain. An alternative to the independence algorithm is to use a random-walk Metropolis algorithm with a fat-tailed innovation such as a t-distribution. The variance can be tuned to insure that the acceptance rates are sufficiently high. In many cases this is an attractive alternative. As mentioned in Section 2.5, it is important to implement multiple algorithms and choose one appropriate for the problem at hand.

5.1.3. A Multivariate Version of Merton's Model

Consider an extension of the geometric model: a multivariate version of Merton (1976) jump-diffusion model. Here a K–vector of asset prices solves

$$\mathrm{d}S_t = \mu S_t \mathrm{d}t + \sigma S_t \mathrm{d}W_t^{\mathbb{P}} + \mathrm{d}\left(\sum_{j=1}^{N_t^{\mathbb{P}}} S_{\tau_{j-}}\left(\mathrm{e}^{Z_j^{\mathbb{P}}} - 1\right)\right),$$

where $W_t(\mathbb{P})$ is a vector standard Brownian motion, $\Sigma = \sigma\sigma'$ is the diffusion matrix, $N_t(\mathbb{P})$ is a Poisson process with constant intensity λ and the jump sizes, $Z_j \in R^K$ are multivariate normal with mean μ_J and variance–covariance matrix Σ_J. This model assumes the prices have common jumps with correlated sizes, although it is easy to add an additional jump process to characterize idiosyncratic jumps.

Solving this SDE, continuously compounded equity returns over a daily interval ($\Delta = 1$) are

$$\log(S_t/S_{t-1}) = \mu + \sigma\left(W_{t+1}^{\mathbb{P}} - W_t^{\mathbb{P}}\right) + \sum_{j=N_t^{\mathbb{P}}+1}^{N_{t+1}^{\mathbb{P}}} Z_j(\mathbb{P}),$$

where, again, we have redefined the drift vector to account for the variance correction. We time discretize the jump component assuming that at most a single jump can occur over each time interval:

$$Y_t \equiv \log(S_t/S_{t-1}) = \mu + \sigma\varepsilon_t + J_t Z_t$$

where $\mathbb{P}[J_t = 1] = \lambda \in (0, 1)$ and the jump sizes retain their structure. Johannes et al. (1999) document that, in the univariate case, the effect of time-discretization in the Poisson arrivals is minimal, as jumps are rare events. To see why, suppose the jump intensity (scaled to daily units) is $\lambda = 0.05$. Since

$$\text{Prob}\left[N_{t+1}^{\mathbb{P}} - N_t^{\mathbb{P}} = j\right] = \frac{e^{-\lambda}\lambda^j}{j!}$$

the probability of two or more jumps occurring over a daily interval is approximately 0.0012 or one-tenth of 1%, which is why the discretization bias is likely to be negligible.

The MCMC algorithm samples from $p(\Theta, X|Y)$, where $\Theta = (\mu, \Sigma, \lambda, \mu_J, \Sigma_J)$ and $X = (J, Z)$, where J, Z, and Y are vectors of jump times, jump sizes, and observed prices. Returns are independent through time, which implies that the full-information likelihood is a product of multivariate normals,

$$p(Y|\Theta, J, Z) = \prod_{t=1}^{T} p(Y_t|\Theta, J_t, Z_t),$$

where

$$p(Y_t|J_t, Z_t, \Theta) \propto |\Sigma|^{-\frac{1}{2}} \exp\left\{-\frac{1}{2}(Y_t - \mu - Z_tJ_t)' \Sigma^{-1} (Y_t - \mu - Z_tJ_t)\right\}.$$

In contrast, the observed likelihood, $p(Y_t|\Theta)$, integrates out Z_t and J_t and is a mixture of multivariate normal distributions. Discrete mixture distributions introduce a number of problems. For example, in the univariate case, it is well known that the observed likelihood has degeneracies as certain parameter values lead an infinite likelihood. Multivariate mixtures are even more complicated and direct maximum likelihood is rarely attempted.

For the parameters, Clifford–Hammersley implies that $p(\mu, \Sigma|J, Z, Y)$, $p(\mu_J, \Sigma_J|J, Z)$, and $p(\lambda|J)$ characterize $p(\Theta|X, Y)$. For the states, $p(Z_t|\Theta, J_t, Y_t)$ and $p(J_t|\Theta, Z_t, Y_t)$ for $t = 1, \ldots, T$ characterize $p(J, Z|\Theta, Y)$. Assuming standard conjugate prior distributions for the parameters, $\mu \sim \mathcal{N}$, $\Sigma \sim \mathcal{IW}$, $\mu_J \sim \mathcal{N}$, $\Sigma_J \sim \mathcal{IW}$, and $\lambda \sim \mathcal{B}$, where $\mathcal{IW}$ is an inverted Wishart (multivariate inverted gamma) and $\mathcal{B}$ is the beta distribution,[9] all of the conditional parameter posteriors are conjugate. We make one adjustment allowing for certain parameters to have conditional priors. We assume that Σ and Σ_J have $\mathcal{IW}$ priors, but that $\mu|\Sigma \sim \mathcal{N}(a, b\Sigma)$ and $\mu_J|\Sigma_J \sim \mathcal{N}(a_J, b_J\Sigma_J)$. This allows us to draw (μ, Σ) and (μ_J, Σ_J) in blocks. Because these parameters are

---

[9]An $n \times n$ matrix Σ has an inverse Wishart distribution, denoted $\mathcal{W}^{-1}(a, A)$, with scaler parameter $a > 0$ and matrix parameter A positive definite, its density is given by:

$$p(\Sigma|a, b) = |A|^{\frac{(a-n-1)}{2}} |\Sigma|^{-\frac{a}{2}} \exp\left(-\frac{1}{2}tr\left(\Sigma^{-1}B\right)\right).$$

The beta distribution, $\mathcal{B}(\alpha, \beta)$ for $\alpha, \beta > 0$, has support over the unit interval and its density is given by

$$p(x|\alpha, \beta) = \frac{\Gamma(\alpha + \beta)}{\Gamma(\alpha)\,\Gamma(\beta)} x^{\alpha-1}(1 - x)^{\beta-1}.$$

likely to be correlated, this will improve the efficiency of the MCMC algorithm. We now derive conditional posteriors for λ, J_t, and Z_t.

The posterior for λ is conjugate and is given by Bayes rule as

$$p(\lambda|J) \propto p(J|\lambda)\,p(\lambda) \propto \left[\lambda^{\sum_{t=1}^{T} J_t}(1-\lambda)^{T-\sum_{t=1}^{T} J_t}\right]\lambda^{\alpha-1}(1-\lambda)^{\beta-1} \sim \mathcal{B}(\alpha^*,\beta^*)$$

where $p(\lambda) = \mathcal{B}(\alpha,\beta)$, $\alpha^* = \sum_{t=1}^{T} J_t + \alpha$ and $\beta^* = T - \sum_{t=1}^{T} J_t + \beta$. The conditional posterior for Z_t is normal:

$$p(Z_t|Y_t,J_t,\Theta) \propto \exp\left(-\frac{1}{2}\left[r_t'\Sigma^{-1}r_t + (Z_t - \mu_Z)'\,\Sigma_J^{-1}(Z_t - \mu_Z)\right]\right)$$

$$\propto \exp\left(-\frac{1}{2}(Z_t - m_t)'\,V_t^{-1}(Z_t - m_t)\right),$$

where $r_t = Y_t - \mu - Z_t J_t$ and

$$V_t = \left(J_t\Sigma^{-1} + \Sigma_J^{-1}\right)^{-1}$$

$$m_t = \Sigma_J^{-1}\left(J_t\Sigma^{-1}(Y_t - \mu) + \Sigma_J^{-1}\mu_Z\right).$$

For the jump times, the conditional posterior is Bernoulli since J_t can only take two values. The Bernoulli probability is

$$p(J_t = 1|\Theta, Z_t, Y_t) \propto p(Y_t|J_t = 1, \Theta, Z_t)\,p(J_t = 1|\Theta)$$

$$\propto \lambda\exp\left(-\frac{1}{2}(Y_t - \mu - Z_t)'\,\Sigma^{-1}(Y_t - \mu - Z_t)\right).$$

Computing $p(J_t = 0|\Theta, Z_t, Y_t)$ then provides the Bernoulli probability. This completes the specification of our MCMC algorithm. The arguments by Rosenthal (1995a,b) show that the algorithm is in fact polynomial time convergent, and thus, converges quickly.

As all of the conditional posteriors can be directly sampled, the MCMC algorithm is a Gibbs sampler iteratively drawing from

$$p(\mu, \Sigma|J, Z, Y) \sim \mathcal{N}/\mathcal{IW}$$

$$p(\mu_J, \Sigma_J|J, Z) \sim \mathcal{N}/\mathcal{IW}$$

$$p(\lambda|J) \sim \mathcal{B}$$

$$p(Z_t|\Theta, J_t, Y_t) \sim \mathcal{N}$$

$$p(J_t|\Theta, Z_t, Y_t) \sim \mathrm{Ber}$$

where $\mathcal{N}/\mathcal{IW}$ is the normal-inverted Wishart joint distribution. Sampling from this distribution requires two steps but it is standard (see, for example, Bernardo and Smith, 1995).

To illustrate the methodology, consider a bivariate jump–diffusion model for S&P 500 and Nasdaq 100 equity index returns from 1986 to 2000. The model is a lower dimensional version of those considered in the work of Duffie and Pan (1999) and it is given by

$$\begin{pmatrix} Y_t^1 \\ Y_t^2 \end{pmatrix} = \begin{pmatrix} \mu_1 \\ \mu_2 \end{pmatrix} + \begin{pmatrix} \sigma_1 & \sigma_{12} \\ \sigma_{12} & \sigma_{22} \end{pmatrix}^{1/2} \begin{pmatrix} \varepsilon_t^1 \\ \varepsilon_t^2 \end{pmatrix} + J_t \begin{pmatrix} Z_t^1 \\ Z_t^2 \end{pmatrix},$$

where $\Sigma = \sigma\sigma'$, $Z_t = [Z_t^1, Z_t^2]' \sim N(\mu_J, \Sigma_J)$ and the jump arrivals, common to both returns, have constant intensity λ.

We run the Gibbs sampler for 1250 iterations and discard the first 250 as a burn-in period, using the last 1000 draws to summarize the posterior distribution. Table 13.1 provides the prior mean and standard deviation and the posterior mean, standard deviation and a $(5, 95)\%$ credible set. The prior on λ is informative, in the sense that it specifies that jumps are rare events. Our prior represents our belief that the variance of jump sizes is larger than the daily diffusive variance. For all parameters, the data is very informative as the posterior standard deviation is much smaller than the prior indicating that the parameters are easily learned from the data. This should not be a surprise as returns in the model are i.i.d. Figure 13.2 provides parameter trace plots and shows how, after burn-in, the Gibbs sampler moves around the posterior distribution.

Table 13.1   Parameter estimates for the bivariate jump-diffusion model for daily S&P 500 and Nasdaq 100 returns from 1986 to 2000

	Prior		Posterior		
	Mean	Std	Mean	Std	(5,95)% Credible set
μ_1	0	$\sqrt{1000}$	0.1417	0.0229	0.1065, 0.1797
μ_2	0	$\sqrt{1000}$	0.0839	0.0148	0.0589, 0.1082
σ_1	1.7770	0.9155	1.2073	0.0191	1.1778, 1.2396
σ_2	1.7770	0.9155	0.7236	0.0369	0.6903, 0.7599
ρ	0	0.1713	0.6509	0.0115	0.6317, 0.6690
λ	0.0476	0.0147	0.0799	0.0081	0.0663, 0.0933
$\mu_{1,J}$	0	$\sqrt{1000}$	-0.5747	0.2131	$-0.9320, -0.2351$
$\mu_{2,J}$	0	$\sqrt{1000}$	-0.3460	0.1765	$-0.6537, -0.0648$
$\sigma_{1,J}$	2.1113	1.1715	2.9666	0.1647	2.7073, 3.2435
$\sigma_{2,J}$	2.1113	1.1715	2.5873	0.1458	2.3540, 2.8233
ρ_J	0	0.1519	0.5190	0.0490	0.4360, 0.5986

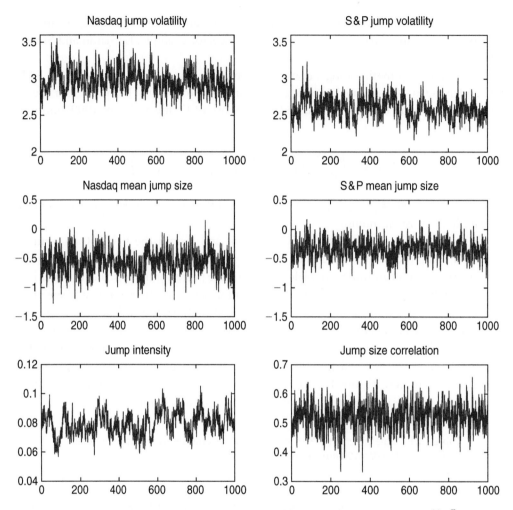

Figure 13.2   Parameter trace plots for the jump parameters. Each panel shows $\left\{\Theta^{(g)}\right\}_{g=1}^{G}$ for the individual parameters.

Figure 13.3 provides Monte Carlo estimates of the jump sizes in returns $(Z_t J_t)$. Because the model has constant volatility, there are periods when jumps are clustered which is clearly capturing time-variation in volatility that the model does not have built in. We address this issue later by introducing time-varying and stochastic volatility.

5.1.4. Time-Varying Equity Premium

The Black–Scholes model assumes that μ and σ are constant. Extensions of the Black–Scholes model allow these parameters to vary over time. In the case of the expected return,

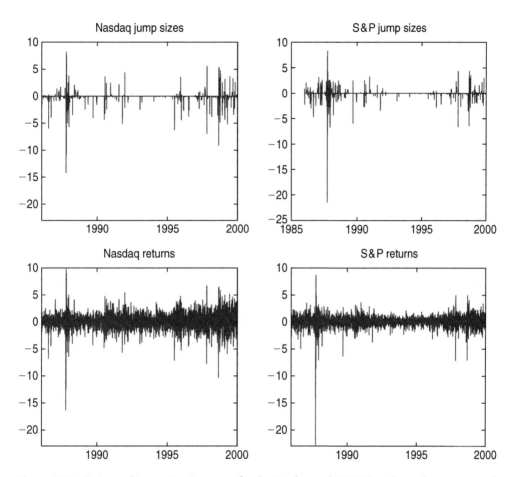

Figure 13.3   Estimated jump sizes in returns for the Nasdaq and S&P 500 and actual returns over the same period.

a straightforward extension posits that the continuously compounded equity premium, μ_t, is time-varying:

$$\frac{\mathrm{d}S_t}{S_t} = \left[r_t + \mu_t + \frac{1}{2}\sigma^2 \right] \mathrm{d}t + \sigma \mathrm{d}W_t^s(\mathbb{P}),$$

where r_t is the spot rate, the equity premium solves

$$\mathrm{d}\mu_t = \kappa_\mu \big(\theta_\mu - \mu_t \big) \, \mathrm{d}t + \sigma_\mu \mathrm{d}W_t^\mu(\mathbb{P})$$

and the Brownian motions could be correlated. The mean-reverting specification for expected returns is popular in the portfolio choice literature and was introduced by

Merton (1971) and recently used by Kim and Omberg (1996), Liu (1999), and Wachter (2000). Brandt and Kang (2000) and Johannes et al. (2001) provide empirical analyses of this model.

Solving the SDE, the increments of μ_t are

$$\mu_t = \mu_{t-1}e^{-\kappa_\mu} + \theta_\mu\left(1 - e^{-\kappa_\mu}\right) + \sigma_\mu \int_{t-1}^{t} e^{-\kappa_\mu(t-s)}\,dW_s^\mu(\mathbb{P})$$

and the model is a discrete-time AR(1):

$$\mu_t = \alpha_\mu + \beta_\mu\mu_{t-1} + \sigma_\mu\varepsilon_t^\mu,$$

where $\alpha_\mu = \theta_\mu\left(1 - e^{-\kappa_\mu}\right)$, $\beta_\mu = e^{-\kappa_\mu}$ and we have redefined σ_μ. The state space form is

$$Y_t = \mu_t + \sigma\varepsilon_t^s$$
$$\mu_t = \alpha_\mu + \beta_\mu\mu_{t-1} + \sigma_\mu\varepsilon_t^\mu,$$

where $Y_t = \log\left(\frac{S_t}{S_{t-1}}\right) - \int_{t-1}^{t} r_s ds$ are excess returns. The parameters are $\Theta = \{\alpha_\mu, \beta_\mu, \sigma_\mu, \sigma\}$, the state variables are $X = \mu = \{\mu_t\}_{t=1}^{T}$, and the posterior distribution is $p(\Theta, \mu|Y)$. Clifford–Hammersley implies that $p(\alpha_\mu, \beta_\mu, \sigma_\mu^2, \sigma^2|\mu, Y)$ and $p(\mu|\alpha_\mu, \beta_\mu, \sigma_\mu^2, \sigma^2, Y)$ are complete conditionals. Assuming normal-inverted Wishart priors conditional priors for the parameters, the parameters can be updated as a single block.

Drawing from $p(\mu|Y, \alpha, \beta, \sigma_v^2)$, a T-dimensional distribution, might appear to be difficult. However, it is possible to use the Kalman filter to obtain this density via the forward-filtering backward sampling (FFBS) algorithm described in Carter and Kohn (1993) and Fruhwirth–Schnatter (1994). This generates the following Gibbs sampler:

$$p(\alpha_\mu, \beta_\mu, \sigma_\mu^2, \sigma^2|\mu, Y) \sim \mathcal{N}/\mathcal{IG}$$
$$p(\mu|\alpha_\mu, \beta_\mu, \sigma_\mu^2, \sigma^2, Y)\ :\ \text{FFBS}.$$

The mechanics of the FFBS algorithm are quite simple. Consider the following decomposition of the joint expected returns posterior:

$$p(\mu|Y, \Theta) \propto p(\mu_T|Y, \Theta) \prod_{t=0}^{T-1} p(\mu_t|\mu_{t+1}, Y^t, \Theta),$$

where $Y^t = [Y_1, \ldots, Y_t]$. To simulate from $p(\mu|Y, \Theta)$, consider the following procedure:

Step 1. Run the Kalman filter for $t = 1, \ldots, T$ to get the moments of $p(\mu_t|Y^t, \Theta)$

Step 2. Sample the last state from $\widehat{\mu}_T \sim p(\mu_T|Y^T, \Theta)$

Step 3. Sample backward through time: $\widehat{\mu}_t \sim p(\mu_t|\widehat{\mu}_{t+1}, Y^t, \Theta)$

The first step is the usual Kalman filtering algorithm (forward filtering) and then the last two steps move backward to unwind the conditioning information (backward sampling). Anderson and Moore (1979, p. 105) and Carter and Kohn (1994, Appendix 1) show that the samples $(\widehat{\mu}_1, \ldots, \widehat{\mu}_T)$ are a direct block draw from $p(\mu|Y, \Theta)$. It is important to recognize that the Kalman filter is just one part of the MCMC algorithm, and the other step (parameter updating) indicates that the algorithm accounts for parameter uncertainty.

To get a sense of some empirical results, we estimate the model aforementioned using S&P 500 returns and Nasdaq 100 returns from 1973 to 2000 and 1987 to 2000, respectively, and report summary statistics of $p(\mu_t|Y)$ over the common period from 1987 to 2000. Figure 13.4 provides posterior estimates of μ_t, $E[\mu_t|Y]$, and 95% confidence bands. Note that the MCMC algorithm provides the entire distribution of the states taking into account estimation risk. Not surprisingly, the risk present in estimating μ_t is quite large. In fact, for many periods of time, the confidence band includes zero, which shows that there is often not a statistically significant equity premium, although the point estimate of the equity premium $E[\mu_t|Y]$ is positive.

Time-Varying Parameter Models   The MCMC algorithm above applies in a slightly modified form to more general time-varying parameter models. Consider the more general setting of Xia (2001):

$$\frac{dS_t}{S_t} = \left[\alpha_t + \beta'_t X_t + \frac{1}{2}\sigma^2\right] dt + \sigma dW_t^s(\mathbb{P}),$$

where the equity premium is $\mu_t = \alpha_t + \beta'_t X_t$, X_t is a vector of predictor variables, and (α_t, β_t) are time-varying coefficients. Xia (2001) assumes they jointly solve

$$d\beta_t = \kappa_\beta(\theta_\beta - \beta_t)\,dt + \sigma_\beta dW_t^\beta(\mathbb{P})$$
$$dX_t = \kappa_x(\theta_x - X_t)\,dt + \sigma_x dW_t^x(\mathbb{P}),$$

where all Brownian motions can be correlated. In discrete-time, this model takes the form of a linear, Gaussian state-space model. The conditional posteriors for the parameters are

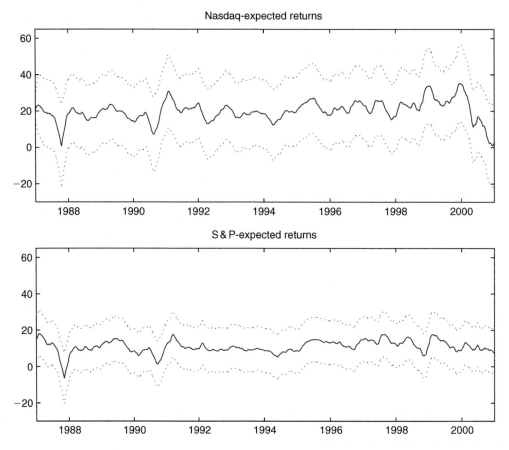

Figure 13.4   Smoothed expected return paths (with confidence bands) for the S&P 500 and Nasdaq 100 from 1987 to 2001.

all standard, while the conditional posterior for the latent variables, α_t and β_t, can be obtained via the FFBS algorithm mentioned earlier.

Merton's Model of Defaultable Debt   The methods in the previous section can be easily adapted to handle Merton's (1974) model of defaultable debt. In this model, a firm has assets with a market value of A_t and has outstanding bond obligations equal to a zero coupon bond expiring at time T with par value B. Equity holders, as residual claimants, receive any excess value over that which is given to the bond holders, that is, at time T the equity holders receive $(A_T - B)_+$. In this case, standard arguments imply that the value of equity, S_t, is given by $S_t = E^Q\left[e^{-\kappa(T-t)}(A_T - B)_+ |A_t\right]$.

Given this, the state space representation for structural models of default implies that

$$S_t = E_t^{\mathbb{Q}}\left[e^{-r(T-t)}(A_T - B)_+ \,|A_t\right]$$

$$dA_t = \mu A_t dt + \sigma A_t dW_t.$$

In the case of geometric Brownian motion for the firm value, the equity price is given by the Black–Scholes formula. It is also important to remember that, from the econometrician's perspective, the firm value, A_t, is an unobserved state variable and estimating it is one of the primary objectives. A time-discretization of this model leads to a combination of the Black–Scholes option pricing model and a time-varying parameter model. Korteweg and Polson (2007) develop MCMC algorithms to estimate these models and investigate the empirics.

5.1.5. Log-Stochastic Volatility Models

Stochastic volatility models are one of the most successful applications of MCMC methods. A wide range of stochastic volatility models appear in the literature, and they all present difficulties for estimation as they are non-Gaussian and nonlinear state space models. We consider a number of different stochastic volatility models: the log-stochastic volatility model, a model incorporating the leverage effect, Heston (1993) square-root stochastic volatility model, and the double-jump model by Duffie et al. (2000).

Log-Volatility   The log-stochastic volatility is arguably the most popular specification for modeling stochastic volatility. In this model, volatility solves a continuous-time AR(1):

$$d\log(S_t) = \mu_t dt + \sqrt{V_t} dW_t^s$$

$$d\log(V_{t+1}) = \kappa_v\big(\theta_v - \log(V_t)\big)\,dt + \sigma_v dW_t^v,$$

where, for simplicity, we assume that the Brownian motions are independent, although this assumption was relaxed by Jacquier et al. (2004). To abstract from conditional mean dynamics, set $\mu_t = 0$. An Euler time discretization implies that

$$Y_t = \sqrt{V_{t-1}}\varepsilon_t^s$$

$$\log(V_t) = \alpha_v + \beta_v \log(V_{t-1}) + \sigma_v \varepsilon_t^v,$$

where Y_t is the continuously compounded returns, $\alpha_v = \kappa_v\theta_v$ and $\beta_v = 1 - \kappa_v$. This reparameterization allows us to use standard conjugate updating theory for the parameters. Define the parameter and state vectors as $\Theta = \{\alpha_v, \beta_v, \sigma_v^2\}$ and $X = V = \{V_t\}_{t=1}^T$.

Jacquier et al. (1994) were the first to use MCMC methods to analyze this model, and since then, there have a been a number of important alternative MCMC algorithms proposed. The Clifford–Hammersley theorem implies that $p(\Theta, V|Y)$ is completely characterized by $p(\alpha_v, \beta_v|\sigma_v, V, Y), p(\sigma_v^2|\alpha_v, \beta_v, V, Y)$, and $p(V|\alpha_v, \beta_v, \sigma_v^2, Y)$. Jacquier et al. (1994) assume conjugate priors for the parameters, $\alpha_v, \beta_v \sim \mathcal{N}$ and $\sigma_v^2 \sim \mathcal{IG}$, which implies that

$$p(\alpha_v, \beta_v|\sigma_v, V, Y) \propto \prod_{t=1}^T p(V_t|V_{t-1}, \alpha_v, \beta_v, \sigma_v)\, p(\alpha_v, \beta_v) \sim \mathcal{N}$$

and for σ_v, we have that

$$p(\sigma_v^2|\alpha_v, \beta_v, V, Y) \propto \prod_{t=1}^T p(V_t|V_{t-1}, \alpha_v, \beta_v, \sigma_v)\, p(\sigma_v^2) \sim \mathcal{IG}.$$

The only difficult step arises in updating the volatility states. The full joint posterior for volatility is

$$p(V|\Theta, Y) \propto p(Y|\Theta, V)\, p(V|\Theta) \propto \prod_{t=1}^T p(Y_t|V_t, \Theta)\, p(V_t|V_{t-1}, \Theta)$$

since $p(Y|\Theta, V) = \prod_{t=1}^T p(Y_t|V_t, \Theta)$ and $p(V|\Theta) \propto \prod_{t=1}^T p(V_t|V_{t-1}, \Theta)$, by the conditional independence and Markov property, respectively. Now the complete conditional are given by $p(V_t|V_{(-t)}, \Theta, Y) = p(V_t|V_{t-1}, V_{t+1}, \Theta, Y)$ by the Markov property: conditional on Y, V_t is only influenced by its local neighbors. By Bayes rule, the conditional is

$$p(V_t|V_{t-1}, V_{t+1}, \Theta, Y) \propto p(V_{t-1}, V_t, V_{t+1}|\Theta, Y)$$
$$\propto p(Y_t|V_t, \Theta)\, p(V_{t-1}, V_t, V_{t+1}|\Theta)$$
$$\propto p(Y_t|V_t, \Theta)\, p(V_t|V_{t-1}, \Theta)\, p(V_{t+1}|V_t, \Theta),$$

where all terms not directly involving V_t are removed. As a function of V_t, the conditional variance posterior is quite complicated:

$$p(V_t|V_{t-1}, V_{t+1}, \Theta, Y) \propto V_t^{-\frac{1}{2}} \exp\left(-\frac{Y_t^2}{2V_t}\right) \exp\left(-\frac{e_t^2}{2\sigma_v^2}\right) V_t^{-1} \exp\left(-\frac{e_{t+1}^2}{2\sigma_v^2}\right),$$

where $e_t = \log(V_t) - \alpha_v - \beta_v \log(V_{t-1})$. Note that V_t enters in four different places. As this distribution is not recognizable, Metropolis–Hastings is required to sample from it.

We first consider a "single-state" Metropolis updating scheme as the joint volatility posterior, $p(V|\Theta, Y)$, cannot directly drawn from without approximations. The MCMC algorithm therefore consists of the following steps:

$$p(\alpha_v, \beta_v|\sigma_v, V, Y) \sim \mathcal{N}$$
$$p(\sigma_v^2|\alpha_v, \beta_v, V, Y) \sim \mathcal{IG}$$
$$p(V_t|V_{t-1}, V_{t+1}, \Theta, Y) \ : \ \text{Metropolis}$$

Jacquier et al. use an independence Metropolis–Hastings algorithm to update the states. This is preferable to a random-walk algorithm because we can closely approximate conditional distribution, $p(V_t|V_{t-1}, V_{t+1}, \Theta, Y)$, especially in the tails. The proposal density is a Gamma proposal density motivated by the observation that the first term in the posterior is an inverse Gamma and the second log-normal term can be approximated (particularly in the tails) by a suitable chosen inverse Gamma. If we refer to the proposal density as $q(V_t)$ and the true conditional density as $\pi(V_t) \triangleq p(V_t|V_{t-1}, V_{t+1}, \Theta, Y)$, this implies the Metropolis–Hastings step is given by:

Step 1. Draw $V_t^{(g+1)}$ from $q(V_t)$

Step 2. Accept $V_t^{(g+1)}$ with probability $\alpha\left(V_t^{(g+1)}, V_t^{(g)}\right)$

where

$$\alpha\left(V_t^{(g)}, V_t^{(g+1)}\right) = \min\left(\frac{\pi\left(V_t^{(g+1)}\right) q\left(V_t^{(g)}\right)}{\pi\left(V_t^{(g)}\right) q\left(V_t^{(g+1)}\right)}\right).$$

As shown by Jacquier et al. (1994) using simulations, this algorithm provides accurate inference. Given that the gamma distribution bounds the tails of the true conditional density, the algorithm is geometrically convergent.

Figure 13.2 provides posterior means, $E(V_t|Y)$, of the latent volatility states with (5,95)% credible sets for the S&P 500 and Nasdaq 100. These are smoothed volatility estimates, as opposed to filtered volatility estimates, and account for estimation risk as they integrate out parameter uncertainty.

Correlated Shocks: The Leverage Effect   One common extension of the model presented earlier relax the assumption that the shocks in volatility and prices are independent and instead assume that $\text{corr}(W_t^v, W_t^s) = \rho$. This "leverage" effect of Black (1976) has been shown to be an important component of returns. For equity returns, this parameters is negative, which indicates that negative returns signal increases in volatility. For MCMC estimation, the leverage effect adds two complications. First, updating volatility is slightly more complicated as equity returns now are directionally correlated with changes in volatility. Second, there is an additional parameter that is present.

Jacquier et al. (2004) consider the log-volatility model and show how to incorporate the leverage effects into the model. In discrete time, they write the model as:

$$Y_t = \sqrt{V_{t-1}}\varepsilon_t^s$$

$$\log(V_t) = \alpha_v + \beta_v \log(V_{t-1}) + \sigma_v\left[\rho\varepsilon_t^s + \sqrt{1-\rho^2}\varepsilon_t^v\right],$$

where ε_t^s and ε_t^v are uncorrelated. Jacquier et al. (2004) reparameterize the model by defining $\phi_v = \sigma_v\rho$ and $\omega_v = \sigma_v^2(1-\rho^2)$. They assume $\alpha_v, \beta_v \sim \mathcal{N}$, $\phi_v \sim \mathcal{N}$, and $\omega_v \sim \mathcal{IG}$. This generates the following MCMC algorithm:

$$p(\alpha_v, \beta_v | \sigma_v, V, Y) \sim \mathcal{N}$$

$$p(\phi_v, \omega_v | \alpha_v, \beta_v, V, Y) \sim \mathcal{N}/\mathcal{IG}$$

$$p(V_t | V_{t-1}, V_{t+1}, \Theta, Y) \; : \text{Metropolis}.$$

We refer the reader to Jacquier et al. (2004) for the details of each of these steps and for extensions to multivariate stochastic volatility models.

Blocking Volatility States   Because the volatility states are correlated, one would ideally like to update them in a block. Unfortunately, direct block updating is extremely difficult and therefore a number of authors have considered an approximation to the model which can then be used to update volatility in a block. One alternative is to approximate the model, in hopes that the approximating model will be negligibly different and will allow black updating. Kim et al. (1998) first square returns and add a small constant, to avoid taking the logarithm of zero. In log-form, the state space model is

$$\log\left((Y_{t+1}^2 + c)\right) = \log(V_t) + \log\left((\varepsilon_{t+1}^s)^2\right)$$

$$\log(V_{t+1}) = \alpha_v + \beta_v \log(V_t) + \sigma_v\varepsilon_{t+1}^v.$$

If we relabel the log-volatilities as $\widetilde{V}_t = \log(V_t)$, we see the model now takes the form of a nonnormal, but linear state space model:

$$\log\left((Y_{t+1}^2 + c)\right) = \widetilde{V}_t + \log\left((\varepsilon_{t+1}^s)^2\right)$$

$$\widetilde{V}_{t+1} = \alpha_v + \beta_v\widetilde{V}_t + \sigma_v\varepsilon_{t+1}^v.$$

This simplifies the model along one line by removing the nonlinearity, but introduces nonnormalities.

Kim et al. (1998) argue that $x_{t+1} = \log\left(\left(\varepsilon_{t+1}^s\right)^2\right)$ can be easily approximated by a 7-component mixture of normals:

$$p[x_t] \approx \sum_{j=1}^{7} q_j \phi\left(x_t | \mu_j, \sigma_j^2\right),$$

where $\phi\left(x | \mu, \sigma^2\right)$ is a normal distribution with mean μ and variance σ^2. The constants q_j, μ_j, and σ_j are chosen to approximate the distribution of $\log\left(\left(\varepsilon_{t+1}^s\right)^2\right)$. Formally, this requires the addition of a latent state variable, s_t, such that

$$x_t | s_t = j \sim \mathcal{N}\left(\mu_j, \sigma_j^2\right)$$

$$\text{Prob}[s_t = j] = q_j.$$

In this transformed model, the posterior $p\left(\alpha_v, \beta_v, \sigma_v^2, \widetilde{V}, s | Y\right)$ has complete conditionals:

$$p\left(\alpha_v, \beta_v | \sigma_v, s, \widetilde{V}, Y\right) \sim \mathcal{N}$$
$$p\left(\sigma_v^2 | \alpha_v, \beta_v, s, \widetilde{V}, Y\right) \sim \mathcal{IG}$$
$$p\left(\widetilde{V} | \alpha_v, \beta_v, \sigma_v, s, Y\right) \ : \ \text{FFBS}$$
$$p\left(s_t | \alpha_v, \beta_v, \sigma_v, \widetilde{V}, Y\right) \sim \text{Multinomial}.$$

The key advantage is that, conditional on the indicators, the model is a linear, normal state space model and the Kalman recursions deliver $p\left(\widetilde{V} | \alpha_v, \beta_v, \sigma_v, s, Y\right)$.

The algorithm generates a Markov Chain with very low autocorrelations. Because of the low autocorrelations, the algorithm is often referred to as a rapidly converging algorithm. This is certainly true of the approximated model, if the shocks to the volatility equation have the postulated mixture representation. If data is simulated from the true distribution, the algorithm could provide inaccurate inference as the state evolution is misspecified. However, this affect appears to be quite small for many financial time series. There are other potential problems with this algorithm. It suffers from the inlier problem when $\varepsilon_{t+1}^s \approx 0$. Moreover, it drastically increases the state space by introducing indicator variables. Rosenthal (1995) discusses potential convergence problems with Markov Chains over discrete state spaces. The algorithm is difficult to extend to other interesting cases, such as the square-root stochastic volatility model, although this is an area of research that certainly deserves further attention.

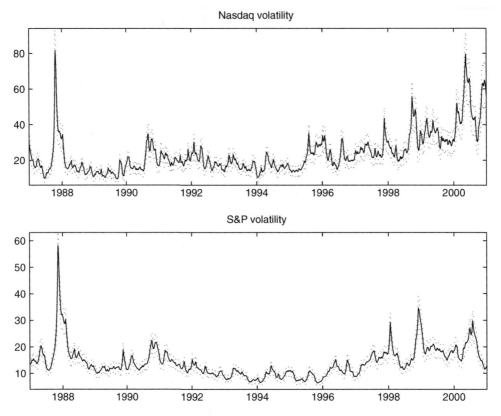

Figure 13.5 Smoothed volatility paths (with posterior confidence bands) for the S&P 500 and Nasdaq 100 from 1987 to 2001.

5.1.6. Alternative Stochastic Volatility Models

Although the log-volatility model is common for many applications, it has a number of potential shortcomings. First, the model falls outside the affine class that implies it is numerically costly to compute option prices or portfolio weights in applications as partial differential equation must be solved. Second, the volatility of volatility is constant, a potentially counterfactual implication. To address these concerns, a number of alternative models have been introduced into the literature.

Heston's Square-Root Volatility Model   In the option pricing and portfolio allocation literature, it is common to use an "affine" model specification for volatility. Heston (1993) introduced the square-root stochastic volatility model

$$dS_t = S_t \left(r_t + \eta_v V_t + \frac{1}{2} V_t \right) dt + S_t \sqrt{V_t} dW_t^s(\mathbb{P}) \tag{5.3}$$

$$dV_t = \kappa_v(\theta_v - V_t) dt + \sigma_v \sqrt{V_t} dW_t^v(\mathbb{P}), \tag{5.4}$$

where the Brownian motions have constant correlation ρ. Discretizing the SDE,

$$Y_t = \eta_v V_{t-1} + \sqrt{V_{t-1}}\varepsilon_t^s$$

$$V_t = \alpha_v + \beta_v V_{t-1} + \sigma_v\sqrt{V_{t-1}}\varepsilon_t^v,$$

where Y_t is excess returns, and we have redefined the parameters in the drift process of the volatility process.

Before continuing with the algorithm, it is important to note that there is a clear problem with the time-discretization of the square-root model. Provided the Feller condition holds, the SDE has a positive solution, that is, starting from an initially positive volatility, the solution remains positive for all t. The time-discretized model does not share this property as the shocks to V_t are normally distributed, which implies that a simulated V_t could be negative. There are three ways to deal with this. First, the original SDE could be transformed by Ito's lemma into logarithms, and the solution simulated in logs. This makes parameter updating more difficult as the volatility appears in both the drift and diffusion. Second, one can ignore the problem and hope that it does not affect the results. For certain time series, such as U.S. equity indices, volatility tends to be rather high and the problem is likely very small as $p(V_t|V_{t-1})$ has very little support below zero, especially when the discretization interval is daily.[10] For other time series, such as exchange rates where volatility is very low, ignoring the problem may not as innocuous. Third, one could fill in missing data points to reduce the impact of discretization.

We assume normal independent priors for η_v and (α_v, β_v), an inverted gamma prior for σ_v^2, and a uniform prior for ρ. Eraker et al. (2003) examine this model using MCMC methods, as well as extensions that include jumps in returns and jump in volatility. The Clifford–Hammersley theorem implies that $p(\alpha_v, \beta_v|\sigma_v, \rho, V, Y)$, $p(\sigma_v^2|\alpha_v, \beta_v, \rho, V, Y)$, $p(\rho|\alpha_v, \beta_v, \sigma_v^2, V, Y)$, and $p(V|\alpha_v, \beta_v, \sigma_v^2, Y)$ are the complete conditionals. The MCMC algorithm is given by:

$$p(\eta_v|\alpha_v, \beta_v, \sigma_v, \rho, V, Y) \sim \mathcal{N}$$

$$p(\alpha_v, \beta_v|\sigma_v, \rho, V, Y) \sim \mathcal{N}$$

$$p(\sigma_v^2|\alpha_v, \beta_v, \rho, V, Y) \sim \mathcal{IG}$$

$$p(\rho|\alpha_v, \beta_v, \sigma_v^2, V, Y) \ : \ \text{Metropolis}$$

$$p(V_t|V_{t-1}, V_{t+1}, \Theta, Y) \ : \ \text{Metropolis}.$$

---

[10]For example, using the estimates in Eraker et al. (2003), we have that

$$V_{t+1}|V_t \sim N\left(V_t + \kappa_v(\theta_v - V_t), \sigma^2 V_t\right)$$

$$\sim N\left(V_t + 0.02(0.9 - V_t), (0.14)^2 V_t\right).$$

If daily volatility is 1%, $V_t = 1$ (roughly 15% annualized), it requires a 50 standard deviation move to make volatility go negative.

The parameter posteriors are similar to those in the previous sections and are omitted. Eraker et al. (2003) use a random-walk Metropolis–Hastings algorithm for both the correlation parameter and the volatility states. The functional form of $p(\rho|\alpha_v, \beta_v, \sigma_v^2, V, Y)$ and $p(V_t|V_{t-1}, V_{t+1}, \Theta, Y)$ are particularly complicated. In both cases, the state dependence in the variance of V_t creates complications and it is difficult to find a good proposal for independence Metropolis. Eraker et al. (2003) provide a simulation study to show the efficacy of their algorithm to estimate the parameters of the underlying continuous-time process. It would be particularly useful if a block-updating scheme were available for updating the volatilities.

Stochastic Volatility with Jumps in Returns and Volatility   As an example, consider the popular double-jump model by Duffie et al. (2000), which assumes the equity price, S_t, and its stochastic variance, V_t, jointly solve

$$dS_t = S_t(r_t + \eta_v V_t)\,dt + S_t\sqrt{V_t}dW_t^s(\mathbb{P}) + d\left(\sum_{j=1}^{N_t(\mathbb{P})} S_{\tau_j^-}\left(e^{Z_j^s(\mathbb{P})} - 1\right)\right) \qquad (5.5)$$

$$dV_t = \kappa_v(\theta_v - V_t)\,dt + \sigma_v\sqrt{V_t}dW_t^v(\mathbb{P}) + d\left(\sum_{j=1}^{N_t(\mathbb{P})} Z_j^v(\mathbb{P})\right), \qquad (5.6)$$

where $W_t^s(\mathbb{P})$ and $W_t^v(\mathbb{P})$ are correlated (ρ) Brownian motions, $N_t(\mathbb{P}) \sim \text{Poisson}(\lambda)$, τ_j are the jump times, $Z_j^s(\mathbb{P})|Z_j^v \sim N\left(\mu_s + \rho_s Z_j^v, \sigma_s^2\right)$ are the return jumps, $Z_j^v(\mathbb{P}) \sim \exp(\mu_v)$ are the variance jumps, and r_t is the spot interest rate. This model plays a prominent role given its importance for practical applications such as option pricing and portfolio analysis. Heston (1993) introduced the square-root stochastic volatility specification, and Bates (1996, 2001), Pan (2001) and Duffie et al. (2000) introduced generalizations with jumps in returns and volatility. Eraker et al. (2003) estimate stochastic volatility models with jumps in returns and volatility using MCMC methods. Eraker (2002) extends Eraker et al. (2003) to incorporate option prices. Liu et al. (2001) analyze the portfolio implications of models with jumps in stock prices and in volatility.

A time discretization of this model

$$Y_t = \mu + \eta_v V_{t-1} + \sqrt{V_{t-1}}\varepsilon_t^s + J_t Z_t^s$$
$$V_t = \alpha_v + \beta_v V_{t-1} + \sigma_v\sqrt{V_{t-1}}\varepsilon_t^v + J_t Z_t^v.$$

Given the time discretization, Clifford–Hammersley implies that we can factor the parameters and states into the following groups, $[(\mu, \eta_v), (\alpha_v, \beta_v), \sigma_v^2, \rho, \lambda, \mu_v, (\mu_s, \rho_s), \sigma_s^2, J, Z^s, Z^v, V]$. We assume normal independent priors for (μ, η_v),

(α_v, β_v), and (μ_s, ρ_s), inverted gamma priors for σ_v^2 and σ_s^2, a Beta prior for λ, an Gamma prior for μ_v, and a uniform prior for ρ.

Although the model has a number of parameters, deriving the conditional posteriors for many of them is straightforward given the results in the previous section. This is due to the modular nature of MCMC algorithms. For example, the conditional posteriors for the "diffusive" parameters are the same as in the previous section, with an adjusted return and volatility series. Conditional on jump times and sizes, we can define the jump-adjusted returns and volatilities to get

$$\tilde{r}_t = Y_t - J_t Z_t^s = \mu + \eta_v V_{t-1} + \sqrt{V_{t-1}} \varepsilon_t^s$$
$$\tilde{V}_t = V_t - J_t Z_t^v = \alpha_v + \beta_v V_{t-1} + \sigma_v \sqrt{V_{t-1}} \varepsilon_t^v,$$

which implies the functional forms conditional posteriors for (μ, η_v), (α_v, β_v), σ_v^2, and ρ are the same as in the previous section. Drawing λ is the same as in previous section. Conditional on the jump sizes, the parameters of the jump distributions are conjugate.

The MCMC algorithm draws from the conditional parameter posteriors

$$p(\mu, \eta_v | \ldots, J, Z, V, Y) \sim \mathcal{N}$$
$$p(\alpha_v, \beta_v | \ldots, J, Z, V, Y) \sim \mathcal{N}$$
$$p(\sigma_v^2 | \ldots, J, Z, V, Y) \sim \mathcal{IG}$$
$$p(\lambda | J) \sim \mathcal{B}$$
$$p(\mu_s, \rho_s | \ldots, J, Z^s, Z^v) \sim \mathcal{N}$$
$$p(\sigma_s^2 | \ldots, J, Z^s, Z^v) \sim \mathcal{IG}$$
$$p(\mu_v | \ldots, J, Z, V, Y) \sim \mathcal{G}$$
$$p(\rho | \alpha_v, \beta_v, \sigma_v^2, V, Y) \; : \; \text{Metropolis}$$

and the conditional state variable posteriors

$$p(Z_t^v | \ldots, Z_t^s, J_t, V_t, V_{t-1}) \sim \mathcal{TN}$$
$$p(Z_t^s | \ldots, Z_t^v, J_t, Y_t, V_t, V_{t-1}) \sim \mathcal{N}$$
$$p(J_t = 1 | \ldots, Z_t^s, Z_t^v, Y_t, V_t, V_{t-1}) \sim \text{Bernoulli}$$
$$p(V_t | V_{t-1}, V_{t+1}, \Theta, Y) \; : \; \text{Metropolis}.$$

For both ρ and the volatilities, Eraker et al. (2003) use a random-walk Metropolis algorithm, properly tuned to deliver acceptance rates in the 30–60% range. Eraker et al. (2003) provide simulation evidence to document the algorithm's ability to estimate the parameters of interest.

5.2. Term Structure Models

One of the great successes of continuous–time asset pricing is term structure models. These models start with a specification for the instantaneous spot rate, r_t, under both the risk–neutral and objective measures, from which bond prices are computed. These models can be justified both on equilibrium (Cox et al., 1985) and arbitrage grounds and provide an excellent framework for understanding the cross-section and dynamics of bond prices.

Term structure models pose a number of difficult problems for estimation. In general, the parameters enter the state space model in a highly nonlinear fashion, often nonanalytically. For example, in general affine models, the parameters appear in ODE's that can only be solved numerically. Second, most models specify a low-dimensional state vector that drives all bond prices. When the number of observed yields or bond prices is greater than the number of state variables, there is a stochastic singularity as the observed yields never conform exactly to the specified model.

5.2.1. Vasicek's Model

The first term structure model we consider is the univariate, Gaussian model of Vasicek (1977) which assumes that r_t solves a continuous–time AR(1) on $(\Omega, \mathcal{F}, \mathbb{P})$:

$$\mathrm{d}r_t = \left(a_r^{\mathbb{P}} - b_r^{\mathbb{P}} r_t\right)\mathrm{d}t + \sigma_r \mathrm{d}W_t^r(\mathbb{P}),$$

where $W_t^r(\mathbb{P})$ is a standard Brownian motion.[11] Assuming a general, "essentially affine" risk–premium specification, (see the review paper by Dai and Singleton, 2003; for details) the spot rate evolves under the equivalent martingale measure $\mathbb{Q}$ via

$$\mathrm{d}r_t = \left(a_r^{\mathbb{Q}} - b_r^{\mathbb{Q}} r_t\right)\mathrm{d}t + \sigma_r \mathrm{d}W_t^r(\mathbb{Q}),$$

where $W_t^r(\mathbb{Q})$ is a standard Brownian motion on $(\Omega, \mathcal{F}, \mathbb{P})$. We label $\Theta^{\mathbb{Q}} = \left(a_r^{\mathbb{Q}}, b_r^{\mathbb{Q}}\right)$ and $\Theta^{\mathbb{P}} = \left(a_r^{\mathbb{P}}, b_r^{\mathbb{P}}, \sigma_r\right)$. To avoid any confusion, we explicitly label $\mathbb{P}$ and $\mathbb{Q}$ measure parameters. Given the risk-premium specifications, the price of a zero coupon, default-free bond maturing at time τ is

$$P(r_t, \tau) = E_t^{\mathbb{Q}}\left[e^{-\int_t^{t+\tau} r_s \mathrm{d}s}\right] = \exp\left(\beta\left(a_r^{\mathbb{Q}}, b_r^{\mathbb{Q}}, \sigma_r, \tau\right) + \beta^r\left(b_r^{\mathbb{Q}}, \sigma_r, \tau\right) r_t\right),$$

---

[11]We note that MCMC easily can accommodate a model of the form in Duarte (2003), which has a nonlinear drift under $\mathbb{P}$ but a linear drift under $\mathbb{Q}$.

where the loading functions are known in closed form:

$$\beta^r\left(b_r^Q, \sigma_r, \tau\right) = \frac{1}{b_r^Q}\left(e^{-b_r^Q \tau} - 1\right)$$

$$\beta\left(a_r^Q, b_r^Q, \sigma_r, \tau\right) = \frac{1}{2}\left[\frac{\sigma_r^2}{\left(b_r^Q\right)^2} + -\frac{a_r^Q}{b_r^Q}\right]\left(\tau - \beta^r\left(b_r^Q, \sigma_r, \tau\right)\right) - \frac{\sigma_r^2}{4b_r^Q}\beta^r\left(b_r^Q, \sigma_r, \tau\right)^2.$$

We assume that there exist a panel of zero coupon, continuously-compounded yields $Y_t = \left[Y_{t,\tau_1}, \ldots, Y_{t,\tau_k}\right]$, where $Y_{t,\tau} = -\log P(\Theta, r_t, \tau)$ and the maturities are $\tau = \tau_1, \ldots, \tau_n$.[12] In this model, if the parameters are known, the spot rate is observable from a single yield. If four yields are observed, the yields can be inverted to compute a_r^Q, b_r^Q, σ_r, and r_t without error, in much the same way volatility is often "implied" from option prices in the Black–Scholes model.

To break this stochastic singularity, it is common to add an additive pricing error:[13]

$$Y_t = \beta\left(a_r^Q, b_r^Q, \sigma_r, \tau\right) + \beta^r\left(b_r^Q, \sigma_r, \tau\right)r_t + \varepsilon_t$$

$$r_{t+1} = r_t + a_r^P + b_r^P r_t + \sigma_r \varepsilon_{t+1}^r,$$

where, for notational simplicity, we relabel $Y_{t,\tau}$ as the log-bond prices, $\varepsilon_t^r \sim \mathcal{N}(0,1)$ is standard normal, and $\varepsilon_t \sim \mathcal{N}(0, \Sigma_\varepsilon)$ is the vector of pricing errors. Because the spot rate evolution is Gaussian, an alternative is to use the exact transitions for the spot rate:

$$r_{t+1} = r_t e^{-b_r^P} + \left(1 - e^{-b_r^P \Delta}\right)\frac{a_r^P}{b_r^P} + \int_t^{t+1} e^{-b_r^P(t-s)}\sigma_r dW_t^r(\mathbb{P}).$$

For parameters typically estimated from data and for common time-intervals such as daily or weekly, the discretization bias is negligible.

Before we discuss MCMC estimation, we provide a brief and informal discussion of parameter identification. Given our risk premium assumptions, it is clear that a_r^Q and b_r^Q are identified solely from the cross-section of bond prices, a_r^P and b_r^P are identified solely by the dynamics of the short rate, and σ_r is identified jointly from the cross-section of bond prices and the dynamics of the short rate. The average slope and curvature of the

---

[12]If discretely compounded bond yields are observed, they can be converted from the discount basis to continuously compounded rates. If par rates or swap rates are observed, it is common to bootstrap these rates using interpolation, if necessary, to obtain zero coupon bond prices.

[13]An alternative justification, which is also plausible, is that the model is misspecified and the pricing error captures some of this misspecification.

yield curve determine the risk premium parameters, as they are assumed to be constant over time. The parameter $a_r^{\mathbb{Q}}$ enters linearly into $\beta(a_r^{\mathbb{Q}}, b_r^{\mathbb{Q}}, \sigma_r, \tau)$, and thus it plays the role of a constant regression parameter. It controls the average long run level of the yield curve. As $(a_r^{\mathbb{P}}, b_r^{\mathbb{P}})$ do not appear in the bond yield expressions, they enter only as regression parameters in the state evolution. Although easy to estimate in principle, interest rates are very persistent which implies that long time series will be required to accurately estimate the drift.

Finally, σ_r enters both in the yields and the dynamics. In principle, either the dynamics of the short rate or the cross-section should identify this parameter as it enters linearly in the bond yields or as a variance parameter in the regression. However, recent research indicates that yield-based information regarding volatility is not necessarily consistent with information based on the dynamics of the spot rate, a time–invariant version of the so–called unspanned volatility puzzle (see, Collin-Dufresne and Goldstein, 2002; Collin-Dufresne et al., 2003). This implies that it may be difficult to reconcile the information regarding spot rate volatility from yields and the dynamics of spot rates. Again, as in the case of Black–Scholes implied volatility, this is not a problem with the model or an estimation scheme per se, rather it is indicative of a sort of misspecification encountered when applying these models to real data.

For the objective measure parameters, we choose standard conjugate priors, $(a_r^{\mathbb{P}}, b_r^{\mathbb{P}}) \sim \mathcal{N}$ and $\sigma_r \sim \mathcal{IG}$. One might also want to impose stationarity, that is, $b_r^{\mathbb{P}} > 0$, which could be imposed by using a truncated prior or just by removing any draws in the MCMC algorithm for which $b_r^{\mathbb{P}} < 0$. We assume that $\Sigma_\varepsilon \sim \mathcal{IW}$ and that $(a_r^{\mathbb{Q}}, b_r^{\mathbb{Q}}) \sim \mathcal{N}$. The posterior distribution is $p(\Theta, r | Y)$ where $\Theta = (a_r^{\mathbb{P}}, b_r^{\mathbb{P}}, a_r^{\mathbb{Q}}, b_r^{\mathbb{Q}}, \sigma_r, \Sigma_\varepsilon)$, $r = (r_1, \ldots, r_T)$, and $Y = (Y_1, \ldots, Y_T)$. The MCMC algorithm consists of the following steps:

$$p\left(a_r^{\mathbb{P}}, b_r^{\mathbb{P}} | \sigma_r, r\right) \sim \mathcal{N}$$

$$p\left(a_r^{\mathbb{Q}} | \sigma_r, \Sigma_\varepsilon, r, Y\right) \sim \mathcal{N}$$

$$p\left(\Sigma_\varepsilon | a_r^{\mathbb{Q}}, b_r^{\mathbb{Q}}, \sigma_r, r, Y\right) \sim \mathcal{IW}$$

$$p\left(b_r^{\mathbb{Q}} | a_r^{\mathbb{Q}}, \sigma_r, \Sigma_\varepsilon, r, Y\right) \; : \; \text{RW Metropolis}$$

$$p\left(\sigma_r^2 | a_r^{\mathbb{P}}, b_r^{\mathbb{P}}, a_r^{\mathbb{Q}}, b_r^{\mathbb{Q}}, \Sigma_\varepsilon, r, Y\right) \; : \; \text{Metropolis}$$

$$p\left(r | a_r^{\mathbb{P}}, b_r^{\mathbb{P}}, a_r^{\mathbb{Q}}, b_r^{\mathbb{Q}}, \sigma_r, \Sigma_\varepsilon, Y\right) \; : \; \text{FFBS.}$$

The updates for $a_r^{\mathbb{P}}, b_r^{\mathbb{P}}, a_r^{\mathbb{Q}}$, and Σ_ε are conjugate and the spot rates can be updated in a single block using the FFBS algorithm developed earlier in Section 5.1.4. It is not possible to directly draw interest rate volatility and the risk-neutral speed of mean reversion as the conditional posterior distributions are not standard due to the complicated manner in which these parameters enter into the loading functions. Because $b_r^{\mathbb{Q}}$ only appears in the yield equation, it can be difficult to generate a reasonable proposal for independence Metropolis, and thus we recommend a fat-tailed random-walk Metropolis step for $b_r^{\mathbb{Q}}$. The Griddy Gibbs sampler would be also be appropriate. For σ_r, the conditional posterior is given as

$$p\left(\sigma_r^2 | a_r^{\mathbb{P}}, b_r^{\mathbb{P}}, a_r^{\mathbb{Q}}, b_r^{\mathbb{Q}}, \Sigma_\varepsilon, r, Y\right) \propto p\left(r | a_r^{\mathbb{P}}, b_r^{\mathbb{P}}, \sigma_r\right) p\left(Y | a_r^{\mathbb{Q}}, b_r^{\mathbb{Q}}, \sigma_r, \Sigma_\varepsilon, r\right) p\left(\sigma_r^2\right)$$

which is not a recognizable distribution. The Griddy Gibbs sampler, random-walk Metropolis or independence Metropolis are all possible for updating $\sigma_r^{\mathbb{P}}$. For independence Metropolis since, as a function of σ_r, $p\left(Y | a_r^{\mathbb{Q}}, b_r^{\mathbb{Q}}, \sigma_r, \Sigma_\varepsilon, r\right)$ is also not a recognizable, one could propose from $p\left(r | a_r^{\mathbb{P}}, b_r^{\mathbb{P}}, \sigma_r^{\mathbb{P}}\right) p\left(\sigma_r^{\mathbb{P}}\right) \sim \mathcal{IG}$ and accept/reject based on the yields. If the information regarding volatility is consistent between the spot rate evolution and yields, this approach will work well. As in all cases when Metropolis is applied, we recommend trying multiple algorithms and choosing the one that has both good theoretical and empirical convergence properties.

5.2.2. Vasicek with Jumps

A number of authors argue that interest rates contain a jump component, in addition to the usual diffusion components. These jumps are often generated by news about the macroeconomy and the jumps arrive at either deterministic or random times. For simplicity, we focus on the latter case, although Piazzesi (2003) addresses the former case. Jumps occurring at predictable times are in fact easier to deal with as there is no timing uncertainty, and in discrete time, the jump component consists of a random size multiplied by a dummy variable indicating the announcement date.

Consider an extension of Vasicek (1977) model to incorporate jumps in the short rate:

$$\mathrm{d}r_t = \left(a_r^{\mathbb{P}} - b_r^{\mathbb{P}} r_t\right) \mathrm{d}t + \sigma_r \mathrm{d}W_t^r\,(\mathbb{P}) + \mathrm{d}\left(\sum_{j=1}^{N_t^{\mathbb{P}}} Z_j^{\mathbb{P}}\right),$$

where $N_t^{\mathbb{P}}$ is a Poisson process with intensity $\lambda_r^{\mathbb{P}}$ and $Z_j^{\mathbb{P}} \sim N\left(\mu_J^{\mathbb{P}}, \left(\sigma_J^{\mathbb{P}}\right)^2\right)$. Assuming essentially affine risk premiums for the diffusive risks and constant risk premiums for the risks associated with the timing and sizes of the jumps, the risk neutral evolution of r_t is

$$\mathrm{d}r_t = \left(a_r^{\mathbb{Q}} - b_r^{\mathbb{Q}} r_t\right) \mathrm{d}t + \sigma_r \mathrm{d}W_t^r\,(\mathbb{Q}) + \mathrm{d}\left(\sum_{j=1}^{N_t^{\mathbb{Q}}} Z_j^{\mathbb{Q}}\right),$$

where $W_t^r(\mathbb{Q})$ is a standard Brownian motion, $N_t^{\mathbb{Q}}$ has intensity $\lambda^{\mathbb{Q}}$, and $Z_j^{\mathbb{Q}} \sim N\big(\mu_J^{\mathbb{Q}}, (\sigma_J^{\mathbb{Q}})^2\big)$, all of which are defined on $\mathbb{Q}$.[14] Jumps affect all of the risk-neutral moments and provide three additional parameters for matching term structure shapes.

This model delivers exponential affine bond prices

$$P(r_t, \tau) = E_t^{\mathbb{Q}}\Big[e^{-\int_t^{t+\tau} r_s ds}|r_t\Big] = \exp\Big(\beta\big(\Theta^{\mathbb{Q}}, \sigma_r, \tau\big) + \beta^r\big(b_r^{\mathbb{Q}}, \tau\big) r_t\Big),$$

where $\Theta^{\mathbb{Q}} = \big(a_r^{\mathbb{Q}}, b_r^{\mathbb{Q}}, \lambda^{\mathbb{Q}}, \mu_J^{\mathbb{Q}}, \sigma_J^{\mathbb{Q}}\big)$ and the loading functions solve the system of ODEs:

$$\frac{\beta^r\big(b_r^{\mathbb{Q}}, \tau\big)}{d\tau} = 1 + \beta^r\big(b_r^{\mathbb{Q}}, \tau\big) b_r^{\mathbb{Q}}$$

$$\frac{d\beta\big(\Theta^{\mathbb{Q}}, \sigma_r, \tau\big)}{d\tau} = \beta^r a_r^{\mathbb{Q}} + \frac{1}{2}(\sigma_r \beta^r)^2 + \lambda^{\mathbb{Q}}\left[\exp\Big(\beta^r \mu_J^{\mathbb{Q}} + \frac{1}{2}\big(\beta^r \sigma_J^{\mathbb{Q}}\big)^2\Big) - 1\right]$$

subject to $\beta^r(b_r^{\mathbb{Q}}, 0) = \beta(\Theta^{\mathbb{Q}}, \sigma_r, 0) = 0$. We have suppressed the dependence of $\beta^r\big(b_r^{\mathbb{Q}}, \tau\big)$ on $b_r^{\mathbb{Q}}$ and τ for notational simplicity on the right-hand side of the second ODE. It is not possible to analytically solve these ordinary differential equations, although it is straightforward to solve them numerically.

Time-discretizing the model gives:

$$Y_{t,\tau} = \beta\big(\Theta^{\mathbb{Q}}, \sigma_r, \tau\big) + \beta^r\big(b_r^{\mathbb{Q}}, \tau\big) r_t + \varepsilon_t$$

$$r_{t+1} = r_t + a_r^{\mathbb{P}} - b_r^{\mathbb{P}} r_t + \sigma_r \varepsilon_{t+1}^r + Z_{t+1}^{\mathbb{P}} J_{t+1}^{\mathbb{P}}$$

$\varepsilon_t^r \sim \mathcal{N}(0, 1)$, $\varepsilon_t \sim \mathcal{N}(0, \Sigma_\varepsilon)$ is the vector of pricing errors, $Z_t^{\mathbb{P}} \sim N\big(\mu_J^{\mathbb{P}}, (\sigma_J^{\mathbb{P}})^2\big)$, and $J_t = 1$ with $\mathbb{P}$-probability $\lambda^{\mathbb{P}}$. With jumps, it is important to explicitly address the issue of potential biases arising from the time-discretization. Empirical estimates indicate that jumps in interest rates occur more often than jumps in equity returns (Johannes et al., 2003). This implies that a simple Bernoulli approximation to the Poisson process could be inaccurate and stresses the importance of using high-frequency data. For the U.S. Treasury market, daily data is available for the past 20 years and reliable daily LIBOR/swap data is available since 1990.

---

[14]These are, of course, very restrictive assumptions on the market prices of risk, especially for the jump components. Provided we allow for affine dynamics under $\mathbb{Q}$, we could specify any dynamics under $\mathbb{P}$. This could include nonlinear drifts, state dependent jump intensities, or state dependent jump distributions.

The posterior distribution is defined over the objective measure jump parameters, $\Theta_J^{\mathbb{P}} = \left(\lambda_r^{\mathbb{P}}, \mu_J^{\mathbb{P}}, \sigma_J^{\mathbb{P}}\right)$, objective measure diffusive parameters, $\Theta_D^{\mathbb{P}} = \left(a_r^{\mathbb{P}}, b_r^{\mathbb{P}}, \sigma_r\right)$, the risk-neutral parameters, $\Theta^{\mathbb{Q}}$, and the latent state variables, (r, Z, J) where $r, Z,$ and J are vectors containing the spot rates, jump sizes, and jump times. For $\Theta^{\mathbb{P}}$ we assume conjugate priors: $a_r^{\mathbb{P}}, b_r^{\mathbb{P}},$ and $\mu_J^{\mathbb{P}}$ are normal, $\sigma_J^{\mathbb{P}}$ and σ_r are inverted gamma, and $\lambda_r^{\mathbb{P}}$ is Beta. For simplicity, we assume the same functional forms for the corresponding risk-neutral parameters. Clifford–Hammersley implies that

$$p\left(\Sigma_\varepsilon, \Theta_D^{\mathbb{P}} | \Theta_J^{\mathbb{P}}, \Theta^{\mathbb{Q}}, r, Z, J, Y\right)$$

$$p\left(\Theta_J^{\mathbb{P}} | \Theta_D^{\mathbb{P}}, \Theta^{\mathbb{Q}}, r, Z, J, Y\right)$$

$$p\left(\Theta^{\mathbb{Q}} | \Theta_D^{\mathbb{P}}, \Theta_J^{\mathbb{P}}, r, Z, J, Y\right)$$

$$p\left(r | \Theta_D^{\mathbb{P}}, \Theta_J^{\mathbb{P}}, \Theta^{\mathbb{Q}}, Z, J, Y\right)$$

$$p\left(Z | \Theta_D^{\mathbb{P}}, \Theta_J^{\mathbb{P}}, \Theta^{\mathbb{Q}}, r, J, Y\right)$$

$$p\left(J | \Theta_D^{\mathbb{P}}, \Theta_J^{\mathbb{P}}, \Theta^{\mathbb{Q}}, r, Z, Y\right)$$

are complete conditionals. We discuss each of these in turn.

The first portion of the MCMC algorithm updates Σ_ε, $\Theta_D^{\mathbb{P}}$, and $\Theta_J^{\mathbb{P}}$. We factor these distributions further via Clifford–Hammersley and sequentially draw $\left(a_r^{\mathbb{P}}, b_r^{\mathbb{P}}\right), \sigma_r, \Sigma_\varepsilon, \lambda_r^{\mathbb{P}},$ and $\left(\mu_J^{\mathbb{P}}, \sigma_J^{\mathbb{P}}\right)$. Because $a_r^{\mathbb{P}}, b_r^{\mathbb{P}},$ and $\Theta_J^{\mathbb{P}}$ do not appear in the ODE's, their conditional posteriors simplify since, conditional on r, the parameter posteriors are independent of Y. To update $\Theta_D^{\mathbb{P}}$ and $\Theta_J^{\mathbb{P}}$, we sequentially draw

$$p\left(a_r^{\mathbb{P}}, b_r^{\mathbb{P}} | \sigma_r, r, Z, J\right) \sim \mathcal{N}$$

$$p\left(\lambda_r^{\mathbb{P}} | J\right) \sim \mathcal{B}$$

$$p\left(\Sigma_\varepsilon | \sigma_r, \Theta^{\mathbb{Q}}, r, Z, J, Y\right) \sim \mathcal{IW}$$

$$p\left(\mu_J^{\mathbb{P}}, \sigma_J^{\mathbb{P}} | \Theta_D^{\mathbb{P}}, Z, J\right) \sim \mathcal{NIW}$$

$$p\left(\sigma_r | a_r^{\mathbb{P}}, b_r^{\mathbb{P}}, \Theta^{\mathbb{Q}}, \Sigma_\varepsilon, r, Z, J, Y\right) \sim \text{Metropolis}.$$

The updates for $a_r^{\mathbb{P}}, b_r^{\mathbb{P}}$ are standard as, conditional on the jump times and sizes, they enter as regression parameters:

$$r_{t+1} - r_t - Z_{t+1}^{\mathbb{P}} J_{t+1}^{\mathbb{P}} = a_r^{\mathbb{P}} - b_r^{\mathbb{P}} r_t + \sigma_r \varepsilon_{t+1}^r.$$

The conditional posteriors for the jump intensity and parameters of the jump size distribution are similar to those in Section 5.1.3. The conditional posterior for σ_r is the same as in the previous section, as this parameter appears in the bond prices and the structural evolution of spot rates.

Next, we update the risk–premium parameters. $a_r^{\mathbb{Q}}$ and $\lambda^{\mathbb{Q}}$ enter linearly and, at least for, $a_r^{\mathbb{Q}}$, a normal prior generates a normal conditional posterior. For $\lambda^{\mathbb{Q}}$, we need to impose positivity, and thus we assume a Beta prior. This has the flexibility to impose that jumps are rare under $\mathbb{Q}$. For $\lambda^{\mathbb{Q}}$ and the other risk–premium parameters, we use a random–walk Metropolis algorithm. This implies the following steps:

$$p\left(a_r^{\mathbb{Q}}|\sigma_r, b_r^{\mathbb{Q}}, \lambda^{\mathbb{Q}}, \mu_J^{\mathbb{Q}}, \sigma_J^{\mathbb{Q}}, \Sigma_\varepsilon, r, Y\right) \sim \mathcal{N}$$

$$p\left(b_r^{\mathbb{Q}}, \lambda^{\mathbb{Q}}, \mu_J^{\mathbb{Q}}, \sigma_J^{\mathbb{Q}}|a_r^{\mathbb{Q}}, \sigma_r, \Sigma_\varepsilon, r, Y\right) \ : \ \text{RW Metropolis.}$$

The final stage updates the state variables. In this model, we are able to draw each vector of state variables in blocks

$$p\left(r|\Theta_D^{\mathbb{P}}, \Theta_J^{\mathbb{P}}, \Theta^{\mathbb{Q}}, \Sigma_\varepsilon, Z, J, Y\right) \ : \ \text{FFBS}$$

$$p\left(Z|\Theta_D^{\mathbb{P}}, \Theta_J^{\mathbb{P}}, r, J\right) \sim \mathcal{N}$$

$$p\left(J|\Theta_D^{\mathbb{P}}, \Theta_J^{\mathbb{P}}, r, Z,\right) \sim \text{Bernoulli.}$$

The FFBS update for spot rates follows directly from the fact that, conditional parameters, jump times, and jump sizes, the model is a linear, Gaussian state space model. The updates from J and Z are, conditional on r, the same as in Section 5.1.3.

The jump–diffusion model can be easily generalized to multiple dimensions. Assume that $r_t = \alpha + \alpha_x' X_t$ where the N–vector of state variables, X_t, solves

$$\mathrm{d}X_t = \left(A_x^{\mathbb{P}} - B_x^{\mathbb{P}} X_t\right)\mathrm{d}t + \sigma_x \mathrm{d}W_t^r(\mathbb{P}) + \mathrm{d}\left(\sum_{j=1}^{N_t^{\mathbb{P}}} Z_j^{\mathbb{P}}\right),$$

where $A_x^{\mathbb{P}} \in R^N$, $\sigma_x, B_x^{\mathbb{P}} \in R^{N\times N}$, $\Sigma_x^{\mathbb{P}} = \sigma_x' \sigma_x$, $W_t^r(\mathbb{P})$ is a N–dimensional standard Brownian motion, and $Z_j^{\mathbb{P}} \in R^N \sim N\left(\mu_J^{\mathbb{P}}, \Sigma_J^{\mathbb{P}}\right)$, and for simplicity we assume that the jump arrivals are coincident across the state variables. In the case of no jumps, this models takes the form of a multifactor Gaussian model.

It is common to assume there are three states, which are typically identified as the short rate, the slope of the curve, and the curvature. This would allow for correlated jumps and generates some potentially interesting issues. For example, while most would agree that the short rate jumps (as it is related to monetary policy), but if one finds that the slope factor also jumps, does this imply that the FED influences the long end of the yield curve? These and other issues can be addressed in a multivariate jump model.

5.2.3. The CIR Model

Gaussian models have three potentially problematic assumptions: (1) interest rate volatility is constant, (2) interest rate increments are normally distributed, and (3) the spot rate can be negative. As r_t is typically assumed to be a nominal rate, this is an unattractive feature. The classic square-root model of Cox et al. (1985) corrects these shortcomings. CIR assume the spot rate follows a Feller (1951) square root process

$$\mathrm{d}r_t = \left(a_r^{\mathbb{P}} - b_r^{\mathbb{P}} r_t \right) \mathrm{d}t + \sigma_r \sqrt{r_t} \mathrm{d}W_t^r(\mathbb{P}),$$

where W_t^r is a Brownian motion under the objective measure, $\mathbb{P}$. As r_t falls to zero, $\sqrt{r_t}$ falls to zero, effectively turning off the randomness in the model. If $b_r^{\mathbb{P}} > 0$ and together the parameters satisfy the Feller condition, the drift will pull r_t up from low rates. Under regularity, this model generates a form of time-varying volatility, (slightly) nonnormal increments, and positive interest rates.

Assuming essentially affine risk premiums, the evolution under $\mathbb{Q}$ is

$$\mathrm{d}r_t = \left(a_r^{\mathbb{Q}} - b_r^{\mathbb{Q}} r_t \right) \mathrm{d}t + \sigma_r \sqrt{r_t} \mathrm{d}W_t^r(\mathbb{Q})$$

and the price of a zero coupon bond maturing at time τ_i is

$$P(r_t, \tau) = \exp \left(\beta\left(a_r^{\mathbb{Q}}, b_r^{\mathbb{Q}}, \sigma_r, \tau \right) + \beta^r\left(b_r^{\mathbb{Q}}, \sigma_r, \tau \right) r_t \right),$$

where again we label $\Theta^{\mathbb{Q}} = \left(a_r^{\mathbb{Q}}, b_r^{\mathbb{Q}} \right)$ and $\Theta^{\mathbb{P}} = \left(a_r^{\mathbb{P}}, b_r^{\mathbb{P}}, \sigma_r \right)$. The loading functions are given by:

$$\beta^r\left(b_r^{\mathbb{Q}}, \sigma_r, \tau \right) = \frac{2\left(1 - \exp(\gamma\tau)\right)}{\left(\gamma + b_r^{\mathbb{Q}}\right)\left(\exp(\gamma\tau) - 1\right) + 2\gamma}$$

$$\beta\left(a_r^{\mathbb{Q}}, b_r^{\mathbb{Q}}, \sigma_r, \tau \right) = \frac{a_r^{\mathbb{Q}}}{\sigma_r^2} \left[2\ln\left(\frac{2\gamma}{\left(b_r^{\mathbb{Q}} + \gamma\right)\left(\exp(\gamma\tau) - 1\right) + 2\gamma} \right) + \left(b_r^{\mathbb{Q}} + \gamma\right)\tau \right]$$

where $\gamma = \left[\left(b_r^{\mathbb{Q}}\right)^2 + 2\sigma_r^2 \right]^{1/2}$.

Given the usual observed panel of yields, and assuming a time-discretization[15] of the interest rate increments, the state space is given by:

$$Y_{t,\tau} = \beta\left(a_r^{\mathbb{Q}}, b_r^{\mathbb{Q}}, \sigma_r, \tau\right) + \beta^r\left(b_r^{\mathbb{Q}}, \sigma_r, \tau\right) r_t + \varepsilon_t$$

$$r_{t+1} = r_t + a_r^{\mathbb{P}} + b_r^{\mathbb{P}} r_t + \sigma_r \sqrt{r_t} \varepsilon_{t+1}^r.$$

The state space is still linear and conditionally Gaussian in the states, but the spot rate evolution has conditional heteroskedasticity.

The posterior distribution is given by $p\left(\Theta^{\mathbb{P}}, \Theta^{\mathbb{Q}}, r | Y\right)$ and the parameter component of the MCMC algorithm we consider is similar to the one in the previous section. For priors, we can choose, for example, $\left(a_r^{\mathbb{P}}, b_r^{\mathbb{P}}\right) \sim \mathcal{N}, \sigma_r \sim \mathcal{IG}, \Sigma_\varepsilon \sim \mathcal{IW}, \left(a_r^{\mathbb{Q}}, b_r^{\mathbb{Q}}\right) \sim \mathcal{N}$. The MCMC algorithm consists of the following steps:

$$p\left(a_r^{\mathbb{P}}, b_r^{\mathbb{P}} | \sigma_r, r\right) \sim \mathcal{N}$$

$$p\left(\Sigma_\varepsilon | a_r^{\mathbb{Q}}, b_r^{\mathbb{Q}}, \sigma_r, r, Y\right) \sim \mathcal{IW}$$

$$p\left(a_r^{\mathbb{Q}}, b_r^{\mathbb{Q}} | \sigma_r, \Sigma_\varepsilon, r, Y\right) \;:\; \text{RW Metropolis}$$

$$p\left(\sigma_r^2 | a_r^{\mathbb{P}}, b_r^{\mathbb{P}}, a_r^{\mathbb{Q}}, b_r^{\mathbb{Q}}, \Sigma_\varepsilon, r, Y\right) \;:\; \text{Metropolis}$$

$$p\left(r | a_r^{\mathbb{P}}, b_r^{\mathbb{P}}, a_r^{\mathbb{Q}}, b_r^{\mathbb{Q}}, \sigma_r, \Sigma_\varepsilon, Y\right) \;:\; \text{Metropolis}.$$

All of these are familiar from the previous sections, with the exception of r. Because the spot rates appear in the conditional variance of the spot rate evolution, the Kalman filter and thus the FFBS algorithm does not apply. To update the spot rates, independence or random walk is required.

It is straightforward to extend this algorithm to multifactor square-root models. Lamoureaux and Whitte (2002) consider a two-factor square-root model and use an alternative approach based on the Griddy-Gibbs sampler for all of the parameters and the state variables. This avoids discretization bias, but is extremely computationally demanding. Polson et al. (2001) analyze a square-root stochastic volatility model using Treasury rates. Bester (2003) analyzes multifactor affine and string models using MCMC.

---

[15]As in the Vasicek model, the exact transitions of the of the interest rate are known and are given by

$$p\left(r_{t+1} | r_t\right) \propto e^{-u-v}\left(\frac{u}{v}\right)^{\frac{q}{2}} I_q\left(2(uv)^{1/2}\right)$$

where $u = c r_t e^{-br}$, $v = c r_{t+1}$, and $c = \dfrac{2br}{\sigma_r^2\left(1 - e^{-br}\right)}$. Lamoureux and Witte (2001) discretize the state space and implement a "Griddy" Gibbs sampler. An attractive alternative to this would be to use a Metropolis algorithm to update the states.

5.3. Regime Switching Models

We first considered the Black–Scholes model, a model with a constant expected return and volatility. In the sections that followed, we considered models that relaxed this constant parameter specification, allowing the expected return and volatility to vary over time. In those models, expected returns or volatility were modeled as diffusions or jump-diffusions, where the jump component was i.i.d. In this section, we consider an alternative: the drift and diffusion are driven by a continuous-time, discrete state Markov Chain. The models are commonly called regime-switching models, Markov switching models, or Markov modulated diffusions.

The general form of the model is

$$dS_t = \mu(\Theta, X_t, S_t)\, dt + \sigma(\Theta, X_t, S_t)\, dW_t,$$

where X_t takes values in a discrete space $X_t = x_1, \ldots, x_k$ with transition matrix $P_{ij}(t)$. $\Theta = (\Theta_1, \ldots, \Theta_J)$. Intuitively, if the process is in state i, the process solves

$$dS_t = \mu(\Theta, i, S_t)\, dt + \sigma(\Theta, i, S_t)\, dW_t.$$

Common specifications assume the drift and diffusion coefficients are parametric functions and the parameters switch over time. In this case, it is common to write the model as

$$dS_t = \mu(\Theta_{X_t}, S_t)\, dt + \sigma(\Theta_{X_t}, S_t)\, dW_t.$$

Term structure models with regime-switches are analyzed in Lee and Naik (1994), Landen (2000), Dai and Singleton (2002), Ang and Bekaert (2000), and Gray (1996). For example, an regime-switching extension of the Vasicek model assumes that the long run mean and the volatility can switch over time:

$$dr_t = \kappa_r(\theta_{X_t} - r_t)\, dt + \sigma_{X_t} dB_t$$

There has been an enormous amount of theoretical and practical work on regime-switching models using MCMC methods. For example, see the monograph by Kim and Nelson (2002) and the earlier papers by Carlin and Polson (1992) and Chib (1996, 1998). We provide a general algorithm, based on Scott (2002) who adapts the FFBS algorithm to the case of regime-switching models. Time discretized, we consider the following model:

$$S_t = \mu(\Theta_{X_t}, S_{t-1}) + \sigma(\Theta_{X_t}, S_{t-1})\, \varepsilon_t.$$

Note that we use the standard notation from discrete-time models where the time index on the Markov state is equal to the current observation. The discrete-time transition probabilities are

$$P_{ij} = P(X_t = i | X_{t-1} = j)$$

and we assume, apriori, that the transition functions are time and state invariant. The joint likelihood is given by

$$p(S|X, \Theta) = \prod_{t=1}^{T} p(S_t|S_{t-1}, X_{t-1}, \Theta),$$

where $p(S_t|S_{t-1}, X_{t-1}, \Theta) = N\big(\mu\big(\Theta_{X_{t-1}}, S_{t-1}\big), \sigma^2\big(\Theta_{X_{t-1}}, S_{t-1}\big)\big)$.

Clifford–Hammersley implies that the complete conditionals are given by $p(\Theta|X, S, P), p(P|X, S, \Theta)$, and $p(X|P, S, \Theta)$. We do not directly address the first step. Conditional on the states and the transition probabilities, updating the parameters is straightforward. Conditional on the states, the transition matrix has a Dirichlet distribution, and updating this is also straightforward. To update the states, define the following quantities

$$\pi^t(X_t = i|\Theta) = p(X_t = i|\Theta, S_{1:t})$$
$$\tilde{\pi}^t(X_t = i|\Theta) = p(X_t = i|\Theta, S_{1:T}).$$

The first distribution is the filtering distribution of the states and the second the smoothing distribution of the states. The updating algorithm is a discrete probability modification of the FFBS algorithm by Carter and Kohn (1994). We first forward filter the states, given the forward filtering distribution, we backward sample. The forward matrices are given by: $P^1, \ldots, P^T$, where $P^t = \big(P_{ij}^t\big)$ is $P_{ij}^t = p\big(X_{t-1} = i, X_t = j|\Theta, S_{1:t}\big)$. To compute the forward matrix, note the recursive structure of the filtering density:

$$P_{ij}^t \propto p\big(S_t, X_{t-1} = i, X_t = j|\Theta, S_{1:t-1}\big)$$
$$\propto p\big(S_t|X_t = j, \Theta\big) p\big(X_t = j|X_{t-1} = i, \Theta\big) \pi^{t-1}(X_{t-1} = i|\Theta).$$

This provides a recursive solution for the forward matrices, P_{ij}^t for $t = 1, \ldots, T$. This is similar to the Kalman filter in Gaussian state space models. Next, we iterate backward in time by finding

$$\tilde{P}_{ij}^t = p\big(X_{t-1} = i, X_t = j|\Theta, S_{1:T}\big).$$

The backward matrices $\tilde{P}_{ij}^t$ are proportional to:

$$P_{ij}^t \frac{\tilde{\pi}^t\big(X_t = j|\Theta\big)}{\pi^t\big(X_t = j|\Theta\big)}$$

which again is computed backward in time for $t = T, \ldots, 1$.

An important component of regime switching models is the prior distribution. Regime switching models (and most mixture models) are not formally identified. For example, in all regime switching models, there is a labeling problem: there is no unique way to identify the states. A common approach to overcome this identification issue is to order the parameters.

6. CONCLUSIONS AND FUTURE DIRECTIONS

This chapter provides an overview of MCMC methods. We discussed the theoretical underpinnings of the algorithms and provided a tutorial on MCMC methods for a number of continuous-time asset pricing models. Although MCMC methods have been used for a number of practical problems, we feel there are numerous additional applications in which MCMC methods will be useful. We now briefly outline a number of future directions.

In many problems, economic theory places constraints on parameter values. For example, pricing kernels must be nonnegative to exclude arbitrage or equilibrium excess expected returns must be positive. Bayesian and MCMC methods are ideally suited to handling these difficult problems, which can be intractable using classical methods. For example, the paper by Wang and Zhang (2003) shows how to use MCMC to characterize the Hansen–Jagannathan distance that imposes positivity on the pricing kernel. As the authors show, these constrains can have major implications regarding our ability to discriminate across models.

Although a number of authors have analyzed term structure models with Gaussian or square-root factors using MCMC, there are a number of other areas that need to be analyzed. There is very little work of jump-diffusion term structure models, and MCMC methods are ideally suited to answering a number of interesting questions. Do multiple factors jump, or is it only the short rate? Does the market price diffusive and jump risks differently in the term structure? How do predictable jumps affect the term structure?

On a mechanical level, there are a number of issues that have not been resolved. First, in many stochastic volatility models (e.g., square-root models), MCMC algorithms update volatility in a single-state manner. Although accurate, it would be preferable to have algorithms to update the volatilities in blocks. If efficient blocking routines were developed, MCMC algorithms would be less computationally intensive and allow a far wider range of models to be analyzed sequentially. Second, in term structure models, the observable yields are often take the form of par rates. These models are nonlinear in the states, but it should be possible to tailor MCMC algorithms to handle this specific form of nonlinearity. Third, there is little work on sequential inference. The filtering distribution of parameters and states is far more relevant than the smoothing distribution for financial applications, and it is important to develop sequential algorithms for practical applications.

ACKNOWLEDGMENTS

We would especially like to thank Chris Sims and the editors, Yacine Ait-Sahalia and Lars Hansen. We also thank Mark Broadie, Mike Chernov, Anne Gron, Paul Glasserman, and Eric Jacquier for their helpful comments.

REFERENCES

Aït-Sahalia, Yacine, 2003, Disentangling Jumps from Volatility, Forthcoming, *Journal of Financial Economics*.

Aldous, David, 1987, On the Markov Chain Simulation Method for Uniform Combinatorial Distributions and Simulated Annealing, *Probability in Engineering Information Systems* 1, 33–46.

Aldous, David, 1989, *Probability Approximations via the Poisson Clumping Heuristic*, Springer-Verlag, New York.

Andersen, Torben, Tim Bollerslev and Frank Diebold, 2002, Parametric and Nonparametric Volatility Measurement, in Lars Peter Hansen and Yacine Ait-Sahalia (editors), *Handbook of Financial Econometrics*, Amsterdam: North-Holland, Forthcoming.

Andersen, Torben, Hyung-Jin Chung and Bent Sorensen, 1999, Efficient Method of Moments Estimation of a Stochastic Volatility Model, *Journal of Econometrics* 91, 61–87.

Anderson, Theodore, 1984, *An Introduction to Multivariate Statistical Analysis*, 2nd Edition, John Wiley & Sons.

Barndorff-Nielsen, Ole Barndorff-Nielson and Neil Shephard, 2003, Impact of Jumps on Returns and Realised Variances: Econometric Analysis of Time-Deformed Lévy Processes, Working Paper, Oxford University.

Bates, David, 1996, Jumps and Stochastic Volatility: Exchange Rate Processes Implicit in Deutsche Mark Options, *Review of Financial Studies* 9, 69–107.

Bates, David, 2000, Post-'87 Crash Fears in S&P 500 Futures Options, *Journal of Econometrics* 94, 181–238.

Bernardo, Jose and Adrian Smith, 1995, *Bayesian Theory*, Wiley, New York.

Besag, Julian and Peter Green, 1993, Spatial Statistics and Bayesian Computation (with Discussion), *Journal of the Royal Statistical Association Series B* 55, 25–37.

Besag, Julian, 1974, Spatial Interaction and the Statistical Analysis of Lattice Systems, *Journal of the Royal Statistical Association Series B* 36, 192–236.

Bester, Alan, 2003, Random Fields and Affine Models of Interest Rates, Working Paper, Duke University.

Black, Fischer and Myron S. Scholes, 1973, The Pricing of Options and Corporate Liabilities, *Journal of Political Economy* 81, 637–654.

Carlin, Bradley and Nicholas Polson, 1991, Inference for Nonconjugate Bayesian Models using the Gibbs sampler, *Canadian Journal of Statistics* 19, 399–405.

Carlin, Bradley and Nicholas Polson, 1992, Monte Carlo Bayesian Methods for Discrete Regression Models and Categorical Time Series, in J.M. Bernardo et al (editors). *Bayesian Statistics 4*, *Oxford University Press*, Oxford, 577–586.

Carlin, Bradley, Nicholas Polson and David Stoffer, 1992, A Monte Carlo Approach to Nonnormal and Nonlinear State-Space Modeling, *Journal of the American Statistical Association* 87, 493–500.

Carlin, Bradley and Sidhartha Chib, 1995, Bayesian Model Choice Through Markov Chain Monte Carlo, *Journal of the Royal Statistical Association Series B 57*, 473–484.

Carter, C.K. and Robert Kohn, 1994, On Gibbs Sampling for State Space Models, *Biometrika* 81, 541–553.

Chib, Sidhartha, 1995, Marginal Likelihood From the Gibbs Output, *Journal of the American Statistical Association* 90, 1313–1321.

Chib, Sidhartha, 1996, Calculating Posterior Distributions and Modal Estimates in Markov Mixture Models, *Journal of Econometrics* 75, 79–97.

Chib, Sidhartha, 1998, Estimation and Comparison of Multiple Change Point Models, *Journal of Econometrics* 86, 221–241.

Clifford, Peter, 1993, Discussion on the Meeting on the Gibbs Sampler and Other Markov Chain Monte Carlo Methods, *Journal of the Royal Statistical Society Series B* 55, 53–54.

Collin-Dufresne, Pierre, Robert Goldstein and Chris Jones, 2003, Identification and Estimation of 'Maximal' Affine Term Structure Models: An Application to Stochastic Volatility, Working Paper, USC.

Cox, John, Jonathan Ingersoll and Stephen Ross, 1985, A Theory of the Term Structure of Interest Rates, *Econometrica* 53, 385–407.

Dai, Qiang and Kenneth Singleton, 2000, Specification Analysis of Affine Term Structure Models, *Journal of Finance* 55, 1943–1978.

Dai, Qiang and Kenneth Singleton, 2003, Term Structure Modeling in Theory and Reality, *Review of Financial Studies* 16, 631–678.

De Finetti, Bruno, 1931, Sul Significato Soggettivo della Probabilità, *Fundamenta Mathematicae* 17, 298–329. Translated into English, On the Subjective Meaning of Probability, in Paola Monari and Daniela Cocchi (editors), *Probabilitá e Induzione*, 1993, Clueb, Bologna, 291–321.

DeGroot, Morris, 1970, *Optimal Statistical Decisions*, McGraw-Hill, New York.

Devroye, Luc, 1986, *Non-Uniform Random Variate Generation*, Springer-Verlag, New York.

Diaconis, Persi and Daniel Stroock, 1991, Geometric Bounds for Eigenvalues of Markov Chains, *Annals of Applied Probability* 1, 36–61.

Doucet, Arnaud, Nando de Freitas, and Neil Gordon, 2001, *Sequential Monte Carlo Methods in Practice*, Springer, New York.

Duarte, Jefferson, 2003, Evaluating an Alternative Risk Preference in Affine Term Structure Models, Forthcoming, *Review of Financial Studies*.

Duffie, Darrell and Jun Pan, 1997, An Overview of Value at Risk, *Journal of Derivatives* 4, 7–49.

Duffie, Darrell, 1996, State-Space Models of the Term Structure of Interest Rates, in H. Körezli-oglu, B. Øksendal, and A. Üstünel (editors) *Stochastic Analysis and Related Topics V: The Silivri Workshop*, Birkhauser, Boston.

Duffie, Darrell, Damir Filipovic, and Walter Schachermayer, 2003, Affine Processes and Applications in Finance, *Annals of Applied Probability* 13, 984–1053.

Duffie, Darrell, Kenneth Singleton and Jun Pan, 2000, Transform Analysis and Asset Pricing for Affine Jump–Diffusions, *Econometrica* 68, 1343–1376.

Elekes, György, 1986, A Geometric Inequality and The Complexity of Computing Volume, *Discrete Computing in Geometry* 1, 289–292.

Elerian, Ola, Sidhartha Chib and Neil Shephard, 2001, Likelihood Inference for Discretely Observed Nonlinear Diffusions, *Econometrica* 69, 959–994.

Eraker, Bjørn, 2001, MCMC Analysis of Diffusion Models with Applications to Finance, *Journal of Business and Economic Statistics* 19–2, 177–191.

Eraker, Bjørn, 2003, Do Equity Prices and Volatility Jump? Reconciling Evidence from Spot and Option Prices, Forthcoming, *Journal of Finance*.

Eraker, Bjorn, Michael Johannes and Nicholas Polson, 2003, The Impact of Jumps in Equity Index Volatility and Returns, *Journal of Finance* 58, 1269–1300.

Frieze, Alan, Ravi Kannan and Nichoals Polson, 1994, Sampling From Log-concave Distributions, *Annals of Applied Probability* 4, 812–834

Gelfand, Alan, Adrian Smith and T.M. Lee, 1992, Bayesian Analysis of Constrained Parameters and Truncated Data Problems Using Gibbs Sampling, *Journal of the American Statistical Association* 87, 523–532.

Gelfand, Alan, Susan Hills, Amy Racine-Poon and Adrian Smith, 1990, Illustration of Bayesian Inference in Normal Data Models Using Gibbs Sampling, *Journal of the American Statistical Association* 85, 972–982.

Gelfand, Alan and Adrian Smith, 1990, Sampling Based Approaches to Calculating Marginal Densities, *Journal of the American Statistical Association* 85, 398–409.

Geman, Stuart and Don Geman, 1984, Stochastic Relaxation, Gibbs Distributions and the Bayesian Restoration of Images, *IEEE Transaction. on Pattern Analysis and Machine Intelligence* 6, 721–741.

Geyer, Charles, 1993, Practical Markov Chain Monte Carlo, *Statistical Science* 7, 473–511.

Glasserman, Paul and Nicholas Merener, 2003, Numerical Solution of Jump-Diffusion LIBOR Market Models, *Finance and Stochastics* 7, 1–27.

Gordon, N., D. Salmond and Adrian Smith, 1993, Novel Approach to Nonlinear/Non-Gaussian Bayesian State Estimation, *IEE Proceedings* F-140, 107–113.

Gray, Stephen, 1996, Modeling the Conditional Distribution of Interest Rates as a Regime-Switching Process, *Journal of Financial Economics* 42, 27–62.

Hammersley, John and Peter Clifford, 1970, Markov Fields on Finite Graphs and Lattices, Unpublished Manuscipt.

Hammersley, John, 1974, Discussion of Besag's Paper, *Journal of the Royal Statistical Society Series B* 36, 230–231.

Han, Cong and Bradley Carlin, 2000, MCMC Methods for Computing Bayes Factors: A Comparative Review, Working Paper, University of Minnesota.

Hastings, W. Keith, 1970, Monte Carlo Sampling Methods Using Markov Chains and their Applications, *Biometrika* 57, 97–109.

Heston, Steven, 1993, A Closed-Form Solution for Options with Stochastic Volatility with Applications to Bond and Currency Options, *Review of Financial Studies* 6, 327–343.

Hobert, J.P. and George Casella, 1996, The Effect of Improper Priors on Gibbs Sampling in Hierarchical Linear Models, *Journal of the American Statistical Association* 91, 1461–1473.

Honore, Peter, 1998, Pitfalls in Estimating Jump-diffusion Models, Working Paper, University of Aarhus.

Jacquier, Eric and Robert Jarrow, 2000, Bayesian Analysis of Contingent Claim Model Error, *Journal of Econometrics* 94, 145–180.

Jacquier, Eric, Nicholas Polson and Peter Rossi, 1994, Bayesian Analysis of Stochastic Volatility Models (with Discussion), *Journal of Business and Economic Statistics* 12, 4.

Jacquier, Eric, Nicholas Polson and Peter Rossi, 1995, Models and Priors for Multivariate Stochastic Volatility Models, Working Paper, University of Chicago.

Jacquier, Eric, Nicholas Polson and Peter Rossi, 2004, Bayesian Inference for SV Models with Correlated Errors, Forthcoming, *Journal of Econometrics*.

Johannes, Michael, 2004, The Statistical and Economic Role of Jumps in Interest Rates, *Journal of Finance*.

Johannes, Michael, Nicholas Polson and Jonathan Stroud, 2002, Volatility Timing and Portfolio Returns, Working Paper.

Johannes, Michael, Nicholas Polson and Jonathan Stroud, 2003, Sequential parameter estimation in stochastic volatility jump-diffusion models, Working Paper.

Johannes, Michael, Nicholas Polson and Jonathan Stroud, 2008, Optimal filtering of jump-diffusions: extracting jumps and volatility from prices, Forthcoming, *Review of Financial Studies*.

Jones, Christopher, 2003, The Dynamics of Stochastic Volatility: Evidence from Underlying and Options Markets, *Journal of Econometrics*.

Kass, Robert and Adrian Raftery, 1995, Bayes Factors, *Journal of the American Statistical Association* 90, 773–795.

Kiefer, Nicholas, 1978, Discrete Parameter Variation: Efficient Estimation of a Switching Regression Mode, *Econometrica* 46, 427–434.

Kim, Sangyoon, Neil Shephard and Siddhartha Chib, 1998, Stochastic Volatility: Likelihood Inference and Comparison with ARCH Models, *Review of Economic Studies* 65, 361–393.

Kim, Tong and Edward Omberg, 1996, Dynamic Non-Myopic Portfolio Behavior, *Review of Financial Studies* 9, 141–161.

Kloeden, Peter and Eckhard Platen, 1995, *Numerical Solution of Stochastic Differential Equations*, Springer Verlag.

Korteweg, Arthur and Nicholas Polson, 2007, Volatility, Liquidity, Credit Spreads and Bankruptcy Prediction, Working Paper, University of Chicago.

Lamoureux, Chris and Doug Witte, 2002, Empirical Analysis of the Yield Curve: The Information in the Data Viewed Through the Window of Cox, Ingersoll, and Ross, *Journal of Finance* 57, 1479–1520.

Landen, Camilla, 2000, Bond Pricing in a Hidden Markov Model of the Short Rate, *Finance and Stochastics* 4, 371–389.

Lindgren, Georg, 1978, Markov Regime Models for Mixed Distributions and Switching Regressions, *Scandanavian Journal of Statistics* 5, 81–91.

Lindley, Dennis, 1971, *Bayesian Statistics: A Review*, SIAM, Philadelphia.

Liu, Jun, 1999, Portfolio Selection in Stochastic Environments, Working Paper, UCLA.

Liu, Jun, Francis Longstaff and Jun Pan, 2003, Dynamic Asset Allocation with Event Risk, *Journal of Finance* 58, 231–259.

Liu, Jun, Wing Wong and Agustine Kong, 1994, Covariance Structure of the Gibbs Sampler with Applications to the Comparisons of Estimators and Sampling Schemes, *Journal of the Royal Statistical Association Series B* 57, 157–169.

Mengersen, Kerrie and Christian Robert, 1998, MCMC Convergence Diagnostics: A Review (With Discussion). in Jose Bernardo et al (editors), *Bayesian Statistics 6*, Oxford University Press, Oxford, 399–432.

Mengersen, Kerrie and Richard Tweedie, 1996, Rates of Convergence of the Hastings and Metropolis Algorithms, *Annals of Statistics* 24, 101–121.

Merton, Robert, 1976, Option pricing when the Underlying Stock Returns are Discontinuous, *Journal of Financial Economics* 3, 125–144.

Merton, Robert, 1980, Estimating the Expected Return on the Market, *Journal of Financial Economics* 8, 323–363.

Metropolis, Nicholas, Rosenbluth, A.W., Rosenbluth, M.N., Teller, A.H., and Teller, Edward, 1953, Equations of State Calculations by Fast Computing Machines, *Journal of Chemical Physics* 21, 1087–1091.

Meyn, Sean and Richard Tweedie, 1995, *Markov Chains and Stochastic Stability*, Springer-Verlag, New York.

Mikulevicius, R., and Eckhart Platen, 1988, Time Discrete Taylor Approximations for Ito Processes with Jump Component, *Mathematische Nachrichten* 138, 93–104.

Naik, Vasant and Moon Hoe Lee, 1997, Yield Curve Dynamics with Discrete Shifts in Economic Regimes: Theory and Estimation, Working Paper, University of British Columbia.

Nummelin, E., 1984, *General Irreducible Markov Chains and Non-Negative Operators*, Cambridge University Press.

Pan, Jun, 2002, The Jump-Risk Premia Implicit in Options: Evidence from an Integrated Time-Series Study, *Journal of Financial Economics* 63, 3–50.

Pastor, Lubos and Robert Stambaugh, 2000, Comparing Asset Pricing Models: An Investment Perspective, with Robert F. Stambaugh, *Journal of Financial Economics* 56, 335–381.

Piazzesi, Monika, 2004, Bond Yields and the Federal Reserve, Forthcoming, *Journal of Political Economy.*

Platen, Echard and Ricardo Rebolledo, 1985, Weak Convergence of Semimartingales and Discretization Methods, *Stochastic Processes and Their Application* 20, 41–58.

Poincare, Henri, 1901, *Science and Hypothesis*, Dover, New York.

Polson, Nicholas and Jonathan Stroud, 2003, Bayesian Inference for Derivative Prices, in Bernardo et al. (editors), *Bayesian Statistics* 7 Oxford University Press, 641–650.

Polson, Nicholas, 1992, Comment on Practical Markov Chain Monte Carlo by Charles Geyer, *Statistical Science* 7, 490–491.

Polson, Nicholas, 1996, Convergence of Markov Chain Monte Carlo Algorithms (with Discussion). in J.M. Bernardo et al (editors), *Bayesian Statistics* 5, Oxford University Press, Oxford, 297–323.

Polson, Nicholas, Jonathan Stroud and Peter Muller, 2002b, Affine State Dependent Variance Models, Working Paper, University of Chicago.

Polson, Nicholas, Jonathan Stroud and Peter Muller, 2002a, Nonlinear State-Space Models with State-Dependent Variances, *Journal of the American Statistical Association* 98, 377–386.

Pritsker, Matt, 1998, Nonparametric Density Estimation and Tests of Continuous Time Interest Rate Models, *Review of Financial Studies* 449–487.

Raiffa, Howard and Robert Schlaifer, 1961, *Applied Statistical Decision Theory*, Harvard University, Boston, MA.

Ramsey, Frank P., 1931, Truth and Probability, *In The Foundations of Mathematics and Other Logical Essays*, Routledge and Kegan Paul, London, 156–198.

Ripley, Brian, 1992, *Stochastic Simulation*, Wiley, New York.

Ritter, Charles and Martin Tanner, 1991, Facilitating the Gibbs Sampler: the Gibbs Stopper and the Griddy-Gibbs Sampler, *Journal of the American Statistical Association* 87, 861–868.

Robert, Christian and George Casella, 1999, Monte Carlo Statistical Methods, Springer, New York.

Roberts, Gareth and Adrian Smith, 1994, Simple Conditions for the Convergence of the Gibbs Sampler and Metropolis-Hastings Algorithms, *Stochastic Processes and Their Application* 49, 207–216.

Roberts, Gareth and Jeffrey Rosenthal, 1998a, Markov Chain Monte Carlo: Some Practical Implications of Theoretical Results, *Canadian Journal of Statistics* 26, 4–31.

Roberts, Gareth and Jeffrey Rosenthal, 1998b, Optimal Scaling of Discrete Approximations to Langevin Diffusions, *Journal of the Royal Statistical Society Series B*, 60, 255–268.

Roberts, Gareth and Jeffrey Rosenthal, 2001, Optimal Scaling for Various Metropolis-Hastings Algorithms, *Statistical Science* 16, 351–367.

Roberts, Gareth and Nicholas Polson, 1994, On the Geometric Convergence of the Gibbs sampler, *Journal of the Royal Statistical Association, Series B*, 377–384.

Roberts, Gareth and Richard Tweedie, 1996, Geometric Convergence and Central Limit Theorems for Multidimensional Hastings and Metropolis Algorithms, *Biometrika* 83, 95–110.

Roberts, Gareth and Richard Tweedie, 1999, Bounds on Regeneration Times and Convergence Rates for Markov Chains, *Stochastic Processes and Their Application* 80, 211–229.

Rosenthal, Jeffrey, 1995a, Rates of Convergence for Gibbs Sampling for Variance Component Models, *Annals of Statistics* 23, 740–761.

Rosenthal, Jeffrey, 1995b, Minorization Conditions and Convergence Rates for MCMC, *Journal of the American Statistical Association* 90, 558–566.

Runggaldier, Wolfgang, 2003, Jump Diffusion Models, in S.T. Rachev, (editors), *Handbook of Heavy Tailed Distributions in Finance Handbooks in Finance, Book 1*, Elesevier/North-Holland, 169–209.

Savage, Leonard, 1964, *The Foundations of Statistics*, John Wiley, New York.

Scott, Steven, 2002, Bayesian Methods for Hidden Markov Models, *Journal of the American Statistical Association* 97, 337–351.

Shimony, Abner, 1955, Coherence and the Axioms of Confirmation, *The Journal of Symbolic Logic* 20, 1–28.

Smith, Adrian and Gareth Roberts, 1993, Bayesian Computation via the Gibbs Sampler and Related Markov Chain Monte Carlo Methods (with Discussion), *Journal of the Royal Statistical Association Series B*, 55, 3–23.

Stanton, Richard, 1997, A Nonparametric Model of Term Structure Dynamics and the Market Price of Interest Rate Risk, *Journal of Finance* 52, 1973–2002.

Stroud, Jonathan, Peter Müller and Nicholas Polson, 2001, Nonlinear State-Space Models with State-Dependent Variance Functions, Forthcoming, *Journal of the American Statistical Association*.

Tanner, Martin and Wing Wong, 1987, The Calculation of Posterior Distributions by Data Augmentation (with Discussion), *Journal of the American Statistical Association* 82, 528–550.

Tierney, Luke, 1994, Markov Chains for Exploring Posterior Distributions (with Discussion), *Annals of Statistics* 22, 1701–1786.

Vasicek, Oldrich, 1977, An Equilibrium Characterization of the Term Structure, *Journal of Financial Economics* 5, 177–188.

Wang, Zhenyu and Xiaoyan Zhang, 2005, Empirical Evaluation of Asset Pricing Models: Arbitrage and Pricing Errors over Contingent Claims, Working Paper, Federal Reserve Bank of New York.

CHAPTER 14

The Analysis of the Cross-Section of Security Returns

Ravi Jagannathan*, Georgios Skoulakis**, *and* Zhenyu Wang***

  * Department of Finance, Kellogg School of Management, Northwestern University, Evanston, IL; and
    NBER, Cambridge, MA
 ** Department of Finance, R. H. Smith School of Business, University of Maryland, College Park, MD
*** Federal Reserve Bank of New York, New York, NY

Contents

Abstract

In this chapter, we offer a comprehensive review of econometric methods used to study the cross-sectional variation of asset returns. The analysis proceeds in a factor asset pricing model framework. We describe three prominent approaches: the cross-sectional regression (CSR) method, the maximum likelihood (ML) method, and the generalized method of moments (GMM). In the context of the CSR method, we review the two-pass procedure of Fama and MacBeth, show how to use security characteristics to test a factor model, and also discuss the N-consistency of the risk premium estimator. In the context of the ML method and under the assumption of multivariate normality, we present tests of factor models with nontraded as well as traded factors. Finally, in the context of the GMM, we show how one can test factor models using either the beta or the stochastic discount factor representation and also discuss how to analyze conditional factor models.

Keywords: factor models; risk premium estimator; two-pass cross-sectional regression; generalized method of moments

1. INTRODUCTION

Financial assets exhibit wide variation in their historical average returns. For example, during the period from 1926 to 1999 large stocks earned an annualized average return of 13.0%, whereas long-term bonds earned only 5.6%. Small stocks earned 18.9%, substantially higher than large stocks. These differences are statistically and economically significant (Ferson and Jagannathan, 1996; Jagannathan and McGrattan, 1995). Furthermore, such significant differences in average returns are also observed among other classes of stocks. If investors were rational, they would have anticipated such differences. Nevertheless, they still preferred to hold financial assets with such widely different expected returns. A natural question that arises is why this is the case. A variety of asset pricing models have been proposed in the literature for understanding why different assets earn different expected rates of return. According to these models, different assets earn different expected returns only because they differ in their systematic risk. The models differ based on the stand they take regarding what constitutes systematic risk. Among them, the linear beta pricing models form an important class.

According to linear beta pricing models, a few economy-wide pervasive factors are sufficient to represent systematic risk, and the expected return on an asset is a linear function of its factor betas (Breeden, 1979; Connor, 1984; Lucas, 1978; Merton, 1973; Ross, 1976). Some beta pricing models specify what the risk factors should be based on theoretical arguments. According to the standard capital asset pricing model (CAPM) by Sharpe (1964) and Lintner (1965), the return on the market portfolio of all assets that are in positive net supply in the economy is the relevant risk factor. Merton (1973) showed that in addition to the return on the market portfolio of all assets in the economy, we need state variables that help forecast future changes in the investment opportunity set. The consumption-based asset pricing model by Lucas (1978) and Breeden (1979) identifies aggregate per capita consumption growth as the relevant risk factor. Epstein and Zin (1989) show that when preferences are recursive, as opposed to time separable, in addition to aggregate per capita consumption growth rate, one also needs the return on the aggregate wealth portfolio to describe economy–wide systematic risk. Other models specify factors based on economic intuition and introspection. For example, Chen et al. (1986) specify unanticipated changes in the term premium, default premium, the growth rate of industrial production, and inflation as the factors, whereas Fama and French (1993) construct factors that capture the size and book-to-market effects documented in the literature and examine if these are sufficient to capture all economy-wide pervasive sources of risk. Campbell (1996) and Jagannathan and Wang (1996) use innovations to labor income as an aggregate risk factor. Another approach is to identify the pervasive risk factors based on systematic statistical analysis of historical return data as in Connor and Korajczyk (1988) and Lehmann and Modest (1988).

In this chapter, we discuss econometric methods that have been used to evaluate linear beta pricing models using historical return data on a large cross-section of stocks. Three approaches have been suggested in the literature for examining linear beta pricing models: (a) the cross-sectional regressions method, (b) the maximum likelihood (ML) methods, and (c) the generalized method of moments (GMM). Shanken (1992) and MacKinlay and Richardson (1991) show that the cross-sectional method is asymptotically equivalent to ML and GMM when returns are identically and independently distributed and conditionally homoskedastic. In view of this, we focus our attention primarily on the cross-sectional regression method because it is more robust and easier to implement in large cross-sections, and provide only a brief overview of the use of ML and GMM.

Fama and MacBeth (1973) developed the two-pass cross-sectional regression method to examine whether the relation between expected return and factor betas are linear. Betas are estimated using time-series regression in the first pass, and the relation between returns and betas is estimated using a second pass cross-sectional regression. The use of estimated betas in the second pass introduces the well-known errors-in-variables (EIV) problem. Note that the EIV problem in the context of the two-pass cross-sectional regression differs from the classical EIV problem studied in statistics and econometrics because the estimation error in the betas is correlated with the residuals in the return regression equation. The standard method for handling the EIV problem is to group stocks into portfolios following Black et al. (1972). Because each portfolio has a large number of individual stocks, portfolio betas are estimated with sufficient precision and this fact allows one to ignore the EIV problem as being of second order in importance. One, however, has to be careful to ensure that the portfolio formation method does not highlight or mask characteristics in the data that have valuable information about the validity of the asset pricing model under examination. Put in other words, one has to avoid data snooping biases discussed by Lo and MacKinlay (1990).

Shanken (1992) provided the first comprehensive analysis of the statistical properties of the classical two-pass estimator under the assumption that returns and factors exhibit conditional homoskedasticity. He demonstrated how to take into account the sampling errors in the betas estimated in the first pass and how to use generalized-least-squares in the second-stage cross-sectional regressions. Given these adjustments, Shanken (1992) conjectured that it may not be necessary to group securities into portfolios to address the EIV problem. Brennan et al. (1998) make the interesting observation that the EIV problem can be avoided without grouping securities into portfolios using risk-adjusted returns as dependent variables in tests of linear beta pricing models, provided all the factors are excess returns on traded assets. However, the relative merits of this approach as compared to portfolio grouping procedures has not been examined in the literature.

Jagannathan and Wang (1998) extended the analysis of Shanken (1992) to allow for conditional heteroskedasticity and consider the case where the model is misspecified. This may happen even when the model holds in the population, if the econometrician uses the wrong factors or misses factors in computing factor betas. When the linear factor pricing model is correctly specified, firm characteristics such as firm size should not be able to explain expected return variations in the cross-section of stocks. In the case of misspecified factor models, Jagannathan and Wang (1998) showed that the t-values associated with firm characteristics will typically be large. Hence, model misspecification can be detected using firm characteristics in the cross-sectional regression. Such a test does not require that the number of assets be small relative to the length of the time-series of observations on asset returns, as is the case with standard multivariate tests of linearity.

Gibbons (1982) showed that the classical ML method can be used to estimate and test linear beta pricing models when stock returns are i.i.d. and jointly normal. Kandel (1984) developed a straightforward computational procedure for implementing the ML method. Shanken (1992) extended it further and showed that the cross-sectional regression approach can be made asymptotically as efficient as the ML method. Kim (1995) developed a ML procedure that allows for the use of betas estimated using past data. Jobson and Korkie (1982) and MacKinlay (1987) developed exact multivariate tests for the CAPM, and Gibbons et al. (1989) developed exact multivariate tests for linear beta pricing models when there is a risk-free asset.

MacKinlay and Richardson (1991) show how to estimate the parameters of the CAPM by applying the GMM to its beta representation. They illustrate the bias in the tests based on standard ML methods when stock returns exhibit conditional heteroskedasticity and show that the GMM estimator and the ML method are equivalent under conditional homoskedasticity. An advantage of using the GMM is that it allows estimation of model parameters in a single pass thereby avoiding the EIV problem. Linear factor pricing models can also be estimated by applying the GMM to their stochastic discount factor (SDF) representation. Jagannathan and Wang (2002) show that parameters estimated by applying the GMM to the SDF representation and the beta representation of linear beta pricing models are asymptotically equivalent.

The rest of the chapter is organized as follows. In Section 2, we set up the necessary notation and describe the general linear beta pricing model. We discuss in detail the two-pass cross-sectional regression method in Section 3 and provide an overview of the ML methods in Section 4 and the GMM in Section 5. We summarize in Section 6.

2. LINEAR BETA PRICING MODELS, FACTORS, AND CHARACTERISTICS

In this section, we first describe the linear beta pricing model and then provide a brief history of its development. We need the following notation. Consider an economy with a large collection of assets. The econometrician has observations on the returns on N of the assets in the economy. Denote by $\mathbf{R}_t = \left[R_t^1 \ R_t^2 \ \cdots \ R_t^N\right]'$ the vector of gross returns on the N securities at time t, by $\mathbf{\Sigma}_R = E\left[(\mathbf{R}_t - E[\mathbf{R}_t])(\mathbf{R}_t - E[\mathbf{R}_t])'\right]$ the covariance matrix of the return vector, and by $\mathbf{f}_t = \left[f_t^1 \ f_t^2 \ \cdots \ f_t^K\right]'$ the vector of time-t values taken by the K factors.

2.1. Linear Beta Pricing Models

Suppose the intertemporal marginal rate of substitution of the marginal investor is a time-variant function of only K economy-wide factors. Further assume that the returns on the N securities are generated according to the following linear factor model with the same K factors:

$$R_t^i = \alpha_i + \mathbf{f}_t'\boldsymbol{\beta}_i + u_{it}, \quad E[u_{it}|\mathbf{f}_t] = 0, \ i = 1, \ldots, N \tag{2.1}$$

where $\boldsymbol{\beta}_i$ is the vector of betas for security i given by

$$\boldsymbol{\beta}_i = \Sigma_F^{-1} E\left[\left(R_t^i - E\left[R_t^i\right]\right)\left(\mathbf{f}_t - E\left[\mathbf{f}_t\right]\right)\right], \tag{2.2}$$

and $\mathbf{\Sigma}_F$ is the covariance matrix of $\mathbf{f}_t$ given by

$$\mathbf{\Sigma}_F = E\left[(\mathbf{f}_t - E[\mathbf{f}_t])(\mathbf{f}_t - E[\mathbf{f}_t])'\right]. \tag{2.3}$$

Under these assumptions, following Connor (1984), it can be shown that the expected return on any asset $i, i = 1, 2, \ldots, N$, is given by the linear beta pricing model as follows

$$E\left[R_t^i\right] = a_0 + \boldsymbol{\lambda}'\boldsymbol{\beta}_i, \quad i = 1, \ldots, N \tag{2.4}$$

where $\boldsymbol{\lambda}$ is the $K \times 1$ vector of constants. The jth element of $\boldsymbol{\lambda}$, λ_j, corresponds to the jth factor risk premium − it is the expected return on a portfolio, p, of the N assets that has the property $\boldsymbol{\beta}_{p,k} = 1$ when $k = j$ and $\boldsymbol{\beta}_{p,k} = 0$ when $k \neq j$.

Sharpe (1964), Lintner (1965), and Mossin (1966) developed the first linear beta pricing model, the standard CAPM. Merton (1973) derived the first linear multibeta pricing model by examining the intertemporal portfolio choice problem of a representative investor in continuous time. Long (1974) proposed a related multibeta pricing model in discrete time. Ross (1976) showed that an approximate version of the linear multibeta pricing model based on the assumptions that returns had a factor structure, the economy was large, and there were no arbitrage opportunities. Chamberlain and Rothschild (1983) extended Ross's result to the case where returns had only an approximate factor structure, i.e., the covariance matrix of asset returns had only K unbounded eigenvalues. Dybvig (1983) and Grinblatt and Titman (1983) provided theoretical arguments supporting the view that deviations from exact linear beta pricing may not be economically important.

2.2. Factor Selection

Three approaches have been followed in the literature for choosing the right factors. The first approach makes use of theory and economic intuition to identify the factors. For example, according to the standard CAPM, there is only one factor and it is the return on the market portfolio of all assets in positive net supply. The intertemporal capital asset pricing model (ICAPM) of Merton (1973) identifies one of the factors as the return on the market portfolio of all assets in positive net supply as in the CAPM. The other factors are those that help predict future changes in investment opportunities. As Campbell (1993) and Jagannathan and Wang (1996) point out, factors that help predict future return on the market portfolio would be particularly suitable as additional factors in an ICAPM setting. The common practice is to use the return on a large portfolio of stocks as a proxy for the return on the market portfolio, and innovations to macroeconomic variables as proxies for the other factors, as in the work of Chen et al. (1986).

The second approach uses statistical analysis of return data for extracting the factors. Factor analysis is one of the statistical approaches used. For expositional purposes, it is convenient to rewrite the linear factor model in matrix notation as follows.

$$\mathbf{R}_t = \boldsymbol{\alpha} + \mathbf{B}\mathbf{f}_t + \mathbf{u}_t \tag{2.5}$$

where $\mathbf{R}_t$ is the $N \times 1$ vector of date t returns on the N assets, $\boldsymbol{\alpha}$ is the N vector of α_i's, $\mathbf{B}$ is the $N \times K$ dimensional matrix of factor betas of the N assets, $\mathbf{f}_t$ is the $K \times 1$ vector of date t factor realizations, and $\mathbf{u}_t$ is the vector of date t linear factor model innovations to the N returns. Let $\boldsymbol{\Sigma}_U$ denote the diagonal covariance matrix of $\mathbf{u}_t$, and $\boldsymbol{\Sigma}_F$ denote the covariance matrix of the factors. The covariance matrix of asset returns $\mathbf{R}_t$, $\boldsymbol{\Sigma}_R$, can be decomposed as follows:

$$\boldsymbol{\Sigma}_R = \mathbf{B}\boldsymbol{\Sigma}_F\mathbf{B}' + \boldsymbol{\Sigma}_U. \tag{2.6}$$

Note that the matrix of factor betas, $\mathbf{B}$, is identified only up to a linear transformation. For example, consider transforming the factors to get $\mathbf{P}^{-1}\mathbf{f}_t$ as a new set of factors and transforming $\boldsymbol{\beta}$ to get $\mathbf{BP}$. Then

$$\boldsymbol{\Sigma}_R = \mathbf{BP}(\mathbf{P}^{-1})\boldsymbol{\Sigma}_F(\mathbf{P}^{-1})'\mathbf{P}'\mathbf{B}' + \boldsymbol{\Sigma}_U = \mathbf{B}\boldsymbol{\Sigma}_F\mathbf{B}' + \boldsymbol{\Sigma}_U. \tag{2.7}$$

The indeterminacy is eliminated by specifying that the factors are orthogonal along with other restrictions. For a discussion the reader is referred to the work of Anderson (2003).

The parameters $\mathbf{B}$ and $\mathbf{\Sigma}_U$ are typically estimated using the ML method under the assumption that stock returns are jointly normal and i.i.d. over time. The estimates of $\mathbf{B}$ obtained in this way are then used in econometric evaluation of the linear beta pricing model given in Eq. (2.4) by applying the cross-sectional regression method described in the next section. When returns on the assets in excess the risk-free rate is used, and the multivariate test proposed by Gibbons et al. (1989) is more convenient after grouping securities into portfolios to reduce the cross-sectional dimension. For many interesting applications, such as portfolio performance evaluation and risk management, it is necessary to have estimates of the factors in addition to the factor betas. There are several approaches to get estimates of the realized value of the factors. The most common is the Fama–MacBeth style GLS cross-sectional regression where the returns are regressed on factor betas obtained through factor analysis. The estimated factors correspond to returns on specific portfolios of the primitive assets used to estimate the factor betas in the first stage using factor analysis. For a detailed discussion of factor selection using factor analysis, the reader is referred to the work of Lehmann and Modest (2005).

Connor and Korajczyk (1986), building on the work of Chamberlain and Rothschild (1983), develop a methodology for identifying the factors using principal components analysis. Let $\mathbf{R}$ denote the $N \times T$ matrix of T returns on the N assets, and define the $T \times T$ matrix $\widehat{\mathbf{\Sigma}}_{RN} = \frac{1}{N}\mathbf{R}'\mathbf{R}$. Connor and Korajczyk (1986) show that, under suitable regularity conditions, the $K \times T$ matrix that has the first K eigenvectors of the matrix $\widehat{\mathbf{\Sigma}}_{RN}$ as rows converges almost surely to the factor matrix $\mathbf{F} = [\mathbf{f}_1 \cdots \mathbf{f}_T]$, as $N \to \infty$, up to a nonsingular linear transformation. Note that a precise estimation of the factors requires the number of securities N to be large. When the number of assets N is much larger than the length of the time-series of return observations T, which is usually the case, Connor and Korajczyk (1986) approach that involves computing the eigenvectors of the $T \times T$ matrix $\widehat{\mathbf{\Sigma}}_{RN}$ is preferable to the other approaches that are equivalent to computing the eigenvectors of the $N \times N$ matrix $\widehat{\mathbf{\Sigma}}_{RT}$, the sample analogue of $\mathbf{\Sigma}_R$. Connor et al. (2007) show that an iterated two-pass procedure, that starts with an arbitrary set of K factors, estimates the factor betas using these factors in the first stage, and then computes the factors using Fama–MacBeth style cross-sectional regressions in the second stage, ultimately converges to the K realized factor values, as the number of asset N becomes large if returns have an approximate K factor structure and some additional regularity conditions are satisfied. The basic intuition behind these methods of estimating factors is that, when returns have an approximate K factor structure, any K distinct well-diversified portfolios span the space of realized values of the K factors as N becomes very large. When the number of assets involved is very large, the sampling errors associated with the factor estimates, as compared to model misspecification errors, are of secondary importance and can be ignored.

The third approach is based on empirical anomalies. Empirical studies in the asset pricing area have documented several well-known anomalies. The size and book-to-price anomalies are the more prominent ones among them. Firms that are relatively small and firms with relatively large book value to market value ratios have historically earned a higher average return after controlling for risk according to the standard CAPM. Banz (1981), Reinganum (1981), and Keim (1983) document the association between size and average returns in the cross-section. Stattman (1980), Rosenberg et al. (1985), and Chan et al. (1991) document the relation between book-to-price ratios and average returns. Schwert (1983) provides a nice discussion of the size and stock return relation and other anomalies. Berk (1995) forcefully argues that relative size and relative book-to-price ratios should be correlated with future returns on average in the cross-section so long as investors have rational expectations. Suppose firms with these characteristics earn a higher return on average to compensate for some pervasive risk factor that is not represented by the standard CAPM. Then the return differential between two portfolios of securities, one with a high score on a characteristic and another that has a low score on the same characteristic, but otherwise similar in all other respects, would mimic the missing risk factor provided the two portfolios have similar exposure to other risk factors. Fama and French (1993) constructed two pervasive risk factors in this way that are now commonly used in empirical studies. One is referred to as the book-to-market factor (HML, short for high minus low) and the other as the size factor (SMB, short for small minus big). Daniel and Titman (1997) present evidence suggesting that these two risk factors constructed by Fama and French may not fully account for the ability of size and book-to-price ratios to predict future returns.

3. CROSS-SECTIONAL REGRESSION METHODS

3.1. Description of the CSR Method

In this subsection, we provide a description of the cross-sectional regression estimator originally developed by Fama and MacBeth (1973) in a slightly different form and present the Fama–MacBeth covariance matrix estimator. We will use succinct vector-matrix notation to ease the exposition. Recall that the $N \times K$ matrix of betas or factor loadings is denoted by $\mathbf{B} = [\boldsymbol{\beta}_1 \; \cdots \; \boldsymbol{\beta}_N]'$. Then Eq. (2.2) can be rewritten compactly as

$$\mathbf{B} = E\left[(\mathbf{R}_t - E[\mathbf{R}_t])\,(\mathbf{f}_t - E[\mathbf{f}_t])'\right] \boldsymbol{\Sigma}_{\mathrm{F}}^{-1}. \tag{3.1}$$

Next, we define the vector of risk premia

$$\mathbf{c} = [a_0 \; \boldsymbol{\lambda}']' \quad ((K+1) \times 1 \text{ vector}) \tag{3.2}$$

and the matrix

$$\mathbf{X} = [\mathbf{1}_N \; \mathbf{B}] \quad (N \times (K+1) \text{ matrix}). \tag{3.3}$$

We assume that $N > K$, as is typically the case in practice. The rank of matrix of $\mathbf{X}$ is assumed to equal $K + 1$, that is, $\mathbf{X}$ is of full rank. The beta representation equation (2.4) is then concisely expressed as

$$E[\mathbf{R}_t] = a_0 \mathbf{1}_N + \mathbf{B}\boldsymbol{\lambda} = \mathbf{X}\mathbf{c} \tag{3.4}$$

and therefore the unknown parameter $\mathbf{c}$ can be expressed as

$$\mathbf{c} = (\mathbf{X}'\mathbf{X})^{-1}\mathbf{X}'E[\mathbf{R}_t]. \tag{3.5}$$

Standard time-series regression yields

$$\mathbf{R}_t = E[\mathbf{R}_t] + \mathbf{B}(\mathbf{f}_t - E[\mathbf{f}_t]) + \mathbf{u}_t \quad \text{with} \quad E[\mathbf{u}_t] = \mathbf{0}_N \quad \text{and} \quad E[\mathbf{u}_t\mathbf{f}_t'] = \mathbf{0}_{N \times K} \tag{3.6}$$

as it follows from the definition of $\mathbf{B}$. Thus, using the beta representation (3.4) we can rewrite Eq. (3.6) as

$$\mathbf{R}_t = a_0 \mathbf{1}_N + \mathbf{B}(\mathbf{f}_t - E[\mathbf{f}_t] + \boldsymbol{\lambda}) + \mathbf{u}_t. \tag{3.7}$$

Equation (3.7) can be viewed as the model describing the return data generating process.

Suppose that the econometrician observes a time-series of length T of security return and factor realizations, denoted as follows

$$\left[\mathbf{R}_t' \ \mathbf{f}_t'\right]' = \left(R_t^1, \ldots, R_t^N, f_t^1, \ldots, f_t^K\right)', \quad t = 1, \ldots, T. \tag{3.8}$$

Some standard econometric assumptions about the dynamics of the preceding time-series are in order. These assumptions will be necessary for the development of the asymptotic theory that follows. We assume that the vector process $\left[\mathbf{R}_t' \ \mathbf{f}_t'\right]'$ is stationary and ergodic and that the law of large numbers applies so that the sample moments of returns and factors converge to the corresponding population moments.

The CSR testing method involves two steps and for this reason it is also referred to as the two-pass procedure. In the first step, we estimate $\boldsymbol{\Sigma}_F$ and $\mathbf{B}$ by the standard sample analog estimates

$$\widehat{\boldsymbol{\Sigma}}_{FT} = \frac{1}{T} \sum_{t=1}^{T} \left(\mathbf{f}_t - \overline{\mathbf{f}}_T\right)\left(\mathbf{f}_t - \overline{\mathbf{f}}_T\right)' \quad \text{where} \quad \overline{\mathbf{f}}_T = \frac{1}{T} \sum_{t=1}^{T} \mathbf{f}_t \tag{3.9}$$

and

$$\widehat{\mathbf{B}}_T = \left[\frac{1}{T} \sum_{t=1}^{T} \left(\mathbf{R}_t - \overline{\mathbf{R}}_T\right)\left(\mathbf{f}_t - \overline{\mathbf{f}}_T\right)'\right]\widehat{\boldsymbol{\Sigma}}_{FT}^{-1} \quad \text{where} \quad \overline{\mathbf{R}}_T = \frac{1}{T} \sum_{t=1}^{T} \mathbf{R}_t. \tag{3.10}$$

Then, in the second step, for each $t = 1, \ldots, T$, we use the estimate $\widehat{\mathbf{B}}_T$ of the beta matrix $\mathbf{B}$ and simple cross-sectional regression to obtain the following ordinary least-squares (OLS) estimates of $\mathbf{c}$

$$\widehat{\mathbf{c}}_t = \left(\widehat{\mathbf{X}}_T' \widehat{\mathbf{X}}_T\right)^{-1} \widehat{\mathbf{X}}_T' \mathbf{R}_t, \quad t = 1, \ldots, T, \tag{3.11}$$

where

$$\widehat{\mathbf{X}}_T = [\mathbf{1}_N \ \widehat{\mathbf{B}}_T] \tag{3.12}$$

as suggested by Eq. (3.4). The standard Fama–MacBeth estimate of $\mathbf{c}$ then is the time-series average of the T estimates

$$\bar{\widehat{\mathbf{c}}}_T = \frac{1}{T}\sum_{t=1}^{T}\widehat{\mathbf{c}}_t = \left(\widehat{\mathbf{X}}_T'\widehat{\mathbf{X}}_T\right)^{-1}\widehat{\mathbf{X}}_T'\overline{\mathbf{R}}_T. \tag{3.13}$$

To conduct inference regarding the parameter of interest $\mathbf{c}$, one also needs estimates of the asymptotic covariance of the estimator $\bar{\widehat{\mathbf{c}}}_T$. Fama and MacBeth (1973) proposed treating the set of the individual CSR estimates $\{\widehat{\mathbf{c}}_t : t = 1, \ldots, T\}$ as a random sample and therefore estimating the covariance matrix of $\sqrt{T}(\bar{\widehat{\mathbf{c}}}_T - \mathbf{c})$ by

$$\widehat{\mathbf{V}}_T = \frac{1}{T}\sum_{t=1}^{T}(\widehat{\mathbf{c}}_t - \bar{\widehat{\mathbf{c}}}_T)(\widehat{\mathbf{c}}_t - \bar{\widehat{\mathbf{c}}}_T)'. \tag{3.14}$$

The Fama–MacBeth procedure has an intuitive appeal and is rather easy to implement. However, one has to use caution when using this procedure because it is subject to the well-known EIV problem. As first pointed out by Shanken (1992), some corrections are required to ensure the validity of the method.

A more flexible estimate that has been suggested in the literature is the feasible GLS version of the foregoing estimate. The following notation for the GLS weighting matrix and the corresponding estimator will be used throughout the Section 3. Let $\mathbf{Q}$ be a symmetric and positive definite $N \times N$ matrix and $\widehat{\mathbf{Q}}_T$ be a consistent estimator of $\mathbf{Q}$ that is also assumed to be symmetric and positive definite for all T. Then the feasible GLS estimator of $\mathbf{c}$ obtained from the cross-sectional regression at time t is

$$\widehat{\mathbf{c}}_t = \left(\widehat{\mathbf{X}}_T'\widehat{\mathbf{Q}}_T\widehat{\mathbf{X}}_T\right)^{-1}\widehat{\mathbf{X}}_T'\widehat{\mathbf{Q}}_T\mathbf{R}_t \tag{3.15}$$

and therefore the Fama–MacBeth estimator of $\mathbf{c}$ is given by

$$\bar{\widehat{\mathbf{c}}}_T = \frac{1}{T}\sum_{t=1}^{T}\left(\widehat{\mathbf{X}}_T'\widehat{\mathbf{Q}}_T\widehat{\mathbf{X}}_T\right)^{-1}\widehat{\mathbf{X}}_T'\widehat{\mathbf{Q}}_T\mathbf{R}_t = \left(\widehat{\mathbf{X}}_T'\widehat{\mathbf{Q}}_T\widehat{\mathbf{X}}_T\right)^{-1}\widehat{\mathbf{X}}_T'\widehat{\mathbf{Q}}_T\overline{\mathbf{R}}_T. \tag{3.16}$$

The subsequent analysis will employ the feasible GLS version of the CSR estimator.

3.2. Consistency and Asymptotic Normality of the CSR Estimator

In this subsection, we address the issues of consistency and asymptotic normality of the two-pass cross-sectional regression estimator that was described in the previous section. Using the law of large numbers and Slutsky's theorem, it follows from (3.10) and (3.9) that $\widehat{\mathbf{X}}_T \overset{P}{\longrightarrow} \mathbf{X}$, as $T \to \infty$. Applying the law of large numbers and Slutsky's theorem once again and using (3.4) we obtain from (3.16) that $\overline{\widehat{\mathbf{c}}}_T$ converges in probability to $(\mathbf{X}'\mathbf{QX})^{-1}\mathbf{X}'\mathbf{Q}E[\mathbf{R}_t] = (\mathbf{X}'\mathbf{QX})^{-1}\mathbf{X}'\mathbf{QXc} = \mathbf{c}$. Thus, we have shown the following

Proposition 1 *The time-series average $\overline{\widehat{\mathbf{c}}}_T$ of the cross-sectional estimates*

$$\widehat{\mathbf{c}}_t = \left(\widehat{\mathbf{X}}_T'\widehat{\mathbf{Q}}_T\widehat{\mathbf{X}}_T\right)^{-1}\widehat{\mathbf{X}}_T'\widehat{\mathbf{Q}}_T\mathbf{R}_t, \quad t = 1, \ldots, T,$$

where $\widehat{\mathbf{X}}_T = [\mathbf{1}_N \ \widehat{\mathbf{B}}_T]$ is a consistent estimator of $\mathbf{c} = \begin{bmatrix} a_0 & \boldsymbol{\lambda}' \end{bmatrix}'$, that is

$$\overline{\widehat{\mathbf{c}}}_T \overset{P}{\longrightarrow} \mathbf{c} \text{ as } T \to \infty. \tag{3.17}$$

Next we proceed to address the issue of precision of the estimator $\overline{\widehat{\mathbf{c}}}_T$ by deriving its asymptotic distribution. The derivation will require some additional mild assumptions. First we need some notation. Define

$$\mathbf{D} = (\mathbf{X}'\mathbf{QX})^{-1}\mathbf{X}'\mathbf{Q} \tag{3.18}$$

and

$$\mathbf{h}_t^1 = \mathbf{R}_t - E[\mathbf{R}_t], \quad \mathbf{h}_t^2 = \left[(\mathbf{f}_t - E[\mathbf{f}_t])'\boldsymbol{\Sigma}_{\mathrm{F}}^{-1}\boldsymbol{\lambda}\right]\mathbf{u}_t, \quad \text{and} \quad \mathbf{h}_t = [(\mathbf{h}_t^1)' \ (\mathbf{h}_t^2)']'. \tag{3.19}$$

Clearly $E[\mathbf{h}_t^1] = \mathbf{0}_N$ and (3.6) implies $E[\mathbf{h}_t^2] = \mathbf{0}_N$. The following assumption will be essential in the derivation of the asymptotic distribution of the CSR estimator.

Assumption A The central limit theorem applies to the random sequence $\mathbf{h}_t$ defined in (3.19), that is $\frac{1}{\sqrt{T}} \sum_{t=1}^T \mathbf{h}_t$ converges in distribution to a multivariate normal with zero mean and covariance matrix given by

$$\boldsymbol{\Sigma}_{\mathbf{h}} = \begin{bmatrix} \boldsymbol{\Psi} & \boldsymbol{\Gamma} \\ \boldsymbol{\Gamma}' & \boldsymbol{\Pi} \end{bmatrix},$$

where

$$\boldsymbol{\Psi} = \sum_{k=-\infty}^{+\infty} E[\mathbf{h}_t^1(\mathbf{h}_{t+k}^1)'], \quad \boldsymbol{\Gamma} = \sum_{k=-\infty}^{+\infty} E[\mathbf{h}_t^1(\mathbf{h}_{t+k}^2)'], \quad \text{and} \quad \boldsymbol{\Pi} = \sum_{k=-\infty}^{+\infty} E[\mathbf{h}_t^2(\mathbf{h}_{t+k}^2)']. \tag{3.20}$$

Assumption A is rather mild and can be obtained under standard stationarity, mixing and moment existence conditions. Related results can be found, for instance, by Hall and Heyde (1980) and Davidson (1994). Note that when the time-series $\begin{bmatrix} \mathbf{R}_t' & \mathbf{f}_t' \end{bmatrix}'$ is stationary and serially independent, we have $\boldsymbol{\Psi} = E[\mathbf{h}_t^1(\mathbf{h}_t^1)'] = \boldsymbol{\Sigma}_{\mathbf{R}}$.

We are now in a position to state and prove the theorem that gives the asymptotic distribution of the CSR estimator. A more general version of this theorem, dealing also with security characteristics, appeared as Theorem 1 in the work of Jagannathan and Wang (1998) with slightly different notation. We will denote $\mathbf{A}_T \overset{LD}{=} \mathbf{B}_T$ when the two multivariate time-series $\mathbf{A}_T$ and $\mathbf{B}_T$ have the same asymptotic distribution as $T \to \infty$.

Theorem 1 *Let* $\mathbf{c} = [a_0 \quad \boldsymbol{\lambda}']'$ *and* $\widehat{\bar{\mathbf{c}}}_T = (\widehat{\mathbf{X}}'_T \widehat{\mathbf{Q}}_T \widehat{\mathbf{X}}_T)^{-1} \widehat{\mathbf{X}}'_T \widehat{\mathbf{Q}}_T \overline{\mathbf{R}}_T$ *where* $\widehat{\mathbf{X}}_T = [\mathbf{1}_N \quad \widehat{\mathbf{B}}_T]$. *Under Assumption A, as* $T \to \infty$, $\sqrt{T}(\widehat{\bar{\mathbf{c}}}_T - \mathbf{c})$ *converges in distribution to a multivariate normal with zero mean and covariance*

$$\boldsymbol{\Sigma}_c = \mathbf{D}\boldsymbol{\Psi}\mathbf{D}' + \mathbf{D}\boldsymbol{\Pi}\mathbf{D}' - \mathbf{D}\left(\boldsymbol{\Gamma} + \boldsymbol{\Gamma}'\right)\mathbf{D}', \tag{3.21}$$

where $\mathbf{D} = (\mathbf{X}'\mathbf{Q}\mathbf{X})^{-1}\mathbf{X}'\mathbf{Q}$ *with* $\mathbf{X} = [\mathbf{1}_N \quad \mathbf{B}]$ *and* $\boldsymbol{\Psi}, \boldsymbol{\Gamma}$, *and* $\boldsymbol{\Pi}$ *are defined in (3.20).*

Proof. First we note that the identity $\mathbf{R}_t = \widehat{\mathbf{X}}_T\mathbf{c} + (\mathbf{B} - \widehat{\mathbf{B}}_T)\boldsymbol{\lambda} + \mathbf{R}_t - \mathbf{Xc}$ holds. Using the pricing equation (3.4) and the foregoing identity we obtain from (3.16)

$$\widehat{\mathbf{c}}_t = \mathbf{c} + (\widehat{\mathbf{X}}'_T\widehat{\mathbf{Q}}_T\widehat{\mathbf{X}}_T)^{-1}\widehat{\mathbf{X}}'_T\widehat{\mathbf{Q}}_T[(\mathbf{B} - \widehat{\mathbf{B}}_T)\boldsymbol{\lambda} + (\mathbf{R}_t - E[\mathbf{R}_t])]$$

from which it follows, using Slutsky's theorem, that

$$\sqrt{T}(\widehat{\bar{\mathbf{c}}}_T - \mathbf{c}) = (\widehat{\mathbf{X}}'_T\widehat{\mathbf{Q}}_T\widehat{\mathbf{X}}_T)^{-1}\widehat{\mathbf{X}}'_T\widehat{\mathbf{Q}}_T\left[\sqrt{T}(\mathbf{B} - \widehat{\mathbf{B}}_T)\boldsymbol{\lambda} + \frac{1}{\sqrt{T}}\sum_{t=1}^{T}(\mathbf{R}_t - E[\mathbf{R}_t])\right]$$

$$\overset{LD}{=} \mathbf{D}\left[\sqrt{T}(\mathbf{B} - \widehat{\mathbf{B}}_T)\boldsymbol{\lambda} + \frac{1}{\sqrt{T}}\sum_{t=1}^{T}(\mathbf{R}_t - E[\mathbf{R}_t])\right]. \tag{3.22}$$

From Eq. (3.7), we have

$$\mathbf{R}_t - \overline{\mathbf{R}}_T = \mathbf{B}(\mathbf{f}_t - \overline{\mathbf{f}}_T) + \mathbf{u}_t - \overline{\mathbf{u}}_T \Rightarrow$$

$$\frac{1}{T}\sum_{t=1}^{T}(\mathbf{R}_t - \overline{\mathbf{R}}_T)(\mathbf{f}_t - \overline{\mathbf{f}}_T)' = \frac{1}{T}\sum_{t=1}^{T}(\mathbf{u}_t - \overline{\mathbf{u}}_T)(\mathbf{f}_t - \overline{\mathbf{f}}_T)' + \mathbf{B}\widehat{\boldsymbol{\Sigma}}_{\mathrm{FT}}$$

and therefore (3.10) yields

$$\widehat{\mathbf{B}}_T - \mathbf{B} = \left[\frac{1}{T}\sum_{t=1}^{T}\mathbf{u}_t(\mathbf{f}_t - \overline{\mathbf{f}}_T)'\right]\widehat{\boldsymbol{\Sigma}}_{\mathrm{FT}}^{-1}.$$

Using the last equation and Slutsky's theorem again we obtain from (3.22) that

$$\sqrt{T}(\bar{\bar{\mathbf{c}}}_T - \mathbf{c}) \overset{\text{LD}}{=} \mathbf{D}\left[-\frac{1}{\sqrt{T}}\sum_{t=1}^{T}\mathbf{u}_t(\mathbf{f}_t - \bar{\mathbf{f}}_T)'\,\boldsymbol{\Sigma}_{\text{F}}^{-1}\boldsymbol{\lambda} + \frac{1}{\sqrt{T}}\sum_{t=1}^{T}(\mathbf{R}_t - E[\mathbf{R}_t])\right]$$

$$\overset{\text{LD}}{=} \mathbf{D}\left[\frac{1}{\sqrt{T}}\sum_{t=1}^{T}\left(\mathbf{h}_t^1 - \mathbf{h}_t^2\right)\right] = \mathbf{DH}\frac{1}{\sqrt{T}}\sum_{t=1}^{T}\mathbf{h}_t,$$

where $\mathbf{H} = [\mathbf{I}_N \quad -\mathbf{I}_N]$. Using Assumption A, which states that the central limit theorem applies to the random sequence $\mathbf{h}_t$, yields the asymptotic distribution of $\bar{\bar{\mathbf{c}}}_T$

$$\sqrt{T}(\bar{\bar{\mathbf{c}}}_T - \mathbf{c}) \overset{\mathcal{D}}{\longrightarrow} N(\mathbf{0}, \boldsymbol{\Sigma}_c),$$

where

$$\boldsymbol{\Sigma}_c = \mathbf{DH}\begin{bmatrix}\boldsymbol{\Psi} & \boldsymbol{\Gamma} \\ \boldsymbol{\Gamma}' & \boldsymbol{\Pi}\end{bmatrix}\mathbf{H}'\mathbf{D}' = \mathbf{D}\boldsymbol{\Psi}\mathbf{D}' + \mathbf{D}\boldsymbol{\Pi}\mathbf{D}' - \mathbf{D}\left(\boldsymbol{\Gamma} + \boldsymbol{\Gamma}'\right)\mathbf{D}'$$

thus completing the proof. ■

Using the previous theorem, we can compute appropriate standard errors and thus test hypotheses of interest, such as $\boldsymbol{\lambda} = \mathbf{0}_K$. Actual application of the theorem, though, requires knowledge of several matrices. Because the matrices are unknown, we use the values of their consistent estimators instead. The matrix $\mathbf{D}$ can be consistently estimated by $(\widehat{\mathbf{X}}_T'\widehat{\mathbf{Q}}_T\widehat{\mathbf{X}}_T)^{-1}\widehat{\mathbf{X}}_T'\widehat{\mathbf{Q}}_T$, while the spectral density matrix $\boldsymbol{\Sigma}_{\mathbf{h}} = \sum_{k=-\infty}^{k=\infty}E\left[\mathbf{h}_t\mathbf{h}_{t+k}'\right]$ can be estimated by the methods proposed by Newey and West (1987), Andrews (1991), and Andrews and Monahan (1992). In large cross-sections, it would be necessary to impose a block diagonal structure on $\boldsymbol{\Sigma}_{\mathbf{h}}$ to ensure that the law of large numbers starts kicking in given the length of the time-series of observations available to the econometrician.

3.3. Fama–MacBeth Variance Estimator

As mentioned in Section 3.1, the Fama–MacBeth estimator of the asymptotic covariance matrix of $\bar{\bar{\mathbf{c}}}_T$ is $\widehat{\mathbf{V}}_T = \frac{1}{T}\sum_{t=1}^{T}(\widehat{\mathbf{c}}_t - \bar{\bar{\mathbf{c}}}_T)(\widehat{\mathbf{c}}_t - \bar{\bar{\mathbf{c}}}_T)'$. In this section, we examine the limiting behavior of $\widehat{\mathbf{V}}_T$. Substituting $\widehat{\mathbf{c}}_t$ from (3.15) into (3.14) we obtain

$$\widehat{\mathbf{V}}_T = \mathbf{D}_T\left[\frac{1}{T}\sum_{t=1}^{T}(\mathbf{R}_t - \bar{\mathbf{R}}_T)(\mathbf{R}_t - \bar{\mathbf{R}}_T)'\right]\mathbf{D}_T', \tag{3.23}$$

where

$$\mathbf{D}_T = (\widehat{\mathbf{X}}_T'\widehat{\mathbf{Q}}_T\widehat{\mathbf{X}}_T)^{-1}\widehat{\mathbf{X}}_T'\widehat{\mathbf{Q}}_T. \tag{3.24}$$

Applying the law of large numbers and the fact that $\widehat{\mathbf{Q}}_T \xrightarrow{P} \mathbf{Q}$ then yields that $\widehat{\mathbf{V}}_T \xrightarrow{P} \mathbf{D}\mathbf{\Sigma}_R\mathbf{D}' = \mathbf{V}$, where $\mathbf{D}$ is defined in (3.18) and $\mathbf{\Sigma}_R$ is the return covariance matrix. Hence, we have established the following

Proposition 2 *The Fama–MacBeth covariance estimator* $\widehat{\mathbf{V}}_T$ *converges in probability to the matrix* $\mathbf{V} = \mathbf{D}\mathbf{\Sigma}_R\mathbf{D}'$, *that is,*

$$\widehat{\mathbf{V}}_T \xrightarrow{P} \mathbf{V} = \mathbf{D}\mathbf{\Sigma}_R\mathbf{D}', \; as \; T \to \infty, \tag{3.25}$$

where $\mathbf{D} = (\mathbf{X}'\mathbf{Q}\mathbf{X})^{-1}\mathbf{X}'\mathbf{Q}$ *with* $\mathbf{X} = [\mathbf{1}_N \; \mathbf{B}]$.

The preceding proposition is the mathematical statement representing the well-known EIV problem. On comparing the expression (3.21) for the asymptotic covariance $\mathbf{\Sigma}_c$ of the estimator $\bar{\bar{\mathbf{c}}}_T$ with the expression for $\mathbf{V}$, it follows that, in general, the standard Fama–MacBeth covariance estimator $\widehat{\mathbf{V}}_T$ is not a consistent estimator of $\mathbf{\Sigma}_c$. In the case of serially uncorrelated returns we have $\mathbf{\Psi} = \mathbf{\Sigma}_R$ and thus $\mathbf{V} = \mathbf{D}\mathbf{\Psi}\mathbf{D}'$ is the first term appearing in the expression (3.21) for the asymptotic covariance of the estimator $\bar{\bar{\mathbf{c}}}_T$. The second term in (3.21) is clearly a positive semidefinite matrix. However, the presence of the last term in (3.21) complicates the situation and makes unclear whether the Fama–MacBeth procedure leads to underestimation or overestimation of the covariance of the CSR estimator, even in the case of serially uncorrelated returns.

In the general case, the bias of the Fama–MacBeth estimator is due to two reasons: the Fama–MacBeth estimator ignores the estimation error in betas as well as serial correlation in returns. To illustrate the point more clearly, consider the following version of the Fama–MacBeth covariance estimator that accounts for serial correlation:

$$\tilde{\mathbf{V}}_T = \tilde{\mathbf{V}}_{0,T} + \sum_{k=1}^{K_T} \left(1 - \frac{k}{K_T + 1}\right)\left(\tilde{\mathbf{V}}_{k,T} + \tilde{\mathbf{V}}'_{k,T}\right), \tag{3.26}$$

where

$$\tilde{\mathbf{V}}_{k,T} = \frac{1}{T}\sum_{t=k+1}^{T}(\widehat{\mathbf{c}}_t - \bar{\bar{\mathbf{c}}}_T)(\widehat{\mathbf{c}}_{t-k} - \bar{\bar{\mathbf{c}}}_T)', \quad k = 0, 1, \ldots$$

The estimator $\tilde{\mathbf{V}}_T$ is constructed in the spirit of heteroskedasticity and autocorrelation consistent (HAC) estimators; see Newey and West (1987) for details. It follows that

$$\tilde{\mathbf{V}}_T = \mathbf{D}_T\widehat{\mathbf{\Psi}}_T\mathbf{D}'_T, \tag{3.27}$$

where $\mathbf{D}_T$ is defined in (3.24), and

$$\widehat{\mathbf{\Psi}}_T = \widehat{\mathbf{\Psi}}_{0,T} + \sum_{k=1}^{K_T} \left(1 - \frac{k}{K_T + 1}\right)\left(\widehat{\mathbf{\Psi}}_{k,T} + \widehat{\mathbf{\Psi}}'_{k,T}\right), \tag{3.28}$$

with

$$\widehat{\mathbf{\Psi}}_{k,T} = \frac{1}{T} \sum_{t=k+1}^{T} \left(\mathbf{R}_t - \overline{\mathbf{R}}_T\right)\left(\mathbf{R}_{t-k} - \overline{\mathbf{R}}_T\right)'. \tag{3.29}$$

Under suitable regularity conditions and if $K_T \to \infty$, as $T \to \infty$, at an appropriate rate, it follows that $\widehat{\mathbf{\Psi}}_T \overset{P}{\longrightarrow} \mathbf{\Psi}$ and, therefore, $\widetilde{\mathbf{V}}_T = \mathbf{D}_T \widehat{\mathbf{\Psi}}_T \mathbf{D}'_T \overset{P}{\longrightarrow} \mathbf{D}\mathbf{\Psi}\mathbf{D}'$. Hence, the generalized Fama–MacBeth estimator $\widetilde{\mathbf{V}}_T$ converges in probability to the first term in (3.21). However, even though it accounts for serial correlation in returns, $\widetilde{\mathbf{V}}_T$ is, in general, not consistent because it ignores the estimation error in betas. The bias is captured by the second and third terms in (3.21). Arguing as mentioned earlier, we conclude that it is not clear whether the generalized estimator $\widetilde{\mathbf{V}}_T$ results in underestimation or overestimation of the covariance of the CSR estimator. The situation becomes more straightforward under the simplifying assumption of conditional homoskedasticity, as we illustrate next.

3.4. Conditionally Homoskedastic Residuals Given the Factors

In this section, we look at the asymptotic behavior of the CSR estimator under the assumption that the time-series residuals $\mathbf{u}_t$ are conditionally homoskedastic given the factors $\mathbf{f}_t$. The assumption of conditional homoskedasticity, which has been employed in the analysis by Shanken (1992) (see Assumption 1 in his paper), holds when the returns and the factors are serially independent, identically distributed and have a joint normal distribution. Some extra notation will enable us to state and prove the related results. Denote by $\mathbf{\Sigma}_{\overline{\mathbf{F}}}$ the asymptotic covariance matrix of $\overline{\mathbf{f}}_T = \frac{1}{T}\sum_{t=1}^{T} \mathbf{f}_t$, that is

$$\mathbf{\Sigma}_{\overline{\mathbf{F}}} = \sum_{k=-\infty}^{\infty} E\left[(\mathbf{f}_t - E[\mathbf{f}_t])\,(\mathbf{f}_{t+k} - E[\mathbf{f}_{t+k}])'\right] \tag{3.30}$$

and further define the so-called bordered version of $\mathbf{\Sigma}_{\overline{\mathbf{F}}}$ by

$$\mathbf{\Sigma}_{\overline{\mathbf{F}}}^* = \begin{bmatrix} 0 & \mathbf{0}'_K \\ \mathbf{0}_K & \mathbf{\Sigma}_{\overline{\mathbf{F}}} \end{bmatrix}. \tag{3.31}$$

Let $\mathcal{F}$ denote the information set generated by the entire factor sequence $\{\mathbf{f}_t : t = 1, 2, \ldots\}$ and let $\mathbf{\Sigma}_U$ be a constant $N \times N$ symmetric and positive definite matrix. Consider the following:

Assumption B Given the information set $\mathcal{F}$, the time-series regression residuals $\mathbf{u}_t$ have zero conditional mean, i.e. $E[\mathbf{u}_t|\mathcal{F}] = \mathbf{0}_N$. Furthermore, given $\mathcal{F}$, the residuals $\mathbf{u}_t$ have constant conditional covariance equal to $\mathbf{\Sigma}_U$ and are conditionally serially uncorrelated, i.e., $E[\mathbf{u}_t\mathbf{u}'_t|\mathcal{F}] = \mathbf{\Sigma}_U$ and $E[\mathbf{u}_t\mathbf{u}'_{t+k}|\mathcal{F}] = \mathbf{0}_{N\times N}$ for all nonzero integers k.

The main result under the conditional homoskedasticity assumption is captured in the following theorem. A more general version of this theorem, directly imposing pricing restrictions to factors that are returns to traded portfolios, appeared as Theorem 1 (iii) in the work of Shanken (1992).

Theorem 2 *Let* $\mathbf{c} = [a_0\ \boldsymbol{\lambda}']'$ *and* $\overline{\widehat{\mathbf{c}}}_T = (\widehat{\mathbf{X}}'_T\widehat{\mathbf{Q}}_T\widehat{\mathbf{X}}_T)^{-1}\widehat{\mathbf{X}}'_T\widehat{\mathbf{Q}}_T\overline{\mathbf{R}}_T$ *with* $\widehat{\mathbf{X}}_T = [\mathbf{1}_N\ \widehat{\mathbf{B}}_T]$. *Assumption B implies* $\boldsymbol{\Psi} = \mathbf{B}\boldsymbol{\Sigma}_{\overline{F}}\mathbf{B}' + \boldsymbol{\Sigma}_U, \boldsymbol{\Pi} = \left(\boldsymbol{\lambda}'\boldsymbol{\Sigma}_F^{-1}\boldsymbol{\lambda}\right)\boldsymbol{\Sigma}_U$, *and* $\boldsymbol{\Gamma} = \mathbf{0}_{N\times N}$ *where* $\boldsymbol{\Psi}, \boldsymbol{\Pi}$, *and* $\boldsymbol{\Gamma}$ *are defined in (3.20). Therefore, under Assumptions A and B, the result in Theorem 1 becomes*

$$\sqrt{T}(\overline{\widehat{\mathbf{c}}}_T - \mathbf{c}) \xrightarrow{\mathcal{D}} N(\mathbf{0}_{K+1}, \boldsymbol{\Sigma}_c) \quad as \quad T \to \infty, \tag{3.32}$$

where

$$\boldsymbol{\Sigma}_c = \boldsymbol{\Sigma}_{\overline{F}}^* + \left(1 + \boldsymbol{\lambda}'\boldsymbol{\Sigma}_F^{-1}\boldsymbol{\lambda}\right)\mathbf{D}\boldsymbol{\Sigma}_U\mathbf{D}' \tag{3.33}$$

with $\boldsymbol{\Sigma}_{\overline{F}}^*$ *being the bordered version of* $\boldsymbol{\Sigma}_{\overline{F}}$ *defined in (3.31) and* $\mathbf{D} = (\mathbf{X}'\mathbf{Q}\mathbf{X})^{-1}\mathbf{X}'\mathbf{Q}$ *with* $\mathbf{X} = [\mathbf{1}_N\ \mathbf{B}]$.

Proof. Let k be any integer. First, we obtain the expression for $\boldsymbol{\Psi}$. Using (3.19), (3.6), the law of iterated expectations and Assumption A we obtain

$$E\left[\mathbf{h}_t^1\left(\mathbf{h}_{t+k}^1\right)'\right] = E\left[[\mathbf{B}(\mathbf{f}_t - E[\mathbf{f}_t]) + \mathbf{u}_t]\left[\mathbf{B}(\mathbf{f}_{t+k} - E[\mathbf{f}_{t+k}]) + \mathbf{u}_{t+k}\right]'\right]$$
$$= \mathbf{B}E\left[(\mathbf{f}_t - E[\mathbf{f}_t])(\mathbf{f}_{t+k} - E[\mathbf{f}_{t+k}])'\right]\mathbf{B}' + \mathbb{I}_{[k=0]}E\left[\mathbf{u}_t\mathbf{u}_t'\right]$$

where $\mathbb{I}$ denotes the indicator function. Therefore from (3.20) and (3.30) it follows that $\boldsymbol{\Psi} = \mathbf{B}\boldsymbol{\Sigma}_{\overline{F}}\mathbf{B}' + \boldsymbol{\Sigma}_U$. Next, we obtain the expression for $\boldsymbol{\Pi}$. From (3.19), the law of iterated expectations and Assumption A, it follows that

$$E\left[\mathbf{h}_t^2\left(\mathbf{h}_{t+k}^2\right)'\right] = E\left[[\boldsymbol{\lambda}'\boldsymbol{\Sigma}_F^{-1}(\mathbf{f}_t - E[\mathbf{f}_t])][\boldsymbol{\lambda}'\boldsymbol{\Sigma}_F^{-1}(\mathbf{f}_{t+k} - E[\mathbf{f}_{t+k}])]\mathbf{u}_t\mathbf{u}_{t+k}'\right]$$
$$= E\left[[\boldsymbol{\lambda}'\boldsymbol{\Sigma}_F^{-1}(\mathbf{f}_t - E[\mathbf{f}_t])][\boldsymbol{\lambda}'\boldsymbol{\Sigma}_F^{-1}(\mathbf{f}_{t+k} - E[\mathbf{f}_{t+k}])]E\left[\mathbf{u}_t\mathbf{u}_{t+k}'|\mathcal{F}\right]\right]$$
$$= \mathbb{I}_{[k=0]}E\left[\boldsymbol{\lambda}'\boldsymbol{\Sigma}_F^{-1}(\mathbf{f}_t - E[\mathbf{f}_t])(\mathbf{f}_t - E[\mathbf{f}_t])'\boldsymbol{\Sigma}_F^{-1}\boldsymbol{\lambda}\right]\boldsymbol{\Sigma}_U$$
$$= \mathbb{I}_{[k=0]}\left(\boldsymbol{\lambda}'\boldsymbol{\Sigma}_F^{-1}\boldsymbol{\Sigma}_F\boldsymbol{\Sigma}_F^{-1}\boldsymbol{\lambda}\right)\boldsymbol{\Sigma}_U = \mathbb{I}_{[k=0]}\left(\boldsymbol{\lambda}'\boldsymbol{\Sigma}_F^{-1}\boldsymbol{\lambda}\right)\boldsymbol{\Sigma}_U.$$

The expression $\boldsymbol{\Pi} = \left(\boldsymbol{\lambda}'\boldsymbol{\Sigma}_F^{-1}\boldsymbol{\lambda}\right)\boldsymbol{\Sigma}_U$ then follows from (3.20). Finally, we obtain the expression for $\boldsymbol{\Gamma}$. From (3.19) and (3.6) we obtain

$$E\left[\mathbf{h}_t^1\left(\mathbf{h}_{t+k}^2\right)'\right] = E\left[(\mathbf{R}_t - E[\mathbf{R}_t])\left[\mathbf{u}_{t+k}(\mathbf{f}_{t+k} - E[\mathbf{f}_{t+k}])'\boldsymbol{\Sigma}_F^{-1}\boldsymbol{\lambda}\right]'\right]$$
$$= E\left[[\boldsymbol{\lambda}'\boldsymbol{\Sigma}_F^{-1}(\mathbf{f}_{t+k} - E[\mathbf{f}_{t+k}])](\mathbf{B}(\mathbf{f}_t - E[\mathbf{f}_t]) + \mathbf{u}_t)\mathbf{u}_{t+k}'\right].$$

Thus, by the assumptions $E[\mathbf{u}_t|\mathcal{F}] = \mathbf{0}_N$ and $E[\mathbf{u}_t\mathbf{u}'_{t+k}|\mathcal{F}] = \mathbf{I}_{[k=0]}\boldsymbol{\Sigma}_U$ and the law of iterated expectations, it follows that $E\left[\mathbf{h}_t^1(\mathbf{h}_{t+k}^2)'\right] = \mathbf{0}_{N\times N}$ for every integer k and therefore (3.20) yields $\boldsymbol{\Gamma} = \mathbf{0}_{N\times N}$. Using the aforementioned expressions for $\boldsymbol{\Psi}, \boldsymbol{\Pi}$, and $\boldsymbol{\Gamma}$, we obtain from Theorem 1 that the asymptotic covariance matrix of $\widehat{\mathbf{c}}_T$ is given by

$$\boldsymbol{\Sigma}_c = \mathbf{D}\left(\mathbf{B}\boldsymbol{\Sigma}_{\overline{F}}\mathbf{B}' + \boldsymbol{\Sigma}_U\right)\mathbf{D}' + \left(\boldsymbol{\lambda}'\boldsymbol{\Sigma}_F^{-1}\boldsymbol{\lambda}\right)\mathbf{D}\boldsymbol{\Sigma}_U\mathbf{D}' = \mathbf{D}\mathbf{B}\boldsymbol{\Sigma}_{\overline{F}}\mathbf{B}'\mathbf{D}' + \left(1 + \boldsymbol{\lambda}'\boldsymbol{\Sigma}_F^{-1}\boldsymbol{\lambda}\right)\mathbf{D}\boldsymbol{\Sigma}_U\mathbf{D}'.$$

Next, note that $\mathbf{DX} = \left(\mathbf{X}'\mathbf{QX}\right)^{-1}\mathbf{X}'\mathbf{QX} = \mathbf{I}_{K+1}$ which implies $\left[\begin{array}{cc} \mathbf{D1}_N & \mathbf{DB} \end{array}\right] = \mathbf{I}_{K+1}$ and so $\mathbf{DB} = \left[\begin{array}{cc} \mathbf{0}_K & \mathbf{I}_K \end{array}\right]'$. It follows that $\mathbf{DB}\boldsymbol{\Sigma}_{\overline{F}}\mathbf{B}'\mathbf{D}' = \left[\begin{array}{cc} \mathbf{0}_K & \mathbf{I}_K \end{array}\right]'$ $\boldsymbol{\Sigma}_{\overline{F}}\left[\begin{array}{cc} \mathbf{0}_K & \mathbf{I}_K \end{array}\right] = \boldsymbol{\Sigma}_{\overline{F}}^*$ upon using the definition (3.31). Using this fact yields the expression for $\boldsymbol{\Sigma}_c$ given in (3.33) and completes the proof. ∎

The preceding theorem and its consequences deserve some further discussion. Consider the commonly used case in which the factors are assumed to be serially uncorrelated, so that $\boldsymbol{\Sigma}_{\overline{F}} = \boldsymbol{\Sigma}_F$. If, in addition, Assumption B is satisfied, then it follows that the returns are also serially uncorrelated and following the lines of the preceding proof one can show that $\boldsymbol{\Sigma}_R = \mathbf{B}\boldsymbol{\Sigma}_F\mathbf{B}' + \boldsymbol{\Sigma}_U$. In this case, the probability limit of the Fama–MacBeth covariance estimator is $\mathbf{V} = \mathbf{D}\boldsymbol{\Sigma}_R\mathbf{D}' = \boldsymbol{\Sigma}_{\overline{F}}^* + \mathbf{D}\boldsymbol{\Sigma}_U\mathbf{D}'$. On comparing the true asymptotic covariance matrix $\boldsymbol{\Sigma}_c$ to $\mathbf{V}$, we observe that, because the matrix $\left(\boldsymbol{\lambda}'\boldsymbol{\Sigma}_F^{-1}\boldsymbol{\lambda}\right)\mathbf{D}\boldsymbol{\Sigma}_U\mathbf{D}'$ is positive definite, the standard errors obtained from the Fama–MacBeth method always overstate the precision of the estimates, under the assumption of conditional homoskedasticity. However, this is generally not true when a time-series is conditionally heteroskedastic.

As mentioned earlier, Assumption B is satisfied when the joint time-series of returns and factors is i.i.d. and normally distributed. However, there is a large body of literature presenting evidence in favor of nonnormality and heteroskedasticity. The early papers by Fama (1965) and Blattberg and Gonedes (1974) document nonnormality, while the papers by Barone-Adesi and Talwar (1983), Schwert and Seguin (1990) and Bollerslev et al. (1988) document conditional heteroskedasticity. Employing an i.i.d. sequence of returns following a multivariate t-distribution with more than four degrees of freedom, MacKinlay and Richardson (1991) demonstrate that returns are conditionally heteroskedastic and the test of mean–variance efficiency will be biased under the assumption of conditional homoskedasticity. They further demonstrate that stock returns are not homoskedastic based on a bootstrapping experiment. For these reasons, MacKinlay and Richardson (1991) advocate the GMM method developed by Hansen (1982), which does not require conditional homoskedasticity.

On the other hand, Assumption A may be satisfied by many stationary time-series that are not conditionally homoskedastic. It follows from Lindeberg–Lèvy central limit theorem that any serially i.i.d. time-series of returns and factors with finite fourth moments satisfies Assumption A, while it might not satisfy the assumption of conditional homoskedasticity unless the time-series is also normally distributed. Clearly, the i.i.d. time-series of returns with t-distribution by MacKinlay and Richardson (1991) is such an example.

3.5. Using Security Characteristics to Test Factor Pricing Models

The methodology developed in the two previous sections can be used to assess the significance of the risk premium associated with a factor under examination. The distribution theory presented in Theorems 1 and 2 allows one to construct t-statistics that have an asymptotic normal distribution. A significantly large t-value indicates that the corresponding factor is indeed priced, while a small t-value suggests that the factor is not priced and should be excluded from the model.

An alternative route that has been taken by several researchers is to use firm characteristics to detect misspecification errors. It has been common practice in empirical studies to identify firm-specific characteristics that help forecast future returns and create portfolios, based on such predictability, that pose the greatest challenge to an asset pricing model. Such portfolios, in a way, summarize what is missing in an asset pricing model. If a linear beta pricing is correctly specified, security characteristics added to the model should not explain the cross-sectional variation of expected returns after the factor betas prescribed by the model have been taken into account. In this case, the t-value of a characteristic reward should be insignificant. On the other hand, a significant t-value of a characteristic reward indicates model misspecification and should lead to rejection of the linear factor model.

Common examples of firm characteristics used in the literature include the relative firm size and the ratio of book value to market value. Banz (1981) first used the firm size to examine the validity of the CAPM. Chan et al. (1991) and Fama and French (1992) use the book-to-market ratio and provide evidence that this variable explains a larger fraction of the cross-sectional variation in expected returns. This evidence led Fama and French (1993) to propose a three-factor model for stock returns. Daniel and Titman (1997) add firm size and book-to-market ratio to the Fama–French three-factor model and find that the t-values associated with these firm characteristics are still significant. Another important characteristic that has received attention in the empirical literature is the relative strength or momentum. It is typically measured by a score that depends on the return on an asset relative to other assets in the comparison group. Jegadeesh and Titman (1993) show how to construct portfolios that earn apparently superior risk-adjusted returns using clever trading strategies that exploit momentum, i.e., the tendency of past winners to continue to win and past losers to continue to lose. Other characteristics that have received attention include liquidity (Brennan and Subrahmanyam, 1996), earnings to price ratio (Basu, 1977), dividend yield (Fama and French, 1988), and leverage (Bhandari, 1988).

Jagannathan and Wang (1998) were the first to provide a rigorous econometric analysis of the cross-sectional regression method when firm characteristics are employed in addition to factors. Their framework assumed that the firm characteristics are constant over time. Let $\mathbf{Z}^i$ denote the vector of M characteristics associated with the ith security. Then the beta pricing model equation (2.4) augmented to include firm characteristics becomes

$$E[R_t^i] = a_0 + \mathbf{a}'\mathbf{Z}^i + \boldsymbol{\lambda}'\boldsymbol{\beta}_i, \quad i = 1, \ldots, N, \tag{3.34}$$

where $\mathbf{a}$ is an M-dimensional constant vector representing the characteristics rewards. Let $L = 1 + M + K$ and define

$$\mathbf{c} = [a_0 \; \mathbf{a}' \; \boldsymbol{\lambda}']' \quad (L \times 1 \text{ vector}), \tag{3.35}$$

$$\mathbf{Z} = [\mathbf{Z}^1 \; \mathbf{Z}^2 \; \cdots \; \mathbf{Z}^N]' \quad (N \times M \text{ matrix}), \tag{3.36}$$

and

$$\mathbf{X} = [\mathbf{1}_N \; \mathbf{Z} \; \mathbf{B}] \quad (N \times L \text{ matrix}), \tag{3.37}$$

where $\mathbf{B}$ is defined in (3.1). Then Eq. (3.34) can be compactly written as

$$E[\mathbf{R}_t] = a_0 \mathbf{1}_N + \mathbf{Z}\mathbf{a} + \mathbf{B}\boldsymbol{\lambda} = \mathbf{X}\mathbf{c}. \tag{3.38}$$

As is typically the case in applications, we assume that $N \geq L$ and that $\mathbf{X}$ is of full rank equal to L. As in Section 3.1, let $\mathbf{Q}$ be a symmetric and positive definite $N \times N$ matrix and $\widehat{\mathbf{Q}}_T$ be a consistent estimator of $\mathbf{Q}$ that is also assumed to be symmetric and positive definite for all T. Following the development in Section 3.1, a GLS estimator of $\mathbf{c}$ is obtained by a cross-sectional regression at each time t as follows

$$\widehat{\mathbf{c}}_t = (\widehat{\mathbf{X}}_T'\widehat{\mathbf{Q}}_T\widehat{\mathbf{X}}_T)^{-1}\widehat{\mathbf{X}}_T'\widehat{\mathbf{Q}}_T\mathbf{R}_t, \tag{3.39}$$

where

$$\widehat{\mathbf{X}}_T = [\mathbf{1}_N \; \mathbf{Z} \; \widehat{\mathbf{B}}_T]. \tag{3.40}$$

Here, $\widehat{\mathbf{B}}_T$ is the sample analog estimator of $\mathbf{B}$ defined in (3.10), and the matrix $\widehat{\mathbf{X}}_T$ is assumed to be of full rank equal to L. As before, the Fama–MacBeth estimator is then obtained by time averaging the T cross-sectional estimates

$$\bar{\widehat{\mathbf{c}}}_T = \frac{1}{T}\sum_{t=1}^{T}\widehat{\mathbf{c}}_t = (\widehat{\mathbf{X}}_T'\widehat{\mathbf{Q}}_T\widehat{\mathbf{X}}_T)^{-1}\widehat{\mathbf{X}}_T'\widehat{\mathbf{Q}}_T\overline{\mathbf{R}}_T. \tag{3.41}$$

3.5.1. Consistency and Asymptotic Normality of the CSR Estimator

It turns out that the consistency and asymptotic normality properties of the Fama–MacBeth estimator are maintained when we include security characteristics in the analysis. Following the steps in the proof of Proposition 1 and using the relation (3.38), one can derive the analogous result for the case in which characteristics are used, which we state next.

Proposition 3 *The time-series average $\bar{\bar{\mathbf{c}}}_T$ of the cross-sectional estimates*

$$\widehat{\mathbf{c}}_t = \left(\widehat{\mathbf{X}}'_T \widehat{\mathbf{Q}}_T \widehat{\mathbf{X}}_T\right)^{-1} \widehat{\mathbf{X}}'_T \widehat{\mathbf{Q}}_T \mathbf{R}_t, \quad t = 1, \dots, T,$$

where $\widehat{\mathbf{X}}_T = [\mathbf{1}_N \ \mathbf{Z} \ \widehat{\mathbf{B}}_T]$ is a consistent estimator of $\mathbf{c} = \begin{bmatrix} a_0 & \mathbf{a}' & \boldsymbol{\lambda}' \end{bmatrix}'$, that is

$$\bar{\bar{\mathbf{c}}}_T \xrightarrow{P} \mathbf{c} \text{ as } T \to \infty. \tag{3.42}$$

The asymptotic behavior of the CSR estimator, when security characteristics are used in the analysis, is captured in the next theorem. The proof of this theorem, which appeared as Theorem 1 in the study of Jagannathan and Wang (1998) with slightly different notation, closely resembles the proof of Theorem 1.

Theorem 3 *Let $\mathbf{c} = [a_0 \ \mathbf{a}' \ \boldsymbol{\lambda}']'$ and $\bar{\bar{\mathbf{c}}}_T = \left(\widehat{\mathbf{X}}'_T \widehat{\mathbf{Q}}_T \widehat{\mathbf{X}}_T\right)^{-1} \widehat{\mathbf{X}}'_T \widehat{\mathbf{Q}}_T \bar{\mathbf{R}}_T$ where $\widehat{\mathbf{X}}_T = [\mathbf{1}_N \ \mathbf{Z} \ \widehat{\mathbf{B}}_T]$. Under Assumption A, as $T \to \infty$, $\sqrt{T}(\bar{\bar{\mathbf{c}}}_T - \mathbf{c})$ converges in distribution to a multivariate normal with zero mean and covariance*

$$\boldsymbol{\Sigma}_c = \mathbf{D}\boldsymbol{\Psi}\mathbf{D}' + \mathbf{D}\boldsymbol{\Pi}\mathbf{D}' - \mathbf{D}\left(\boldsymbol{\Gamma} + \boldsymbol{\Gamma}'\right)\mathbf{D}', \tag{3.43}$$

where $\mathbf{D} = (\mathbf{X}'\mathbf{Q}\mathbf{X})^{-1}\mathbf{X}'\mathbf{Q}$ with $\mathbf{X} = [\mathbf{1}_N \ \mathbf{Z} \ \mathbf{B}]$ and $\boldsymbol{\Psi}, \boldsymbol{\Gamma}$, and $\boldsymbol{\Pi}$ are defined in (3.20).

A result, similar to Proposition 2, can be shown in the present context stating that the Fama–MacBeth covariance matrix estimator is not a consistent estimator of the asymptotic covariance matrix of the cross-sectional regression estimator.

Under the additional assumption of conditional homoskedastic residuals given the factors (Assumption B), proceeding as in the proof of Theorem 2, we can obtain the following theorem as a consequence of the preceding Theorem 3.

Theorem 4 *Let $\mathbf{c} = [a_0 \ \mathbf{a}' \ \boldsymbol{\lambda}']'$ and $\bar{\bar{\mathbf{c}}}_T = \left(\widehat{\mathbf{X}}'_T \widehat{\mathbf{Q}}_T \widehat{\mathbf{X}}_T\right)^{-1} \widehat{\mathbf{X}}'_T \widehat{\mathbf{Q}}_T \bar{\mathbf{R}}_T$ where $\widehat{\mathbf{X}}_T = [\mathbf{1}_N \ \mathbf{Z} \ \widehat{\mathbf{B}}_T]$. Then, under Assumptions A and B, the result in Theorem 3 becomes*

$$\sqrt{T}(\bar{\bar{\mathbf{c}}}_T - \mathbf{c}) \xrightarrow{D} N(\mathbf{0}_{K+M+1}, \boldsymbol{\Sigma}_c) \text{ as } T \to \infty, \tag{3.44}$$

where

$$\boldsymbol{\Sigma}_c = \boldsymbol{\Sigma}_{\bar{\mathbf{F}}}^{**} + \left(1 + \boldsymbol{\lambda}'\boldsymbol{\Sigma}_{\mathbf{F}}^{-1}\boldsymbol{\lambda}\right)\mathbf{D}\boldsymbol{\Sigma}_{\mathbf{U}}\mathbf{D}', \tag{3.45}$$

$\mathbf{D} = (\mathbf{X}'\mathbf{QX})^{-1}\mathbf{X}'\mathbf{Q}$ with $\mathbf{X} = [\mathbf{1}_N \quad \mathbf{Z} \quad \mathbf{B}]$, and $\mathbf{\Sigma}_{\overline{\mathbf{F}}}^{**}$ is the bordered version of $\mathbf{\Sigma}_{\overline{\mathbf{F}}}$ given by

$$\mathbf{\Sigma}_{\overline{\mathbf{F}}}^{**} = \begin{bmatrix} \mathbf{0}_{(M+1)\times(M+1)} & \mathbf{0}_{(M+1)\times K} \\ \mathbf{0}_{K\times(M+1)} & \mathbf{\Sigma}_{\overline{\mathbf{F}}} \end{bmatrix}. \tag{3.46}$$

3.5.2. Misspecification Bias and Protection Against Spurious Factors

The main assumption of the preceding analysis was that the null hypothesis model is correctly specified. When the model is correctly specified, the CSR estimator is consistent under very general conditions that we stated earlier. However, if the null hypothesis model is misspecified, the estimator in cross-sectional regression will be asymptotically biased. Assume that $\tilde{\mathbf{f}}$ is a different vector of factors than $\mathbf{f}$, that is, at least some of the factors in $\tilde{\mathbf{f}}$ and $\mathbf{f}$ are different. Suppose the true factor vector is $\tilde{\mathbf{f}}$ and thus the true model is

$$E[\mathbf{R}_t] = a_0 \mathbf{1}_N + \mathbf{Za} + \tilde{\mathbf{B}}\boldsymbol{\lambda}, \tag{3.47}$$

where

$$\tilde{\mathbf{B}} = E[(\mathbf{R}_t - E[\mathbf{R}_t])(\tilde{\mathbf{f}} - E[\tilde{\mathbf{f}}])']\tilde{\mathbf{\Sigma}}_{\mathbf{F}}^{-1} \quad \text{and} \quad \tilde{\mathbf{\Sigma}}_{\mathbf{F}} = E[(\tilde{\mathbf{f}}_t - E[\tilde{\mathbf{f}}_t])(\tilde{\mathbf{f}}_t - E[\tilde{\mathbf{f}}_t])']. \tag{3.48}$$

A researcher who incorrectly specifies the model as

$$E[\mathbf{R}_t] = a_0 \mathbf{1}_N + \mathbf{Za} + \mathbf{B}\boldsymbol{\lambda}, \tag{3.49}$$

where

$$\mathbf{B} = E\left[(\mathbf{R}_t - E[\mathbf{R}_t])(\mathbf{f}_t - E[\mathbf{f}_t])'\right]\mathbf{\Sigma}_{\mathbf{F}}^{-1} \quad \text{and} \quad \mathbf{\Sigma}_{\mathbf{F}} = E\left[(\mathbf{f}_t - E[\mathbf{f}_t])(\mathbf{f}_t - E[\mathbf{f}_t])'\right], \tag{3.50}$$

will estimate betas by regressing returns on the vector of misspecified factors $\mathbf{f}$ and then estimate the risk premia in cross-sectional regression. The resulting bias is presented in the following theorem. We make the standard assumption that the time-series $\begin{bmatrix} \mathbf{R}'_t & \mathbf{f}'_t \end{bmatrix}'$ is stationary and ergodic so that the law of large numbers applies and sample moments converge to population moments.

Theorem 5 *Assume that* $\mathbf{X} = [\mathbf{1}_N \ \mathbf{Z} \ \mathbf{B}]$ *has full rank equal to* L. *If Eq. (3.47) holds for the time-series* $\begin{bmatrix} \mathbf{R}'_t & \tilde{\mathbf{f}}'_t \end{bmatrix}'$ *but betas are estimated using the time-series* $[\mathbf{R}'_t \ \mathbf{f}'_t]'$, *then the cross-sectional estimator* $\overline{\hat{\mathbf{c}}}_T = \left(\widehat{\mathbf{X}}'_T \widehat{\mathbf{Q}}_T \widehat{\mathbf{X}}_T\right)^{-1} \widehat{\mathbf{X}}'_T \widehat{\mathbf{Q}}_T \overline{\mathbf{R}}_T$ *with* $\widehat{\mathbf{X}}_T = [\mathbf{1}_N \ \mathbf{Z} \ \widehat{\mathbf{B}}_T]$ *converges to* $\mathbf{c} + (\mathbf{X}'\mathbf{QX})^{-1}\mathbf{X}'\mathbf{Q}(\tilde{\mathbf{B}} - \mathbf{B})\boldsymbol{\lambda}$ *in probability as* $T \to \infty$.

Proof. Using Eq. (3.47) and appropriately rearranging the terms yields

$$\overline{\mathbf{R}}_T = (\overline{\mathbf{R}}_T - E[\mathbf{R}_t]) + \widehat{\mathbf{X}}_T \mathbf{c} - (\widehat{\mathbf{B}}_T - \mathbf{B})\boldsymbol{\lambda} + (\tilde{\mathbf{B}} - \mathbf{B})\boldsymbol{\lambda}.$$

On multiplying the above equation by $\left(\widehat{\mathbf{X}}'_T\widehat{\mathbf{Q}}_T\widehat{\mathbf{X}}_T\right)^{-1}\widehat{\mathbf{X}}'\widehat{\mathbf{Q}}_T$, one obtains the following expression for the cross-sectional regression estimator

$$\overline{\widehat{\mathbf{c}}}_T = \mathbf{c} + \left(\widehat{\mathbf{X}}'_T\widehat{\mathbf{Q}}_T\widehat{\mathbf{X}}_T\right)^{-1}\widehat{\mathbf{X}}'_T\widehat{\mathbf{Q}}\left[(\overline{\mathbf{R}}_t - E[\mathbf{R}_t]) - (\widehat{\mathbf{B}}_T - \mathbf{B})\boldsymbol{\lambda}\right]$$
$$+ \left(\widehat{\mathbf{X}}'_T\widehat{\mathbf{Q}}_T\widehat{\mathbf{X}}_T\right)^{-1}\widehat{\mathbf{X}}'_T\widehat{\mathbf{Q}}_T(\widetilde{\mathbf{B}} - \mathbf{B})\boldsymbol{\lambda}.$$

Using the law of large numbers, the assumption that $\mathbf{X}$ has full rank and Slutsky's theorem, it follows from the last equation that

$$\overline{\widehat{\mathbf{c}}}_T \overset{P}{\longrightarrow} \mathbf{c} + (\mathbf{X}'\mathbf{Q}\mathbf{X})^{-1}\mathbf{X}'\mathbf{Q}(\widetilde{\mathbf{B}} - \mathbf{B})\boldsymbol{\lambda}.$$

This completes the proof. ∎

In view of this theorem, the estimator in cross-sectional regression is asymptotically biased if and only if $\mathbf{X}'\mathbf{Q}(\widetilde{\mathbf{B}} - \mathbf{B})\boldsymbol{\lambda} \neq \mathbf{0}_L$. Notice that not only the estimates for the premium on the misspecified factors can be biased, but the estimates for the premium on those correctly specified betas can also be biased when some other factor is misspecified.

3.6. Time-Varying Security Characteristics

Jagannathan et al. (2003) extend the analysis of Jagannathan and Wang (1998) to allow for time-varying firm characteristics. They study the case in which no pricing restrictions are imposed on the traded factors – if there are any such factors – and the case in which all factors are traded and pricing restrictions are imposed on all of them. Their main result is that using the observed time-varying characteristics in each cross-sectional regression induces a bias making the cross-sectional regression estimator generally inconsistent. They provide an expression for the bias and derive the asymptotic theory for the CSR estimator in both cases. They also show how one can avoid the bias problem by using time-averages of the firm characteristics. In the next three sections, we state some of the more important results while we refer the interested reader to Jagannathan et al. (2003) for the full analysis including proofs and details.

3.6.1. No Pricing Restrictions Imposed on Traded Factors

In this section, we proceed without directly imposing any pricing restrictions on traded factors, if any such factors are employed in the analysis. In other words, we do not distinguish between traded and nontraded factors. On the other hand, we allow for time-varying firm-specific characteristics. Let $\mathbf{Z}_t^i$ be a vector of M characteristics associated with the ith asset observed at time $t - 1$. The factor pricing equation (2.4) is expanded to include the firm characteristics as follows:

$$E[R_t^i] = a_0 + \mathbf{a}'E[\mathbf{Z}_t^i] + \boldsymbol{\lambda}'\boldsymbol{\beta}_i \quad \text{for} \quad i = 1, \dots, N, \tag{3.51}$$

where $\mathbf{a}$ is the M-dimensional constant vector of characteristics rewards. Note that under the above representation (3.51), the hypothesis $\mathbf{a} = \mathbf{0}_M$ is equivalent to the factor pricing equation $E[R_t^i] = a_0 + \boldsymbol{\lambda}'\boldsymbol{\beta}_i$, $\iota = 1, \ldots, N$. As in Section 3.5, we let $L = 1 + M + K$, $\mathbf{c} = [a_0 \; \mathbf{a}' \; \boldsymbol{\lambda}']'$ ($L \times 1$ vector) and define the time-varying characteristics matrix

$$\mathbf{Z}_t = \begin{bmatrix} \mathbf{z}_t^1 \; \mathbf{z}_t^2 \; \cdots \; \mathbf{z}_t^N \end{bmatrix}' \quad (N \times M \text{ matrix}) \tag{3.52}$$

and

$$\mathbf{X}_t = [\mathbf{1}_N \; \mathbf{Z}_t \; \mathbf{B}] \quad (N \times L \text{ matrix}), \tag{3.53}$$

where $\mathbf{B}$ is defined in (3.1). Then Eq. (3.51) can be written as

$$E[\mathbf{R}_t] = a_0\mathbf{1}_N + E[\mathbf{Z}_t]\mathbf{a} + \mathbf{B}\boldsymbol{\lambda} = E[\mathbf{X}_t]\mathbf{c}. \tag{3.54}$$

Again assume that $N \geq L$ and that $\mathbf{X}_t$ is of full rank equal to L for all t. Following the development in Section 3.1, a GLS estimate of $\mathbf{c}$ is obtained by a cross-sectional regression at each time t as follows

$$\widehat{\mathbf{c}}_t = \left(\widehat{\mathbf{X}}'_{T,t}\widehat{\mathbf{Q}}_T\widehat{\mathbf{X}}_{T,t}\right)^{-1}\widehat{\mathbf{X}}'_{T,t}\widehat{\mathbf{Q}}_T\mathbf{R}_t, \tag{3.55}$$

where

$$\widehat{\mathbf{X}}_{T,t} = [\mathbf{1}_N \; \mathbf{Z}_t \; \widehat{\mathbf{B}}_T] \tag{3.56}$$

and $\widehat{\mathbf{B}}_T$ is the sample analog estimate of $\mathbf{B}$ defined in (3.10). The matrix $\widehat{\mathbf{X}}_{T,t}$ is assumed to be of full rank equal to L for all t. As before, the time average of the T cross-sectional estimates provides the Fama–MacBeth CSR estimate

$$\overline{\mathbf{c}}_T = \frac{1}{T}\sum_{t=1}^{T}\widehat{\mathbf{c}}_t = \frac{1}{T}\sum_{t=1}^{T}\left(\widehat{\mathbf{X}}'_{T,t}\widehat{\mathbf{Q}}_T\widehat{\mathbf{X}}_{T,t}\right)^{-1}\widehat{\mathbf{X}}'_{T,t}\widehat{\mathbf{Q}}_T\mathbf{R}_t. \tag{3.57}$$

Our goal is to obtain the probability limit and the asymptotic distribution of the CSR estimator in the case of time-varying firm characteristics. We make the standard assumption that the vector process $\left[(\mathbf{R}_t)' \; (\mathbf{f}_t)' \; (\text{vec}(\mathbf{Z}_t))'\right]'$ is stationary and ergodic so that the law of large numbers applies. The derivation of the results that follow requires a few mild technical assumptions, the first of which is stated next.

Assumption C Consider an arbitrarily small $\delta > 0$ and assume that, for all t, the smallest eigenvalue of the matrix $\mathbf{X}_t'\mathbf{Q}\mathbf{X}_t$ is greater than δ, where $\mathbf{X}_t = [\mathbf{1}_N \; \mathbf{Z}_t \; \mathbf{B}]$. In addition, assume that all elements of the characteristics matrix $\mathbf{Z}_t$ are bounded uniformly in t.

Under the usual assumption that, for a given t, the matrix $\mathbf{X}_t$ is of full rank, namely L, we have that the $L \times L$ matrix $\mathbf{X}_t'\mathbf{Q}\mathbf{X}_t$ also has rank L and is positive definite because $\mathbf{Q}$ is positive definite. In this case, the smallest eigenvalue of $\mathbf{X}_t'\mathbf{Q}\mathbf{X}_t$ will be strictly positive. Assumption C requires a slightly stronger condition, namely that the smallest eigenvalue of $\mathbf{X}_t'\mathbf{Q}\mathbf{X}_t$ is outside a fixed small neighborhood of 0 for all t. On the other hand, it turns out that if the OLS estimator of $\mathbf{c}$ is used, instead of the feasible GLS estimator, the analysis still goes through without the boundedness assumption on $\mathbf{Z}_t$.

The derivation of the results stated in this section relies heavily on the following lemma, the proof of which is based on Assumption C. We state the lemma to give the reader an idea of how the proofs proceed in the present setting of time-varying firm characteristics.

Lemma 1 *Under Assumption C, the matrix random sequence $\mathbf{A}_{T,t} = (\widehat{\mathbf{X}}_{T,t}'\widehat{\mathbf{Q}}_T\widehat{\mathbf{X}}_{T,t})^{-1}$ $\widehat{\mathbf{X}}_{T,t}'\widehat{\mathbf{Q}}_T - (\mathbf{X}_t'\mathbf{Q}\mathbf{X}_t)^{-1}\mathbf{X}_t'\mathbf{Q}$ converges in probability to $\mathbf{0}_{L \times N}$ as $T \to \infty$ uniformly in t.*

An important result about the CSR estimator in the present setting is that the use of time-varying firm characteristics in the fashion described by Eqs. (3.55) and (3.56) produces an estimator that is not necessarily a consistent estimator of the unknown parameter $\mathbf{c}$. The following proposition describes the limiting behavior of the CSR estimator and its asymptotic bias, as $T \to \infty$.

Proposition 4 *Let $\mathbf{c} = [a_0 \quad \mathbf{a}' \quad \boldsymbol{\lambda}']'$. Under Assumption C, the probability limit of the cross-sectional regression estimator $\bar{\widehat{\mathbf{c}}}_T = \frac{1}{T}\sum_{t=1}^{T}\left(\widehat{\mathbf{X}}_{T,t}'\widehat{\mathbf{Q}}_T\widehat{\mathbf{X}}_{T,t}\right)^{-1}\widehat{\mathbf{X}}_{T,t}'\widehat{\mathbf{Q}}_T\mathbf{R}_t$ is given by*

$$\bar{\widehat{\mathbf{c}}}_T \xrightarrow{P} \mathbf{c} + \boldsymbol{\gamma}, \quad as \quad T \to \infty,$$

where the asymptotic bias is given by

$$\boldsymbol{\gamma} = E\left[\left(\mathbf{X}_t'\mathbf{Q}\mathbf{X}_t\right)^{-1}\mathbf{X}_t'\mathbf{Q}\left(\mathbf{R}_t - \mathbf{X}_t\mathbf{c}\right)\right] \tag{3.58}$$

assuming that the expectation that defines $\boldsymbol{\gamma}$ exists and is finite. Under the null hypothesis H_0 : $\mathbf{a} = \mathbf{0}_M$ the bias is given by $\boldsymbol{\gamma} = E\left[\left(\mathbf{X}_t'\mathbf{Q}\mathbf{X}_t\right)^{-1}\mathbf{X}_t'\mathbf{Q}\left(\mathbf{R}_t - E[\mathbf{R}_t]\right)\right]$.

From Proposition 4, one can see that the cross-sectional estimator $\bar{\widehat{\mathbf{c}}}_T$ is an asymptotically biased estimator of $\mathbf{c}$ unless $\boldsymbol{\gamma} = \mathbf{0}_L$. Because the firm characteristics will presumably be correlated with the returns, it follows from the expression $\boldsymbol{\gamma} = E[(\mathbf{X}_t'\mathbf{Q}\mathbf{X}_t)^{-1}\mathbf{X}_t'\mathbf{Q}(\mathbf{R}_t - \mathbf{X}_t\mathbf{c})]$ that, in principle, the bias $\boldsymbol{\gamma}$ will not be equal to the zero vector. Therefore, ignoring this potential bias of the CSR estimator might lead to erroneous inferences. However, when the firm characteristics $\mathbf{Z}_t$ used in the study are constant over time, say equal to $\mathbf{Z}$, then $\mathbf{X}_t = \mathbf{X} \equiv [\mathbf{1}_N \quad \mathbf{Z} \quad \mathbf{B}]$ and so (3.54) implies that $\boldsymbol{\gamma} = (\mathbf{X}'\mathbf{Q}\mathbf{X})^{-1}\mathbf{X}'\mathbf{Q}E[\mathbf{R}_t - \mathbf{X}\mathbf{c}] = \mathbf{0}_L$, which is equivalent to $\bar{\widehat{\mathbf{c}}}_T$ being a consistent estimator of $\mathbf{c}$. Thus we obtain Proposition 3 as a corollary to Proposition 4.

3.6.2. Traded Factors with Imposed Pricing Restrictions

In this section, we study the behavior of the cross-sectional regression two-pass estimator when all factors are returns on traded portfolios and the relevant pricing restrictions are imposed on the factors. In particular, we examine the approach that Brennan et al. (1998) proposed to handle the EIV problem without the requirement of grouping securities into portfolios. As in Section 3.5, we assume that there are N risky securities, K economy-wide factors, M security-specific characteristics with the addition of a riskless asset. The expected excess return on the jth asset can be written as

$$E[R_j - R_f] = a_0 + \sum_{m=1}^{M} E[Z_m^j]a_m + \sum_{k=1}^{K} \beta_{jk}\lambda_k, \quad j = 1,\ldots,N \tag{3.59}$$

where λ_k is the risk premium of factor k, β_{jk} is the factor loading of factor k for the jth security, Z_m^j is the value of the mth characteristic specific to the jth security, and a_m is the reward or premium per unit of the mth characteristic. Examples of factors that are returns on portfolios of traded securities include the first five principal components of Connor and Korajczyk (1988) and the three factors of Fama and French (1993). Examples of security characteristics used include relative firm size, relative book-to-market ratio, dividend yield, relative strength, and turnover. To test the validity of the factor pricing model, one needs to construct a test of the null hypothesis $H_0 : a_0 = a_1 = \cdots = a_M = 0$.

The notation of the previous sections is employed except that we now denote $\mathbf{c} = [a_0 \ \mathbf{a}']'$, where $\mathbf{a} = (a_1,\ldots,a_M)'$ is the vector of characteristics rewards. We further use superscript e to denote excess returns on the assets and the factors: $\mathbf{R}_t^e = \mathbf{R}_t - R_{ft}\mathbf{1}_N$ and $\mathbf{f}_t^e = \mathbf{f}_t - R_{ft}\mathbf{1}_K$. Then we can define the factor loading matrix as

$$\mathbf{B}^e = E\left[\left(\mathbf{R}_t^e - E[\mathbf{R}_t^e]\right)\left(\mathbf{f}_t^e - E[\mathbf{f}_t^e]\right)'\right]\mathbf{\Sigma}_F^{e\,-1}, \tag{3.60}$$

where the covariance matrix of the factor excess returns is given

$$\mathbf{\Sigma}_F^e = E[(\mathbf{f}_t^e - E[\mathbf{f}_t^e])(\mathbf{f}_t^e - E[\mathbf{f}_t^e])']. \tag{3.61}$$

Similarly to (3.6), but now using excess returns, we let $\mathbf{u}_t^e = \mathbf{R}_t^e - E[\mathbf{R}_t^e] - \mathbf{B}^e(\mathbf{f}_t^e - E[\mathbf{f}_t^e])$ to obtain the time-series regression

$$\mathbf{R}_t^e = E[\mathbf{R}_t^e] + \mathbf{B}(\mathbf{f}_t^e - E[\mathbf{f}_t^e]) + \mathbf{u}_t^e \quad \text{with} \quad E[\mathbf{u}_t^e] = \mathbf{0}_N \quad \text{and} \quad E[\mathbf{u}_t^e\mathbf{f}_t^{e'}] = \mathbf{0}_{N\times K}. \tag{3.62}$$

Therefore, the model can be written in vector-matrix notation form as $E[\mathbf{R}_t^e] = a_0\mathbf{1}_N + E[\mathbf{Z}_t]\mathbf{a} + \mathbf{B}^e\boldsymbol{\lambda}$ that allows to rewrite Eq. (3.62) as

$$\mathbf{R}_t^e = a_0\mathbf{1}_N + E[\mathbf{Z}_t]\mathbf{a} + \mathbf{B}^e(\mathbf{f}_t^e - E[\mathbf{f}_t^e] + \boldsymbol{\lambda}) + \mathbf{u}_t^e.$$

Because the factors are assumed to be returns on traded assets, it follows that the factor risk premia equal expected excess returns, that is $\boldsymbol{\lambda} = E[\mathbf{f}_t^e]$, and so the last equation becomes

$$\mathbf{R}_t^e = a_0 \mathbf{1}_N + \mathbf{B}^e \mathbf{f}_t^e + \mathbf{Z}_t \mathbf{a} + \mathbf{e}_t, \quad \text{where} \quad \mathbf{e}_t = -(\mathbf{Z}_t - E[\mathbf{Z}_t])\mathbf{a} + \mathbf{u}_t^e. \tag{3.63}$$

Following Brennan et al. (1998), we define the risk-adjusted returns as

$$\mathbf{R}_t^* = \mathbf{R}_t^e - \mathbf{B}^e \mathbf{f}_t^e \tag{3.64}$$

and write the previous equation as

$$\mathbf{R}_t^* = \mathbf{X}_t \mathbf{c} + \mathbf{e}_t, \quad \text{where} \quad \mathbf{X}_t = [\mathbf{1}_N \ \mathbf{Z}_t] \quad \text{and} \quad \mathbf{c} = [a_0 \ \mathbf{a}']'. \tag{3.65}$$

The estimation and testing procedure proposed by Brennan et al. (1998) consists of the following steps. First, a set of factors is selected. Two sets of factors are used: the principal component factors of Connor and Korajczyk (1988) and the Fama and French (1993) factors. Second, the factor betas are estimated using standard time-series regressions as follows:

$$\widehat{\mathbf{B}}_T^e = \left[\frac{1}{T} \sum_{t=1}^T \left(\mathbf{R}_t^e - \overline{\mathbf{R}_T^e} \right) \left(\mathbf{f}_t^e - \overline{\mathbf{f}_T^e} \right)' \right] \widehat{\boldsymbol{\Sigma}}_{FT}^{e-1}, \quad \text{where} \quad \widehat{\boldsymbol{\Sigma}}_{FT}^e = \frac{1}{T} \sum_{t=1}^T \left(\mathbf{f}_t^e - \overline{\mathbf{f}_T^e} \right) \left(\mathbf{f}_t^e - \overline{\mathbf{f}_T^e} \right)'. \tag{3.66}$$

Third, using the estimates of the factor betas from the second step, the estimated risk-adjusted returns are formed:

$$\widehat{\mathbf{R}}_t^* = \mathbf{R}_t^e - \widehat{\mathbf{B}}_T^e \mathbf{f}_t^e. \tag{3.67}$$

Then the risk-adjusted returns are used in the following cross-sectional regressions

$$\widehat{R}_{jt}^* = c_0 + \sum_{m=1}^M c_m Z_{m,t}^j + \tilde{e}_{jt}, \quad j = 1, \dots, N \tag{3.68}$$

or in vector-matrix notation $\widehat{\mathbf{R}}_t^* = \mathbf{X}_t \mathbf{c} + \tilde{\mathbf{e}}_t$ for all $t = 1, \dots, T$. Thus, in the fourth step, for each t, cross-sectional simple regression is used to obtain the following estimates $\widehat{\mathbf{c}}_t$ of the vector $\mathbf{c}$ of characteristic rewards

$$\widehat{\mathbf{c}}_t = (\mathbf{X}_t' \mathbf{X}_t)^{-1} \mathbf{X}_t' \widehat{\mathbf{R}}_t^*, \quad t = 1, \dots, T. \tag{3.69}$$

Finally, in the spirit of Fama and MacBeth, the time-series average of the estimates is formed to obtain what Brennan et al. (1998) term the raw estimate of $\mathbf{c}$ as follows

$$\overline{\mathbf{c}}_T = \frac{1}{T} \sum_{t=1}^T \widehat{\mathbf{c}}_t. \tag{3.70}$$

Alternatively, the use of GLS would allow us obtain more efficient estimates. Employing the previously used notation, we can write the GLS raw estimate of $\mathbf{c}$ as

$$\overline{\overline{\mathbf{c}}}_T = \frac{1}{T} \sum_{t=1}^{T} \left(\mathbf{X}_t' \widehat{\mathbf{Q}}_T \mathbf{X}_t\right)^{-1} \mathbf{X}_t' \widehat{\mathbf{Q}}_T \widehat{\mathbf{R}}_t^*. \tag{3.71}$$

Next, we describe the probability limit and the asymptotic distribution of the GLS version of the estimator proposed by Brennan et al. (1998). We make the standard assumption that the vector process $\left[\left(\mathbf{R}_t^e\right)' \left(\mathbf{f}_t^e\right)' \left(\mathrm{vec}(\mathbf{Z}_t)\right)'\right]'$ is stationary and ergodic so that the law of large numbers applies. As before, some additional assumptions will ensure the validity of the results. The first assumption, which we state next, is the suitable modification of Assumption C that was made in Section 3.6.1.

Assumption D Consider an arbitrarily small $\delta > 0$ and assume that, for all t, the smallest eigenvalue of the matrix $\mathbf{X}_t' \mathbf{Q} \mathbf{X}_t$ is greater than δ, where $\mathbf{X}_t = [\mathbf{1}_N \ \mathbf{Z}_t]$. In addition, assume that all elements of the characteristics matrix $\mathbf{Z}_t$ are bounded uniformly in t.

It turns out that the cross-sectional regression estimator $\overline{\overline{\mathbf{c}}}_T$, obtained by regressing the estimated risk-adjusted returns on a constant and the time-varying firm characteristics as described by Eq. (3.68), is not a consistent estimator of the parameter $\mathbf{c}$. This is a property we encountered in Proposition 4 under a different setting. The next proposition presents the asymptotic bias of $\overline{\overline{\mathbf{c}}}_T$.

Proposition 5 *Let $\mathbf{c} = [a_0 \ \mathbf{a}']'$. Under Assumption D, the probability limit of the cross-sectional regression raw estimate $\overline{\overline{\mathbf{c}}}_T = \frac{1}{T} \sum_{t=1}^{T} (\mathbf{X}_t' \widehat{\mathbf{Q}}_T \mathbf{X}_t)^{-1} \mathbf{X}_t' \widehat{\mathbf{Q}}_T \widehat{\mathbf{R}}_t^*$ is given by*

$$\overline{\overline{\mathbf{c}}}_T \xrightarrow{P} \mathbf{c} + \boldsymbol{\gamma}^*, \quad \text{as } T \to \infty,$$

where the asymptotic bias is given by

$$\boldsymbol{\gamma}^* = E[(\mathbf{X}_t' \mathbf{Q} \mathbf{X}_t)^{-1} \mathbf{X}_t' \mathbf{Q} \mathbf{e}_t] \tag{3.72}$$

assuming that the expectation that defines $\boldsymbol{\gamma}^*$ exists and is finite. Under the null hypothesis $H_0 : \mathbf{c} = \mathbf{0}$ the bias is given by $\boldsymbol{\gamma}^* = E[(\mathbf{X}_t' \mathbf{Q} \mathbf{X}_t)^{-1} \mathbf{X}_t' \mathbf{Q} \mathbf{u}_t]$.

The foregoing proposition illustrates that the issue of potential bias in the CSR parameter estimates is still a concern even if one imposes pricing restrictions, as long as time-varying characteristics are used in the cross-sectional regression. In the following section, we show that one can deal with this issue by employing time-average characteristics.

3.6.3. Using Time-Average Characteristics to Avoid the Bias
In this section, we reconsider the framework of Section 3.6.1 and demonstrate how we can overcome the problem of the asymptotic bias using time-average firm characteristics

instead of the spot values of characteristics in the cross-sectional regression. We adopt the notation of Section 3.6.1, namely, we denote $\mathbf{X}_t = [\mathbf{1}_N \ \mathbf{Z}_t \ \mathbf{B}]$, where $\mathbf{Z}_t$ is the $N \times M$ matrix of t-time characteristics and $\mathbf{c} = [a_0 \ \mathbf{a}' \ \boldsymbol{\lambda}']'$. Cross-sectional regression using the time-average $\overline{\mathbf{Z}}_T$ of the firm characteristics yields the following estimates of $\mathbf{c}$

$$\widehat{\mathbf{c}}_t = (\widehat{\mathbf{X}}'_T \widehat{\mathbf{Q}}_T \widehat{\mathbf{X}}_T)^{-1} \widehat{\mathbf{X}}'_T \widehat{\mathbf{Q}}_T \mathbf{R}_t, \quad t = 1, \ldots, T, \tag{3.73}$$

where

$$\widehat{\mathbf{X}}_T = [\mathbf{1}_N \ \overline{\mathbf{Z}}_T \ \widehat{\mathbf{B}}_T], \tag{3.74}$$

which is assumed to be of full rank equal to $L = 1 + M + K$. The use of time-average $\overline{\mathbf{Z}}_T$ ensures the consistency of the CSR estimator as the next proposition illustrates.

Proposition 6 *The time-series average $\overline{\overline{\mathbf{c}}}_T$ of the cross-sectional estimates*

$$\widehat{\mathbf{c}}_t = (\widehat{\mathbf{X}}'_T \widehat{\mathbf{Q}}_T \widehat{\mathbf{X}}_T)^{-1} \widehat{\mathbf{X}}'_T \widehat{\mathbf{Q}}_T \mathbf{R}_t, \quad t = 1, \ldots, T,$$

where $\widehat{\mathbf{X}}_T = [\mathbf{1}_N \ \overline{\mathbf{Z}}_T \ \widehat{\mathbf{B}}_T]$ is a consistent estimator of $\mathbf{c} = [a_0 \ \mathbf{a}' \ \boldsymbol{\lambda}']'$, that is

$$\overline{\overline{\mathbf{c}}}_T \xrightarrow{P} \mathbf{c} \text{ as } T \to \infty. \tag{3.75}$$

Next, we describe the asymptotic distribution of the CSR estimator using the time-average characteristics. For this we need some additional assumptions and notation. We assume that $E[\mathbf{X}_t] = [\mathbf{1}_N \ E[\mathbf{Z}_t] \ \mathbf{B}]$ is of full rank equal to L and define

$$\mathbf{D} = (E[\mathbf{X}_t]' \mathbf{Q} E[\mathbf{X}_t])^{-1} E[\mathbf{X}_t]' \mathbf{Q} \tag{3.76}$$

and

$$\mathbf{k}_t^1 = \mathbf{R}_t - E[\mathbf{R}_t] - (\mathbf{Z}_t - E[\mathbf{Z}_t])\mathbf{a}, \ \mathbf{k}_t^2 = \left[(\mathbf{f}_t - E[\mathbf{f}_t])' \boldsymbol{\Sigma}_F^{-1} \boldsymbol{\lambda} \right] \mathbf{u}_t, \quad \text{and} \quad \mathbf{k}_t = [(\mathbf{k}_t^1)'(\mathbf{k}_t^2)']'. \tag{3.77}$$

By definition, we have $E[\mathbf{k}_t^1] = \mathbf{0}_N$. Moreover, from the decomposition given in (3.6) it follows that $E[\mathbf{k}_t^2] = \mathbf{0}_N$. In the present context, we need the following assumption.

Assumption E The central limit theorem applies to the random sequence $\mathbf{k}_t$ defined in (3.77), that is $\frac{1}{\sqrt{T}} \sum_{t=1}^T \mathbf{k}_t$ converges in distribution to a multivariate normal with zero mean and covariance matrix given by

$$\begin{bmatrix} \mathbf{K} & \boldsymbol{\Xi} \\ \boldsymbol{\Xi}' & \mathbf{N} \end{bmatrix},$$

where

$$\mathbf{K} = \sum_{k=-\infty}^{+\infty} E\left[\mathbf{k}_t^1 \ (\mathbf{k}_{t+k}^1)'\right], \ \mathbf{\Xi} = \sum_{k=-\infty}^{+\infty} E\left[\mathbf{k}_t^1 (\mathbf{k}_{t+k}^2)'\right], \text{ and } \mathbf{N} = \sum_{k=-\infty}^{+\infty} E\left[\mathbf{k}_t^2 (\mathbf{k}_{t+k}^2)'\right]. \quad (3.78)$$

We are now in a position to state the theorem that gives the asymptotic distribution of the cross-sectional regression estimator using time-average characteristics.

Theorem 6 *Let* $\mathbf{c} = [a_0 \quad \mathbf{a}' \quad \boldsymbol{\lambda}']'$ *and* $\overline{\widehat{\mathbf{c}}}_T = (\widehat{\mathbf{X}}'_T \widehat{\mathbf{Q}}_T \widehat{\mathbf{X}}_T)^{-1} \widehat{\mathbf{X}}'_T \widehat{\mathbf{Q}}_T \overline{\mathbf{R}}_T$ *where* $\widehat{\mathbf{X}}_T = [\mathbf{1}_N \quad \overline{\mathbf{Z}}_T \quad \widehat{\mathbf{B}}_T]$. *Under Assumption E, as* $T \to \infty$, $\sqrt{T}(\overline{\widehat{\mathbf{c}}}_T - \mathbf{c})$ *converges in distribution to a multivariate normal with zero mean and covariance*

$$\mathbf{\Sigma}_c = \mathbf{DKD}' + \mathbf{DND}' - \mathbf{D}\left(\mathbf{\Xi} + \mathbf{\Xi}'\right)\mathbf{D}', \quad (3.79)$$

where $\mathbf{D} = (E[\mathbf{X}_t]'\mathbf{Q}E[\mathbf{X}_t])^{-1}E[\mathbf{X}_t]'\mathbf{Q}$ *with* $\mathbf{X}_t = [\mathbf{1}_N \quad \mathbf{Z}_t \quad \mathbf{B}]$ *and* $\mathbf{K}, \mathbf{\Xi},$ *and* $\mathbf{N}$ *are defined in (3.78).*

3.7. N-Consistency of the CSR Estimator

The preceding sections present an extensive discussion of the asymptotic properties, as $T \to \infty$, of the cross-sectional regression estimator in a number of different formulations. In this section, we examine the CSR estimator from a different perspective. We assume that the length of the available time-series T is fixed and consider the limiting behavior of the estimator as the number of individual assets N increases without bound. This perspective is of particular interest given the availability of rather large cross-sections of return data.

Consider an economy with N traded assets and a linear pricing factor model with K factors $f^1, \ldots, f^K$. Consider the following pricing equation

$$E[\mathbf{R}_t] = \gamma_0 \mathbf{1}_N + \mathbf{B}\boldsymbol{\gamma}_1 = \mathbf{X}_N \mathbf{\Gamma}, \quad (3.80)$$

where the beta matrix $\mathbf{B}$ is given by $\mathbf{B} = E[(\mathbf{R}_t - E[\mathbf{R}_t])(\mathbf{f}_t - E[\mathbf{f}_t])']\mathbf{\Sigma}_\mathrm{F}^{-1}$ with $\mathbf{\Sigma}_\mathrm{F}$ denoting the factor covariance matrix $E[(\mathbf{f}_t - E[\mathbf{f}_t])(\mathbf{f}_t - E[\mathbf{f}_t])']$, $\mathbf{X}_N = [\mathbf{1}_N \quad \mathbf{B}]$ $(N \times (1 + K)$ matrix), and $\mathbf{\Gamma} = (\gamma_0, \boldsymbol{\gamma}'_1)'$ $((1 + K) \times 1$ vector). The factors could be either traded or nontraded. However, even if they are traded we do not impose any pricing restriction implied by the model.

Recall from (3.6) the following time-series regression equation $\mathbf{R}_t = E[\mathbf{R}_t] + \mathbf{B}(\mathbf{f}_t - E[\mathbf{f}_t]) + \mathbf{u}_t$, $t = 1, \ldots, T$ with $E[\mathbf{u}_t] = \mathbf{0}_N$ and $E[\mathbf{u}_t \mathbf{f}'_t] = \mathbf{0}_{N \times K}$. Taking time average in the last regression and incorporating (3.80) we obtain

$$\overline{\mathbf{R}}_T = \gamma_0 \mathbf{1}_N + \mathbf{B}\left(\boldsymbol{\gamma}_1 + \overline{\mathbf{f}}_T - E[\mathbf{f}_t]\right) + \overline{\mathbf{u}}_T = \mathbf{X}_N \overline{\mathbf{\Gamma}}_T + \overline{\mathbf{u}}_T, \quad (3.81)$$

where $\overline{\boldsymbol{\Gamma}}_T = (\gamma_0, \overline{\boldsymbol{\gamma}}'_{1T})'$ and $\overline{\boldsymbol{\gamma}}_{1T} = \boldsymbol{\gamma}_1 + \overline{\mathbf{f}}_T - E[\mathbf{f}_t]$. In Shanken (1992), the vector $\overline{\boldsymbol{\Gamma}}_T$ is referred to as the vector of "ex-post prices of risk."

Assume the time-series length T is fixed and consider limiting behavior as the number of assets N goes to ∞. Because T is fixed it is clear that we cannot estimate the vector of "ex-ante prices of risk" $\boldsymbol{\Gamma}$. Instead, we can estimate the vector of "ex-post prices of risk" $\overline{\boldsymbol{\Gamma}}_T$. Following Shanken (1992), we define an estimator to be N-consistent if it converges in probability to the ex-post parameter vector $\overline{\boldsymbol{\Gamma}}_T$ as $N \to \infty$.

To ease the exposition, let us suppose for a moment that the beta matrix $\mathbf{B}$ is known. Then Eq. (3.81) suggests $\left(\mathbf{X}'_N \mathbf{X}_N\right)^{-1} \mathbf{X}'_N \overline{\mathbf{R}}_T$ as an estimator for $\overline{\boldsymbol{\Gamma}}_T$. Indeed from (3.81) we have

$$\left(\mathbf{X}'_N \mathbf{X}_N\right)^{-1} \mathbf{X}'_N \overline{\mathbf{R}}_T = \overline{\boldsymbol{\Gamma}}_T + \left(\mathbf{X}'_N \mathbf{X}_N\right)^{-1} \mathbf{X}'_N \overline{\mathbf{u}}_T. \tag{3.82}$$

Then, under appropriate assumptions that are stated below, we have that as $N \to \infty$

$$\frac{1}{N}\mathbf{X}'_N \mathbf{X}_N = \begin{bmatrix} 1 & \frac{1}{N}\sum_{i=1}^N \boldsymbol{\beta}'_i \\ \frac{1}{N}\sum_{i=1}^N \boldsymbol{\beta}_i & \frac{1}{N}\sum_{i=1}^N \boldsymbol{\beta}_i \boldsymbol{\beta}'_i \end{bmatrix} \xrightarrow{P} \begin{bmatrix} 1 & \boldsymbol{\mu}'_\beta \\ \boldsymbol{\mu}_\beta & \boldsymbol{\Sigma}_\beta + \boldsymbol{\mu}_\beta \boldsymbol{\mu}'_\beta \end{bmatrix} \tag{3.83}$$

and

$$\frac{1}{N}\mathbf{X}'_N \overline{\mathbf{u}}_T = \begin{bmatrix} 1 & \cdots & 1 \\ \boldsymbol{\beta}_1 & \cdots & \boldsymbol{\beta}_N \end{bmatrix} \begin{bmatrix} \overline{u}_{1T} \\ \vdots \\ \overline{u}_{NT} \end{bmatrix} = \begin{bmatrix} \frac{1}{T}\sum_{t=1}^T \left(\frac{1}{N}\sum_{i=1}^N u_{it}\right) \\ \frac{1}{T}\sum_{t=1}^T \left(\frac{1}{N}\sum_{i=1}^N u_{it}\boldsymbol{\beta}_i\right) \end{bmatrix} \xrightarrow{P} \mathbf{0}_{1+K} \tag{3.84}$$

and so

$$\left(\mathbf{X}'_N \mathbf{X}_N\right)^{-1} \mathbf{X}'_N \overline{\mathbf{R}}_T \xrightarrow{P} \overline{\boldsymbol{\Gamma}}_T.$$

However, in practice the beta matrix $\mathbf{B}$ is unknown and has to be estimated using the available data. The two-pass procedure uses time-series regressions to estimate $\mathbf{B}$. The estimate $\widehat{\mathbf{B}}_T$ is given in (3.10). Replacing $\mathbf{B}$ by $\widehat{\mathbf{B}}_T$ we obtain $(\widehat{\mathbf{X}}'_N \widehat{\mathbf{X}}_N)^{-1}\widehat{\mathbf{X}}'_N \overline{\mathbf{R}}_T$ as an estimator for $\overline{\boldsymbol{\Gamma}}_T$ where $\widehat{\mathbf{X}}'_N = [\mathbf{1}_N \ \ \widehat{\mathbf{B}}_T]$. However, this estimator is subject to the well-known EIV problem and needs to be modified to maintain the property of N-consistency. Before we proceed with the illustration of the appropriate modification, we present a set of conditions that will guarantee the validity of our claim. The first condition ensures that there is sufficiently weak cross-sectional dependence as required in the statement of Theorem 5 in the study of Shanken (1992). The second condition requires that average betas and their squares converge to well-defined quantities as $N \to \infty$.

Assumption F *The time-series residuals* $\mathbf{u}_t$ *satisfy the following cross-sectional properties:*

(a)

$$\frac{1}{N} \sum_{i=1}^{N} u_{it} \xrightarrow{P} 0 \text{ as } N \to \infty \text{ for all } t = 1, 2, \ldots, \tag{3.85}$$

(b)

$$\frac{1}{N} \sum_{i=1}^{N} u_{it} \boldsymbol{\beta}_i \xrightarrow{P} \mathbf{0}_K \text{ as } N \to \infty \text{ for all } t = 1, 2, \ldots, \tag{3.86}$$

(c)

$$\frac{1}{N} \sum_{i=1}^{N} u_{is} u_{it} \xrightarrow{P} 0 \text{ as } N \to \infty \text{ for all } t, s = 1, 2, \ldots \text{ with } s \neq t. \tag{3.87}$$

Denote by $\boldsymbol{\Sigma}_U$ *the covariance matrix of* $\mathbf{u}_t$ *and by* σ_i^2 *the ith diagonal element of* $\boldsymbol{\Sigma}_U$, $i = 1, \ldots, N$. *Define* $v_{it} = u_{it}^2 - \sigma_i^2$ *which implies* $E[v_{it}] = 0$ *for all i and t. Then the following hold*

(d)

$$\frac{1}{N} \sum_{i=1}^{N} v_{it} \xrightarrow{P} 0 \text{ as } N \to \infty \text{ for all } t = 1, 2, \ldots, \tag{3.88}$$

(e)

$$\frac{1}{N} \sum_{i=1}^{N} \sigma_i^2 \to \bar{\sigma}^2 \text{ as } N \to \infty. \tag{3.89}$$

Assumption G *The sequence of betas* $\{\boldsymbol{\beta}_i : i = 1, 2, \ldots\}$ *satisfies the following two conditions:*

(a)

$$\frac{1}{N} \sum_{i=1}^{N} \boldsymbol{\beta}_i \to \boldsymbol{\mu}_\beta \text{ as } N \to \infty \tag{3.90}$$

(b)

$$\frac{1}{N} \sum_{i=1}^{N} \boldsymbol{\beta}_i \boldsymbol{\beta}_i' \to \boldsymbol{\Sigma}_\beta + \boldsymbol{\mu}_\beta \boldsymbol{\mu}_\beta' \text{ as } N \to \infty \tag{3.91}$$

where $\boldsymbol{\mu}_\beta$ *is a* $K \times 1$ *vector and* $\boldsymbol{\Sigma}_\beta$ *is positive-definite symmetric* $K \times K$ *matrix.*

Returning to our calculation, we have

$$\frac{1}{N}\widehat{\mathbf{X}}'_N\overline{\mathbf{R}}_T = \left[\begin{array}{ccc} \frac{1}{\widehat{\boldsymbol{\beta}}_{1T}} & \cdots & \frac{1}{\widehat{\boldsymbol{\beta}}_{NT}} \end{array}\right]\left[\begin{array}{c} \overline{R}_{1T} \\ \vdots \\ \overline{R}_{NT} \end{array}\right] = \left[\begin{array}{c} \frac{1}{N}\sum_{i=1}^N \overline{R}_{iT} \\ \frac{1}{N}\sum_{i=1}^N \overline{R}_{iT}\widehat{\boldsymbol{\beta}}_{iT} \end{array}\right]. \tag{3.92}$$

It follows from (3.81) that

$$\frac{1}{N}\sum_{i=1}^N \overline{R}_{iT} = \gamma_0 + \left(\frac{1}{N}\sum_{i=1}^N \boldsymbol{\beta}_i\right)'(\boldsymbol{\gamma}_1 + \overline{\mathbf{f}}_T - E[\mathbf{f}_t]) + \frac{1}{T}\sum_{t=1}^T\left(\frac{1}{N}\sum_{i=1}^N u_{it}\right)$$

and so

$$\frac{1}{N}\sum_{i=1}^N \overline{R}_{iT} \xrightarrow{P} \gamma_0 + \boldsymbol{\mu}'_\beta(\boldsymbol{\gamma}_1 + \overline{\mathbf{f}}_T - E[\mathbf{f}_t]) \text{ as } N \to \infty \tag{3.93}$$

as it follows from Assumptions F and G. Recall that

$$\widehat{\boldsymbol{\beta}}_{iT} = \widehat{\boldsymbol{\Sigma}}_{FT}^{-1}\left[\frac{1}{T}\sum_{t=1}^T (\mathbf{f}_t - \overline{\mathbf{f}}_T)(R_{it} - \overline{R}_{iT})\right]$$

and

$$R_{it} - \overline{R}_{iT} = \boldsymbol{\beta}'_i(\mathbf{f}_t - \overline{\mathbf{f}}_T) + (u_{it} - \overline{u}_{iT}) \tag{3.94}$$

which combined deliver

$$\widehat{\boldsymbol{\beta}}_{iT} = \boldsymbol{\beta}_i + \boldsymbol{\xi}_{iT} \tag{3.95}$$

where

$$\boldsymbol{\xi}_{iT} = \widehat{\boldsymbol{\Sigma}}_{FT}^{-1}\left[\frac{1}{T}\sum_{t=1}^T u_{it}(\mathbf{f}_t - \overline{\mathbf{f}}_T)\right]. \tag{3.96}$$

Thus,

$$\frac{1}{N}\sum_{i=1}^N \overline{R}_{iT}\widehat{\boldsymbol{\beta}}_{iT} = \frac{1}{N}\sum_{i=1}^N (\boldsymbol{\beta}_i + \boldsymbol{\xi}_{iT})\left[\gamma_0 + \boldsymbol{\beta}'_i(\boldsymbol{\gamma}_1 + \overline{\mathbf{f}}_T - E[\mathbf{f}_t]) + \overline{u}_{iT}\right]$$

$$= \gamma_0\left(\frac{1}{N}\sum_{i=1}^N \boldsymbol{\beta}_i + \frac{1}{N}\sum_{i=1}^N \boldsymbol{\xi}_{iT}\right)$$

$$+ \left(\frac{1}{N} \sum_{i=1}^{N} \boldsymbol{\beta}_i \boldsymbol{\beta}_i' + \frac{1}{N} \sum_{i=1}^{N} \boldsymbol{\xi}_{iT} \boldsymbol{\beta}_i' \right) (\boldsymbol{\gamma}_1 + \bar{\mathbf{f}}_T - E[\mathbf{f}_t]) \tag{3.97}$$

$$+ \frac{1}{T} \sum_{t=1}^{T} \left(\frac{1}{N} \sum_{i=1}^{N} u_{it} \boldsymbol{\beta}_i + \frac{1}{N} \sum_{i=1}^{N} u_{it} \boldsymbol{\xi}_{iT} \right).$$

We consider the limiting behavior of each term in the last equation. It follows from (3.96), 3.85 and Assumption F $\frac{1}{N} \sum_{i=1}^{N} \boldsymbol{\xi}_{iT} \xrightarrow{P} \mathbf{0}_K$ as $N \to \infty$. Similarly, from (3.96) and (3.86) we obtain $\frac{1}{N} \sum_{i=1}^{N} \boldsymbol{\xi}_{iT} \boldsymbol{\beta}_i' \xrightarrow{P} \mathbf{0}_{K \times K}$ as $N \to \infty$. Further we have

$$\sum_{t=1}^{T} \frac{1}{N} \sum_{i=1}^{N} u_{it} \boldsymbol{\xi}_{iT} = \widehat{\boldsymbol{\Sigma}}_{FT}^{-1} \left[\frac{1}{T} \sum_{t=1}^{T} \sum_{s=1}^{T} \left(\frac{1}{N} \sum_{i=1}^{N} u_{is} u_{it} \right) (\mathbf{f}_s - \bar{\mathbf{f}}_T) \right]$$

$$\xrightarrow{P} \widehat{\boldsymbol{\Sigma}}_{FT}^{-1} \left[\frac{1}{T} \sum_{t=1}^{T} \bar{\sigma}^2 (\mathbf{f}_t - \bar{\mathbf{f}}_T) \right] = \mathbf{0}_K \text{ as } N \to \infty, \tag{3.98}$$

which follows from (3.87), (3.88), and (3.89). Using (3.90), (3.91), and (3.86), we now obtain from Eq. (3.97) that

$$\frac{1}{N} \sum_{i=1}^{N} \overline{R}_{iT} \widehat{\boldsymbol{\beta}}_{iT} \xrightarrow{P} \gamma_0 \boldsymbol{\mu}_\beta + (\boldsymbol{\Sigma}_\beta + \boldsymbol{\mu}_\beta \boldsymbol{\mu}_\beta')(\boldsymbol{\gamma}_1 + \bar{\mathbf{f}}_T - E[\mathbf{f}_t]) \text{ as } N \to \infty. \tag{3.99}$$

Finally, the combination (3.92), (3.93), and (3.99) yields

$$\frac{1}{N} \widehat{\mathbf{X}}_N' \overline{\mathbf{R}}_T \xrightarrow{P} \begin{bmatrix} \gamma_0 + \boldsymbol{\mu}_\beta' (\boldsymbol{\gamma}_1 + \bar{\mathbf{f}}_T - E[\mathbf{f}_t]) \\ \\ \gamma_0 \boldsymbol{\mu}_\beta + (\boldsymbol{\Sigma}_\beta + \boldsymbol{\mu}_\beta \boldsymbol{\mu}_\beta')(\boldsymbol{\gamma}_1 + \bar{\mathbf{f}}_T - E[\mathbf{f}_t]) \end{bmatrix} \text{ as } N \to \infty. \tag{3.100}$$

Next we study the limiting behavior of $\frac{1}{N} \widehat{\mathbf{X}}_N' \widehat{\mathbf{X}}_N$. This will enable us to appropriately modify the proposed estimator to achieve N-consistency. We have

$$\frac{1}{N} \widehat{\mathbf{X}}_N' \widehat{\mathbf{X}}_N = \begin{bmatrix} 1 & \frac{1}{N} \sum_{i=1}^{N} \widehat{\boldsymbol{\beta}}_i' \\ \\ \frac{1}{N} \sum_{i=1}^{N} \widehat{\boldsymbol{\beta}}_i & \frac{1}{N} \sum_{i=1}^{N} \widehat{\boldsymbol{\beta}}_i \widehat{\boldsymbol{\beta}}_i' \end{bmatrix}. \tag{3.101}$$

The calculations aforementioned imply that, as $N \to \infty$, $\frac{1}{N} \sum_{i=1}^{N} \widehat{\boldsymbol{\beta}}_i \xrightarrow{P} \boldsymbol{\mu}_\beta$ and $\frac{1}{N} \sum_{i=1}^{N} \widehat{\boldsymbol{\beta}}_i \widehat{\boldsymbol{\beta}}_i' \xrightarrow{P} \boldsymbol{\Sigma}_\beta + \boldsymbol{\mu}_\beta \boldsymbol{\mu}_\beta' + \text{p-}\lim_{N \to \infty} \frac{1}{N} \sum_{i=1}^{N} \boldsymbol{\xi}_{iT} \boldsymbol{\xi}_{iT}'$. Using (3.96) and

(3.88) and (3.89) we obtain

$$
\frac{1}{N}\sum_{i=1}^{N}\boldsymbol{\xi}_{iT}\boldsymbol{\xi}_{iT}' = \widehat{\boldsymbol{\Sigma}}_{FT}^{-1}\left[\frac{1}{T^2}\sum_{t=1}^{T}\sum_{s=1}^{T}\left(\frac{1}{N}\sum_{i=1}^{N}u_{it}u_{is}\right)(\mathbf{f}_t - \bar{\mathbf{f}}_T)(\mathbf{f}_s - \bar{\mathbf{f}}_T)'\right]\widehat{\boldsymbol{\Sigma}}_{FT}^{-1}
$$

$$
\xrightarrow{P}\widehat{\boldsymbol{\Sigma}}_{FT}^{-1}\left[\frac{1}{T^2}\sum_{t=1}^{T}\bar{\sigma}^2(\mathbf{f}_t - \bar{\mathbf{f}}_T)(\mathbf{f}_t - \bar{\mathbf{f}}_T)'\right]\widehat{\boldsymbol{\Sigma}}_{FT}^{-1} = \bar{\sigma}^2\frac{1}{T}\widehat{\boldsymbol{\Sigma}}_{FT}^{-1} \text{ as } N \to \infty.
$$

(3.102)

Thus, from (3.101) it follows that

$$
\frac{1}{N}\widehat{\mathbf{X}}_N'\widehat{\mathbf{X}}_N \xrightarrow{P} \begin{bmatrix} 1 & \boldsymbol{\mu}_\beta' \\ \boldsymbol{\mu}_\beta & \boldsymbol{\Sigma}_\beta + \boldsymbol{\mu}_\beta\boldsymbol{\mu}_\beta' + \bar{\sigma}^2\frac{1}{T}\widehat{\boldsymbol{\Sigma}}_{FT}^{-1} \end{bmatrix}.
$$

(3.103)

Using the expression for the inverse of a partitioned matrix and a few steps of algebra, we now obtain

$$
\begin{bmatrix} 1 & \boldsymbol{\mu}_\beta' \\ \boldsymbol{\mu}_\beta & \boldsymbol{\Sigma}_\beta + \boldsymbol{\mu}_\beta\boldsymbol{\mu}_\beta' \end{bmatrix}^{-1} \begin{bmatrix} \gamma_0 + \boldsymbol{\mu}_\beta'(\boldsymbol{\gamma}_1 + \bar{\mathbf{f}}_T - E[\mathbf{f}_t]) \\ \gamma_0\boldsymbol{\mu}_\beta + (\boldsymbol{\Sigma}_\beta + \boldsymbol{\mu}_\beta\boldsymbol{\mu}_\beta')(\boldsymbol{\gamma}_1 + \bar{\mathbf{f}}_T - E[\mathbf{f}_t]) \end{bmatrix}
$$

$$
= \begin{bmatrix} 1 + \boldsymbol{\mu}_\beta'\boldsymbol{\Sigma}_\beta^{-1}\boldsymbol{\mu}_\beta & -\boldsymbol{\mu}_\beta'\boldsymbol{\Sigma}_\beta^{-1} \\ -\boldsymbol{\Sigma}_\beta^{-1}\boldsymbol{\mu}_\beta & \boldsymbol{\Sigma}_\beta^{-1} \end{bmatrix} \begin{bmatrix} \gamma_0 + \boldsymbol{\mu}_\beta'(\boldsymbol{\gamma}_1 + \bar{\mathbf{f}}_T - E[\mathbf{f}_t]) \\ \gamma_0\boldsymbol{\mu}_\beta + (\boldsymbol{\Sigma}_\beta + \boldsymbol{\mu}_\beta\boldsymbol{\mu}_\beta')(\boldsymbol{\gamma}_1 + \bar{\mathbf{f}}_T - E[\mathbf{f}_t]) \end{bmatrix} = \bar{\boldsymbol{\Gamma}}_T.
$$

Thus, to obtain an N-consistent estimator we need to subtract a term from $\widehat{\mathbf{X}}_N'\widehat{\mathbf{X}}_N$ to eliminate the term $\bar{\sigma}^2\frac{1}{T}\widehat{\boldsymbol{\Sigma}}_{FT}^{-1}$ in the probability limit in (3.103). (3.89) states that

$$
\frac{\text{tr}(\boldsymbol{\Sigma}_U)}{N} = \frac{\sum_{i=1}^{N}\sigma_i^2}{N} \to \bar{\sigma}^2 \text{ as } N \to \infty
$$

which, in the light of (3.103), suggests that we should replace $\widehat{\mathbf{X}}_N'\widehat{\mathbf{X}}_N$ by

$$
\widehat{\mathbf{X}}_N'\widehat{\mathbf{X}}_N - \begin{bmatrix} 0 & \mathbf{0}_K' \\ \mathbf{0}_K & \text{tr}(\widehat{\boldsymbol{\Sigma}}_{UT})\frac{1}{T}\widehat{\boldsymbol{\Sigma}}_{FT}^{-1} \end{bmatrix} = \widehat{\mathbf{X}}_N'\widehat{\mathbf{X}}_N - \frac{\text{tr}(\widehat{\boldsymbol{\Sigma}}_{UT})}{T}\mathbf{M}'\widehat{\boldsymbol{\Sigma}}_{FT}^{-1}\mathbf{M},
$$

where $\mathbf{M} = [\mathbf{0}_K \ \mathbf{I}_K]$ $(K \times (1 + K)$ matrix) and

$$
\widehat{\boldsymbol{\Sigma}}_{UT} = \frac{1}{T - K - 1}\sum_{t=1}^{T}\mathbf{e}_t\mathbf{e}_t', \quad \mathbf{e}_t = \mathbf{R}_t - \widehat{\mathbf{a}} - \widehat{\mathbf{B}}_T\mathbf{f}_t = (\mathbf{R}_t - \bar{\mathbf{R}}_T) - \widehat{\mathbf{B}}_T(\mathbf{f}_t - \bar{\mathbf{f}}_T). \quad (3.104)
$$

That is, $\widehat{\boldsymbol{\Sigma}}_{\mathrm{UT}}$ is the unbiased estimator of $\boldsymbol{\Sigma}_{\mathrm{U}}$ based on the sample of size T. It remains to show that

$$\frac{\mathrm{tr}(\widehat{\boldsymbol{\Sigma}}_{\mathrm{UT}})}{N} \to \bar{\sigma}^2 \text{ as } N \to \infty. \tag{3.105}$$

Using (3.104) and the decomposition in (3.94) we obtain

$$\frac{\mathrm{tr}(\widehat{\boldsymbol{\Sigma}}_{\mathrm{UT}})}{N} = \frac{1}{N}\mathrm{tr}\left(\frac{1}{T-K-1}\sum_{t=1}^{T}\mathbf{e}_t\mathbf{e}_t'\right)$$

$$= \frac{1}{N(T-K-1)}\sum_{t=1}^{T}\sum_{i=1}^{N}\left[(R_{it}-\bar{R}_{iT})-\widehat{\boldsymbol{\beta}}_{iT}'\left(\mathbf{f}_t-\bar{\mathbf{f}}_T\right)\right]^2$$

$$= \frac{1}{N(T-K-1)}\sum_{t=1}^{T}\sum_{i=1}^{N}\left[\left(\boldsymbol{\beta}_i-\widehat{\boldsymbol{\beta}}_{iT}\right)'\left(\mathbf{f}_t-\bar{\mathbf{f}}_T\right)+(u_{it}-\bar{u}_{iT})\right]^2$$

$$= \frac{1}{T-K-1}\sum_{t=1}^{T}\left(\mathbf{f}_t-\bar{\mathbf{f}}_T\right)'\left(\frac{1}{N}\sum_{i=1}^{N}\boldsymbol{\xi}_{iT}\boldsymbol{\xi}_{iT}'\right)\left(\mathbf{f}_t-\bar{\mathbf{f}}_T\right)$$

$$-\frac{2}{T-K-1}\sum_{t=1}^{T}\left(\mathbf{f}_t-\bar{\mathbf{f}}_T\right)'\left(\frac{1}{N}\sum_{i=1}^{N}u_{it}\boldsymbol{\xi}_{iT}\right)$$

$$+\frac{T}{T-K-1}\frac{1}{N}\sum_{i=1}^{N}\left(\frac{1}{T}\sum_{t=1}^{T}(u_{it}-\bar{u}_{iT})^2\right). \tag{3.106}$$

Following the calculation in (3.98) we obtain that $\frac{1}{N}\sum_{i=1}^{N}u_{it}\boldsymbol{\xi}_{iT} \xrightarrow{P} \frac{\bar{\sigma}^2}{T}\widehat{\boldsymbol{\Sigma}}_{\mathrm{FT}}^{-1}\left(\mathbf{f}_t-\bar{\mathbf{f}}_T\right)$ as $N \to \infty$. Further, using (3.87), (3.88), and (3.89), we have

$$\frac{1}{N}\sum_{i=1}^{N}\left(\frac{1}{T}\sum_{t=1}^{T}(u_{it}-\bar{u}_{iT})^2\right) = \frac{1}{N}\sum_{i=1}^{N}\left(\frac{1}{T}\sum_{t=1}^{T}u_{it}^2 - \frac{1}{T^2}\sum_{t=1}^{T}\sum_{s=1}^{T}u_{it}u_{is}\right) \xrightarrow{P} \frac{T-1}{T}\bar{\sigma}^2.$$

Combining the aforementioned probability limits and the result in (3.102), we obtain from (3.106) that

$$\frac{\mathrm{tr}(\widehat{\boldsymbol{\Sigma}}_{\mathrm{UT}})}{N} \xrightarrow{P} \frac{T-1}{T-K-1}\bar{\sigma}^2 - \frac{1}{T-K-1}\bar{\sigma}^2\left[\frac{1}{T}\sum_{t=1}^{T}\left(\mathbf{f}_t-\bar{\mathbf{f}}_T\right)'\widehat{\boldsymbol{\Sigma}}_{\mathrm{FT}}^{-1}\left(\mathbf{f}_t-\bar{\mathbf{f}}_T\right)\right] = \bar{\sigma}^2, \tag{3.107}$$

where $\frac{1}{T}\sum_{t=1}^{T}\left(\mathbf{f}_t-\bar{\mathbf{f}}_T\right)'\widehat{\boldsymbol{\Sigma}}_{\mathrm{FT}}^{-1}\left(\mathbf{f}_t-\bar{\mathbf{f}}_T\right) = K$ because $\widehat{\boldsymbol{\Sigma}}_{\mathrm{FT}}$ is assumed to be positive definite. The last equality follows from the following matrix algebraic result that is based on the properties of the trace operator for matrices. Suppose $\mathbf{x}_t$, $t = 1, \ldots, T$ are K-dimensional vectors and let $\mathbf{X} = \sum_{t=1}^{T} \mathbf{x}_t \mathbf{x}_t'$. If $\mathbf{X}$ is nonsingular, then $\sum_{t=1}^{T} \mathbf{x}_t' \mathbf{X}^{-1} \mathbf{x}_t = K$. Thus, we have completed the proof of the following theorem.

Theorem 7 *Suppose Assumptions F and G hold. Then*

$$\left(\widehat{\mathbf{X}}_N' \widehat{\mathbf{X}}_N - tr(\widehat{\mathbf{\Sigma}}_{\mathrm{UT}}) \mathbf{M}' \widehat{\mathbf{\Sigma}}_{\mathrm{FT}}^{-1} \mathbf{M}/T \right)^{-1} \widehat{\mathbf{X}}_N' \overline{\mathbf{R}}_T \tag{3.108}$$

is an N-consistent estimator of the vector of the ex-post prices of risk $\overline{\mathbf{\Gamma}}_T$ where $\widehat{\mathbf{X}}_N = [\mathbf{1}_N \ \widehat{\mathbf{B}}_T]$, $\mathbf{M} = [\mathbf{1}_K \ \mathbf{I}_K]$, and $\widehat{\mathbf{B}}_T$, $\widehat{\mathbf{\Sigma}}_{\mathrm{FT}}$, $\widehat{\mathbf{\Sigma}}_{\mathrm{UT}}$ are defined by (3.10), (3.9), and (3.104), respectively.

4. MAXIMUM LIKELIHOOD METHODS

When the researcher is willing to make distributional assumptions on the joint dynamics of the asset returns and the factors, the likelihood function is available and the ML method provides a natural way to estimate and test the linear beta pricing model. The earliest application of the ML method was described by Gibbons (1982). Given the computational difficulties involved at that time, Gibbons linearized the restriction imposed by the linear beta pricing model. He estimated the model and tested the hypothesis that the restrictions imposed by the pricing model holds using the likelihood-ratio test statistic, which has a central chi-square distribution with the number of degrees of freedom equal to the number of constraints. In what follows, we first describe the ML method for estimating and testing the general linear beta-pricing model under the assumption that none of the factors are traded and then relax the assumption to allow some factors to be traded. We then consider the more special case where there is a risk-free asset.

4.1. Nontraded Factors

Consider the linear factor model given in Eq. (2.5) reproduced below for convenience

$$\mathbf{R}_t = \boldsymbol{\alpha} + \mathbf{B}\mathbf{f}_t + \mathbf{u}_t \quad \text{with} \quad \boldsymbol{\alpha} = \boldsymbol{\mu}_{\mathrm{R}} - \mathbf{B}\boldsymbol{\mu}_{\mathrm{F}} \tag{4.1}$$

where the alternative notation $\boldsymbol{\mu}_{\mathrm{R}} = E[\mathbf{R}_t]$ and $\boldsymbol{\mu}_{\mathrm{F}} = E[\mathbf{f}_t]$ is used. We are first concerned with the case in which the factors are not returns on traded portfolios. Assume that the innovations $\mathbf{u}_t$ are i.i.d. multivariate normal conditional on contemporaneous and past realizations of the factors, and denote by $\mathbf{\Sigma}_{\mathrm{U}}$ the covariance matrix of the innovations and by $\mathcal{L}_{\mathrm{F}}$ the marginal likelihood of the factors.

The linear beta pricing model in Eq. (2.4) imposes the restriction that

$$\boldsymbol{\alpha} = a_0 \mathbf{1} + \mathbf{B}(\boldsymbol{\lambda} - \boldsymbol{\mu}_{\mathrm{F}}) \tag{4.2}$$

where $\boldsymbol{\lambda}$ and $\boldsymbol{\mu}_F$ denote the vector of the risk premia and the vector of expected values of the K factors, respectively. In the special case where there is only one factor and it is the return on the market portfolio, R_{mt}, this gives the well-known intercept restriction,

$$\alpha_i = a_0(1 - \beta_{mi}), i = 1, \ldots, N.$$

The loglikelihood function of the unconstrained model is given by

$$\mathcal{L} = -\frac{NT}{2}\log(2\pi) - \frac{T}{2}\log(|\boldsymbol{\Sigma}_U|) - \frac{1}{2}\sum_{t=1}^{T}(\mathbf{R}_t - \boldsymbol{\alpha} - \mathbf{B}\mathbf{f}_t)'\boldsymbol{\Sigma}_U^{-1}(\mathbf{R}_t - \boldsymbol{\alpha} - \mathbf{B}\mathbf{f}_t) + \log(\mathcal{L}_F).$$

It can be verified that the ML estimator of the parameter vector is given by

$$\widehat{\boldsymbol{\mu}}_R = \frac{1}{T}\sum_{t=1}^{T}\mathbf{R}_t; \quad \widehat{\boldsymbol{\mu}}_F = \frac{1}{T}\sum_{t=1}^{T}\mathbf{f}_t;$$

$$\widehat{\boldsymbol{\Sigma}}_F = \frac{1}{T}\sum_{t=1}^{T}(\mathbf{f}_t - \widehat{\boldsymbol{\mu}}_F)(\mathbf{f}_t - \widehat{\boldsymbol{\mu}}_F)'; \quad \widehat{\mathbf{B}} = \left[\frac{1}{T}\sum_{1}^{T}(\mathbf{R}_t - \widehat{\boldsymbol{\mu}}_R)(\mathbf{f}_t - \widehat{\boldsymbol{\mu}}_F)'\right]\widehat{\boldsymbol{\Sigma}}_F^{-1}; \qquad (4.3)$$

$$\widehat{\boldsymbol{\alpha}} = \widehat{\boldsymbol{\mu}}_R - \widehat{\mathbf{B}}\widehat{\boldsymbol{\mu}}_F; \quad \widehat{\boldsymbol{\Sigma}}_U = \frac{1}{T}\sum_{t=1}^{T}(\mathbf{R}_t - \widehat{\boldsymbol{\alpha}} - \widehat{\mathbf{B}}\mathbf{f}_t)(\mathbf{R}_t - \widehat{\boldsymbol{\alpha}} - \widehat{\mathbf{B}}\mathbf{f}_t)'.$$

When the beta pricing model holds $\boldsymbol{\alpha}$ is given by Eq. (4.2), substituting the right side of Eq. (4.2) for $\boldsymbol{\alpha}$ into the linear factor model in Eq. (4.1) and rearranging the terms gives

$$\mathbf{R}_t - a_0\mathbf{1} = \mathbf{B}(\mathbf{a}_1 + \mathbf{f}_t) + \mathbf{u}_t, \qquad (4.4)$$

where $\mathbf{a}_1 = \boldsymbol{\lambda} - \boldsymbol{\mu}_F$. Let $\mathbf{a} = [a_0 \ \mathbf{a}_1']'$. It can then be verified that the constrained ML estimators are given by

$$\widehat{\boldsymbol{\alpha}}_c = \widehat{\boldsymbol{\mu}}_R - \mathbf{B}^c\widehat{\boldsymbol{\mu}}_F; \quad \widehat{\mathbf{a}}_c = \left(\widehat{\mathbf{B}}_c'\widehat{\boldsymbol{\Sigma}}_{Uc}^{-1}\widehat{\mathbf{B}}_c\right)^{-1}\left(\widehat{\mathbf{B}}_c'\widehat{\boldsymbol{\Sigma}}_{Uc}^{-1}\widehat{\boldsymbol{\alpha}}_c\right)$$

$$\widehat{\mathbf{B}}_c = \left[\frac{1}{T}\sum_{t=1}^{T}(\mathbf{R}_t - \widehat{a}_{0c}\mathbf{1})(\widehat{\mathbf{a}}_{1c} + \mathbf{f}_t)'\right]\left[\frac{1}{T}\sum_{t=1}^{T}(\widehat{\mathbf{a}}_{1c} + \mathbf{f}_t)(\widehat{\mathbf{a}}_{1c} + \mathbf{f}_t)'\right]^{-1} \qquad (4.5)$$

$$\widehat{\boldsymbol{\Sigma}}_{Uc} = \frac{1}{T}\sum_{t=1}^{T}[\mathbf{R}_t - \widehat{a}_{0c}\mathbf{1} - \widehat{\mathbf{B}}_c(\widehat{\mathbf{a}}_{1c} + \mathbf{f}_t)][\mathbf{R}_t - \widehat{a}_{0c}\mathbf{1} - \widehat{\mathbf{B}}_c(\widehat{\mathbf{a}}_{1c} + \mathbf{f}_t)]'$$

where the subscript c indicates that these are the constrained ML estimates.

The aforementioned equations can be solved by successive iteration. The unconstrained estimates of $\boldsymbol{\alpha}$ and $\boldsymbol{\Sigma}_U$ are used to obtain an initial estimate of $\mathbf{a}$. The asymptotic variance of the estimators can be obtained using standard ML procedures. When the linear beta pricing model restriction holds, the likelihood-ratio test statistic (minus twice the logarithm of the likelihood ratio) given by

$$J_{LR} = -T\left[\log(|\widehat{\boldsymbol{\Sigma}}_U|) - \log(|\widehat{\boldsymbol{\Sigma}}_{Uc}|)\right] \qquad (4.6)$$

has an asymptotic chi-square distribution with $N - (K + 1)$ degrees of freedom. Jobson and Korkie (1982) suggest replacing T in Eq. (4.6) with $T - \frac{N}{2} - K - 1$ for faster convergence to the asymptotic chi-square distribution.

4.2. Some Factors Are Traded

When all the factors are returns on some benchmark portfolios, $\boldsymbol{\lambda} - \boldsymbol{\mu}_F$ is the vector of expected return on the benchmark portfolios in excess of the zero-beta return. In this case, Shanken (1985) shows that the exact constrained ML can be computed without iteration. It is an extension of the method worked out by Kandel (1984) for the standard CAPM. For the general case in which a subset of the factors are returns on portfolios of traded securities, Shanken (1992) shows that the ML and the two-pass GLS cross-sectional regression estimators are asymptotically equivalent under the standard regularity conditions assumed in empirical studies as the number of observations T becomes large. Hence, the two-pass cross-sectional regression approach is asymptotically efficient as T becomes large.

Shanken (1985) establishes the connection between the likelihood-ratio test for the restrictions imposed by the pricing model to the multivariate T^2 test that examines whether the vector of model expected return errors are zero after allowing for sampling errors. Zhou (1991) derives the exact finite sample distribution of the likelihood-ratio test statistic and shows that the distribution depends on a nuisance parameter.

Suppose the mean–variance frontier of returns generated by a given set of N assets is spanned by the returns on a subset of K benchmark assets only. This is a stronger assumption than the assumption that the K factor linear beta pricing model holds. In this case, there is an additional restriction on the parameters in the linear factor model given in Equation (4.1). The β_{ik}'s should sum to 1 for each asset i, that is $\sum_{k=1}^{K} \beta_{ik} = 1$ for all $i = 1, \ldots, N$ and the intercept term $\boldsymbol{\alpha}$ should equal the zero vector. Under the assumption that the returns are i.i.d. with a multivariate normal distribution, Huberman and Kandel (1987) and Kan and Zhou (2001) show that the statistic $\frac{T-N-K}{N} \left[\left(\frac{|\widehat{\Sigma}_{Uc}|}{|\widehat{\Sigma}_{U}|} \right)^{\frac{1}{2}} - 1 \right]$ has a central F distribution with $(2N, 2(T - N - K))$ degrees of freedom.

When a factor is a return on a traded asset, the ML estimate of the factor risk premium is its average return in the sample minus the ML estimate of the zero-beta return. For a nontraded factor, the ML estimate of the expected value of the factor is its sample average.

4.3. Single Risk-Free Lending and Borrowing Rates with Portfolio Returns as Factors

When there is a risk-free asset and borrowing and lending is available at the same rate, it is convenient to work with returns in excess of the risk-free return. Let us denote by $\mathbf{R}_t^e$ the vector of date t excess returns on the N assets and by $\mathbf{f}_t^e$ the vector of excess returns on the K factor portfolios. The linear factor model in this case assumes the form

$$\mathbf{R}_t^e = \boldsymbol{\alpha} + \mathbf{B}\mathbf{f}_t^e + \mathbf{u}_t. \tag{4.7}$$

As before, we assume that the innovations $\mathbf{u}_t$ are i.i.d. with a multivariate normal distribution conditionally on contemporaneous and past factor excess returns, and $\mathcal{L}_F$ denotes the marginal likelihood of the factor excess returns. The beta pricing model implies that the vector of intercepts, $\boldsymbol{\alpha}$, equals the zero vector. Let us denote by $\widehat{\boldsymbol{\alpha}}, \widehat{\mathbf{B}}$ the OLS estimates of $\boldsymbol{\alpha}, \mathbf{B}$, by $\widehat{\boldsymbol{\mu}}_F$ the sample mean of the vector of excess returns on the factor portfolios, and by $\widehat{\boldsymbol{\Sigma}}_U, \widehat{\boldsymbol{\Sigma}}_F$ the sample covariance matrices of the linear factor model residuals and the excess returns on the factor portfolios, respectively. Under the null hypothesis the statistic

$$J_{\text{LR}} = \frac{T - N - K}{N} \left(\frac{\widehat{\boldsymbol{\alpha}}' \widehat{\boldsymbol{\Sigma}}_U^{-1} \widehat{\boldsymbol{\alpha}}}{1 + \widehat{\boldsymbol{\mu}}_F' \widehat{\boldsymbol{\Sigma}}_F \widehat{\boldsymbol{\mu}}_F} \right) \tag{4.8}$$

has an exact F distribution with $(N, T - N - K)$ degrees of freedom. The reader is referred to Jobson and Korkie (1985), MacKinlay (1987), and Gibbons et al. (1989) for further details, analysis of the test statistic under the alternative that $\boldsymbol{\alpha} \neq 0$, a geometric interpretation of the test when $K = 1$ and a discussion of the power of the tests.

5. THE GENERALIZED METHOD OF MOMENTS

One major shortcoming of the ML method is that the econometrician has to make strong assumptions regarding the joint distribution of stock returns. The common practice is to assume that returns are drawn from an i.i.d. multivariate normal distribution. The GMM has made econometric analysis of stock returns possible under more realistic assumptions regarding the nature of the stochastic process governing the temporal evolution of economic variables. In this section, we discuss how to use the GMM to analyze the cross-section of stock returns. After giving an overview of the GMM, we discuss the estimation and testing of linear beta pricing models using their beta as well as the SDF representation. Finally, we discuss the various issues related to the GMM tests of conditional models with time-varying parameters.

The use of the GMM in finance started with Hansen and Hodrick (1980) and Hansen and Singleton (1982). Subsequent developments have made it a reliable and robust econometric methodology for studying the implications of not only linear beta pricing models but also dynamic asset-pricing models in general, allowing stock returns and other economic variables to be serially correlated, leptokurtic, and conditionally heteroskedastic. The works by Newey and West (1987), Andrews (1991), and Andrews and Monahan (1992) on estimating covariance matrices in the presence of autocorrelation and heteroskedasticity are the most significant among these developments. We refer the reader to Jagannathan et al. (2002) for a review of financial econometric applications of the GMM.

The major disadvantage of the GMM when compared to the ML method is that the sampling theory has only asymptotic validity. We therefore require a long history of observations on returns relative to the number of assets. When the number of assets is large, it is difficult to estimate the covariance matrix of returns precisely. Two approaches have been suggested in the literature to address this issue. The first approach is to group the primitive assets into a small number of portfolios and then evaluate the pricing models using return data on the portfolios. However, even when the econometrician is working with only 10 or 20 portfolios, the length of the time-series of observations available may not be sufficient for appealing to the law of large numbers. Therefore, Monte Carlo simulation is often used to check if GMM estimators and test statistics that rely on asymptotic theory have any biases. Using Monte Carlo simulations, Ferson and Foerster (1994) found that the GMM tends to overreject models when the number of observations, T, corresponds to values typically used in empirical studies. The second approach is to make additional assumptions so that the covariance matrix of the residuals in the linear factor generating model for the vector of asset returns takes a diagonal or block diagonal form. Some even suggest assuming it to be a scaled identity matrix. These assumptions usually reduce the GMM estimator to an OLS estimator in linear regressions.

5.1. An Overview of the GMM

Let $\mathbf{x}_t$ be a vector of m variables observed in the tth period. Let $\mathbf{g}(\mathbf{x}_t, \boldsymbol{\theta})$ be a vector of n functions, where $\boldsymbol{\theta}$ is a vector of k unknown parameters. Suppose when $\boldsymbol{\theta} = \boldsymbol{\theta}_0$ the following moment restriction holds

$$E[\mathbf{g}(\mathbf{x}_t, \boldsymbol{\theta}_0)] = \mathbf{0}_n, \tag{5.1}$$

where $\mathbf{0}_n$ is the column vector of n zeros. For any $\boldsymbol{\theta}$, the sample analog of $E[\mathbf{g}(\mathbf{x}_t, \boldsymbol{\theta})]$ is

$$\mathbf{g}_T(\boldsymbol{\theta}) = \frac{1}{T} \sum_{t=1}^{T} \mathbf{g}(\mathbf{x}_t, \boldsymbol{\theta}). \tag{5.2}$$

Suppose $\mathbf{x}_t$ satisfies the necessary regularity conditions so that the central limit theorem can be applied to $\mathbf{g}(\mathbf{x}_t, \boldsymbol{\theta}_0)$. Then

$$\sqrt{T}\mathbf{g}_T(\boldsymbol{\theta}_0) \xrightarrow{\mathcal{D}} N(\mathbf{0}_n, \mathbf{S}), \quad \text{as } T \to \infty, \tag{5.3}$$

where $\mathbf{S}$ is the spectral density matrix of $\mathbf{g}(\mathbf{x}_t, \boldsymbol{\theta}_0)$, i.e.,

$$\mathbf{S} = \sum_{j=-\infty}^{\infty} E\big[\mathbf{g}(\mathbf{x}_t, \boldsymbol{\theta}_0)\mathbf{g}(\mathbf{x}_{t+j}, \boldsymbol{\theta}_0)'\big]. \tag{5.4}$$

A natural estimation strategy for $\boldsymbol{\theta}_0$ would be to choose those values that make $\mathbf{g}_T(\boldsymbol{\theta})$ as close to the zero vector as possible. For that reason we choose $\boldsymbol{\theta}$ to solve

$$\min_{\boldsymbol{\theta}}\ \mathbf{g}_T(\boldsymbol{\theta})'\mathbf{S}_T^{-1}\mathbf{g}_T(\boldsymbol{\theta}), \tag{5.5}$$

where $\mathbf{S}_T$ is a consistent estimator of $\mathbf{S}$. The solution to the minimization problem, denoted by $\widehat{\boldsymbol{\theta}}_T$, is the GMM estimator of $\boldsymbol{\theta}$. We assume that $\mathbf{g}$ satisfies the regularity conditions laid out in the work of Hansen (1982) so that $\boldsymbol{\theta}_0$ is identified. In that case the following probability limit

$$\mathbf{D} = \text{p-}\lim_{T\to\infty}\frac{\partial\mathbf{g}_T(\boldsymbol{\theta}_0)}{\partial\boldsymbol{\theta}'} = E\left[\frac{\partial\mathbf{g}(\mathbf{x}_t,\boldsymbol{\theta}_0)}{\partial\boldsymbol{\theta}'}\right] \tag{5.6}$$

exists and has rank k. Hansen (1982) shows that the asymptotic distribution of the GMM estimator is given by

$$\sqrt{T}(\widehat{\boldsymbol{\theta}}_T - \boldsymbol{\theta}_0) \xrightarrow{\mathcal{D}} N\left(0_k, (\mathbf{D}'\mathbf{S}^{-1}\mathbf{D})^{-1}\right),\ \text{as}\ T\to\infty. \tag{5.7}$$

In general, $\mathbf{g}_T(\widehat{\boldsymbol{\theta}}_T)$ will be different from the zero vector because of sampling errors. A natural test for model misspecification would be to examine whether $\mathbf{g}_T(\widehat{\boldsymbol{\theta}}_T)$ is indeed different from the zero vector only because of sampling errors. For that, we need to know the asymptotic distribution of $\mathbf{g}_T(\widehat{\boldsymbol{\theta}}_T)$, which is provided by

$$\sqrt{T}\mathbf{g}_T(\widehat{\boldsymbol{\theta}}_T) \xrightarrow{\mathcal{D}} N\left(0_n, \mathbf{S} - \mathbf{D}(\mathbf{D}'\mathbf{S}^{-1}\mathbf{D})^{-1}\mathbf{D}'\right). \tag{5.8}$$

The covariance matrix $\mathbf{S} - \mathbf{D}(\mathbf{D}'\mathbf{S}^{-1}\mathbf{D})^{-1}\mathbf{D}'$ is positive semidefinite and can be degenerate. To test the moment restriction, Hansen (1982) suggests using the following J-statistic

$$J_T = T\mathbf{g}_T(\widehat{\boldsymbol{\theta}}_T)'\mathbf{S}_T^{-1}\mathbf{g}_T(\widehat{\boldsymbol{\theta}}_T). \tag{5.9}$$

He shows that the asymptotic distribution of J_T is a central χ^2 distribution with $n - k$ degrees of freedom, that is

$$J_T \xrightarrow{\mathcal{D}} \chi^2(n - k),\ \text{as}\ T\to\infty. \tag{5.10}$$

The key to using the GMM is the specification of the moment restrictions, involving the observable variables $\mathbf{x}_t$, the unknown parameters $\boldsymbol{\theta}$, and the function $\mathbf{g}(\cdot)$. Once a decision regarding which moment restrictions are to be used is made, estimating the model parameters and testing the model specifications are rather straightforward.

5.2. Evaluating Beta Pricing Models Using the Beta Representation

Let $\mathbf{R}_t$ be a vector of N stock returns during period t in excess of the risk-free rate. Let $\mathbf{f}_t$ be a vector of K economy-wide pervasive risk factors during period t. The mean and variance of the factors are denoted by $\boldsymbol{\mu}$ and $\boldsymbol{\Omega}$. The standard linear beta pricing model, also referred to as the beta representation, is given by:

$$E[\mathbf{R}_t] = \mathbf{B}\boldsymbol{\delta}, \tag{5.11}$$

where $\boldsymbol{\delta}$ is the vector of factor risk premia, and $\mathbf{B}$ is the matrix of factor loadings defined as

$$\mathbf{B} \equiv E[\mathbf{R}_t(\mathbf{f}_t - \boldsymbol{\mu})']\boldsymbol{\Omega}^{-1}. \tag{5.12}$$

The factor loadings matrix, $\mathbf{B}$, can be equivalently defined as a parameter in the time-series regression: $\mathbf{R}_t = \boldsymbol{\phi} + \mathbf{B}\mathbf{f}_t + \boldsymbol{\varepsilon}_t$. The residual $\boldsymbol{\varepsilon}_t$ has zero mean and is uncorrelated with the factor $\mathbf{f}_t$. The beta pricing model (5.11) imposes the following restriction on the intercept: $\boldsymbol{\phi} = \mathbf{B}(\boldsymbol{\delta} - \boldsymbol{\mu})$. By substituting this expression for $\boldsymbol{\phi}$ in the regression equation, we obtain:

$$\mathbf{R}_t = \mathbf{B}(\boldsymbol{\delta} - \boldsymbol{\mu} + \mathbf{f}_t) + \boldsymbol{\varepsilon}_t \tag{5.13}$$

$$E[\boldsymbol{\varepsilon}_t] = \mathbf{0}_N \tag{5.14}$$

$$E[\boldsymbol{\varepsilon}_t \mathbf{f}_t'] = \mathbf{0}_{N \times K}. \tag{5.15}$$

As we have pointed out, the key step in using GMM is to specify the moment restrictions. Equations (5.13), (5.14), and (5.15) in addition to the definition of $\boldsymbol{\mu}$ yield the following equations

$$E[\mathbf{R}_t - \mathbf{B}(\boldsymbol{\delta} - \boldsymbol{\mu} + \mathbf{f}_t)] = \mathbf{0}_N \tag{5.16}$$

$$E\left[[\mathbf{R}_t - \mathbf{B}(\boldsymbol{\delta} - \boldsymbol{\mu} + \mathbf{f}_t)]\mathbf{f}_t'\right] = \mathbf{0}_{N \times K} \tag{5.17}$$

$$E[\mathbf{f}_t - \boldsymbol{\mu}] = \mathbf{0}_K. \tag{5.18}$$

Notice that we need Eq. (5.18) to identify the vector of risk premium $\boldsymbol{\delta}$. In this case, the vector of unknown parameters is $\boldsymbol{\theta} = [\boldsymbol{\delta}' \quad \text{vec}(\mathbf{B})' \quad \boldsymbol{\mu}']'$, the vector of observable variables is $\mathbf{x}_t = [\mathbf{R}_t' \quad \mathbf{f}_t']'$, and the function $\mathbf{g}$ in the moment restriction is given by

$$\mathbf{g}(\mathbf{x}_t, \boldsymbol{\theta}) = \begin{pmatrix} \mathbf{R}_t - \mathbf{B}(\boldsymbol{\delta} - \boldsymbol{\mu} + \mathbf{f}_t) \\ \text{vec}\left([\mathbf{R}_t - \mathbf{B}(\boldsymbol{\delta} - \boldsymbol{\mu} + \mathbf{f}_t)]\mathbf{f}_t'\right) \\ \mathbf{f}_t - \boldsymbol{\mu} \end{pmatrix}. \tag{5.19}$$

Then, the precision of the GMM estimate can be assessed using the sampling distribution (5.7), and the model can be tested using the J-statistic with asymptotic χ^2 distribution given in (5.10). The degree of freedom is $N - K$ because there are $N + NK + K$ equations in the moment restriction and $K + NK + K$ unknown parameters.

Often we are interested in finding out the extent to which a beta pricing model assigns the correct expected return to a particular collection of assets. For that purpose it is helpful to examine the vector of pricing errors associated with a model, given by

$$\boldsymbol{\alpha} = E[\mathbf{R}_t] - \mathbf{B}\boldsymbol{\delta}. \tag{5.20}$$

The pricing error associated with the CAPM is usually referred to as Jensen's alpha. When the model holds, we should have $\boldsymbol{\alpha} = \mathbf{0}_N$. The sample analog of the pricing error is

$$\boldsymbol{\alpha}_T = \frac{1}{T} \sum_{t=1}^{T} \mathbf{R}_t - \widehat{\mathbf{B}\boldsymbol{\delta}}, \tag{5.21}$$

which can serve as a consistent estimator of the pricing error. To obtain the sampling distribution of $\boldsymbol{\alpha}_T$, we express it in terms of $\mathbf{g}_T(\widehat{\boldsymbol{\theta}}_T)$ as follows:

$$\boldsymbol{\alpha}_T = \widehat{\mathbf{Q}}\mathbf{g}_T(\widehat{\boldsymbol{\theta}}_T), \quad \text{where} \quad \widehat{\mathbf{Q}} = \begin{bmatrix} \mathbf{I}_N & \mathbf{0}_{N \times NK} & \widehat{\mathbf{B}} \end{bmatrix}. \tag{5.22}$$

Obviously, we have

$$\text{p-}\lim_{T \to \infty} \widehat{\mathbf{Q}} = \begin{bmatrix} \mathbf{I}_N & \mathbf{0}_{N \times K} & \mathbf{B} \end{bmatrix}. \tag{5.23}$$

Let us use $\mathbf{Q}$ to denote the matrix on the right-hand side of the aforementioned equation. It follows from (5.8) that, under the null hypothesis that the asset pricing model holds and so $\boldsymbol{\alpha} = \mathbf{0}_N$, the asymptotic distribution of $\boldsymbol{\alpha}_T$ should be

$$\sqrt{T}\boldsymbol{\alpha}_T \xrightarrow{\mathcal{D}} N(\mathbf{0}_N, \mathbf{Q}(\mathbf{S} - \mathbf{D}(\mathbf{D}'\mathbf{S}^{-1}\mathbf{D})^{-1}\mathbf{D}')\mathbf{Q}') \tag{5.24}$$

where $\mathbf{S}$ and $\mathbf{D}$, given by (5.4) and (5.6), respectively, should be estimated using the function $\mathbf{g}$ in (5.19).

When an economy-wide factor, say f_{jt}, is the return on a portfolio of traded assets, we call it a traded factor. An example of a traded factor would be the return on the value-weighted portfolio of stocks used in empirical studies of the CAPM by Sharpe (1964). Examples of nontraded factors can be found by Chen et al. (1986), who use the growth rate of industrial production and the rate of inflation, and Breeden et al. (1989) who use the growth rate in per capita consumption as a factor. When a factor f_{jt} is the excess return on a traded asset, Eqs. (5.11) and (5.12) imply $\delta_j = \mu_j$, i.e., the risk premium is the mean of the factor. In that case it can be verified that the sample mean of the factor is the estimator of the risk premium. If the factor is not traded, this restriction does not hold, and we have to estimate the risk premium using stock returns.

If all the factors in the model are traded, Eqs. (5.16) and (5.17) become

$$E[\mathbf{R}_t - \mathbf{Bf}_t] = \mathbf{0}_N \tag{5.25}$$

$$E[(\mathbf{R}_t - \mathbf{Bf}_t)\mathbf{f}_t'] = \mathbf{0}_{N\times K}. \tag{5.26}$$

In that case, we can estimate $\boldsymbol{\beta}$ and test the model restrictions (5.25) and (5.26) without the need to estimate the risk premium $\boldsymbol{\delta}$. If one needs the estimate of risk premium, it can be obtained from Eq. (5.18). When all the factors are traded, the restriction imposed on the risk premium gives extra degrees of freedom – the number of degrees of freedom in (5.25) and (5.26) is N while the number of degrees of freedom in (5.16)–(5.18) is $N - K$. With traded factors, we can evaluate pricing errors of the model in the same way as done with nontraded factors.

The traded factors, however, allow us to estimate the pricing errors more conveniently as unknown parameters. For this purpose, we use the following moment restrictions

$$E[\mathbf{R}_t - \boldsymbol{\alpha} - \mathbf{Bf}_t] = \mathbf{0}_N \tag{5.27}$$

$$E[(\mathbf{R}_t - \boldsymbol{\alpha} - \mathbf{Bf}_t)\mathbf{f}_t'] = \mathbf{0}_{N\times K}, \tag{5.28}$$

and investigate the hypothesis $\boldsymbol{\alpha} = \mathbf{0}_N$. The preceding system is exactly identified because there are $N + NK$ equations and $N + NK$ unknown parameters. With these moment restrictions, we have $\mathbf{x}_t = [\mathbf{R}_t' \ \mathbf{f}_t']'$, $\boldsymbol{\theta} = [\boldsymbol{\alpha}' \ \text{vec}(\mathbf{B})']'$ and

$$\mathbf{g}(\mathbf{x}_t, \boldsymbol{\theta}) = \begin{pmatrix} \mathbf{R}_t - \boldsymbol{\alpha} - \mathbf{Bf}_t \\ \text{vec}\left([\mathbf{R}_t - \boldsymbol{\alpha} - \mathbf{Bf}_t]\mathbf{f}_t'\right) \end{pmatrix}. \tag{5.29}$$

Because the aforementioned GMM system is exactly identified, the GMM estimator $\widehat{\boldsymbol{\theta}}_T = \left[\widehat{\boldsymbol{\alpha}}_T' \ \text{vec}\left(\widehat{\mathbf{B}}_T\right)'\right]'$ can be obtained in closed form as follows

$$\widehat{\mathbf{B}}_T = \left[\frac{1}{T}\sum_{t=1}^{T}(\mathbf{R}_t - \overline{\mathbf{R}}_T)(\mathbf{f}_t - \overline{\mathbf{f}}_T)'\right]\left[\frac{1}{T}\sum_{t=1}^{T}(\mathbf{f}_t - \overline{\mathbf{f}}_T)(\mathbf{f}_t - \overline{\mathbf{f}}_T)'\right]^{-1}, \tag{5.30}$$

and

$$\widehat{\boldsymbol{\alpha}}_T = \overline{\mathbf{R}}_T - \widehat{\mathbf{B}}_T\overline{\mathbf{f}}_T. \tag{5.31}$$

Note, the GMM estimators $\widehat{\mathbf{B}}_T$ and $\widehat{\boldsymbol{\alpha}}_T$ given above coincide with the sample analogs of $\mathbf{B}$ and $\boldsymbol{\alpha}$, respectively. It follows that the GMM estimator of $\boldsymbol{\alpha}$ is $\widehat{\boldsymbol{\alpha}}_T = \mathbf{P}\widehat{\boldsymbol{\theta}}_T$, where $\mathbf{P} = [\mathbf{I}_N \ \mathbf{0}_{N\times NK}]$. The above function $\mathbf{g}$ defines the matrix $\mathbf{S}$ and $\mathbf{D}$ through Eqs. (5.4) and (5.6). Let $\mathbf{S}_T$ and $\mathbf{D}_T$ be their consistent estimators. Under the null hypothesis $\boldsymbol{\alpha} = \mathbf{0}_N$, it follows from (5.7) that

$$T\widehat{\boldsymbol{\alpha}}_T'\left(\mathbf{P}\left(\mathbf{D}_T'\mathbf{S}_T^{-1}\mathbf{D}_T\right)^{-1}\mathbf{P}'\right)^{-1}\widehat{\boldsymbol{\alpha}}_T \xrightarrow{D} \chi^2(N), \text{ as } T \to \infty. \tag{5.32}$$

Some remarks are in order. As shown earlier, for the case of traded factors, we can use the J-statistic to test the moment restrictions given by (5.25) and (5.26). However, we cannot do so for the moment restrictions given by (5.27) and (5.28) because the exactly identified system implies $J_T \equiv 0$. In that case, we can only examine whether $\widehat{\boldsymbol{\alpha}}_T$ is statistically different from zero using the distribution in (5.32). Therefore, for the case of traded factors, we have two choices. The first is to test (5.25) and (5.26) using the J-statistic, and the second is to test $\boldsymbol{\alpha} = \mathbf{0}_N$ using (5.27) and (5.28). MacKinlay and Richardson (1991) refer to the first as restricted test and the second as unrestricted test. It is important to notice that we cannot add $\boldsymbol{\alpha}$ as unknown parameters to Eqs. (5.16) and (5.17) when factors are nontraded because there will be more unknown parameters than equations. The pricing error has to be obtained from $\mathbf{g}_T(\widehat{\boldsymbol{\theta}}_T)$. In this case, we have to use the J-statistic to test the moment restriction (5.16)–(5.18). Therefore, we can only do the restricted test when factors are nontraded.

Note that the factor risk premium does not appear in Eqs. (5.27) and (5.28). To estimate the factor risk premium, it is necessary to add the additional moment restriction that the factor risk premium is the expected value of the factor, which is the excess return on some benchmark portfolio of traded assets. As mentioned earlier, it can be verified that the best estimate of the factor risk premium is the sample average of the factor realizations.

When returns and factors exhibit conditional homoskedasticity and independence over time, the GMM estimator is equivalent to the ML estimator suggested by Gibbons et al. (1989). For details, we refer the reader to MacKinlay and Richardson (1991). This implies that GMM estimator of the risk premia in the linear beta pricing model is the most efficient unbiased estimator when stock returns and factors are homoskedastic and independent over time. More importantly, MacKinlay and Richardson (1991) demonstrate that the ML estimation and test are biased when stock returns are conditionally heteroskedastic. They argue that the advantage of GMM is its robustness to the presence of conditional heteroskedasticity and thus recommend estimating the parameters in beta models using GMM.

5.3. Evaluating Beta Pricing Models Using the Stochastic Discount Factor Representation

We can derive a different set of moment restrictions from the linear beta pricing model. Substituting Eq. (5.12) into Eq. (5.11) and appropriately rearranging terms, we obtain

$$E\left[\mathbf{R}_t\left(1 + \boldsymbol{\delta}'\boldsymbol{\Omega}^{-1}\boldsymbol{\mu} - \boldsymbol{\delta}'\boldsymbol{\Omega}^{-1}\mathbf{f}_t\right)\right] = \mathbf{0}_N. \tag{5.33}$$

If the factors are traded, we have $1 + \boldsymbol{\delta}'\boldsymbol{\Omega}^{-1}\boldsymbol{\mu} = 1 + \boldsymbol{\mu}'\boldsymbol{\Omega}^{-1}\boldsymbol{\mu} \geq 1$. If the factors are not traded, we assume $1 + \boldsymbol{\delta}'\boldsymbol{\Omega}^{-1}\boldsymbol{\mu} \neq 0$. Then, we can use it to divide both sides of Eq. (5.33) and obtain

$$E\left[\mathbf{R}_t\left(1 - \frac{\boldsymbol{\delta}'\boldsymbol{\Omega}^{-1}}{1 + \boldsymbol{\delta}'\boldsymbol{\Omega}^{-1}\boldsymbol{\mu}}\mathbf{f}_t\right)\right] = \mathbf{0}_N. \tag{5.34}$$

If we transform the vector of risk premia, $\boldsymbol{\delta}$, into a vector of new parameters $\boldsymbol{\lambda}$ as follows

$$\boldsymbol{\lambda} = \frac{\boldsymbol{\Omega}^{-1}\boldsymbol{\delta}}{1 + \boldsymbol{\delta}'\boldsymbol{\Omega}^{-1}\boldsymbol{\mu}}, \tag{5.35}$$

then Eq. (5.34) becomes

$$E\left[\mathbf{R}_t\left(1 - \boldsymbol{\lambda}'\mathbf{f}_t\right)\right] = \mathbf{0}_N. \tag{5.36}$$

Because the GMM equation is linear in $\boldsymbol{\lambda}$, one can use the first-order condition to obtain the GMM estimator of $\boldsymbol{\lambda}$ in closed form as follows

$$\widehat{\boldsymbol{\lambda}}_T = \left(\mathbf{D}_T'\mathbf{S}_T^{-1}\mathbf{D}_T\right)^{-1}\mathbf{D}_T'\mathbf{S}_T^{-1}\overline{\mathbf{R}}_T, \tag{5.37}$$

where $\mathbf{D}_T = \frac{1}{T}\sum_{t=1}^{T}\mathbf{R}_t\mathbf{f}_t'$, $\mathbf{S}_T$ is a consistent estimator of the asymptotic covariance matrix $\mathbf{S}$ of the sequence $\mathbf{h}_t(\boldsymbol{\lambda}_0) = \mathbf{R}_t\left(1 - \boldsymbol{\lambda}_0'\mathbf{f}_t\right)$ that satisfies $\frac{1}{\sqrt{T}}\sum_{t=1}^{T}\mathbf{h}_t(\boldsymbol{\lambda}_0) \xrightarrow{\mathcal{D}} N(\mathbf{0}_N, \mathbf{S})$, as $T \to \infty$, and $\boldsymbol{\lambda}_0$ is the true parameter value.

The moment restriction (5.36) is often referred to as the SDF representation of the beta pricing model. The variable $m_t \equiv 1 - \boldsymbol{\lambda}'\mathbf{f}_t$ is the SDF because $E[\mathbf{R}_t m_t] = \mathbf{0}_N$. In general, a number of random variables m_t satisfying $E[\mathbf{R}_t m_t] = \mathbf{0}_N$ exist and thus, there are more than one SDF. The linear factor pricing model (5.36) designates the random variable m_t to be a linear function of the factors $\mathbf{f}_t$.

Dybvig and Ingersoll (1982) derive the SDF representation of the CAPM, and Ingersoll (1987) derives the SDF representation for a number of theoretical asset pricing models. Hansen and Richard (1987) coined the term "stochastic discount factor."

Most asset pricing models have a convenient SDF representation – not just the linear beta pricing model. The SDF representation typically follows from the Euler equation (first order condition) for the portfolio choice problem faced by an investor. In general, the Euler equation can be written as, $E_{t-1}[\mathbf{R}_t m_t] = \mathbf{0}_N$ for *excess* returns, where E_{t-1} is the expectation conditional on the information at the end of period $t - 1$. This is often referred to as conditional SDF representation. When the utility function in the economic model depends on a vector of parameters, denoted by $\boldsymbol{\theta}$, the SDF m_t is a function of $\boldsymbol{\theta}$ and a vector of economic variables $\mathbf{f}_t$. Then, the SDF has the form of $m(\boldsymbol{\theta}, \mathbf{f}_t)$. For example, in the representative agent and endowment economy of Lucas (1978), $m(\boldsymbol{\theta}, f_t) = \rho c_t^a$, where $f_t = c_t$, the growth rate of aggregate consumption, and $\boldsymbol{\theta} = [\rho \ a]'$. The linear beta model implies $m(\boldsymbol{\theta}, \mathbf{f}_t) = 1 - \boldsymbol{\lambda}'\mathbf{f}_t$, where $\boldsymbol{\theta} = \boldsymbol{\lambda}$ and $\mathbf{f}_t$ is the vector of factors.

Bansal et al. (1993) and Bansal and Viswanathan (1993) specify m as a polynomial function of the factors $\mathbf{f}_t$. We will write the general conditional SDF representation of the pricing model as follows

$$E_{t-1}[\mathbf{R}_t m(\boldsymbol{\theta}, \mathbf{f}_t)] = \mathbf{0}_N. \tag{5.38}$$

Taking the unconditional expectation, we have

$$E[\mathbf{R}_t m(\boldsymbol{\theta}, \mathbf{f}_t)] = \mathbf{0}_N, \tag{5.39}$$

which includes Eq. (5.36) as a special case.

We can test the pricing model using its conditional SDF representation (5.38) by incorporating conditional information. Let $\mathbf{z}_{t-1}$ be a vector of economic variables observed by the end of period $t - 1$. Consider a $M \times N$ matrix denoted $\mathbf{H}(\mathbf{z}_{t-1})$, the elements of which are functions of $\mathbf{z}_{t-1}$. Multiplying $\mathbf{H}(\mathbf{z}_{t-1})$ to both sides of (5.38) and taking the unconditional expectation, we obtain

$$E\left[\mathbf{H}(\mathbf{z}_{t-1})\mathbf{R}_t m(\boldsymbol{\theta}, \mathbf{f}_t)\right] = \mathbf{0}_M. \tag{5.40}$$

In testing (5.38) using $\mathbf{z}_{t-1}$, the common practice is to multiply the returns by the instrumental variables to get $\text{vec}(\mathbf{z}_{t-1} \otimes \mathbf{R}_t)$, generally referred to as the vector of scaled returns. If we choose $\mathbf{H}(\mathbf{z}_{t-1}) = \mathbf{z}_{t-1} \otimes \mathbf{I}_N$, then $\mathbf{H}(\mathbf{z}_{t-1})\mathbf{R}_t = \text{vec}(\mathbf{z}_{t-1} \otimes \mathbf{R}_t)$. If we are only interested in testing the unconditional SDF model (5.39), we choose the conditional portfolios to be the original assets by setting $\mathbf{H}(\mathbf{z}_{t-1}) = \mathbf{I}_N$. If $m(\boldsymbol{\theta}, \mathbf{f}_t)$ satisfies Eq. (5.40), we say $m(\boldsymbol{\theta}, \mathbf{f}_t)$ prices the portfolios correctly and call it a valid SDF. The idea of scaling stock returns by conditional variables was first proposed by Hansen and Singleton (1982).

If we normalize each row of $\mathbf{H}(\mathbf{z}_{t-1})$ to a vector of weights that sum to 1, then the vector $\widetilde{\mathbf{R}}_t = \mathbf{H}(\mathbf{z}_{t-1})\mathbf{R}_t$ is, in fact, the vector of returns on conditional portfolios of stocks. The weights in these portfolios are time-varying. We thus obtain an unconditional SDF representation of the beta pricing model, i.e., the SDF representation becomes $E[\widetilde{\mathbf{R}}_t m(\boldsymbol{\theta}, \mathbf{f}_t)] = \mathbf{0}_M$. Therefore, testing a conditional SDF representation using conditional variables is equivalent to testing an unconditional SDF representation using portfolios managed with conditioning information. For example, portfolios constructed using firm size or book-to-market ratio are portfolios whose weights are managed to vary over time in a particular way, and tests of the unconditional SDF representation using these portfolios can be viewed as tests of conditional SDF representation using firm size or book-to-market ratio as conditioning variables. Therefore, in principle we do not lose any information by testing unconditional moment restrictions because we can always augment the set of assets with portfolios that are managed in clever ways using conditioning information.

The application of GMM to the SDF representation is straightforward. Let $\mathbf{x}_t = \left[\mathbf{R}_t'\ \mathbf{f}_t'\ \mathbf{z}_{t-1}'\right]'$ and

$$\mathbf{g}(\mathbf{x}_t, \boldsymbol{\theta}) = \widetilde{\mathbf{R}}_t m(\boldsymbol{\theta}, \mathbf{f}_t) = \mathbf{H}(\mathbf{z}_{t-1})\mathbf{R}_t m(\boldsymbol{\theta}, \mathbf{f}_t). \tag{5.41}$$

We can provide consistent estimates of matrices $\mathbf{S}$ and $\mathbf{D}$ using the definition of the function $\mathbf{g}$. We obtain the GMM estimator $\widehat{\boldsymbol{\theta}}_T$ by solving (5.5), and test the restrictions (5.40), using the framework in Section 5.1. The sample analog of the vector of pricing errors, $\mathbf{g}_T(\widehat{\boldsymbol{\theta}}_T)$, is defined by Eq. (5.2). This pricing error is analyzed extensively by Hansen and Jagannathan (1997). Jagannathan and Wang (2002) examine the relation between pricing error and Jensen's alpha. It is shown that the former is a linear transformation of the latter in linear beta pricing models. Hodrick and Zhang (2001) compare the pricing errors across a variety of model specifications. The statistic J_T is calculated as in (5.9). The approach outlined here applies to SDF representation of asset pricing models in general – not just the linear beta pricing model which is the focus of our study in this chapter. In addition, the entries of the matrix $\mathbf{H}(\mathbf{z}_{t-1})$ do not have to correspond to portfolio weights.

Because the SDF representation can be used to represent an arbitrary asset pricing model, not just the beta pricing model, it is of interest to examine the relative efficiency and power of applying the GMM to the SDF and beta representations of the pricing model. Jagannathan and Wang (2002) find that using the SDF representation provides as precise an estimate of the risk premium as that obtained using the beta representation. Using Monte Carlo simulations, they demonstrate that the two methods provide equally precise estimates in finite samples as well. The sampling errors in the two methods are similar, even when returns have fatter tails relative to the normal distribution allowing for conditional heteroskedasticity. They also examine the specification tests associated with the two approaches and find that these tests have similar power. Skoulakis (2006) extends the theoretical results of Jagannathan and Wang (2002), that are obtained under the assumption that the joint process of returns and factors is normally distributed and i.i.d. over time, to a general class of stationary processes.

Although the J-statistic is useful for testing for model misspecification, comparing the J-statistics across different model specifications may lead to wrong conclusions. One model may do better than another not because the vector of average pricing errors, $\mathbf{g}_T$, associated with it are smaller, but because the inverse of the optimal weighting matrix, $\mathbf{S}_T$, associated with it is smaller. To overcome this difficulty, Hansen and Jagannathan (1997) suggested examining the pricing error of the most mispriced portfolio among those whose second moments of returns are normalized to 1. This corresponds to using the inverse of the second moment matrix of returns, $\mathbf{G}^{-1} = \left(E[\widetilde{\mathbf{R}}_t\widetilde{\mathbf{R}}_t']\right)^{-1}$, as the weighting matrix under the assumption that $\mathbf{G}$ is positive definite. Hansen and Jagannathan (1997) demonstrate that

$$d(\boldsymbol{\theta}) = \left[E[\mathbf{g}(\mathbf{x}_t, \boldsymbol{\theta})]'\mathbf{G}^{-1}E[\mathbf{g}(\mathbf{x}_t, \boldsymbol{\theta})]\right]^{\frac{1}{2}} \tag{5.42}$$

equals the least-square distance between the candidate SDF and the set of all valid SDFs. Further, they show that $d(\boldsymbol{\theta})$ is the maximum pricing error on normalized portfolios of the N assets, generally referred to as the HJ-distance.

For given $\boldsymbol{\theta}$, the sample estimate of the HJ-distance is

$$\hat{d}(\boldsymbol{\theta}) = \left[\mathbf{g}_T(\boldsymbol{\theta})'\mathbf{G}_T^{-1}\mathbf{g}_T(\theta)\right]^{\frac{1}{2}}, \tag{5.43}$$

where $\mathbf{G}_T$ is a consistent estimate of $\mathbf{G}$. An obvious choice for the consistent estimate is

$$\mathbf{G}_T = \frac{1}{T}\sum_{t=1}^{T}\widetilde{\mathbf{R}}_t\widetilde{\mathbf{R}}_t' = \frac{1}{T}\sum_{t=1}^{T}\mathbf{H}(\mathbf{z}_{t-1})\mathbf{R}_t\mathbf{R}_t'\mathbf{H}(\mathbf{z}_{t-1})'. \tag{5.44}$$

To check the model's ability to price stock returns, it is natural to choose the parameter $\boldsymbol{\theta}$ that minimizes the estimated HJ-distance. This leads us to choose

$$\widetilde{\boldsymbol{\theta}}_T = \arg\min_{\boldsymbol{\theta}} \mathbf{g}_T(\boldsymbol{\theta})'\mathbf{G}_T^{-1}\mathbf{g}_T(\boldsymbol{\theta}). \tag{5.45}$$

It is important to note that $\widetilde{\boldsymbol{\theta}}_T$ is not the same as the GMM estimator $\widehat{\boldsymbol{\theta}}_T$ because $\mathbf{G}$ is not equal to $\mathbf{S}$. Also, the T-scaled estimate of the square of HJ-distance, $T[\hat{d}(\widetilde{\boldsymbol{\theta}}_T)]^2$, is not equal to the J-statistic, and thus does not follow the distribution $\chi^2(M-K)$ asymptotically.

Following Jagannathan and Wang (1996), it can be shown that the limiting distribution of $T[\hat{d}(\widetilde{\boldsymbol{\theta}}_T)]^2$ is a linear combination of χ^2 distributions, each of which has one degree of freedom. More precisely,

$$T[\hat{d}(\widetilde{\boldsymbol{\theta}}_T)]^2 \xrightarrow{\mathcal{D}} \sum_{j=1}^{M-K} a_j\xi_j, \quad \text{as } T \to \infty, \tag{5.46}$$

where $\xi_1, \ldots, \xi_{M-K}$ are independent random variables following $\chi^2(1)$ distributions. The coefficients, $a_1, \ldots, a_{M-K}$, are the nonzero eigenvalues of the matrix

$$\mathbf{A} = \mathbf{S}^{1/2}\mathbf{G}^{-1/2}\left(\mathbf{I}_M - (\mathbf{G}^{-1/2})'\mathbf{D}(\mathbf{D}'\mathbf{G}^{-1}\mathbf{D})^{-1}\mathbf{D}'\mathbf{G}^{-1/2}\right)\mathbf{G}^{-1/2})'(\mathbf{S}^{1/2})', \tag{5.47}$$

where $\mathbf{S}^{1/2}$ and $\mathbf{G}^{1/2}$ are the upper triangular matrices in the Cholesky decompositions of $\mathbf{S}$ and $\mathbf{G}$. The distribution in (5.46) can be used to test the hypothesis $d(\boldsymbol{\theta}) = 0$. Applications of the sampling distribution in (5.46) can be found by Jagannathan and Wang (1996), Buraschi and Jackwerth (2001), and Hodrick and Zhang (2001).

5.4. Models with Time-Varying Betas and Risk Premia

In analysis of stock returns in the cross-section, financial economists often consider conditional linear models with time-varying beta and factor risk premia. In that case, we need to consider conditional moments of stock returns and factors in generating the moment restrictions. We need the following additional notation to denote the conditional means and variances of the factors and the conditional betas of the assets.

$$\boldsymbol{\mu}_{t-1} = E_{t-1}[\mathbf{f}_t] \tag{5.48}$$

$$\boldsymbol{\Omega}_{t-1} = E_{t-1}\big[(\mathbf{f}_t - \boldsymbol{\mu}_{t-1})(\mathbf{f}_t - \boldsymbol{\mu}_{t-1})'\big] \tag{5.49}$$

$$\mathbf{B}_{t-1} = E_{t-1}\big[\mathbf{R}_t(\mathbf{f}_t - \boldsymbol{\mu}_{t-1})'\big]\boldsymbol{\Omega}_{t-1}^{-1}. \tag{5.50}$$

The conditional analog of the linear beta pricing model with time-varying risk premia, $\boldsymbol{\delta}_{t-1}$, is then given by

$$E_{t-1}[\mathbf{R}_t] = \mathbf{B}_{t-1}\boldsymbol{\delta}_{t-1}. \tag{5.51}$$

Obviously, it is impossible to estimate and test the aforementioned time-varying model without imposing additional assumptions. In general, we need to reduce the time-varying unknown parameters to a small number of constant parameters. In this section, we discuss five ways of introducing testable hypotheses for GMM in conditional linear beta models with time-varying parameters.

Suppose either the betas or the risk premia, but not both, are constants. To see the implication of this assumption, take the unconditional expectation of both sides of Eq. (5.51) to obtain

$$E[\mathbf{R}_t] = E[\mathbf{B}_{t-1}]\,E[\boldsymbol{\delta}_{t-1}] + \mathrm{Cov}[\mathbf{B}_{t-1}, \boldsymbol{\delta}_{t-1}], \tag{5.52}$$

where $E[\boldsymbol{\beta}_{t-1}]$ and $E[\boldsymbol{\delta}_{t-1}]$ can be interpreted as the average beta and the risk premium. The covariance between beta and the risk premium is $\mathrm{Cov}(\mathbf{B}_{t-1}, \boldsymbol{\delta}_{t-1}) = E[\mathbf{B}_{t-1}(\boldsymbol{\delta}_{t-1} - E[\boldsymbol{\delta}_{t-1}])]$. If either beta or premium is constant, the covariance term is zero. Then, the unconditional expected return is simply the product of the average beta and the average premium. More generally, if the conditional beta and premium are uncorrelated, the model is essentially equivalent to an unconditional or static model. However, it does not make good economic sense to assume that the conditional beta and the risk premium are uncorrelated because both risk and risk premia are affected by the same pervasive forces that affect the economy as a whole. As a matter of fact, Ang and Liu (2005) demonstrate that this correlation is rather high.

The unconditional correlation between conditional betas and conditional risk premia induces stock returns to be unconditionally correlated with conditional factor risk premia. Therefore, when a conditional linear beta pricing model holds, the unconditional expected return on an asset will be a linear function of the asset's unconditional factor betas and the asset's unconditional betas with respect to the conditional factor risk premia. For example, when the conditional version of the CAPM holds, Jagannathan and Wang (1996) show that the following unconditional two-beta model would obtain:

$$E[\mathbf{R}_t] = \mathbf{B}\mathbf{a} + \mathbf{B}_\delta\mathbf{b}, \tag{5.53}$$

where the two vector of betas are defined as

$$\mathbf{B} = E[\mathbf{R}_t(\mathbf{f}_t - \boldsymbol{\mu})]\,\boldsymbol{\Omega}^{-1} \tag{5.54}$$

$$\mathbf{B}_\delta = E[\mathbf{R}_t(\boldsymbol{\delta}_{t-1} - \boldsymbol{\mu}_\delta)]\,\boldsymbol{\Omega}_\delta^{-1}. \tag{5.55}$$

In the aforementioned equations, $\boldsymbol{\mu}$ and $\boldsymbol{\mu}_\delta$ are unconditional mean of the factors and risk premia, and $\boldsymbol{\Omega}$ and $\boldsymbol{\Omega}_\delta$ are their unconditional variances. The vectors $\mathbf{a}$ and $\mathbf{b}$ are unknown coefficients.

Because the risk premia are not observable, we still cannot estimate and test the model without additional assumptions. A convenient assumption that is often made in empirical studies is that the risk premium is a function of a prespecified set of observable economic variables, i.e.,

$$\boldsymbol{\delta}_{t-1} = \mathbf{h}_\delta(\boldsymbol{\gamma}_\delta, \mathbf{z}_{t-1}), \tag{5.56}$$

where $\mathbf{z}_{t-1}$ is a vector of economic variables observed at the end of period $t-1$, and $\boldsymbol{\gamma}_\delta$ is a vector of unknown parameters. For example, when studying the conditional CAPM, Jagannathan and Wang (1996) choose $\mathbf{z}_{t-1}$ to be the default spread of corporate bonds and $\mathbf{h}_\delta$ a linear function. Then, Eqs. (5.53)–(5.56) can be transformed into an unconditional SDF model:

Hypothesis 1 $E\big[\mathbf{R}_t\big(1 + \boldsymbol{\vartheta}'\mathbf{f}_t + \boldsymbol{\vartheta}_\delta'\mathbf{h}_\delta(\boldsymbol{\gamma}_\delta, \mathbf{z}_{t-1})\big)\big] = \mathbf{0}_N, \tag{5.57}$

where $\boldsymbol{\vartheta}$ and $\boldsymbol{\vartheta}_\delta$ are vectors of unknown parameters. This model can be estimated and tested using GMM as discussed in Section 5.3. When factors are traded, the time-varying risk premia are equal to the conditional expectation of factors, i.e., $\boldsymbol{\delta}_{t-1} = \boldsymbol{\mu}_{t-1}$. Then, we can replace Eq. (5.56) by a prediction model for factors such as

$$\boldsymbol{\mu}_{t-1} = \mathbf{h}_\mu(\boldsymbol{\gamma}_\mu, \mathbf{z}_{t-1}), \tag{5.58}$$

where $\boldsymbol{\gamma}_\mu$ is a vector of unknown parameters. The prediction model can be estimated and tested together with Eq. (5.57). That is, we can use GMM to estimate and test the following moment restriction:

$$E\left[\begin{pmatrix} \mathbf{f}_t - \mathbf{h}_\mu(\boldsymbol{\gamma}_\mu, \mathbf{z}_{t-1}) \\ \mathbf{R}_t\big(1 + \boldsymbol{\vartheta}'\mathbf{f}_t + \boldsymbol{\vartheta}_\delta'\mathbf{h}_\mu(\boldsymbol{\gamma}_\mu, \mathbf{z}_{t-1})\big) \end{pmatrix}\right] = \mathbf{0}_{K+N}. \tag{5.59}$$

The first part of the equation is the restriction implied by the prediction model $\boldsymbol{\mu}_{t-1} = \mathbf{h}_\mu(\boldsymbol{\gamma}_\mu, \mathbf{z}_{t-1})$.

Instead of testing the unconditional SDF representation of the conditional linear beta pricing model using Hypothesis 1, we can directly obtain a conditional SDF representation from Eq. (5.51) and derive an alternative test by making additional assumptions about the time-varying parameters. Equation (5.57) implies

$$E_{t-1}\left[\mathbf{R}_t\left(1 + \boldsymbol{\delta}'_{t-1}\boldsymbol{\Omega}^{-1}_{t-1}\boldsymbol{\mu}_{t-1} - \boldsymbol{\delta}'_{t-1}\boldsymbol{\Omega}^{-1}_{t-1}\mathbf{f}_t\right)\right] = \mathbf{0}_N. \tag{5.60}$$

To make this model testable, assume that (5.58) holds and,

$$\boldsymbol{\Omega}^{-1}_{t-1}\boldsymbol{\delta}_{t-1} = \mathbf{h}_\omega(\boldsymbol{\gamma}_\omega, \mathbf{z}_{t-1}), \tag{5.61}$$

where $\boldsymbol{\gamma}_\omega$ is a vector of unknown parameters. When there is only one factor, $\boldsymbol{\Omega}^{-1}_{t-1}\boldsymbol{\delta}_{t-1}$ is the reward-to-variability ratio. Then, Eq. (5.60) becomes

$$E_{t-1}\left[\mathbf{R}_t\left(1 + \mathbf{h}_\omega(\boldsymbol{\gamma}_\omega, \mathbf{z}_{t-1})'\mathbf{h}_\mu(\boldsymbol{\gamma}_\mu, \mathbf{z}_{t-1}) + \mathbf{h}_\omega(\boldsymbol{\gamma}_\omega, \mathbf{z}_{t-1})'\mathbf{f}_t\right)\right] = \mathbf{0}_N. \tag{5.62}$$

We can estimate and test the conditional moment restriction given below using the GMM as described in Section 5.3:

$$\textbf{Hypothesis 2} \quad E_{t-1}\left[\begin{pmatrix} \mathbf{f}_t - \mathbf{h}_\mu\left(\boldsymbol{\gamma}_\mu, \mathbf{z}_{t-1}\right) \\ \mathbf{R}_t m_t \end{pmatrix}\right] = \mathbf{0}_{K+N}, \tag{5.63}$$

where $m_t = 1 + \mathbf{h}_\omega(\boldsymbol{\gamma}_\omega, \mathbf{z}_{t-1})'\mathbf{h}_\mu(\boldsymbol{\gamma}_\mu, \mathbf{z}_{t-1}) + \mathbf{h}_\omega(\boldsymbol{\gamma}_\omega, \mathbf{z}_{t-1})'\mathbf{f}_t$. The advantage of this approach is that we make use of the information in the conditioning variables $\mathbf{z}_{t-1}$. The cost is that we have to make assumption (5.61), which is rather difficult to justify. In empirical studies using this approach, it is commonly assumed that $\mathbf{h}_\mu$ is a linear function of $\mathbf{z}_{t-1}$ and that $\mathbf{h}_\omega$ is constant. When factors are traded, assumption (5.61) implies

$$\mathbf{h}_\mu(\boldsymbol{\gamma}_\mu, \mathbf{z}_{t-1}) = \boldsymbol{\Omega}_{t-1}\mathbf{h}_\omega(\boldsymbol{\gamma}_\omega, \mathbf{z}_{t-1}). \tag{5.64}$$

Letting $\mathbf{u}_t = \mathbf{f}_t - \mathbf{h}_\mu(\boldsymbol{\gamma}_\mu, \mathbf{z}_{t-1})$, we can rewrite the aforementioned equation as

$$E_t\left[\mathbf{u}_t\mathbf{u}'_t\mathbf{h}_\omega(\boldsymbol{\gamma}_\omega, \mathbf{z}_{t-1}) - \mathbf{h}_\mu(\boldsymbol{\gamma}_\mu, \mathbf{z}_{t-1})\right] = \mathbf{0}_K, \tag{5.65}$$

which can be added to the moment restriction in Hypothesis 2. Harvey (1989) rejects the hypothesis under the assumption that $\mathbf{h}_\mu$ is linear and $\mathbf{h}_\omega$ is constant.

The third approach uses the conditional SDF representation and simply assumes that all the time-varying parameters are functions of a few chosen observable conditioning variables observed by the econometrician. In that case the conditional beta model (5.51) implies the following conditional SDF representation

$$E_{t-1}\big[\mathbf{R}_t(1 - \boldsymbol{\lambda}_{t-1}'\mathbf{f}_t)\big] = \mathbf{0}_N \quad \text{where} \quad \boldsymbol{\lambda}_{t-1} = \frac{\boldsymbol{\Omega}_{t-1}^{-1}\boldsymbol{\delta}_{t-1}}{1 + \boldsymbol{\delta}_{t-1}'\boldsymbol{\Omega}_{t-1}^{-1}\boldsymbol{\mu}_{t-1}}. \tag{5.66}$$

In this approach, we assume that $\boldsymbol{\lambda}_{t-1}$ is a function of $\mathbf{z}_{t-1}$ up to some unknown parameters denoted by $\boldsymbol{\gamma}_\lambda$. That is, we assume

$$\frac{\boldsymbol{\delta}_{t-1}'\boldsymbol{\Omega}_{t-1}^{-1}}{1 + \boldsymbol{\delta}_{t-1}'\boldsymbol{\Omega}_{t-1}^{-1}\boldsymbol{\mu}_{t-1}} = \mathbf{h}_\lambda(\boldsymbol{\gamma}_\lambda, \mathbf{z}_{t-1}). \tag{5.67}$$

Using GMM, we can test the conditional moment restriction:

Hypothesis 3 $E_{t-1}\big[\mathbf{R}_t(1 - \mathbf{h}_\lambda(\boldsymbol{\gamma}_\lambda, \mathbf{z}_{t-1})\mathbf{f}_t)\big] = \mathbf{0}_N. \tag{5.68}$

Cochrane (1996) assumes a linear function $\boldsymbol{\lambda}' = \mathbf{a}' + \mathbf{z}_{t-1}'\mathbf{C}$, where $\mathbf{a}$ is a vector of unknown parameters and $\mathbf{C}$ is a matrix of unknown parameters. Then, the hypothesis becomes

$$E_{t-1}\big[\mathbf{R}_t(1 - \mathbf{a}'\mathbf{f}_t - (\mathbf{f}_t' \otimes \mathbf{z}_{t-1})\text{vec}(\mathbf{C}))\big] = \mathbf{0}_N. \tag{5.69}$$

In the empirical literature the convention is to refer to $\mathbf{f}_t' \otimes \mathbf{z}_{t-1}$ as the scaled factors. Equation (5.69) can be viewed as a linear conditional SDF representation with scaled factors included as a subset of the factors. Estimation and testing of this model can be carried out using GMM as described in Section 5.3. The advantage of this approach is that it is straightforward and simple. The disadvantage of this approach is that assumption (5.67) often lacks economic intuition, and it is not clear how to test the assumption.

  None of the approaches discussed so far involve making assumptions about the laws governing the temporal evolution of $\mathbf{B}_{t-1}$ and $E_{t-1}[\mathbf{R}_t]$. However, assumptions about the dynamics of the conditional factor risk premia impose restrictions on the joint dynamics of the conditional expected stock returns and the conditional factor betas. Here onwards, for convenience, we will assume that all the factors are traded. Then, we have $\boldsymbol{\delta}_{t-1} = \boldsymbol{\mu}_{t-1}$. Equation (5.58) and the conditional beta pricing model (5.51) implies

$$E_{t-1}[\mathbf{R}_{t-1}] = \mathbf{B}_{t-1}\mathbf{h}_\mu(\boldsymbol{\gamma}_\mu, \mathbf{z}_{t-1}) \tag{5.70}$$

$$\mathbf{B}_{t-1} = E_{t-1}\big[\mathbf{R}_t\mathbf{u}_{t-1}'\big]\big(E_{t-1}\big[\mathbf{u}_{t-1}\mathbf{u}_{t-1}'\big]\big)^{-1}, \tag{5.71}$$

where $\mathbf{u}_{t-1} = \mathbf{f}_t - \mathbf{h}_\mu(\boldsymbol{\gamma}_\mu, \mathbf{z}_{t-1})$. It would be rather difficult to verify whether assumptions about the dynamics of conditional betas and conditional expected stock returns are consistent with the restrictions imposed by the aforementioned equations. Hence, it would be advisable to make assumptions regarding the dynamics of only two of the three groups of variables, conditional factor risk premia, conditional factor betas, and conditional expected return on assets.

Some empirical studies assume that $E_{t-1}[\mathbf{R}_t]$ is a prespecified function of only a few conditioning variables, $\mathbf{z}_{t-1}$, i.e.,

$$E_{t-1}[\mathbf{R}_t] = \mathbf{h}_r(\boldsymbol{\gamma}_r, \mathbf{z}_{t-1}). \tag{5.72}$$

In empirical studies, $\mathbf{z}_{t-1}$ usually contains only a small number of macroeconomic variables that help predict future factor realizations. Note that Eq. (5.72) is a rather strong assumption, because it requires these variables to be sufficient for predicting future returns on every stock. Therefore, before testing a conditional beta pricing model we need to examine whether assumptions (5.72) and (5.58) are reasonable. For this purpose we may use the GMM to test the following moment restrictions:

$$E\left[\mathbf{H}(\mathbf{z}_{t-1})\begin{pmatrix}\mathbf{R}_t - \mathbf{h}_r(\boldsymbol{\gamma}_r, \mathbf{z}_{t-1}) \\ \mathbf{f}_t - \mathbf{h}_\mu(\boldsymbol{\gamma}_\mu, \mathbf{z}_{t-1})\end{pmatrix}\right] = \mathbf{0}_M, \tag{5.73}$$

where $\mathbf{H}(\mathbf{z}_{t-1})$ is an $M \times (N + K)$ matrix of functions of $\mathbf{z}_{t-1}$, as described in Section 5.3.

Equation (5.72) imposes the following restrictions on the dynamics of conditional factor betas through the beta pricing model (5.51)

$$\mathbf{h}_r(\boldsymbol{\gamma}_r, \mathbf{z}_{t-1}) = \mathbf{B}_{t-1}\mathbf{h}_\mu(\boldsymbol{\gamma}_\mu, \mathbf{z}_{t-1}). \tag{5.74}$$

Some empirical studies of conditional beta pricing models assume that conditional factor betas are specific functions of a few prespecified conditioning variables, i.e.,

$$\mathbf{B}_{t-1} = \mathbf{h}_\beta(\boldsymbol{\gamma}_\beta, \mathbf{z}_{t-1}). \tag{5.75}$$

In that case it is necessary to ensure that this assumption does not conflict with Eq. (5.74). For example, Ferson and Korajczyk (1995) assume (5.58) and (5.72) and take $\mathbf{h}_\mu$ and $\mathbf{h}_r$ as linear functions. Then, the dynamics of conditional betas in (5.75) cannot be captured by a linear function of the conditioning variables $\mathbf{z}_{t-1}$ because $\mathbf{h}_r$ would then be a quadratic function. To understand the nature of the restrictions on the dynamics of conditional betas, let us consider the special case where $\mathbf{z}_{t-1}$ is a scalar and $\mathbf{h}_r(\boldsymbol{\gamma}_r, \mathbf{z}_{t-1}) = \boldsymbol{\gamma}_r \mathbf{z}_{t-1}$, and $\mathbf{h}_\mu(\boldsymbol{\gamma}_\mu, \mathbf{z}_{t-1}) = \boldsymbol{\gamma}_\mu \mathbf{z}_{t-1}$, where $\boldsymbol{\gamma}_r$ and $\boldsymbol{\gamma}_\mu$ are $N \times 1$ and $K \times 1$ vectors, respectively. In that case, $\mathbf{B}_{t-1}$ is a constant and does not vary with time because $\mathbf{z}_{t-1}$ can be canceled out from both sides of Eq. (5.74) yielding $\boldsymbol{\gamma}_r = \mathbf{B}_{t-1}\boldsymbol{\gamma}_\mu$. We can use GMM to test the following moment restrictions implied by (5.58) and (5.51)

Hypothesis 4 $E_{t-1}\left[\begin{pmatrix}\mathbf{f}_t - \mathbf{h}_\mu(\boldsymbol{\gamma}_\mu, \mathbf{z}_{t-1}) \\ \mathbf{R}_t - \mathbf{h}_r(\boldsymbol{\gamma}_r, \mathbf{z}_{t-1}) \\ \mathbf{h}_r(\boldsymbol{\gamma}_r, \mathbf{z}_{t-1}) - \mathbf{h}_\beta(\boldsymbol{\gamma}_\beta, \mathbf{z}_{t-1})\mathbf{h}_\mu(\boldsymbol{\gamma}_\mu, \mathbf{z}_{t-1})\end{pmatrix}\right] = \mathbf{0}_{K+2N}.$ (5.76)

The main problem with this approach is that the specification for $\mathbf{h}_\beta$ can be inconsistent with the specifications for $\mathbf{h}_\mu$ and $\mathbf{h}_r$. Using international stocks, Ferson and Harvey (1993) reject the above hypothesis under the assumption that all the three functions, $\mathbf{h}_r$, $\mathbf{h}_\delta$, and $\mathbf{h}_\beta$, are linear. For the one-factor CAPM, Ghysels (1998) compares the mean square prediction error of various model specifications. Not surprisingly, the assumption of linear dynamics for conditional beta gives the worst results. This suggests that assumption (5.72) may not be appropriate. We may therefore test Eqs. (5.75) and (5.70) and omit the second group of equations in (5.76).

When there is only one factor in the model, the restriction on conditional beta can be tested without specifying beta dynamics – i.e., Eqs. (5.74), (5.58), and (5.72) can be estimated and tested without using Eq. (5.75). Substituting (5.71) into Eq. (5.74) and using the fact that f_t is a scalar, we obtain

$$\mathbf{h}_r(\boldsymbol{\gamma}_r, \mathbf{z}_{t-1}) = E_{t-1}\left[\mathbf{R}_t u_t\right]\left(E_{t-1}\left[u_t^2\right]\right)^{-1} h_\mu(\boldsymbol{\gamma}_\mu, \mathbf{z}_{t-1}), \tag{5.77}$$

where $u_t = f_t - h_\mu(\boldsymbol{\gamma}_\mu, \mathbf{z}_{t-1})$. Multiplying $E_{t-1}[u_t^2]$ to both sides and rearranging terms, we get

$$E_{t-1}\left[u_t^2 \mathbf{h}_r(\boldsymbol{\gamma}_r, \mathbf{z}_{t-1}) - \mathbf{R}_t u_t h_\mu(\boldsymbol{\gamma}_\mu, \mathbf{z}_{t-1})\right] = \mathbf{0}_N. \tag{5.78}$$

Therefore, we can use GMM to test the following conditional moment restrictions:

$$\textbf{Hypothesis 5} \quad E_{t-1}\left[\begin{pmatrix} f_t - h_\mu(\boldsymbol{\gamma}_\mu, \mathbf{z}_{t-1}) \\ \mathbf{R}_t - \mathbf{h}_r(\boldsymbol{\gamma}_r, \mathbf{z}_{t-1}) \\ u_t^2 \mathbf{h}_r(\boldsymbol{\gamma}_r, \mathbf{z}_{t-1}) - \mathbf{R}_t u_t h_\mu(\boldsymbol{\gamma}_\mu, \mathbf{z}_{t-1}) \end{pmatrix}\right] = \mathbf{0}_{1+2N}. \tag{5.79}$$

Although this hypothesis has the advantage that a stand on beta dynamics does not have to be taken, it has two disadvantages. First, it assumes Eq. (5.72), which is a prediction model for stock returns. Second, the asset pricing model can only have one factor. Using both U.S. stock returns, Harvey (1989) rejects the hypothesis under the assumption that $\mathbf{h}_r$ and $\mathbf{h}_\mu$ are both linear functions.

Ghysels (1998) points out that we should be cautious about overfitting data when evaluating beta pricing models with time-varying parameters. When overfitting happens, the GMM test would not able to reject the model. In that case, it is likely that the constant parameters specified in the model would exhibit structural breaks. Therefore, Ghysels suggests using the supLM test developed by Andrews (1993) to check the stability of all constant coefficients when a model specification passes the GMM test, and as an illustration tests linear versions of Hypotheses 4 and 5. To ensure that overfitting does not occur in the examples he considers, he uses only one asset in each test. He shows that most of the J-statistics are not significant, but many supLM statistics are

Table 14.1   Comparison of testable hypotheses for GMM

Type of hypothesis	Additional assumption on	Moment restrictions	Factor type and dimension	Example of studies
1	δ_{t-1}	Unconditional	Nontraded/multi	Jagannathan and Wang (1996)
2	$\mu_{t-1}, \Omega_{t-1}^{-1}\delta_{t-1}$	Conditional	Nontraded/multi	Harvey (1989)
3	$\dfrac{\delta_{t-1}'\Omega_{t-1}^{-1}}{1+\delta_{t-1}'\Omega_{t-1}^{-1}\mu_{t-1}}$	Conditional	Nontraded/multi	Cochrane (1996)
4	$\mu_{t-1}, E_{t-1}[\mathbf{R}_t], \mathbf{B}_{t-1}$	Conditional	Traded/multi	Ferson and Harvey (1993)
5	$\mu_{t-1}, E_{t-1}[\mathbf{R}_t]$	Conditional	Traded/single	Harvey (1991)

significant. These results suggest that it would be advisable to conduct GMM tests using a large number of assets to rule out over fitting, especially for models containing many factors. Because empirical studies in this area typically use returns on a large collection of assets, over fitting is unlikely to be an issue in practice. For example, Ferson and Harvey (1993) and Harvey (1989) reject the linear versions of Hypotheses 4 and 5 using GMM.

Table 14.1 compares features of the five types of hypothesis we discussed. As can be seen, Hypothesis 1 involves minimal assumptions, but the moment restriction does not make use of conditioning information. As we have argued earlier, this need not be a serious limitation when the collection of assets available to the econometrician include portfolios managed in clever ways using conditioning information. The most important distinction of Hypotheses 1–3 from Hypotheses 4 and 5 is that they do not require additional assumptions regarding the dynamics of conditional expected stock returns $E_{t-1}[\mathbf{R}_t]$. Hypotheses 1–3 allow the conditional expected stock returns to be completely determined by the conditional beta pricing model relation. When Hypotheses 4 and 5 are rejected by GMM, further investigation is necessary to identify whether the rejection is due to the prediction model or the asset pricing model being wrong. Another important difference is that Hypotheses 1–3 can be viewed as special cases of the SDF representation of the conditional linear beta pricing model.

6. CONCLUSION

Linear beta pricing models have received wide attention in the asset pricing literature. In this chapter, we reviewed econometric methods that are available for empirical evaluation of linear beta pricing models using time-series observations on returns and characteristics on a large collection of financial assets. The econometric methods can be grouped into three classes: the two-stage cross-sectional regression method, the ML method, and the GMM. Shanken (1992) showed that the cross-sectional method and the ML method are asymptotically equivalent when returns are drawn from an i.i.d. joint normal distribution. Under that condition MacKinlay and Richardson (1991) showed that the ML method and the GMM are also asymptotically equivalent. The GMM, however, has advantages when returns are not jointly normal and exhibit conditional heteroskedasticity.

In general, the number of assets will be large relative to the length of the time-series of return observations. The classical approach to reducing the dimensionality, without losing too much information, is to use the portfolio grouping procedure by Black et al. (1972). Because portfolio betas are estimated more precisely than individual security betas, the portfolio grouping procedure attenuates the EIV problem faced by the econometrician when using the classical two-stage cross-sectional regression method. The portfolio formation method can highlight or mask characteristics in the data that have valuable information about the validity or otherwise of the asset pricing model being examined. Hence, the econometrician has to exercise care to avoid the data snooping biases discussed in the study of Lo and MacKinlay (1990).

As Brennan et al. (1998) observe, it is not necessary to group securities into portfolios to minimize the EIV problem when all the factors are excess returns on traded assets by working with risk adjusted returns as dependent variables. However, the advantages to working directly with security returns instead of first grouping securities into portfolios have not been fully explored in the literature.

When the linear beta pricing model holds, the expected return on every asset is a linear function of factor betas. The common practice for examining model misspecification using the cross-sectional regression method is to include security characteristics like relative size and book-to-price ratios as additional explanatory variables. These characteristics should not have any explanatory power when the pricing model is correctly specified. An alternative approach would be to test for linearity using multivariate tests. The former tests have the advantage that the alternative hypotheses provide valuable information as to what may be missing in the model. The latter tests, on the other hand, will have more power in general to detect any type of model misspecification. Hence both types of tests may have to be used in conjunction, to understand the dimensions along which a given model performs well when confronted with data.

ACKNOWLEDGMENTS

The authors wish to thank Bob Korajczyk, Ernst Schaumburg, and Jay Shanken for comments and Aiyesha Dey for editorial assistance.

REFERENCES

Anderson, T. W. (2003) *An Introduction to Multivariate Statistical Analysis* (3rd Ed.). New York, NY: John Wiley.

Andrews, D. W. K. (1991) "Heteroskedasticity and Autocorrelation Consistent Covariance Matrix Estimation," *Econometrica*, 59, 817–858.

Andrews, D. W. K. (1993) "Tests for Parameter Instability and Structural Change with Unknown Change Point," *Econometrica*, 61, 821–856.

Andrews, D. W. K., and J. C. Monahan. (1992) "An Improved Heteroskedasticity and Autocorrelation Consistent Covariance Matrix Estimator," *Econometrica*, 60, 953–966.

Ang, A., and J. Liu. (2005) "How to Discount Cash Flows with Time-Varying Expected Returns," *Journal of Finance*, 59, 2745–2783.

Bansal, R., D. A. Hsieh, and S. Viswanathan. (1993) "A New Approach to International Arbitrage Pricing," *Journal of Finance*, 48, 1719–1747.

Bansal, R., and S. Viswanathan. (1993) "No Arbitrage and Arbitrage Pricing: A New Approach," *Journal of Finance*, 48, 1231–1262.

Banz, R. W. (1981) "The Relationship Between Returns and Market Value of Common Stocks," *Journal of Financial Economics*, 9, 3–18.

Barone-Adesi, G., and P. P. Talwar. (1983) "Market Models and Heteroskedasticity of Security Returns," *Journal of Business and Economic Statistics*, 4, 163–168.

Basu, S. (1977) "Investment Performance of Common Stocks in Relation to Their Price-Earnings Ratios: A Test of the Efficient Market Hypothesis," *Journal of Finance*, 32, 663–682.

Berk, J. B. (1995) "A Critique of Size-Related Anomalies," *Review of Financial Studies*, 8, 275–286.

Bhandari, L. C. (1988) "Debt/Equity Ratio and Expected Common Stock Returns: Empirical Evidence," *Journal of Finance*, 43, 507–528.

Black, F., M. C. Jensen, and M. Scholes. (1972) "The Capital Asset Pricing Model: Some Empirical Tests," In M. C. Jensen (Ed.), *Studies in the Theory of Capital Markets* (pp. 79–121). New York, NY: Praeger.

Blattberg, R. C., and N. J. Gonedes. (1974) "A Comparison of the Stable and Student Distributions as Statistical Models of Stock Prices," *Journal of Business*, 47, 244–280.

Bollerslev, T., R. F. Engle, and J. M. Wooldridge. (1988) "A Capital Asset Pricing Model with Time-Varying Covariances," *Journal of Political Economy*, 96, 116–131.

Breeden, D. T. (1979) "An Intertemporal Asset Pricing Model with Stochastic Consumption and Investment Opportunities," *Journal of Financial Economics*, 7, 265–296.

Breeden, D. T., M. R. Gibbons, and R. H. Litzenberger. (1989) "Empirical Tests of the Consumption-Oriented CAPM," *Journal of Finance*, 44, 231–262.

Brennan, M. J., T. Chordia, and A. Subrahmanyam. (1998) "Alternative Factor Specifications, Security Characteristics, and the Cross Section of Expected Returns," *Journal of Financial Economics*, 49, 345–373.

Brennan, M. J., and A. Subrahmanyam. (1996) "Market Microstructure and Asset Pricing: On the Compensation for Illiquidity in Stock Returns," *Journal of Financial Economics*, 41, 441–464.

Buraschi, A., and J. Jackwerth. (2001) "The Price of a Smile: Hedging and Spanning in Option Markets," *Review of Financial Studies*, 49, 495–527.

Campbell, J. Y. (1993) "Intertemporal Asset Pricing Without Consumption Data," *American Economic Review*, 83, 487–512.

Campbell, J. Y. (1996) "Understanding Risk and Return," *Journal of Political Economy*, 104, 298–345.

Chamberlain, G., and M. Rothschild. (1983) "Arbitrage, Factor Structure, and Mean-Variance Analysis on Large Asset Markets," *Econometrica*, 51, 1281–1304.

Chan, L. K. C., Y. Hamao, and J. Lakonishok. (1991) "Fundamentals and Stock Returns in Japan," *Journal of Finance*, 46, 1739–1764.

Chen, N.-F., R. Roll, and S. A. Ross. (1986) "Economic Forces and the Stock Market," *Journal of Business*, 59, 383–404.

Cochrane, J. H. (1996) "A Cross-Sectional Test of an Investment-Based Asset Pricing Model," *Journal of Political Economy*, 104, 572–621.

Connor, G. (1984) "A Unified Beta Pricing Theory," *Journal of Economic Theory*, 34, 13–31.

Connor, G., and R. A. Korajczyk. (1986) "Performance Measurement with the Arbitrage Pricing Theory: A New Framework for Analysis," *Journal of Financial Economics*, 15, 373–394.

Connor, G., and R. A. Korajczyk. (1988) "Risk and Return in an Equilibrium APT: Application of a New Test Methodology," *Journal of Financial Economics*, 21, 255–289.

Connor, G., R. A. Korajczyk, and R. T. Uhlaner. (2007) "Sunspots, Iterative Two-Pass Cross-Sectional Regressions, and Asymptotic Principal Components," *Working Paper*, Northwestern University.

Daniel, K., and S. Titman. (1997) "Evidence on the Characteristics of Cross Sectional Variation of Stock Returns," *Journal of Finance*, 52, 1–33.

Davidson, J. (1994) *Stochastic Limit Theory: An Introduction for Econometricians*. New York, NY: Oxford University Press.

Dybvig, P. H. (1983) "An Explicit Bound on Individual Assets' Deviations from APT Pricing in a Finite Economy," *Journal of Financial Economics*, 12, 483–496.

Dybvig, P. H., and J. E. Ingersoll. (1982) "Mean-Variance Theory in Complete Markets," *Journal of Business*, 55, 233–251.

Epstein, L. G., and S. Zin. (1989) "Substitution, Risk Aversion and the Temporal Behavior of Consumption and Asset Returns: A Theoretical Framework," *Econometrica*, 57, 937–969.

Fama, E. F. (1965) "The Behavior of Stock Market Prices," *Journal of Business*, 38, 34–105.

Fama, E. F., and K. R. French. (1988) "Dividend Yields and Expected Stock Returns," *Journal of Financial Economics*, 22, 3–25.

Fama, E. F., and K. R. French. (1992) "The Cross-Section of Expected Stock Returns," *Journal of Finance*, 47, 427–465.

Fama, E. F., and K. R. French. (1993) "Common Risk Factors in the Returns on Bonds and Stocks," *Journal of Financial Economics*, 33, 3–56.

Fama, E. F., and J. D. MacBeth. (1973) "Risk, Return, and Equilibrium: Empirical Tests," *Journal of Political Economy*, 81, 607–636.

Ferson, W. E., and S. R. Foerster. (1994) "Finite Sample Properties of the Generalized Method of Moments Tests of Conditional Asset Pricing Models," *Journal Financial Economics*, 36, 29–55.

Ferson, W. E., and C. R. Harvey. (1993) "The Risk and Predictability of International Equity Returns," *Review Financial Studies*, 6, 527–566.

Ferson, W. E., and R. Jagannathan. (1996) "Econometric Evaluation of Asset Pricing Models," In G. S. Maddala, and C. R. Rao (Eds.), *Handbook of Statistics, Vol. 14: Statistical Methods in Finance* (pp. 1–30). Amsterdam, The Netherlands: Elsevier.

Ferson, W. E., and R. A. Korajczyk. (1995) "Do Arbitrage Pricing Models Explain the Predictability of Stock Returns?," *Journal of Business*, 68, 309–349.

Ghysels, E. (1998) "On Stable Factor Structures in the Pricing of Risk: Do Time-Varying Betas Help or Hurt?," *Journal of Finance*, 53, 549–573.

Gibbons, M. R. (1982) "Multivariate Tests of Financial Models: A New Approach," *Journal of Financial Economics*, 10, 3–27.

Gibbons, M. R., S. A. Ross, and J. Shanken. (1989) "A Test of the Efficiency of a Given Portfolio," *Econometrica*, 57, 1121–1152.

Grinblatt, M., and S. Titman. (1983) "Factor pricing in a Finite Economy," *Journal of Financial Economics*, 12, 497–507.

Hall, P., and C. C. Heyde. (1980) *Martingale Limit Theory and its Application*. New York, NY: Academic Press.

Hansen, L. P. (1982) "Large Sample Properties of Generalized Method of Moments Estimators," *Econometrica*, 50, 1029–1054.

Hansen, L. P., and R. J. Hodrick. (1980) "Forward Exchange Rates as Optimal Predictors of Future Spot Rates: An Econometric Analysis," *Journal of Political Economy*, 88, 829–853.

Hansen, L. P., and R. Jagannathan. (1997) "Assessing Specification Errors in Stochastic Discount Factor Models," *Journal of Finance*, 62, 557–590.

Hansen, L. P., and S. F. Richard. (1987) "The Role of Conditioning Information in Deducing Testable Restrictions Implied by Dynamic Asset Pricing Models," *Econometrica*, 55, 587–613.

Hansen, L. P., and K. J. Singleton. (1982) "Generalized Instrumental Variables Estimation of Nonlinear Rational Expectations Models," *Econometrica*, 50, 1269–1286.

Harvey, C. R. (1989) "Time-Varying Conditional Covariances in Tests of Asset Pricing Models," *Journal of Financial Economics*, 24, 289–317.

Harvey, C. R. (1991) "The World Price of Covariance Risk," *Journal of Finance*, 46, 111–157.

Hodrick, R. J., and X. Zhang. (2001) "Evaluating Specification Errors in Stochastic Discount Factor Models," *Journal of Financial Economics*, 62, 327–376.

Huberman, G., and S. Kandel. (1987) "Mean-Variance Spanning," *Journal of Finance*, 42, 873–888.

Ingersoll, J. E. (1987) *Theory of Financial Decision Making*. Totowa, NJ: Rowman & Littlefield.

Jagannathan, R., and E. R. McGrattan. (1995) "The CAPM Debate," *Federal Reserve Bank of Minneapolis Quarterly Review*, 19, 2–17.

Jagannathan, R., G. Skoulakis, and Z. Wang. (2002) "Generalized Method of Moments: Applications in Finance," *Journal of Business and Economic Statistics*, 20, 470–481.

Jagannathan, R., G. Skoulakis, and Z. Wang. (2003) "Testing Linear Asset Pricing Factor Models using Cross-Sectional Regressions and Security Characteristics: Asymptotic Theory," Working Paper, Northwestern University.

Jagannathan, R., and Z. Wang. (1996) "The Conditional CAPM and the Cross-Section of Expected Returns," *Journal of Finance*, 51, 3–53.

Jagannathan, R., and Z. Wang. (1998) "An Asymptotic Theory for Estimating Beta-Pricing Models using Cross-Sectional Regression," *Journal of Finance*, 53, 1285–1309.

Jagannathan, R., and Z. Wang. (2002) "Empirical Evaluation of Asset-Pricing Models: A Comparison of the SDF and Beta Methods," *Journal of Finance*, 57, 2337–2367.

Jegadeesh, N., and S. Titman. (1993) "Returns to Buying Winners and Selling Losers: Implications for Stock Market Efficiency," *Journal of Finance*, 48, 65–91.

Jobson, J. D., and B. Korkie. (1982) "Potential Performance and Tests of Portfolio Efficiency," *Journal of Financial Economics*, 10, 433–466.

Jobson, J. D., and B. Korkie. (1985) "Some Tests of Linear Asset Pricing with Multivariate Normality," *Canadian Journal of Administrative Sciences*, 2, 114–138.

Kan, R., and G. Zhou. (2001) "Tests of Mean-Variance Spanning," Working Paper, University of Toronto.

Kandel, S. (1984) "The Likelihood Ratio Test Statistic of Mean-Variance Efficiency Without a Riskless Asset," *Journal of Financial Economics*, 13, 575–592.

Keim, D. B. (1983) "Size-Related Anomalies and Stock Return Seasonality: Further Empirical Evidence," *Journal of Financial Economics*, 12, 13–32.

Kim, D. (1995) "The Errors in the Variables Problem in the Cross-Section of Expected Stock Returns," *Journal of Finance*, 50, 1605–1634.

Lehmann, B. N., and D. M. Modest. (1988) "The Empirical Foundations of the Arbitrage Pricing Theory," *Journal of Financial Economics*, 21, 213–254.

Lehmann, B. N., and D. M. Modest. (2005) "Diversification and the Optimal Construction of Basis Portfolios," *Management Science*, 51, 581–598.

Lintner, J. (1965) "The Valuation of Risky Assets and the Selection of Risky Investments in Stock Portfolios and Capital Budgets," *Review of Economics and Statistics*, 47, 13–37.

Lo, A. W., and A. C. MacKinlay. (1990) "Data-Snooping Biases in Tests of Financial Asset Pricing Models," *Review of Financial Studies*, 3, 431–467.

Long, J. B. (1974) "Stock Prices, Inflation and the Term Structure of Interest Rates," *Journal of Financial Economics*, 1, 131–170.

Lucas, R. E. (1978) "Asset Prices in an Exchange Economy," *Econometrica*, 46, 1429–1445.

MacKinlay, A. C. (1987) "On Multivariate Tests of the CAPM," *Journal of Financial Economics*, 18, 341–371.

MacKinlay, A. C., and M. P. Richardson. (1991) "Using Generalized Method of Moments to Test Mean-Variance Efficiency," *Journal of Finance*, 46, 511–527.

Merton, R. C. (1973) "An Intertemporal Asset Pricing Model," *Econometrica*, 41, 867–888.

Mossin, J. (1966) "Equilibrium in a Capital Asset Market," *Econometrica*, 34, 768–783.

Newey, W. K., and K. D. West. (1987) "A Simple, Positive Semi-definite, Heteroskedasticity and Autocorrelation Consistent Covariance Matrix," *Econometrica*, 55, 703–708.

Reinganum, M. R. (1981) "Misspecification of Capital Asset Pricing: Empirical Anomalies Based on Earnings' Yields and Market Values," *Journal of Financial Economics*, 9, 19–46.

Rosenberg, B., K. Reid, and R. Lanstein. (1985) "Persuasive Evidence of Market Inefficiency," *Journal of Portfolio Management*, 11, 9–17.

Ross, S. A. (1976) "The Arbitrage Theory of Capital Asset Pricing," *Journal of Economic Theory*, 13, 341–360.

Schwert, G. W. (1983) "Size and Stock Returns and other Empirical Regularities," *Journal of Financial Economics*, 12, 3–12.

Schwert, G. W., and P. J. Seguin. (1990) "Heteroskedasticity in Stock Returns," *Journal of Finance*, 45, 1129–1155.

Shanken, J. (1985) "Multivariate Tests of the Zero-Beta CAPM," *Journal of Financial Economics*, 14, 327–348.

Shanken, J. (1992) "On the Estimation of Beta-Pricing Models," *Review of Financial Studies*, 5, 1–33.

Sharpe, W. F. (1964) "Capital Asset Prices: A Theory of Market Equilibrium under Conditions of Risk," *Journal of Finance*, 19, 425–442.

Skoulakis, G. (2006) "Essays in Asset Pricing and Financial Econometrics," Doctoral Dissertation, Northwestern University.

Stattman, D. (1980) "Book Values and Stock Returns," *The Chicago MBA: A Journal of Selected Papers*, 4, 25–45.

Zhou, G. (1991) "Small Sample Tests of Portfolio Efficiency," *Journal of Financial Economics*, 30, 165–191.

CHAPTER 15

Option Pricing Bounds and Statistical Uncertainty: Using Econometrics to Find an Exit Strategy in Derivatives Trading

Per A. Mykland
Department of Statistics, The University of Chicago, Chicago, IL

Contents

Abstract

In the presence of statistical uncertainty, what bounds can one set on derivatives prices? We let P be the actual probability distribution of the underlying processes and distinguish between two problems: the "probabilistic problem," in which P is fixed and known but there is incompleteness or other barriers to perfect hedging; and the "statistical problem," in which P is not known. We shall be interested in the statistical problem as seen from the perspective of a single actor in the market, who could be either an investor or a regulator. In our development, we shall mostly not distinguish between parameter uncertainty and model uncertainty. In most cases, the model will implicitly be uncertain. We are mainly interested in the forecasting problem (standing at time $t = 0$ and looking into the future). There are additional issues involved in actually observing quantities like volatility contemporaneously.

Keywords: options hedging; prediction sets; trading strategies; interest rates; European options

1. INTRODUCTION

1.1. Pricing Bounds, Trading Strategies, and Exit Strategies

In the presence of statistical uncertainty, what bounds can one set on derivatives prices? This is particularly important when setting reserve requirements for derivatives trading.

To analyze this question, suppose we find ourselves at a time $t = 0$, with the following situation:

The Past: Information has been collected up to and including time $t = 0$. For the purpose of this chapter, this is mainly historical statistical/econometric information (we use the terms interchangeably). It could also, however, include cross-sectional implied quantities or well-informed subjective quantifications.

The Present: We wish to value a derivative security, or portfolio of securities, whose final payoff is η. This could be for a purchase or sale, or just to value a book. In addition to other valuations of this instrument, we would like a safe bound on its value. If the derivative is a liability, we need an upper bound, which we call $\mathbb{A}$. If it is an asset, the relevant quantity is a lower bound, call it $\mathbb{B}$. We wish to attach probability $1 - \alpha$, say 95%, to such a bound.

The standard approach of options theory is to take as starting point the (distribution of the) prices of a set of market-traded "primary" or "underlying" securities $S_t^{(1)}, \ldots, S_t^{(p)}$, as well as of a money market bond $\beta_t = \exp\{\int_0^t r_u du\}$. Prices of options on these primary securities are then based on self-financing trading strategies in the underlying securities. (In this setting, price formation for the primary securities is usually seen as a separate problem, see, e.g., Duffie (1996). This dichotomy is not necessarily useful in incomplete markets, but we shall follow it here as we wish to create bounds that only depend on the behavior of underlying securities. We shall, however, take the probability distribution for the primary securities prices as unknown.)

This leads to a consideration of the following:

The Future: Consider the case of the upper bound $\mathbb{A}$. We consider lower bounds later. A trading-based approach would be the following. $\mathbb{A}$ would be the smallest value for which there would exist a portfolio A_t, self-financing in the underlying securities, so that $A_0 = \mathbb{A}$ and $A_T \geq \eta$ with probability at least $1 - \alpha$. We shall see important examples in Sections 3, 6, and 7 and give precise mathematical meaning to these concepts in Sections 4 and 5.

The bound $\mathbb{A}$ is what it would cost to liquidate the liability η through delta hedging. It is particularly relevant as it provides an exit strategy in the event of model failure when using standard calibration methods. This is discussed in Section 2.3.

Our approach, therefore, is to find $\mathbb{A}$ by finding a trading strategy. How to do the latter is the problem we are trying to solve.

The question of finding such a bound might also come up without any statistical uncertainty. In fact, one can usefully distinguish between two cases, as follows. We let P be the actual probability distribution of the underlying processes. Now distinguish between

1. the "probabilistic problem": P is fixed and known, but there is incompleteness or other barriers to perfect hedging. Mostly, this means that the "risk neutral probability" P^* (Delbaen and Schachermayer, 1994, 1995; Harrison and Kreps, 1979; Harrison and Pliskà, 1981) is unknown (see Section 1.2 for further discussion); and
2. the "statistical problem": P is not known.

This chapter is about problem (2). We shall be interested in the problem seen from the perspective of a single actor in the market, who could be either an investor, or a regulator. In our development, we shall mostly not distinguish between parameter uncertainty and model uncertainty. In most cases, the model will implicitly be uncertain. We are mainly interested in the forecasting problem (standing at time $t = 0$ and looking into the future). There are additional issues involved in actually observing quantities like volatility contemporaneously. These are discussed in Sections 3.4 and 3.5 but are not the main focus in the following.

There are, in principle, several ways of approaching Problem (2). There are many models and statistical methods available to estimate features of the probability P (see the end of Section 1.2) and hence the value $\mathbb{A}$ (see Section 8). We shall here mainly be concerned with the use of prediction sets, as follows. A prediction set C is established at time $t = 0$ and concerns the behavior of, say, volatility in the time interval $[0, T]$. One possible form of C is the set $\{\Xi^- \leq \int_0^T \sigma_t^2 dt \leq \Xi^+\}$ (cf. (2.3) below), and this will be our main example throughout. Another candidate set is given in (2.2) below, and any number of forms are possible. Further examples, involving interest rates, are discussed in Section 6. One can also incorporate other observables (such as the leverage effect) into a prediction set. The set C (in the example, Ξ^- and Ξ^+) is formed using statistical methods based on the information up to and including time zero. The prediction set has (Bayesian or frequentist) probability at least $1 - \alpha$ (say, 95%) of being realized. In our approach, the upper bound of the price of a derivative security is the minimal starting value (at time $t = 0$) for a nonparametric trading strategy that can cover the value of the security so long as prediction set is realized. The lower bound is similarly defined. In this setup, therefore, the communication between the statistician and the trader happens via the prediction set. Our main candidate for setting prediction intervals from data is the "decoupled" procedure described in Section 5.3. The procedure is consistent with any (continuous process) statistical model and set of investor beliefs so long as one is willing to communicate them via a prediction set. Investor preferences (as expressed, say, via a risk neutral probability) do not enter into the procedure. The approach is based in large part on Avellaneda et al. (1995), Lyons (1995), and Mykland (2000, 2003a,b, 2005).

The philosophical stance in this chapter is conceptually close to that of Hansen and Sargent (2001, 2008, and the references therein), who in a series of articles (and their recent book) have explored the application of robust control theory as a way of coping with model uncertainty. As in their work, we stand at time zero and are facing model uncertainty. Uncertainty is given by a bound (see, for example, the constraint (2.2.4) on p. 27 of Hansen and Sargent (2008), and compare to (2.2), (2.3) and the definition of super-replication below). We assume a possibly malevolent nature, and take a worst case approach to solving the problem [ibid, Chapter 1.10 and 2.2, compare to (2.5) below]. Also, we do not assume that there is learning while the replication process is going on, between time 0 and T, and rationales for this are discussed in ibid, Chapter 1.12. An additional rationale in our case is that learning during the process may create a multiple-comparison situation when setting the prediction set, and this may actually widen the price bounds at time zero. In contrast with Hansen and Sargent's work, our bound is imposed either on a future realization or on the probability thereof (probability of failure), while Hansen and Sargent impose bounds on entropy. It would be a nice future project to try to compare these two approaches in more depth, including the study of possible ambiguity premia for volatilities.

The set of possible probabilities P that we consider is highly nonparametric. Some regularity conditions aside, it will only be required that securities prices are continuous semimartingales under P, and that the conditional probability of the prediction set C given the information at time $t = 0$ is at least $1 - \alpha$. In particular, it should be emphasized that volatility is allowed to be stochastic with unknown governing equations.

We emphasize that our approach is different from trying to estimate options prices either through econometrics or calibration. There is a substantial model-based literature, including Heston (1993), Bates (2000), Duffie et al. (2000), Pan (2002), Carr et al. (2004), see also the study by Bakshi et al. (1997). Alternatively, one can proceed nonparametrically, as in Aït-Sahalia and Lo (1998). A rigorous econometric framework for assessing prices is in development, and for this we refer to Garcia et al. (2009) in this volume for further discussion and references.

Perhaps the most standard approach, as practiced by many banks and many academics, uses calibration. It goes as follows. Pick a suitable family of risk neutral distributions P^* (normally corresponding to several actual P's), and *calibrate* it cross-sectionally to the current value of relevant market-traded options. The upside to the calibration approach is that it attempts to mark derivatives prices to market. The downside is that a cross-section of todays' prices does not provide much information about the behavior over time of price processes, a point made (in greater generality) by Bibby et al. (2005). The problem is also revealed in that "implied" parameters in models typically change over time, even when the model supposes that they are constant. This problem does not seem to have led to severe difficulties in the case of simple European options on market-traded securities, and this is perhaps in part because of the robustness documented in Section 3.2 below. However, the calibration procedure would seem to have been partly to blame for the (at the time of writing) recent meltdown in the market for collateralized debt obligations, which are less transparent and where valuations may thus have been more dependent on arbitrary model choices.

The decision problems faced by the investor and the regulator may therefore require the use of multiple approaches. The bounds in this chapter need not necessarily be used to set prices, they can alternatively be used to determine reserve requirements that are consistent with an exit strategy, see Section 2.3 below. One possible form of organization may be that regulators use our bounds to impose such reserve requirements, while investors rely on the calibration approach to take decisions to maximize their utility. As shown in Section 2.3, the bound-based reserves permit the investor to fall back on a model free strategy in the case where the more specific (typically parametric) model fails. The main contribution of this chapter is thus perhaps to provide an exit strategy when traditional calibration has gone wrong.

It would be desirable if the setting of prices and the setting of reserves could be integrated into a single procedure. For example, in a fully Bayesian setting, this may possible. Concerns that would have to be overcome to set up such a procedure include the difficulty in setting priors on very large spaces (see, for example, Diaconis and Freedman, 1986a,b), and our space is large indeed (the set of all $\mathbb{R}^q$ valued continuous functions on $[0, T]$). Further difficulties arising from an economics perspective can be found in Lucas (1976), see also Chapter 1.11 in Hansen and Sargent (2008). We do not rule out, however, the possibility that such an approach will eventually be found. Also, we once again emphasize that Bayesian methods can be used to find the prediction set in our method. See Section 3.5 for an example.

1.2. Related Problems and Related Literature

In addition to the work cited earlier, there is a wealth of problems related to the one considered in this chapter. The following is a quick road map to a number of research areas. The papers cited are just a small subset of the work that exists in these areas.

First of all, a substantial area of study has been concerned with the *"probabilistic"* problem (1) mentioned earlier. P is known, but due to some form of incompleteness or other barrier to perfect hedging, there are either several P^*s, or one has to find methods of pricing that do not involve a risk-neutral measure. The situation (1) most basically arises when there are not enough securities to complete the market, in particular, when there are too many independent Brownian motions driving the market, when there are jumps of unpredictable size in the prices of securities, or in some cases when there is bid-ask spread (see, e.g., Jouini and Kallal, 1995). This situation can also arise due to transaction cost, differential cost of borrowing and lending, and so on. Strategies in such circumstances include *super-hedging* (Cvitanić and Karatzas, 1992, 1993; Cvitanić et al., 1998, 1999; Eberlein and Jacod, 1997; El Karoui and Quenez, 1995; Karatzas, 1996; Karatzas and Kou, 1996, 1998; Kramkov, 1996), *mean variance hedging* (Föllmer and Schweizer, 1991; Föllmer and Sondermann, 1986; Schweizer, 1990, 1991, 1992, 1993, 1994; and later also Delbaen and Schachermayer, 1996; Delbaen et al., 1997; Laurent and Pham, 1999; Pham et al., 1998), and *quantile style hedging* (see, in particular, Föllmer and Leukert, 1999, 2000; Külldorff, 1993; Spivak and Cvitanić, 1998).

It should be noted that the P known and P unknown cases *can* overlap in the case of Bayesian statistical inference. Thus, if P is a statistical posterior distribution, quantile hedging can accomplish similar aims to those of this chapter. Also, the methods from super-hedging are heavily used in the development here.

Closely connected to super-hedging (whether for P known or unknown) is the study of *robustness*, in a different sense from Hansen and Sargent (2001, 2008). In this version of robustness, one does not try to optimize a starting value, but instead one takes a reasonable strategy and sees when it will cover the final liability. Papers focusing on the latter include Bergman et al. (1996), El Karoui et al. (1998), and Hobson (1998a).

There are also several other methods for considering bounds that reflect the riskiness of a position. Important work includes Lo (1987), Bergman (1995), Constantinides and Zariphopoulou (1999, 2001), Friedman (2000), and Fritelli (2000). A main approach here is to consider risk measures (Artzner et al., 1999; Cont, 2006; Cvitanić and Karatzas, 1999; Föllmer and Schied, 2002). In general, such measures can cover either the P known or or P unknown cases. In particular, Cont (2006) addresses the latter, with a development which is close to Mykland (2003a). Of particular interest are so-called coherent risk measures (going back to Artzner et al. (1999)), and it should be noted that the bounds in the current chapter are indeed coherent when seen as measures of risk. [This is immediate from (2.5) below.] Another kind of risk measure is *Value at Risk*. We here refer to Gourieroux and Jasiak (2009) in this volume for further elaboration and references.

This chapter assumes that securities prices are continuous processes. Given the increasing popularity of models with jumps (such as in several of the papers cited in connection with calibration in Section 1.1), it would be desirable to extend the results to the discontinuous case. We conjecture that the technology in this chapter can be extended thus, in view of the work of Kramkov (1996) in the P-known setting. It should also be noted that the worst case scenario often happens along continuous paths, cf. the work of Hobson (1998b). This is because of the same Dambis (1965)/Dubins–Schwartz (1965) time change that is used in this chapter.

Finally, this chapter is mostly silent on what methods of statistical inference that should be used to set the prediction intervals that are at the core of this methodology. Our one application with data (in Section 3.5) is meant to be a toy example. Because our main recommendation is to set prediction intervals for volatility, a large variety of econometric methods can be used. This includes the ARCH- and GARCH-type models, going back to the seminal papers of Engle (1982) and Bollerslev (1986). There is a huge literature in this area, see, for example the surveys by Bollerslev et al. (1992, 1994) and Engle (1995). See also Engle and Sun (2005). One can also do inference directly in a continuous-time model, and here important papers include Aït-Sahalia (1996, 2002), Aït-Sahalia and Mykland (2003), Barndorff-Nielsen and Shephard (2001), Bibby and Sørensen (1995, 1996a,b), Conley et al. (1997), Dacunha-Castelle and Florens-Zmirou (1986), Danielsson (1994), Florens-Zmirou (1993), Genon-Catalot and Jacod (1994), Genon-Catalot et al. (1999, 2000), Hansen and Scheinkman (1995), Hansen et al. (1998), Jacod (2000), Kessler and Sørensen (1999), and Küchler and Sørensen (1998). Inference in continuous versions of the GARCH model is studied by Drost and Werker (1996), Haug et al. (2007), Meddahi and Renault (2004), Meddahi et al. (2006), Nelson (1990), and Stelzer (2008); see also the review by Lindner (2008). On the other hand, the econometrics of discrete time stochastic volatility models is discussed in the works of Harvey and Shephard (1994), Jacquier et al. (1994), Kim et al. (1998), Ruiz (1994), and Taylor (1994). A review of GMM-based (Hansen, 1982) inference by such models is given by Renault (2008). The cited papers are, of course, only a small sample of the literature available.

An alternative has begun to be explored in the works of Andersen and Bollerslev (1998), Meddahi (2001), Andersen et al. (2001, 2003), Dacorogna et al. (2001), Aït-Sahalia and Mancini (2006), Andersen et al. (2009), and Ghysels and Sinko (2009), which takes estimated daily volatilities as "data." This scheme may not be as efficient as fitting a model directly to the data, but it may be more robust. This procedure is, in turn, based on recent developments in the estimation of volatility from high-frequency data, which is discussed, with references, in Section 3.4 below. In summary, however, the purpose of this chapter is to *enable* econometric methods as a device to set bounds on derivatives prices, and we do not particularly endorse one method over another.

The approach based on prediction sets is outlined in the next section. Section 3 provides the original examples of such sets. A more theoretical framework is laid in Sections 4 and 5. Section 6 considers interest rates, and Section 7 the effect of market-traded options. The incorporation of econometric or statistical conclusions is discussed in Sections 5.3 and 8.

2. OPTIONS HEDGING FROM PREDICTION SETS: BASIC DESCRIPTION

2.1. Setup and Super-Self-Financing Strategies

The situation is described in the introduction. We have collected data. On the basis of these, we are looking for trading strategies in $S_t^{(1)}, \ldots, S_t^{(p)}, \beta_t$, where $0 \le t \le T$, that will super-replicate the payoff with probability at least $1 - \alpha$.

The way we will mostly go about this is to use the data to set a prediction set C, and then to super-replicate the payoff on C. A prime instance would be to create such sets for volatilities, cross-volatilities, or interest rates. If we are dealing with a single continuous security S, with random and time varying volatility σ_t at time t, we could write

$$dS_t = m_t S_t dt + \sigma_t S_t dB_t, \tag{2.1}$$

where B is a Brownian motion. The set C could then get the form

- Extremes-based bounds (Avellaneda et al., 1995; Lyons, 1995):

$$C = \{\sigma_- \le \sigma_t \le \sigma_+, \quad \text{for all } t \in [0, T]\} \tag{2.2}$$

- Integral-based bounds (Mykland, 2000, 2003a,b, 2005):

$$C = \left\{ \Xi^- \le \int_0^T \sigma_t^2 dt \le \Xi^+ \right\}. \tag{2.3}$$

There is a wide variety of possible prediction sets, in particular, when also involving the interest rate, cf. Section 6. We emphasize that C is a set of outcomes (not a set of probabilities). For a rigorous description of the formation of the set C, please consult the beginning of Section 5.2.

It will be convenient to separate the two parts of the concept of super-replication, as we see in the following.

As usual, we call X_t^* the discounted process X_t. In other words, $X_t^* = \beta_t^{-1} X_t$, and vice versa. In certain explicitly defined cases, discounting may be done differently, for example by a zero coupon bond (cf. Section 6 in this chapter, and El Karoui et al., 1998).

A process $V_t, 0 \leq t \leq T$, representing a dynamic portfolio of the underlying securities, is said to be a *super-self-financing portfolio* provided there are processes H_t and D_t, so that, for all $t, 0 \leq t \leq T$,

$$V_t = H_t + D_t, \quad 0 \leq t \leq T, \tag{2.4}$$

where D_t^* is a nonincreasing process and H_t is self-financing in the traded securities $S_t^{(1)}, \ldots, S_t^{(p)}$. In other words, one may extract dividend from a super-self-financing portfolio, but one cannot add funds.

"Self-financing" means, by numeraire invariance (see, for example, Section 6B of Duffie, 1996), that H_t^* can be represented as a stochastic integral with respect to the $S_t^{(i)*}$'s, subject to regularity conditions to eliminate doubling strategies. There is some variation in how to implement this (see, e.g., Duffie, 1996; Chapter 6C (pp. 103–105)). In our case, a "hard" credit restriction is used in Section 5.1, and a softer constraint is used in Section 4.2.

On the other hand, V_t is a *sub-self-financing portfolio* if it admits the representation (2.4) with D_t^* as nondecreasing instead.

For portfolio V to super-replicate η on the set C, we would then require

(i) V is a super-self-financing strategy and
(ii) solvency: $V_T \geq \eta$ on C

If one can attach a probability, say, $1 - \alpha$, to the realization of C, then $1 - \alpha$ is the *prediction probability*, and C is a $1 - \alpha$ prediction set. The probability can be based on statistical methods, and it can be either frequentist or Bayesian.

Definition 1 *Specifically, C is a $1 - \alpha$ prediction set, provided $P(C|\mathcal{H}) \geq 1 - \alpha$, $P - a.s..$ Here either (i) $P(\cdot|\mathcal{H})$ is a Bayesian posterior given the data at time zero, or (ii) in the frequentist case, P describes a class of models and $\mathcal{H}$ represents an appropriate subset of the information available at time zero (the values of securities and other financial quantities, and possibly ancillary material). α can be any number in $[0, 1)$.*

The above definition is deliberately vague. This is for reasons that will become clear in Sections 5.3 and 8, where the matter is pursued further.

For example, a prediction set will normally be random. Given the information at time zero, however, C is fixed, and we treat it as such until Section 5.3. Also, note that if we extend "Bayesian probability" to cover general belief, our definition of a prediction set does not necessarily imply an underlying statistical procedure.

The problem we are trying to solve is as follows. We have to cover a liability η at a nonrandom time T. Because of our comparative lack of knowledge about the relevant set of probabilities, a full super-replication (that works with probability one for all P) would be prohibitively expensive, or undesirable for other reasons. Instead, we require that we can cover the payoff η with, at least, the same (Bayesian or frequentist) probability $1 - \alpha$.

Given the above, if the set C has probability $1 - \alpha$, then also $V_T \geq \eta$ with probability at least $1 - \alpha$, and hence this is a solution to our problem.

Technical Point 1 *All processes, unless otherwise indicated, will be taken to be càdlàg, i.e., right continuous with left limits. In Sections 1–3, we have ignored what probabilities are used when defining stochastic integrals, or even when writing statements like "$V_T \geq \eta$," which tend to only be "almost sure." Also, the set C is based on volatilities that are only defined relative to a probability measure. And there is no mention of filtrations. Discussion of these matters is deferred until Sections 4 and 5.*

2.2. The Bounds $\mathbb{A}$ and $\mathbb{B}$

Having defined super-replication for a prediction set, we would now like the cheapest super-replication. This defines $\mathbb{A}$.

Definition 2 *The* conservative ask price *(or offer price) at time 0 for a payoff η to be made at a time T is*

$$\mathbb{A} = \inf\{V_0 : \ (V_t) \text{ is a super-replication on } C \text{ of the liability } \eta\}. \tag{2.5}$$

The definition is in analogy to that used by Cvitanić and Karatzas (1992, 1993), El Karoui and Quenez (1995), and Kramkov (1996). It is straightforward to see that $\mathbb{A}$ is a version of "value at risk" (see Chapter 14 (pp. 342–365) of Hull, 1999) that is based on dynamic trading. At the same time, $\mathbb{A}$ is coherent in the sense of Artzner et al. (1999).

It would normally be the case that there is a super-replication A_t so that $A_0 = \mathbb{A}$, and we argue this in Section 4.1. Note that in the following, V_t denotes the portfolio value of any super-replication, while A_t is the cheapest one, provided it exists.

Similarly, the *conservative bid price* can be defined as the supremum over all subreplications of the payoff, in the obvious sense. For payoff η, one would get

$$\mathbb{B}(\eta) = -\mathbb{A}(-\eta), \tag{2.6}$$

in obvious notation, and subject to mathematical regularity conditions, it is enough to study ask prices. More generally, if one already has a portfolio of options, one may wish to charge or set reserves $\mathbb{A}(\text{portfolio} + \eta) - \mathbb{A}(\text{portfolio})$ for the payoff η.

But is $\mathbb{A}$ the starting value of a trading strategy? And how does one find $\mathbb{A}$?

As a first stab at this, let a probability distribution P^* be risk neutral if all of $S_t^{(1)*}, \ldots, S_t^{(p)*}$ are P^* martingales. (Slightly varying definitions of "risk neutral" are used in different places, for technical reasons. See, for example, Section 5.1. In general, the existence of such measures is implied by assumptions concerning the non-existence of arbitrage, see, in particular, Delbaen and Schachermayer (1995).) Suppose that $\mathcal{P}^*$ is the set of all risk neutral probabilities that allocate probability one to the set C. And suppose that $\mathcal{P}^*$ is nonempty. If we set

$$\eta^* = \beta_T^{-1}\eta, \tag{2.7}$$

and if $P^* \in \mathcal{P}^*$, then $E^*(\eta^*)$ is a possible price that is consistent with the prediction set C. Hence a lower bound for $\mathbb{A}$ is

$$\mathbb{A}' = \sup_{P^* \in \mathcal{P}^*} E^*(\eta^*). \tag{2.8}$$

Technical Point 2 *Specifically, the reason for this is as follows. By the definition of $\mathbb{A}$ in (2.5), for any $\epsilon > 0$, there must exist a super-self-financing strategy V_t (in particular, it must be super-self-financing for all probability distributions which admit an equivalent martingale measure) so that $V_0 \leq \mathbb{A} + \epsilon$, and so that $V_T \geq \eta$ on the set C. For any fixed $P^* \in \mathcal{P}^*$, therefore, V_t is super-self-financing, and hence V_t^* is a P^*-supermartingale. Also $V_T^* \geq \eta^*$ with P^*-probability one (since $P^*(C) = 1$). These two last properties gives rise to $E_{P^*}(\eta^*) \leq E_{P^*}(V_{T^*}) \leq V_0^* = V_0 \leq \mathbb{A} + \epsilon$. Since P^* is arbitrary, it follows that $\mathbb{A}' \leq \mathbb{A} + \epsilon$. Since ϵ was arbitrary nonnegative, it follows that $\mathbb{A}' \leq \mathbb{A}$.*

It will turn out that in many cases, $\mathbb{A} = \mathbb{A}'$. But $\mathbb{A}'$ is also useful in a more primitive way. Suppose one can construct a super-replication V_t on C so that $V_0 \leq \mathbb{A}'$. Then V_t can be taken as our super-replication A_t, and $\mathbb{A} = V_0 = \mathbb{A}'$.

We shall see two cases of this in Section 3.

2.3. The Practical Rôle of Prediction Set Trading: Reserves and Exit Strategies

How does one use this form of trading? If the prediction probability $1 - \alpha$ is set too high, the starting value may be too high given the market price of contingent claims.

There are, however, at least three other ways of using this technology. First of all, it is not necessarily the case that α need to be set all that small. A reasonable way of setting hedges might be to use a 60 or 70% prediction set, and then implement the resulting strategy. It should also be emphasized that an economic agent can use this approach without necessarily violating market equilibrium, cf. Heath and Ku (2004).

On the other hand, one can analyze a possible transaction by finding out what is the smallest α for which a conservative strategy exists with the proposed price as starting value. If this α is too large, the transaction might be better avoided.

A main way of using conservative trading, however, is as a backup device for other strategies, and this is what we shall discuss in the following.

We suppose that a financial institution sells a payoff η (to occur at time T), and that a trading strategy is established on the basis of whatever models, data, or other considerations that the trader or the institution wishes to make. We shall call this the "preferred" strategy, and refer to its current value as V_t.

On the other hand, we also suppose that we have established a conservative strategy, with current value A_t, where the relevant prediction interval has probability $1 - \alpha$. We also assume that a reserve is put in place in the amount of K units of account, where

$$K > A_0 - V_0.$$

The overall strategy is then as follows. One uses the preferred strategy unless or until it eats up the excess reserve over the conservative one. If or when that happens, one switches to the conservative strategy. In other words, one uses the preferred strategy until

$$\tau = \inf\{t : K = A_t^* - V_t^*\} \wedge T$$

where the superscript "$*$" refers, as before, to discounting with respect to whatever security the reserve is invested in. This will normally be a money market account or the discount bond Λ_t. The symbol $a \wedge b$ means $\min(a, b)$.

This trading strategy has the following desirable properties:

• If the prediction set is realized, the net present value of the maximum loss is

$$V_0 + K - \text{ actual sales price of the contingent claim.}$$

• If the reserves allocated to the position are used up, continuing a different sort of hedge would often be an attractive alternative to liquidating the book.
• The trader or the institution does not normally have to use conservative strategies. Any strategy can be used, and the conservative strategy is just a backup.

The latter is particularly important because it does not require any interference with any institution's or trader's standard practice unless the reserve is used up. The trader can use what she (or Risk Management) thinks of as an appropriate model and can even take a certain amount of directional bets until time τ.

The question of how to set the reserve K remains. From a regulatory point of view, it does not matter how this is done, and it is more a reflection of the risk preferences of the trader or the institution. There will normally be a trade-off in that expected return goes up with reserve level K. To determine an appropriate reserve level one would have to look at the actual hedging strategy used. For market-traded or otherwise liquid options one common strategy is to use implied volatility (Beckers, 1981; Bick and Reisman, 1993), or other forms of calibration. The level K can then be evaluated by empirical data. If a strategy is based on theoretical considerations, one can evaluate the distribution of the return for given K based on such a model.

3. OPTIONS HEDGING FROM PREDICTION SETS: THE ORIGINAL CASES

Suppose that a stock follows (2.1) and pays no dividends, and that there is a risk free interest rate r_t. *Both σ_t and r_t can be stochastic and time varying.* We put ourselves in the context of European options, with payoff $f(S_T)$. For future comparison, note that when r and σ are constant, the Black–Scholes (1973) and Merton (1973) price of this option is $B(S_0, \sigma^2 T, rT)$, where

$$B(S, \Xi, R) = \exp(-R) Ef(S \exp(R - \Xi/2 + \sqrt{\Xi}Z)), \tag{3.1}$$

and where Z is standard normal (see, for example, Ch. 6 of Duffie, 1996). In particular, for the call payoff $f(s) = (s - K)^+$,

$$B(S, \Xi, R) = S\Phi(d_1) - K \exp(-R)\Phi(d_2), \tag{3.2}$$

where

$$d_1 = \left(\log(S/K) + R + \Xi/2\right)/\sqrt{\Xi} \tag{3.3}$$

and $d_2 = d_1 - \sqrt{\Xi}$. This will have some importance in the future discussion.

3.1. Pointwise Bounds

This goes back to Avellaneda et al. (1995) and Lyons (1995). See also Frey and Sin (1999) and Frey (2000). In the simplest form, one lets C be the set for which

$$\sigma_t \epsilon [\sigma_-, \sigma_+] \quad \text{for all } t \epsilon [0, T], \tag{3.4}$$

and we let r_t be nonrandom, but possibly time varying. More generally, one can consider bounds on the form

$$\sigma_-(S_t, t) \le \sigma_t \le \sigma_+(S_t, t) \tag{3.5}$$

A super-replicating strategy can now be constructed for European options based on the "Black–Scholes–Barenblatt" equation (cf. Barenblatt, 1978). The price process $V(S_t, t)$ is found using the Black–Scholes partial differential equation, but the term containing the volatility takes on either the upper or lower limit in (3.5), depending on the sign of the second derivative $V_{SS}(s, t)$. In other words, V solves the equation

$$r(V - V_S S) = \frac{\partial V}{\partial t} + \frac{1}{2}S^2 \max_{(3.5)}(\sigma_t^2 V_{SS}), \tag{3.6}$$

with the usual boundary condition $V(S_T, T) = f(S_T)$.

The *rationale* for this is the following. By Itô's Lemma, and assuming that the actual realized σ_t satisfies (3.5), dV_t becomes:

$$
dV(S_t, t) = V_S dS_t + \frac{\partial V}{\partial t} dt + \frac{1}{2} V_{SS} S_t^2 \sigma_t^2 dt
$$

$$
\leq V_S dS_t + \frac{\partial V}{\partial t} dt + \frac{1}{2} S^2 \max_{(3.5)}(\sigma_t^2 V_{SS}) dt \tag{3.7}
$$

$$
= V_S dS_t + (V - V_S S_t)\beta_t^{-1} d\beta_t,
$$

in view of (3.6). Hence $V_t = V(S_t, t)$ is the value of a super-self-financing portfolio, and it covers the option liability by the boundary condition.

To see the relationship to (2.4), note that the process D_t has the form

$$
D_t^* = -\frac{1}{2} \int_0^t S_u^2 \left(\max_{(3.5)}(\sigma_t^2 V_{SS}) - \sigma_t^2 V_{SS} \right) du. \tag{3.8}
$$

This is easily seen by considering (3.6)–(3.7) on the discounted scale.

The reason why V_0 can be taken to be $\mathbb{A}$, is that the stated upper bound coincides with the price for one specific realization of σ_t that is inside the prediction region. Hence, also, V_t can be taken to be A_t.

Pointwise bounds have also been considered by Bergman et al. (1996), El Karoui et al. (1998), and Hobson (1998a), but these papers have concentrated more on robustness than on finding the lowest price $\mathbb{A}$.

3.2. Integral Bounds

This goes back to Mykland (2000), and for the moment, we only consider convex payoffs f (as in puts and calls). The interest rate can be taken to be random, in which case f must also be increasing (as in calls). More general formulae are given in Sections 6.3 and 6.4. The prediction set C has the form

$$
R_0 \geq \int_0^T r_u du \quad \text{and} \quad \Xi_0 \geq \int_0^T \sigma_u^2 du. \tag{3.9}
$$

Following Section 2.2, we show that $\mathbb{A} = B(S_0, \Xi_0, R_0)$ and that a super-replication A_t exists.

Consider the instrument whose value at time t is

$$
V_t = B(S_t, \Xi_t, R_t), \tag{3.10}
$$

where

$$R_t = R_0 - \int_0^t r_u du \quad \text{and} \quad \Xi_t = \Xi_0 - \int_0^t \sigma_u^2 du. \tag{3.11}$$

In Eq. (3.11), r_t and σ_t are the actual observed quantities. As mentioned earlier, they can be time varying and random.

Our claim is that V_t is exactly self-financing. Note that, from differentiating (3.1),

$$\frac{1}{2}B_{SS}S^2 = B_{\Xi} \quad \text{and} \quad -B_R = B - B_S S. \tag{3.12}$$

Also, for calls and puts, the first of the two equations in (3.12) is the well-known relationship between the "gamma" and the "vega" (cf., for example, Chapter 14 of Hull, 1997).

Hence, by Itô's Lemma, dV_t equals:

$$\begin{aligned}
dB(S_t, \Xi_t, R_t) &= B_S dS_t + \frac{1}{2}B_{SS}S_t^2\sigma_t^2 dt + B_{\Xi}d\Xi_t + B_R dR_t \\
&= B_S dS_t + (B - B_S S_t)r_t dt \\
&\quad + \left[\frac{1}{2}B_{SS}S_t^2 - B_{\Xi}\right]\sigma_t^2 dt \\
&\quad + [B - B_S S_t - B_R]r_t dt.
\end{aligned} \tag{3.13}$$

In view of (3.12), the last two lines of (3.13) vanish, and hence there is a self-financing hedging strategy for V_t in S_t and β_t. The "delta" (the number of stocks held) is $B'_S(S_t, \Xi_t, R_t)$.

Furthermore, since $B(S, \Xi, R)$ is increasing in Ξ and R, (3.9) yields that

$$\begin{aligned}
V_T &= B(S_T, \Xi_T, R_T) \\
&\geq \lim_{\Xi\downarrow 0, R\downarrow 0} B(S_T, \Xi, R) \\
&= f(S_T)
\end{aligned} \tag{3.14}$$

almost surely. In other words, one can both synthetically create the security V_t, and one can use this security to cover one's obligations. Note that if r_t is nonrandom (but can be time varying), there is no limit in R in (3.14), and so f does not need to be increasing.

The reason why V_0 can be taken to be $\mathbb{A}$ is the same as in Section 3.1. Also, the stated upper bound coincides with the Black–Scholes (1973) and Merton (1973) price for constant coefficients $r = R_0/T$ and $\sigma^2 = \Xi_0/T$. This is one possible realization satisfying the constraint (3.9). Also, V_t can be taken to be A_t.

3.3. Comparison of Approaches

The main feature of the two approaches described earlier is how similar they are. Apart from having all the features from Section 2, they also have in common that they work "independently of probability." This, of course, is not quite true, because stochastic integrals require the usual probabilistic setup with filtrations and distributions. It does mean, however, that one can think of the set of possible probabilities as being exceedingly large. A stab at an implementation of this is given in Section 5.1.

And then we should discuss the differences. To start on a one-sided note, consider first the results in Table 15.1 for convex European payoffs.

To compare these approaches, note that the function $B(S, \Xi, R)$ is increasing in the argument Ξ. It will therefore be the case that the ordering in Table 15.1 places the lowest value of A_0 at the top and the highest at the bottom. This is since $\sigma^2 T \leq \Xi^+ \leq \sigma_+^2 T$. The latter inequality stems from the fact that Ξ^+ is a prediction bound for an integral of a process, while σ_+^2 is the corresponding bound for the maximum of the same process. In this case, therefore, the average-based interval is clearly better than the extremes-based one in that it provides a lower starting value A_0.

But Table 15.1 is not the full story. This ordering of intervals may not be the case for options that are not of European type. For example, *caplets* (see Hull, 1999; p. 538) on volatility would appear be better handled through extremes-based intervals, though we have not investigated this issue. The problem is, perhaps, best understood in the interest rate context, when comparing caplets with European options on swaps ("swaptions," see Hull, 1999; p. 543). See Carr et al. (2001) and Heath and Ku (2004) for a discussion in terms of coherent measures of risk. To see the connection, note that the average-based procedure, with starting value $A_0 = B(S_0, \Xi^+, rT)$, delivers an actual payoff $A_T = B(S_T, , 0, \Xi^+ - \int_0^T \sigma_u^2 du)$. Hence A_T not only dominates the required payoff

Table 15.1   Comparative prediction sets for convex European options: r constant.

Device	Prediction set	A_0 at time 0	Delta at time t
Black–Scholes	σ constant	$B(S_0, \sigma^2 T, rT)$	$\frac{\partial B}{\partial S}(S_t, \sigma^2(T-t), r(T-t))$
Average-based	$\Xi^- \leq \int_0^T \sigma_u^2 du \leq \Xi^+$	$B(S_0, \Xi^+, rT)$	$\frac{\partial B}{\partial S}(S_t, \Xi^+ - \int_0^t \sigma_u^2 du, r(T-t))$
Extremes-based	$\sigma_- \leq \sigma_t \leq \sigma_+$	$B(S_0, (\sigma^+)^2 T, rT)$	$\frac{\partial B}{\partial S}(S_t, \sigma_+^2(T-t), r(T-t))$

B is defined in (3.2) and (3.3) for call options, and more generally in (3.1). A_0 is the conservative price (2.5). Delta is the hedge ratio (the number of stocks held at time t to super-hedge the option).

$f(S_T)$ on C, but the actual A_T is a combination of option on the security S and swaption on the volatility, in both cases European.

Another issue when comparing the two approaches is how one sets the hedge in each case. In Section 3.2, one uses the actual σ_t (for the underlying security) to set the hedge. In Section 3.1, on the other hand, the hedge itself is based on the worst case nonobserved volatility. In both cases, of course, the price is based on the worst case scenario.

3.4. Trading with Integral Bounds and the Estimation of Consumed Volatility

Volatility is not strictly speaking observable. If one wishes to trade based on the integral-based bounds from Section 3.2, the hedge ratio (delta) at time t, $\frac{\partial B}{\partial S}(S_t, \Xi^+ - \int_0^t \sigma_u^2 du, r(T-t))$, is also not quite observable, but only approximable to a high degree of accuracy.

We here tie in to the literature on *realized volatility*. It is natural to approximate the integral of σ_t^2 by the observed quadratic variation of log S. Specifically, suppose at time t that one has recorded log S_{t_i} for $0 = t_0 < \cdots < t_n \leq t$ (the t_i can be transaction times, or times of quote changes, or from some more regular grid). The observed quadratic variation, a.k.a. the realized volatility, is then given by

$$\hat{\Xi}_t = \sum_{i=1}^{n} (\log S_{t_i} - \log S_{t_{i-1}})^2. \tag{3.15}$$

See Andersen and Bollerslev (1998), Andersen (2000), and Dacorogna et al. (2001) for early econometric contributions on this. The quantity $\hat{\Xi}_t$ converges in probability to $\int_0^t \sigma_u^2 du$ as the points t_i become dense in $[0, t]$, cf. Theorem I.4.47 (p. 52) of Jacod and Shiryaev (1987). Note that the limit of (3.15) is often taken as the definition of the integrated volatility, and it is then denoted by $[\log S, \log S]_t$. This is also called the (theoretical) quadratic variation of log S. More generally, the quadratic covariation between processes X and Y is given by

$$[X, Y]_t = \text{limit in probability of} \sum_{i=1}^{n} (X_{t_i} - X_{t_{i-1}})(Y_{t_i} - Y_{t_{i-1}}) \tag{3.16}$$

as $\Delta t \to 0$. The convergence of $\hat{\Xi}_t$ to Ξ has been heavily investigated in recent years, see, in particular, Jacod and Protter (1998), Barndorff-Nielsen and Shephard (2002), Zhang (2001), and Mykland and Zhang (2006). Under mild regularity conditions, it is shown that $\hat{\Xi}_t - \int_0^t \sigma_u^2 du = O_p(\Delta t^{1/2})$, where Δt is the average distance t/n. It is furthermore the the case that $\Delta t^{-1/2}(\hat{\Xi}_t - \int_0^t \sigma_u^2 du)$ converges, as a process, to a limit which is an integral over a Brownian motion. The convergence in law is "stable." For further details, consult the cited papers.

Subsequent research has revealed that these orders of convergence are optimistic, because of microstructure noise in prices. In this case, rates of convergence of $\Delta^{1/6}$ (Zhang et al., 2005) and $\Delta^{1/4}$ (Barndorff-Nielsen et al., 2008; Jacod et al., 2008; Zhang, 2006) have been found. The estimator $\hat{\Xi}_t$ is also more complicated in these cases, and we refer to the cited papers for details. We also refer to Andersen et al. (2009) in this volume for further discussion and references on realized volatility.

Given a suitable estimator $\hat{\Xi}_t$, the natural hedge ratio at time t for the average-based procedure would therefore be

$$\frac{\partial B}{\partial S}(S_t, \Xi^+ - \hat{\Xi}_t,, r(T-t)). \tag{3.17}$$

The order or convergence of $\hat{\Xi}_t - \Xi_t$ would also be the order of the hedging error relative to using the delta given in Table 15.1. How to adjust the prediction interval accordingly remains to be investigated.

The fact that volatility is only approximately observable may also have an impact on how to define the set of risk neutral measures. In fact, under discrete observation, the set of risk neutral measures that survive even asymptotically as $\Delta t \to 0$ is quite a bit larger than the standard set of such measures. An investigation of this phenomenon in the econometric context is provided by Mykland and Zhang (2007), but the ramifications for financial engineering remain to be explored.

3.5. An Implementation with Data

We here demonstrate by example how one can take data, create a prediction set, and then feed this into the hedging schemes mentioned earlier. We use the band from Section 3.2, and the data analysis of Jacquier et al. (1994), which analyses (among other series) the S&P 500 data recorded daily. The authors consider a stochastic volatility model that is linear on the log scale:

$$d \log(\sigma_t^2) = (a + b \log(\sigma_t^2)) dt + c \, dW_t,$$

in other words, by exact discretization,

$$\log(\sigma_{t+1}^2) = (\alpha + \beta \log(\sigma_t^2)) + \gamma \epsilon_t,$$

where W is a standard Brownian motion and the ϵs are consequently i.i.d. standard normal. In the following we shall suppose that the effects of interest rate uncertainty are negligible. With some assumptions, their posterior distribution, as well as our

Table 15.2   S&P 500: Posterior distribution of $\Xi = \int_0^T \sigma_t^2 dt$ for $T = 1$ year conservative price A_0 corresponding to relevant coverage for at the money call option.

Posterior coverage	50%	80%	90%	95%	99%
Upper end $\sqrt{\Xi}$ of posterior interval	0.168	0.187	0.202	0.217	0.257
Conservative price A_0	9.19	9.90	10.46	11.03	12.54

Posterior is conditional on $\log(\sigma_0^2)$ taking the value of the long run mean of $\log(\sigma^2)$. A_0 is based on prediction set (2.3) with $\Xi^- = 0$. A 5% p.a. known interest rate is assumed. $S_0 = 100$.

corresponding options price, are given in Table 15.2. We follow the custom of stating the volatility *per annum* and on a square root scale.

In the above, we are bypassing the issue of conditioning on σ_0. Our excuse for this is that σ_0 appears to be approximately observable in the presence of high frequency data. Following Foster and Nelson (1996), Zhang (2001), and Mykland and Zhang (2008), the error in observation is of the order $O_p(\Delta t^{1/4})$, where Δt is the average distance between observations. This is in the absence of microstructure; if there is microstructure, Mykland and Zhang (2008) obtains a rate of $O_p(\Delta t^{1/12})$, and conjecture that the best achievable rate will be $O_p(\Delta t^{1/8})$. Comte and Renault (1998) obtain yet another set of rates when σ_t is long-range dependent. What modification has to be made to the prediction set in view of this error remains to be investigated. It may also be that it would be better to condition on some other quantity than σ_0, such as an observable $\hat{\sigma}_0$.

The above does not consider the possibility of also hedging in market-traded options. We return to this in Section 7.

4. PROPERTIES OF TRADING STRATEGIES

4.1. Super-Self-Financing and Supermartingale

The analysis in the preceding sections has been heuristic. To more easily derive results, it is useful to set up a somewhat more theoretical framework. In particular, we are missing a characterization of what probabilities can be applicable, both for the trading strategies, and for the candidate upper bound (2.8).

The discussion in this section will be somewhat more general than what is required for pure prediction sets. We also make use of this development in Section 7 on interpolation, and in Section 8 on (frequentist) confidence and (Bayesian) credible sets. Sharper results, that pertain directly to the pure prediction set problem, will be given in Section 5.

We consider a filtered space $(\Omega, \mathcal{F}, \mathcal{F}_t)_{0 \leq t \leq T}$. The processes $S_t^{(1)}, \ldots, S_t^{(p)}$, r_t, and $\beta_t = \exp\{\int_0^t r_u du\}$ are taken to be adapted to this filtration. The $S^{(i)}$'s are taken to be continuous, though similar theory can most likely be developed in more general cases.

$\mathcal{P}$ is a set of probability distributions on $(\Omega, \mathcal{F})$.

Definition 3 *A property will be said to hold $\mathcal{P} - a.s.$ if it holds $P - a.s.$ for all $P \in \mathcal{P}$.*

"Super-self-financing" now means that the decomposition (2.4) must be valid for all $P \in \mathcal{P}$, but note that H and D may depend on P. The stochastic integral is defined with respect to each P, cf. Section 4.2.

To give the general form of the ask price $\mathbb{A}$, we consider an appropriate set $\mathcal{P}^*$ of "risk neutral" probability distributions P^*.

Definition 4 *Set*

$$\mathcal{N} = \{C \subseteq \Omega : \forall P \in \mathcal{P} \, \exists E \epsilon \mathcal{F} : \ C \subseteq E \quad and \quad P(E) = 0\}. \tag{4.1}$$

$\mathcal{P}^*$ is now defined as the set of probability measures P^* on $\mathcal{F}$ whose null sets include those in $\mathcal{N}$, and for which $S_t^{(1)*}, \ldots, S_t^{(p)*}$ are martingales. We also define $\mathcal{P}^e$ as the set of extremal elements in $\mathcal{P}^*$. P^e is extremal in $\mathcal{P}^*$ if $P^e \in \mathcal{P}^*$ and if, whenever $P^e = a_1 P_1^e + a_2 P_2^e$ for a_1, $a_2 > 0$ and P_1^e, $P_2^e \in \mathcal{P}^*$, it must be the case that $P^e = P_1^e = P_2^e$. Note that $\mathcal{P}^*$ is (typically) not a family of mutually equivalent probability measures.

Subject to regularity conditions, we shall show that there is a super-replicating strategy A_t with initial value $\mathbb{A}$ from (2.5).

First, however, a more basic result, which is useful for understanding super-self-financing strategies.

Theorem 1 *Subject to the regularity conditions stated below, (V_t) is a super-self-financing strategy if and only if (V_t^*) is a càdlàg supermartingale for all $P^* \in \mathcal{P}^*$.*

For example, the set $\mathcal{P}^*$ can be the set of all risk neutral measures satisfying (2.2) or (2.3). For further elaboration, see the longer example below in this section. Also, note that due to possibly stochastic volatility, the approximate observability of local volatility (Section 3.5) does not preclude a multiplicity of risk neutral measures P^*.

A similar result to Theorem 1, obviously, applies to the relationship between subself-financing strategies and submartingales. We return to the regularity conditions below, but for the moment we will focus on the impact of this result. Note that the minimum of two, or even a countable number, of supermartingales, remains a supermartingale. By Theorem 1, the same must then apply to super-self-financing strategies.

Corollary 1 *Subject to the regularity conditions stated below, suppose that there exists a super-replication of η on Ω (the entire space). Then there is a super-replication A_t so that $A_0 = \mathbb{A}$.*

The latter result will be important even when dealing with prediction sets, as we shall see in Section 5.

Technical Conditions 1 *The assumptions required for Theorem 1 and Corollary 1 are as follows. The system: $(\mathcal{F}_t)$ is right continuous; $\mathcal{F}_0$ is the smallest σ-field containing $\mathcal{N}$; the $S_t^{(i)}$ are $\mathcal{P} - a.s.$ continuous and adapted; the short-rate process r_t is adapted, and integrable $\mathcal{P} - a.s.$; every $P \in \mathcal{P}$ has an equivalent martingale measure, that is to say that there is a $P^* \in \mathcal{P}^*$ that is equivalent to P. Define the following conditions. (E_1): "if X is a bounded random variable and there is a $P^* \in \mathcal{P}^*$ so that $E^*(X) > 0$, then there is a $P^e \in \mathcal{P}^e$ so that $E^e(X) > 0$." (E_2): "there is a real number K so that $\{V_T^* \geq -K\}^c \in \mathcal{N}$."*

Theorem 1 now holds supposing that (V_t) is an adapted process, and assuming either

- *condition (E_1) and that the terminal value of the process satisfies:*

$$\sup_{P^* \epsilon \mathcal{P}^*} E^* V_T^{*-} < \infty; \text{ or}$$

- *condition (E_2); or*
- *that (V_t) is continuous.*

Corollary 1 holds under the same system assumptions, and provided either (E_1) and $\sup_{P^* \epsilon \mathcal{P}^*} E^*|\eta^*| < \infty$, or provided $\eta^* \geq -K \, \mathcal{P} - a.s.$ for some K.

Note that under condition (E_2), Theorem 1 is a corollary to Theorem 2.1 (p. 461) of Kramkov (1996). This is because $\mathcal{P}^*$ includes the union of the equivalent martingale measures of the elements in $\mathcal{P}$. For reasons of symmetry, however, we have also sought to study the case where η^* is not bounded below, whence the condition (E_1). The need for symmetry arises from the desire to also study bid prices, cf. (2.6). For example, neither a short call not a short put are bounded below. See Section 4.2.

A requirement in the above results that does need some comment is the one involving extremal probabilities. Condition (E_1) is actually quite weak, as it is satisfied when $\mathcal{P}^*$ is the convex hull of its extremal points. Sufficient conditions for a result of this type are given in Theorems 15.2, 15.3, and 15.12 (pp. 496–498) by Jacod (1979). For example, the first of these results gives the following as a special case (see Section 6). This will cover our examples.

Proposition 1 *Assume the conditions of Theorem 1. Suppose that r_t is bounded below by a nonrandom constant (greater than $-\infty$). Suppose that $(\mathcal{F}_t)$ is the smallest right continuous filtration for which $(\beta_t, S_t^{(1)}, \ldots, S_t^{(p)})$ is adapted and so that $\mathcal{N} \subseteq \mathcal{F}_0$. Let $C \in \mathcal{F}_T$. Suppose that $\mathcal{P}^*$ equals the set of all probabilities P^* so that $(S_t^{(1)*}), \ldots, (S_t^{(p)*})$ are P^*-martingales, and so that $P^*(C) = 1$. Then Condition (E_1) is satisfied.*

Example 1 *To see how the above Proposition works, consider systems with only one stock $(p = 1)$. We let (β_t, S_t) generate $(\mathcal{F}_t)$. A set $C \in \mathcal{F}_T$ will describe our restrictions. For example, C can be* the set given by (2.2) or (2.3). The fact that σ_t is only defined given a probability distribution is not a difficulty here: we consider Ps so that the set C has probability 1 (where quantities like σ_t are defined under P).

One can also work with other types of restrictions. For example, C can be the set of probabilities so that (3.9) is satisfied, and also $\Pi^- \le [r, \sigma]_T \le \Pi^+$, where the covariation "[,]" is defined in (3.16) in Section 3.4. Only the imagination is the limit here.

Hence, $\mathcal{P}$ is the set of all probability distributions P so that $S_0 = s_0$ (the actual value),

$$dS_t = \mu_t S_t dt + \sigma_t S_t dW_t, \tag{4.2}$$

with r_t integrable $P - a.s.$, and bounded below by a nonrandom constant, so that $P(C) = 1$, and so that

$$\exp\left\{ -\int_0^t \lambda_u dW_u - \frac{1}{2}\int_0^t \lambda_u^2 du \right\} \qquad \text{is a P-martingale,} \tag{4.3}$$

where $\lambda_u = (\mu_u - r_u)/\sigma_u$. The condition (4.3) is what one needs for Girsanov's Theorem (see, for example, Karatzas and Shreve, 1991; Theorem 3.5.1) to hold, which is what assures the required existence of equivalent martingale measure. Hence, in view of Proposition 1, Condition (E_1) is taken care of.

To gain more flexibility, one can let $(\mathcal{F}_t)$ be generated by more than one stock, and just let these stocks remain "anonymous." One can then still use condition (E_1). Alternatively, if the payoff is bounded below, one can use condition (E_2).

4.2. Defining Self-Financing Strategies

In essence, H_t being self-financing means that we can represent H_t^* by

$$H_t^* = H_0^* + \sum_{i=1}^{p} \int_0^t \theta_s^{(i)} dS_s^{(i)*}. \tag{4.4}$$

This is in view of numeraire invariance (see, e.g., Section 6B of Duffie, 1996).

Fix $P \in \mathcal{P}$, and recall that the $S_t^{(i)*}$ are continuous. We shall take the stochastic integral to be defined when $\theta_t^{(1)}, \ldots, \theta_t^{(p)}$ is an element in $L_{\text{loc}}^2(P)$, which is the set of p-dimensional predictable processes so that $\int_0^t \theta_u^{(i)2} d[S^{(i)*}, S^{(i)*}]_u$ is locally integrable $P-a.s.$ The stochastic integral (4.4) is then defined by the process in Theorems I.4.31 and I.4.40 (pp. 46–48) by Jacod and Shiryaev (1987).

A restriction is needed to be able to rule out doubling strategies. The two most popular ways of doing that are to insist either that H_t^* be in an L^2-space, or that it be bounded below (Delbaen and Schachermayer, 1995; Dybvig and Huang, 1988; Harrison and Kreps,

1979; Karatzas, 1996; see also Duffie, 1996; Section 6C). We shall here go with a criterion that encompasses both.

Definition 5 *A process H_t, $0 \leq t \leq T$, is self-financing with respect to $S_t^{(1)}, \ldots, S_t^{(p)}$ if H_t^* satisfies (4.4), and if $\{H_\lambda^{*-}, \ 0 \leq \lambda \leq T, \ \lambda$ stopping time$\}$ is uniformly integrable under all $P^* \in \mathcal{P}^*$ that are equivalent to P.*

The reason for seeking to avoid the requirement that H_t^* be bounded below is that, to the extent possible, the same theory should apply equally to bid and ask prices. Because the bid price is normally given by (2.6), securities that are unbounded below will be a common phenomenon. For example, $\mathbb{B}((S - K)^+) = -\mathbb{A}(-(S - K)^+)$, and $-(S - K)^+$ is unbounded below.

It should be emphasized that our definition does, indeed, preclude doubling-type strategies. The following is a direct consequence of optional stopping and Fatou's Lemma.

Proposition 2 *Let $P \in \mathcal{P}$, and suppose that there is at least one $P^* \in \mathcal{P}^*$ that is equivalent to P. Suppose that H_t^* is self-financing in the sense given above. Then, if there are stopping times λ and μ, $0 \leq \lambda \leq \mu \leq T$, so that $H_\mu^* \geq H_\lambda^*$, $P-a.s.$, then $H_\mu^* = H_\lambda^*$, $P-a.s.$*

Note that Proposition 2 is, in a sense, an equivalence. If the conclusion holds for all H_t^*, it must in particular hold for those that Delbaen and Schachermayer (1995) term admissible. Hence, by Theorem 1.4 (p. 929) of their work, P^* exists.

4.3. Proofs for Section 4.1
4.3.1. Proof of Theorem 1

The "only if" part of the result is obvious, so it remains to show the "if" part.

(a) Structure of the Doob–Meyer decomposition of (V_t^*). Fix $P^* \in \mathcal{P}^*$. Let

$$V_t^* = H_t^* + D_t^*, \quad D_0 = 0 \tag{4.5}$$

be the Doob–Meyer decomposition of V_t^* under this distribution. The decomposition is valid by, for example, Theorem 8.22 (p. 83) in Elliot (1982). Then $\{H_\lambda^{*-}, \ 0 \leq \lambda \leq T, \ \lambda$ stopping time$\}$ is uniformly integrable under P^*. This is because $H_t^{*-} \leq V_t^{*-} \leq E^*(|\eta^*| \mid \mathcal{F}_t)$, the latter inequality because $V_t^{*-} = (-V_t^*)^+$, which is a submartingale since V_t^* is a supermartingale. Hence uniform integrability follows by, say, Theorem I.1.42(b) (p. 11) of Jacod and Shiryaev (1987).

(b) Under condition (E$_1$), (V_t) can be written $V_t^* = V_t^{*c} + V_t^{*d}$, where (V_t^{*c}) is a continuous supermartingale for all $P^* \in \mathcal{P}^*$, and (V_t^{*d}) is a nonincreasing process. Consider the set C of $\omega \in \Omega$ so that $\Delta V_t^* \leq 0$ for all t, and so that $V_t^{*d} = \sum_{s \leq t} \Delta V_s^*$ is well defined. We want to show that the complement $C^c \in \mathcal{N}$. To this end, invoke Condition (E$_1$), which means that we only have to prove that $P^e(C) = 1$ for all $P^e \in \mathcal{P}^e$.

Fix, therefore, $P^e \in \mathcal{P}^e$, and let H_t^* and D_t^* be given by the Doob–Meyer decomposition (4.5) under this distribution. By Proposition 11.14 (p. 345) in Jacod (1979), P^e is extremal in the set $M(\{S^{(1)*}, \ldots, S^{(p)*}\})$ (in Jacod's notation), and so it follows from Theorem 11.2 (p. 338) in the same work, that (H_t^*) can be represented as a stochastic integral over the $(S_t^{(i)*})$'s, whence (H_t^*) is continuous. $P^e(C) = 1$ follows.

To see that (V_t^{*c}) is a supermartingale for any given $P^* \in \mathcal{P}^*$, note that Condition (E_1) again means that we only have to prove this for all $P^e \in \mathcal{P}^e$. The latter, however, follows from the decomposition in the previous paragraph. (b) follows.

(c) (V_t^*) is a super-replication of η. Under condition (E_2), the result follows directly from Theorem 2.1 (p. 461) of Kramkov (1996). Under the other conditions stated, by (b) above, one can take (V_t^*) to be continuous without losing generality. Hence, by local boundedness, the result also in this case follows from the cited theorem of Kramkov's.

4.3.2. Proof of Corollary 1

Let $(V_t^{(n)})$ be a super-replication satisfying $V_0^{(n)} \le \mathbb{A} + 1/n$. Set $V_t = \inf_n V_t^{(n)}$. (V_t) is a supermartingale for all $P^* \in \mathcal{P}^*$. By Proposition 1.3.14 (p. 16) in Karatzas and Shreve (1991), (V_{t+}^*) (taken as a limit through rationals) exists and is a càdlàg supermartingale except on a set in $\mathcal{N}$. Hence (V_{t+}^*) is a super-replication of η, with initial value no greater than $\mathbb{A}$. The result follows from Theorem 1.

4.3.3. Proof of Proposition 1

Suppose that $r_t \ge -c$ for some $c < \infty$. We use Theorem (15.2c) (p. 496) by Jacod (1979). This theorem requires the notation $Ss^1(X)$, which is the set of probabilities under which the process X_t is indistinguishable from a submartingale so that $E \sup_{0 \le s \le t} |X_s| < \infty$ for all t (in our case, t is bounded, so things simplify). (cf. p. 353 and 356 of Jacod, 1979).

Jacod's result (15.2c) studies, among other things, the set (in Jacod's notation) $S = \bigcap_{X \in \mathcal{X}} Ss^1(X)$, and under conditions which are satisfied if we take $\mathcal{X}$ to consist of our processes $S_t^{(1)*}, \ldots, S_t^{(p)*}, -S_t^{(1)*}, \ldots, -S_t^{(p)*}, \beta_t e^{ct}, Y_t$. Here, $Y_t = 1$ for $t < T$, and I_C for $t = T$. (If necessary, $\beta_t e^{ct}$ can be localized to be bounded, which makes things messier but yields the same result). In other words, S is the set of probability distributions so that the $S_t^{(1)*}, \ldots, S_t^{(p)*}$ are martingales, r_t is bounded below by c, and the probability of C is one.

Theorem 15.2(c) now asserts a representation of all the elements in the set S in terms of its extremal points. In particular, any set that has probability zero for the extremal elements of S also has probability zero for all other elements of S.

However, $S = \widetilde{M}(\{S^{(1)*}, \ldots, S^{(p)*}\})$ (again in Jacod's notation, see p. 345 of that work) – this is the set of extremal probabilities among those making $S^{(1)*}, \ldots, S^{(p)*}$ a martingale. Hence, our Condition (E_1) is proved.

5. PREDICTION SETS: GENERAL THEORY

5.1. The Prediction Set Theorem

In the preceding section, we did not take a position on the set of possible probabilities. As mentioned at the beginning of Section 3.3, one can let this set be exceedingly large. Here is one stab at this, in the form of the set Q.

Assumption A (System assumptions): *Our probability space is the set* $\Omega = \mathbb{C}[0, T]^{p+1}$, *and we let* $(\beta_t, S_t^{(1)}, \ldots, S_t^{(p)})$ *be the coordinate process,* $\mathcal{B}$ *is the Borel* σ-*field, and* $(\mathcal{B}_t)$ *is the corresponding Borel filtration. We let* Q^* *be the set of all distributions* P^* *on* $\mathcal{B}$ *so that*

(i) $(\log \beta_t)$ *is absolutely continuous* P^*−*a.s., with derivative* r_t *bounded (above and below) by a nonrandom constant,* P^*−*a.s.;*

(ii) *the* $S_t^{(i)*} = \beta_t^{-1} S_t^{(i)}$ *are martingales under* P^*;

(iii) $[\log S^{(i)*}, \log S^{(i)*}]_t$ *is absolutely continuous* P^*−*a.s. for all i, with derivative (above and below) by a nonrandom constant,* P^*−*a.s. As before, "[,]" is the quadratic variation of the process, see our definition in (3.16) in Section 3.4;*

(iv) $\beta_0 = 1$ *and* $S_0^{(i)} = s_0^{(i)}$ *for all i.*

We let $(\mathcal{F}_t)$ *be the smallest right continuous filtration containing* $(\mathcal{B}_{t+})$ *and all sets in* $\mathcal{N}$, *given by*

$$\mathcal{N} = \{F \subseteq \Omega : \forall P^* \in Q^* \; \exists E \epsilon \mathcal{B} : \; F \subseteq E \text{ and } P^*(E) = 0\}. \tag{5.1}$$

and we let the information at time t be given by $\mathcal{F}_t$. *Finally, we let* Q *be all distributions on* $\mathcal{F}_T$ *that are equivalent (mutually absolutely continuous) to a distribution in* Q^*. *If we need to emphasize the dependence of* Q *on* $s_0 = (s_0^{(1)}, \ldots, s_0^{(p)})$, *we write* Q_{s_0}.

Remark *An important fact is that* $\mathcal{F}_t$ *is analytic for all t, by Theorem III.10 (p. 42) in Dellacherie and Meyer (1978). Also, the filtration* $(\mathcal{F}_t)$ *is right continuous by construction.* $\mathcal{F}_0$ *is a noninformative (trivial)* σ-*field. The relationship of* $\mathcal{F}_0$ *to information from the past (before time zero) is established in Section 5.3.*

The reason for considering this set Q as our world of possible probability distributions is the following. Stocks and other financial instruments are commonly assumed to follow processes of the form (2.1) or a multidimensional equivalent. The set Q now corresponds to all probability laws on this form, subject only to certain integrability requirements (for details, see, for example, the version of Girsanov's Theorem given by Karatzas and Shreve, 1991; Theorem 3.5.1). Also, if these requirements fail, the S's do not have an equivalent martingale measure, and it can therefore not normally model a traded security (see Delbaen and Schachermayer, 1995; for precise statements). In other words, roughly speaking, the set Q covers all distributions of traded securities that have a form (2.1).

Typical forms of the prediction set C would be those discussed in Section 3. If there are several securities $S_t^{(i)}$, one can also set up prediction sets for the quadratic variations and covariations (volatilities and cross-volatilities, in other words). It should be noted that one has to exercise some care in how to formally define the set C corresponding to (2.1) – see the development in Sections 5.2 and 5.3 below.

The price A_0 is now as follows. A subset of $\mathcal{Q}^*$ is given by

$$\mathcal{P}^* = \{P^* \in \mathcal{Q}^* \; : \; P^*(C) = 1\}. \tag{5.2}$$

The price is then, from Theorem 2 below,

$$A_0 = \sup \left\{ E^*(\eta^*) : P^* \epsilon \mathcal{P}^* \right\}, \tag{5.3}$$

where E^* is the expectation with respect to P^*, and

$$\eta^* = \exp \left\{ -\int_0^T r_u du \right\} \eta. \tag{5.4}$$

It should be emphasized that though (5.2) only involves probabilities that give measure 1 to the set C, this is *only a computational device*. The prediction set C can have any real prediction probability $1 - \alpha$, cf. statement (5.7) below. The point of Theorem 2 is to reduce the problem from $1 - \alpha$ to 1, and hence to the discussion in Sections 3 and 4.

We assume the following structure for C.

Definition 6 *A set C in $\mathcal{F}_T$ is $\mathcal{Q}^*$-closed if, whenever P_n^* is a sequence in $\mathcal{Q}^*$ for which P_n^* converges weakly to P^* and so that $P_n^*(C) \to 1$, then $P^*(C) = 1$. Weak convergence is here relative to the usual supremum norm on $\mathbb{C}^{p+1} = \mathbb{C}^{p+1}[0, T]$, the coordinate space for $(\beta., S_.^{(1)}, \ldots, S_.^{(p)})$.*

Obviously, C is $\mathcal{Q}^*$-closed if it is closed in the supremum norm, but the opposite need not be true. See Section 5.2 below.

The precise result is as follows. Note that $-K$ is a credit constraint; see below in this section.

Theorem 2 (Prediction Region Theorem): *Let Assumptions (A) hold. Let C be a $\mathcal{Q}^*$-closed set, $C \in \mathcal{F}_T$. Suppose that $\mathcal{P}^*$ is nonempty. Let*

$$\eta = \theta(\beta., S_.^{(1)}, \ldots, S_.^{(p)}), \tag{5.5}$$

where θ is continuous on Ω (with respect to the supremum norm) and bounded below by $-K\beta_T$, where K is a nonrandom constant ($K \geq 0$). We suppose that

$$\sup_{P^* \in \mathcal{P}^*} E^* |\eta^*| < \infty \tag{5.6}$$

Then there is a super-replication (A_t) of η on C, valid for all $Q \in \mathcal{Q}$, whose starting value is A_0 given by (5.3). Furthermore, $A_t \geq -K\beta_t$ for all t, $\mathcal{Q}$–a.s.

In particular,

$$Q(A_T \geq \eta) \ \geq \ Q(C) \text{ for all } Q \in \mathcal{Q} \,, \tag{5.7}$$

and this is, roughly, how a $1 - \alpha$ prediction set can be converted into a trading strategy that is valid with at least the same probability. This works both in the frequentist and Bayesian cases, as described in Section 5.2. Note that both in Theorem 2 and in Eq. (5.7), Q refers to all probabilities in $\mathcal{Q}$, and not only the "risk neutral" ones in $\mathcal{Q}^*$.

The form of A_0 and the super-replicating strategy is discussed earlier in Section 3 and later in Sections 6 and 7 for European options.

The condition that θ be bounded below can be seen as a restriction on credit. Since K is arbitrary, this is not severe. Note that the credit limit is more naturally stated on the discounted scale: $\eta^* \geq -K$ and $A_t^* \geq K$. See also Section 4.2, where a softer bound is used.

The finiteness of credit has another implication. The portfolio (A_t), because it is bounded below, also solves another problem. Let I_C and $I_{\tilde{C}}$ be the indicator functions for C and its complement. A corollary to the statement in Theorem 2 is that (A_t) super-replicates the random variable $\eta' = \eta I_C - K\beta_T I_{\tilde{C}}$. And here we refer to the more classical definition: the super-replication is $\mathcal{Q} - a.s.$, on the entire probability space. This is for free: A_0 has not changed.

It follows that A_0 can be expressed as $\sup_{P^* \in \mathcal{Q}^*} E^*((\eta')^*)$, in obvious notation. Of course, this is a curiosity, because this expression depends on K while A_0 does not.

5.2. Prediction Sets: A Problem of Definition

A main example of this theory is where one has prediction sets for the cumulative interest $-\log \beta_T = \int_0^T r_u du$ and for quadratic variations $[\log S^{(i)*}, \log S^{(j)*}]_T$. For the cumulative interest, the application is straightforward. For example, $\{R^- \leq -\log \beta_T \leq R^+\}$ is a well defined and closed set. For the quadratic (co-)variations, however, one runs into the problem that these are only defined relative to the probability distribution under which they live. In other words, if F is a region in $\mathbb{C}[0, T]^q$, and

$$C_Q = \{(-\log \beta_t, [\log S^{(i)*}, \log S^{(j)*}]_t, i \leq j)_{0 \leq t \leq T} \in F\}, \tag{5.8}$$

then, as the notation suggests, C_Q will depend on $Q \in \mathcal{Q}$. This is not permitted by Theorem 2. The trading strategy cannot be allowed to depend on an unknown $Q \in \mathcal{Q}$, and so neither can the set C. To resolve this problem, and to make the theory more directly operational, the following Proposition 3 shows that C_Q has a modification that is independent of Q, and that satisfies the conditions of Theorem 2.

Proposition 3 *Let F be a set in $\mathbb{C}[0, T]^q$, where $q = \frac{1}{2}p(p-1) + 1$. Let F be closed with respect to the supremum norm on $\mathbb{C}[0, T]^q$. Let C_Q be given by (5.8). Then there is a Q^*-closed set C in $\mathcal{F}_T$ so that, for all $Q \in \mathcal{Q}$,*

$$Q\left(C \Delta C_Q\right) = 0, \tag{5.9}$$

where Δ refers to the symmetric difference between sets.

Only the existence of C matters, not its precise form. The reason for this is that relation (5.9) implies that C_{P*} and C_Q can replace C in (5.2) and (5.7), respectively. For the two prediction sets on which our discussion is centered, (2.3) uses

$$F = \{(x_t)_{0 \le t \le T} \in \mathbb{C}[0, T], \text{ nondecreasing} : x_0 = 0 \text{ and } \Xi^- \le x_T \le \Xi^+\},$$

whereas (3.5) relies on

$$F = \{(x_t)_{0 \le t \le T} \in \mathbb{C}[0, T], \text{ nondecreasing} : x_0 = 0 \text{ and}$$
$$\forall s, t \in [0, T], \ s \le t : \ \sigma_-^2(t-s) \le x_t - x_s \le \sigma_+^2(t-s)\}.$$

One can go all the way and jettison the set C altogether. Combining Theorem 2 and Proposition 3 immediately yields such a result:

Theorem 3 (Prediction Region Theorem, without Prediction Region): *Let Assumptions (A) hold. Let F be a set in $\mathbb{C}[0, T]^q$, where $q = \frac{1}{2}p(p-1) + 1$. Suppose that F is closed with respect to the supremum norm on $\mathbb{C}[0, T]^q$. Let C_Q be given by (5.8), for every $Q \in \mathcal{Q}$. Replace C by C_{P*} in Eq. (5.2), and suppose that $\mathcal{P}^*$ is nonempty. Impose the same conditions on $\theta(\cdot)$ and $\eta = \theta(\beta., S.^{(1)}, \ldots, S.^{(p)})$ as in Theorem 2. Then there exists a self-financing portfolio (A_t), valid for all $Q \in \mathcal{Q}$, whose starting value is A_0 given by (5.3), and which satisfies (5.7). Furthermore, $A_t \ge -K\beta_t$ for all t, Q–a.s.*

It is somewhat unsatisfying that there is no prediction region anymore, but, of course, C is there, underlying Theorem 3. The latter result, however, is easier to refer to in practice.

It should be emphasized that it is possible to extend the original space to include a volatility coordinate. Hence, if prediction sets are given on forms like (2.2) or (2.3), one *can* take the set to be given independently of probability. In fact, this is how Proposition 3 is proved.

In the case of European options, this may provide a "probability free" derivation of Theorem 2. Under the assumption that the volatility is defined independently of probability distribution, Föllmer (1979) and Bick and Willinger (1994) provide a nonprobabilistic derivation of Itô's formula, and this can be used to show Theorem 2 in the European case. Note, however, that this nonprobabilistic approach would have a harder time with exotic options, because there is (at this time) no corresponding martingale representation theorem, either for the known probability case [as in Jacod (1979)] or in the unknown probability case (as in Kramkov, 1996; Mykland, 2000). Also, the probability free approach exhibits a dependence on subsequences (see the discussion starting in the last paragraph on p. 350 of Bick and Willinger, 1994).

5.3. Prediction Regions from Historical Data: A Decoupled Procedure

Until now, we have behaved as if the prediction sets or prediction limits were nonrandom, fixed, and not based on data. This, of course, would not be the case with statistically obtained sets.

Consider the situation where one has a method giving rise to a prediction set $\widehat{C}$. For example, if $C(\Xi^-, \Xi^+)$ is the set from (2.3), then, a prediction set might look like $\widehat{C} = C(\widehat{\Xi}^-, \widehat{\Xi}^+)$, where $\widehat{\Xi}^-$ and $\widehat{\Xi}^+$ are quantities that are determined (and observable) at time 0.

At this point, one runs into a certain number of difficulties. First of all, C, as given by (2.2) or (2.3), is not well defined, but this is solved through Proposition 3 and Theorem 3. In addition, there is a question of whether the prediction set(s), A_0, and the process (A_t) are measurable when the functions of data available at time zero. We return to this issue at the end of this section.

From an applied perspective, however, there is a considerably more crucial matter that comes up. It is the question of connecting the model for statistical inference with the model for trading.

What we advocate is the following two-stage procedure: (1) find a prediction set C by statistical or other methods, and then (2) trade conservatively using the portfolio that has value A_t. When statistics is used, there are two probability models involved, one for each stage.

We have so far been explicit about the model for Stage (2). This is the nonparametric family $\mathcal{Q}$. For the purpose of inference – Stage (1) – the statistician may, however, wish to use a different family of probabilities. It could also be nonparametric, or it could be any number of parametric models. The choice might depend on the amount and quality of data, and on other information available.

Suppose that one considers an overall family Θ of probability distributions P. If one collects data on the time interval $[T_-, 0]$, and sets the prediction interval based on these data, the $P \in \Theta$ could be probabilities on $\mathbb{C}[T_-, T]^{p+1}$. More generally, we suppose that the P's are distributions on $\mathcal{S} \times \mathbb{C}[0, T]$, where $\mathcal{S}$ is a complete and separable metric space. This permits more general information to go into the setting of the prediction interval. We let $\mathcal{G}_0$ be the Borel σ-field on $\mathcal{S}$. As a matter of notation, we assume that $S_0 = (S_0^{(1)}, \ldots, S_0^{(p)})$ is $\mathcal{G}_0$-measurable. Also, we let P_ω be the regular conditional probability on $\mathbb{C}[0, T]^{p+1}$ given $\mathcal{G}_0$. (P_ω is well defined; see, for example p. 265 in Ash, 1972). A meaningful passage from inference to trading then requires the following.

Nesting Condition 1 *For all $P \in \Theta$, and for all $\omega \in \mathcal{S}$, $P_\omega \in \mathcal{Q}_{S_0}$.*

In other words, we do not allow the statistical model Θ to contradict the trading model $\mathcal{Q}$.

The inferential procedure might then consist of a mapping from the data to a random closed set $\hat{F}$. The prediction set is formed using (5.8), yielding

$$\hat{C}_Q = \{(-\log \beta_t, [\log S^{(i)*}, \log S^{(j)*}]_t, i \leq j)_{0 \leq t \leq T} \in \hat{F}\},$$

for each $Q \in \mathcal{Q}_{S_0}$. Then proceed via Proposition 3 and Theorem 2, or use Theorem 3 for a shortcut. In either case, obtain a conservative ask price and a trading strategy. Call these $\hat{A}_0$ and $\hat{A}_t$. For the moment, suspend disbelief about measurability.

To return to the definition of prediction set, it is now advantageous to think of this set as being $\hat{F}$. This is because there are more than one C_Q, and because C is only defined up to measure zero. The definition of a $1 - \alpha$ prediction set can then be taken as a requirement that

$$P(\{(-\log \beta_t, [\log S^{(i)*}, \log S^{(j)*}]_t, i \leq j)_{0 \leq t \leq T} \in \hat{F}\} \mid \mathcal{H}) \geq 1 - \alpha. \tag{5.10}$$

In the frequentist setting, (5.10) must hold for all $P \in \Theta$. $\mathcal{H}$ is a sub-σ-field of $\mathcal{G}_0$, and in the purely unconditional case, it is trivial. By (5.7), $P(\hat{A}_T \geq \eta \mid \mathcal{H}) \geq 1 - \alpha$, again for all $P \in \Theta$.

In the Bayesian setting, $\mathcal{H} = \mathcal{G}_0$, and $P(\cdot \mid \mathcal{H})$ is a mixture of P_ω's with respect to the posterior distribution $\hat{\pi}$ at time zero. As mentioned after Eq. (5.7), the mixture would again be in $\mathcal{Q}_{S_0}$, subject to some regularity. Again, (5.7) would yield that $P(\hat{A}_T \geq \eta \mid \mathcal{H}) \geq 1 - \alpha$, a.s.

In this discussion, we do not confront the questions that are raised by setting prediction sets by asymptotic methods. Such approximation is almost inevitable in the frequentist setting. For important contributions to the construction of prediction sets, see Barndorff-Nielsen and Cox (1996) and Smith (1999), and the references therein.

It may seem odd to argue for an approach that uses different models for inference and trading, even if the first is nested in the other. We call this the *decoupled prediction approach*. A main reason for doing this is that we have taken inspiration from the cases studied in Sections 3, 6, and 7. One can consider alternatives, however, cf. Section 8 below.

To round off this discussion, we return to the question of measurability. There are (at least) three functions of the data where the measurability is in question: (i) the prediction set $\hat{F}$, (ii) the prediction probabilities (5.10), and (iii) the starting value ($\hat{A}_0$).

We here only consider (ii) and (iii), as the first question is heavily dependent on Θ and $\mathcal{S}$. In fact, we shall take the measurability of $\hat{F}$ for granted.

Let $\boldsymbol{F}$ be the collection of closed subsets F of $\mathbb{C}[0, T]^q$. We can now consider the following two maps:

$$\boldsymbol{F} \times \mathcal{S} \to \mathbb{R} : (F, \omega) \to P_\omega(\{(-\log \beta_t, [\log S^{(i)*}, \log S^{(j)*}]_t, i \leq j)_{0 \leq t \leq T} \in F) \tag{5.11}$$

and

$$\boldsymbol{F} \times \mathbb{R}^{p+1} \to \mathbb{R} : (F, x) \to A_0 = A_0^F(x). \tag{5.12}$$

Oh, yes, and we need a σ-field on $\boldsymbol{F}$. How can we otherwise do measurability? Make the detour via convergence; $F_n \to F$ if $\limsup F_n = \liminf F_n = F$, which is the same as saying that the indicator functions I_{F_n} converge to I_F pointwise. On $\boldsymbol{F}$, this convergence is metrizable (see the Proof of Proposition 4 for one such metric). Hence $\boldsymbol{F}$ has a Borel σ-field. This is our σ-field.

Proposition 4 *Let Assumptions (A) hold. Impose the same conditions on $\theta(\cdot)$ and $\eta = \theta(\beta., S.^{(1)}, \ldots, S.^{(p)})$ as in Theorem 2. Then the maps (5.11) and (5.12) are measurable.*

If we now *assume* that the map $\mathcal{S} \to \boldsymbol{F}, \omega \to \hat{F}$, is measurable, then standard considerations yield the measurability of $\mathcal{S} \to \mathbb{R}, \omega \to P_\omega(\{(-\log \beta_t, [\log S^{(i)*}, \log S^{(j)*}]_t, i \leq j)_{0 \leq t \leq T} \in \hat{F})$, and $\mathcal{S} \times \mathbb{R}^{p+1} \to \mathbb{R}, (\omega, x) \to \hat{A}_0 = A_0^{\hat{F}}$. Hence problem (iii) is solved, and the resolution of (ii) follows since (5.11) equals the expected value of $P_\omega(\{(-\log \beta_t, [\log S^{(i)*}, \log S^{(j)*}]_t, i \leq j)_{0 \leq t \leq T} \in \hat{F})$, given $\mathcal{H}$, both in the Bayesian and frequentist cases.

5.4. Proofs for Section 5
5.4.1. Proof of Theorem 2
Assume the conditions of Theorem 2. Let $m \geq K$, and define $\theta^{(m)}$ by

$$\theta^{(m)}(\beta., S.^{(1)}, \ldots, S.^{(p)}) = \theta(\beta., S.^{(1)}, \ldots, S.^{(p)}) I_C(\beta., S.^{(1)}, \ldots, S.^{(p)})$$
$$- m\beta_T I_{\tilde{C}}(\beta., S.^{(1)}, \ldots, S.^{(p)}),$$

where $\tilde{C}$ is the complement of C.

On the other hand, for given probability $P^* \in \mathcal{Q}^*$, define σ_u^{ij} by

$$[\log S^{(i)*}, \log S^{(j)*}]_t = \int_0^t \sigma_u^{ij} du.$$

Also, for c as a positive integer, or $c = +\infty$, set

$$\mathcal{Q}_c^* = \left\{ P^* \in \mathcal{Q}^* : \sup_t |r_t| + \sum_i \sigma_t^{ii} \leq c \right\}.$$

Let $\mathcal{P}_c^*$ be the set of all distributions in $\mathcal{Q}_c^*$ that vanish outside C. Under Assumptions (A), there is a $c_0 < +\infty$ so that $\mathcal{P}_c^*$ is nonempty for $c \geq c_0$. Also, consider the set $\mathcal{Q}_c^*(t)$ of distributions on $\mathbb{C}[t, T]^{p+1}$ satisfying the same requirements as those above, but instead of (iv) (in Assumption A) that, for all $u \in [0, t]$, $\beta_u = 1$ and $S_u^{(i)} = 1$ for all i.

(1) First, let $c_0 \leq c < +\infty$. Below, we shall make substantial use of the fact that the space $\mathcal{Q}_c^*(t)$ is compact in the weak topology. To see this, invoke Propositons VI.3.35, VI.3.36, and Theorem VI.4.13 (pp. 318 and 322) by Jacod and Shiryaev (1987)).

Consider the functional $\mathbb{C}[0, t]^{p+1} \times \mathcal{Q}_c^*(t) \to \mathbb{R}$ given by

$$\theta_t^{(m)}\left(b_., s_.^{(1)}, \ldots, s_.^{(p)}, P^*\right) = E^* b_t \beta_T^{-1} \theta^{(m)}\left(b.\beta_., s_.^{(1)} S_.^{(1)}, \ldots, s_.^{(p)} S_.^{(p)}\right).$$

Also, set, for $m \geq K$,

$$\theta_t^{(m)} = \left(b_., s_.^{(1)}, \ldots, s_.^{(p)}\right) = \sup_{P^* \in \mathcal{Q}_c^*(t)} \theta_t^{(m)}\left(b_., s_.^{(1)}, \ldots, s_.^{(p)}, P^*\right).$$

The supremum is $\mathcal{F}_t$-measurable since this σ-field is analytic (see Remark 1), and since the space $\mathcal{Q}_c^*(t)$ is compact in the weak topology. The result then follows from Theorems III.9 and III.13 (pp. 42–43) by Dellacherie and Meyer (1978); see also the treatment in Pollard (1984), pp. 196–197.

Since, again, the space $\mathcal{Q}_c^*(t)$ is compact in the weak topology, it follows that the supremum is a bounded. By convergence, $A_t^{(m)*} = \beta_t^{-1} \theta_t^{(m)}(\beta_., S_.^{(1)}, \ldots, S_.^{(p)})$ is an $(\mathcal{F}_t)$-supermartingale for all $P^* \in \mathcal{Q}_c^*$. Also, in consequence, $(A_t^{(m)*})$ can be taken to be càdlàg, since $(\mathcal{F}_t)$ is right continuous. This is by the construction in Proposition I.3.14 (pp. 16–17) of Karatzas and Shreve (1991). Set $A_t^{(m)} = \beta_t A_t^{(m)*}$ (the càdlàg version).

(2) Consider the special case where $\eta = -K\beta_T$, and call $\widetilde{A}_t^{(m)*}$ the resulting supermartingale. Note that $\widetilde{A}_t^{(m)*} \leq -K$ on the entire space, and set

$$\tau = \inf\{t : \widetilde{A}_t^{(m)*} < -K\}.$$

τ is an $\mathcal{F}_t$ stopping time by Example I.2.5 (p. 6) of Karatzas and Shreve (1991).

By definition, $A_t^{(m)*} \geq \widetilde{A}_t^{(m*)}$ everywhere. Because both are supermartingales, we can consider a modified version of $A_t^{(m)*}$ so that it takes new value

$$A_t^{(m)} = \lim_{u \uparrow \tau} A_u^{(m)} \quad \text{for } \tau \leq t \leq T$$

In view of Proposition I.3.14 (again) by Karatzas and Shreve (1991), this does not interfere with the supermartingale property of $A_t^{(m)*}$.

Now observe two particularly pertinent facts: (i) The redefinition of $A^{(m)}$ does not affect the initial value, since $\mathcal{P}_c^*$ is nonempty, and (ii) $A_t^{(m)} = A_t^{(K)}$ for all t, since $m \geq K$.

(3) On the basis of this, one can conclude that

$$A_0^{(K)} = \sup_{P^* \in \mathcal{P}_c^*} E^*(\eta^*), \tag{5.13}$$

as follows. By the weak compactness of $\mathcal{Q}_c^*$, there is a P_m^* be such that for given $(b_0, s_0^{(1)}, \ldots, s_0^{(p)}), \theta_0^{(m)}(b., s.^{(1)}, \ldots, s.^{(p)}) \le \theta_0^{(m)}(b., s.^{(1)}, \ldots, s.^{(p)}, P_m^*) + m^{-1}$.

Also, there is a subsequence $P_{m_k}^*$ that converges weakly to some P^*.

Recall that m is fixed, and $-$ is greater than K. It is then true that, for $m_k \ge m$, and with $\tilde{C}$ denoting the complement of C,

$$
\begin{aligned}
A_0^{(K)*} = A_0^{(m)*} &= \theta_0^{(m)}\left(b_0, s_0^{(1)}, \ldots, s_0^{(p)}\right) \\
&\le \theta_0^{(m_k)}\left(b_0, s_0^{(1)}, \ldots, s_0^{(p)}, P_{m_k}^*\right) + m_k^{-1} \\
&\le E_{m_k}^* \beta_T^{-1} \theta\left(\beta., S.^{(1)}, \ldots, S.^{(p)}\right) + P_{m_k}^*(\tilde{C})(K - m_k) + m_k^{-1} \qquad (5.14) \\
&\le E_{m_k}^* \beta_T^{-1} \theta\left(\beta., S.^{(1)}, \ldots, S.^{(p)}\right) + P_{m_k}^*(\tilde{C})(K - m) + m_k^{-1} \\
&\le E^* \beta_T^{-1} \theta\left(\beta., S.^{(1)}, \ldots, S.^{(p)}\right) + \limsup_{m \to +\infty} P_{m_k}^*(\tilde{C})(K - m) + o(1)
\end{aligned}
$$

as $k \to \infty$. The first term on the right-hand side of (5.14) is bounded by the weak compactness of $\mathcal{Q}_c^*$. The left-hand side is a fixed, finite, number. Hence, $\limsup P_{m_k}^*(\tilde{C}) = 0$. By the $\mathcal{Q}^*$-closedness of C, it follows that $P^*(C) = 1$.

Hence, (5.14) yields that the right-hand side in (5.13) is an upper bound for $A_0^{(K)*} = A_0^{(m)*}$. Since this is also trivially a lower bound, (5.13) follows.

(4) Now make $A_t^{(m)}$ dependent on c, by writing $A_t^{(m,c)}$. For all $Q^* \in \mathcal{Q}^*$, the $A_t^{(m,c)*}$ are all Q^*-supermartingales, bounded below by $-m$. $A_t^{(m,c)*}$ is nondecreasing in c. Let $A_t^{(m,\infty)}$ denote the limit as $c \to +\infty$. By Fatou's Lemma, for $Q^* \in \mathcal{Q}^*$, and for $s \le t$,

$$E^*\left(A_t^{(m,\infty)*} | \mathcal{F}_s\right) \le \liminf_{c \to +\infty} E^*\left(A_t^{(m,c)*} | \mathcal{F}_s\right) = \liminf_{c \to +\infty} A_s^{(m,c)*} = A_s^{(m,\infty)*}.$$

Hence, $A_t^{(m,\infty)*}$ is a supermartingale for all $m \ge K$. Also, by construction, $A_T^{(m,\infty)*} \ge \eta^*$. By the results of Kramkov (1996) or Mykland (2000), $A_{t+}^{(m,\infty)}$ is, therefore, a super-replication of η.

For the case of $t = 0$, (5.13) yields that

$$A_0^{(m,\infty)} = \sup_{P^* \in \mathcal{P}^*} E^*(\eta^*), \tag{5.15}$$

where the nonobvious inequality ($\ge$) follows from the monotone convergence, and assumption (5.7). Since one can choose $m = K$, Theorem 2 is proved.

5.4.2. Proof of Proposition 3

Extend the space $\mathbb{C}^{p+1}$ to $\mathbb{C}^{p+q}$. Consider the set $\widetilde{Q}$ of probabilities Q on $\mathbb{C}^{p+q}$ for which the projection onto $\mathbb{C}^{p+1}$ is in Q^* and so that $([\log S^{(i)*}, \log S^{(j)*}]_t, i \leq j)$ are indistinguishable from $(x_t^{(k)}, k = p+2, \ldots, p+q)$. Now consider the set $F' = \{\omega : (-\log \beta, x^{(p+2)}, \ldots, x^{(p+q)}) \in F\}$. Note that F' is in the completion of $\mathcal{F}_t \otimes \{\mathbb{C}^{q-1}, \emptyset\}$ with respect to $\widetilde{Q}$. Hence, there is a C in $\mathcal{F}_T$ so that $P^*(C \Delta F') = 0$ for all $\mathcal{P}^* \in Q^*$. This is our C.

To show that C is Q^*-closed, suppose that a sequence (in Q^*) $P_n^* \to P^*$ weakly. Construct the corresponding measures $\widetilde{P}_n^*$ and $\widetilde{P}^*$ in $\widetilde{Q}$. By corollary VI.6.7 (p. 342) in Jacod and Shiryaev (1987), $\widetilde{P}_n^* \to \widetilde{P}^*$ weakly. Since F and hence F' is closed, it follows from the weak convergence that if $\widetilde{P}_n^*(F') \to 1$, then $\widetilde{P}^*(F') = 1$. The same property must then also hold for C.

5.4.3. Proof of Proposition 4

Let d be the uniform metric on C^q, i.e., $d(x, y) = \sum_{i=1,\ldots,q} \sup_{t \in [0,T]} |x_t^i - y_t^i|$. Let $\{z_n\}$ be a countable dense set in C^q with respect to this metric. It is then easy to see that

$$\rho(F, G) = \sum_{n \in \mathbb{N}} \frac{1}{2^n} (|d(z_n, F) - d(z_n, G)| \wedge 1)$$

is a metric on $\mathbf{F}$ whose associated convergence is the pointwise one.

We now consider the functions $f_m(F, x) = (1 - md(x, F))^+$. These are continuous as maps $\mathbf{F} \times \mathbb{C}[0, T]^q \to \mathbb{R}$. From this, the indicator function $I_F(x) = \inf_{m \in \mathbb{N}} f(x)$ is upper semicontinuous, and hence measurable. The result for (5.11) then follows from Exercise 1.5.5 (p. 43) by Strook and Varadhan (1979). The development for (5.12) is similar.

6. PREDICTION SETS: THE EFFECT OF INTEREST RATES AND GENERAL FORMULAE FOR EUROPEAN OPTIONS

6.1. Interest Rates: Market Structure and Types of Prediction Sets

When evaluating options on equity, interest rates are normally seen by practitioners as a second-order concern. In the following, however, we shall see how to incorporate such uncertainty if one so wishes. It should be emphasized that the following does not discuss interest rate derivatives as such. We suppose that intervals are set on integral form, in the style of (2.3). One could then consider the incorporation of interest rate uncertainty in several ways.

One possibility would be to use a separate interval for the interest rate:

$$R^- \leq \int_0^T r_u du \leq R^+. \tag{6.1}$$

In combination with (2.3), this gives $\mathbb{A} = B(S_0, \Xi^+, R^+)$, for convex increasing payoff $f(S_T)$ cf. Section 3.2.

For more general European payoffs f, set

$$h(s) = \sup_{R^- \leq R \leq R^+} \exp\{-R\} f(\exp\{R\}s). \tag{6.2}$$

The bound $\mathbb{A}$ then becomes the bound for hedging payoff $h(S_T)$ under interval (2.3). This is seen by the same methods as those used to prove Theorem 5 below. Note that when f is convex or concave, then so is h, and so in this case $\mathbb{A} = B(S_0, \Xi^{\pm}, 0; h)$. Here B is as in (3.1), but based on h instead of f. The $\pm$ on Ξ depends on whether f is convex (+) or concave (−). A more general formula is given by (6.13) in Section 6.3.

This value of A_0, however, comes with an important qualification. It is the value one gets by only hedging in the stock S and the money market bond β. But usually one would also have access to longer term bonds. In this case, the value of $\mathbb{A}$ would be flawed because it does not respect put-call parity (see p. 167 in Hull, 1997). To remedy the situation, we now also introduce the zero coupon treasury bond Λ_t. This bond matures with the value one dollar at the time T, which is also the expiration date of the European option.

If such a zero coupon bond exists, and if one decides to trade in it as part of the super-replicating strategy, the price A_0 will be different. We emphasize that there are two if's here. For example, Λ could exist, but have such high transaction cost that one would not want to use it. Or maybe one would encounter legal or practical constraints on its use. These problems would normally not occur for zero coupon bonds, but can easily be associated with other candidates for "underlying securities." Market-traded call and put options, for example, can often exist while being too expensive to use for dynamic hedging. There may also be substantial room for judgment.

We emphasize, therefore, that the price A_0 depends not only on one's prediction region, but also on the market structure. Both in terms of what exists and in terms of what one chooses to trade in. To reflect the ambiguity of the situation, in the following we shall describe Λ as *available* if it is traded and if it is practicable to hedge in it.

If we assume that Λ is, indeed, available, then as one would expect from Section 3, different prediction regions give different values of A_0. If one combines (2.3) and (6.1), the form of A_0 is somewhat unpleasant. We give the details in Section 6.4. Also, one suffers from the problem of setting a two-dimensional prediction region, which will require prediction probabilities in each dimension that will be higher than $1 - \alpha$.

A better approach is the following. This elegant way of dealing with uncertain interest was first encountered by this author in the work of El Karoui et al. (1998). Consider the stock price discounted (or rather, blown up) by the zero coupon bond:

$$S_t^{(*)} = S_t / \Lambda_t. \tag{6.3}$$

Table 15.3   Comparative prediction sets: r nonconstant convex European options, including calls

Λ_t available?	A_0 from (2.3) and (6.1)	A_0 from (6.4)
No	$B(S_0, \Xi^+, R^+)$	Not available
Yes	see Section 6.4	$B(S_0, \Xi^{*+}, -\log \Lambda_0)$

B is defined in (3.2) and (3.3) for call options, and more generally in (3.1).

In other words, $S_t^{(*)}$ is the price of the forward contract that delivers S_T at time T. Suppose that the process $S^{(*)}$ has volatility σ_t^*, and that we now have prediction bounds similar to (2.3), in the form

$$\Xi^{*-} \leq \int_0^T \sigma_t^{*2} dt \leq \Xi^{*+}. \tag{6.4}$$

We shall see in Section 6.3 that the second interval gives rise to a nice form for the conservative price A_0. For convex European options such as puts and calls, $A_0 = B(S_0, \Xi^{*+}, -\log \Lambda_0)$. The main gain from using this approach, however, is that it involves a scalar prediction interval. There is only one quantity to keep track of. And no multiple comparison type problems.

The situation for the call option is summarized in Table 15.3. The value A_0 depends on two issues: is the zero coupon bond available, and which prediction region should one use?

Table 15.3 follows directly from the development in Section 6.3. The hedge ratio corresponding to (6.4) is given in (6.12) below.

6.2. The Effect of Interest Rates: The Case of the Ornstein-Uhlenbeck Model

We here discuss a particularly simple instance of incorporating interest rate uncertainty into the interval (6.4). In the following, we suppose that interest rates follow a linear model (introduced in the interest rate context by Vasicek, 1977),

$$dr_t = a_r(b_r - r_t)dt + c_r dV_t, \tag{6.5}$$

where V is a Brownian motion independent of B in (2.1).

The choice of interest rate model highlights the beneficial effects of the "decoupled" prediction procedure (Section 5.3): this model would be undesirable for hedging purposes as it implies that any government bond can be hedged in any other government bond, but on the other hand it may not be so bad for statistical purposes. Incidentally, the other main conceptual criticism of this model is that rates can go negative. Again, this is something that is less bothersome for a statistical analysis than for a hedging operation. This issue, as far as interest rates are concerned, may have become obsolete after the apparent occurrence of negative rates in Japan [see, e.g., "Below zero" (*The Economist*, Nov. 14, 1998, p. 81)]. Similar issues remain, however, if one wishes to use linear models for volatilities.

Suppose that the time T to maturity of the discount bond Λ is sufficiently short that there is no risk adjustment, in other words, $\Lambda_0 = E \exp\{-\int_0^T r_t dt\}$. One can then parametrize the quantities of interest as follows: there are constants v and γ so that

$$\int_0^T r_t dt \text{ has distribution } N(v, \gamma^2). \tag{6.6}$$

It follows that

$$\log \Lambda_0 = -v + \frac{1}{2}\gamma^2. \tag{6.7}$$

In this case, if we suppose that the stock follows (2.1), then

$$\int_0^T \sigma_u^{*2} du = \int_0^T \sigma_u^2 du + \gamma^2. \tag{6.8}$$

Prediction intervals can now be adjusted from (2.3) to (6.4) by incorporating the estimation uncertainty in γ^2. Nonlinear interest rate models, such as the one from Cox et al. (1985), require, obviously, a more elaborate scheme.

It may seem confusing to declare the Vasicek model (6.5) to be unsuitable in one paragraph, and then set prediction intervals with it in the next. To first order, this is because the distribution for the integral may be approximately correct even if the trading implications of the model are not. Also, a small error in (6.8), when used through a prediction interval, does not have very severe consequences.

6.3. General European Options

We here focus on the single prediction set (6.4). The situation of constant interest rate (Table 15.1 in Section 3.3) is a special case of this, where the prediction set reduces to (2.3).

Theorem 4 *Under the Assumptions (A), and with prediction set (6.4), if one hedges liability* $\eta = g(S_T)$ *in* S_t *and* Λ_t*, the quantity* $\mathbb{A}$ *has the form*

$$A_0 = \sup_\tau \tilde{E} \Lambda_0 f\left(\frac{1}{\Lambda_0}\tilde{S}_\tau\right), \tag{6.9}$$

where the supremum is over all stopping times τ that take values in $[\Xi^{*-}, \Xi^{*+}]$, and where $\widetilde{P}$ is a probability distribution on $\mathbb{C}[0, T]$ so that

$$d\widetilde{S}_t = \widetilde{S}_t d\widetilde{W}_t, \quad \text{with } \widetilde{S}_0 = s_0, \tag{6.10}$$

where s_0 is the actual observed value of S_0.

If one compares this with the results concerning nonconstant interest below in Section 6.4, the above would seem to be more elegant, and it typically yields lower values for A_0. It is also easier to implement since $\widetilde{S}$ is a martingale.

Now consider the case of convex or concave options. The martingale property of $\widetilde{S}$ yields that the A_0 in (6.9) has the value

$$A_0 = B(S_0, \Xi^{*\pm}, -\log \Lambda_0). \tag{6.11}$$

As in Section 6.1, $\pm$ depends on whether f is convex of concave.

It is shown in Section 6.5 that the delta hedge ratio for convex g is

$$\frac{\partial B}{\partial S}\left(S_t, \Xi^{*+} - \int_0^t \sigma_u^{*2} du, -\log \Lambda_t\right). \tag{6.12}$$

In practice, one has to make an adjustment similar to that at the end of Section 3.3.

As a consequence of Theorem 4, we can also state the form of the value $\mathbb{A}$ when hedging only in stock and the money market bond. If h is defined as in (6.2), one gets similarly to (6.9) that

$$A_0 = \sup_\tau \widetilde{E}h(\widetilde{S}_\tau), \tag{6.13}$$

6.4. General European Options: The Case of Two Intervals and a Zero-Coupon Bond

Now assume that we have a prediction set consisting of the two intervals (2.3) and (6.1). We can now incorporate the uncertainty due to interest rates as follows. First, form the auxiliary function

$$h(s, \lambda; f) = \sup_{R^- \leq R \leq R^+} \exp\{-R\}[f(\exp\{R\}s) - \lambda] + \lambda \Lambda_0 \tag{6.14}$$

Our result is now that the price for the dynamic hedge equals the price for the best static hedge, and that it has the form of the price of an American option.

Theorem 5 *Under the assumptions above, if one hedges in S_t and Λ_t, the quantity $\mathbb{A}$ has the form*

$$A_0(f) = \inf_\lambda \sup_\tau \widetilde{E}h(\widetilde{S}_\tau, \lambda; f) \tag{6.15}$$

where $\widetilde{P}$ is the probability distribution for which

$$d\widetilde{S}_t = \widetilde{S}_t d\widetilde{W}_t, \quad \widetilde{S}_0 = S_0 \tag{6.16}$$

and τ is any stopping time between Ξ^- and Ξ^+.

As above, if f is convex or concave, then so is the h in (6.14). In other words, because convex functions of martingales are submartingales and concave ones are supermartingales (see, for example, Karatzas and Shreve, 1991; Proposition I.3.6 (p. 13)), the result in Theorem 5 simplifies in those cases:

$$f \text{ convex: } A_0 = \inf_\lambda \widetilde{E}h\left(\widetilde{S}_{\Xi^+}, \lambda; f\right), \quad \text{and}$$

$$\tag{6.17}$$

$$f \text{ concave: } A_0 = \inf_\lambda \widetilde{E}h\left(\widetilde{S}_{\Xi^-}, \lambda; f\right),$$

both of the expressions are analytically computable.

We emphasize that what was originally cumulative volatilities (Ξ^-, Ξ^+) have now become measures of time when computing (6.15). This is because of the Dambis (1965)/Dubins–Schwartz (1965) time change, which leads to time being measured on the volatility scale.

Remark 2 *Note that in Theorem 5, the optimization involving R and λ can be summarized by replacing (6.15) with $A_0(f) = \sup_\tau \widetilde{E}g(\widetilde{S}_\tau; f)$, where $g(s; f)$ is the supremum of $Eh(s, \lambda; f)$ over (random variables) $R \in [R^-, R^+]$, subject to $E(\exp\{-R\}) = \Lambda_0$. R becomes a function of s, which in the case of convex f will take values R^- and R^+. This type of development is further pursued in Section 7 below.*

Remark 3 *Bid prices are formed similarly. In Theorem 5,*

$$B_0(f) = \sup_\lambda \inf_\tau \widetilde{E}h(\widetilde{S}_\tau, \lambda; f).$$

This is as in Eq. (2.6).

The expression for $\mathbb{A}(f)$ for the call option, $f(s) = (s - K)^+$, is the following. If v_0 solves

$$\Phi(d_2(S_0, v_0, \Xi^+)) = \frac{\exp(-R^-) - \Lambda_0}{\exp(-R^-) - \exp(-R^+)},$$

where Φ is the cumulative normal distribution and in the same notation as in (3.2) and (3.3), then one can start a super-replicating strategy with the price at time zero given in the following:

$$\nu_0 \geq R^+ : B(S_0, \Xi^+, R^+)$$

$$R^+ > \nu_0 > R^- : B(S_0, \Xi^+, \nu_0) + K\left(\exp(-\nu_0) - \exp(-R^+)\right)\Phi\left(d_2(S_0, \Xi^+, \nu_0)\right)$$

$$\nu_0 \leq R^- : B(S_0, \Xi^+, R^-) + K\left(\exp(-R^-) - \Lambda_0\right)$$

6.5. Proofs for Section 6
6.5.1. Proof of Theorem 4

The A_t be a self-financing trading strategy in S_t and Λ_t that covers payoff $g(S_T)$. In other words,

$$\mathrm{d}A_t = \theta_t^{(0)}\mathrm{d}\Lambda_t + \theta_t^{(1)}\mathrm{d}S_t \text{ and } A_t = \theta_t^{(0)}\Lambda_t + \theta_t^{(1)}S_t$$

If $S_t^{(*)} = \Lambda_t^{-1}S_t$, and similarly for $A_t^{(*)}$, this is the same as asserting that

$$\mathrm{d}A_t^{(*)} = \theta_t^{(1)}\mathrm{d}S_t^{(*)}.$$

This is by numeraire invariance and/or Itô's formula. In other words, for a fixed probability P, under suitable regularity conditions, the price of payoff $g(S_T)$ is $A_0 = \Lambda_0 A_0^{(*)} = \Lambda_0 E^{(*)}A_T^{(*)} = \Lambda_0 E^{(*)}g(S_T^{(*)})$, where $P^{(*)}$ is a probability distribution equivalent to P under which $S^{(*)}$ is a martingale.

It follows that Theorem 2 can be applied as if $r = 0$ and one wishes to hedge in security $S_t^{(*)}$. Hence, it follows that

$$A_0 = \sup_{P^* \in \mathcal{P}^*} \Lambda_0 E^{(*)}g\left(S_T^{(*)}\right)$$

By using the Dambis (1965)/Dubins–Schwartz (1965) time change, the result follows.

Derivation of the hedging strategy (6.12). As discussed in Section 3.2, the function $B(S, \Xi, R)$ defined in (3.1) satisfies two partial differential equations, viz., $\frac{1}{2}B_{SS}S^2 = B_\Xi$ and $-B_R = B - B_S S$. It follows that $B_{RR} = B_R - B_{SR}S$ and $B_{RS} = B_{SS}S$.

Now suppose that Ξ_t is a process with no quadratic variation. We then get the following from Itô's Lemma:

$$\mathrm{d}B(S_t, \Xi_t, -\log\Lambda_t) = B_S \mathrm{d}S_t - B_R \frac{1}{\Lambda_t}\mathrm{d}\Lambda_t \tag{6.18}$$
$$+ B_\Xi(d < \log S^* >_t + d\Xi_t)$$

If one looks at the right-hand side of (6.18), the first line is the self-financing component in the trading strategy. One should hold $B_S(S_t, \Xi_t, -\log\Lambda_t)$ units of stock, and $B_R(S_t, \Xi_t, -\log \Lambda_t)/\Lambda_t$ units of the zero coupon bond Λ. For this strategy to not require additional input during the life of the option, one needs the second line in (6.18) to be nonpositive. In the case of a convex or concave payoff, one just uses $d\Xi_t = -d < \log S^* >_t$, with Ξ_0 as Ξ^{*+} or Ξ^{*-}, as the case may be.

6.5.2. Proof of Theorem 5

By Theorem 2,

$$A_0 = \sup_{P^* \in \mathcal{P}^*} E_{P^*} \exp\left\{ -\int_0^T r_u du \right\} f\left(\exp\left\{ \int_0^T r_u du \right\} S_T^* \right).$$

For a given $P^* \in \mathcal{P}^*$, define $P^{(1)}$, also in $\mathcal{P}^*$, by letting $v > 1$, $\sigma_t^{\text{new}} = \sigma_{vt}$ for $vt \le T$ and zero thereafter until T. whereas we let $r_t^{\text{new}} = 0$ until T/v, and thereafter let $r_t^{\text{new}} = r_{(vt-T)/(v-1)}$. On the other hand, define $P^{(2)}$, also in $\mathcal{P}^*$, by letting $r_t^{(2)} = 0$ for $t < T/v$, and $r_t^{(2)} = Rv/T(1-v)$, where R maximizes the right-hand side of (6.14) given $s = S_T^*$ and subject to $E\exp\{-R\} = \Lambda_0$.

Obviously,

$$E_{P^*} \exp\left\{ -\int_0^T r_u du \right\} f\left(\exp\left\{ \int_0^T r_u du \right\} S_T^* \right)$$

$$= E_{P^{(1)}} \exp\left\{ -\int_0^T r_u du \right\} f\left(\exp\left\{ \int_0^T r_u du \right\} S_T^* \right)$$

$$\le E_{P^{(2)}} \exp\left\{ -\int_0^T r_u du \right\} f\left(\exp\left\{ \int_0^T r_u du \right\} S_T^* \right)$$

$$\le \inf_\lambda E_{P^{(2)}} h\left(S_T^*, \lambda; f \right)$$

by a standard constrained optimization argument.

By using the Dambis (1965)/Dubins–Schwartz (1965) time change (see, e.g., Karatzas and Shreve (1991), pp. 173–179), (6.15) and (6.16) follows.

7. PREDICTION SETS AND THE INTERPOLATION OF OPTIONS

7.1. Motivation

A major problem with a methodology that involves intervals for prices is that these can, in many circumstances, be too wide to be useful. There is scope, however, for narrowing these intervals by hedging in auxiliary securities, such as market-traded derivatives. The purpose of this section is to show that this can be implemented for European options. A general framework is briefly described in Section 7.2. To give a concise illustration, we show how to interpolate call options in Section 7.3. As we shall see, this interpolation substantially lowers the upper interval level $\mathbb{A}$ from (2.8).

Similar work with different models has been carried out by Bergman (1995), and we return to the connection at the end of Section 7.3. Our reduction of the option value to an optimal stopping problem, both in Theorem 6 and above in Theorem 4, mirrors the development in Frey (2000). Frey's paper uses the bounds of Avellaneda et al. (cf. Assumption 3 (p. 166) in his paper; the stopping result is Theorem 2.4 (p. 167)). In this context, Frey (2000) goes farther than the present paper in that it also considers certain types of non-European options. See also Frey and Sin (1999).

7.2. Interpolating European Payoffs

We first describe the generic case where restrictions on the volatility and interest rates are given by

$$\Xi^- \leq \int_0^T \sigma_t^2 dt \leq \Xi^+ \text{ and } R^- \leq \int_0^T r_u du \leq R^+. \tag{7.1}$$

We suppose that there market contains a zero coupon bond, there are p market-traded derivatives $V_t^{(i)}$ $(i = 1, \ldots, p)$ whose payoffs are $f_i(S_T)$ at time T. Again, it is the case that the price for the dynamic hedge equals the best price for a static hedge in the auxiliary securities, with a dynamic one in S_t only:

Theorem 6 *Under the assumptions above, if one hedges in S_t, Λ_t, and the $V_t^{(i)}$ $(i = 1, \ldots, p)$, the quantity A_0 has the form*

$$A_0(f, f_1, \ldots, f_p) = \inf_{\lambda_1 \ldots, \lambda_p} A_0(f - \lambda_1 f_1 - \ldots \lambda_p f_p) + \sum_{i=1}^p \lambda_i V_0^{(i)}, \tag{7.2}$$

where $A_0(f - \lambda_1 f_1 - \ldots \lambda_p f_p)$ is as given by (6.15) and (6.16).

A special case that falls under the above is one where one has a prediction interval for the volatility of the future S^* on S. Set $S_t^* = S_t/\Lambda_t$, and replace equation (2.1) by $dS_t^* = \mu_t S_t^* dt + \sigma_t S_t^* dW_t^*$. S^* is then the value of S in numeraire Λ, and the interest rate is zero in this numeraire. By numeraire invariance, one can now treat the problem in this unit of account. If one has an interval or the form (6.4), this is therefore the same as the problem posed in the form (7.1), with $R^- = R^+ = 0$. There is no mathematical difference, but (6.4) is an interval for the volatility of the future S^* rather than the actual stock price S. This is similar to what happens in Theorem 4.

Still with numeraire Λ, the Black–Scholes price is $B(S_0, \Xi, -\log \Lambda_0; f)/\Lambda_0 = B(S_0^*, \Xi, 0; f)$. In this case, h (from (6.14)) equals f. Theorems 6 and 7, the Algorithm, and Corollary 2 go through unchanged. For example, Eq. (6.15) becomes (after reconversion to dollars) $A_0(f) = \Lambda_0 \sup_\tau \tilde{E}f(\tilde{S}_\tau)$, where the initial value in (6.16) is $\tilde{S}_0 = S_0^* = S_0/\Lambda_0$.

7.3. The Case of European Calls

To simplify our discussion, we shall in the following assume that the short-term interest rate r is known, so that $R^+ = R^- = rT$. This case also covers the case of the bound (6.4). We focus here on the volatility only because this seems to be the foremost concern as far as uncertainty is concerned. In other words, our prediction interval is

$$\Xi^+ \geq \int_0^T \sigma_u^2 du \geq \Xi^-. \tag{7.3}$$

Consider, therefore, the case where one wishes to hedge an option with payoff $f_0(S_T)$, where f_0 is (nonstrictly) convex. We suppose that there are, in fact, market-traded call options $V_t^{(1)}$ and $V_t^{(2)}$ with strike prices K_1 and K_2. We suppose that $K_1 < K_2$, and set $f_i(s) = (s - K_i)^+$.

From Theorem 6, the price A_0 at time 0 for payoff $f_0(S_T)$ is

$$A_0(f_0, f_1, f_2) = \inf_{\lambda_1, \lambda_2} \; \sup_\tau \tilde{E}(h - \lambda_1 h_1 - \lambda_2 h_2)(\tilde{S}_\tau) + \sum_{i=1}^2 \lambda_i V_0^{(i)}, \tag{7.4}$$

where, for $i = 1, 2$, $h_i(s) = \exp\{-rT\} f_i(\exp\{rT\}s) = (s - K_i')^+$, with $K_i' = \exp\{-rT\}K_i$.

We now give an algorithm for finding A_0.

For this purpose, let $B(S, \Xi, R, K)$ be as defined in (3.1) for $f(s) = (s - K)^+$ (in other words, the Black–Scholes–Merton price for a European call with strike price K). Also define, for $\Xi \leq \tilde{\Xi}$,

$$\tilde{B}(S, \Xi, \tilde{\Xi}, K, \tilde{K}) = \tilde{E}((\tilde{S}_\tau - \tilde{K})^+ \mid S_0 = S), \tag{7.5}$$

where τ is the minimum of $\tilde{\Xi}$ and the first time after Ξ that $\tilde{S}_t$ hits K. An analytic expression for (7.5) is given as Eq. (7.15) in Section 7.5.

Algorithm 1

(i) *Find the implied volatilities* Ξ_i^{impl} *of the options with strike price* K_i. *In other words,*
$\tilde{B}(S_0, \Xi_i^{\text{impl}}, rT, K_i) = V_0^{(i)}$.

(ii) *If* $\Xi_1^{\text{impl}} < \Xi_2^{\text{impl}}$, *set* $\Xi_1 = \Xi_1^{\text{impl}}$, *but adjust* Ξ_2 *to satisfy* $\tilde{B}(S_0, \Xi_1^{\text{impl}}, \Xi_2, K_1', K_2') = V_0^{(2)}$. *If* $\Xi_1^{\text{impl}} > \Xi_2^{\text{impl}}$, *do the opposite, in other words, keep* $\Xi_2 = \Xi_2^{\text{impl}}$, *and adjust* Ξ_1 *to satisfy* $\tilde{B}(S_0, \Xi_2^{\text{impl}}, \Xi_1, K_2', K_1') = V_0^{(1)}$. *If* $\Xi_1^{\text{impl}} = \Xi_2^{\text{impl}}$, *leave them both unchanged, i.e.,* $\Xi_1 = \Xi_2 = \Xi_1^{\text{impl}} = \Xi_2^{\text{impl}}$.

(iii) *Define a stopping time τ as the minimum of Ξ^+, the first time $\tilde{S}_t$ hits K_1' after Ξ_1, and the first time $\tilde{S}_t$ hits K_2' after Ξ_2. Then $\mathbb{A}$ has the form*

$$A_0(f_0; f_1, f_2) = \tilde{E}h_0(\tilde{S}_\tau).$$

Note in particular that if f_0 is also a call option, with strike K_0, and still with the convention $K_0' = \exp\{-rT\}K_0$, one obtains

$$\mathbb{A} = \tilde{E}(\tilde{S}_\tau - K_0')^+. \tag{7.6}$$

This is the sense in which one could consider the above, an interpolation or even extrapolation: the strike prices K_1 and K_2 are given, and K_0 can now vary.

Theorem 7 *Suppose that* $\Xi^- \le \Xi_1^{\text{impl}}, \Xi_2^{\text{impl}} \le \Xi^+$. *Then the A_0 found in Algorithm 1 coincides with the one given by (7.4). Furthermore, for $i = 1, 2$,*

$$\Xi_i^{\text{impl}} \le \Xi_i. \tag{7.7}$$

Note that the condition $\Xi^- \le \Xi_1^{\text{impl}}, \Xi_2^{\text{impl}} \le \Xi^+$ must be satisfied to avoid arbitrage, assuming one believes the bound (7.3). Also, though Theorem 7 remains valid, no-arbitrage considerations impose constraints on Ξ_1 and Ξ_2, as follows.

Corollary 2 *Assume* $\Xi^- \le \Xi_1^{\text{impl}}, \Xi_2^{\text{impl}} \le \Xi^+$. *Then Ξ_1 and Ξ_2 must not exceed Ξ^+. Otherwise there is arbitrage under the condition (7.3).*

We prove the algorithm and the corollary in Section 7.5. Note that $\tilde{B}(S, \Xi, \tilde{\Xi}, K, \tilde{K})$ in (7.5) is a down-and-out type call for $\tilde{K} \ge K$, and can be rewritten as an up-and-out put for $\tilde{K} < K$, and is hence obtainable in closed form – cf. Eq. (7.15) in Section 7.5. $\mathbb{A}$ in (7.6) has a component that is on the form of a double barrier option, so the analytic expression (which can be found using the methods in Chapter 2.8 (pp. 94–103) in Karatzas and Shreve (1991)) will involve an infinite sum (as in ibid, Proposition 2.8.10 (p. 98)). See also Geman and Yor (1996) for analytic expressions. Simulations can be carried out using theory by Asmussen et al. (1995) and Simonsen (1997).

The pricing formula does not explicitly involve Ξ^-. It is implicitly assumed, however, that the implied volatilities of the two market-traded options exceed Ξ^-. Otherwise, there would be arbitrage opportunities. This, obviously, is also the reason why one can assume that $\Xi_i^{\text{impl}} \le \Xi^+$ for both i.

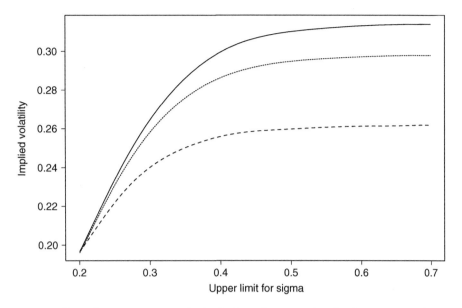

Figure 15.1 Effect of interpolation: Implied volatilities for interpolated call options as a function of the upper limit of the prediction interval. We consider various choices of strike price K_0 (from top to bottom: K_0 is 130, 120, and 110) for the option to be interpolated. The options that are market traded have strike prices $K_1 = 100$ and $K_2 = 160$. The graph shows the implied volatility of the options price A (σ_{impl} given by $B(S_0, \sigma_{\text{impl}}^2, rT, K_0) = A$ as a function of $\sqrt{\Xi^+}$. We are using square roots as this is the customary reporting form. The other values defining the graph are $S_0 = 100$, $T = 1$, and $r = 0.05$, and $\sqrt{\Xi_1^{\text{impl}}} = \sqrt{\Xi_2^{\text{impl}}} = 0.2$. The asymptotic value of each curve corresponds to the Merton bound for that volatility.

How does this work in practice? We consider an example scenario in Figs. 15.1 and 15.2. We suppose that market-traded calls are sparse, so that there is nothing between $K_1 = 100$ (which is at the money) and $K_2 = 160$. Figure 15.1 gives implied volatilities of $\mathbb{A}$ as a function of the upper limit Ξ^+. Figure 15.2 gives the implied volatilities as a function of K_0. As can be seen from the plots, the savings over using volatility Ξ^+ are substantial.

All the curves in Fig. 15.1 have an asymptote corresponding to the implied volatility of the price $\mathbb{A}_{\text{crit}} = \lambda_1^{(0)} V_0^{(1)} + (1 - \lambda_1^{(0)}) V_0^{(2)}$, where $\lambda_1^{(0)} = (K_2 - K_0)/(K_2 - K_1)$. This is known as the Merton bound, and holds since, obviously, $\lambda_1^{(0)} S_t^{(1)} + (1 - \lambda_1^{(0)}) S_t^{(2)}$ dominates the call option with strike price K_0 and is the cheapest linear combination of $S_t^{(1)}$ and $S_t^{(2)}$ with this property. In fact, if one denotes as $\mathbb{A}_{\Xi^+}$ the quantity from (7.6), and if the Ξ_i^{impl} are kept fixed, it is easy to see that, for (7.6),

$$\lim_{\Xi^+ \to +\infty} \mathbb{A}_{\Xi^+} = \mathbb{A}_{\text{crit}}. \tag{7.8}$$

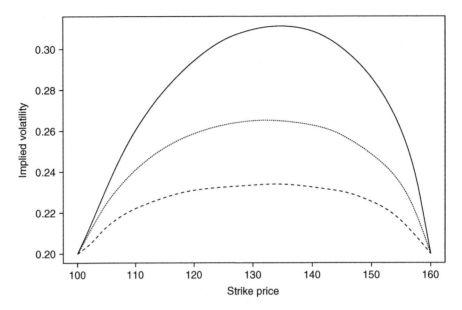

Figure 15.2   Effect of interpolation: implied volatilities for interpolated call options as a function of the strike price K_0 for the option to be interpolated. We consider various choices of maximal volatility values $\sqrt{\Xi^+}$ (from top to bottom: $\sqrt{\Xi^+}$ is 0.50, 0.40, and 0.25). Other quantities are as in Fig. 15.1. Note that the curve for $\sqrt{\Xi^+} = 0.50$ is graphically indistinguishable from that of the Merton bound.

Figures 15.1 and 15.2 presuppose that the implied volatility of the two market-traded options are the same $\left(\sqrt{\Xi_1^{impl}} = \sqrt{\Xi_2^{impl}} = 0.2\right)$. To see what happens when the out of the money option increases its implied volatility, we fix $\sqrt{\Xi_1^{impl}} = 0.2$, and we show in the following the plot of $\sqrt{\Xi_2}$ as a function of $\sqrt{\Xi_2^{impl}}$ (Fig. 15.3). Also, we give the implied volatilities for the interpolated option (7.6) with strike price $K_0 = 140$ (Fig. 15.4). We see that except for high $\sqrt{\Xi_2^{impl}}$, there is still gain by a constraint on the form (7.3).

It should be noted that there is similarity between the current paper and the work by Bergman (1995). This is particularly so in that he finds an arbitrage relationship between the value of two options (see his Section 3.2 (pp. 488–494), and in particular Proposition 4). Our development, similarly, finds an upper limit for the price of a third option given two existing ones. As seen in Corollary 2, it can also be applied to the relation between two options only.

The similarity, however, is mainly conceptual, as the model assumptions are substantially different. An interest rate interval [Bergman's equations (1) and (2) on p. 478] is obtained by differentiating between lending and borrowing rates (as also in Cvitanić and Karatzas, 1993), and the stock price dynamic is given by differential equations (3) and (4) on p. 479.

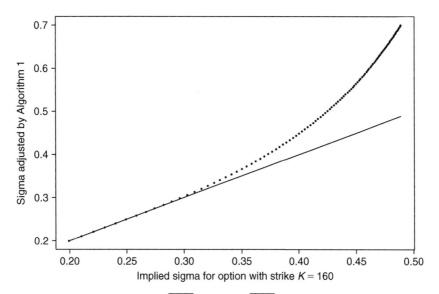

Figure 15.3 $\tilde{C}$: $\sqrt{\Xi_2}$ as a function of $\sqrt{\Xi_2^{impl}}$, for fixed $\sqrt{\Xi_1^{impl}} = \sqrt{\Xi_2} = 0.2$. A diagonal line is added to highlight the functional relationship.

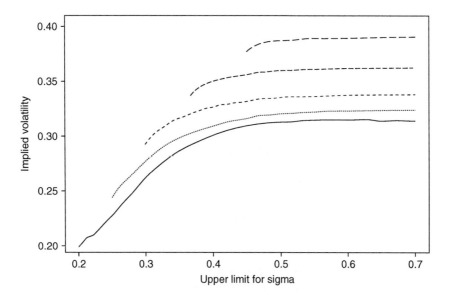

Figure 15.4 Implied volatility for interpolated call option with strike price $K_0 = 140$, as the upper bound $\sqrt{\Xi^+}$ varies. The curves assume $\sqrt{\Xi_1^{impl}} = 0.2$ and, in ascending order, correspond to $\sqrt{\Xi_2^{impl}} = 0.2, 0.25, 0.3, 0.35,$ and 0.4. The starting point for each curve is the value $\sqrt{\Xi^+}$ (on the x-axis) so that the no-arbitrage condition of Corollary 2 is not violated. As in Fig. 15.1, the asymptotic value of each curve corresponds to the Merton bound for that volatility.

This is in contrast to our assumptions (7.1). It is, therefore, hard to compare Bergman's and our results in other than conceptual terms.

7.4. The Usefulness of Interpolation

We have shown in the above that the interpolation of options can substantially reduce the length of intervals for prices that are generated under uncertainty in the predicted volatility and interest rates. It would be natural to extend the approach to the case of several options, and this is partially carried out in Mykland (2005). It is seen in that paper that there is a state price distribution which gives rise to the bound $\mathbb{A}$ for all convex European options, in a way that incorporates both all traded options and a statistical prediction interval.

Further research in this area should confront the common reality that the volatility itself is quite well pinned down, whereas correlations are not. Another interesting question is whether this kind of nonparametrics can be used in connection with the interest rate term structure, where the uncertainty about models is particularly acute.

7.5. Proofs for Section 7
7.5.1. Proof of Theorem 6

This result follows in a similar way to the proof of Theorem 5, with the modification that $\mathcal{Q}^*$ is now the set of all probability distributions Q^* so that (7.1) is satisfied, so that Λ_t^* and the $V_t^{(i)*}$ $(i = 1, \ldots, p)$ are martingales, and so that $dS_t^* = \sigma_t S_t^* dW_t$, for given S_0. ∎

Before we proceed to the proof of Theorem 7, let us establish the following set of inequalities for $\Xi < \widetilde{\Xi}$,

$$B(S, \Xi, R, K_2) < \tilde{B}(S, \Xi, \widetilde{\Xi}, K_1', K_2') < B(S, \widetilde{\Xi}, R, K_2). \tag{7.9}$$

The reason for this is that $\tilde{B}(S, \Xi, \widetilde{\Xi}, K_1', K_2') = \widetilde{E}((\widetilde{S}_\tau - K_2')^+)$ is nondecreasing in both Ξ and $\widetilde{\Xi}$, because $\widetilde{S}$ is a martingale and $x \to x^+$ is convex, and also that $\tilde{B}(S, \Xi, \Xi, K_1', K_2') = B(S, \Xi, 0, K_2') = B(S, \Xi, R, K_2)$. The inequalities are obviously strict otherwise.

7.5.2. Proof of Theorem 7 (and Algorithm 1)

We wish to find (7.4). First fix λ_1 and λ_2, in which case we are seeking $\sup_\tau \widetilde{E} h_{\lambda_1, \lambda_2}(\widetilde{S}_\tau)$, where $h_{\lambda_1, \lambda_2} = h_0 - \lambda_1 h_1 - \lambda_2 h_2$. This is because the $V_0^{(i)}$ are given. We recall that h_0 is (nonstrictly) convex because f_0 has this property, and that $h_i(s) = (s - K_i')^+$. It follows that h_{λ_1, λ_2} is convex except at points $s = K_1'$ and $= K_2'$.

Because $\widetilde{S}_t$ is a martingale, $h_{\lambda_1, \lambda_2}(\widetilde{S}_t)$ is therefore a submartingale so long as $\widetilde{S}_t$ does not cross K_1' or K_2' (see Proposition I.3.6 (p. 13) in Karatzas and Shreve, 1991). It follows that if τ_0 is a stopping time, $\Xi^- \leq \tau_0 \leq \Xi^+$, and we set

$$\tau = \inf\{\, t \geq \tau_0 : \widetilde{S}_t = K_1' \text{ or } K_2' \,\} \wedge \Xi^+,$$

then $\widetilde{E}h_{\lambda_1,\lambda_2}(\widetilde{S}_{\tau_0}) \leq \widetilde{E}h_{\lambda_1,\lambda_2}(\widetilde{S}_\tau)$. It follows that the only possible optimal stopping points would be $\tau = \Xi^+$ and τs for which $\widetilde{S}_\tau = K_i'$ for $i = 1, 2$.

Further inspection makes it clear that the rule must be on the form given in part (iii) of the algorithm, but with Ξ_1 and Ξ_2 as yet undetermined. This comes from standard arguments for American options (see Karatzas, 1988; Myneni, 1992; and the references therein), as follows. Define the *Snell envelope* for h_{λ_1,λ_2} by

$$\text{SE}(s, \Xi) = \sup_{\Xi \leq \tau \leq \Xi^+} \widetilde{E}(h_{\lambda_1,\lambda_2}(\widetilde{S}_\tau) \mid S_\Xi = s).$$

The solution for American options is then that

$$\tau = \inf\{\xi \geq \Xi^- \; : \; \text{SE}(\widetilde{S}_\xi, \xi) = h_{\lambda_1,\lambda_2}(\widetilde{S}_\xi)\}$$

Inspection of the preceding formula yields that $\tau = \tau_1 \wedge \tau_2$, where

$$\tau_i = \inf\{\, \xi \geq \Xi^- \; : \; \{\, \text{SE}(\widetilde{S}_\xi, \xi) = h_{\lambda_1,\lambda_2}(\widetilde{S}_\xi)\, \} \cap \{\, \widetilde{S}_\xi = K_i'\, \}\, \} \wedge \Xi^+$$

$$= \inf\{\, \xi \geq \Xi^- \; : \; \{\, \text{SE}(K_i', \xi) = h_{\lambda_1,\lambda_2}(K_i')\, \} \cap \{\, \widetilde{S}_\xi = K_i'\, \}\, \} \wedge \Xi^+$$

$$= \inf\{\, \xi \geq \Xi_i \; : \; \widetilde{S}_\xi = K_i'\, \} \wedge \Xi^+,$$

where $\Xi_i = \inf\{\, \xi \geq \Xi^- \; : \; \text{SE}(K_i', \xi) = h_{\lambda_1,\lambda_2}(K_i')\} \wedge \Xi^+$.

Because the system is linear in λ_1 and λ_2, it must be the case that

$$\widetilde{E}(\widetilde{S}_\tau - K_i')^+ = V_0^{(i)} \quad \text{for } i = 1, 2. \tag{7.10}$$

Hence, the form of A_0 given in part (iii) of the algorithm must be correct, and one can use (7.10) to find Ξ_1 and Ξ_2. Note that the left-hand side of (7.10) is continuous and increasing in Ξ_1 and Ξ_2, (again since $\widetilde{S}$ is a martingale and $x \to x^+$ is convex). Combined with our assumption in Theorem 7 that $\Xi^- \leq \Xi_1^{\text{impl}}, \Xi_2^{\text{impl}} \leq \Xi^+$, we are assured that (7.10) has solutions Ξ_1 and Ξ_2 in $[\Xi^-, \Xi^+]$.

Let (Ξ_1, Ξ_2) be a solution for (7.10) (we have not yet decided what values they take, or even that they are in the interval $[\Xi^-, \Xi^+]$).

Suppose first that $\Xi_1 < \Xi_2$.

It is easy to see that

$$\widetilde{E}[(\widetilde{S}_\tau - K_1')^+ \mid \widetilde{S}_{\Xi_1}] = (\widetilde{S}_{\Xi_1} - K_1')^+. \tag{7.11}$$

This is immediate when $\widetilde{S}_{\Xi_1} \leq K_1'$; in the opposite case, note that $(\widetilde{S}_\tau - K_1')^+ = \widetilde{S}_\tau - K_1'$ when $\widetilde{S}_{\Xi_1} > K_1'$, and one can then use the martingale property of $\widetilde{S}_t$. Taking expectations in (7.11) yields from (7.10) that Ξ_1 must be the implied volatility of the call with strike price K_1.

Conditioning on $\mathcal{F}_{\Xi_2}$ is a little more complex. Suppose first that $\inf_{\Xi_1 \leq t \leq \Xi_2} \tilde{S}_t > K_1'$. This is equivalent to $\tau > \Xi_2$, whence

$$\tilde{E}[(\tilde{S}_\tau - K_2')^+ \mid \mathcal{F}_{\Xi_2}] = (\tilde{S}_{\Xi_2} - K_2')^+,$$

as in the previous argument (separate into the two cases $\tilde{S}_{\Xi_2} \leq K_2'$ and $\tilde{S}_{\Xi_2} > K_2'$). Hence, incorporating the case where $\tau \leq \Xi_2$, we find that

$$\tilde{E}(\tilde{S}_\tau - K_2')^+ = \tilde{E}(\tilde{S}_{\Xi_2 \wedge \tau} - K_2')^+,$$

thus showing that Ξ_2 can be obtained from $\tilde{B}(S_0, \Xi_1^{\text{impl}}, \Xi_2, K_1', K_2') = V_0^{(2)}$. In consequence, from the left-hand inequality in (7.9),

$$B(S_0, \Xi_1^{\text{impl}}, rT, K_2) < \tilde{B}(S_0, \Xi_1^{\text{impl}}, \Xi_2, K_1', K_2')$$
$$= V_0^{(2)} = B(S_0, \Xi_2^{\text{impl}}, rT, K_2)$$

Since, for call options, $B(S, \Xi, R, K_2)$ is increasing in Ξ, it follows that $\Xi_2^{\text{impl}} > \Xi_1^{\text{impl}}$.

Hence, under the assumption that $\Xi_1 < \Xi_2$, Algorithm 1 produces the right result.

The same arguments apply in the cases $\Xi_1 > \Xi_2$ and $\Xi_1 = \Xi_2$, in which cases, respectively, $\Xi_1^{\text{impl}} > \Xi_2^{\text{impl}}$ and $\Xi_1^{\text{impl}} = \Xi_2^{\text{impl}}$. Hence, also in these cases, Algorithm 1 provides the right solution.

Hence the solution to (7.10) is unique and is given by Algorithm 1.

The uniqueness of solution, combined with the above established fact that there are solutions in $[\Xi^-, \Xi^+]$, means that our solution must satisfy this constraint. Hence, the rightmost inequality in (7.7) must hold. The other inequality in (7.7) follows because the adjustment in (ii) increases the value of the Ξ_i that is adjusted. This is because of the rightmost inequality in (7.9).

The result follows.

An analytic expression for Eq. (7.5). To calculate the expression (7.5), note first that

$$\tilde{B}(S, \Xi, \tilde{\Xi}, K, \tilde{K}) = \tilde{E}[\tilde{B}(S_\Xi, 0, \tilde{\Xi} - \Xi, K, \tilde{K}) \mid S_0 = S]$$

We therefore first concentrate on the expression for $\tilde{B}(s, 0, T, K, \tilde{K})$. For $K < \tilde{K}$, this is the price of a down-and-out call, with strike $\tilde{K}$, barrier K, and maturity T. We are still under the $\tilde{P}$ distribution, in other words, $\sigma = 1$ and all interest rates are zero. The formula for this price is given on p. 462 by Hull (1997), and because of the unusual values of the parameters, one gets

$$\tilde{B}(s, 0, T, K, \tilde{K}) = \tilde{E}((S_T - \tilde{K})^+ \mid S_0 = s) - \frac{\tilde{K}}{K}\tilde{E}((S_T - H)^+ \mid S_0 = s) + \frac{\tilde{K}}{K}(s - H)$$

for $s > K$, while the value is zero for $s \leq K$. Here, $H = K^2/\tilde{K}$.

Now set

$$D(s, \Xi, \tilde{\Xi}, K, X) = \tilde{E}[(S_{\tilde{\Xi}} - X)^+ I\{S_{\Xi} \geq K\}|S_0 = s]$$

and let BS_0 be the Black–Scholes formula for zero interest rate and unit volatility, $BS_0(s, \Xi, X) = \tilde{E}[(S_{\Xi} - X)^+|S_0 = s]$, in other words,

$$BS_0(s, \Xi, X) = s\Phi(d_1(s, X, \Xi)) - X\Phi(d_2(s, X, \Xi)), \tag{7.12}$$

where Φ is the cumulative standard normal distribution, and

$$d_i = d_i(s, X, \Xi) = (\log(s/X) \pm \Xi/2)/\sqrt{\Xi} \quad \text{where } \pm \text{ is } + \text{ for } i = 1 \text{ and } - \text{ for } i = 2. \tag{7.13}$$

Then, for $K < \tilde{K}$,

$$\tilde{B}(s, \Xi, \tilde{\Xi}, K, \tilde{K}) = D(s, \Xi, \tilde{\Xi}, K, \tilde{K}) - \frac{\tilde{K}}{K}D(s, \Xi, \tilde{\Xi}, K, H) + \frac{\tilde{K}}{K}BS_0(s, \Xi, K)$$
$$+ (\tilde{K} - K)\Phi(d_2(s, K, \Xi)). \tag{7.14}$$

Similarly, for $K \geq \tilde{K}$, a martingale argument and the formula on p. 463 by Hull (1997) gives that

$$\tilde{B}(s, 0, T, K, \tilde{K}) = s - \tilde{K} + \text{value of up-and-out put option with strike } \tilde{K} \text{ and barrier } K,$$
$$= \tilde{E}((S_T - \tilde{K})^+|S_0 = s) - \text{value of up-and-in put option with strike } \tilde{K},$$
$$\text{and barrier } K$$
$$= \tilde{E}((S_T - \tilde{K})^+|S_0 = s) - \frac{\tilde{K}}{K}\tilde{E}((S_T - H)^+|S_0 = s) \text{ for } s < K.$$

On the other hand, obviously, for $s \geq K$, $\tilde{B}(s, 0, T, K, \tilde{K}) = (s - \tilde{K})$ by a martingale argument.

Hence, for $K \geq \tilde{K}$, we get

$$\tilde{B}(s, \Xi, \tilde{\Xi}, K, \tilde{K}) = BS_0(s, \tilde{\Xi}, \tilde{K}) - \frac{\tilde{K}}{K}BS_0(s, \tilde{\Xi}, H) - D(s, \Xi, \tilde{\Xi}, K, \tilde{K})$$
$$+ \frac{\tilde{K}}{K}D(s, \Xi, \tilde{\Xi}, K, H) + BS_0(s, \Xi, K) + (K - \tilde{K})\Phi(d_2(s, K, \Xi)). \tag{7.15}$$

The formula for D is

$$D(s, \Xi, \tilde{\Xi}, K, X) = s\Phi(d_1(s, X, \tilde{\Xi}), d_1(s, K, \Xi); \Sigma) - X\Phi(d_2(s, X, \tilde{\Xi}), d_2(s, K, \Xi); \Sigma), \tag{7.16}$$

where

$$\Phi(x, y; \Sigma) = \text{cumulative bivariate normal c.d.f. with covariance matrix } \Sigma \qquad (7.17)$$

and Σ is the matrix with diagonal elements 1 and off diagonal elements ρ,

$$\rho = \sqrt{\frac{\Xi}{\tilde{\Xi}}}. \qquad (7.18)$$

7.5.3. Proof of Corollary

It is easy to see that Theorem 7 goes through with $K_1 = K_2$ (in the case where the implied volatilities are the same). Using formula (7.7), we get from Algorithm 1 that

$$\mathbb{A}((s - K_0)^+; (s - K_1)^+) = \tilde{C}(S_0, \Xi_1^{\text{impl}}, \Xi^+, K_1', K_1'). \qquad (7.19)$$

The result then follows by replacing "0" by "2" in (7.19).

8. BOUNDS THAT ARE NOT BASED ON PREDICTION SETS

It may seem odd to argue, as we have in Section 5.3, for an approach that uses different models for inference and trading, even if the first is nested in the other. To see it in context, recall that we referred to this procedure as the *decoupled prediction approach*. Now consider two alternative devices. One is a *consistent prediction approach*: use the prediction region obtained earlier, but also insist for purposes of trading that $P \in \Theta$. Another alternative would be to find a *confidence or credible set* $\hat{\Theta} \subseteq \Theta$, and then do a super-replication that is valid for all $P \in \hat{\Theta}$. The starting values for these schemes are considered below.

Table 15.4 suggests the operation of the three schemes.

Table 15.4   Three approaches for going from data to hedging strategies.

Approach	Product of statistical analysis	Hedging is valid and solvent for
Confidence or credible sets	Set $\hat{\Theta}$ of probabilities	Probabilities in $\hat{\Theta}$
Consistent prediction set method	Set C of possible outcomes	Probabilities in Θ outcomes in C
Decoupled prediction set method	Set C of possible outcomes	Probabilities in $\mathcal{Q}$ outcomes in C

Θ is the parameter space used in the statistical analysis, which can be parametric or nonparametric. $\mathcal{Q}$ is the set of distributions defined in Assumption (A). C is a prediction set, and $\hat{\Theta}$ is a confidence or credible set.

The advantages of the decoupled prediction set approach are the following. First, transparency. It is easy to monitor, *en route*, how good the set is. For example, in the case of (2.3), one can at any time t see how far the realized $\int_0^t \sigma_u^2 du$ (or, rather, the estimated volatility $\hat{\Xi}_t$ in Section 3.4) is from the prediction limits Ξ^- and Ξ^+. This makes it easy for both traders and regulators to anticipate any disasters, and, if possible, to take appropriate action (such as liquidating the book).

Second, the transparency of the procedure makes this approach ideal as an exit strategy when other schemes have gone wrong. This can be seen from the discussion in Section 2.3.

Third, and perhaps most importantly, the decoupling of the inferential and trading models respects how these two activities are normally carried out. The statistician's mandate is, usually, to find a model Θ, and to estimate parameters, on the basis of whether these reasonably fit the data. This is different from finding a structural model of asset prices, one which also works well for trading. For example, consider modeling interest rates with an Ornstein–Uhlenbeck process. In many cases, this will give a perfectly valid fit to the data. For trading purposes, however, this model has severe drawbacks, as outlined in Section 6.2 mentioned earlier.

The gold standard, of course, is to look for good structural asset price models, and this is an ongoing topic of research, cf. many of the references in the Introduction. One should not, however, expect market participants to always use such models. Furthermore, the possibility of regime shifts somewhat curtails the predictive power of most models in finance.

With the decoupling of the two stages the statistical process can concentrate on good inference, without worrying about the consequences of the model on trading. For inference, one can use the econometrics literature cited at the end of the Introduction, and new methods become available over time.

To sum up, the decoupled prediction set approach is, in several ways, robust.

Is it efficient? The other two approaches, using the model Θ for both stages, would seem to give rise to lower starting values A_0, just by being consistent and by using a smaller family Θ for trading. We have not investigated this question in any depth, but tentative evidence suggests that the consistent prediction approach will yield a cheaper A_0, while the confidence/credible approach is less predictable in this respect. Consider the following.

Using Kramkov (1996) and Mykland (2000), one can obtain the starting value for a true super-replication over a confidence/credible set $\hat{\Theta}$ for conditional probabilities P_ω. Assume the nesting condition. Let $\hat{\Theta}^*$ be the convex hull of distributions $Q^* \in \mathcal{Q}^*$ for which Q^* is mutually absolutely continuous with a $P_\omega \in \hat{\Theta}$. The starting value for the super-replication would then normally have the form

$$A_0 = \sup\{E^*(\eta^*) \ : \ P^* \in \hat{\Theta}^*\}.$$

Whether this A_0 is cheaper than the one from (5.3) may, therefore, vary according to Θ and to the data. This is because $\hat{\Theta}^*$ and $\mathcal{P}^* = \mathcal{P}^*_{S_0}$ (from 5.2) are not nested one in the other, either way.

For the consistent prediction approach, we have not investigated how one can obtain a result like Theorem 2 for subsets of $\mathcal{Q}$, so we do not have an explicit expression for A_0. However, the infimum in (2.5) is with respect to a smaller class of probabilities, and hence a larger class of super-replications on C. The resulting price, therefore, can be expected to be smaller than the conservative ask price from (5.2). As outlined earlier, however, this approach is not as robust as the one we have been advocating.

ACKNOWLEDGMENTS

I would like to thank Marco Avellaneda, Eric Renault, and the editors and referees both for this volume, and for my 2000 and 2003 papers, and everyone who has helped me understand this area. This research was supported in part by National Science Foundation grants DMS 99–71738, 02–04639, 06–04758, and SES 06–31605.

REFERENCES

Aït-Sahalia, Y. (1996). nonparametric pricing of interest rate derivative securities. *Econometrica* **64** 527–560.

Aït-Sahalia, Y. (2002). Maximum-likelihood estimation of discretely-sampled diffusions: A closed-form approximation approach. *Econometrica* **70** 223–262.

Aït-Sahalia, Y., and Lo, A. (1998). Nonparametric estimation of state-price densities implicit in financial asset prices. *Journal of Finance* **53** 499–547.

Aït-Sahalia, Y., and Mancini, L. (2008). Out of sample forecasts of quadratic variation. *Journal of Econometrics* **147** 17–33.

Aït-Sahalia, Y., and Mykland, P.A. (2003). The effects of random and discrete sampling when estimating continuous-time diffusions. *Econometrica* **71** 483–549.

Andersen, T.G. (2000). Some reflections on analysis of high frequency data, *Journal of Business and Economic Statistics* **18** 146–153.

Andersen, T.G., and Bollerslev, T. (1998). Answering the skeptics: Yes, standard volatility models do provide accurate forecasts. *International Economic Review* **39** 885–905.

Andersen, T.G., Bollerslev, T., and Diebold, F.X. (2009) Parametric and Nonparametric Volatility Measurement. In: Aït-Sahalia, Y., and Hansen, L.P. (eds.) *Handbook of Financial Econometrics* (In press).

Andersen, T.G., Bollerslev, T., Diebold, F.X., and Labys, P. (2001). The distribution of realized exchange rate volatility. *Journal of the American Statistical Association* **96** 42–55.

Andersen, T.G., Bollerslev, T., Diebold, F.X., and Labys, P. (2003). Modeling and forecasting realized volatility. *Econometrica* **71** 579–625.

Andersen, T.G., Bollerslev, T., and Meddahi, N. (2009). Market microstructure noise and realized volatility forecasting. *Journal of Econometrics* (In press).

Artzner, P.H., Delbaen, F., Eber, J.M., and Heath, D. (1999). Coherent measures of risk. *Mathematical Finance* **9** 203–228.

Ash, R.B. (1972). *Real Analysis and Probability*. Academic Press, New York.

Asmussen, S., Glynn, P., and Pitman, J. (1995). Discretization error in simulation of one-dimensional reflecting Brownian motion. The Annals of Applied Probability **5** 875–896.

Avellaneda, M., Levy, A., and Paras, A. (1995). Pricing and hedging derivative securities in markets with uncertain volatilities. *Applied Mathematical Finance* **2** 73–88.

Bakshi, G., Cao, C., and Chen, Z. (1997). Empirical performance of alternative option pricing models. *Journal of Finance* **52** 2003–2049.

Barenblatt, G.I. (1978). *Similarity, Self-similarity and Intermediate Asymptotics*. Consultants Bureau, New York.

Barndorff-Nielsen, O.E., and Cox, D.R. (1996). Prediction and asymptotics. *Bernoulli* **2** 319–340.

Barndorff-Nielsen, O.E., and Shephard, N. (2001). Non-gaussian ornstein-Uhlenbeck-based modes and some of their uses in financial economics. *Journal of the Royal Statistical Society, B* **63** 167–241.

Barndorff-Nielsen, O.E., and Shephard, N. (2002). Econometric analysis of realized volatility and its use in estimating stochastic volatility models. *Journal of the Royal Statistical Society, B* **64** 253–280.

Barndorff-Nielsen, O.E., Hansen, P.R., Lunde, A., and Shephard, N. (2008). Designing realized kernels to measure ex-post variation of equity prices in the presence of noise. *Econometrica* **76** 1481–1536.

Bates, D.S. (2000). Post-'87 crash fears in the S&P 500 futures option market. *Journal of Econometrics* **94** 181–238.

Beckers, S. (1981). Standard deviations implied in option prices as predictors of future stock price variability. *Journal of Banking and Finance* **5** 363–382.

Bergman, Y.Z. (1995). Options pricing with differential interest rates. *Review of Financial Studies* **8** 475–500.

Bergman, Y.Z., Grundy, B.D., and Wiener, Z. (1996). General properties of option prices. *Journal of Finance* **5** 1573–1610.

Bibby, B.M., Skovgaard, I.M., and Sørensen, M. (2005). Diffusion-type models with given marginal and autocorrelation function. *Bernoulli* **11** 191–220.

Bibby, B.M., and Sørensen, M. (1995). Martingale estimating functions for discretely observed diffusion processes. *Bernoulli* **1** 17–39.

Bibby, B.M., and Sørensen, M. (1996a). On estimation for discretely observed diffusions: A review. *Theory of Stochastic Processes* **2** 49–56.

Bibby, B.M., and Sørensen, M. (1996b). A hyperbolic diffusion model for stock prices. *Finance and Stochastics* **1** 25–41.

Bick, A., and Reisman, H. (1993). Generalized implied volatility. (Preprint).

Bick, A., and Willinger, W. (1994). Dynamic spanning without probabilities. *Stochastic Processes and their Applications* **50** 349–374.

Black, F., and Scholes, M. (1973). The pricing of options and corporate liabilities. *Journal of Political Economy* **81** 637–654.

Bollerslev, T. (1986). Generalized autoregressive conditional heteroscedasticity. *Journal of Econometrics* **31** 307–327.

Bollerslev, T., Chou, R.Y., and Kroner, K.F. (1992). ARCH modeling in Finance. *Journal of Econometrics* **52** 5–59.

Bollerslev, T., Engle, R.F., and Nelson, D.B. (1994). ARCH Models. In: Engle, R.F., and McFadden, D. (eds.) *Handbook of Econometrics*, vol IV, pp. 2959–3038. North-Holland, Amsterdam.

Carr, P., Geman, H., and Madan, D. (2001). Pricing and hedging in incomplete markets. *Journal of Financial Economics* **62** 131–167.

Carr, P., Madan, D., Geman, H., and Yor, M. (2004). From local volatility to local Levy models. *Quantitative Finance* **4** 581–588.

Comte, F., and Renault, E. (1998). Long memory in continuous-time stochastic volatility models. *Mathematical Finance* **8** 291–323.

Conley, T.G., Hansen, L.P., Luttmer, E.G.J., and Scheinkman, J. (1997). Short-term interest rates as subordinated diffusions. *Review of Financial Studies* **10** 525–577.

Constantinides, G.M., and Zariphopoulou, T. (1999). Bounds on prices of contingent claims in an intertemporal economy with proportional transaction cost and general preferences. *Finance and Stochastics* **3** 345–369.

Constantinides, G.M., and Zariphopoulou, T. (2001). Bounds on derivative prices in an intertemporal setting with proportional transaction cost and multiple securities. *Mathematical Finance* **11** 331–346.

Cont, R. (2006). Model uncertainty and its impact on the pricing of derivative instruments. *Mathematical Finance* **16** 519–547.

Cox, J., Ingersoll, J., and Ross, S. (1985). A theory of the term structure of interest rates. *Econometrica* **53** 385–408.

Cvitanić, J., and Karatzas, I. (1992). Convex duality in constrained portfolio optimization. *The Annals of Applied Probability* **2** 767–818.

Cvitanić, J., and Karatzas, I. (1993). Hedging of contingent claims with constrained portfolios. *The Annals of Applied Probability* **3** 652–681.

Cvitanić, J., and Karatzas, I. (1999). On dynamic measures of risk. *Finance and Stochastics* **3** 451–482.

Cvitanić, J., Pham, H., and Touzi, N. (1998). A closed form solution to the problem of super-replication under transaction cost. *Finance and Stochastics* **3** 35–54.

Cvitanić, J., Pham, H., and Touzi, N. (1999). Super-replication in stochastic volatility models under portfolio constraints. *Journal of Applied Probability* **36** 523–545.

Dacorogna, M.M., Gençay, R., Müller, U., Olsen, R.B., and Pictet, O.V. (2001). *An Introduction to High-Frequency Finance*. Academic Press, San Diego.

Dacunha-Castelle, D., and Florens-Zmirou, D. (1986). Estimation of the coefficients of a diffusion from discrete observations. *Stochastics* **19** 263–284.

Dambis, K. (1965). On the decomposition of continuous sub-martingales. *Theory of Probability and its Applications* **10** 401–410.

Danielsson, J. (1994). Stochastic volatility in asset prices: Estimation with simulated maximum likelihood. *Journal of Econometrics* **64** 375–400.

Delbaen, F., Monat, P., Schachermayer, W., Schweizer, M., and Stricker, C. (1997). Weighted norm inequalities and hedging in incomplete markets. *Finance and Stochastics* **1** 181–227.

Delbaen, F., and Schachermayer, W. (1994). Arbitrage and free lunch with bounded risk for unbounded continuous processes. *Math. Finance* **4** 343-348.

Delbaen, F., and Schachermayer, W. (1995). The existence of absolutely continuous local martingale measure. *Annals of Applied Probability* **5** 926–945.

Delbaen, F., and Schachermayer, W. (1996). The variance-optimal martingale measure for continuous processes. *Bernoulli* **2** 81–105.

Dellacherie, C., and Meyer, P.A. (1978). *Probabilities and Potential.* Amsterdam, New York.

Diaconis, P.W., and Freedman, D. (1986a). On the consistency of Bayes estimators. *Annals of Statistics* **14** 1–26.

Diaconis, P.W., and Freedman, D. (1986b). On inconsistent Bayes estimates of location. *Annals of Statistics* **14** 68–87.

Drost, F., and Werker, B. (1996). Closing the GARCH gap: Continuous time GARCH modeling. *Journal of Econometrics* **74** 31–58.

Dubins, L.E., and Schwartz, G. (1965). On continuous martingales. *Proceedings of the National Academy of Sciences of United States of America* **53** 913–916.

Duffie, D. (1996). *Dynamic Asset Pricing Theory* (2nd ed.) Princeton, N. J.

Duffie, D., Pan, J., and Singleton, K.J. (2000). Transform analysis and asset pricing for affine jump-diffusions. *Econometrica* **68** 1343–1376.

Dybvig, P., and Huang, C.-F. (1988). Nonnegative wealth, absence of arbitrage, and feasible consumption plans. *Rev. Financial Studies* **1** 337–401.

Eberlein, E., and Jacod, J. (1997). On the range of options prices. *Finance and Stochastics* **1** 131–140.

El Karoui, N., Jeanblanc-Picqué, M., and Shreve, S.E. (1998). Robustness of the Black and Scholes formula. *Mathematical Finance* **8** 93–126.

El Karoui, N., and Quenez, M.-C. (1995). Dynamic programming and pricing of contingent claims in an incomplete market. *SIAM Journal on Control and Optimization* **33** 29–66.

Elliot, R.J. (1982). *Stochastic Calculus and Applications.* Springer, New York.

Engle, R.F. (1982). Autoregressive conditional heteroscedasticity with estimates of U.K. inflation. *Econometrica* **50** 987–1008.

Engle, R.F. (1995). *ARCH: Selected Readings.* Oxford University Press, New York, N.Y.

Engle, R.F., and Sun, Z. (2005). Forecasting volatility using tick by tick data. Technical report, New York University.

Florens-Zmirou, D. (1993). On estimating the diffusion coefficient from discrete observations. *Journal of Applied Probability* **30** 790–804.

Föllmer, H., (1979). Calcul d'Itô sans probabilités, *Seminaire de Probabilités XV*, Lect. Notes in Math. Springer-Verlag.

Föllmer, H., and Leukert, P. (1999). Quantile hedging. *Finance and Stochastics* **3** 251–273.

Föllmer, H., and Leukert, P. (2000). Efficient hedging: Cost versus shortfall risk. *Finance and Stochastics* **4** 117–146.

Föllmer, H., and Schied, A. (2002). *Stochastic Finance: An Introduction in Discrete Time*, deGruyter Studies in Mathematics, Berlin.

Föllmer, H., and Schweizer, M. (1991). Hedging of Contingent Claims under Incomplete Information. In: Davis, M.H.A., and Elliot, R.J. (eds.) *Applied Stochastic Analysis*, Gordon and Breach Science Publisher, New York.

Föllmer, H., and Sondermann, D. (1986). Hedging of Non-Redundant Contingent Claims. In: Hildebrand,W., and Mas-Colell,A. (eds.) *Contributions to Mathematical Economics*, pp. 205–223, Amsterdam: North-Holland.

Foster, D.P., and Nelson, D.B. (1996). Continuous record asymptotics for rolling sample variance estimators. *Econometrica* **64** 139–74.

Frey, R. (2000). Superreplication in stochastic volatility models and optimal stopping. *Finance and Stochastics* **4** 161–188.

Frey, R., and Sin, C. (1999). Bounds on European options prices under stochastic volatility. *Mathematical Finance* **9** 97–116.

Friedman, C. (2000). Confronting model misspecification in finance: Tractable collections of scenario probability measures for robust financial optimization problems (preprint).

Fritelli, M. (2000). Introduction to a theory of value coherent with the no-arbitrage principle. *Finance and Stochastics* **4** 275–297.

Garcia, R., Ghysels, E., and Renault, E. (2009). The Econometrics of Option Pricing. In: Aït-Sahalia,Y., and Hansen, L.P. (eds.) *Handbook of Financial Econometrics* (Inpress).

Geman, H., and Yor, M. (1996). Pricing and hedging double-barrier options: A probabilistic approach. *Mathematical Finance* **6** 365–378.

Genon-Catalot, V., and Jacod, J. (1994). Estimation of the diffusion coefficient of diffusion processes: Random sampling. *Scandinavian Journal of Statistics* **21** 193–221.

Genon-Catalot, V., Jeantheau, T., and Laredo, C. (1999). Parameter estimation for discretely observed stochastic volatility models. *Bernoulli* **5** 855–872.

Genon-Catalot, V., Jeantheau, T., and Laredo, C. (2000). Stochastic volatility models as hidden Markov models and statistical applications. *Bernoulli* **6** 1051–1079.

Ghysels, E., and Sinko, A. (2009). Volatility forecasting and microstructure noise. *Journal of Econometrics* (Inpress).

Gourieroux, C., and Jasiak, J. (2009). Value at Risk. In: Aït-Sahalia, Y., and Hansen, L.P. (eds.) *Handbook of Financial Econometrics* (to appear).

Hansen, L.P. (1982). Large sample properties of generalized-method of moments estimators. *Econometrica* **50** 1029–1054.

Hansen, L.P., and Sargent, T.J. (2001). Robust control and model uncertainty. *American Economic Review* **91** 60–66.

Hansen, L.P., and Sargent, T.J. (2008). *Robustness*. Princeton University Press, Princeton, NJ.

Hansen, L.P., and Scheinkman, J.A. (1995). Back to the future: Generating moment implications for continuous-time Markov processes. *Econometrica* **63** 767–804.

Hansen, L.P., Scheinkman, J.A., and Touzi, N. (1998). Spectral methods for identifying scalar diffusions. *Journal of Econometrics* **86** 1–32.

Harrison, J.M., and Kreps, D.M. (1979). Martingales and arbitrage in multiperiod securities markets. *Journal of Econometrics Theory* **20** 381–408.

Harrison, J.M., and Pliskà, S.R. (1981). Martingales and stochastic integrals in the theory of continuous trading. *Stochastic Processes and their Applications* **11** 215–260.

Harvey, A.C., and Shephard, N. (1994). Estimation of an asymmetric stochastic volatility model for asset returns. *Journal of Business and Economic Statistics* **14** 429–434.

Haug, S., Klüppelberg, C., Lindner, A., and Zapp, M. (2007) Method of moment estimation in the COGARCH(1,1) model. *The Econometrics Journal* **10** 320–341.

Heath, D., and Ku, H. (2004). Pareto equilibria with coherent measures of risk. *Mathematical Finance* **14** 163–172.

Heston, S. (1993). A closed-form solution for options with stochastic volatility with applications to bonds and currency Options. *Review of Financial Studies* **8** 327–343.

Hobson, D.G. (1998a). Volatility misspecification, option pricing and superreplication via coupling. The *Annals of Applied Probability* **8** 193–205.

Hobson, D.G. (1998b) Robust hedging of the lookback option. *Finance and Stochastics* **2** 329–347.

Hofmann, N., Platen, E., and Schweizer, M. (1992). Option pricing under incompleteness and stochastic volatility. *Mathematical Finance* **2** 153–187.

Hull, J.C. (1997). *Options, Futures and Other Derivatives*, 3rd Ed. Prentice Hall, Englewood Cliffs, NJ.

Hull, J.C. (1999). *Options, Futures and Other Derivatives* (4rd eds.). Prentice Hall, Englewood Cliffs, NJ.

Jacod, J. (1979). *Calcul Stochastique et Problèmes de Martingales*, Lect. N. Math. 714 (Springer-Verlag).

Jacod, J. (2000). Non-parametric kernel estimation of the coefficient of a diffusion. *Scandinavion Journal of Statistics* **27** 83–96.

Jacod, J., Li, Y., Mykland, P.A., Podolskij, M., and Vetter, M. (2008). Microstructure noise in the continuous case: The Pre-Averaging Approach (to appear in *Stochastic Processes and Applications*).

Jacod, J., and Protter, P.(1998). Asymptotic error distributions for the Euler method for stochastic differential equations. *Annals of Probability* **26** 267–307.

Jacod, J., and Shiryaev, A.N. (1987). *Limit Theory for Stochastic Processes*. Springer-Verlag, New York.

Jacquier, E., Polson, N., and Rossi, P.E. (1994). Bayesian analysis of stochastic volatility models. *Journal Business and Economic Statistics* **12** 371–389.

Jouini, E., and Kallal, H. (1995). Martingale and arbitrage in securities markets with transaction costs. *Journal of Economic Theory* **66** 178–197.

Karatzas, I. (1988). On the pricing of American options. Applied Mathematics and Optimization **17** 37–60 (1988)

Karatzas, I. (1996). *Lectures on the Mathematics of Finance* (CRM monograph series).

Karatzas, I., and Kou, S.G. (1996). On the pricing of contingent claims under constraints, *Annals of Applied Probability* **6** 321–369.

Karatzas, I., and Kou, S.G. (1998). Hedging American contingent claims with constrained portfolios. *Finance and Stochastics* **2** 215–258.

Karatzas, I., and Shreve, S.E. (1991). *Brownian Motion and Stochastic Calculus* (2nd ed). Springer-Verlag, New York.

Kessler, M., and Sørensen, M. (1999). Estimating equations based on eigenfunctions for a discretely observed diffusion process. *Bernoulli* **5** 299–314.

Kim, S., Shephard, N., and Chib, S. (1998). Stochastic volatility: Likelihood inference and comparison with ARCH models. *Review of Economic Studies* **65** 361–393.

Kramkov, D.O. (1996). Optional decompositions of supermartingales and hedging in incomplete security markets. *Probability Theory and Related Fields* **105** 459–479.

Külldorff, M. (1993). Optimal control of favorable games with a time limit. *SIAM J. Control Optim.* **31** 52–69.

Küchler, U., and Sørensen, M. (1998). *Exponential Families of Stochastic Processes*. Springer-Verlag, New York.

Laurent, J.P., and Pham, H. (1999). Dynamic programming and mean-variance hedging. *Finance Stochast* **3** 83–110.

Lindner, A.M. (2008). Continuous Time Approximations to GARCH and Stochastic Volatility Models. In: Andersen, T.G., Davis, R.A., Kreiβ, J.-P., and Mikosch, TH. (eds.), *Handbook of Financial Time Series*, Springer, Berlin and Heidelberg, 481–496.

Lo, A.W. (1987). Semi-parametric upper bounds for option prices and expected payoffs. *Journal of Financial Economics* **19** 373–387.

Lucas, R.E., Jr. (1976). Econometric Policy Evaluation: A Critique. In: Brunner, K., and Meltzer, A.H. (eds.) *The Phillips Curve and Labor Markets.* North-Holland, Amsterdam.

Lyons, T.J. (1995). Uncertain volatility and the risk-free synthesis of derivatives. *Applied Mathematical Finance* **2** 117–133.

Meddahi, N. (2001). An Eigenfunction Approach for Volatility Modeling. Techical Report 29–2001, Centre de recherche et développment en économique, Université de Montréal.

Meddahi, N., and Renault, E. (2004). Temporal aggregation of volatility models. *Journal of Econometrics* **119** 355–379.

Meddahi, N., Renault, E., and Werker, B. (2006). GARCH and irregularly spaced data. *Economic Letters* **90** 200–204.

Merton, R.C. (1973). Theory of rational options pricing. *Bell Journal of Economics and Measurement Science* **4** 141–183.

Mykland, P.A. (2000). Conservative delta hedging. The *Annals of Applied Probability* **10** 664–683.

Mykland, P.A. (2003a). The interpolation of options. *Finance and Stochastics* **7** 417–432.

Mykland, P.A. (2003b). Financial options and statistical prediction intervals. *Annals of Statistics* **31** 1413–1438.

Mykland, P.A. (2005). Combining statistical intervals and market prices: The worst case state price distribution, TR 553, Department of Statistics, The University of Chicago.

Mykland, P.A., and Zhang, L. (2006). ANOVA for diffusions and Itô processes. *Annals of Statistics* **34** 1931–1963.

Mykland, P.A., and Zhang, L. (2007). Inference for continuous semimartingales observed at high frequency (to appear in *Econometrica*).

Mykland, P.A., and Zhang, L. (2008). Inference for volatility-type objects and implications for hedging. *Statistics and Its Interface* **1** 255–278.

Myneni, R. (1992). The pricing of the American option. The *Annals of Applied Probability* **2** 1–23.

Nelson, D.B. (1990). ARCH models as diffusion approximations. *Journal of Econometrics* **45** 7–38.

Pan, J. (2002). The jump-risk premia implicit in options: Evidence from an integrated time-series study. *Journal of Financial Economics* **63** 3–50.

Pollard, D. (1984). *Convergence of Stochastic Processes.* Springer-Verlag, New York.

Pham, H., Rheinländer, T., and Schweizer, M. (1998). Mean-variance hedging for continuous processes: New proofs and examples. *Finance and Stochastics* **2** 173–198.

Renault, E. (2008). Moment-Based Estimation of Stochastic Volatility Models. In: Andersen, T.G., Davis, R.A., Krei., J.-P., and Mikosch, TH. (eds.), 269–312. *Handbook of Financial Time Series* Springer, Berlin and Heidelberg.

Ruiz, E. (1994). Quasi-maximum likelihood estimation of stochastic volatility models. *Journal of Econometrics* **63** 289–306.

Schweizer, M. (1990). Risk-minimality and orthogonality of martingales. *Stochastics* **30** 123–131.

Schweizer, M. (1991). Option hedging for semimartingales. *Stochastic Processes and their Application* **37** 339–363.

Schweizer, M. (1992). Mean-variance hedging for general claims. The *Annals of Applied Probility* **2** 171–179.

Schweizer, M. (1993). Semimartingales and hedging in incomplete markets *Theory of Probability and its Applications* **37** 169–171.

Schweizer, M. (1994). Approximating random variables by stochastic integrals. *Annals of Probability* **22** 1536–1575.

Simonsen, K.K. (1997). Simulating First Passage Times and the Maximum of Stochastic Differential Equations: An Error Analysis. Ph.D. dissertation, Department of Statistics, The University of Chicago.

Smith, R.L. (1999). Bayesian and Frequentist Approaches to Parametric Predictive Inference (with discussion). In: *Bayesian Statistics*, Bernardo, J.M., Berger, J.O., Dawid, A.P., and Smith, A.F.M., (eds.), **6** 589–612. Oxford University Press, Oxford.

Spivak, G., and Cvitanić (1998). Maximizing the probability of a perfect hedge. The *Annals of Applied Probability* **9** 1303–1328.

Stelzer, R. (2008). Multivariate Continuous Time Lvvy-Driven GARCH(1,1) Processes. (Technical report, Technische Universität München).

Strook, D.W., and Varadhan, S.R.S. (1979). *Multidimensional Diffusion Processes*. Springer, New York.

Taylor, S.J. (1994). Modeling stochastic volatility: A review and comparative study. *Mathematical Finance* **4** 183–204.

Vasicek, O.A. (1977). An equilibrium characterization of the term structure. *Journal of Financial Economics* **5** 177–188.

Willinger, W., and Taqqu, M.S. (1991). Toward a convergence theory for continuous stochastic securities market models. *Mathematical Finance* **1** 55–99.

Zhang, L. (2001). From martingales to ANOVA: Implied and realized volatility. Ph.D. dissertation, Department of Statistics, University of Chicago.

Zhang, L. (2006). Efficient estimation of stochastic volatility using noisy observations: A multiscale approach. *Bernoulli* **12** 1019–1043.

Zhang, L., Mykland, P.A., and Aït-Sahalia, Y. (2005). A tale of two time scales: Determining integrated volatility with noisy high-frequency data. *Journal of the American Statistical Association* **100** 1394–1411.

CHAPTER 16

Inference for Stochastic Processes

Jean Jacod

Institut de Mathématiques de Jussieu, Université P. et M. Curie (Paris-6), Paris, France

Contents

Abstract

We present a review, without proofs, of some of the methods used for estimating an unknown parameter occurring in the coefficients of a diffusion process, under various observation schemes. These schemes are mostly discrete in time, along a regular grid, with say n observations, and we are mainly interested in asymptotically good (or even optimal) statistical procedures, in various limiting situations: the mesh of the grid is constant, or it goes to 0 at some rate in function of the number n. We make an attempt to compare the pro and con of those methods. We also consider a situation where each observation is made with a measurement error, in two cases: the error is an additive error or it is a round-off error.

Keywords: diffusion processes; asymptotic statistical theory; LAN property; estimating functions

1. INTRODUCTION

The title of this chapter is clearly overoptimistic and a bit misleading: another appropriate title, perhaps more to the point, would have been "discretely sampled diffusions," but this was already used by other contributors to this volume, and somehow our title stresses our ambition, which is to write a sort of commented review of the topic of inference for diffusion processes.

The reader should ask himself right away whether it is really possible to describe such a topic in any sort of depth within a score of pages? For example, Prakasa Rao devoted two thick books [1, 2] to this, without exhausting the subject. But here our aim is much more modest and also slightly different in spirit: we essentially consider parametric inference for diffusion processes observed at discrete times, and for each setting, we usually describe a single estimation method, sometimes very quickly, and of course no proof is given; on the other hand, we describe a variety of observation schemes and we try to compare these various schemes when it comes to applying the methods to concrete data.

Considering only diffusion processes is motivated by their wide use in finance and also by the fact that essentially nothing is known about statistics for other continuous-time processes, apart from point processes that occur in quite other contexts, very far from finance. Considering only parametric inference is motivated mainly by the fact that so far most models used in finance are parametric models but also by the facts that relatively little is known about nonparametric inference for one-dimensional diffusions, whereas for multidimensional diffusions, nonparametric inference is perhaps even meaningless as soon as one wants to infer the diffusion coefficient (the volatility) from data coming form the observation of a single path of the process on a finite time interval. Concerning this statement, I should emphasize that a large number of papers about inference of the integrated volatility or other characteristics (spot volatility, jumps, and so on) have been written, in most cases in a nonparametric setting, for one- or multidimensional processes: but the aim is radically different. In these papers, one wants to estimate, for example, the (random) path of the volatility and not an unknown deterministic function which can at the best be estimated at the points which have been visited by the single observed path of the underlying process.

As in most statistical contexts, the first concern of the statistician is the structure of the available data. This is more important for continuous-time processes because many different observation schemes might be thought of. One may observe the whole path of the process over some time interval (a very rare occurrence indeed) or the exact values taken by the process at some "discrete" times, either regularly spaced or not, or even at random times; one may also observe a "regularization" of the path (this is certainly the case in physical applications, probably much less the case in finance) or the values taken by the process at some times, but blurred by some kind of error, and so on. Here, we mainly consider the case where n observations are given, regularly spaced on a grid with mesh Δ_n. The number n is usually very large, and this is why we are interested in asymptotic properties as n goes to infinity; as for the mesh Δ_n, it might be "small" (relatively to the characteristics of the diffusion process) or not. So, we study both the case where $\Delta_n \to 0$ and the case where $\Delta_n = \Delta$ is fixed; in practice, though, n and Δ_n are given, and we have to decide whether one can consider Δ_n as small or not.

Another question will be closely looked at in this chapter: what happens when the data are blurred with measurement errors? Surprisingly enough, very few papers have been devoted so far to this topic, which we feel to be of much importance. Two kinds of errors will be considered, both of them quite likely to occur in finance and in other situations: first when each value of the process is measured with an additive independent error and next when each value is measured with a round-off error. We also put a lot of emphasis on the asymptotic "optimality," or lack of optimality, of the procedures we describe.

The structure of this chapter is as follows: we start with a very brief account on diffusion processes (Section 2) and another short reminder about asymptotic optimality in statistics (Section 3). In Section 4, we give some general facts about statistics of diffusions. Sections 5 and 6 are devoted to regularly spaced observations, with a mesh Δ_n going to 0 or being fixed, respectively. In Section 7, we study the situation when the process is observed with measurement errors. Finally, Section 8 is devoted to some concluding remarks and some hints about discontinuous processes.

2. ABOUT DIFFUSION PROCESSES

There is a large literature on diffusion processes, and one can, for example, refer to Øksendal [3] for an introductory account or to "classical" books like Stroock and Varadhan [4], Liptser and Shiryayev [5], Ikeda and Watanabe [6], or Revuz and Yor [7]. Of special interest for finance is of course the book of Karatzas and Shreve [8]. For likelihood ratios, we refer to [5] or [9].

In most of this section, we consider only a single given diffusion process: this is in contrast with the rest of the paper, where a whole family of diffusion processes, depending on some parameter θ, is given.

2.1. The Basic Setting

By a "diffusion process," we mean the solution $X = (X_t)$ of the following stochastic differential equation (SDE):

$$dX_t = a(t, X_t)dt + \sigma(t, X_t)dW_t, \quad X_0 = U. \tag{2.1}$$

Here, time t typically ranges through the real half-line $\mathbf{R}_+ = (0, \infty)$; the process X takes its values in $\mathbf{R}^d$ for some integer d, so X_t has d components $(X_t^i)_{1 \leq i \leq d}$; next, $W = (W_t)_{t \geq 0}$ stands for a d'-dimensional standard Wiener process. The other ingredients of Eq. (2.1) are

(i) The *initial condition* $U = (U^i)_{1 \leq i \leq d}$, which is a random vector with values in $\mathbf{R}^d$ and independent from the Wiener process W.

(ii) The *drift coefficient* $a = (a^i)_{1 \leq i \leq d}$, which is a measurable function from $\mathbf{R}_+ \times \mathbf{R}^d$ into $\mathbf{R}^d$.

(iii) The *diffusion coefficient* $\sigma = (\sigma^{i,j})_{1 \leq i \leq d, 1 \leq j \leq d'}$, which is a $d \times d'$-matrix-valued measurable function on $\mathbf{R}_+ \times \mathbf{R}^d$. We also associate with σ the $d \times d$ symmetrical nonnegative matrix $c(t, x) = \sigma(t, x)\sigma(t, x)^\star$ (where "$\star$" stands for the transpose): sometimes c is also called "diffusion coefficient."

Now that the basic terms are defined, we can introduce the notion(s) of a "solution." The simplest notion is called a solution-process: in addition to the data a and σ, we start with a given initial condition U and a given Wiener process W, all defined on some probability space $(\Omega, \mathcal{F}, \mathbf{P})$ endowed with a *filtration* $(\mathcal{F}_t)$. This space supports a d-dimensional random vector U (the initial condition), which is $\mathcal{F}_0$-measurable. It also supports a d'-dimensional Wiener process W, which is in fact an $(\mathcal{F}_t)$-Wiener process: it is *adapted* to the filtration $(\mathcal{F}_t)$ (each variable W_t is $\mathcal{F}_t$-measurable), and for any $0 \leq s \leq t$, the variable $W_t - W_s$ is independent of $\mathcal{F}_s$. The term $(\Omega, \mathcal{F}, (\mathcal{F}_t), U, W, \mathbf{P})$ will be called an *SDE basis*. Then a *solution-process* of (2.1) on this SDE basis is any $\mathbf{R}^d$-valued process X which is continuous in time, adapted to the filtration $(\mathcal{F}_t)$, and which satisfies the following (written componentwise):

$$X_t^i = U^i + \int_0^t a(s, X_s)^i ds + \sum_{j=1}^{d'} \int_0^t \sigma(s, X_s)^{i,j} dW_s^j, \quad i = 1, \ldots, d. \tag{2.2}$$

The second integrals above are stochastic integrals with respect to the one-dimensional Wiener processes W^j, uniquely defined up to a null set only; of course, writing (2.2) supposes that all the integrals make sense. When the filtration $(\mathcal{F}_t)$ is the one "generated by" the Wiener process W and the initial condition U, then a solution-process is called a *strong solution*.

Let us now recall a set of hypotheses that yields *existence and uniqueness* of a solution process for our SDE (the uniqueness is to be understood up to null sets, that is, if X and

X' are two solutions, then the set of all ω for which the paths $t \mapsto X_t(\omega)$ and $t \mapsto X'_t(\omega)$ do not agree is of probability 0). These hypotheses are

(L) Local Lipschitz condition: For all $T > 0, K > 0$, there is a constant $C(T, K)$ such that (with $|.|$ being the Euclidian norm on any relevant space)

$$t \in [0, T], \quad |x|, |y| \leq K \quad \Rightarrow \quad |a(t, x) - a(t, y)| + |\sigma(t, x) - \sigma(t, y)| \leq C(T, K)|x - y| \tag{2.3}$$

(G) Linear growth condition: For all $T > 0$, there is a constant $C(T)$ such that

$$t \in [0, T] \quad \Rightarrow \quad |a(t, x)| + |\sigma(t, x)| \leq C(T)(1 + |x|). \tag{2.4}$$

If (L) holds but (G) fails, then a (unique) solution exists up to the "explosion" time: there is a stopping time T such that (2.2) holds for $t < T$, and $\lim \sup_{t \uparrow T} |X_t| = \infty$ on the set $\{T < \infty\}$.

So far, the Wiener process W and the initial condition U were given. In financial applications, though, the actual Wiener process does not really matter. Similarly the actual variable U has no importance, only its law μ matters. Hence, it is meaningful to speak about X when the coefficients a and c and the law μ of the initial condition are given, without reference to any predefined Wiener process W and random variable U. Mathematically, this means that we are interested in the *law* of X. And, in statistics also, one is usually interested in the laws of the data and not in the actual probability space on which these data are defined.

A *weak solution* to Eq. (2.1) is the law of any solution-process of this equation. As the law of any random variable, the law of X will be a probability measure on the space in which X takes its values. So, let us denote by Ω the space of all continuous functions from $\mathbf{R}_+$ into $\mathbf{R}^d$ (here d is fixed and does not appear in our notation). We endow this space with the so-called "canonical process" Y, defined by $Y_t(\omega) = \omega(t)$ when $\omega \in \Omega$, with the Kolmogorov σ-field $\mathcal{Y} = \sigma(Y_t : t \geq 0)$ and with the canonical filtration $\mathcal{Y}_t = \cap_{s>t}\sigma(Y_r : r \leq s)$. Then if X is a solution-process on any given SDE basis, its law is a *weak solution*. The law μ of the initial condition U (which is also the law of Y_0 under the weak solution) is called the "initial condition" of the weak solution.

Studying weak solutions seems to be a rather difficult task because a priori different solution-processes, possibly defined on different spaces, lead to different weak solutions. However, due to two remarkable results, weak solutions are indeed quite tractable:

Theorem 1 (Yamada and Watanabe): *Let μ be a probability measure on $\mathcal{R}^d$, and suppose that on any SDE basis such that $\mathcal{L}(U) = \mu$, Eq. (2.1) admits a unique solution-process. Then, the weak solution with initial condition μ (which of course exists !) is unique.* [This holds in particular under (L) and (G).]

Theorem 2 (Stroock and Varadhan): *Suppose that the coefficients a and σ satisfy the linear growth condition (G) and are continuous in x, and also that the matrix $c(t, x) = \sigma(t, x)\sigma(t, x)^*$ is everywhere invertible. Then, for any probability measure μ on $\mathbf{R}^d$, there is one and only one weak solution with initial condition μ.*

2.2. The Markov Property and the Infinitesimal Generator

In the sequel, we assume that our SDE admits, for every initial measure μ, a unique weak solution. Denote by $\mathbf{P}_\mu$ the weak solution associated with the initial measure μ. A crucial property of our diffusion is that the process Y is, under each $\mathbf{P}_\mu$, a Markov process. Of course, it is in general nonhomogeneous, and it becomes homogeneous when the coefficients a and c do not depend on time.

We will denote by $(P_{s,t})_{0 \leq s \leq t}$ the (nonhomogeneous) transition semigroup, that is, $P_{s,t}(x, .)$ is the law of Y_t, under each $\mathbf{P}_\mu$, conditionally on the fact that $Y_s = x$. In the homogeneous case, we get a one-parameter semigroup, denoted by $(P_t)_{t \geq 0}$.

Another characteristic of our diffusion is its infinitesimal generator, which is useful mainly in the homogeneous case. So, assuming that the coefficients a and c do not depend on time, we introduce the following second-order elliptic operator:

$$Af(x) = \sum_{i=1}^{d} a(x)^i \frac{\partial}{\partial x_i} f(x) + \frac{1}{2} \sum_{i,j=1}^{d} c(x)^{i,j} \frac{\partial^2}{\partial x_i \partial x_j} f(x). \tag{2.5}$$

Then one can show that a probability measure $\mathbf{P}$ on the canonical space is a weak solution to our SDE if and only if, for any twice continuously differentiable function f on $\mathbf{R}^d$, the following processes

$$M_t^f = f(Y_t) - f(Y_0) - \int_0^t Af(Y_s)\mathrm{d}s \tag{2.6}$$

are local martingales under $\mathbf{P}$.

This "martingale characterization" of weak solutions is most useful (a similar statement holds in the nonhomogeneous case). We will call the operator A the *infinitesimal generator* of the diffusion process, although this is a slight abuse of terminology (our operator A is more like the so-called "extended generator" of Kunita, except that we do not bother here about the actual domain of this unbounded linear operator, using only the fact that C^2 functions are in the domain).

2.3. Examples – Diffusions on a Domain

Below we list a number of examples, some of them having an explicit solution in terms of the driving Wiener process: this is rather rare, but such situations are worth mentioning because they provide some of the most commonly used diffusion processes in finance, and also they provide simple case studies in which various statistical procedures can be tested. All these simple examples below concern the one-dimensional case, $d = d' = 1$. The reader will observe that in all examples, there are parameters coming naturally within the coefficients.

Example 1 (Wiener process with drift): *This is Eq. (2.1) with the coefficients $a(x) = \mu$ and $\sigma(x) = \sigma$, where $\mu \in \mathbf{R}$ and $\sigma > 0$ are given constants. The "solution" is of course $X_t = X_0 + \mu t + \sigma W_t$.*

Example 2 (Geometric Brownian motion or Black–Scholes model): *This is Eq. (2.1) with the coefficients $a(x) = \mu x$ and $\sigma(x) = \sigma x$, where $\mu \in \mathbf{R}$ and $\sigma > 0$:*

$$dX_t = \mu X_t dt + \sigma X_t dW_t, \quad X_0 = U. \tag{2.7}$$

This equation is a "linear" equation, which admits an "explicit" solution given by

$$X_t = U \exp\left(\left(\mu - \frac{\sigma^2}{2}\right)t + \sigma W_t\right). \tag{2.8}$$

Example 3 (Ornstein–Uhlenbeck process): *This is the equation*

$$dX_t = -\mu X_t dt + \sigma dW_t, \quad X_0 = U, \tag{2.9}$$

where $\mu \in \mathbf{R}$ and $\sigma > 0$. This is again a linear equation with an explicit solution given by

$$X_t = U e^{-\mu t} + \sigma \int_0^t e^{-\mu(t-s)} dW_s. \tag{2.10}$$

The above stochastic integral is a Wiener integral (the integrand is a deterministic function), so it gives a centered normal variable with variance $\int_0^t e^{-2\mu(t-s)} ds = (1 - e^{-2\mu t})/2\mu$ if $\mu \neq 0$ and t if $\mu = 0$.

Example 4 (The Vasicek model): *This is the equation*

$$dX_t = \mu(\nu - X_t) dt + \sigma dW_t, \quad X_0 = U, \tag{2.11}$$

where $\mu, \nu \in \mathbf{R}$, and $\sigma > 0$. This generalizes the Ornstein–Uhlenbeck equation and is again a linear equation with an explicit solution given by

$$X_t = U e^{-\mu t} + \sigma \int_0^t e^{-\mu(t-s)} dW_s + \nu(1 - e^{-\mu t}). \tag{2.12}$$

Example 5 (The Cox–Ingersoll–Ross model): *This is the equation*

$$dX_t = \mu(\nu - X_t) dt + \sigma \sqrt{X_t} dW_t, \quad X_0 = U, \tag{2.13}$$

where $\mu, \nu \in \mathbf{R}, \sigma > 0$, and U is a positive random variable. In this case, (G) is satisfied but not (L); however, a "version" of (L) holds on $(0, \infty)$, namely (2.3) holds for x and y in any compact subset K of $(0, \infty)$, and we have a unique solution process up to the first time when this solution hits 0. In other words, there is a unique solution process on the whole half-line as soon as we are sure that this solution never hits 0: this is the case if and only if $2\mu\nu > \sigma^2$ and $\mu > 0$.

In the last example, it is crucial that the solution remains positive. In the Black–Scholes model, we see from (2.8) that if the initial condition U is positive, then X remains always positive: in both cases, we can consider that the state space is $(0, \infty)$ instead of $\mathbf{R}$.

These are examples where the solution takes its values in a domain D of $\mathbf{R}^d$. Considering, for example, Eq. (2.1) on such a domain D means that the functions a and σ are defined on $\mathbf{R}_+ \times D$ and that the solution takes its values in D. Two extreme cases are possible:

1. The domain D is open: one extends a and σ over the whole set $\mathbf{R}_+ \times \mathbf{R}^d$ in an arbitrary fashion and considers initial conditions U taking values in D only. One solves the equation in $\mathbf{R}^d$ and with some luck the solution will not leave D. However, it is not always easy (nor even possible) to extend a and σ in such a way that (L) and (G) or the conditions for Theorem 2 hold, and further, there is no general criterion yielding that X will stay in D; only ad hoc arguments for each special case, as for the Cox–Ingersoll–Ross model, will (sometimes) do the job.

2. The domain D is closed. This case is more difficult because one has to specify what happens when the solution X hits the boundary ∂D: it can reflect instantaneously toward the interior of D, stick for a while on the boundary ∂D at the hitting point, or diffuse over the boundary itself for a while before bouncing back inside the interior of D. All these behaviors necessitate additional specifications.

And, of course, there are "mixed" cases, where D is neither open nor closed, and the specifications of the process are even harder in these cases. However, in Case 1 above, all what we have said for diffusions over $\mathbf{R}^d$ remains true for diffusions over an open domain as soon as we know that the process never exits the domain. As a matter of fact, in this chapter, we will always assume that we are in Case 1, whenever the state space is a domain D of $\mathbf{R}^d$, that is, we can and will *always* do as if the state space were the whole of $\mathbf{R}^d$ (this is an important remark because when a diffusion hits its boundary, the statistical properties might be radically modified, and in particular, the rates of convergence of estimators might be greatly improved, or on the opposite, the asymptotic variance of the estimators can be increased). That means for the Cox–Ingersoll–Ross process, for example, we restrict our attention to the set of parameters $\{(\mu, \nu, \sigma) : \mu > 0, \ 2\mu\nu > \sigma^2\}$.

2.4. Likelihood Ratio
One of the main tools in statistics is the likelihood ratios for the solutions of Eq. (2.1) associated with various coefficients.

Let us consider two sets of coefficients (a, σ) and (a', σ') with the same dimensionality, and $c = \sigma\sigma^*$ and $c' = \sigma'\sigma'^*$, and consider solutions X and X' corresponding to these coefficients and starting at the same point x_0 for simplicity. The likelihood ratio "of X' w.r.t. X" is the likelihood ration (or Radon–Nikodym derivative) of the law P' of X' w.r.t. the law P of X, that is, we consider the weak solutions P and P' of our equations, and we want to compute the likelihood ratio in terms of the coefficients.

Two preliminary remarks are in order: first, as seen, for example, in Theorem 2, the weak solution P depends on a and c, but not on σ itself (we may have different functions σ with the same "square" $\sigma\sigma^*$). So the likelihood ration can at the best be expressed in terms of a, a', c, c'. For example, the two equations $dX_t = dW_t$ and $dX'_t = -dW_t$ have the same unique weak solution, and thus we cannot discriminate between the two equations upon observing even the whole processes X and X'. Second, we obviously need that P and P' be completely characterized by the pairs (a, c) and (a', c'), that is, we need existence and uniqueness of the weak solutions to our two equations. And, the likelihood ratio will be computed *on the canonical space* $(\Omega, \mathcal{Y})$.

Next, an extremely important observation: before computing any likelihood ratio, we need to specify on which σ-field this ratio will be computed (in statistical terms: what is the form of the actual observations). This is because on the largest σ-field $\mathcal{Y}$, the measures P and P' are – typically – mutually singular. In statistical terms, if the whole process is observed (up to infinity!), then one can discriminate for sure between (a, c) and (a', c').

Although one may think of several other possibilities (some of them considered later on), we mainly consider two main schemes:

1. The σ-field is $\mathcal{G} = \mathcal{Y}_T$ for some given $T < \infty$; this corresponds to observing the path of the solution over the interval $[0, T]$.
2. The σ-field is $\mathcal{G} = \sigma(Y_{t_i} : i = 0, 1, \ldots, n)$ for some times $0 \le t_0 < t_1 < \cdots < t_n$: this corresponds to observing the solution at discrete times t_i.

Let us consider first (1). We need to assume that

$$c(t, x) = c'(t, x), \quad a'(t, x) - a(t, x) = c(t, x)b(t, x) \tag{2.14}$$

for some measurable vector-valued function b. This is because if $c(t, Y_t)$ and $c'(t, Y_t)$ do not coincide P-almost surely for all $t \in [0, T]$, or if they do but $a'(t, Y_t) - a(t, Y_t)$ is not P-almost surely of the form $c(t, Y_t)b(t, Y_t)$ when $t \in [0, T]$, then P' is not absolutely continuous w.r.t. P on the σ-field $\mathcal{G}$ (see, for example, [5]): so assuming (2.14) is quite natural in this context. Then, provided the integrals in the next equation make sense, the likelihood ratio of P' w.r.t. P, in restriction to $\mathcal{G} = \mathcal{Y}_T$, takes the form

$$Z_T = \exp\left\{ \int_0^T b(t, Y_t)^* dY_t - \frac{1}{2} \int_0^T b(t, Y_t)^\star (a(t, Y_t) + a'(t, Y_t)) dt \right\}. \tag{2.15}$$

Next we consider (2). The σ-field $\mathcal{G}$ is much smaller now, so it is much easier for $\boldsymbol{P}'$ to be absolutely continuous w.r.t. $\boldsymbol{P}$ in restriction to $\mathcal{G}$: in particular, we no longer need something like $c' = c$. In fact, as soon as for instance c is invertible on the domain D where the diffusion process lives (an hypothesis usually satisfied by financial models), the transition semigroup admits positive densities w.r.t. Lebesgue measure on D: that means the measures $P_{s,t}(x, .)$ admit positive probability densities $y \mapsto p_{s,t}(x, y)$ for all $x \in D$ and all $s < t$.

Suppose that our two diffusion processes live on the same domain D, with transition semigroups admitting positive densities $p_{s,t}$ and $p'_{s,t}$, respectively. Then, because of the Markov structure, the likelihood ratio in restriction to $\mathcal{G} = \sigma(Y_{t_i} : i = 0, 1, \ldots, n)$ is

$$Z = \prod_{i=1}^{n} \frac{p'_{t_{i-1}, t_i}(Y_{t_{i-1}}, Y_{t_i})}{p_{t_{i-1}, t_i}(Y_{t_{i-1}}, Y_{t_i})}. \tag{2.16}$$

3. PARAMETRIC ESTIMATION: ASYMPTOTIC OPTIMALITY CRITERIA

Let us now come to statistical estimation from the asymptotic point of view. We have a parameter set $\Theta \subset \boldsymbol{R}^q$, and for each $\theta \in \Theta$ a probability measure $\boldsymbol{P}_\theta$ on our basic space $(\Omega, \mathcal{Y})$ (for diffusions, each $\boldsymbol{P}_\theta$ is the weak solution of an Eq. (2.1) with coefficients depending on the value θ).

Typically (at least in the diffusion setting) one does not observe the whole σ-field $\mathcal{Y}$ but some sub-σ-field $\mathcal{G}_n$: here n stands for the "number" of available data, it is large, and we are looking at what happens when $n \to \infty$. More precisely, we want to construct for each n an estimator $\widehat{\theta}_n$ for θ, in such a way that the sequence $(\widehat{\theta}_n)_n$ behaves as well as possible when n grows. This question of asymptotic optimality in estimation for general statistical models was taken on essentially by LeCam (see [10] or LeCam and Yang [11] and also the book of Ibragimov and Khashminski [12]).

We suppose that all measures $\boldsymbol{P}_\theta$ are equivalent on the σ-field $\mathcal{G}_n$, and we use the following notation for the likelihood ratios:

$$Z_n(\zeta/\theta) = \frac{d\boldsymbol{P}_\zeta}{d\boldsymbol{P}_\theta}\Big|_{\mathcal{G}_n}.$$

Let us assume that the "true" value of the parameter is θ, some point in the interior of $\Theta \subset \boldsymbol{R}^q$. For each ζ, the sequence of random variables $(Z_n(\zeta/\theta))_n$ is tight, so it is not a drastic assumption to assume that these sequences converge in law (under $\boldsymbol{P}_\theta$). Two extreme phenomena can arise:

1. For all ζ in Θ, the limit of $Z_n(\zeta/\theta)$ under $\boldsymbol{P}_\theta$ is a strictly positive variable; then "in the limit," we still have a statistical model where all measures are equivalent. For diffusions, this arises, for example, if at stage n one observes the values $Y_{i/n}$ for

$i = 0, \ldots, n$, and when all measures $\boldsymbol{P}_\zeta$ are equivalent on the σ-field $\mathcal{Y}_1$ (typically when the diffusion coefficient c does not depend on the parameter): in the limit, we have the full observation of the diffusion over the time interval $[0, 1]$, and the likelihood is then given by (2.15).

2. For any ζ, the sequence $Z_n(\zeta/\theta)$ goes to 0 in $\boldsymbol{P}_\theta$-measure: that means "in the limit," the measures become mutually singular and a "perfect" estimation becomes possible. For diffusions, this arises, for example, if at stage n one observes the values $Y_{i/n}$ for $i = 0, \ldots, n$, and when all measures $\boldsymbol{P}_\zeta$ are mutually singular on the σ-field $\mathcal{Y}_1$ (typically when the diffusion coefficient $c(\theta, .)$ are distinct for different values of θ): in the limit, we have the full observation of the diffusion over the time interval $[0, 1]$, which gives us the function c, hence the value θ.

In case (1) above, there is nothing more to say, except to wish good luck to the statistician (observe that there is no consistent sequences of estimators). In case (2), on the opposite, we can go much further because it is possible to find weakly consistent sequences of estimators $(\widehat{\theta}_n)_n$: this means that $\widehat{\theta}_n \to \theta$ in $\boldsymbol{P}_\theta$-probability for any θ. Then, one can look for rates of convergence, and this is what the so-called "local behavior" around the "true" value θ is all about. More precisely consider a sequence u_n going to 0 (and which may depend of course on the value θ). Here, again several situations are possible:

(i) $u_n \to 0$ "slowly": then $Z_n(\theta + u_n h/\theta)$ goes to 0 in $\boldsymbol{P}_\theta$-measure, and exactly as in (2) above, one can "asymptotically" estimate perfectly the parameter at the scale u_n.

(ii) $u_n \to 0$ "fast": then $Z_n(\theta + u_n h/\theta)$ goes to 1 in $\boldsymbol{P}_\theta$-measure. This means that the measures $\boldsymbol{P}_\theta$ and $\boldsymbol{P}_{\theta+u_n h}$ become more and more indistinguishable as n increases and we cannot do any sensible estimation at the scale u_n.

(iii) In between, there is hopefully a choice of u_n such that for any choice $h_1, \ldots, h_r$ of vectors in $\boldsymbol{R}^q$ the sequence $(Z_n(\theta + u_n h_i/\theta)_n)_{1 \leq i \leq r}$ converges in law under $\boldsymbol{P}_\theta$ to a limit whose components take their values in $(0, \infty)$ and have expectation equal to 1.

Suppose now that we can find a sequence u_n such that (iii) above holds. The value θ is fixed here. One can find a statistical model $\mathcal{B}' = (\Omega', \mathcal{G}', (\boldsymbol{P}'_h)_{h \in \boldsymbol{R}^q})$ (everything depends on θ) such that the measures $\boldsymbol{P}'_h$ are all equivalent, and the likelihood ratios $Z'(h/0) = \mathrm{d}\boldsymbol{P}'_h/\mathrm{d}\boldsymbol{P}'_0$ are limits in law of the variables $Z(\theta + u_n h/\theta)_n$ under $\boldsymbol{P}_\theta$. Then one says that the *local models* $\mathcal{B}^\theta_n = (\Omega, \mathcal{G}_n, (\boldsymbol{P}_{\theta+u_n h})_{h \in \boldsymbol{R}^q})$ *converge weakly* to $\mathcal{B}'$.

In the limit, we can identify $\mathcal{B}^\theta_n$ with $\mathcal{B}'$, and LeCam showed interesting properties, which we state in a rather heuristic way: if $\widehat{h}$ is an estimator of h for $\mathcal{B}'$, there is a sequence $\widehat{\theta}_n$ of estimators for θ such that $\frac{1}{u_n}(\widehat{\theta}_n - (\theta + u_n h))$ converges in law under $\boldsymbol{P}_{\theta+u_n h}$ toward the law of $\widehat{h} - h$ under $\boldsymbol{P}'_h$ for any h. Conversely for any sequence of estimators $\widehat{\theta}_n$ such that the sequence $\frac{1}{u_n}(\widehat{\theta}_n - (\theta + u_n h))$ converges in law under $\boldsymbol{P}_{\theta+u_n h}$ to a variable U_h

for all h, then there exists an estimator $\widehat{h}$ on $\mathcal{B}'$ such that the law of U_h is the same as the law of $\widehat{h} - h$ under $\boldsymbol{P}'_h$. Further, at least in a neighborhood of θ (shrinking to 0 at speed u_n), the "asymptotically best" estimators $\widehat{\theta}_n$ converge to the true value of the parameter with the rate $1/u_n$ and $\frac{1}{u_n}(\widehat{\theta}_n - \theta)$ converges in law under $\boldsymbol{P}_\theta$ to the "best" estimator $\widehat{h}$ of h at point 0 for the model $\mathcal{B}'$, if such a best estimator exists.

In particular, if the weak convergence of local models holds at any point θ, with a rate $u_n(\theta)$ which in principle may depend on θ, we will say that a sequence $\widehat{\theta}_n$ of estimators is *rate-efficient* if for any value θ the sequence $\frac{1}{u_n(\theta)}(\widehat{\theta}_n - \theta)$ is tight under $\boldsymbol{P}_\theta$.

Remarks *When the parameter is multidimensional, there is also the possibility that the rate differs according to the components of the parameter. So we can do the same analysis with a q-dimensional vector u_n whose components decrease to 0, and the change of parameter becomes componentwise: $\zeta^i = \theta^i + u_n^i h^i$, for $i = 1, \ldots, q$. We will see such an example for ergodic diffusions later.*

3.1. The Local Asymptotic Normality Property

Finding rate-efficient estimators is good, but in some cases, we can even go further: when it is possible to derive "best" estimators for the limiting model $\mathcal{B}'$, we can in principle find accordingly "best" estimators, in the asymptotic sense, for the original model.

The simplest of these cases is by far when $\mathcal{B}'$ is the so-called *Gaussian shift*: let I be an invertible symmetric $q \times q$-matrix; the associated Gaussian shift experiment consists in taking $\Omega' = \boldsymbol{R}^q$ and $\mathcal{G}' = \mathcal{R}^q$ (the Borel σ-field) and $\boldsymbol{P}'_h = \mathcal{N}(h, I^{-1})$ (the Gaussian distribution with mean h and covariance matrix I^{-1}). With the notation $X(\omega') = \omega'$, we thus have

$$Z'(h/0) = \exp\left(h^* IX - \frac{1}{2} h^* Ih \right). \tag{3.1}$$

Observe that the matrix I is also the Fisher information matrix of the model $\mathcal{B}'$, for all values $h \in \boldsymbol{R}^q$.

We will say that *the local asymptotic normality (LAN) property holds at point θ, with rate u_n*, if the sequence of local models $\mathcal{B}_n^\theta$ around θ converges weakly to the Gaussian shift experiment $\mathcal{B}'$ described above. Of course, the matrix I depends on θ and is usually written $I = I(\theta)$.

Because of the Gaussian property of the limit, we have LAN at point θ as soon as the following convergence in law holds true:

$$Z_n(\theta + u_n h/\theta) \xrightarrow{\mathcal{L}(\boldsymbol{P}_\theta)} \exp\left(h^* X - \frac{1}{2} h^* I(\theta)h \right) \tag{3.2}$$

for all h. Equivalently, we have LAN as soon as we can write

$$\log Z_n(\theta + u_n h/\theta) = h^* U_n - \frac{1}{2} h^* \Gamma_n(\theta)h + R_n(h), \tag{3.3}$$

where $\Gamma_n(\theta) \to I(\theta)$ and $R_n(h) \to 0$ in P_θ-probability and U_n converges in law under P_θ to $\mathcal{N}(0, I(\theta))$.

Now the model $\mathcal{B}'$ is the simplest of all possible models, for which the best estimator for h (recall that $I(\theta)$ is known) is obviously $\widehat{h} = X$, in all possible senses of "best." Moreover under P'_h, the variable $\widehat{h} - h$ has the law $\mathcal{N}(0, I(\theta)^{-1})$.

Therefore, if the LAN property holds at a point θ, a sequence $\widehat{\theta}_n$ will be asymptotically optimal in a neighborhood of θ if

$$\left.\begin{array}{l} \dfrac{1}{u_n}(\widehat{\theta}_n - \theta) \xrightarrow{\mathcal{L}(P_\theta)} \mathcal{N}(0, I(\theta)^{-1}), \quad \text{or equivalently} \\[3mm] \dfrac{\sqrt{\Gamma_n(\theta)}}{u_n}(\widehat{\theta}_n - \theta) \xrightarrow{\mathcal{L}(P_\theta)} \mathcal{N}(0, I_q), \end{array}\right\} \tag{3.4}$$

where I_q is the $q \times q$ identity matrix. Observe that these estimators achieve asymptotically the Cramer–Rao bound for the estimation variance. Moreover, such estimators will also satisfy for all h:

$$\frac{1}{u_n}(\widehat{\theta}_n - (\theta + u_n h)) \xrightarrow{\mathcal{L}(P_{\theta+u_n h})} \mathcal{N}(0, I(\theta)^{-1}) \tag{3.5}$$

as well. Finally, such estimators are, in principle, easy to get: it suffices to set $\widehat{\theta}_n = \Gamma_n(\theta)^{-1} U_n$; however, in practice, finding $\Gamma_n(\theta)$ and U_n is quite a different matter!

Sequences of stimators having the property (3.4) are called *asymptotically efficient* around θ and simply "asymptotically efficient" if this holds for each θ [with $u_n = u_n(\theta)$ if it happens that u_n actually depends on θ].

3.2. Local Asymptotic Mixed Normality and Local Asymptotic Quadraticity

Of course, there are other limiting models than Gaussian shifts. Two of them are of particular interest and are sometimes obtained when dealing with diffusion processes.

Suppose that the likelihood ratios of the local model $\mathcal{B}_n^\theta$ satisfy (3.3). Suppose also that the pair $(U_n, \Gamma_n(\theta))$ converge in law, under P_θ, to a limit $(U, I(\theta))$ and that the (random) matrix $I(\theta)$ is everywhere invertible. Then,

(a) We have *the local asymptotic mixed normality (LAMN) property at point θ with rate u_n* if further we can write $U = I(\theta)^{1/2} U'$, where U' is independent of $I(\theta)$ and distributed according to $\mathcal{N}(0, I_q)$. The matrix $I(\theta)$ is called the *random Fisher information matrix*.

(b) We have *the local asymptotic quadraticity (LAQ) property at point θ with rate u_n* if further for any $h \in \mathbf{R}^q$ we have

$$E\left(e^{h^* U - \frac{1}{2} h^* I(\theta) h}\right) = 1. \tag{3.6}$$

"Quadraticity" means that the log-likelihood is approximately a quadratic form in h [in (3.3)], whereas mixed normality means that the variable U has a mixed Gaussian distribution. Obviously, LAN $\Rightarrow$ LAMN $\Rightarrow$ LAQ.

The LAMN property was introduced by Jeganathan [13], see also [11]. The LAQ property has been introduced by a number of different authors: see LeCam and Yang [11], Shiryaev, Spokoiny, and so on.

Exactly as for LAN, if the LAMN property holds at a point θ, a sequence $\widehat{\theta}_n$ will be asymptotically optimal in a neighborhood of θ if we have the analog of (3.4) [note that the first line in (3.4) makes no sense here]:

$$\frac{\sqrt{\Gamma_n(\theta)}}{u_n}(\widehat{\theta}_n - \theta) \xrightarrow{\mathcal{L}(\mathbf{P}_\theta)} \mathcal{N}(0, I_q). \tag{3.7}$$

Equivalently, one says the sequence $\frac{1}{u_n}(\widehat{\theta}_n - \theta)$ converges in law, under $\mathbf{P}_\theta$, toward a centered mixed Gaussian variable, with conditional covariance matrix $I(\theta)^{-1}$.

4. DIFFUSIONS AND STATISTICS

Let us now come back to our diffusion processes. We have a parameter set $\Theta \subset \mathbf{R}^q$ and, for each $\theta \in \Theta$, a pair $(a(\theta, .), \sigma(\theta, .))$ of coefficients with the same dimensionality, and a given starting point x_0. We set $c(\theta, .) = \sigma(\theta, .)\sigma(\theta, .)^\star$. We suppose that the equation

$$dX_t = a(\theta, t, X_t)dt + \sigma(\theta, t, X_t)dW_t, \quad X_0 = x_0 \tag{4.1}$$

has a unique weak solution $\mathbf{P}_\theta$ for every $\theta \in \Theta$. Our statistical model is $(\Omega, \mathcal{Y}, (\mathbf{P}_\theta)_{\theta \in \Theta})$, where Ω is the canonical space with the canonical process Y. Recall that according to the end of Subsection 2.3, we assume that the state space of our diffusions is the whole of $\mathbf{R}^d$. Taking a deterministic and known starting point x_0 is just for convenience, most of what follows accommodates random initial conditions (in most observation schemes, anyway the value of the process at time 0 is observed and may thus be considered as known).

We also have a set of data, which generates a sub-σ-field $\mathcal{G}_n$ of $\mathcal{Y}$, where n here stands for the size of the data set. On the basis of these data, we want to construct an estimate $\widehat{\theta}_n$ for θ, and we are particularly interested in the asymptotic optimality as $n \to \infty$. As a matter of fact, estimation procedures and even rates of convergence may greatly differ for the drift coefficient and for the diffusion coefficient. So it might be useful to label the parameters on which a and σ depend with different symbols. This leads to write the equation as

$$dX_t = a(\theta_1, X_t)dt + \sigma(\theta_2, X_t)dW_t, \quad X_0 = x_0. \tag{4.2}$$

The full parameter is then $\theta = (\theta_1, \theta_2)$. The two Eqs. (4.1) and (4.2) are two ways of writing the same thing, and the most convenient one depends on the problem at hand and especially on the structure of the set Θ: in the extreme case where $\theta_1 = \theta_2$ for all $(\theta_1, \theta_2) \in \Theta$, one prefers (4.1), whereas (4.2) is handier in the other extreme case where $\Theta = \Theta_1 \times \Theta_2$.

Because we want to have at least consistent sequences of estimators, we obviously need a minimal *identifiability assumption*, which can be expressed as follows: the measures $\boldsymbol{P}_\theta$ should be mutually singular for different values of θ, in restriction to the σ-field $\mathcal{G}_\infty = \bigvee_n \mathcal{G}_n$ which represents the biggest possible observed σ-field (note that the sequence $(\mathcal{G}_n)$ is not necessarily increasing, though). Of course this is not fully satisfactory because checking this property on the coefficients a and c themselves is not always a trivial matter. So in practice, we sometimes impose more restrictive identifiability assumptions, which are not necessary but much handier than the minimal one.

Let us now quickly review below a number of more or less commonly encountered observation schemes, which amounts to specify the observed σ-field $\mathcal{G}_n$. Some of these schemes are studied more leisurely in the forthcoming sections. But, all throughout we apply the methods to a special case to make comparisons, namely to the Ornstein–Uhlenbeck process, due to its Gaussian properties, it is particularly amenable to explicit computations. In accordance with the notation of (4.2), we write it as

$$dX_t = -\theta_1 X_t dt + \sqrt{\theta_2} dW_t, \quad X_0 = x_0, \tag{4.3}$$

and the natural parameter space is $\Theta = \Theta_1 \times \Theta_2$, with $\Theta_1 = \boldsymbol{R}$ and $\Theta_2 = (0, \infty)$.

4.1. Observation Over a Whole Interval

Problem A: The mathematically simplest case is when the whole path $t \mapsto Y_t$ is observed over an interval $[0, T_n]$, that is, $\mathcal{G}_n = \mathcal{Y}_{T_n} := \sigma(Y_s : 0 \le t \le T_n)$. The theory has been established mainly by Kutoyants (see [14] and many subsequent papers by this author).

This observation scheme has an immediate and obvious drawback: it is *stricto sensu* impossible to achieve because any conceivable mean of observation will end up with a finite set of numbers. And even if this set of numbers is very large, it is difficult to obtain a good approximation of the path $t \mapsto X_t$, which is quite irregular: it is Hölder continuous with arbitrary index $\alpha < 1/2$ but not with index $1/2$. Nevertheless, it is in principle possible to achieve an approximation of the path which is as good as one wishes by, say, discrete observations on a grid with sufficiently small mesh. So, even if this continuous–time observation scheme is not feasible strictly speaking, it can be viewed as an idealization of real observation schemes. In this sense, it has a lot of mathematical interest because it gives an "upper limit" of what can be achieved by observing X on any (regular or irregular) grid inside the interval $[0, T_n]$.

As seen in Subsection 2.4, the measures P_θ are mutually singular if the diffusion coefficients $c(\theta, .)$ differ for distinct values of θ. And, by computing the quadratic variation $\int_0^{T_n} c(\theta, s, Y_s) ds$ (a theoretically possible computation if the whole path is known), we can compute exactly the true value of θ. In other words, the statistical problem is completely solved, with no estimation error.

The situation is totally different for the drift coefficient. So let us assume that $c(\theta, .) = c(.)$ does not depend on θ, and further that it is invertible and that the functions $b_{\zeta/\theta}(.) = c(.)^{-1}(a(\zeta, .) - a(\theta, .))$ are, say, locally bounded for all θ, ζ. Then, the measures P_θ are all equivalent on $\mathcal{G}_n$, and the likelihood $Z_n(\zeta/\theta)$ is given by (2.15) with $b_{\zeta/\theta}$ instead of b and $T = T_n$.

The asymptotic is then $T_n \to \infty$: for getting any kind of results, we need some nice behavior of the diffusion process at infinity. In practice, we need our diffusion processes to be *homogeneous and positive recurrent*, with an invariant probability measure μ_θ whose support is R^d (or the domain D over which all our diffusions live). Then, using the ergodic theorem and the associated central limit theorem, and if further the matrix c is everywhere invertible, one can prove that, under mild smoothness assumptions on the coefficients, *we have the LAN property with rate* $1/\sqrt{T_n}$ and with asymptotic Fisher information matrix

$$I(\theta)_{i,j} = \int \frac{\partial}{\partial \theta_i} a(\theta, x)^* c(x)^{-1} \frac{\partial}{\partial \theta_j} a(\theta, x) \mu_\theta(dx). \tag{4.4}$$

Further the maximum likelihood estimators (MLEs) are asymptotically efficient, as soon as, for example, the parameter set Θ is compact. Using the explicit expression (2.15), we can in principle compute the MLE, but this involves computing two integrals, one being a stochastic integral; for this one needs to do some approximation, like a Riemann-type approximation, and it is difficult to keep track of the errors introduced through these approximations. A lot of papers have been devoted to methods allowing practical approximations of the likelihood or to alternative methods.

But, apart from the drawback stated at the beginning and from the difficulty of concrete calculations involving (2.15), one should emphasize the assumption that our diffusions are positive recurrent (one often say "ergodic," despite the fact the initial value is not drawn from the invariant probability and so the process is not stationary). The Examples 3, 4, and 5 of Section 2 have this property if and only if the parameter μ is positive, while the Black–Scholes diffusion is never ergodic; more important even, all these examples are one-dimensional, but if the diffusion is multidimensional, it is much more difficult to have ergodic properties. And further, it is very unlikely that accurate models in finance can be at all ergodic (or even homogeneous) because there are obvious trends, at least for assets prices: so modeling with a Vasicek model or a Cox–Ingersoll–Ross model can probably be good only over a finite horizon, and this is of course totally contradictory with the fact that $T_n \to \infty$ above.

The Ornstein–Uhlenbeck Process: For the process (4.3), with θ_2 fixed and θ_1 unknown, we can write explicitly the likelihood ratio and find the MLE, which takes the form

$$\widehat{\theta}_{1,n} = -\int_0^{T_n} Y_s dY_s \Big/ \int_0^{T_n} Y_s^2 ds. \tag{4.5}$$

The process is ergodic if and only if $\theta_1 > 0$, in which case the stationary measure is $\mu_\theta = \mathcal{N}(0, \theta_2/2\theta_1)$. As said before, we have the LAN property with rate $1/\sqrt{T_n}$ at each point $\theta_1 > 0$, and the asymptotic Fisher information is $I(\theta) = 1/2\theta_1$, and of course, the MLE is then asymptotically efficient.

What is interesting here is that we can also derive the local asymptotic properties of this model at the points $\theta_1 \leq 0$:

(a) At point $\theta_1 = 0$, we have the LAQ property with rate $1/T_n$, and the variable $I(\theta)$ in (3.6) has the law of the variable $\int_0^1 W_s^2 dW_s$, where W is a Brownian motion. Observe that for $\theta_1 = 0$, the diffusion is just a nonstandard Brownian motion, recurrent but not positive recurrent.

(b) At all points $\theta_1 < 0$, we have the LAMN property with rate $e^{\theta_1 T_n}$, and the conditional Fisher information $I(\theta)$ has the law of the square of an $\mathcal{N}\left(\frac{x_0}{\sqrt{-2\theta_1\theta_2}}, \frac{1}{4\theta_1^2}\right)$ random variable. Observe that for $\theta_1 < 0$, the diffusion is transient: this explains why the starting point x_0 has an impact on the asymptotic behavior.

In all cases, the MLE is asymptotically efficient. But the rate of convergence of $\widehat{\theta}_{1,n}$ to θ_1, which is $\sqrt{T_n}$ in the ergodic case, is *much faster* in the other cases, especially in the transient case. This is very specific to the Ornstein–Uhlenbeck process, and for other transient or null-recurrent diffusions, very little is known, and in particular not the rates of convergence if they exist at all (see however [1], [2] for some worked out examples in these situations).

Problem B: A closely related asymptotic problem is as follows. Instead of (4.1), we consider the equation

$$dX_t = a(\theta, X_t)dt + \varepsilon_n \sigma(X_t)dW_t, \quad X_0 = x_0, \quad t \in [0, T]. \tag{4.6}$$

Here, T is fixed and σ is a known function, and the known parameter ε_n is supposed to be small, so the above equation is a "noisy" version of the ordinary differential equations

$$dX_t = a(\theta, X_t)dt, \quad X_0 = x_0, \quad t \in [0, T] \tag{4.7}$$

with a "small noise" $\varepsilon_n W$. Then as $\varepsilon_n \to 0$ the, solutions of (4.6), say, converge to the (deterministic) solution of (4.7), under appropriate assumptions on a.

There is a big difference between the two settings (4.1) as $T_n \to \infty$ and (4.6) as $\varepsilon_n \to 0$: the first one corresponds to modeling an intrinsically random phenomenon, whereas the second one corresponds to modeling a deterministic phenomenon with a small random noise. However, although the second problem is somewhat easier to handle and requires much less assumptions on a and almost no assumption on σ, both problems present many mathematical similarities. For instance we get (under appropriate assumptions) the LAN property for the model associated with (4.6) with rate ε_n.

4.2. Discrete Observations

Now we proceed to more realistic observation schemes. The process is observed on a regular grid, at n regularly spaced values in time, say at times $(0, \Delta_n, 2\Delta_n, \ldots, n\Delta_n)$. The observed σ-field is $\mathcal{G}_n = \sigma(Y_{i\Delta_n} : 0 \le i \le n)$. Then, as seen in Subsection 2.5, under mild assumptions the measures $\mathbf{P}_\theta$ are all equivalent on $\mathcal{G}_n$, and the likelihood ratios $Z_n(\zeta/\theta)$ are given by (2.16), which here take the following form ($p_{s,t}^\theta$ denoting the transition densities for the parameter θ):

$$Z_n(\zeta/\theta) = \prod_{i=1}^{n} \frac{p_{(i-1)\Delta_n,i\Delta_n}^{\zeta}(Y_{(i-1)\Delta_n}, Y_{i\Delta_n})}{p_{(i-1)\Delta_n,i\Delta_n}^{\theta}(Y_{(i-1)\Delta_n}, Y_{i\Delta_n})}. \tag{4.8}$$

Mathematically speaking, we are observing a realization of a Markov chain, and asymptotic statistical theory for Markov chains is well established, at least in the homogeneous and positive recurrent case. However, we have two main problems here: first, it may happen that Δ_n actually depends on n, so indeed we observe different Markov chains for different values of n; and more important, *we do not know explicitly the transition densities* of our Markov chain, so the classical techniques for Markov chains *cannot be used* here.

Let us review the most important situations:

(a) Constant stepsize: The stepsize is $\Delta_n = \Delta$, independent on n. This setting is the most natural one (apparently at least) but also the most difficult because the transitions are not explicitly known. Further, to provide asymptotic results, we need homogeneity and positive recurrence, a set of assumptions that is probably rather rare in finance, as already said before. We study this case in Section 6.

(b) Decreasing stepsize: Another possibility is to let $\Delta_n \to 0$ as $n \to \infty$: this will be studied in detail in Section 5. Then, although we do not know the densities $p_{s,t}^\theta$, we have good approximations for them as soon as $t - s$ is small: the first-order approximation is a Gaussian kernel, and there exist approximations at any order under enough smoothness of the coefficients. So we have approximate expressions for the likelihood, which are good when Δ_n is small, and we can expect to find concrete estimators which perform as well, or almost as well, as the MLE.

In fact, we can single out two very different situations:

1. The first one is when $n\Delta_n$ (that is, the maximal length of the observed interval) is also big. This amounts to say that $n\Delta_n \to \infty$. The drawback is again that we need homogeneity and positive recurrence. Let us mention right away that in the setting of Eq. (4.2), the rates of convergence differ for θ_1 and θ_2.

2. The second one is when $n\Delta_n$ stays bounded, in which case we can as well suppose that $n\Delta_n = T$ is constant. In this situation, we of course cannot do better than if we were observing the whole path of the diffusion over the interval $[0, T]$, and consequently, we cannot have even consistent estimators for θ_1 in (4.2): so only θ_2 (that is, the volatility which fortunately is the most crucial parameter in finance) can be consistently estimated. On the other hand, we need neither homogeneity nor any form of recurrence.

Yet another situation that frequently occurs in practice is when the process is observed on a regular grid but with missing observations. This is akin with the situation where the observations are made on an irregular grid. The mathematics for theses situations is not really more complicated than in the regular grid case, and we will not touch upon this topic here.

4.3. Observations with Errors

So far we have examined the cases with complete observation on an interval (an idealized situation) or observation along a regular grid. Even this is an idealization of the reality because it is not so often than one can observe exactly the values at any particular time. More realistic schemes are as follows and will be studied in Section 7 in the setting of discrete observations:

(a) **Additive errors:** Each observation suffers from an additive (random) error: instead of $Y_{i\Delta_n}$ one observes $Y_{i\Delta_n} + \varepsilon_{n,i}$, where the variables $\varepsilon_{n,i}$ are independent of Y and usually i.i.d. and centered when i varies. Rates of convergence of estimators then depend on the variances of the additive errors.

(b) **Round-off errors:** Another kind of errors can occur, especially in financial data: instead of observing Y_t, one observes a rounded-off value (this is also called space quantization). More precisely one fixes a step $\alpha_n > 0$, and instead of $Y_{i\Delta_n}$ one observes the smallest multiple of α_n, which is smaller or equal (or alternatively closest) to $Y_{i\Delta_n}$. The rate of convergence of estimators then depends on α_n.

(c) **Partially observed diffusion:** Another situation is when the diffusion X is, say, two-dimensional and one observes only the first component X^1 of X (according to one the schemes mentioned above). This happens for example in finance, where X^1 is the price of the asset and X^2 represents the "volatility" of this price. Such a setting is somehow related to Problem A) above. This is quite difficult to study on the mathematical level, is more or less hinges upon filtering theory, and may also be viewed as an avatar of the theory of *hidden Markov chains*. Very few definitive results are known here, and one has to resort on procedures that are not known to be optimal. We will not touch upon this problem here.

5. DISCRETE OBSERVATIONS WITH DECREASING STEPSIZE

We start studying the Problem B of Subsection 4.2: we are in the setting of Section 4, and we observe our diffusion at times $i\Delta_n$ for $i = 0, 1, \ldots, n$, without any measurement error, and $\Delta_n \to 0$. As said before, we should single out the two cases where $T_n = n\Delta_n$ goes to infinity or stays constant, and we begin with the second one, which is somewhat easier to grasp (although the proofs are more difficult).

5.1. Observations on a Fixed Interval

Here, we suppose that $\Delta_n = T/n$ for some $T > 0$. The observed σ-fields $\mathcal{G}_n = \sigma(Y_{iT/n} : i = 0, \ldots, n)$ are not increasing, but "in the limit," the σ-field $\mathcal{G}_\infty$ is $\mathcal{Y}_T$: so we have no consistent estimators for θ_1, but only for θ_2 in (4.2), and it is natural to look at the following equations

$$dX_t = a(t, X_t)dt + \sigma(\theta, t, X_t)dW_t, \quad X_0 = x_0. \tag{5.1}$$

The coefficient a is not specified at all (we are in a *semiparametric* setting), except that we assume it is continuous. The coefficient σ (or equivalently $c = \sigma\sigma^*$) is smooth enough and with linear growth in x: for example, twice continuously differentiable in all variables is more than enough for most results below. For simplicity, we suppose that Θ is a compact interval of $\mathbf{R}$, but everything would work as well in the multidimensional case for θ.

We need also an identifiability assumption: there are several possibilities, but again for simplicity we assume the simplest one to check, namely that

$$\theta \neq \zeta \quad \Rightarrow \quad c(\theta, 0, x_0) \neq c(\zeta, 0, x_0) \tag{5.2}$$

(the minimal one would be that for any $\zeta \neq \theta$, the $\mathbf{P}_\theta$-probability that the two processes $t \mapsto c(\theta, t, Y_t)$ and $t \mapsto c(\zeta, t, Y_t)$ agree on the interval $[0, T]$ equals 0).

The first (theoretical rather than practical) question which arises is whether the local models around some value $\theta \in \Theta$ converge in the sense of Subsection 3.1, with an appropriate rate. To solve this, and in addition to the smoothness of c, we need two extra assumptions: first, a mild assumption is that $\dot{c}$, the derivative of c in θ, is not identically 0 along the path of Y, for example, we have $\dot{c}(\theta, 0, x_0) \neq 0$ [to be compared with (5.2)]; second, a much stronger assumption is that the matrix $c(\theta, t, x)$ is invertible for all (t, x). Then, one can show the LAMN property, with rate $u_n = \frac{1}{\sqrt{n}}$ and random Fisher information given by (because $\Theta \subset \mathbf{R}$, the random Fisher information is not a matrix but a random number)

$$I(\theta) = \frac{1}{2T} \int_0^T \text{trace}(\dot{c}c^{-1}\dot{c}c^{-1})(\theta, s, Y_s)ds. \tag{5.3}$$

This result has been shown by Dohnal [15] when X is one-dimensional, using an explicit expression of the densities of the transitions in terms of the scale function and of an extra Brownian bridge; it was next extended in [16] in the d-dimensional case when the coefficient c derives from a potential (the same explicit expression being still available), and it was given its final form by Gobet [17], using Malliavin calculus.

Hence, the rate-efficient estimators will converge at rate $\sqrt{n}$, and asymptotically efficient estimators will further be asymptotically mixed Gaussian centered around the true value and with conditional variance $I(\theta)^{-1}$.

The second question which arises, and *is* of much practical interest, is to find such rate-efficient or even asymptotically efficient estimators. This turns out to be relatively easy. We can, for example, construct the following *contrasts*:

$$V_n(\zeta) = \sum_{i=1}^n \left(\log \det \left(c \left(\zeta, \frac{i-1}{n}, Y_{\frac{(i-1)T}{n}} \right) \right) \right.$$
$$\left. + \frac{n}{T} \left(Y_{\frac{iT}{n}} - Y_{\frac{(i-1)T}{n}} \right)^* c^{-1} \left(\zeta, \frac{i-1}{n}, Y_{\frac{(i-1)T}{n}} \right) \left(Y_{\frac{iT}{n}} - Y_{\frac{(i-1)T}{n}} \right) \right). \tag{5.4}$$

Then, one takes the following estimator:

$$\widehat{\theta}_n = \text{ArgMin } V_n(.) \tag{5.5}$$

[the function $\zeta \mapsto V_n(\zeta)$, being continuous, admits an absolute minimum on the compact set Θ; if there are several, take any one of them in (5.5)]. It can then be proved that the sequence $\sqrt{n}(\widehat{\theta}_n - \theta)$ converges in law under P_θ toward a centered mixed Gaussian variable with conditional variance $I(\theta)^{-1}$, provided θ is in the interior of Θ. The proofs are a bit complicated, but the reasons for both the LAMN property and the optimality of the above estimators are simple enough:

- If $c(\theta, t, x) = c(\theta, t)$ does not depend on x at all and if $a \equiv 0$, then under each P_θ the process Y is Gaussian, with mean x_0, and the densities $p_{s,t}^\theta$ are explicitly known. Then a tedious but elementary computation shows that the LAN property holds, with rate $\frac{1}{\sqrt{n}}$ and limiting Fisher information $\frac{1}{2T} \int_0^T \text{trace}(\dot{c}c^{-1}\dot{c}c^{-1})(\theta, s)ds$. In addition, the variable $V_n(\zeta)$ in (5.4) is $-\log Z_n(\zeta/\theta)$, up to a multiplicative constant; hence (5.5) gives the MLE, which in the Gaussian case is known to be the best estimator.

- Coming back to the general case, under $\boldsymbol{P}_\theta$ and conditionally on $\mathcal{Y}_{(i-1)T/n}$, the variable $Y_{iT/n}$ is approximately Gaussian with mean $Y_{(i-1)T/n} + O_P(1/n)$ and variance $c(\theta, (i-1)T/n, Y_{(i-1)T/n})/n$. Then, our statistical model behaves asymptotically like another model constructed as such: first, we have our canonical process Y and the law $\boldsymbol{P}_\theta$; then we have another process U which, conditionally on the path $t \mapsto Y_t$, is Gaussian with mean x_0 and covariance $E(U_s U_t^*) - x_0 x_0^* = \int_0^s c(\theta, r, Y_r)dr$ for $s \leq t$; finally, we observe the variables $U_{iT/n}$. Therefore, one can argue "conditionally on the process Y," and at the heuristic level, we can apply the (elementary) results valid for Gaussian processes.

The previous results hold under the crucial hypothesis that the matrix c is everywhere invertible. If this fails, the formulae (5.3) and (5.4) make no sense. However, it is still possible to obtain reasonable estimators, as shown in [18]. For instance, instead of defining V_n by (5.4), we can set

$$V_n(\zeta) = \sum_{i=1}^n \left(\left| Y_{\frac{iT}{n}} - Y_{\frac{(i-1)T}{n}} \right|^2 - \frac{T}{n} \sum_{i=1}^d c^{ii}\left(\zeta, \frac{(i-1)T}{n}, Y_{\frac{(i-1)T}{n}} \right) \right)^2 \tag{5.6}$$

and still define $\widehat{\theta}_n$ by (5.5). Then, $\sqrt{n}(\widehat{\theta}_n - \theta)$ converges in law under $\boldsymbol{P}_\theta$ to a centered mixed Gaussian variable with conditional variance

$$\frac{2T \int_0^T \left(\left(\sum_i c^{ii} \right)^2 \sum_{i,j} \left(c^{ij} \right)^2 \right)(\theta, s, Y_s)ds}{\left(\int_0^T \left(\sum_i c^{ii} \right)^2 (\theta, s, Y_s)ds \right)^2}. \tag{5.7}$$

One can check that as it should be, this quantity is always bigger than $1/I(\theta)$ when c is invertible. Once more, the contrast (5.6) is only one among many different possibilities.

Remarks

1. *The same method accommodates the case where there are missing data or where the observations take place at an irregular grid. For example, if the observations are at times $0 = t(n, 0) < t(n, 1) < \cdots < t(n, n) = T_n$, we can take the following contrast [extending (5.4) and with the notation $\Delta(n, i) = t(n, i) - t(n, i - 1)$]:*

$$V_n(\zeta) = \sum_{i=1}^n \Big(\log \det \big(c\left(\zeta, t(n, i - 1), Y_{t(n,i-1)} \right) \big)$$

$$+ \frac{1}{\Delta(n, i)} \left(Y_{t(n,i)} - Y_{t(n,i-1)} \right)^* c^{-1} \left(\zeta, t(n, i - 1), Y_{t(n,i-1)} \right) \left(Y_{t(n,i)} - Y_{t(n,i-1)} \right) \Big). \tag{5.8}$$

Then, we have exactly the same asymptotic result for $\widehat{\theta}_n$ given by (5.5), provided $T_n \to T$, and the "empirical" measure $\frac{1}{n}\sum_{i=1}^{n}\varepsilon_{t(n,i)}$ of the observation times converges weakly to the uniform measure over the interval $[0, T]$.

2. *When c is not invertible, the estimators minimizing (5.6) converge with the rate $\sqrt{n}$, but this does not mean that they are rate-efficient: although this remains an open question, it might happen that the singularity of c induces the LAMN property with a smaller rate, that is, a rate u_n such that $u_n\sqrt{n} \to 0$: then rate-efficient estimators $\widehat{\theta}'_n$ are such that the sequence $\frac{1}{u_n}(\widehat{\theta}'_n - \theta)$ is tight under P_θ, whereas of course the sequence $\frac{1}{u_n}(\widehat{\theta}_n - \theta)$ with $\widehat{\theta}_n$ as above is not tight under P_θ, and $\widehat{\theta}_n$ is not rate-efficient. Nevertheless, the estimators $\widehat{\theta}_n$ stay "reasonable" in all cases.*

The Ornstein–Uhlenbeck Process: Let us consider the process (4.3). In the present setting, θ_1 is a nuisance parameter and θ_2 is the parameter we wish to estimate. It turns out that we have not only the LAMN but even the LAN property, with rate $\frac{1}{\sqrt{n}}$ and Fisher information $I(\theta) = 1/2\theta_2^2$. The contrast (5.4) takes the form

$$V_n(\zeta_2) = n\left(\log \zeta_2 + \frac{1}{T\zeta_2}\sum_{i=1}^{n}\left(Y_{\frac{iT}{n}} - Y_{\frac{(i-1)T}{n}}\right)^2\right),$$

and the minimum contrast estimator is

$$\widehat{\theta}_{2,n} = \frac{1}{T}\sum_{i=1}^{n}\left(Y_{\frac{iT}{n}} - Y_{\frac{(i-1)T}{n}}\right)^2.$$

Note that this works whenever the value of θ_1 is. Now, if further θ_1 is known, one can derive the genuine MLE, say $\widehat{\theta}'_{2,n}$, which takes the following form to be compared with $\widehat{\theta}_{2,n}$ above:

$$\widehat{\theta}'_{2,n} = \begin{cases} \dfrac{2\theta_1}{n(1 - e^{-2\theta_1 T/n})}\sum_{i=1}^{n}\left(Y_{\frac{iT}{n}} - e^{-\theta_1 T/n}Y_{\frac{(i-1)T}{n}}\right)^2 & \text{if } \theta_1 \neq 0 \\ \dfrac{1}{T}\sum_{i=1}^{n}\left(Y_{\frac{iT}{n}} - Y_{\frac{(i-1)T}{n}}\right)^2 & \text{if } \theta_1 = 0. \end{cases}$$

The sequence $(\widehat{\theta}'_{2,n})$ is also asymptotically efficient, and indeed $\sqrt{n}(\widehat{\theta}_{2,n} - \widehat{\theta}'_{2,n})$ goes to 0 in P_θ-probability.

5.2. Observations on an Increasing Interval

Now we suppose that at the same time $\Delta_n \to 0$ and $T_n = n\Delta_n \to \infty$. Here again the observed σ-fields $\mathcal{G}_n = \sigma(Y_{i\Delta_n} : i = 0, 1, \ldots, n)$ are not increasing, but "in the limit" $\mathcal{G}_\infty = \mathcal{Y}$: so as soon as the minimal identifiability assumption is met, namely that the measures $\boldsymbol{P}_\theta$ are all mutually singular on the largest σ-field $\mathcal{Y}$, we can hope for consistent estimators for θ.

Constructing estimators that are, first, consistent and further with a reasonable (or optimal) rate of convergence is however a very different matter. This is where the place where the parameter comes in (in the drift term or in the diffusion term) makes a lot of differences. This is why we write the equations in the form (4.2), and some preliminary remarks are more or less obvious:

(a) For θ_2, we can apply the previous method; by keeping only the first $l_n = [1/\Delta_n]$ observations (where $[x]$ denotes the integer part of x) and discarding the others, we are in the previous setting with l_n observations, and we can construct estimators that converge to the true value θ_2 with the rate $\sqrt{l_n} \sim 1/\sqrt{\Delta_n}$. This is of course not very good if Δ_n goes slowly to 0, but at least it gives consistent estimators.

Using all the data, we can of course hope for better estimators for θ_2, but then to derive any kind of asymptotic properties, we have to assume that our diffusions are homogeneous and positive recurrent.

(b) For θ_1, it is quite another matter: first, to obtain any kind of reasonable result, we must again assume that our diffusions are homogeneous positive recurrent. Second, we cannot do better than if the whole path of our process had been observed over the interval $[0, T_n]$, and we have seen already that the best possible rate in the later case is $\sqrt{T_n}$.

Therefore, in the rest of this subsection, we assume that the coefficients a and c depend on θ_1 and θ_2, respectively, and on x, but not on time. We suppose that the set Θ of all possible values for $\theta = (\theta_1, \theta_2)$ is a compact subset of $\boldsymbol{R}^2$ (higher dimension for θ is purely a notational problem). Finally, we assume that the diffusions are positive recurrent, and that the unique invariant probabilities $\mu_\theta = \mu_{\theta_1,\theta_2}$ all have $\boldsymbol{R}^d$ as their support. Within this setting, the minimal identifiability assumption stated above has a simple expression in terms of the coefficient:

$$\left.\begin{array}{ll} a(\theta_1, x) = a(\zeta_1, x) & \text{for all } x \quad \Rightarrow \quad \theta_1 = \zeta_1 \\ c(\theta_2, x) = c(\zeta_2, x) & \text{for all } x \quad \Rightarrow \quad \theta_2 = \zeta_2. \end{array}\right\} \tag{5.9}$$

There are several ways of finding good estimators in this setting: see, for example, Florens-Zmirou [19] or Yoshida [20]; here, we expound a method due to Kessler [21]: this method has been derived for the one-dimensional case, so we suppose here that our diffusions are one-dimensional, but there would be no difficulty to extend it to the multidimensional case, except for very cumbersome notation. It is based on the consideration of the (extended) infinitesimal generator A_θ of the diffusion, which takes the form [see (2.5)]

$$A_\theta f(x) = a(\theta_1, x)f'(x) + \frac{1}{2}c(\theta_2, x)f''(x),$$

and its iterates A_θ^m for $m = 2, \ldots,$ and A_θ^0 is by convention the identity operator. For taking $A_\theta^m f$, we need of course f to be of class C^{2m}, whereas the coefficients a and c should be at least of class $C^{2(m-1)}$ in x: for simplicity, we assume that they are infinitely differentiable in x and also three times differentiable in θ, with all derivatives of polynomial growth and the first derivatives in x bounded. Finally, we assume that $\varepsilon \leq c(\theta_2, x) \leq 1/\varepsilon$ for some $\varepsilon > 0$ and all θ_2, x, and that the measure μ_θ has moments of all orders and that $\sup_t \mathbf{E}_\theta(|Y_t|^p) < \infty$ for all $p < \infty$. All these assumptions are satisfied in most applications, as soon as the processes are ergodic.

Let us introduce a number of notation. We denote by $\phi(x) = x$ the identity on $\mathbf{R}$. Then, we define the functions

$$\eta_l(h, \theta, x) = \sum_{i=0}^{l} \frac{h^i}{i!} A_\theta^i \phi(x),$$

$$g_{\theta,x}^0(y) = (y - x)^2,$$

$$j \geq 1 \quad \Rightarrow \quad g_{\theta,x}^j(y) = 2(y - x)\frac{A_\theta^j \phi(x)}{j!} + \sum_{r,s \geq 1, r+s=j} \frac{A_\theta^r \phi(x)}{r!} \frac{A_\theta^s \phi(x)}{s!},$$

$$\Gamma_l(h, \theta, x) = \sum_{j=0}^{l} h^j \sum_{r=0}^{l-j} \frac{h^r}{r!} A_\theta^r g_{\theta,x}^j(x).$$

Γ_l is a polynomial of degree l in h, with no constant term and first-order term equal to $hc(\theta_2, x)$, so $\Gamma_l'(h, \theta, x) = \frac{\Gamma_l(h,\theta,x)}{hc(\theta_2,x)}$ is a polynomial of degree $l - 1$ in h with constant term equal to 1. Then, we can denote by $d_{j,l}(\theta, x)$ and $e_{j,l}(\theta, x)$ the coefficients of order $j \geq 0$ of the Taylor expansion in h, around 0, of the functions $1/\Gamma_l'(h, \theta, x)$ and $\log \Gamma_l'(h, \theta, x)$, respectively. Finally, we consider the contrast

$$V_{l,n}(\zeta) = \sum_{i=1}^{n} \left(\log c(\zeta_2, Y_{(i-1)\Delta_n}) + \sum_{j=1}^{l} \Delta_n^j e_{j,l+1}(\theta, Y_{(i-1)\Delta_n}) \right.$$

$$\left. + \frac{1}{\Delta_n c(\zeta_2, Y_{(i-1)\Delta_n})}(Y_{i\Delta_n} - \eta_l(\Delta_n, \zeta, Y_{(i-1)\Delta_n}))^2 \left(1 + \sum_{j=1}^{l} \Delta_n^j d_{j,l+1}(\zeta, Y_{(i-1)\Delta_n}) \right) \right)$$

(5.10)

This expression looks complicated, all the more when l is large, but it must be observed that it is "explicit" in the sense that if one knows the functions a and c, everything in (5.4) can be explicitly computed. Then, one consider the estimator

$$\widehat{\theta}_n^l = (\widehat{\theta}_{1,n}^l, \widehat{\theta}_{2,n}^l) = \text{ArgMin } V_{l,n}(.),$$

(5.11)

which exists because Θ is compact and $V_{l,n}$ is a continuous function.

Now the result is as follows: suppose that Δ_n is such that $n\Delta_n^{l/2} \to 0$ for some integer $l \geq 2$ and also that θ is in the interior of Θ. Then, the pair $\left(\sqrt{n\Delta_n}\left(\widehat{\theta}_{1,n}^l - \theta_1\right), \sqrt{n}\left(\widehat{\theta}_{2,n}^l - \theta_2\right)\right)$ converges in law, under $\mathbb{P}_\theta$, toward a pair (U, V) of independent centered Gaussian variables with respective variances given by

$$\left(\int \frac{\dot{a}(\theta_1, x)^2}{c(\theta_2, x)} \mu_\theta(dx)\right)^{-1}, \quad 2\left(\int \frac{\dot{c}(\theta_2, x)^2}{c(\theta_2, x)^2} \mu_\theta(dx)\right)^{-1}. \tag{5.12}$$

Remarks

1. *The contrast (5.10) is an approximation of the log-likelihood (up to a multiplicative negative constant), which converges to the true log-likelihood as $l \to \infty$ for each fixed n. This is why the estimators based on this contrast work well when l is large enough relatively to the size of Δ_n, a fact expressed by the property $n\Delta_n^{l/2} \to 0$.*

2. *We do not know about the optimality of the second component $\widehat{\theta}_{2,n}^l$, although it is certainly rate-efficient at least. But the first component $\widehat{\theta}_{1,n}^l$ is asymptotically efficient: in fact, if instead of the values $Y_{i\Delta_n}$, one observes the whole path of Y over $[0, T_n]$; from the results of Subsection 4.1, we know that θ_2 is known exactly and that for θ_1 the LAN property holds with rate $1/\sqrt{n\Delta_n}$ and asymptotic Fisher information being the inverse of the first expression in (5.12) [compare with (4.4)]: so $\widehat{\theta}_{1,n}^l$ performs as well as the asymptotically efficient estimators for θ_1 when we observe the whole path over $[0, T_n]$.*

3. *Let us emphasize once more the two different rates we get for the estimation of the two components θ_1 and θ_2.*

4. *How to apply the previous method, and in particular how to choose l? This is of course a crucial point. On the theoretical level, the sequence Δ_n is given, and we have $n\Delta_n^{l/2} \to 0$ for all l bigger than some l_0, in which case one should take $l = l_0$, or it may also happen that $n\Delta_n^p \to \infty$ for all $p < \infty$, in which case the previous method breaks down. In practice, it is quite a different matter because indeed n and Δ_n are given ! Hopefully n is large and Δ_n is small, and one may perform the previous estimations for increasing values of l, until the estimators $\widehat{\theta}_{1,n}^l$ and $\widehat{\theta}_{2,n}^l$ more or less stabilize.*

   To accommodate more precisely this sequential procedure, one may also give an adaptive version of the previous estimators (see the thesis of Kessler [22] for a precise definition), where the computation of $\widehat{\theta}_n^l$ is based on the previous value $\widehat{\theta}_n^{l-1}$: then one stops when $\widehat{\theta}_{1,n}^l - \widehat{\theta}_{1,n}^{l-1}$ is small w.r.t. $1/\sqrt{T_n}$ and $\widehat{\theta}_{2,n}^l - \widehat{\theta}_{2,n}^{l-1}$ is small w.r.t. $1/\sqrt{n}$.

5. *There are also some results in the null-recurrent case and even the transient case, which give estimators based on contrast functions and having reasonable rates, see for example the recent papers [23] or [24] (both written after the first draft of this chapter was started) and the references therein.*

The Ornstein–Uhlenbeck Process: Let us consider the process (4.3). By looking at the explicit form for the likelihoods, one can prove that in our setting (the ergodic case, so

that $\theta_1 > 0$), the LAN property holds, with rate $\frac{1}{\sqrt{T_n}}$ for the θ_1-component and $\frac{1}{\sqrt{n}}$ for the θ_2-component, and with asymptotic Fisher information matrix

$$I(\theta)_{1,1} = \frac{1}{2\theta_1}, \quad I(\theta)_{2,2} = \frac{1}{2\theta_2^2}, \quad I(\theta)_{1,2} = I(\theta)_{2,1} = 0. \tag{5.13}$$

Comparing with (5.12), we observe that the covariance matrix of the centered Gaussian variable (U, V) introduced just before this formula is exactly $I(\theta)^{-1}$: in other words, as soon as $n\Delta_n^{1/2} \to 0$, the sequence of estimators $(\widehat{\theta}_n)$ is *asymptotically efficient* for estimating θ (with of course different rates for the two components).

Now, it turns out that we have also local asymptotic properties when $\theta_1 \leq 0$, exactly as for observations over a whole interval (Section 4): if $\theta_1 = 0$, we have the LAQ property with rates $\frac{1}{T_n}$ for θ_1 and $\frac{1}{\sqrt{n}}$ for θ_2; if $\theta_1 < 0$, we have the LAMN property with rates $e^{\theta_1 T_n}$ for θ_1 and $\frac{1}{\sqrt{n}}$ for θ_2; further the components $I(\theta)_{i,j}$ of the associated random matrix $I(\theta)$ are given by (5.13) if (i, j) is either $(1, 2)$, $(2, 1)$, or $(2, 2)$, whereas $I(\theta)_{1,1}$ is as given in Section 4. As a matter of fact, one could prove that the MLE is asymptotically efficient in these two cases as well.

6. DISCRETE OBSERVATIONS WITH CONSTANT STEPSIZE

The setting is the same as in Section 5, except that here $\Delta_n = \Delta$. In a sense, this scheme of observations seems the most natural one when observations are discrete in time. However, as in Subsection 5.2, we must assume that the diffusions are homogeneous positive recurrent, with unique invariant probability measures μ_θ whose supports are $\mathbb{R}^d$ (or D if all diffusions live on the domain D). Observe that here, in accordance with the results of this subsection, the rates for θ_1 and θ_2 should both be $\sqrt{n}$: so there is no reason to single out these two components, and we come back to Eq. (4.1), with coefficients not depending on time, and some given starting point x_0 (the same for all θs).

Next, about the necessary identifiability assumption: at first glance, one should take the analog of (5.9), that is,

$$a(\zeta, x) = a(\theta, x) \quad \text{and} \quad c(\zeta, x) = c(\theta, x) \quad \text{for all } x \quad \Rightarrow \quad \zeta = \theta. \tag{6.1}$$

However, this turns out to be not enough: indeed "at the limit," we have $\mathcal{G}_\infty = \sigma(Y_{i\Delta} : i = 0, 1, \ldots)$, and the restriction of $\mathbb{P}_\theta$ to $\mathcal{G}_\infty$ is entirely characterized by the kernel P_Δ^θ, where $(P_t^\theta)_{t \geq 0}$ is the semigroup of the diffusion with parameter θ. So the right identifiability assumption is in fact

$$P_\Delta^\zeta(x, .) = P_\Delta^\theta(x, .) \quad \text{for all } x \quad \Rightarrow \quad \zeta = \theta, \tag{6.2}$$

an assumption that is strictly stronger than (6.1) and that unfortunately cannot be read in a simple way from the coefficients (in the Examples 3, 4, and 5 of Section 2, however, this identifiability assumption is satisfied).

Apparently the problem is much simpler here than before because we observe the sequence $(Y_{i\Delta})_{0 \le i \le n}$, an homogeneous Markov chain with transition P_Δ^θ under each $\mathbf{P}_\theta$. And as soon as the matrices $c(\theta, x)$ are invertible, these transitions admit positive densities $p_\Delta^\theta(x, .)$ w.r.t. Lebesgue measure. So the likelihood on the σ-field $\mathcal{G}_n$ is given by (4.8), that is,

$$Z_n(\zeta/\theta) = \prod_{i=1}^n \frac{p_\Delta^\zeta(Y_{(i-1)\Delta}, Y_{i\Delta})}{p_\Delta^\theta(Y_{(i-1)\Delta}, Y_{i\Delta})}. \tag{6.3}$$

Then, because our Markov chains are in addition ergodic, it is well known since a long time ago (see, for example, the book of Roussas [25]) that under some reasonable smoothness assumptions on the densities p_Δ^θ (implied by suitable smoothness of a and c), we have the LAN property with rate $1/\sqrt{n}$, with asymptotic Fisher information matrix at point θ given by

$$I(\theta)_{i,j} = \int \frac{\frac{\partial}{\partial \theta_i} p_\Delta^\theta(x, y) \frac{\partial}{\partial \theta_j} p_\Delta^\theta(x, y)}{p_\Delta^\theta(x, y)} \mu_\theta(dx) dy. \tag{6.4}$$

Now the problems begin because we aim to getting asymptotically efficient estimators, if possible. The MLE is of course asymptotically efficient, but it is also unavailable because we have no explicit expression for the densities p_Δ^θ in terms of the coefficients of the equations. So, we have to resort on other methods.

6.1. Approximating the Likelihood

A first method consists in computing an approximation of the likelihood (6.3) and then maximizing in ζ this approximation; more precisely, we have to compute an approximation $\tilde{p}_\Delta^\zeta(x, y)$ for all pairs of the form $(x, y) = (Y_{(i-1)\Delta}, Y_{i\Delta})$ and all values of ζ and minimize

$$\zeta \mapsto \tilde{V}_n(\zeta) = \prod_{i=1}^n n \tilde{p}_\Delta^\zeta(Y_{(i-1)\Delta}, Y_{i\Delta}).$$

The key point is to compute $\tilde{p}_\Delta^\zeta$: for this, we can use expansions of p_Δ^ζ as a power series in Δ and stop the expansion at some prescribed degree. This is, for example, the point of view taken by Aït-Sahalia [26]: he first makes a space transform that renders p_Δ relatively close to a Gaussian kernel and then uses an expansion in Hermite polynomials; other expansions are also possible. But in a sense, this is not much different from the underlying idea behind the method explained in Subsection 5.2, and it is likely to work only for relatively "small" values of Δ.

The nice thing about such methods is that they give right away the function $\tilde{p}_\Delta^\zeta(x, y)$ (as a function of x, y, and ζ) and often also allow to keep track of the error $p_\Delta^\zeta - \tilde{p}_\Delta^\zeta$.

Another possibility is to use Monte–Carlo techniques to approximate p_Δ^ζ: this has been developed by Pedersen in [27], [28]: these work for any value of Δ, but the error $\tilde{P}_\Delta^\zeta - p_\Delta^\zeta$ is difficult to control.

This method is relatively efficient, but its main drawback is that it allows to nicely approximate $p_\Delta^\zeta(x, y)$ for any given individual value of (x, y, ζ) but not as a function of these variables, which we need because we have to maximize $\tilde{V}_n$. So we can either compute $\tilde{p}_\Delta^\zeta$ for all ζ in a finite set Θ_n consisting in grid with a mesh much smaller than $\frac{1}{\sqrt{n}}$ (because we want an estimate whose error is of order $\frac{1}{\sqrt{n}}$) or use a gradient method or more sophisticated minimization methods, which necessitate, for example, the approximation of the derivatives of p_Δ^ζ in ζ. All these are again much computing-intensive. And once again, it is extremely difficult to keep track of the approximation errors of the method.

Let us also mention that because the first draft of this chapter was written, quite new Bayesian and "exact" Monte–Carlo methods have been developed for tackling the problem of approximating the densities p_Δ^ζ, see for example [29]. These methods seem to be computationally quite efficient, though rates are usually not provided explicitly.

6.2. Contrast Functions and Estimating Functions

Another idea, which has many similarities with the method explained in Section 5, consists in using a contrast function of the form

$$V_n(\zeta) = \sum_{i=1}^{n} F(Y_{(i-1)\Delta}, Y_{i\Delta}, \zeta) \tag{6.5}$$

for a suitable smooth function F, and to take for estimator $\widehat{\theta}_n$ the value, or one of the values, which minimize $V_n(.)$, as in (5.5).

When F is differentiable in ζ and when $\widehat{\theta}_n$ above is not on the boundary of Θ, then $\widehat{\theta}_n$ also solves the system of equations $\frac{\partial}{\partial \zeta_i} V_n(\zeta) = 0$ for $i = 1, \ldots, q$ (q is the dimension of θ). That is, with G denoting the gradient of F (as a function of the parameter), $\widehat{\theta}_n$ solves the following equation called *an estimating equation*:

$$W_n(\widehat{\theta}_n) = 0, \tag{6.6}$$

where W_n is

$$W_n(\zeta) = \sum_{i=1}^{n} G(Y_{(i-1)\Delta}, Y_{i\Delta}, \zeta). \tag{6.7}$$

In the sequel, we suppose for simplicity that θ is one-dimensional, so the function G above is also one-dimensional; but everything would work in the multidimensional case as well. First, the ergodic theorem says that

$$\frac{1}{n}W_n(\zeta) \;\rightarrow\; W(\theta,\zeta) := \int \mu_\theta(dx)P_\Delta^\theta(x,dy)G(x,y,\zeta) \tag{6.8}$$

in $\boldsymbol{P}_\theta$-probability. Therefore, if G is smooth enough and chosen in such a way that

$$\int \mu_\theta(dx)P_\Delta^\theta(x,dy)G(x,y,\zeta) = 0 \;\Leftrightarrow\; \theta = \zeta, \tag{6.9}$$

then the sequence $\widehat{\theta}_n$ of (6.6) converge in $\boldsymbol{P}_\theta$-probability to θ, for every $\theta \in \Theta$: that is, the estimators are weakly consistent. Similarly one has that

$$\frac{1}{n}\dot{W}_n(\zeta) \;\rightarrow\; \dot{W}(\theta,\zeta) := \int \mu_\theta(dx)P_\Delta^\theta(x,dy)\dot{G}(x,y,\zeta) \tag{6.10}$$

in $\boldsymbol{P}_\theta$-probability, and this convergence holds even uniformly in ζ (for each fixed θ; as usual a "dot" means taking the derivative in θ).

Suppose next that G satisfies in addition

$$\int G(x,y,\theta)P_\Delta^\theta(x,dy) = 0 \quad \text{for all } x,\theta. \tag{6.11}$$

We then say that the estimating function W_n is a *martingale estimating function* because the summands in (6.7) are martingale increments [note that (6.11) yields the implication from right to left in (6.9)]. Then, the central limit theorem for ergodic Markov chains and the martingale property imply that the sequence $\frac{1}{\sqrt{n}}W_n(\theta)$ converges in law under $\boldsymbol{P}_\theta$ to a centered Gaussian variable with variance $\int \mu_\theta(dx)P_\Delta^\theta(x,y)G(x,y,\theta)^2$, under suitable assumptions. Now, suppose that θ is in the interior of Θ; for n large enough, $\widehat{\theta}_n$ is also in the interior of Θ, so we can write $0 = W_n(\widehat{\theta}_n) = W_n(\theta) + (\widehat{\theta}_n - \theta)\dot{W}_n(\zeta_n)$, where ζ_n is between θ and $\widehat{\theta}_n$ (and random). These facts, together with (6.10), yield that the sequence $\sqrt{n}(\widehat{\theta}_n - \theta)$ converges in law under $\boldsymbol{P}_\theta$ to a centered Gaussian variable with variance

$$\alpha = \int \mu_\theta(dx)P_\Delta^\theta(x,y)G(x,y,\theta)^2 \Big/ \left(\int \mu_\theta(fx)P_\Delta^\theta(x,y)\dot{G}(x,y,\theta)\right)^2. \tag{6.12}$$

In other words, the sequence of estimators $\widehat{\theta}_n$ defined by (6.6) is rate-efficient, provided the function G is smooth enough and satisfies (6.9) and (6.11). Then, among all possible choices for G, one should choose one which minimizes the variance α in (6.12).

Of course (6.9) and (6.11) are not so easy to fulfill, and especially the last one, because one still does not know the transitions P_Δ^ζ! One may think of several possibilities:

1. For each θ, take a function $\phi(.,\theta)$, which is an eigenfunction of the generator A_θ of our diffusion, with eigenvalue $\lambda(\theta)$ (note that $\lambda(\theta) < 0$). Then $G(x, y, \theta) = g(x, \theta)(\phi(y, \theta) - e^{-\lambda(\theta)}\phi(x, \theta))$ will satisfies (6.11), whichever the function g is. Linear combinations of such functions also do the job. This is done, for example, by Hansen et al. [30] and by Kessler and Sørensen [31]. Observe that because A_θ is given in terms of the coefficients $a(\theta, .)$ and $c(\theta, .)$, finding eigenfunctions for A_θ is in principle easier than finding P_Δ^θ.

2. We take an arbitrary smooth function f on $\mathbf{R}^d \times \mathbf{R}^d$ and let $G(x, y, \theta) = f(x, y) - f'(x, \theta)$, where $f'(x, \theta) = \int P_\Delta^\theta(x, dy)f(x, y)$, so (6.11) is obvious. The function f' is, once more, not explicit, but it is possible to approximate it by Monte–Carlo techniques, for example, with the same drawbacks than the method using approximated likelihoods. This method is akin with the so–called "simulated moments method" developed by many authors in practical studies.

3. One can relax (6.11), for instance by taking $G(x, y, \theta) = g(x, \theta)$ not depending on y, but such that $\int \mu_\theta(dx)g(x, \theta) = 0$ for all θ: this property replaces (6.11) and is enough to obtain that $\sqrt{n}(\widehat{\theta}_n - \theta)$ converges in law under $\mathbf{P}_\theta$ to some centered Gaussian variable, although with a variance having a much more complicated form than (6.12). The advantage is that finding functions g satisfying $\int \mu_\theta(dx)g(x, \theta) = 0$ is much easier than finding functions satisfying both (6.10) and (6.11) because μ_θ is reasonably often explicitly known (when the diffusion process is one-dimensional, for example). The main disadvantage is that the minimal variance we can thus obtain by appropriately choosing g is always bigger than the minimal variance α in (6.12) when G is appropriately chosen. This was done by Kessler [32], who in particular studied the Ornstein–Uhlenbeck case completely.

Many other possibilities are indeed available in the literature: one can consult Prakasa Rao [2] for an extensive account on this and of course the paper [33] of Bibby et al. in this volume for many more details about estimating functions. But one must say that indeed there is no universal method in this setting, working for all diffusions: the comparison between the various methods is largely empirical and done only for special diffusion processes.

A last remark: if one wants to get rid of the identifiability problem stated at the beginning (that is, replace (6.2) by (6.1)), a possibility is to assume that the observations take place at times $T_1, T_2, \ldots, T_n$, the occurrence times of a Poisson process independent of the diffusion, and with parameter $1/\Delta$: this seems strange at first glance, but in fact, it is compatible with many sets of data, in which the inter-observation times are not really regularly spaced (see Duffie and Singleton [34]).

7. OBSERVATIONS WITH ERRORS

When there are errors of various kinds, or incomplete observations, very little is known so far. The problem becomes difficult because we loose the Markov structure of the process and introduce complicated dependencies between the observed variables.

We will give very few elements here and only for a single observation scheme: namely when the process is observed at times iT/n for $i = 0, 1, \ldots, n$. In view of the discussion in Subsection 5.1, we consider Eq. (5.1):

$$dX_t = a(t, X_t)dt + \sigma(\theta, t, X_t)dW_t, \quad X_0 = x_0$$

with a not depending on θ. For simplicity, we also assume that X and θ as well are one-dimensional, that σ (or $c = \sigma^2$) does not vanish, and that a and c are smooth enough in all variables. Further, we assume some kind of identifiability assumption, say that $c(\theta, 0, x_0) \neq c(\zeta, 0, x_0)$ whenever $\theta \neq \zeta$ (as said before this could be much weakened). This choice of our observation scheme is due to the fact that this is almost the only situation for which the influence of error measurements has been studied so far.

We also consider only two "extreme" types of errors, namely errors that are i.i.d. and independent of the process, and "pure rounding" so that one might perhaps call this a form of incomplete observation rather than an error. Because this chapter was first written, a relatively large literature has been appearing on this subject, accommodating more general types of error, but in a situation which is not really parametric estimation for diffusions but rather the estimations of *random* quantities related to the volatility (squared-volatility, quarticity, and so on); see, for example, [35–40] and the references therein.

7.1. Additive Errors

The simplest possible kind of error, if not the most natural one, is when each observation is blurred with an additive error, all errors being i.i.d. and independent of the diffusion itself and with a known distribution. As a matter of fact, we can only deal with Gaussian errors. So we suppose that the actual observations are of the form

$$Z_i^n = Y_{iT/n} + \sqrt{\rho_n}\varepsilon_i, \tag{7.1}$$

where ρ_n is a known positive number and the ε_i are i.i.d. variables with law $\mathcal{N}(0, 1)$, independent of the process X.

We let the error variance ρ_n depend on n: this is because we are interested again in asymptotic properties, and it may seem natural that the measurement error be small when there are many observations; on the other hand, the case where $\rho_n = \rho$ does not depend on n may also seem quite natural.

Mathematically speaking, the statistical model at hand may be described as follows: let still $(\Omega, \mathcal{Y}, (\boldsymbol{P}_\theta)_{\theta \in \Theta})$ be the canonical space with the canonical process Y and the weak solutions P_θ of our diffusion equations; let $(\Omega'', \mathcal{Y}'', Q)$ be another probability space on which are defined i.i.d. $\mathcal{N}(0, 1)$ variables ε_n; then we take the statistical model $(\Omega', \mathcal{Y}', (P'_\theta)_{\theta \in \Theta})$, where

$$\Omega' = \Omega \times \Omega'', \quad \mathcal{Y}' = \mathcal{Y} \otimes \mathcal{Y}'', \quad P'_\theta = P_\theta \otimes Q.$$

Further we define the variables Z_i^n on this space by (7.1). The observed σ-field at stage n is then $\mathcal{G}_n = \sigma(Z_i^n : i = 0, 1, \ldots, n)$. Here, not only the σ-fields $\mathcal{G}_n$ are not increasing but as said before we have lost the Markov property for the chain $(Z_i^n)_{i \geq 0}$.

7.1.1. Neglecting the Errors

The first try to estimate might be to neglect the measurement errors and to use the method explained in Subsection 5.1. Let us try this in the *very simple* case where $x_0 = 0$ and $a \equiv 0$ and $c(\theta, t, x) = \theta$ and $\Theta = (0, \infty)$. Then of course our Eq. (5.1) reduces to $X = \sqrt{\theta} W$, where W is a Brownian motion.

If we observe without error (which amounts to taking $\rho_n = 0$), we have the LAN property with rate $\frac{1}{\sqrt{n}}$ and asymptotic Fisher information $I(\theta) = \frac{1}{2\theta^2}$; this can be seen from (5.3), but it also reduces to very old results because here we observe equivalently the normalized increments $U_i^n = \sqrt{\frac{n}{T}}(Y_{(i-1)T/n} - Y_{iT/n})$, which are i.i.d. $\mathcal{N}(0, \theta)$. The contrast (5.4) writes as

$$V_n(\zeta) = n \log \zeta + \frac{n}{T} \sum_{i=1}^{n} \frac{(Y_{iT/n} - Y_{(i-1)T/n})^2}{\zeta},$$

whose minimum is achieved at the point

$$\widehat{\theta}_n = \frac{1}{T} \sum_{i=1}^{n} (Y_{iT/n} - Y_{(i-1)T/n})^2 = \sum_{i=1}^{n} (U_i^n)^2. \tag{7.2}$$

Because the U_i^n are i.i.d. $\mathcal{N}(0, \theta)$, it is also well known that $\widehat{\theta}_n$ is optimal for estimating θ in all possible senses, not only asymptotically but for every n.

Now we have measurement errors, but we still use the contrast above, just replacing the unobserved $Y_{iT/n}^n$ by the variables Z_i^n of (7.1). This amounts to taking the estimate $\widehat{\theta}_n$ of (7.2) with Z_i^n instead of $Y_{iT/n}^n$. Because all variables are Gaussian, it is elementary to check that

- $\widehat{\theta}_n \to \theta$ in P'_θ-probability if and only if $n\rho_n \to 0$: so if $n\rho_n$ does not go to 0, the sequence $\widehat{\theta}_n$ is not even consistent, and in fact it goes to $+\infty$!
- $\sqrt{n}(\widehat{\theta}_n - \theta)$ converges in law under P'_θ to an $\mathcal{N}(0, 2\theta^2) = \mathcal{N}(0, 1/I(\theta))$ random variable if and only if $n^{3/2}\rho_n \to 0$: in this case, the sequence $\widehat{\theta}_n$ is asymptotically efficient.

- $\sqrt{n}(\widehat{\theta}_n - \theta)$ converges in law under P'_θ to an $\mathcal{N}(v, 2\theta^2) = \mathcal{N}(v, 1/I(\theta))$ random variable if and only if $n^{3/2}\rho_n \to v \in (0, \infty)$: if $v > 0$, the sequence $\widehat{\theta}_n$ is rate-efficient but not asymptotically efficient because of the bias.
- If $n^{3/2}\rho_n \to \infty$, then the sequence $\sqrt{n}(\widehat{\theta}_n - \theta)$ is not tight under P'_θ: so in this case, the sequence $\widehat{\theta}_n$ is not rate-efficient.

The main point coming out from this analysis is that it is *very dangerous* to forget about measurement errors: if these are "small enough," meaning that $n^{3/2}\rho_n$ is small, then there is no harm (this is obvious from a heuristic point of view, except for the power $3/2$ which comes from precise calculations), but otherwise one gets bad estimators and even *inconsistent* estimators when $n\rho_n$ does not go to 0.

7.1.2. Taking Care of the Errors
In view of what precedes, we should take the errors into consideration, at least to get consistent estimators, and if possible to find asymptotically efficient estimators. For this, we reproduce some (unfortunately not quite complete) results from [41, 48].

Let us first single out three cases corresponding to different asymptotic behavior of ρ_n (Case 3 below accommodates the situation where $\rho_n = \rho$ does not depend on n) and introduce some notation:

$$
\left.
\begin{array}{llll}
\textbf{Case 1:} & n\rho_n \to u = 0, & \text{then set} \quad u_n = 1/\sqrt{n} \\[4pt]
\textbf{Case 2:} & n\rho_n \to u \in (0, \infty), & \text{then set} \quad u_n = 1/\sqrt{n} \\[4pt]
\textbf{Case 3:} & n\rho_n \to u = \infty, \quad \sup_n \rho_n < \infty, & \text{then set} \quad u_n = (\rho_n/n)^{1/4},
\end{array}
\right\} \quad (7.3)
$$

$$
\phi_u(x, y) = \begin{cases}
\dfrac{y^2}{2x^2} & \text{if} \quad u = 0 \\[10pt]
\dfrac{y^2(2+x/u)}{2\sqrt{u}x^{3/2}(4+x/u)^{3/2}} & \text{if} \quad 0 < u < \infty. \\[10pt]
\dfrac{y^2}{8x^{3/2}} & \text{if} \quad u = \infty
\end{cases} \quad (7.4)
$$

Next, in agreement with the case without errors, we can hope for the LAMN property to hold, perhaps. We have been unable to prove this, but we can prove it in the particular case where $a \equiv 0$ and $c(\theta, t, x) = c(\theta, t)$ does not depend on x [then the solution of (5.1) is a Gaussian process with constant mean x_0]. We also assume that c is smooth and that both c and $\dot{c}$ do not vanish (the last assumption may be somehow relaxed, but we want to keep things simple here). In this case, and if further $\rho_n = 0$, according to Subsection 5.1, we have the LAN property with asymptotic Fisher information

$$
I(\theta) = \frac{1}{2T} \int_0^T \frac{\dot{c}(\theta, s)^2}{c(\theta, s)^2} ds. \quad (7.5)
$$

If measurement errors are present and if ρ_n is such that we are in one of the three cases above, one can then prove that the LAN property hold *with rate* u_n and asymptotic Fisher information

$$I(\theta) = \frac{1}{T} \int_0^T \phi_u(T\dot{c}(\theta, s), T\dot{c}(\theta, s))ds. \tag{7.6}$$

Observe that (7.6) and (7.5) agree when $u = 0$. Observe also that the rate is $\frac{1}{\sqrt{n}}$ as soon as $n\rho_n \to u < \infty$: in this case, and even when $n^{3/2}\rho_n$ does not go to 0, one should be able to find asymptotically efficient estimators with this rate $\frac{1}{\sqrt{n}}$, a property not enjoyed by the estimators (7.2).

Now, let us turn to constructing estimators. We go back to the general situation of Eq. (5.1). We first choose a sequence k_n of integers in such a way that $nu_n^2/k_n \to 0$ and $k_n/nu_n \to 0$, by taking, for example,

$$k_n = \begin{cases} \left[n^{1/4} \right] & \text{in Cases 1 and 2} \\ \left[n^{5/8}\rho_n^{3/8} \right] & \text{in Case 3.} \end{cases}$$

We also set $l_n = [n/k_n]$, and we take n large enough to have $k_n \geq 2$ and $l_n \geq 2$. Next we consider the $(k_n - 1) \times (k_n - 1)$-matrix D^n whose entries are

$$D_{i,j}^n = \begin{cases} 2\rho_n & \text{if } i = j \\ -\rho_n & \text{if } |i - j| = 1 \\ 0 & \text{otherwise} \end{cases}$$

and whose eigenvalues are

$$\lambda_i^n = 2\rho_n \left(1 - \cos\frac{i\pi}{k_n} \right), \quad i = 1, \ldots, k_n - 1,$$

and we write $D^n = P^n L^n P^{n,\star}$, where L^n is diagonal with entries given above and P^n is orthogonal. Next we set $s_m^n = \frac{k_n(m-1)T}{n}$ for $m = 1, \ldots, l_n$, and recalling the observations Z_i^n of (7.1),

$$F_j^{n,m} = \sum_{i=1}^{k_n-1} P_{ij}^n \left(Z_{k_n(m-1)+j}^n - Z_{k_n(mp-1)+j-1}^n \right), \quad j = 1, \ldots, k_n - 1, \quad m = 1, \ldots, l_n,$$

$$S_m^n = \frac{1}{k_n - 1} \sum_{i=1}^{k_n-1} Z_{k_n(m-2)+i}^n, \quad m = 2, \ldots, l_n,$$

$$\Phi_j^{n,m}(\zeta) = 2 \left(1 - \cos\frac{j\pi}{k_n} \right) + \frac{T\dot{c}(\zeta, s_m^n, S_m^n)}{n\rho_n}, \quad j = 1, \ldots, k_n - 1, \quad m = 2, \ldots, l_n.$$

Then at this point, we can write a contrast function as

$$W_n(\zeta) = \sum_{m=2}^{l_n} \sum_{j=1}^{k_n-1} \left(\frac{\left(F_j^{n,m}\right)^2}{\rho_n \Phi_j^{n,m}(\zeta)} + \log \Phi_j^{n,m}(\zeta) \right). \tag{7.7}$$

Finally $\widehat{\theta}_n$ is a point achieving the minimum of $W_n(.)$ over Θ: observe that $W_n(\zeta)$, hence $\widehat{\theta}_n$, can actually be computed (in principle) from the observations.

Then one can prove that provided θ is in the interior of Θ, the sequence $\frac{1}{u_n}(\widehat{\theta}_n - \theta)$ converges in law under P'_θ toward a centered mixed Gaussian variable with conditional variance $I(\theta)^{-1}$, where

$$I(\theta) = \frac{1}{T} \int_0^T \phi_u(T\dot{c}(\theta, s, Y_s), T\dot{c}(\theta, s, Y_s)) \mathrm{d}s. \tag{7.8}$$

Remarks

1. *When $c(\theta, t, x) = c(\theta, t)$ does not depend on x, then (7.6) and (7.8) agree; so if further $a \equiv 0$, the estimators $\widehat{\theta}_n$ above are asymptotically efficient.*
2. *Although we cannot prove the LAMN property in general, a comparison with the case $c(\theta, t, x) = c(\theta, t)$ strongly supports the fact that we indeed have the LAMN property with rate u_n and asymptotic conditional Fisher information $I(\theta)$ given by (7.8), together with the fact that the estimators $\widehat{\theta}_n$ are asymptotically efficient, also in the case of genuine diffusions (5.1).*
3. *It is noteworthy to observe that all ingredients above use the known value ρ_n and of course the observations themselves, but they do not depend on the case we are in [see (7.3)]. This is of big practical importance because, although we know n and ρ_n, it is difficult to decide whether the product $n\rho_n$ is "very small" or moderate or big. In fact, in all cases, our estimators will be optimal (asymptotically speaking), within the relevant asymptotic framework.*
4. *Assuming that the errors are Gaussian is rather strong, but we know nothing about more general errors.*

The Ornstein–Uhlenbeck Process: We just mention here the case of the process (4.3), to see more explicitly on an example the value taken by the conditional Fisher information (7.8). We get in fact a deterministic quantity, given by

$$I(\theta) = \begin{cases} \frac{1}{2\theta_2^2} & \text{if } u = 0 \\[2ex] \frac{\sqrt{T}(2+T\theta_2/u)}{4\sqrt{u}\theta_2^{3/2}(4+T\theta_2/u)^{3/2}} & \text{if } 0 < u < \infty \\[2ex] \frac{\sqrt{T}}{8\theta_2^{3/2}} & \text{if } u = \infty \end{cases}$$

One can observe that T comes in explicitly, except when $u = 0$.

7.2. Round-Off Errors

Another sort of error consists in round-off errors: instead of the true value x of the diffusion at some time, only a rounded-off value of x, at some level $\alpha > 0$, is available to the statistician: that is, instead of x one observes the value $\alpha[x/\alpha]$ (recall that $[v]$ denotes the integer part of $v \in \mathbf{R}$). This sort of measurement is particularly relevant for financial data, where one models prices or interest rates with a diffusion, although the actual values in the market are always multiples of some basic currency (dollars, cents, or 0.1%s, and so on).

Recall that everything here is one-dimensional (θ as well as the diffusion), and a and c are smooth, and c does not vanish. Exactly as in the previous subsection where the error level ρ_n was possibly depending on n, here the round-off level will also possibly depend on n, say α_n. That is, at stage n, we observe the variables

$$Z_i^n = \alpha_n \left[Y_{\frac{iT}{n}} / \alpha_n \right]. \tag{7.9}$$

Contrarily to the previous case, there is no need to enlarge our probability space: the statistical model is thus $(\Omega, \mathcal{Y}, (\mathbf{P}_\theta)_{\theta \in \Theta})$ (the canonical space with the canonical process Y), but the observed σ-field is $\mathcal{G}_n = \sigma(Z_i^n : i = 0, 1, \dots, n)$.

7.2.1. Neglecting the Errors

Here again we can first try to use the method of Subsection 5.1 without taking care of the errors, and we again do this in the simple case where $x_0 = 0$ and $a \equiv 0$ and $c(\theta, t, x) = \theta$ and $\Theta = (0, \infty)$, that is, $X = \sqrt{\theta}W$, where W is a Brownian motion.

Recall again that without round-off error, we have the LAN property with rate $\frac{1}{\sqrt{n}}$ and asymptotic Fisher information $I(\theta) = \frac{1}{2\theta^2}$, and the optimal estimators are given by (7.2), that is,

$$\widehat{\theta}_n = \frac{1}{T} \sum_{i=1}^n (Y_{iT/n} - Y_{(i-1)T/n})^2. \tag{7.10}$$

Now we have round-off errors. If we just use $\widehat{\theta}_n$ above with Z_i^n given by (7.9) instead of $Y_{iT/n}^n$, we get the following asymptotic behavior [see [42]]:

- If $\alpha_n \sqrt{n} \to 0$, then $\widehat{\theta}_n \to \theta$ in $\mathbf{P}_\theta$-probability.
- The sequence $\sqrt{n}(\widehat{\theta}_n - \theta)$ converges in law under $\mathbf{P}_\theta$ toward an $\mathcal{N}(0, 2\theta^2)$ random variable if and only if $\alpha_n n \to 0$; it is tight if and only if the sequence $\alpha_n n$ is bounded.
- If $\alpha_n \sqrt{n} \to \beta \in (0, \infty)$, then $\widehat{\theta}_n$ converges in $\mathbf{P}_\theta$-probability to some constant depending on β, which is strictly bigger than θ: so the estimators $\widehat{\theta}_n$ are not consistent.
- If $\alpha_n \sqrt{n} \to \infty$ and $\alpha_n \to 0$, then $\frac{1}{\alpha_n \sqrt{n}} \widehat{\theta}_n$ converges in $\mathbf{P}_\theta$-probability to some positive constant: so the estimators $\widehat{\theta}_n$ are not consistent and even converge to $+\infty$.

- If $\alpha_n \to \alpha \in (0, \infty)$, then the sequence $\frac{1}{\sqrt{n}}\widehat{\theta}_n$ converges in P_θ-probability toward a constant times the sum of the values of the local time of Y taken at all level $k\alpha$ for $k \in \mathbf{Z}$, taken at time T.

We can draw the same conclusion from this analysis than for additive errors: it is *very dangerous* to forget about round-off errors: if these are "small enough," meaning that $n\alpha_n$ is small, then there is no harm in doing that, but otherwise one gets bad estimators and even *inconsistent* estimators when $\alpha_n\sqrt{n}$ does not go to 0.

7.2.2. Taking Care of the Errors

Now we take the round-off errors into consideration and we exhibit asymptotically efficient estimators. The method explained below is due to Delattre, see [43] and [44].

First, it is possible to prove the LAMN property when $\alpha_n\sqrt{n} \to \beta \in (0, \infty)$. Describing the asymptotic random Fisher information is a bit lengthy, and we need some preliminary notation. First, consider a Brownian motion W over $\mathbf{R}$ (such that $W_0 = 0$) and a random variable U, which is uniform over $[0, 1]$ and independent from W; for $\alpha > 0$, let $\mathcal{H}_\alpha$ be the σ-field generated by all variables of the form $\alpha\left[U + \frac{W_i}{\alpha}\right]$, $i \in \mathbf{Z}$; then for all $i \in \mathbf{N}$ and all $\alpha \in (0, \infty)$, we define the random variables $\xi_i^\alpha = E((W_i - W_{i-1})^2 - 1 | \mathcal{H}_\alpha)$. The following formula defines a positive function over $\mathbf{R}_+$:

$$J(\alpha) = E((\xi_1^\alpha)^2) + 2\sum_{i=2}^{\infty} E(\xi_1^\alpha \xi_i^\alpha),$$

and $J(0) := \lim_{\alpha \downarrow 0} J(\alpha)$ equals 2 and J strictly decreases from 2 to 0 when α increases from 0 to ∞. Then, assuming that a and c are smooth enough and that c does not vanish, if $\alpha_n\sqrt{n} \to \beta \in (0, \infty)$, we have the LAMN property with rate $\frac{1}{\sqrt{n}}$ and conditional Fisher information given by

$$I(\theta) = \frac{1}{4T}\int_0^T \frac{\dot{c}(\theta, s, Y_s)^2}{c(\theta, s, Y_s)^2} J\left(\frac{\beta}{\sqrt{c(\theta, s, Y_s)}}\right) ds. \tag{7.11}$$

Observe that if $\beta = 0$, and because $J(0) = 2$, the above $I(\theta)$ is also the value given in (5.3), corresponding to observations without errors. If $\beta > 0$, then the above $I(\theta)$ is strictly smaller than the value given in (5.3), which corresponds to the intuitive idea that if the round-off error is "big," then we obtain less information on the process.

When $\alpha_n\sqrt{n} \to \infty$ and $\alpha_n \to 0$, it is also possible to prove the LAMN property, but the rate is now α_n and the conditional Fisher information takes yet another form.

Now let us come to constructing estimators. Here again, $\widehat{\theta}_n$ will be a point achieving the minimum of a contrast function, which takes the form

$$W_n(\zeta) = \sum_{i=1}^{n} F\left(\alpha_n\sqrt{n}, c(\zeta, \frac{(i-1)T}{n}, Z_i^n + \frac{\alpha_n}{2}), \sqrt{n}(Z_i^n - Z_{i-1}^n)\right), \tag{7.12}$$

where F is a suitable (known) function on $\mathbf{R}_+ \times \mathbf{R}_+ \times \mathbf{R}$, so $\widehat{\theta}_n$ can actually be computed (in principle) from the observations.

Then, when $\alpha_n \sqrt{n} \to \beta \in (0, \infty)$, one can prove the following, as soon as the function F is smooth, with polynomial growth at most, even in the last variable [that is, $F(\alpha, z, x) = F(\alpha, z, -x)$], and such that the function $z \mapsto \int_0^1 du \int h(y) F(\alpha, z, \alpha[u + z'y/\alpha])h(y)dy$ [where h is the density of the law $\mathcal{N}(0, 1)$] admits a unique minimum at point $z' = z$: provided θ is in the interior of Θ, the sequence $\sqrt{n}(\widehat{\theta}_n - \theta)$ converges in law under $\mathbf{P}_\theta$ toward a centered mixed Gaussian variable with conditional variance $\Sigma_{F,\beta}(\theta)$ [an expression in terms of F and its derivatives and of β looking a bit like (5.7) in a more complicated way]. Examples of possible such functions F are

$$F_p(\alpha, z, x) = \frac{|x|^p}{\gamma_p(z, \alpha)} + \log \gamma_p(z, \alpha), \quad \text{where} \quad \gamma_p(z, \alpha) = \int\limits_0^1 du \int h(y) \left| \alpha \left[u + \frac{z}{\alpha} \right] \right|^p dy.$$

The estimators such constructed are thus rate-efficient; they are usually nor asymptotically efficient, and indeed one does not know how to choose F in such a way that $\widehat{\theta}_n$ becomes asymptotically efficient [that is, $\Sigma_{F,\beta} = I(\theta)^{-1}$, see (7.11)]. However with F_2 as above, we obtain $\Sigma_{F,0} = I(\theta)^{-1}$, so the associated estimators are asymptotically efficient when $\alpha_n \sqrt{n} \to 0$ at least.

When $\alpha_n \sqrt{n} \to \infty$ and $\alpha_n \to 0$, one can use the same contrasts, except that we need some additional assumptions on the behavior of the function $F(\alpha, z, x)$ as $\alpha \to \infty$. Then the sequence $\frac{1}{\alpha_n}(\widehat{\theta}_n - \theta)$ converges in law under $\mathbf{P}_\theta$ toward a centered mixed Gaussian variable with conditional variance $\Sigma_{F,\infty}(\theta)$ (which indeed is the limit of $\frac{1}{\alpha^2}\Sigma_{F,\alpha}$ as $\alpha \to \infty$). So again these estimators are rate-efficient.

An example of function F that works for all cases ($\alpha_n \sqrt{n}$ bounded or going to infinity) is

$$F(\alpha, z, x) = \frac{1}{1 \bigvee \alpha} \frac{|x|^2}{\gamma_2(z, \alpha)} + \log \frac{\gamma_2(z, \alpha)}{1 \bigvee \alpha}. \tag{7.13}$$

Remarks

1. *One sees that with, for example, the function in (7.13) we have estimators $\widehat{\theta}_n$ that do not depend on the asymptotic behavior of the sequence $\alpha_n \sqrt{n}$: this is again of big practical importance.*

2. *The fact that α_n goes to 0 is crucial to all what precedes. If, for example, we take $\alpha_n = \alpha$ not depending on n, then apart from the convergence in probability of $\widehat{\theta}_n/\sqrt{n}$ for the estimators in (7.10) toward a sum of local times, essentially nothing is known, but even the identifiability of the parameter in this case could be a problem.*

The Ornstein–Uhlenbeck Process: Again, we mention the case of the process (4.3) to see more explicitly on an example the value taken by the conditional Fisher information

(7.11). We get again a deterministic quantity, which is $I(\theta) = \frac{1}{2\theta_2^2} J(\beta/\sqrt{\theta_2})$: we see clearly on this formula the influence of the "asymptotic" round-off factor β, and that the key quantity is the quotient $\beta/\sqrt{\theta_2}$, as it should be by scaling arguments. And, contrarily to the case with additive errors, the quantity T does not come into the picture.

8. CONCLUDING REMARKS

We now have seen a series of methods for estimating parameters in diffusion processes, mainly when the observations are regularly spaced at times $i\Delta_n$ for $i = 0, \ldots, n$. Obviously we have let aside a number of problems, even in this setting: first we have made assumptions on the coefficients, which are not necessarily met in practice, like in particular the invertibility of the diffusion coefficient which plays an important role in several cases. Second, and probably more importantly, we have not really studied the case where the diffusions live on a domain D and especially the case where the boundary ∂D can be attained. Third, the case where there are measurement errors has been studied in quite specific situations only, and there is obviously a need to go further in this topic.

Let us stick to the case of perfect observations on a regular grid. In a concrete situation, we have a number n of observations and a stepsize $\Delta = \Delta_n$. Then, which one among the various methods should we choose? Because in practice n is (relatively) large, this question boils down to determining in which asymptotic situation we can reasonably assume we are: is Δ small, in which case we may assume that $\Delta = \Delta_n \to 0$? is it "really" small, in which case we can suppose that $n\Delta_n$ is more or less constant? Related with this problem is, of course, the kind of parameter we wish to estimate: in the setting of Eq. (4.2), is it θ_1 or θ_2 or both? Keeping in mind that the volatility is probably the most important parameter, we can think that in most cases we are interested essentially in θ_2; keeping in mind that as soon as $T_n = n\Delta_n \to \infty$ we essentially need the process to be ergodic, is it reasonable to believe that our phenomenon is truly stationary?

All these questions are crucial in a sense, and so far there is no definitive answers. In fact, there is a need for numerical experimentations on some case studies (for models more involved than the Ornstein–Uhlenbeck process which, because of its Gaussian property, might present too much specific structure to be truly representative of general diffusions): one should check the validity of the different methods with the same set of data, perhaps with simulated data to be sure of the underlying model. And also, before using a method that necessitates ergodicity, we should perhaps make a test of the stationarity of the process or at least do the estimation on disjoint pieces of data and check whether the estimates on each piece are more or less consistent with one another or whether there is a clear trend.

It might of course be the case that all reasonable methods give more or less the same results, at least as far as the second component θ_2 is concerned: a close examination of the methods suggests such a nice property (except for the methods using simulated moments or simulated likelihoods), but there is of course no guarantee for that.

Finally, we end this chapter with some words about inference for discontinuous processes, letting apart the case of point processes, which has been extensively studied but is not relevant for finance. There is a number of papers about general estimation problems for possibly discontinuous semimartingales, but mainly when the whole path of the process is observed on an interval $[0, T_n]$, the asymptotic being $T_n \to \infty$. More interesting would be to look at discontinuous processes observed on a regular grid, just as above: but the problems seem then to be quite difficult, and very few results have been obtained so far.

More precisely, if the grid has a constant stepsize Δ and provided our discontinuous processes are Markov, we are again in the situation of observing n successive values taken by a Markov chain, and if it is ergodic, the methods of Section 6 can still be applied, with obvious modifications. If our processes are Lévy processes and although they are never ergodic, some reasonably complete answers are available, see Jedidi [45].

However, if the stepsize Δ_n goes to 0, then very unexpected phenomena appear. Assume, for example, that $\Delta_n = T/n$ and that the observed processes are $X_t = \theta Z_t$, where Z is a given process whose law is known and θ is the parameter to estimate ($\theta \in (0, \infty)$). If Z is a stable process with index $\alpha \in (0, 2)$, then by the scaling property we easily find that the LAN property holds with rate $\frac{1}{\sqrt{n}}$. If now Z is the sum of a symmetric stable process of index $\alpha \in (0, 2)$ and of a standard Poisson process, then Far [46] proved that when $\alpha = 2$ (that is, Z is the sum of a Brownian motion and a Poisson process) we have the LAMN property with rate $\frac{1}{\sqrt{n}}$ (and asymptotically efficient estimators can be derived and behave better than if we had a Brownian motion alone); if $\alpha < 2$, then we have convergence of the local model with a "random rate" which is $\frac{1}{\sqrt{n}}$ with positive probability and $\frac{1}{n^{1/\alpha}}$ with also positive probability. So asymptotically efficient estimators converge to the true value at a random rate which is $\sqrt{n}$ with positive probability and $n^{1/\alpha}$ (much bigger than $\sqrt{n}$) also with positive probability. And of course nothing is known when the observed process is the solution of an SDE driven by, say, a Lévy process and with a coefficient depending on the parameter of interest.

REFERENCES

[1] Prakasa Rao, B.L.S. (1999a) *Semimartingales and Their Statistical Inference*. Boca Raton: Chapman & Hall.
[2] Prakasa Rao, B.L.S. (1999b) *Statistical Inference for Diffusion Type Processes*. London: Arnold.
[3] Øksendal, B. (1985) *Stochastic Differential Equations*. Berlin: Springer Verlag.
[4] Stroock, D.W., and Varadhan, S.R.S. (1979) *Multidimensional Diffusion Processes*. Berlin: Springer Verlag.

[5] Liptser, R.S., and Shiryayev, A.N. (1978) *Statistics of Stochastic Processes*. Berlin: Springer Verlag.

[6] Ikeda, N., and Watanabe, S. (1981) *Stochastic differential equations and diffusion processes*. North Holland: New York.

[7] Revuz, D., and Yor, M. (1991) *Continuous Martingales and Brownian Motion*. Berlin: Springer Verlag.

[8] Karatzas, I., and Shreve, S. (1988) *Brownian Motion and Stochastic Calculus*. Berlin: Springer Verlag.

[9] Jacod, J., and Shiryaev, A.N. (1987) *Limit Theorems for Stochastic Processes*. Berlin: Springer Verlag.

[10] LeCam, L. (1986) *Asymptotic Methods in Statistical Decision Theory*. Berlin: Springer Verlag.

[11] LeCam, L., and Yang, G.L. (1990) *Asymptotics in Statistics: Some Basic Concepts*. Berlin: Springer Verlag.

[12] Ibragimov, I.A., and Has'minskii, R.Z. (1981) *Statistical Estimation: Asymptotic Theory*. Berlin: Springer Verlag.

[13] Jeganathan, P. (1982) On the asymptotic theory of estimation when the limit of the loglikelihood ration is mixed normal. *Sankhya A* **44**: 173–212.

[14] Kutoyants, Yu.A. (1984) *Parameter Estimation for Stochastic Processes*. Berlin: Heldermann Verlag.

[15] Dohnal, G. (1987) On estimating the diffusion coefficient. *J Appl Probab* **34**: 105–114.

[16] Genon-Catalot, V., and Jacod, J. (1994) Estimation of the diffusion coefficient for diffusion processes; random sampling. *Scand J Stat* **21**: 193–221.

[17] Gobet, E. (2001) Local asymptotic mixed normality property for elliptic diffusion: a malliavin calculus approach. *Bernoulli* **7**: 899–912.

[18] Genon-Catalot, V., and Jacod, J. (1993) On the estimation of the diffusion coefficient for multi-dimensional diffusion processes. *Ann IHP Probab* **29**: 119–151.

[19] Florens-Zmirou, D. (1989) Approximate discrete time schemes for statistics of diffusion processes. *Statistics* **20**: 547–557.

[20] Yoshida, N. (1992) Estimation for diffusion processes from discrete observations. *J Multivar Anal* **41**: 220–242.

[21] Kessler, M. (1997) Estimation of an ergodic diffusion from discrete observations. *Scand J Stat* **24**: 211–229.

[22] Kessler, M. (1996) Estimation paramétrique des coefficients d'une diffusion ergodique à partir d'observations discrètes. *Thesis*, Université Paris-6.

[23] Jacod, J. (2006) Parametric inference for discretely observed non–ergodic diffusions. *Bernoulli* **12**: 383–403.

[24] Bandi, F.M., and Phillips, P.C.P. (2007) A simple approach to the parametric estimation of potentially nonstationary diffusions. *J Econom* **137**: 354–395.

[25] Roussas, G. (1972) *Contiguity of Probability Measures*. London: Cambridge University Press.

[26] Aït-Sahalia, Y. (2002) Maximum likelihood estimation of discretely sampled diffusions: a Closed-form approximation approach. *Econometrica* **70**: 223–262.

[27] Pedersen, A.R. (1995) A new approach to maximum likelihood estimation for stochastic differential equations based on discrete observations. *Scand J Stat* **22**: 55–71.

[28] Pedersen, A.R. (1995) Consistency and asymptotic normality of an approximate maximum likelihood estimator for discretely observed diffusion processes. *Bernoulli* **1**: 257–279.

[29] Beskos, A., Papaspiliopoulos, O., and Roberts, G. (2009) Monte Carlo maximum likelihood estimation for discretely observed diffusion processes. *Ann Stat* **37**: 223–245.

[30] Hansen, L.P., Scheinkman, J.A., and Touzi, N. (1998) Spectral methods for identifying scalar diffusions. *J Econom* **86**: 1–32.

[31] Kessler, M., and Sørensen, M. (1999) Estimating equations based on eigenfunctions for a discretely observed diffusion process. *Bernoulli* **5**: 299–314.

[32] Kessler, M. (1997) Simple and explicit estimating functions for a discretely observed diffusion process. *Scand J Stat* **27**: 65–82.

[33] Bibby, B.M., Jacobsen, M., and Sørensen, M. (2010) Estimating functions for discretely sampled diffusions-type models, in Y. Ait-Sahalia, L.P. Hansen (eds.), *Handbook of Financial Econometrics*. Amsterdam: North-Holland.

[34] Duffie, D., and Glynn, P. (2004) Estimation of continuous-time Markov processes sampled at random time intervals. *Econometrica* **72**: 1773–1808.

[35] Aït-Sahalia, Y., Mykland, P.A., and Zhang, L. (2005) How often to sample a continuous-time process in the presence of market microstructure noise. *Rev Financ Stud* **18**: 351–416.

[36] Zhang, L., Mykland, P., and Aït-Sahalia, Y. (2005) A tale of two time scales: determining integrated volatility with noisy high-frequency data. *JASA* **100**: 1394–1411.

[37] Bandi, F.M., and Russell, J.R. (2006) Separating microstructure noise from volatility. *J Financ Econ* **79**: 655–692.

[38] Zhang, L. (2006) Efficient estimation of stochastic volatility using noisy observations: a multi-scale approach. *Bernoulli* **12**: 1019–1043.

[39] Barndorff-Nielsen, O.E., Hansen, P.R., Lunde, A., and Shephard, N. (2008) Designing realised kernels to measure ex-post variation of equity prices in the presence of noise. *Tech. Report.*

[40] Jacod, J., Li, Y., Mykland, P.A., Podolskij, M., and Vetters, M. (2009) Microstructure noise in the continuous case: the pre-averaging approach. *Stoch Process Appl.*

[41] Gloter, A., and Jacod, J. (2001) Diffusions with measurements errors, I-Local Asymptotic Normality. *ESAIM-PS* **5**: 225–242.

[42] Jacod, J. (1996) La variation quadratique du brownien en présence d'erreurs d'arrondi. *Astérisque* **236**: 155–162.

[43] Delattre, S. (1997) Estimation du coefficient de diffusion pour un processus de diffusion en présence d'erreurs d'arrondi. *Thesis*, Université Paris-6.

[44] Delattre, S. (1998) Estimation for a diffusion in the presence of round-off errors. Tech. *Report.*

[45] Jedidi, W. (2001) Local asymptotic normality of statistical models associated with discrete observations of Lévy Processes. *Preprint.*

[46] Far, H. (2001) Propeiétés asymptotiques de modèmes paramétriques associés à l'observation discrétisée de processus de sauts. *Thesis*, Université Paris-6.

[47] Florens-Zmirou, D. (1993). On estimating the diffusion coefficient from discrete observations. *J Appl Probab* **30**: 790–804.

[48] Gloter, A., and Jacod, J. (2001) Diffusions with measurements errors, II-Optimal estimators. *ESAIM-PS* **5**: 243–260.

[49] Höpfner, R., Jacod, J., and Ladelli, L. (1990) Local asymptotic normality and mixed normality for Markov statistical models. PTRF **86**: 105–129.

CHAPTER 17

Stock Market Trading Volume

Andrew W. Lo *and* Jiang Wang

Sloan School of Management, Massachusetts Institute of Technology, Cambridge, MA; NBER, Cambridge, MA

Contents

Abstract

If price and quantity are the fundamental building blocks of any theory of market interactions, the importance of trading volume in understanding the behavior of financial markets is clear. However, while many economic models of financial markets have been developed to explain the behavior of prices – predictability, variability, and information content – far less attention has been devoted to explaining the behavior of trading volume. In this chapter, we hope to expand our understanding of trading volume by developing well-articulated economic models of asset prices and volume and empirically estimating them using recently available daily volume data for individual securities from the University of Chicago's Center for Research in Securities Prices. Our theoretical contributions include (1) an economic definition of volume that is most consistent with theoretical models of trading activity; (2) the derivation of volume implications of basic portfolio theory; and (3) the development of an intertemporal equilibrium model of asset market in which the trading process is determined endogenously by liquidity needs and risk-sharing motives. Our empirical contributions include (1) the construction of a volume/returns database extract of the CRSP volume data; (2) comprehensive exploratory data analysis of both the time-series and cross-sectional properties of trading volume; (3) estimation and inference for price/volume relations implied by asset pricing models; and (4) a new approach for empirically identifying factors to be included in a linear factor model of asset returns using volume data.

Keywords: volume; turnover; trading; asset pricing; liquidity

1. INTRODUCTION

One of the most fundamental notions of economics is the determination of prices through the interaction of supply and demand. The remarkable amount of information contained in equilibrium prices has been the subject of countless studies, both theoretical and empirical, and with respect to financial securities, several distinct literatures devoted solely to prices have developed.[1] Indeed, one of the most well developed and most highly cited strands of modern economics is the asset *pricing* literature.

However, the intersection of supply and demand determines not only equilibrium prices but also equilibrium quantities, yet quantities have received far less attention, especially in the asset pricing literature (Is there a parallel asset *quantities* literature?).

In this chapter, we hope to balance the asset pricing literature by reviewing the quantity implications of a dynamic general equilibrium model of asset markets under uncertainty and by investigating those implications empirically. Through theoretical and empirical analysis, we seek to understand the motives for trade, the process by which trades are consummated, the interaction between prices and volume, and the roles that risk preferences and market frictions play in determining trading activity as well as price dynamics. We begin in Section 2 with the basic definitions and notational conventions of our volume

---

[1] For example, the *Journal of Economic Literature* classification system includes categories such as Market Structure and Pricing (D4), Price Level, Inflation, and Deflation (E31), Determination of Interest Rates and Term Structure of Interest Rates (E43), Foreign Exchange (F31), Asset Pricing (G12), and Contingent and Futures Pricing (G13).

investigation – not a trivial task given the variety of volume measures used in the extant literature, e.g., shares traded, dollars traded, number of transactions, etc. We argue that turnover – shares traded divided by shares outstanding – is a natural measure of trading activity when viewed in the context of standard portfolio theory and equilibrium asset pricing models.

Using weekly turnover data for individual securities on the New York and American Stock Exchanges from 1962 to 1996 – made available by the Center for Research in Security Prices (CRSP) – we document in Sections 3 and 4 the time-series and cross-sectional properties of turnover indexes, individual turnover, and portfolio turnover. Turnover indexes exhibit a clear time trend from 1962 to 1996, beginning at less than 0.5% in 1962, reaching a high of 4% in October 1987, and dropping to just over 1% at the end of our sample in 1996. The cross section of turnover also varies through time: fairly concentrated in the early 1960s, much wider in the late 1960s, narrow again in the mid-1970s, and wide again after that. There is some persistence in turnover deciles from week to week: the largest- and smallest-turnover stocks in one week are often the largest- and smallest-turnover stocks, respectively, the next week; however, there is considerable diffusion of stocks across the intermediate turnover deciles from one week to the next. To investigate the cross-sectional variation of turnover in more detail, we perform cross-sectional regressions of average turnover on several regressors related to expected return, market capitalization, and trading costs. With R^2's ranging from 29.6 to 44.7%, these regressions show that stock-specific characteristics do explain a significant portion of the cross-sectional variation in turnover. This suggests the possibility of a parsimonious linear factor representation of the turnover cross section.

In Section 5, we derive the volume implications of basic portfolio theory, showing that two-fund separation implies that turnover is identical across all assets, and that $(K + 1)$-fund separation implies that turnover has an approximately linear K-factor structure. To investigate these implications empirically, we perform a principal component decomposition of the covariance matrix of the turnover of ten portfolios, where the portfolios are constructed by sorting on turnover betas. Across five-year subperiods, we find that a one-factor model for turnover is a reasonable approximation, at least in the case of turnover-beta-sorted portfolios, and that a two-factor model captures well over 90% of the time-series variation in turnover.

Finally, to investigate the dynamics of trading volume, in Section 6, we propose an intertemporal equilibrium asset pricing model and derive its implications for the joint behavior of volume and asset returns. In this model, assets are exposed to two sources of risks: market risk and the risk of changes in market conditions.[2] As a result, investors wish to hold two distinct portfolios of risky assets: the market portfolio and a hedging portfolio.

---

[2] One example of changes in market conditions is changes in the investment opportunity set considered by Merton (1973).

The market portfolio allows them to adjust their exposure to market risk, and the hedging portfolio allows them to hedge the risk of changes in market conditions. In equilibrium, investors trade in only these two portfolios, and expected asset returns are determined by their exposure to these two risks, i.e., a two-factor linear pricing model holds, where the two factors are the returns on the market portfolio and the hedging portfolio, respectively. We then explore the implications of this model on the joint behavior of volume and returns using the same weekly turnover data as in the earlier sections. From the trading volume of individual stocks, we construct the hedging portfolio and its returns. We find that the hedging-portfolio returns consistently outperform other factors in predicting future returns to the market portfolio, an implication of the intertemporal equilibrium model. We then use the returns to the hedging and market portfolios as two risk factors in a cross-sectional test along the lines of Fama and MacBeth (1973), and find that the hedging portfolio is comparable to other factors in explaining the cross-sectional variation of expected returns.

Our extensive analysis was based on data from 1962 to 1996, when it was first available from CRSP. We later updated our analysis on the tests of volume–return implications of the intertemporal asset pricing model to include the data from 1997 to 2004. These results are reported at the end of Section 6.

We conclude with suggestions for future research in Section 7.

2. MEASURING TRADING ACTIVITY

Any empirical analysis of trading activity in the market must start with a proper measure of volume. The literature on trading activity in financial markets is extensive and a number of measures of volume have been proposed and studied.[3] Some studies of aggregate trading activity use the total number of shares traded as a measure of volume (see Epps and Epps, 1976; Gallant et al., 1992; Hiemstra and Jones, 1994; Ying, 1966). Other studies use aggregate *turnover* – the total number of shares traded divided by the total number of shares outstanding – as a measure of volume (see Campbell et al., 1993; LeBaron, 1992; Smidt, 1990; the *1996 NYSE Fact Book*). Individual share volume is often used in the analysis of price/volume and volatility/volume relations (see Andersen, 1996; Epps and Epps, 1976; Lamoureux and Lastrapes, 1990, 1994). Studies focusing on the impact of information events on trading activity use individual turnover as a measure of volume (see Bamber, 1986, 1987; Lakonishok and Smidt, 1986; Morse, 1980; Richardson et al., 1986; Stickel and Verrecchia, 1994). Alternatively, Tkac (1999) considers individual dollar volume normalized by aggregate market dollar volume. Even the total number of trades (Conrad et al., 1994) and the number of trading days per year (James and Edmister, 1983) have been used as measures of trading activity. Table 17.1 provides a

---

[3]See Karpoff (1987) for an excellent introduction to and survey of this burgeoning literature.

Table 17.1   Selected volume studies grouped according to the volume measure used

Volume measure	Study
Aggregate share volume	Gallant et al. (1992), Hiemstra and Jones (1994), Ying (1966)
Individual share volume	Andersen (1996), Epps and Epps (1976), James and Edmister (1983), Lamoureux and Lastrapes (1990, 1994)
Aggregate dollar volume	—
Individual dollar volume	James and Edmister (1983), Lakonishok and Smidt (1986)
Relative individual dollar volume	Tkac (1999)
Individual turnover	Bamber (1986, 1987), Hu (1997), Lakonishok and Smidt (1986), Morse (1980), Richardson et al. (1986), Stickel and Verrecchia (1994)
Aggregate turnover	Campbell et al. (1993), LeBaron (1992), Smidt (1990), NYSE Fact Book
Total number of trades	Conrad et al. (1994)
Trading days per year	James and Edmister (1983)
Contracts traded	Tauchen and Pitts (1983)

summary of the various measures used in a representative sample of the recent volume literature. These differences suggest that different applications call for different volume measures.

To proceed with our analysis, we first need to settle on a measure of volume. After developing some basic notation in Section 2.1, we review several volume measures in Section 2.2 and provide some economic motivation for turnover as a canonical measure of trading activity. Formal definitions of turnover – for individual securities, portfolios, and in the presence of time aggregation – are given in Sections 2.3 and 2.4. Theoretical justifications for turnover as a volume measure are provided in Sections 5 and 6. Based on these considerations, in Section 2.5 we describe our approach to constructing the volume variables used throughout the rest of this chapter.

2.1. Notation

Our analysis begins with I investors indexed by $i = 1, \ldots, I$ and J stocks indexed by $j = 1, \ldots, J$. We assume that all the stocks are risky and nonredundant. For each stock j, let N_{jt} be its total number of shares outstanding, D_{jt} its dividend, and P_{jt} its ex-dividend price at date t. For notational convenience and without loss of generality, we assume throughout that the total number of shares outstanding for each stock is constant over time, i.e., $N_{jt} = N_j, j = 1, \ldots, J$.

For each investor i, let S_{jt}^i denote the number of shares of stock j he holds at date t. Let $P_t \equiv [P_{1t} \cdots P_{Jt}]^{\mathsf{T}}$ and $S_t \equiv [S_{1t} \cdots S_{Jt}]^{\mathsf{T}}$ denote the vector of stock prices and shares held in a given portfolio, where A^{T} denotes the transpose of a vector or matrix A. Let the return on stock j at t be $R_{jt} \equiv (P_{jt} - P_{jt-1} + D_{jt})/P_{jt-1}$. Finally, denote by V_{jt} the total number of shares of security j traded at time t, i.e., share volume, hence

$$V_{jt} = \frac{1}{2} \sum_{i=1}^{I} |S_{jt}^i - S_{jt-1}^i|, \tag{2.1}$$

where the coefficient $\frac{1}{2}$ corrects for the double counting when summing the shares traded over all investors.

2.2. Motivation

To motivate the definition of volume used in this chapter, we begin with a simple numerical example drawn from portfolio theory (a formal discussion is given in Section 5). Consider a stock market comprised of only two securities, A and B. For concreteness, assume that security A has 10 shares outstanding and is priced at $100 per share, yielding a market value of $1000, and security B has 30 shares outstanding and is priced at $50 per share, yielding a market value of $1500, hence $N_{at} = 10$, $N_{bt} = 30$, $P_{at} = 100$, $P_{bt} = 50$. Suppose there are only two investors in this market – call them investor 1 and 2 – and let two-fund separation hold so that both investors hold a combination of risk-free bonds and a stock portfolio with A and B in the same relative proportion. Specifically, let investor 1 hold 1 share of A and 3 shares of B, and let investor 2 hold 9 shares of A and 27 shares of B. In this way, all shares are held and both investors hold the same *market* portfolio (40% A and 60% B).

Now suppose that investor 2 liquidates $750 of his portfolio – 3 shares of A and 9 shares of B – and assume that investor 1 is willing to purchase exactly this amount from investor 2 at the prevailing market prices.[4] After completing the transaction, investor 1 owns 4 shares of A and 12 shares of B, and investor 2 owns 6 shares of A and 18 shares of B. What kind of trading activity does this transaction imply?

---

[4]This last assumption entails no loss of generality but is made purely for notational simplicity. If investor 1 is unwilling to purchase these shares at prevailing prices, prices will adjust so that both parties are willing to consummate the transaction, leaving two-fund separation intact. See Section 6 for a more general treatment.

For individual stocks, we can construct the following measures of trading activity:

- Number of trades per period
- Share volume, V_{jt}
- Dollar volume, $P_{jt} V_{jt}$
- Relative dollar volume, $P_{jt} V_{jt} / \sum_j P_{jt} V_{jt}$
- Share turnover,

$$\tau_{jt} \equiv \frac{V_{jt}}{N_{jt}}$$

- Dollar turnover,

$$v_{jt} \equiv \frac{P_{jt} V_{jt}}{P_{jt} N_{jt}} = \tau_{jt},$$

where $j = a, b$.[5] To measure aggregate trading activity, we can define similar measures:

- Number of trades per period
- Total number of shares traded, $V_{at} + V_{bt}$
- Dollar volume, $P_{at} V_{at} + P_{bt} V_{bt}$
- Share-weighted turnover,

$$\tau_t^{\text{SW}} \equiv \frac{V_{at} + V_{bt}}{N_a + N_b} = \frac{N_a}{N_a + N_b} \tau_{at} + \frac{N_b}{N_a + N_b} \tau_{bt}$$

- Equal-weighted turnover,

$$\tau_t^{\text{EW}} \equiv \frac{1}{2} \left(\frac{V_{at}}{N_a} + \frac{V_{bt}}{N_a} \right) = \frac{1}{2} (\tau_{at} + \tau_{bt})$$

- Value-weighted turnover,

$$\tau_t^{\text{VW}} \equiv \frac{P_{at} N_a}{P_{at} N_a + P_{bt} N_b} \frac{V_{at}}{N_a} + \frac{P_{bt} N_b}{P_{at} N_a + P_{bt} N_b} \frac{V_{bt}}{N_b} = \omega_{at} \tau_{at} + \omega_{bt} \tau_{bt}.$$

Table 17.2 reports the values that these various measures of trading activity take on for the hypothetical transaction between investors 1 and 2. Though these values vary considerably − 2 trades, 12 shares traded, \$750 traded − one regularity does emerge: the turnover measures are all identical. This is no coincidence but is an implication of

---

[5]Although the definition of dollar turnover may seem redundant since it is equivalent to share turnover, it will become more relevant in the portfolio case below (see Section 2.3).

Table 17.2   Volume measures for a two-stock, two-investor example when investors only trade in the market portfolio

Volume measure	A	B	Aggregate
Number of trades	1	1	2
Shares traded	3	9	12
Dollars traded	$300	$450	$750
Share turnover	0.3	0.3	0.3
Dollar turnover	0.3	0.3	0.3
Share-weighted turnover	—	—	0.3
Equal-weighted turnover	—	—	0.3
Value-weighted turnover	—	—	0.3

two-fund separation. If all investors hold the same relative proportions of risky assets at all times, then it can be shown that trading activity, as measured by turnover, must be identical across all risky securities (see Section 5). Although the other measures of volume do capture important aspects of trading activity, if the focus is on the relation between volume and equilibrium models of asset markets [such as the capital asset pricing model (CAPM) and Intertemporal CAPM (ICAPM)], turnover yields the sharpest empirical implications and is the most natural measure. For this reason, we will use turnover as the measure of volume throughout this chapter. In Sections 5 and 6, we formally show this point in the context of classic portfolio theory and ICAPMs.

2.3. Defining Individual and Portfolio Turnover

For each individual stock j, let turnover be defined by

Definition 1 *The turnover τ_{jt} of stock j at time t is*

$$\tau_{jt} \equiv \frac{V_{jt}}{N_j},\tag{2.2}$$

where V_{jt} is the share volume of security j at time t and N_j is the total number of shares outstanding of stock j.

Although we define the turnover ratio using the total number of shares traded, it is obvious that using the total dollar volume normalized by the total market value gives the same result.

Given that investors, particularly institutional investors, often trade portfolios or *baskets* of stocks, a measure of portfolio trading activity would be useful. But even after settling on turnover as the preferred measure of an individual stock's trading activity, there is still some ambiguity in extending this definition to the portfolio case. In the absence of a theory for which portfolios are traded, why they are traded, and how they are traded, there is no natural definition of portfolio turnover.[6] For the specific purpose of investigating the implications of portfolio theory and ICAPM for trading activity (see Sections 5 and 6), we propose the following definition.

Definition 2 *For any portfolio p defined by the vector of shares held $S_t^p = [S_{1t}^p \cdots S_{Jt}^p]^\top$ with nonnegative holdings in all stocks, i.e., $S_{jt}^p \geq 0$ for all j, and strictly positive market value, i.e., $S_t^{p\top} P_t > 0$, let $\omega_{jt}^p \equiv S_{jt}^p P_{jt}/(S_t^{p\top} P_t)$ be the fraction invested in stock $j, j = 1, \ldots, J$. Then its turnover is defined to be*

$$\tau_t^p \equiv \sum_{j=1}^J \omega_{jt}^p \tau_{jt}. \tag{2.3}$$

Under this definition, the turnover of value-weighted and equal-weighted indexes are well-defined as

$$\tau_t^{VW} \equiv \sum_{j=1}^J \omega_{jt}^{VW} \tau_{jt} \quad \text{and} \quad \tau_t^{EW} \equiv \frac{1}{J} \sum_{j=1}^J \tau_{jt}, \tag{2.4}$$

respectively, where $\omega_{jt}^{VW} \equiv N_j P_{jt}/\left(\sum_j N_j P_{jt}\right)$, for $j = 1, \ldots, J$.

Although (2.3) seems to be a reasonable definition of portfolio turnover, some care must be exercised in interpreting it. Although τ_t^{VW} and τ_t^{EW} are relevant to the theoretical implications derived in Sections 5 and 6, they should be viewed only as particular weighted averages of individual turnover, not necessarily as the turnover of any specific trading strategy.

In particular, Definition 2 cannot be applied too broadly. Suppose, e.g., shortsales are allowed so that some portfolio weights can be negative. In that case, (2.3) can be quite misleading since the turnover of short positions will offset the turnover of long positions. We can modify (2.3) to account for short positions by using the absolute values of the portfolio weights

$$\tau_t^p \equiv \sum_{j=1}^J \frac{|\omega_{jt}^p|}{\sum_k |\omega_{kt}^p|} \tau_{jt}, \tag{2.5}$$

but this can yield some anomalous results as well. For example, consider a two-asset portfolio with weights $\omega_{at} = 3$ and $\omega_{bt} = -2$. If the turnover of both stocks are identical

---

[6]Although it is common practice for institutional investors to trade baskets of securities, there are few regularities in how such baskets are generated or how they are traded, i.e., in piece-meal fashion and over time or all at once through a *principal bid*. Such diversity in the trading of portfolios makes it difficult to define single measure of portfolio turnover.

and equal to τ, the portfolio turnover according to (2.5) is also τ, yet there is clearly a great deal of more trading activity than this implies. Without specifying *why* and *how* this portfolio is traded, a sensible definition of portfolio turnover cannot be proposed.

Neither (2.3) nor (2.5) is a completely satisfactory measure of trading activities of a portfolio in general. Until we introduce a more specific context in which trading activity is to be measured, we shall have to satisfy ourselves with Definition 2 as a measure of trading activities of a portfolio.

2.4. Time Aggregation

Given our choice of turnover as a measure of volume for individual securities, the most natural method of handling time aggregation is to sum turnover across dates to obtain time-aggregated turnover. Although there are several other alternatives, e.g., summing share volume and then dividing by average shares outstanding, summing turnover offers several advantages. Unlike a measure based on summed shares divided by average shares outstanding, summed turnover is cumulative and linear; each component of the sum corresponds to the actual measure of trading activity for that day, and it is unaffected by "neutral" changes of units such as stock splits and stock dividends.[7] Therefore, we shall adopt this measure of time aggregation in our empirical analysis below.

Definition 3 *If the turnover for stock j at time t is given by τ_{jt}, the turnover between $t - 1$ and $t + q$ for any $q \geq 0$ is given by*

$$\tau_{jt}(q) \equiv \tau_{jt} + \tau_{jt+1} + \cdots + \tau_{jt+q}. \tag{2.6}$$

2.5. The Data

Having defined our measure of trading activity as turnover, we use the University of Chicago's (CRSP) Daily Master File to construct weekly turnover series for individual NYSE and AMEX securities from July 1962 to December 1996 (1800 weeks) using the time-aggregation method discussed in Section 2.4, which we call the "MiniCRSP" volume data extract.[8] We choose a weekly horizon as the best compromise between maximizing sample size while minimizing the day-to-day volume and return fluctuations that have less direct economic relevance. Since our focus is the implications of portfolio theory for volume behavior, we confine our attention to ordinary common shares on the

---

[7]This last property requires one minor qualification: a "neutral" change of units is, by definition, one where trading activity is unaffected. However, stock splits can have nonneutral effects on trading activity such as enhancing liquidity (this is often one of the motivations for splits), and in such cases, turnover will be affected (as it should be).

[8]To facilitate research on turnover and to allow others to easily replicate our analysis, we have produced daily and weekly "MiniCRSP" data extracts comprised of returns, turnover, and other data items for each individual stock in the CRSP Daily Master file, stored in a format that minimizes storage space and access times. We have also prepared a set of access routines to read our extracted data sets via either sequential and random access methods on almost any hardware platform, as well as a user's guide to MiniCRSP (see Lim et al., 1998). More detailed information about MiniCRSP can be found at http://www.lfe.mit.edu/volume/.

NYSE and AMEX (CRSP sharecodes 10 and 11 only), omitting ADRs, SBIs, REITs, closed-end funds, and other such exotica whose turnover may be difficult to interpret in the usual sense.[9] We also omit NASDAQ stocks altogether since the differences between NASDAQ and the NYSE/AMEX (market structure, market capitalization, etc.) have important implications for the measurement and behavior of volume (see, e.g., Atkins and Dyl, 1997), and this should be investigated separately.

Throughout our empirical analysis, we report turnover and returns in units of percent per week – they are *not* annualized.

Finally, in addition to the exchange and sharecode selection criteria imposed, we also discard 37 securities from our sample because of a particular type of data error in the CRSP volume entries.[10]

3. TIME-SERIES PROPERTIES

Although it is difficult to develop simple intuition for the behavior of the entire time-series/cross-section volume data set – a data set containing between 1700 and 2200 individual securities per week over a sample period of 1800 weeks – some gross characteristics of volume can be observed from value-weighted and equal-weighted turnover indexes.[11] These characteristics are presented in Fig. 17.1 and in Tables 17.3 and 17.4.

Figure 17.1a shows that value-weighted turnover has increased dramatically since the mid-1960s, growing from less than 0.20% to over 1% per week. The volatility of value-weighted turnover also increases over this period. However, equal-weighted turnover behaves somewhat differently: Fig. 17.1b shows that it reaches a peak of nearly 2% in 1968, then declines until the 1980s when it returns to a similar level (and goes well beyond it during October 1987). These differences between the value-weighted and equal-weighted indexes suggest that smaller-capitalization companies can have high turnover.

Since turnover is, by definition, an asymmetric measure of trading activity – it cannot be negative – its empirical distribution is naturally skewed. Taking natural logarithms may provide more (visual) information about its behavior and this is done in Figs. 17.1c

---

[9]The bulk of NYSE and AMEX securities are ordinary common shares; hence, limiting our sample to securities with sharecodes 10 and 11 is not especially restrictive. For example, on January 2, 1980, the entire NYSE/AMEX universe contained 2307 securities with sharecode 10, 30 securities with sharecode 11, and 55 securities with sharecodes other than 10 and 11. Ordinary common shares also account for the bulk of the market capitalization of the NYSE and AMEX (excluding ADRs, of course).

[10]Briefly, the NYSE and AMEX typically report volume in round lots of 100 shares – "45" represents 4500 shares – but on occasion, volume is reported in shares, and this is indicated by a "Z" flag attached to the particular observation. This Z status is relatively infrequent, is usually valid for at least a quarter, and may change over the life of the security. In some instances, we have discovered daily share volume increasing by a factor of 100 only to decrease by a factor of 100 at a later date. While such dramatic shifts in volume are not altogether impossible, a more plausible explanation – one that we have verified by hand in a few cases – is that the Z flag was inadvertently omitted when in fact the Z status was in force. See Lim et al. (1998) for further details.

[11]These indexes are constructed from weekly individual security turnover, where the value-weighted index is reweighted each week. Value-weighted and equal-weighted return indexes are also constructed in a similar fashion. Note that these return indexes do not correspond exactly to the time-aggregated CRSP value-weighted and equal-weighted return indexes because we have restricted our universe of securities to ordinary common shares. However, some simple statistical comparisons show that our return indexes and the CRSP return indexes have very similar time-series properties.

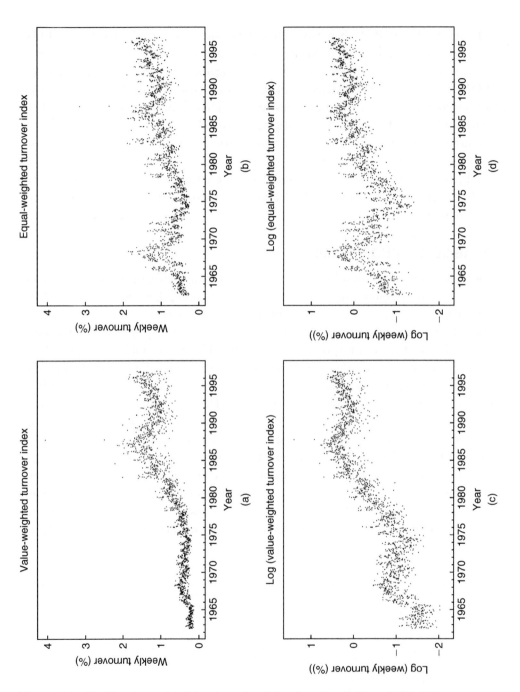

Figure 17.1   Weekly value-weighted and equal-weighted turnover indexes, 1962–1996.

Table 17.3   Summary statistics for value-weighted and equal-weighted turnover and return indexes of NYSE and AMEX ordinary common shares (CRSP share codes 10 and 11, excluding 37 stocks containing Z-errors in reported volume) for July 1962–December 1996 (1800 weeks) and subperiods

Statistic	τ^{VW}	τ^{EW}	R^{VW}	R^{EW}
Mean	0.78	0.91	0.23	0.32
S.D.	0.48	0.37	1.96	2.21
Skewness	0.66	0.38	−0.41	−0.46
Kurtosis	0.21	−0.09	3.66	6.64
Percentiles:				
Min	0.13	0.24	−15.64	−18.64
5%	0.22	0.37	−3.03	−3.44
10%	0.26	0.44	−2.14	−2.26
25%	0.37	0.59	−0.94	−0.80
50%	0.64	0.91	0.33	0.49
75%	1.19	1.20	1.44	1.53
90%	1.44	1.41	2.37	2.61
95%	1.57	1.55	3.31	3.42
Max	4.06	3.16	8.81	13.68
Autocorrelations:				
ρ_1	91.25	86.73	5.39	25.63
ρ_2	88.59	81.89	−0.21	10.92
ρ_3	87.62	79.30	3.27	9.34
ρ_4	87.44	78.07	−2.03	4.94
ρ_5	87.03	76.47	−2.18	1.11
ρ_6	86.17	74.14	1.70	4.07
ρ_7	87.22	74.16	5.13	1.69
ρ_8	86.57	72.95	−7.15	−5.78
ρ_9	85.92	71.06	2.22	2.54
ρ_{10}	84.63	68.59	−2.34	−2.44
Box–Pierce Q_{10}	13,723.0	10,525.0	23.0	175.1
	(0.000)	(0.000)	(0.010)	(0.000)

Turnover and returns are measured in percent per week and p values for Box–Pierce statistics are reported in parentheses.

and 17.1d. Although a trend is still present, there is more evidence for cyclical behavior in both indexes.

Table 17.3 reports various summary statistics for the two indexes over the 1962–1996 sample period, and Table 17.4 reports similar statistics for five-year subperiods. Over the entire sample, the average weekly turnover for the value-weighted and equal-weighted

Table 17.4   Summary statistics for weekly value-weighted and equal-weighted turnover and return indexes of NYSE and AMEX ordinary common shares (CRSP share codes 10 and 11, excluding 37 stocks containing Z-errors in reported volume) for July 1962–December 1996 (1800 weeks) and subperiods

Statistic	τ^{VW}	τ^{EW}	R^{VW}	R^{EW}	τ^{VW}	τ^{EW}	R^{VW}	R^{EW}
	1962–1966 (234 weeks)				1982–1986 (261 weeks)			
Mean	0.25	0.57	0.23	0.30	1.20	1.11	0.37	0.39
S.D.	0.07	0.21	1.29	1.54	0.30	0.29	2.01	1.93
Skewness	1.02	1.47	−0.35	−0.76	0.28	0.45	0.42	0.32
Kurtosis	0.80	2.04	1.02	2.50	0.14	−0.28	1.33	1.19
	1967–1971 (261 weeks)				1987–1991 (261 weeks)			
Mean	0.40	0.93	0.18	0.32	1.29	1.15	0.29	0.24
S.D.	0.08	0.32	1.89	2.62	0.35	0.27	2.43	2.62
Skewness	0.17	0.57	0.42	0.40	2.20	2.15	−1.51	−2.06
Kurtosis	−0.42	−0.26	1.52	2.19	14.88	12.81	7.85	16.44
	1972–1976 (261 weeks)				1992–1996 (261 weeks)			
Mean	0.37	0.52	0.10	0.19	1.25	1.31	0.27	0.37
S.D.	0.10	0.20	2.39	2.78	0.23	0.22	1.37	1.41
Skewness	0.93	1.44	−0.13	0.41	−0.06	−0.05	−0.38	−0.48
Kurtosis	1.57	2.59	0.35	1.12	−0.21	−0.24	1.00	1.30
	1977–1981 (261 weeks)							
Mean	0.62	0.77	0.21	0.44				
S.D.	0.18	0.22	1.97	2.08				
Skewness	0.29	0.62	−0.33	−1.01				
Kurtosis	−0.58	−0.05	0.31	1.72				

Turnover and returns are measured in percent per week and p values for Box–Pierce statistics are reported in parentheses.

indexes is 0.78 and 0.91%, respectively. The standard deviation of weekly turnover for these two indexes is 0.48 and 0.37%, respectively, yielding a coefficient of variation of 0.62 for the value-weighted turnover index and 0.41 for the equal-weighted turnover index. In contrast, the coefficients of variation for the value-weighted and equal-weighted *returns* indexes are 8.52 and 6.91, respectively. Turnover is not nearly so variable as returns, relative to their means.

Table 17.4 illustrates the nature of the secular trend in turnover through the five-year subperiod statistics. Average weekly value-weighted and equal-weighted turnover is 0.25 and 0.57%, respectively, in the first subperiod (1962–1966); they grow to 1.25 and 1.31%, respectively, by the last subperiod (1992–1996). At the beginning of the sample, equal-weighted turnover is three to four times more volatile than value-weighted turnover (0.21% versus 0.07% in 1962–1966, 0.32% versus 0.08% in 1967–1971), but by the end of the sample, their volatilities are comparable (0.22% versus 0.23% in 1992–1996).

The subperiod containing the October 1987 crash exhibits a few anomalous properties: excess skewness and kurtosis for both returns and turnover, average value-weighted turnover slightly higher than average equal-weighted turnover, and slightly higher volatility for value-weighted turnover. These anomalies are consistent with the extreme outliers associated with the 1987 crash (see Fig. 17.1).

3.1. Seasonalities

In Tables 17.5–17.7, we check for seasonalities in daily and weekly turnover, e.g., day-of-the-week, quarter-of-the-year, turn-of-the-quarter, and turn-of-the-year effects. Table 17.5 reports regression results for the entire sample period, Table 17.6 reports day-of-the-week regressions for each subperiod, and Table 17.7 reports turn-of-the-quarter and turn-of-the-year regressions for each subperiod. The dependent variable for each regression is either turnover or returns and the independent variables are indicators of the particular seasonality effect. No intercept terms are included in any of these regressions.

Table 17.5 shows that, in contrast to returns that exhibit a strong day-of-the-week effect, daily turnover is relatively stable over the week. Mondays and Fridays have slightly lower average turnover than the other days of the week, Wednesdays the highest, but the differences are generally small for both indexes: the largest difference is 0.023% for value-weighted turnover and 0.018% for equal-weighted turnover, both between Mondays and Wednesdays.

Table 17.5 also shows that turnover is relatively stable over quarters – the third quarter has the lowest average turnover, but it differs from the other quarters by less than 0.15% for either turnover index. Turnover tends to be lower at the beginning-of-quarters, beginning-of-years, and end-of-years, but only the end-of-year effect for value-weighted turnover (-0.189%) and the beginning-of-quarter effect for equal-weighted turnover (-0.074%) are statistically significant at the 5% level.

Table 17.6 reports day-of-the-week regressions for the five-year subperiods and shows that the patterns in Table 17.6 are robust across subperiods: turnover is slightly lower on Mondays and Fridays. Interestingly, the return regressions indicate that the "weekend" effect – large negative returns on Mondays and large positive returns on Fridays – is *not* robust across subperiods.[12] In particular, in the 1992–1996 subperiod, average Monday returns for the value-weighted index is positive, statistically significant, and the highest of all the five days' average returns.

[12]The weekend effect has been documented by many. See, for instance, Cross (1973), French (1980), Gibbons and Hess (1981), Harris (1986), Jaffe and Westerfield (1985), Keim and Stambaugh (1984), and Lakonishok and Levi (1982), and Lakonishok and Smidt (1988).

Table 17.5 Seasonality regressions for daily and weekly value-weighted and equal-weighted turnover and return indexes of NYSE and AMEX ordinary common shares (CRSP share codes 10 and 11, excluding 37 stocks containing Z-errors in reported volume) from July 1962 to December 1996

Regressor	τ^{VW}	τ^{EW}	R^{VW}	R^{EW}
Daily: 1962–1996 (8686 days)				
MON	0.147	0.178	−0.061	−0.095
	(0.002)	(0.002)	(0.019)	(0.019)
TUE	0.164	0.192	0.044	0.009
	(0.002)	(0.002)	(0.019)	(0.018)
WED	0.170	0.196	0.112	0.141
	(0.002)	(0.002)	(0.019)	(0.018)
THU	0.167	0.196	0.050	0.118
	(0.002)	(0.002)	(0.019)	(0.018)
FRI	0.161	0.188	0.091	0.207
	(0.002)	(0.002)	(0.020)	(0.018)
Weekly: 1962–1996 (1800 weeks)				
Q1	0.842	0.997	0.369	0.706
	(0.025)	(0.019)	(0.102)	(0.112)
Q2	0.791	0.939	0.232	0.217
	(0.024)	(0.018)	(0.097)	(0.107)
Q3	0.741	0.850	0.201	0.245
	(0.023)	(0.018)	(0.095)	(0.105)
Q4	0.807	0.928	0.203	−0.019
	(0.024)	(0.019)	(0.099)	(0.110)
BOQ	−0.062	−0.074	−0.153	−0.070
	(0.042)	(0.032)	(0.171)	(0.189)
EOQ	0.008	−0.010	−0.243	−0.373
	(0.041)	(0.032)	(0.170)	(0.187)
BOY	−0.109	−0.053	0.179	1.962
	(0.086)	(0.067)	(0.355)	(0.392)
EOY	−0.189	−0.085	0.755	1.337
	(0.077)	(0.060)	(0.319)	(0.353)

Q1–Q4 are quarterly indicators, BOQ and EOQ are beginning-of-quarter and end-of-quarter indicators, and BOY and EOY are beginning-of-year and end-of-year indicators.

Table 17.6 Seasonality regressions over subperiods for daily value-weighted and equal-weighted turnover and return indexes of NYSE or AMEX ordinary common shares (CRSP share codes 10 and 11, excluding 37 stocks containing Z-errors in reported volume) for subperiods of the sample period from July 1962 to December 1996

Regressor	τ^{VW}	τ^{EW}	R^{VW}	R^{EW}	τ^{VW}	τ^{EW}	R^{VW}	R^{EW}
	1962–1966 (1134 days)				1967–1971 (1234 days)			
MON	0.050	0.116	−0.092	−0.073	0.080	0.192	−0.157	−0.135
	(0.001)	(0.003)	(0.037)	(0.038)	(0.001)	(0.005)	(0.045)	(0.056)
TUE	0.053	0.119	0.046	0.012	0.086	0.200	0.021	0.001
	(0.001)	(0.003)	(0.037)	(0.037)	(0.001)	(0.005)	(0.044)	(0.054)
WED	0.054	0.122	0.124	0.142	0.087	0.197	0.156	0.204
	(0.001)	(0.003)	(0.036)	(0.037)	(0.001)	(0.005)	(0.046)	(0.057)
THU	0.054	0.121	0.032	0.092	0.090	0.205	0.039	0.072
	(0.001)	(0.003)	(0.037)	(0.037)	(0.001)	(0.005)	(0.044)	(0.055)
FRI	0.051	0.117	0.121	0.191	0.084	0.198	0.127	0.221
	(0.001)	(0.003)	(0.037)	(0.037)	(0.001)	(0.005)	(0.044)	(0.055)
	1972–1976 (1262 days)				1977–1981 (1263 days)			
MON	0.069	0.102	−0.123	−0.122	0.118	0.153	−0.104	−0.127
	(0.001)	(0.003)	(0.060)	(0.057)	(0.003)	(0.003)	(0.051)	(0.050)
TUE	0.080	0.110	0.010	−0.031	0.131	0.160	0.029	0.007
	(0.001)	(0.003)	(0.059)	(0.056)	(0.002)	(0.003)	(0.050)	(0.048)
WED	0.081	0.111	0.066	0.063	0.135	0.166	0.116	0.166
	(0.001)	(0.003)	(0.058)	(0.055)	(0.002)	(0.003)	(0.049)	(0.048)
THU	0.081	0.111	0.087	0.122	0.134	0.164	0.018	0.143
	(0.001)	(0.003)	(0.059)	(0.056)	(0.002)	(0.003)	(0.050)	(0.048)
FRI	0.076	0.106	0.056	0.215	0.126	0.158	0.136	0.277
	(0.001)	(0.003)	(0.059)	(0.056)	(0.002)	(0.003)	(0.050)	(0.049)
	1980–1984 (1264 days)				1987–1991 (1263 days)			
MON	0.224	0.212	−0.030	−0.107	0.246	0.221	−0.040	−0.132
	(0.004)	(0.004)	(0.053)	(0.043)	(0.005)	(0.004)	(0.073)	(0.062)
TUE	0.251	0.231	0.070	0.040	0.269	0.241	0.119	0.028
	(0.004)	(0.004)	(0.051)	(0.041)	(0.005)	(0.004)	(0.071)	(0.059)
WED	0.262	0.239	0.093	0.117	0.276	0.246	0.150	0.193
	(0.004)	(0.004)	(0.051)	(0.041)	(0.005)	(0.004)	(0.071)	(0.059)
THU	0.258	0.236	0.111	0.150	0.273	0.246	0.015	0.108
	(0.004)	(0.004)	(0.052)	(0.042)	(0.005)	(0.004)	(0.071)	(0.060)
FRI	0.245	0.226	0.122	0.226	0.273	0.237	0.050	0.156
	(0.004)	(0.004)	(0.052)	(0.042)	(0.005)	(0.004)	(0.072)	(0.060)

(Continued)

Table 17.6 (*Continued*)

Regressor	τ^{VW}	τ^{EW}	R^{VW}	R^{EW}	τ^{VW}	τ^{EW}	R^{VW}	R^{EW}
	1992–1996 (1265 days)							
MON	0.232	0.249	0.117	0.033				
	(0.003)	(0.003)	(0.036)	(0.031)				
TUE	0.261	0.276	0.009	0.003				
	(0.003)	(0.003)	(0.035)	(0.030)				
WED	0.272	0.283	0.080	0.105				
	(0.003)	(0.003)	(0.035)	(0.030)				
THU	0.266	0.281	0.050	0.138				
	(0.003)	(0.003)	(0.035)	(0.030)				
FRI	0.259	0.264	0.026	0.164				
	(0.003)	(0.003)	(0.035)	(0.030)				

The subperiod regression results for the quarterly and annual indicators in Table 17.7 are consistent with the findings for the entire sample period in Table 17.5: on average, turnover is slightly lower in third quarters, during the turn-of-the-quarter, and during the turn-of-the-year.

3.2. Secular Trends and Detrending

It is well known that turnover is highly persistent. Table 17.3 shows the first 10 autocorrelations of turnover and returns and the corresponding Box–Pierce Q-statistics. Unlike returns, turnover is strongly autocorrelated, with autocorrelations that start at 91.25% and 86.73% for the value-weighted and equal-weighted turnover indexes, respectively, decaying very slowly to 84.63% and 68.59%, respectively, at lag 10. This slow decay suggests some kind of nonstationarity in turnover – perhaps a stochastic trend or *unit root* (see Hamilton, 1994 for example) – and this is confirmed at the usual significance levels by applying the Kwiatkowski et al. (1992) Lagrange Multiplier test of stationarity versus a unit root to the two turnover indexes.[13]

For these reasons, many empirical studies of volume use some form of detrending to induce stationarity. This usually involves either taking first differences or estimating the trend and subtracting it from the raw data. To gauge the impact of various methods of detrending on the time-series properties of turnover, we report summary

---

[13] In particular, two LM tests were applied: a test of the level-stationary null and a test of the trend-stationary null, both against the alternative of difference stationarity. The test statistics are 17.41 (level) and 1.47 (trend) for the value-weighted index and 9.88 (level) and 1.06 (trend) for the equal-weighted index. The 1% critical values for these two tests are 0.739 and 0.216, respectively. See Hamilton (1994) and Kwiatkowski et al. (1992) for further details concerning unit root tests, and Andersen (1996) and Gallant et al. (1992) for highly structured (but semiparametric) procedures for detrending individual and aggregate daily volume.

Table 17.7 Seasonality regressions for weekly value-weighted and equal-weighted turnover and return indexes of NYSE or AMEX ordinary common shares (CRSP share codes 10 and 11, excluding 37 stocks containing Z-errors in reported volume) for subperiods of the sample period from July 1962 to December 1996 (1800 weeks)

Regressor	τ^{VW}	τ^{EW}	R^{VW}	R^{EW}	τ^{VW}	τ^{EW}	R^{VW}	R^{EW}
	1962–1966 (234 weeks)				1967–1971 (261 weeks)			
Q1	0.261	0.649	0.262	0.600	0.421	0.977	0.216	0.463
	(0.011)	(0.030)	(0.192)	(0.224)	(0.010)	(0.042)	(0.258)	(0.355)
Q2	0.265	0.615	0.072	0.023	0.430	1.022	−0.169	−0.118
	(0.010)	(0.029)	(0.184)	(0.215)	(0.010)	(0.041)	(0.247)	(0.341)
Q3	0.229	0.478	0.185	0.187	0.370	0.840	0.307	0.512
	(0.009)	(0.026)	(0.165)	(0.193)	(0.010)	(0.040)	(0.245)	(0.338)
Q4	0.272	0.595	0.413	0.363	0.415	0.928	0.097	0.000
	(0.010)	(0.027)	(0.173)	(0.202)	(0.010)	(0.042)	(0.255)	(0.352)
BOQ	−0.026	−0.055	0.388	0.304	−0.029	−0.097	0.407	0.327
	(0.017)	(0.049)	(0.310)	(0.364)	(0.017)	(0.070)	(0.425)	(0.586)
EOQ	0.017	0.028	−0.609	−0.579	−0.011	−0.051	0.076	0.029
	(0.017)	(0.048)	(0.304)	(0.357)	(0.018)	(0.073)	(0.442)	(0.610)
BOY	−0.008	−0.074	0.635	2.009	−0.021	0.111	−0.751	0.812
	(0.037)	(0.107)	(0.674)	(0.790)	(0.037)	(0.151)	(0.919)	(1.269)
EOY	−0.064	−0.049	0.190	0.304	−0.022	0.063	0.782	1.513
	(0.030)	(0.087)	(0.548)	(0.642)	(0.033)	(0.133)	(0.811)	(1.119)
	1972–1976 (261 weeks)				1977–1981 (261 weeks)			
Q1	0.441	0.677	0.513	1.079	0.613	0.738	−0.034	0.368
	(0.012)	(0.025)	(0.325)	(0.355)	(0.024)	(0.030)	(0.269)	(0.280)
Q2	0.364	0.513	0.019	−0.323	0.629	0.787	0.608	0.948
	(0.012)	(0.024)	(0.308)	(0.337)	(0.023)	(0.029)	(0.255)	(0.266)
Q3	0.334	0.436	−0.267	−0.166	0.637	0.805	0.309	0.535
	(0.012)	(0.023)	(0.306)	(0.335)	(0.023)	(0.029)	(0.253)	(0.264)
Q4	0.385	0.500	0.083	−0.416	0.643	0.779	0.117	−0.024
	(0.012)	(0.024)	(0.319)	(0.349)	(0.024)	(0.030)	(0.265)	(0.276)
BOQ	−0.034	−0.057	−0.569	−0.097	−0.012	−0.023	−0.200	−0.322
	(0.021)	(0.042)	(0.543)	(0.593)	(0.042)	(0.052)	(0.458)	(0.478)
EOQ	0.013	−0.013	0.301	0.003	−0.011	−0.009	−0.588	−0.716
	(0.021)	(0.042)	(0.554)	(0.606)	(0.041)	(0.051)	(0.449)	(0.469)
BOY	−0.047	−0.024	1.440	4.553	−0.028	0.074	0.412	1.770
	(0.042)	(0.084)	(1.098)	(1.200)	(0.083)	(0.103)	(0.912)	(0.952)
EOY	−0.101	−0.019	0.300	1.312	−0.144	−0.123	1.104	1.638
	(0.040)	(0.081)	(1.055)	(1.153)	(0.079)	(0.098)	(0.868)	(0.906)

(Continued)

Table 17.7 (*Continued*)

Regressor	τ^{VW}	τ^{EW}	R^{VW}	R^{EW}	τ^{VW}	τ^{EW}	R^{VW}	R^{EW}
	1982–1986 (261 weeks)				1987–1991 (261 weeks)			
Q1	1.258	1.177	0.389	0.524	1.416	1.254	0.823	1.202
	(0.039)	(0.039)	(0.274)	(0.262)	(0.046)	(0.035)	(0.330)	(0.343)
Q2	1.173	1.115	0.313	0.356	1.317	1.159	0.424	0.305
	(0.037)	(0.037)	(0.262)	(0.251)	(0.044)	(0.034)	(0.313)	(0.325)
Q3	1.188	1.058	0.268	0.164	1.252	1.105	0.099	−0.081
	(0.037)	(0.037)	(0.262)	(0.251)	(0.043)	(0.034)	(0.310)	(0.323)
Q4	1.320	1.190	0.625	0.526	1.317	1.160	−0.228	−0.787
	(0.039)	(0.039)	(0.274)	(0.262)	(0.045)	(0.035)	(0.325)	(0.338)
BOQ	−0.123	−0.132	−0.329	−0.336	−0.108	−0.060	0.117	0.316
	(0.065)	(0.065)	(0.462)	(0.442)	(0.078)	(0.061)	(0.562)	(0.584)
EOQ	−0.042	−0.052	0.222	0.158	−0.003	−0.013	−0.548	−0.655
	(0.065)	(0.065)	(0.462)	(0.442)	(0.077)	(0.060)	(0.551)	(0.573)
BOY	−0.202	−0.114	−0.395	1.033	−0.293	−0.207	−0.118	1.379
	(0.139)	(0.139)	(0.985)	(0.942)	(0.156)	(0.121)	(1.120)	(1.165)
EOY	−0.280	−0.158	−0.477	−0.160	−0.326	−0.104	2.259	3.037
	(0.121)	(0.122)	(0.861)	(0.823)	(0.148)	(0.115)	(1.065)	(1.108)
	1992–1996 (261 weeks)							
Q1	1.362	1.432	0.388	0.687				
	(0.029)	(0.028)	(0.182)	(0.183)				
Q2	1.253	1.302	0.328	0.292				
	(0.028)	(0.027)	(0.176)	(0.176)				
Q3	1.170	1.223	0.521	0.570				
	(0.028)	(0.027)	(0.174)	(0.175)				
Q4	1.298	1.353	0.322	0.219				
	(0.029)	(0.028)	(0.182)	(0.183)				
BOQ	−0.058	−0.078	−0.890	−0.705				
	(0.051)	(0.050)	(0.321)	(0.322)				
EOQ	0.036	0.006	−0.567	−0.840				
	(0.047)	(0.046)	(0.297)	(0.298)				
BOY	−0.149	−0.102	0.012	1.857				
	(0.105)	(0.103)	(0.663)	(0.664)				
EOY	−0.348	−0.220	1.204	1.753				
	(0.090)	(0.088)	(0.568)	(0.570)				

Q1–Q4 are quarterly indicators, BOQ and EOQ are beginning-of-quarter and end-of-quarter indicators, and BOY and EOY are beginning-of-year and end-of-year indicators.

statistics of detrended turnover in Table 17.8 where we detrend according to the following six methods:

$$\tau_{1t}^d = \tau_t - \left(\widehat{\alpha}_1 + \widehat{\beta}_1 t\right) \tag{3.1a}$$

$$\tau_{2t}^d = \log \tau_t - \left(\widehat{\alpha}_2 + \widehat{\beta}_2 t\right) \tag{3.1b}$$

$$\tau_{3t}^d = \tau_t - \tau_{t-1} \tag{3.1c}$$

$$\tau_{4t}^d = \frac{\tau_t}{(\tau_{t-1} + \tau_{t-2} + \tau_{t-3} + \tau_{t-4})/4} \tag{3.1d}$$

$$\tau_{5t}^d = \tau_t - \left(\widehat{\alpha}_4 + \widehat{\beta}_{3,1} t + \widehat{\beta}_{3,2} t^2\right.$$

$$+ \widehat{\beta}_{3,3}\mathrm{DEC1}_t + \widehat{\beta}_{3,4}\mathrm{DEC2}_t + \widehat{\beta}_{3,5}\mathrm{DEC3}_t + \widehat{\beta}_{3,6}\mathrm{DEC4}_t$$

$$+ \widehat{\beta}_{3,7}\mathrm{JAN1}_t + \widehat{\beta}_{3,8}\mathrm{JAN2}_t + \widehat{\beta}_{3,9}\mathrm{JAN3}_t + \widehat{\beta}_{3,10}\mathrm{JAN4}_t$$

$$\left. + \widehat{\beta}_{3,11}\mathrm{MAR}_t + \widehat{\beta}_{3,12}\mathrm{APR}_t + \cdots + \widehat{\beta}_{3,19}\mathrm{NOV}_t\right) \tag{3.1e}$$

$$\tau_{6t}^d = \tau_t - \widehat{K}(\tau_t), \tag{3.1f}$$

where (3.1a) denotes linear detrending, (3.1b) denotes log-linear detrending, (3.1c) denotes first-differencing, (3.1d) denotes a four-lag moving-average normalization, (3.1e) denotes linear-quadratic detrending and deseasonalization (in the spirit of Gallant et al., 1992),[14] and (3.1f) denotes nonparametric detrending via kernel regression (where the bandwidth is chosen optimally via cross validation).

The summary statistics in Table 17.8 show that the detrending method can have a substantial impact on the time-series properties of detrended turnover. For example, the skewness of detrended value-weighted turnover varies from 0.09 (log linear) to 1.77 (kernel), and the kurtosis varies from −0.20 (log linear) to 29.38 (kernel). Linear, log-linear, and Gallant, Rossi, and Tauchen (GRT) detrending seem to do little to eliminate the persistence in turnover, yielding detrended series with large positive autocorrelation coefficients that decay slowly from lags 1 to 10. However, first-differenced value-weighted turnover has an autocorrelation coefficient of −34.94% at lag 1, which becomes positive at lag 4, and then alternates sign from lag 6 through 10. In contrast, kernel-detrended

---

[14]In particular, in (3.1e), the regressors $\mathrm{DEC1}_t, \ldots, \mathrm{DEC4}_t$ and $\mathrm{JAN1}_t, \ldots, \mathrm{JAN4}_t$ denote weekly indicator variables for the weeks in December and January, respectively, and $\mathrm{MAR}_t, \ldots, \mathrm{NOV}_t$ denote monthly indicator variables for the months of March through November (we have omitted February to avoid perfect collinearity). This does not correspond exactly to the Gallant et al. (1992) procedure – they detrend and deseasonalize the volatility of volume as well.

Table 17.8 Impact of detrending on the statistical properties of weekly value-weighted and equal-weighted turnover indexes of NYSE and AMEX ordinary common shares (CRSP share codes 10 and 11, excluding 37 stocks containing Z-errors in reported volume) for July 1962 to December 1996 (1800 weeks)

Statistic	Value-weighted turnover index							Equal-weighted turnover index						
	Raw	Linear	Log linear	First difference	MA(4) ratio	GRT	Kernel	Raw	Linear	Log linear	First difference	MA(4) ratio	GRT	Kernel
R^2 (%)	—	70.6	78.6	82.6	81.9	72.3	88.6	—	36.9	37.2	73.6	71.9	42.8	78.3
Mean	0.78	0.00	0.00	0.00	1.01	0.00	0.00	0.91	0.00	0.00	0.00	1.01	0.00	0.00
S.D.	0.48	0.26	0.31	0.20	0.20	0.25	0.16	0.37	0.30	0.35	0.19	0.20	0.28	0.17
Skewness	0.66	1.57	0.09	0.79	0.73	1.69	1.77	0.38	0.90	0.00	0.59	0.67	1.06	0.92
Kurtosis	0.21	10.84	−0.20	17.75	3.02	11.38	29.38	−0.09	1.80	0.44	7.21	2.51	2.32	6.67
Percentiles:														
Min	0.13	−0.69	−0.94	−1.55	0.45	−0.61	−0.78	0.24	−0.62	−1.09	−0.78	0.44	−0.59	−0.59
5%	0.22	−0.34	−0.51	−0.30	0.69	−0.32	−0.26	0.37	−0.44	−0.63	−0.32	0.70	−0.38	−0.27
10%	0.26	−0.29	−0.38	−0.19	0.76	−0.28	−0.15	0.44	−0.36	−0.43	−0.21	0.76	−0.32	−0.20
25%	0.37	−0.18	−0.21	−0.08	0.89	−0.17	−0.06	0.59	−0.19	−0.20	−0.09	0.88	−0.20	−0.10
50%	0.65	−0.01	−0.02	−0.00	1.00	−0.02	0.00	0.91	−0.04	−0.00	−0.00	1.01	−0.05	−0.01
75%	1.19	0.13	0.23	0.07	1.12	0.12	0.06	1.20	0.16	0.20	0.09	1.12	0.16	0.09
90%	1.44	0.30	0.41	0.20	1.25	0.29	0.16	1.41	0.42	0.46	0.21	1.25	0.38	0.21
95%	1.57	0.45	0.50	0.31	1.35	0.46	0.23	1.55	0.55	0.63	0.32	1.35	0.54	0.28
Max	4.06	2.95	1.38	2.45	2.48	2.91	2.36	3.16	2.06	1.11	1.93	2.44	2.08	1.73

Autocorrelations:

ρ_1	91.25	70.15	74.23	−34.94	22.97	70.24	23.11	86.73	79.03	83.07	−31.94	29.41	77.80	39.23
ρ_2	88.59	61.21	66.17	−9.70	−6.48	64.70	0.54	81.89	71.46	77.27	−8.69	0.54	71.60	17.95
ρ_3	87.62	58.32	63.78	−4.59	−19.90	60.78	−6.21	79.30	67.58	74.25	−5.07	−13.79	66.89	8.05
ρ_4	87.44	58.10	63.86	1.35	−20.41	60.96	−5.78	78.07	65.84	72.60	1.45	−16.97	65.14	4.80
ρ_5	87.03	56.79	62.38	2.58	−6.12	60.31	−7.79	76.47	63.41	70.64	2.68	−4.87	62.90	−0.11
ρ_6	86.17	54.25	59.37	−10.96	−4.35	58.78	−12.93	74.14	59.95	67.29	−8.79	−4.23	60.03	−7.54
ρ_7	87.22	58.20	60.97	9.80	4.54	61.46	−1.09	74.16	60.17	66.27	4.60	0.17	59.28	−3.95
ρ_8	86.57	56.30	59.83	−0.10	1.78	59.39	−4.29	72.95	58.45	64.76	2.52	−0.37	57.62	−5.71
ρ_9	85.92	54.54	57.87	3.73	−2.43	59.97	−7.10	71.06	55.67	62.54	2.25	−2.27	56.48	−10.30
ρ_{10}	84.63	50.45	53.57	−11.95	−13.46	55.85	−15.86	68.59	51.93	58.81	−10.05	−10.48	53.06	−17.59

Six detrending methods are used: linear, log linear, first differencing, normalization by the trailing four-week moving average, linear–quadratic and seasonal detrending proposed by Gallant et al. (1992) (GRT), and kernel regression.

value-weighted turnover has an autocorrelation of 23.11% at lag 1, which becomes negative at lag 3 and remains negative through lag 10. Similar disparities are also observed for the various detrended equal-weighted turnover series.

Despite the fact that the R^2s of the six detrending methods are comparable for the value-weighted turnover index – ranging from 70.6% to 88.6% – the basic time-series properties vary considerably from one detrending method to the next.[15] To visualize the impact that various detrending methods can have on turnover, compare the various plots of detrended value-weighted turnover in Fig. 17.2, and detrended equal-weighted turnover in Fig. 17.3.[16] Even linear and log-linear detrending yield differences that are visually easy to detect: linear detrended turnover is smoother at the start of the sample and more variable towards the end, whereas log-linearly detrended turnover is equally variable but with lower frequency fluctuations. The moving-average series looks like white noise, the log-linear series seems to possess a periodic component, and the remaining series seem heteroskedastic.

For these reasons, we shall continue to use raw turnover rather than its first difference or any other detrended turnover series in much of our empirical analysis (the sole exception is the eigenvalue decomposition of the first differences of turnover in Table 17.14). To address the problem of the apparent time trend and other nonstationarities in raw turnover, the empirical analysis in the rest of the chapter is conducted within five-year subperiods only (the exploratory data analysis of this section contains entire-sample results primarily for completeness).[17] This is no doubt a controversial choice and, therefore, requires some justification.

From a purely statistical point of view, a nonstationary time series is nonstationary over *any* finite interval – shortening the sample period cannot induce stationarity. Moreover, a shorter sample period increases the impact of sampling errors and reduces the power of statistical tests against most alternatives.

However, from an empirical point of view, confining our attention to five-year sub-periods is perhaps the best compromise between letting the data "speak for itself" and imposing sufficient structure to perform meaningful statistical inference. We have very little confidence in our current understanding of the trend component of turnover, yet a well-articulated model of the trend is a prerequisite to detrending the data. Rather than

---

[15] The R^2 for each detrending method is defined by

$$R_j^2 \equiv 1 - \frac{\sum_t (\tau_{jt}^d - \overline{\tau}_j^d)^2}{\sum_t (\tau_t - \overline{\tau})^2}.$$

Note that the R^2s for the detrended equal-weighted turnover series are comparable to those of the value-weighted series except for linear, log-linear, and GRT detrending – evidently, the high turnover of small stocks in the earlier years creates a "cycle" that is not as readily explained by linear, log-linear, and quadratic trends (see Fig. 17.1).

[16] To improve legibility, only every 10th observation is plotted in each of the panels of Figs. 17.2 and 17.3.

[17] However, we acknowledge the importance of stationarity in conducting formal statistical inferences – it is difficult to interpret a t-statistic in the presence of a strong trend. Therefore, the summary statistics provided in this section are intended to provide readers with an intuitive feel for the behavior of volume in our sample, not to be the basis of formal hypothesis tests.

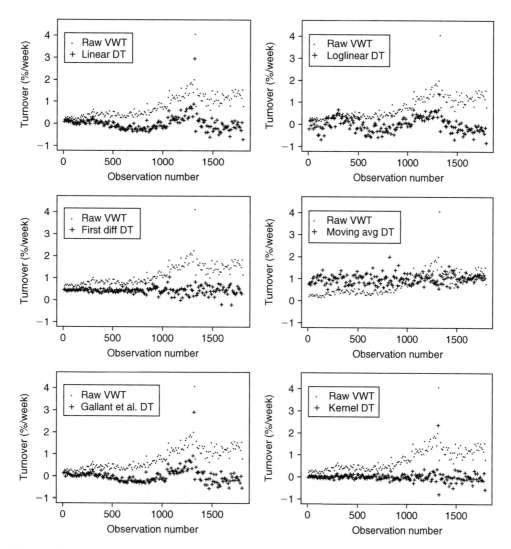

Figure 17.2   Raw and detrended weekly value-weighted turnover indexes, 1962–1996.

filter our data through a specific trend process that others might not find as convincing, we choose instead to analyze the data with methods that require minimal structure, yielding results that may be of broader interest than those of a more structured analysis.[18]

---

[18]See Andersen (1996) and Gallant et al. (1992) for an opposing view – they propose highly structured detrending and deseasonalizing procedures for adjusting raw volume. Andersen (1996) uses two methods: nonparametric kernel regression and an equally weighted moving average. Gallant et al. (1992) extract quadratic trends and seasonal indicators from both the mean and variance of log volume.

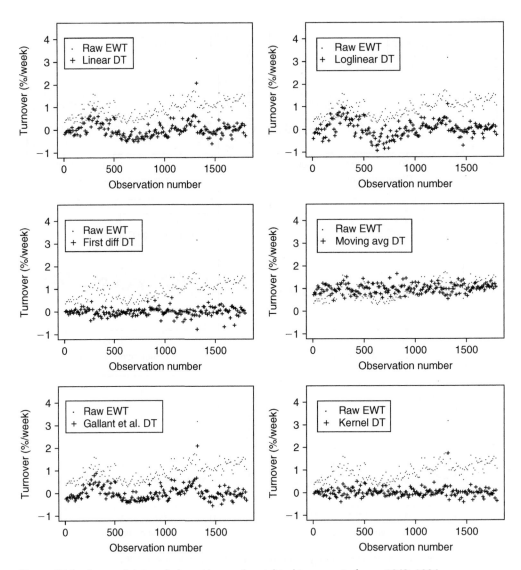

Figure 17.3   Raw and detrended weekly equal-weighted turnover indexes, 1962–1996.

Of course, *some* structure is necessary for conducting any kind of statistical inference. For example, we must assume that the mechanisms governing turnover are relatively stable over five-year subperiods, otherwise even the subperiod inferences may be misleading. Nevertheless, for our current purposes – exploratory data analysis and tests of the implications of portfolio theory and ICAPMs – the benefits of focusing on subperiods are likely to outweigh the costs of larger sampling errors.

4. CROSS-SECTIONAL PROPERTIES

To develop a sense for cross-sectional differences in turnover over the sample period, we turn our attention from turnover indexes to the turnover of individual securities. Figure 17.4 provides a compact graphical representation of the cross section of turnover: Fig. 17.4a plots the deciles for the turnover cross section – nine points, representing the 10th percentile, the 20th percentile, and so forth – for each of the 1800 weeks in the sample period; Fig. 17.4b simplifies this by plotting the deciles of the cross section of *average* turnover, averaged within each year; and Figs. 17.4c and 17.4d plot the same data but on a logarithmic scale.

Figures 17.4a and 17.4b show that while the median turnover (the horizontal bars with vertical sides in Fig. 17.4b) is relatively stable over time – fluctuating between 0.2% and just over 1% over the 1962–1996 sample period – there is considerable variation in the cross-sectional dispersion over time. The range of turnover is relatively narrow in the early 1960s, with 90% of the values falling between 0 and 1.5%, but there is a dramatic increase in the late 1960s, with the 90th percentile approaching 3% at times. The cross-sectional variation of turnover declines sharply in the mid-1970s and then begins a steady increase until a peak in 1987, followed by a decline and then a gradual increase until 1996.

The logarithmic plots in Figs. 17.4c and 17.4d seem to suggest that the cross-sectional distribution of log-turnover is similar over time up to a location parameter. This implies a potentially useful statistical or "reduced-form" description of the cross-sectional distribution of turnover: an identically distributed random variable multiplied by a time-varying scale factor.

To explore the dynamics of the cross section of turnover, we ask the following question: if a stock has high turnover this week, how likely will it continue to be a high-turnover stock next week? Is turnover persistent or are there reversals from one week to the next?

To answer these questions, Table 17.9a reports the estimated transition probabilities for turnover deciles in adjacent weeks. For example, the first entry of the first row, 54.74, implies that 54.74% of the stocks that have turnover in the first decile this week will, on average, still be in the first turnover decile next week. The next entry, 21.51, implies that 21.51% of the stocks in the first turnover decile this week will, on average, be in the second turnover decile next week.

These entries indicate some persistence in the cross section of turnover for the extreme deciles, but considerable movement *across* the intermediate deciles. For example, there is only an 18.47% probability that stocks in the fifth decile (40–50%) in one week remain in the fifth decile the next week, and a probability of 12.18 and 11.53% of jumping to the third and seventh deciles, respectively.

For purposes of comparison, Tables 17.9b and 17.9c report similar transition probabilities estimates for market capitalization deciles and return deciles, respectively. Market

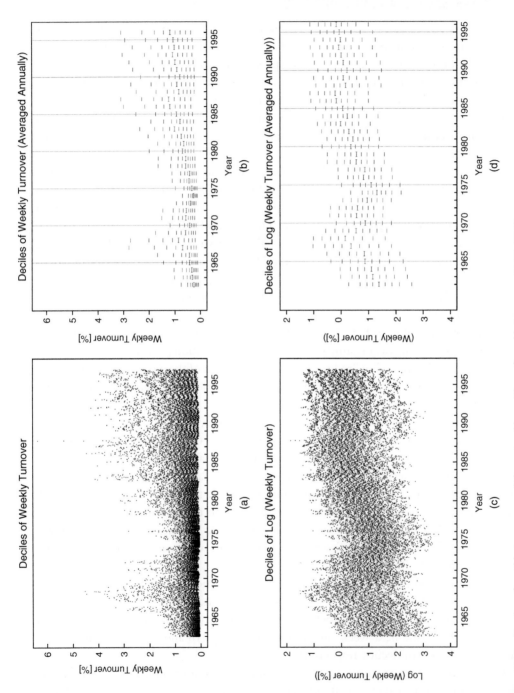

Figure 17.4 Deciles of weekly turnover and the natural logarithm of weekly turnover, 1962–1996.

Table 17.9a Transition probabilities for weekly turnover deciles (in percent), estimated with weekly turnover of NYSE or AMEX ordinary common shares (CRSP share codes 10 and 11, excluding 37 stocks containing Z-errors in reported volume) from July 1962 to December 1996 (1800 weeks)

Turnover transition	Next week decile									
	0–10	10–20	20–30	30–40	40–50	50–60	60–70	70–80	80–90	90–100
0–10	54.74 (0.12)	21.51 (0.06)	9.82 (0.05)	5.32 (0.04)	3.17 (0.03)	2.02 (0.03)	1.31 (0.02)	0.93 (0.02)	0.66 (0.01)	0.46 (0.01)
10–20	22.12 (0.06)	28.77 (0.10)	19.36 (0.06)	11.48 (0.05)	6.93 (0.05)	4.42 (0.04)	2.95 (0.03)	1.91 (0.03)	1.26 (0.02)	0.75 (0.02)
20–30	10.01 (0.05)	20.09 (0.07)	22.37 (0.09)	17.19 (0.06)	11.43 (0.05)	7.50 (0.05)	4.91 (0.04)	3.22 (0.03)	2.05 (0.03)	1.16 (0.02)
30–40	5.31 (0.04)	11.92 (0.05)	17.91 (0.07)	19.70 (0.08)	16.21 (0.06)	11.49 (0.05)	7.69 (0.05)	4.97 (0.04)	3.09 (0.03)	1.65 (0.02)
This week 40–50	3.15 (0.04)	7.15 (0.05)	12.18 (0.05)	16.81 (0.06)	18.47 (0.08)	15.77 (0.06)	11.53 (0.05)	7.74 (0.05)	4.75 (0.04)	2.40 (0.03)
50–60	1.94 (0.03)	4.42 (0.04)	7.82 (0.05)	12.22 (0.05)	16.59 (0.06)	18.37 (0.08)	16.02 (0.06)	11.64 (0.05)	7.33 (0.04)	3.60 (0.03)
60–70	1.22 (0.02)	2.79 (0.03)	4.91 (0.04)	8.10 (0.05)	12.41 (0.05)	16.99 (0.07)	19.10 (0.07)	16.84 (0.06)	11.72 (0.05)	5.87 (0.04)
70–80	0.81 (0.02)	1.72 (0.03)	3.05 (0.03)	5.10 (0.04)	8.27 (0.05)	12.73 (0.05)	18.15 (0.07)	21.30 (0.08)	18.69 (0.07)	10.13 (0.05)
80–90	0.51 (0.01)	1.04 (0.02)	1.78 (0.03)	2.85 (0.03)	4.58 (0.04)	7.77 (0.05)	13.02 (0.05)	20.78 (0.07)	27.18 (0.09)	20.43 (0.06)
90–100	0.29 (0.01)	0.53 (0.01)	0.79 (0.02)	1.18 (0.02)	1.83 (0.03)	2.97 (0.03)	5.31 (0.04)	10.62 (0.05)	23.28 (0.07)	53.14 (0.12)

Each week, all securities with nonmissing returns are sorted into turnover deciles, and the frequencies of transitions from decile i in one week to decile j in the next week are tabulated for each consecutive pair of weeks and for all (i, j) combinations, $i, j = 1, \ldots, 10$, and then normalized by the number of consecutive pairs of weeks. The number of securities with nonmissing returns in any given week varies between 1700 and 2200. Standard errors, computed under the assumption of i.i.d. transitions, are given in parentheses.

Table 17.9b Transition probabilities for weekly market-capitalization deciles (in percent), estimated with weekly market capitalization of NYSE or AMEX ordinary common shares (CRSP share codes 10 and 11, excluding 37 stocks containing Z-errors in reported volume) from July 1962 to December 1996 (1800 weeks)

Market cap transition	Next week decile									
This week	0–10	10–20	20–30	30–40	40–50	50–60	60–70	70–80	80–90	90–100
0–10	96.75 (0.06)	3.18 (0.03)	0.01 (0.00)	0.00 (0.00)	0.00 (0.00)	0.00 (0.00)	0.00 (0.00)	0.00 (0.00)	0.00 (0.00)	0.00 (0.00)
10–20	3.31 (0.03)	92.61 (0.07)	4.01 (0.03)	0.01 (0.00)	0.00 (0.00)	0.00 (0.00)	0.00 (0.00)	0.00 (0.00)	0.00 (0.00)	0.00 (0.00)
20–30	0.00 (0.00)	4.09 (0.03)	91.61 (0.07)	4.23 (0.03)	0.01 (0.00)	0.00 (0.00)	0.00 (0.00)	0.00 (0.00)	0.00 (0.00)	0.00 (0.00)
30–40	0.00 (0.00)	0.01 (0.00)	4.26 (0.03)	91.36 (0.08)	4.31 (0.04)	0.01 (0.00)	0.00 (0.00)	0.00 (0.00)	0.00 (0.00)	0.00 (0.00)
40–50	0.00 (0.00)	0.00 (0.00)	0.01 (0.00)	4.29 (0.03)	91.80 (0.07)	3.85 (0.03)	0.00 (0.00)	0.00 (0.00)	0.00 (0.00)	0.00 (0.00)
50–60	0.00 (0.00)	0.00 (0.00)	0.00 (0.00)	0.01 (0.00)	3.77 (0.03)	92.77 (0.07)	3.39 (0.03)	0.00 (0.00)	0.00 (0.00)	0.00 (0.00)
60–70	0.00 (0.00)	0.00 (0.00)	0.00 (0.00)	0.00 (0.00)	0.01 (0.00)	3.31 (0.03)	93.76 (0.07)	2.86 (0.03)	0.00 (0.00)	0.00 (0.00)
70–80	0.00 (0.00)	0.00 (0.00)	0.00 (0.00)	0.00 (0.00)	0.00 (0.00)	0.00 (0.00)	2.78 (0.02)	95.01 (0.06)	2.14 (0.02)	0.00 (0.00)
80–90	0.00 (0.00)	0.00 (0.00)	0.00 (0.00)	0.00 (0.00)	0.00 (0.00)	0.00 (0.00)	0.00 (0.00)	2.08 (0.02)	96.38 (0.06)	1.48 (0.02)
90–100	0.00 (0.00)	0.00 (0.00)	0.00 (0.00)	0.00 (0.00)	0.00 (0.00)	0.00 (0.00)	0.00 (0.00)	0.00 (0.00)	1.45 (0.02)	98.49 (0.06)

Each week, all securities with nonmissing returns are sorted into market-capitalization deciles, and the frequencies of transitions from decile i in one week to decile j in the next week are tabulated for each consecutive pair of weeks and for all (i,j) combinations, $i,j = 1,\ldots,10$, and then normalized by the number of consecutive pairs of weeks. The number of securities with nonmissing returns in any given week varies between 1700 and 2200. Standard errors, computed under the assumption of i.i.d. transitions, are given in parentheses.

Table 17.9c Transition probabilities for weekly return deciles (in percent), estimated with weekly returns of NYSE or AMEX ordinary common shares (CRSP share codes 10 and 11, excluding 37 stocks containing Z-errors in reported volume) from July 1962 to December 1996 (1800 weeks)

Return transition		Next week decile									
		0–10	10–20	20–30	30–40	40–50	50–60	60–70	70–80	80–90	90–100
	0–10	12.70 (0.09)	8.57 (0.06)	7.20 (0.06)	7.23 (0.07)	7.58 (0.07)	7.77 (0.07)	8.00 (0.07)	9.28 (0.06)	12.13 (0.07)	19.50 (0.11)
	10–20	9.51 (0.06)	9.95 (0.06)	9.60 (0.05)	9.42 (0.05)	9.24 (0.05)	9.44 (0.05)	9.84 (0.05)	10.63 (0.06)	11.38 (0.06)	10.93 (0.06)
	20–30	8.03 (0.06)	9.74 (0.05)	10.43 (0.05)	10.40 (0.06)	10.38 (0.06)	10.51 (0.06)	10.77 (0.06)	10.78 (0.06)	10.33 (0.06)	8.56 (0.06)
	30–40	7.60 (0.06)	9.33 (0.05)	10.35 (0.06)	10.85 (0.07)	11.20 (0.07)	11.28 (0.07)	11.22 (0.07)	10.55 (0.06)	9.66 (0.05)	7.90 (0.06)
This week	40–50	7.62 (0.07)	9.07 (0.05)	10.21 (0.06)	10.99 (0.07)	11.70 (0.08)	11.68 (0.07)	11.22 (0.07)	10.38 (0.06)	9.40 (0.05)	7.69 (0.06)
	50–60	7.43 (0.07)	9.16 (0.05)	10.44 (0.06)	11.11 (0.07)	11.55 (0.07)	11.63 (0.07)	11.29 (0.07)	10.52 (0.06)	9.30 (0.06)	7.52 (0.06)
	60–70	7.44 (0.06)	9.61 (0.05)	10.70 (0.06)	11.15 (0.07)	11.17 (0.07)	11.23 (0.07)	11.10 (0.07)	10.45 (0.06)	9.51 (0.06)	7.59 (0.05)
	70–80	8.30 (0.06)	10.40 (0.06)	10.88 (0.06)	10.84 (0.07)	10.46 (0.06)	10.40 (0.06)	10.44 (0.06)	10.37 (0.06)	9.78 (0.06)	8.07 (0.05)
	80–90	10.92 (0.07)	11.70 (0.06)	10.86 (0.06)	9.93 (0.06)	9.34 (0.06)	9.15 (0.06)	9.30 (0.06)	9.61 (0.06)	9.82 (0.06)	9.32 (0.06)
	90–100	20.49 (0.11)	12.39 (0.06)	9.34 (0.06)	8.03 (0.06)	7.28 (0.05)	6.95 (0.05)	6.82 (0.05)	7.38 (0.05)	8.68 (0.05)	12.59 (0.08)

Each week, all securities with nonmissing returns are sorted into return deciles, and the frequencies of transitions from decile i in one week to decile j in the next week are tabulated for each consecutive pair of weeks and for all (i,j) combinations, $i,j = 1, \ldots, 10$, and then normalized by the number of consecutive pairs of weeks. The number of securities with nonmissing returns in any given week varies between 1700 and 2200. Standard errors, computed under the assumption of i.i.d. transitions, are given in parentheses.

capitalization is considerably more persistent: none of the diagonal entries in Table 17.9b are less than 90%. However, returns are considerably less persistent – indeed, Table 17.9c provides strong evidence of reversals. For example, stocks in the first return decile this week have a 19.50% probability of being in the tenth return decile next week; stocks in the tenth return decile this week have a 20.49% probability of being in the first return decile next week. These weekly transition probabilities are consistent with the longer horizon return reversals documented by Chopra et al. (1992), DeBondt and Thaler (1985), and Lehmann (1990).

In summary, the turnover cross-section exhibits considerable variation, some persistence in extreme deciles, and significant movement across intermediate deciles.

4.1. Specification of Cross-Sectional Regressions

It is clear from Fig. 17.4 that turnover varies considerably in the cross section. In Sections 5 and 6, we propose formal models for the cross section of volume. But before doing so, we first consider a less formal, more exploratory analysis of the cross-sectional variation in turnover. The results we report here are from Lo and Wang (2000) (see also Lim et al. (1998)).

In particular, we wish to examine the explanatory power of several economically motivated variables such as expected return, volatility, and trading costs in explaining the cross section of turnover. To do this, we estimate cross-sectional regressions over five-year subperiods where the dependent variable is the median turnover $\tilde{\tau}_j$ of stock j and the explanatory variables are the following stock-specific characteristics[19]:

$\widehat{\alpha}_{r,j}$: Intercept coefficient from the time-series regression of stock j's return on the value-weighted market return.

$\widehat{\beta}_{r,j}$: Slope coefficient from the time-series regression of stock j's return on the value-weighted market return.

$\widehat{\sigma}_{\epsilon,r,j}$: Residual standard deviation of the time-series regression of stock j's return on the value-weighted market return.

v_j: Average of natural logarithm of stock j's market capitalization.

p_j: Average of natural logarithm of stock j's price.

d_j: Average of dividend yield of stock j, where dividend yield in week t is defined by

$$d_{jt} = \max\big[0, \ \log\big((1 + R_{jt})V_{jt-1}/V_{jt}\big)\big],$$

and V_{jt} is j's market capitalization in week t.

SP500$_j$: Indicator variable for membership in the S&P 500 Index.

$\widehat{\gamma}_{r,j}(1)$: First-order autocovariance of returns.

---

[19] We use median turnover instead of mean turnover to minimize the influence of outliers (which can be substantial in this data set). Also, within each five-year period, we exclude all stocks that are missing turnover data for more than two-thirds of the subsample.

The inclusion of these regressors in our cross-sectional analysis is loosely motivated by various intuitive "theories" that have appeared in the volume literature.

The motivation for the first three regressors comes partly from linear asset pricing models such as the CAPM and APT; they capture excess expected return $(\widehat{\alpha}_{r,j})$, systematic risk $(\widehat{\beta}_{r,j})$, and residual risk $(\widehat{\sigma}_{\epsilon,r,j})$, respectively. To the extent that expected excess return $(\widehat{\alpha}_{r,j})$ may contain a premium associated with liquidity (see, e.g., Amihud and Mendelson, 1986a,b; Hu, 1997) and heterogeneous information (see, e.g., He and Wang, 1995; Wang, 1994), it should also give rise to cross-sectional differences in turnover. Although a higher premium from lower liquidity should be inversely related to turnover, a higher premium from heterogeneous information can lead to either higher or lower turnover, depending on the nature of information heterogeneity. The two risk measures of an asset, $\widehat{\beta}_{r,j}$ and $\widehat{\sigma}_{\epsilon,r,j}$, also measure the volatility in its returns, which is associated with systematic risk and residual risk, respectively. Given that realized returns often generate portfolio-rebalancing needs, the volatility of returns should be positively related to turnover.

The motivation for log market capitalization (v_j) and log price (p_t) is two-fold. On the theoretical side, the role of market capitalization in explaining volume is related to Merton (1987) model of capital market equilibrium in which investors hold only the assets they are familiar with. This implies that larger capitalization companies tend to have more diverse ownership, which can lead to more active trading. The motivation for log price is related to trading costs. Given that part of trading costs comes from the bid-ask spread, which takes on discrete values in dollar terms, the actual costs in percentage terms are inversely related to price levels. This suggests that volume should be positively related to prices.

On the empirical side, there is an extensive literature documenting the significance of log market capitalization and log price in explaining the cross-sectional variation of expected returns, e.g., Banz (1981), Black (1976), Brown et al. (1993), Marsh and Merton (1987), and Reinganum (1992). If size and price are genuine factors driving expected returns, they should drive turnover as well (see Lo and Wang, 1998, for a more formal derivation and empirical analysis of this intuition).

Dividend yield (d_j) is not only motivated by its (empirical) ties to expected returns but also by *dividend-capture* trades – the practice of purchasing stock just before its ex-dividend date and then selling it shortly thereafter.[20] Often induced by differential taxation of dividends versus capital gains, dividend-capture trading has been linked to short-term increases in trading activity, e.g., Karpoff and Walkling (1988, 1990), Lakonishok and Smidt (1986), Lakonishok and Vermaelen (1986), Lynch-Koski (1996),

---

[20] Our definition of d_j is meant to capture net corporate distributions or outflows (recall that returns R_{jt} are inclusive of all dividends and other distributions). The purpose of the nonnegativity restriction is to ensure that inflows, e.g., new equity issues, are not treated as negative dividends.

Michaely (1991), Michaely and Vila (1995, 1996), and Stickel (1991). Stocks with higher dividend yields should induce more dividend-capture trading activity, and this may be reflected in higher median turnover.

The effects of membership in the S&P 500 have been documented in many studies, e.g., Dhillon and Johnson (1991), Goetzmann and Garry (1986), Harris and Gurel (1986), Jacques (1988), Jain (1987), Lamoureux and Wansley (1987), Pruitt and Wei (1989), Shleifer (1986), Tkac (1999), and Woolridge and Ghosh (1986). In particular, Harris and Gurel (1986) document increases in volume just after inclusion in the S&P 500, and Tkac (1999) uses an S&P 500 indicator variable to explain the cross-sectional dispersion of relative turnover (relative dollar volume divided by relative market capitalization). The obvious motivation for this variable is the growth of indexation by institutional investors and by the related practice of *index arbitrage*, in which disparities between the index futures price and the spot prices of the component securities are exploited by taking the appropriate positions in the futures and spot markets. For these reasons, stocks in the S&P 500 index should have higher turnover than others. Indexation began its rise in popularity with the advent of the mutual fund industry in the early 1980s, and index arbitrage first became feasible in 1982 with the introduction of the Chicago Mercantile Exchange's S&P 500 futures contracts. Therefore, the effects of S&P 500 membership on turnover should be more dramatic in the later subperiods. Another motivation for S&P 500 membership is its effect on the publicity of member companies, which leads to more diverse ownership and more trading activity in the context of Merton (1987).

The last variable, the first-order return autocovariance ($\widehat{\gamma}_{r,j}(1)$), serves as a proxy for trading costs, as in Roll (1984) model of the "effective" bid-ask spread. In that model, Roll shows that in the absence of information-based trades, prices bouncing between bid and ask prices imply the following approximate relation between the spread and the first-order return autocovariance:

$$\frac{s_{r,j}^2}{4} \approx -\mathrm{Cov}[R_{jt}, R_{jt-1}] \equiv -\gamma_{r,j}(1), \qquad (4.1)$$

where $s_{r,j} \equiv s_j / \sqrt{P_{aj} P_{bj}}$ is the percentage effective bid-ask spread of stock j as a percentage of the geometric average of the bid and ask prices P_{bj} and P_{aj}, respectively, and s_j is the dollar bid-ask spread.

Rather than solve for $s_{r,j}$, we choose instead to include $\widehat{\gamma}_{r,j}(1)$ as a regressor to sidestep the problem of a positive sample first-order autocovariance, which yields a complex number for the effective bid-ask spread. Of course, using $\widehat{\gamma}_{r,j}(1)$ does not eliminate this problem, which is a symptom of a specification error, but rather is a convenient heuristic that allows us to estimate the regression equation (complex observations for even one regressor can yield complex parameter estimates for all the other regressors as well!). This heuristic is not unlike Roll's method for dealing with positive autocovariances; however, it is more direct.[21]

Under the trading-cost interpretation for $\widehat{\gamma}_{r,j}(1)$, we should expect a positive coefficient in our cross-sectional turnover regression – a large negative value for $\widehat{\gamma}_{r,j}(1)$ implies a large bid-ask spread, which should be associated with lower turnover. Alternatively, Roll (1984) interprets a positive value for $\widehat{\gamma}_{r,j}(1)$ as a negative bid-ask spread; hence, turnover should be higher for such stocks.

These eight regressors yield the following regression equation to be estimated:

$$\tilde{\tau}_j = \gamma_0 + \gamma_1 \widehat{\alpha}_{r,j} + \gamma_2 \widehat{\beta}_{r,j} + \gamma_3 \widehat{\sigma}_{\epsilon,r,j} + \gamma_4 v_j + \gamma_5 p_j + \gamma_6 d_j + \gamma_7 \text{SP500}_j + \gamma_8 \widehat{\gamma}_{r,j}(1) + \epsilon_j. \quad (4.2)$$

4.2. Summary Statistics for Regressors

Table 17.10 reports summary statistics for these regressors, as well as for three other variables relevant to Sections 5 and 6:

$\widehat{\alpha}_{\tau,j}$: Intercept coefficient from the time-series regression of stock j's turnover on the value-weighted market turnover.

$\widehat{\beta}_{\tau,j}$: Slope coefficient from the time-series regression of stock j's turnover on the value-weighted market turnover.

$\widehat{\sigma}_{\epsilon,\tau,j}$: Residual standard deviation of the time-series regression of stock j's turnover on the value-weighted market turnover.

These three variables are loosely motivated by a one-factor linear model of turnover, i.e., a market model for turnover, which will be discussed in Section 5.

Table 17.10 contains means, medians, and standard deviations for these variables over each of the seven subperiods. The entries show that return betas are approximately 1.0 on average, with a cross-sectional standard deviation of about 0.5. Observe that return betas have approximately the same mean and median in all subperiods, indicating an absence of dramatic skewness and outliers in their empirical distributions.

In contrast, turnover betas have considerably higher means, starting at 2.2 in the first subperiod (1962–1966) to an all-time high of 3.1 in the second subperiod (1967–1971), and declining steadily thereafter to 0.7 (1987–1991) and 0.8 (1992–1996). Also, the means and medians of turnover betas differ dramatically, particularly in the earlier subperiods, e.g., 2.2 mean versus 0.7 median (1962–1966) and 3.1 mean versus 1.9 median (1967–1971), implying a skewed empirical distribution with some outliers in the right tail. Turnover betas are also more variable than return betas, with cross-sectional standard deviations that range from 2–10 times those of return betas.

---

[21] In a parenthetical statement in footnote a of Table I, Roll (1984) writes "The sign of the covariance was preserved after taking the square root."

Table 17.10   Summary statistics of variables for cross-sectional analysis of weekly turnover of NYSE or AMEX ordinary common shares (CRSP share codes 10 and 11, excluding 37 stocks containing Z-errors in reported volume) for subperiods of the sample period from July 1962 to December 1996

	$\bar{\tau}_j$	$\tilde{\tau}_j$	$\hat{\alpha}_{\tau,j}$	$\hat{\beta}_{\tau,j}$	$\hat{\sigma}_{\epsilon,\tau,j}$	$\hat{\alpha}_{r,j}$	$\hat{\beta}_{r,j}$	$\hat{\sigma}_{\epsilon,r,j}$	v_j	p_j	d_j	$\mathrm{SP}^{500}{}_j$	$\hat{\gamma}_{r,j}(1)$
					1962–1966 (234 weeks)								
μ	0.576	0.374	0.009	2.230	0.646	0.080	1.046	4.562	17.404	1.249	0.059	0.175	−2.706
m	0.397	0.272	0.092	0.725	0.391	0.064	1.002	3.893	17.263	1.445	0.058	0.000	−0.851
s	0.641	0.372	1.065	5.062	0.889	0.339	0.529	2.406	1.737	0.965	0.081	0.380	8.463
					1967–1971 (261 weeks)								
μ	0.900	0.610	−0.361	3.134	0.910	0.086	1.272	5.367	17.930	1.442	0.049	0.178	−1.538
m	0.641	0.446	−0.128	1.948	0.612	0.081	1.225	5.104	17.791	1.522	0.042	0.000	−0.623
s	0.827	0.547	0.954	3.559	0.940	0.383	0.537	1.991	1.566	0.685	0.046	0.382	4.472
					1972–1976 (261 weeks)								
μ	0.521	0.359	−0.025	1.472	0.535	0.085	0.986	6.252	17.574	0.823	0.072	0.162	−3.084
m	0.420	0.291	0.005	1.040	0.403	0.086	0.955	5.825	17.346	0.883	0.063	0.000	−1.007
s	0.408	0.292	0.432	1.595	0.473	0.319	0.429	2.619	1.784	0.890	0.067	0.369	8.262
					1977–1981 (261 weeks)								
μ	0.780	0.553	0.043	1.199	0.749	0.254	0.950	5.081	18.155	1.074	0.099	0.176	−1.748
m	0.629	0.449	0.052	0.818	0.566	0.215	0.936	4.737	18.094	1.212	0.086	0.000	−0.622
s	0.561	0.405	0.638	1.348	0.643	0.356	0.428	2.097	1.769	0.805	0.097	0.381	5.100
					1982–1986 (261 weeks)								
μ	1.160	0.833	0.005	0.957	1.135	0.113	0.873	5.419	18.629	1.143	0.090	0.181	−1.627
m	0.998	0.704	0.031	0.713	0.902	0.146	0.863	4.813	18.512	1.293	0.063	0.000	−0.573
s	0.788	0.605	0.880	1.018	0.871	0.455	0.437	2.581	1.763	0.873	0.126	0.385	8.405
					1987–1991 (261 weeks)								
μ	1.255	0.888	0.333	0.715	1.256	−0.007	0.977	6.450	18.847	0.908	0.095	0.191	−5.096
m	0.995	0.708	0.171	0.505	0.899	0.014	0.998	5.174	18.778	1.108	0.062	0.000	−0.386
s	1.039	0.773	1.393	1.229	1.272	0.543	0.414	5.417	2.013	1.097	0.134	0.393	44.246
					1992–1996 (261 weeks)								
μ	1.419	1.032	0.379	0.833	1.378	0.147	0.851	5.722	19.407	1.081	0.063	0.182	−3.600
m	1.114	0.834	0.239	0.511	0.997	0.113	0.831	4.674	19.450	1.297	0.042	0.000	−1.136
s	1.208	0.910	1.637	1.572	1.480	0.482	0.520	3.901	2.007	1.032	0.095	0.386	21.550

The variables are $\bar{\tau}_j$ (average turnover); $\tilde{\tau}_j$ (median turnover); $\hat{\alpha}_{\tau,j}$, $\hat{\beta}_{\tau,j}$, and $\hat{\sigma}_{\epsilon,\tau,j}$ (the intercept, slope, and residual, respectively, from the time-series regression of an individual security's turnover on market turnover); $\hat{\alpha}_{r,j}$, $\hat{\beta}_{r,j}$, and $\hat{\sigma}_{\epsilon,r,j}$ (the intercept, slope, and residual, respectively, from the time-series regression of an individual security's return on the market return); v_j (natural logarithm of market capitalization); p_j (natural logarithm of price); d_j (dividend yield); SP^{500}_j (S&P 500 indicator variable); and $\hat{\gamma}_{r,j}(1)$ (first-order return autocovariance). The statistics are μ (mean); m (median); and s (standard deviation).

The summary statistics for the first-order return autocovariances show that they are negative on average, which is consistent with the trading-cost interpretation, though there is considerable skewness in their distribution as well given the differences between means and medians. The means and medians vary from subperiod to subperiod in a manner also consistent with the trading-cost interpretation – the higher the median of median turnover $\tilde{\tau}_j$, the closer to 0 is the median autocovariance.[22] In particular, between the first and second subperiods, median autocovariance decreases (in absolute value) from -0.851 to -0.623, signaling lower trading costs, while median turnover increases from 0.272 to 0.446. Between the second and third subperiods, median autocovariance increases (in absolute value) from -0.623 to -1.007 while median turnover decreases from 0.446 to 0.291, presumably due to the Oil Shock of 1973–1974 and the subsequent recession. The 1977–1981 subperiod is the first subperiod after the advent of negotiated commissions (May 1, 1975), and median turnover increases to 0.449 while median autocovariance decreases (in absolute value) to -0.622. During the 1982–1986 subperiod when S&P 500 index futures began trading, median autocovariance declines (in absolute value) to -0.573 while median turnover increases dramatically to 0.704. During the 1987–1991 subperiod, which includes the October 1987 Crash, median turnover is essentially unchanged (0.708 versus 0.704 from the previous subperiod), median autocovariance decreases (in absolute value) from -0.573 in the previous subperiod to -0.386, but mean autocovariance increases (in absolute value) dramatically from -1.627 in the previous subperiod to -5.096, indicating the presence of outliers with very large trading costs.

We have also estimated correlations among the variables in Table 17.10, which are reported in Table 17.11. It shows that median turnover is highly correlated with both turnover beta and return beta, with correlations that exceed 50% in most subperiods, hinting at the prospect of two or more factors driving the cross-sectional variation in turnover. We shall address this issue more formally in Section 5.

Median turnover is not particularly highly correlated with S&P 500 membership during the first four subperiods, with correlations ranging from -10.6 (1967–1971) to 8.6% (1972–1976). However, with the advent of S&P 500 futures and the growing popularity of indexation in the early 1980s, median turnover becomes more highly correlated with S&P 500 membership, jumping to 22.7% in 1982–1986, 25.4% in 1987–1991, and 15.9% in 1992–1996.

Turnover betas and return betas are highly positively correlated, with correlations ranging from 25.5 (1987–1991) to 55.4% (1967–1971). Not surprisingly, log price p_j is highly positively correlated with log market capitalization v_j, with correlations exceeding 75% in every subperiod. Dividend yield is positively correlated with both log price and

---

[22] Recall that $\tilde{\tau}_j$ is the median turnover of stock j during the five-year subperiod; the median of $\tilde{\tau}_j$ is the median across all stocks j in the five-year subsample.

Table 17.11 Correlation matrix of variables for cross-sectional analysis of weekly turnover of NYSE or AMEX ordinary common shares (CRSP share codes 10 and 11, excluding 37 stocks containing Z-errors in reported volume) for subperiods of the sample period from July 1962 to December 1996

	$\bar{\tau}_j$	$\tilde{\tau}_j$	$\widehat{\alpha}_{\tau,j}$	$\widehat{\beta}_{\tau,j}$	$\widehat{\sigma}_{\epsilon,\tau,j}$	$\widehat{\alpha}_{r,j}$	$\widehat{\beta}_{r,j}$	$\widehat{\sigma}_{\epsilon,r,j}$	v_j	p_j	d_j	SP_j^{500}
					1962–1966 (2073 stocks)							
$\tilde{\tau}_j$	93.1											
$\widehat{\alpha}_{\tau,j}$	−8.6	1.9										
$\widehat{\beta}_{\tau,j}$	56.6	43.9	−86.9									
$\widehat{\sigma}_{\epsilon,\tau,j}$	88.8	70.3	−11.8	54.1								
$\widehat{\alpha}_{r,j}$	14.9	10.7	−12.0	16.9	14.8							
$\widehat{\beta}_{r,j}$	56.3	59.3	−15.8	40.8	43.2	1.5						
$\widehat{\sigma}_{\epsilon,r,j}$	36.1	25.4	−19.5	34.0	45.8	16.3	29.2					
v_j	−19.2	−11.4	9.6	−17.5	−28.9	−3.0	1.9	−62.7				
p_j	−7.6	1.7	14.6	−16.0	−20.1	1.6	3.2	−77.1	78.7			
d_j	−11.4	−9.3	9.3	−13.2	−12.2	0.4	−17.0	−27.9	13.1	20.7		
SP_j^{500}	−5.0	−0.6	4.8	−6.4	−10.2	−6.6	2.4	−24.2	43.1	32.0	4.8	
$\widehat{\gamma}_{r,j}(1)$	−0.6	3.0	5.7	−5.1	−7.6	−14.4	1.9	−63.2	31.1	52.7	12.9	10.7
					1967–1971 (2292 stocks)							
$\tilde{\tau}_j$	96.8											
$\widehat{\alpha}_{\tau,j}$	−30.9	−23.0										
$\widehat{\beta}_{\tau,j}$	77.6	70.6	−83.8									
$\widehat{\sigma}_{\epsilon,\tau,j}$	92.2	80.7	−38.2	77.9								
$\widehat{\alpha}_{r,j}$	10.3	8.7	4.2	1.9	12.5							
$\widehat{\beta}_{r,j}$	59.2	60.4	−31.2	55.4	50.0	−12.6						
$\widehat{\sigma}_{\epsilon,r,j}$	56.3	49.5	−36.7	57.0	60.7	−1.5	61.3					
v_j	−32.5	−25.3	32.7	−40.5	−41.1	1.1	−23.7	−67.6				
p_j	−19.8	−11.9	35.6	−35.3	−30.1	16.7	−22.1	−68.9	77.0			
d_j	−38.2	−37.2	19.8	−35.3	−35.2	3.0	−51.9	−57.1	28.0	28.3		
SP_j^{500}	−14.0	−10.6	11.9	−16.1	−18.2	2.2	−11.5	−30.9	47.9	35.2	13.3	
$\widehat{\gamma}_{r,j}(1)$	−8.7	−6.8	11.7	−12.8	−11.4	8.8	−14.9	−40.7	30.7	43.8	18.2	12.3
					1972–1976 (2084 stocks)							
$\tilde{\tau}_j$	96.5											
$\widehat{\alpha}_{\tau,j}$	2.5	8.9										
$\widehat{\beta}_{\tau,j}$	67.4	60.2	−72.0									
$\widehat{\sigma}_{\epsilon,\tau,j}$	83.9	69.4	−5.9	62.6								
$\widehat{\alpha}_{r,j}$	8.5	7.2	−7.7	11.1	7.5							
$\widehat{\beta}_{r,j}$	54.3	54.3	−16.4	49.4	39.7	−14.8						
$\widehat{\sigma}_{\epsilon,r,j}$	22.2	12.7	−2.9	17.9	35.7	−11.3	29.9					
v_j	0.6	12.0	3.8	−2.7	−21.7	5.3	12.6	−65.2				
p_j	8.1	17.4	8.8	−1.0	−11.7	14.6	1.8	−76.1	83.7			
d_j	−20.9	−18.3	7.0	−19.8	−20.9	9.4	−34.2	−41.6	19.4	25.0		
SP_j^{500}	1.2	8.6	1.5	−0.4	−13.1	−2.2	9.1	−28.2	50.5	37.9	2.6	
$\widehat{\gamma}_{r,j}(1)$	0.0	3.2	6.4	−5.2	−5.6	5.3	−8.3	−57.1	32.9	50.6	23.8	11.6

Table 17.11 (*Continued*)

	$\bar{\tau}_j$	$\tilde{\tau}_j$	$\hat{\alpha}_{\tau,j}$	$\hat{\beta}_{\tau,j}$	$\hat{\sigma}_{\epsilon,\tau,j}$	$\hat{\alpha}_{r,j}$	$\hat{\beta}_{r,j}$	$\hat{\sigma}_{\epsilon,r,j}$	v_j	p_j	d_j	SP_j^{500}
					1977–1981 (2352 stocks)							
$\tilde{\tau}_j$	96.4											
$\hat{\alpha}_{\tau,j}$	6.7	11.0										
$\hat{\beta}_{\tau,j}$	61.9	55.1	−72.9									
$\hat{\sigma}_{\epsilon,\tau,j}$	83.0	67.4	3.5	54.9								
$\hat{\alpha}_{r,j}$	10.6	2.8	−8.2	16.9	22.7							
$\hat{\beta}_{r,j}$	59.8	63.8	−11.0	47.1	35.6	3.2						
$\hat{\sigma}_{\epsilon,r,j}$	28.5	18.3	−8.2	25.6	42.8	30.8	24.9					
v_j	5.3	15.7	6.7	−2.0	−16.5	−26.8	16.4	−63.4				
p_j	8.1	17.1	11.7	−3.6	−10.8	−9.0	12.2	−70.1	80.8			
d_j	−18.4	−18.2	3.8	−15.2	−14.7	1.4	−27.9	−27.3	9.9	13.0		
SP_j^{500}	2.5	8.4	−0.4	2.5	−8.9	−19.0	8.5	−28.5	51.6	35.1	2.8	
$\hat{\gamma}_{r,j}(1)$	0.2	3.0	1.8	−1.3	−5.3	−3.6	−2.3	−55.6	31.5	52.1	14.7	10.5
					1982–1986 (2644 stocks)							
$\tilde{\tau}_j$	96.2											
$\hat{\alpha}_{\tau,j}$	−12.0	−5.6										
$\hat{\beta}_{\tau,j}$	71.3	64.3	−77.8									
$\hat{\sigma}_{\epsilon,\tau,j}$	80.0	62.8	−19.8	64.7								
$\hat{\alpha}_{r,j}$	−7.4	−10.9	−14.5	6.2	2.4							
$\hat{\beta}_{r,j}$	46.4	50.6	−12.6	38.3	24.8	−32.5						
$\hat{\sigma}_{\epsilon,r,j}$	15.4	7.3	12.3	0.7	25.2	−17.7	15.6					
v_j	19.0	29.7	−8.3	18.8	−5.0	−3.1	27.6	−55.7				
p_j	9.0	16.5	−12.4	15.3	−5.9	22.3	10.3	−76.1	75.3			
d_j	−6.7	−7.6	−4.1	−0.5	−2.5	15.5	−12.6	−21.4	16.6	20.5		
SP_j^{500}	15.5	22.7	−2.0	12.1	−1.6	−3.8	18.2	−24.7	57.3	37.5	8.0	
$\hat{\gamma}_{r,j}(1)$	5.2	5.6	−8.9	9.5	4.1	18.9	−0.4	−39.2	15.7	32.6	7.1	5.2
					1987–1991 (2471 stocks)							
$\tilde{\tau}_j$	94.1											
$\hat{\alpha}_{\tau,j}$	17.1	25.8										
$\hat{\beta}_{\tau,j}$	50.8	39.2	−76.0									
$\hat{\sigma}_{\epsilon,\tau,j}$	79.1	56.6	−1.0	53.0								
$\hat{\alpha}_{r,j}$	7.1	5.1	16.8	−9.7	9.2							
$\hat{\beta}_{r,j}$	45.4	49.4	5.0	25.5	22.3	−15.0						
$\hat{\sigma}_{\epsilon,r,j}$	3.1	−3.6	−0.7	2.5	12.7	24.4	−2.6					
v_j	20.3	31.7	3.3	10.4	−2.0	5.6	22.4	−48.1				
p_j	12.3	22.0	6.4	2.5	−5.7	10.8	11.2	−62.0	80.4			
d_j	−1.2	−1.9	−1.8	0.8	1.6	2.9	−4.7	−10.9	12.9	15.7		
SP_j^{500}	16.1	25.4	−1.4	11.6	−3.8	−2.4	19.1	−20.7	58.7	39.1	5.9	
$\hat{\gamma}_{r,j}(1)$	4.2	5.5	2.7	0.5	0.4	−39.5	11.7	−76.1	14.4	23.0	2.9	4.4

(*Continued*)

Table 17.11 (Continued)

	$\bar{\tau}_j$	$\tilde{\tau}_j$	$\widehat{\alpha}_{\tau,j}$	$\widehat{\beta}_{\tau,j}$	$\widehat{\sigma}_{\epsilon,\tau,j}$	$\widehat{\alpha}_{r,j}$	$\widehat{\beta}_{r,j}$	$\widehat{\sigma}_{\epsilon,r,j}$	v_j	p_j	d_j	SP_j^{500}
					1992–1996 (2520 stocks)							
$\tilde{\tau}_j$	94.8											
$\widehat{\alpha}_{\tau,j}$	6.8	10.8										
$\widehat{\beta}_{\tau,j}$	55.8	49.1	−78.9									
$\widehat{\sigma}_{\epsilon,\tau,j}$	79.1	58.6	6.0	43.8								
$\widehat{\alpha}_{r,j}$	−2.8	−6.4	−13.5	9.6	3.8							
$\widehat{\beta}_{r,j}$	46.6	49.1	0.0	28.7	27.8	−14.4						
$\widehat{\sigma}_{\epsilon,r,j}$	18.6	6.4	5.4	7.4	36.3	24.2	4.2					
v_j	10.1	23.8	−7.1	12.0	−18.8	−15.7	27.8	−61.5				
p_j	5.8	17.2	−3.3	6.1	−17.4	−8.4	16.2	−76.8	81.5			
d_j	−9.5	−8.3	−1.5	−4.5	−9.3	0.4	−6.4	−14.6	13.3	15.4		
SP_j^{500}	6.6	15.9	−8.8	11.5	−12.3	−9.1	17.5	−24.2	56.7	37.7	11.0	
$\widehat{\gamma}_{r,j}(1)$	2.3	4.9	−2.3	3.2	−3.8	1.2	12.1	−23.2	19.1	29.3	5.0	4.5

The variables are $\bar{\tau}_j$ (average turnover); $\tilde{\tau}_j$ (median turnover); $\widehat{\alpha}_{\tau,j}$, $\widehat{\beta}_{\tau,j}$, and $\widehat{\sigma}_{\epsilon,\tau,j}$ (the intercept, slope, and residual, respectively, from the time-series regression of an individual security's turnover on market turnover); $\widehat{\alpha}_{r,j}$, $\widehat{\beta}_{r,j}$, and $\widehat{\sigma}_{\epsilon,r,j}$ (the intercept, slope, and residual, respectively, from the time-series regression of an individual security's return on the market return); v_j (natural logarithm of market capitalization), p_j (natural logarithm of price); SP_j^{500} (S&P 500 indicator variable); and $\widehat{\gamma}_{r,j}(1)$ (first-order return autocovariance).

log market capitalization, though the correlation is not particularly large. This may seem counterintuitive at first, but recall that these are cross-sectional correlations, not time-series correlations, and the level of dividends per share varies cross-sectionally, as well as average log price.

4.3. Regression Results

Table 17.12 contains the estimates of the cross-sectional regression model (4.2). We estimated three regression models for each subperiod: one with all eight variables and a constant term included, one excluding log market capitalization, and one excluding log price. Since the log price and log market capitalization regressors are so highly correlated (see Lim et al., 1998), regressions with only one or the other included were estimated to gauge the effects of multicollinearity. The exclusion of either variable does not affect the qualitative features of the regression – no significant coefficients changed sign other than the constant term – though the quantitative features were affected to a small degree. For example, in the first subperiod v_j has a negative coefficient (−0.064) and p_j has a positive coefficient (0.150), both significant at the 5% level. When v_j is omitted, the coefficient of p_j is still positive but smaller (0.070), and when p_j is omitted, the coefficient of v_j is still negative and also smaller in absolute magnitude (−0.028). In both of these cases, the coefficients retain their significance.

Table 17.12 Cross-sectional regressions of median weekly turnover of NYSE and AMEX ordinary common shares (CRSP share codes 10 and 11, excluding 37 stocks containing Z-errors in reported volume) for five-year subperiods of the sample period from July 1962 to December 1996

c	$\widehat{\alpha}_{r,j}$	$\widehat{\beta}_{r,j}$	$\widehat{\sigma}_{\epsilon,r,j}$	v_j	p_j	d_j	SP_j^{500}	$\widehat{\gamma}_{r,j}(1)$	R^2 (%)
			1962–1966 (234 weeks, 2073 stocks)						
0.742	0.059	0.354	0.043	−0.064	0.150	0.071	0.048	0.004	41.8
(0.108)	(0.019)	(0.014)	(0.006)	(0.006)	(0.014)	(0.081)	(0.018)	(0.001)	
−0.306	0.068	0.344	0.053	—	0.070	0.130	−0.006	0.006	38.8
(0.034)	(0.020)	(0.015)	(0.006)		(0.012)	(0.083)	(0.018)	(0.001)	
0.378	0.111	0.401	0.013	−0.028	—	0.119	0.048	0.005	38.7
(0.105)	(0.019)	(0.014)	(0.005)	(0.005)		(0.083)	(0.019)	(0.001)	
			1967–1971 (261 weeks, 2292 stocks)						
0.289	0.134	0.448	0.095	−0.062	0.249	0.027	0.028	0.006	44.7
(0.181)	(0.024)	(0.023)	(0.009)	(0.010)	(0.023)	(0.235)	(0.025)	(0.002)	
−0.797	0.152	0.434	0.112	—	0.173	0.117	−0.026	0.007	43.7
(0.066)	(0.024)	(0.023)	(0.009)		(0.020)	(0.237)	(0.024)	(0.002)	
−0.172	0.209	0.507	0.057	−0.009	—	−0.108	0.023	0.011	41.9
(0.180)	(0.023)	(0.023)	(0.009)	(0.009)		(0.241)	(0.026)	(0.002)	
			1972–1976 (261 weeks, 2084 stocks)						
0.437	0.102	0.345	0.027	−0.041	0.171	−0.031	0.031	0.001	38.0
(0.092)	(0.015)	(0.013)	(0.003)	(0.005)	(0.012)	(0.079)	(0.015)	(0.001)	
−0.249	0.111	0.320	0.032	—	0.114	−0.058	−0.007	0.002	36.5
(0.027)	(0.015)	(0.013)	(0.003)		(0.009)	(0.080)	(0.014)	(0.001)	
−0.188	0.141	0.367	0.008	0.008	—	−0.072	0.020	0.003	32.7
(0.085)	(0.015)	(0.014)	(0.003)	(0.004)		(0.082)	(0.015)	(0.001)	
			1977–1981 (261 weeks, 2352 stocks)						
−0.315	−0.059	0.508	0.057	−0.001	0.139	0.015	0.013	0.005	44.2
(0.127)	(0.020)	(0.018)	(0.006)	(0.007)	(0.017)	(0.069)	(0.019)	(0.002)	
−0.344	−0.058	0.508	0.057	—	0.137	0.015	0.011	0.005	44.2
(0.035)	(0.019)	(0.017)	(0.005)		(0.013)	(0.069)	(0.018)	(0.002)	
−0.810	−0.008	0.534	0.040	0.037	—	−0.001	−0.001	0.009	42.6
(0.114)	(0.019)	(0.018)	(0.005)	(0.006)		(0.070)	(0.020)	(0.002)	
			1982–1986 (261 weeks, 2644 stocks)						
−1.385	0.051	0.543	0.062	0.071	0.085	−0.223	0.091	0.006	31.6
(0.180)	(0.025)	(0.027)	(0.007)	(0.010)	(0.023)	(0.081)	(0.031)	(0.001)	
−0.193	0.018	0.583	0.057	—	0.170	−0.182	0.187	0.005	30.4
(0.051)	(0.024)	(0.027)	(0.007)		(0.020)	(0.081)	(0.028)	(0.001)	

(Continued)

Table 17.12 (*Continued*)

c	$\widehat{\alpha}_{r,j}$	$\widehat{\beta}_{r,j}$	$\widehat{\sigma}_{\epsilon,r,j}$	v_j	p_j	d_j	SP^{500}_j	$\widehat{\gamma}_{r,j}(1)$	R^2 (%)
				1982–1986 (261 weeks, 2644 stocks)					
−1.602	0.080	0.562	0.048	0.091	—	−0.217	0.085	0.006	31.3
(0.170)	(0.023)	(0.027)	(0.005)	(0.009)		(0.081)	(0.031)	(0.001)	
				1987–1991 (261 weeks, 2471 stocks)					
−1.662	0.155	0.791	0.038	0.078	0.066	−0.138	0.131	0.003	31.9
(0.223)	(0.027)	(0.034)	(0.005)	(0.013)	(0.024)	(0.097)	(0.041)	(0.001)	
−0.313	0.153	0.831	0.035	—	0.158	−0.128	0.252	0.003	30.9
(0.052)	(0.027)	(0.033)	(0.005)		(0.019)	(0.098)	(0.036)	(0.001)	
−1.968	0.171	0.795	0.031	0.100	—	−0.122	0.119	0.003	31.7
(0.195)	(0.026)	(0.034)	(0.005)	(0.010)		(0.097)	(0.041)	(0.001)	
				1992–1996 (261 weeks, 2520 stocks)					
−1.004	−0.087	0.689	0.077	0.040	0.262	−0.644	0.029	0.000	29.6
(0.278)	(0.034)	(0.033)	(0.007)	(0.016)	(0.033)	(0.164)	(0.049)	(0.001)	
−0.310	−0.095	0.708	0.076	—	0.314	−0.641	0.087	−0.001	29.4
(0.061)	(0.034)	(0.032)	(0.007)		(0.026)	(0.164)	(0.043)	(0.001)	
−2.025	−0.025	0.711	0.046	0.115	—	−0.590	−0.005	0.000	27.8
(0.249)	(0.034)	(0.033)	(0.006)	(0.012)		(0.166)	(0.049)	(0.001)	

The explanatory variables are $\widehat{\alpha}_{r,j}$, $\widehat{\beta}_{r,j}$, and $\widehat{\sigma}_{\epsilon,r,j}$ (the intercept, slope, and residual, respectively, from the time-series regression of an individual security's return on the market return); v_j (natural logarithm of market capitalization), p_j (natural logarithm of price); d_j (dividend yield); SP500$_j$ (S&P 500 indicator variable); and $\widehat{\gamma}_{r,j}(1)$ (first-order return autocovariance).

The fact that size has a negative impact on turnover while price has a positive impact is an artifact of the earlier subperiods. This can be seen heuristically in the time-series plots of Fig. 17.1 – compare the value-weighted and equal-weighted turnover indexes during the first two or three subperiods. Smaller capitalization stocks seem to have higher turnover than larger capitalization stocks.

This begins to change in the 1977–1981 subperiod: the size coefficient is negative but not significant, and when price is excluded, the size coefficient changes sign and becomes significant. In the subperiods after 1977–1981, both size and price enter positively. One explanation of this change is the growth of the mutual fund industry and other large institutional investors in the early 1980s. As portfolio managers manage larger asset bases, it becomes more difficult to invest in smaller capitalization companies because of liquidity and corporate-control issues. Therefore, the natural economies of scale in investment management coupled with the increasing concentration of investment capital make small stocks less actively traded than large stocks. Of course, this effect should have implications for the equilibrium return of small stocks versus large stocks.

The first-order return autocovariance has a positive coefficient in all subperiods except the second regression of the last subperiod (in which the coefficient is negative but insignificant), and these coefficients are significant at the 5% level in all subperiods except 1972–1976 and 1992–1996. This is consistent with the trading-cost interpretation of $\widehat{\gamma}_{r,j}(1)$: a large negative return autocovariance implies a large effective bid-ask spread which, in turn, should imply lower turnover.

Membership in the S&P 500 also has a positive impact on turnover in all subperiods as expected, and the magnitude of the coefficient increases dramatically in the 1982–1986 subperiod, from 0.013 in the previous period to 0.091, also as expected given the growing importance of indexation and index arbitrage during this period, and the introduction of S&P 500 futures contracts in April 1982. Surprisingly, in the 1992–1996 subperiod, the S&P 500 coefficient declines to 0.029 because of the interactions between this indicator variable and size and price (all three variables are highly positively correlated with each other; see Lim et al., 1998 for further details). When size is omitted, S&P 500 membership becomes more important, yet when price is omitted, size becomes more important and S&P 500 membership becomes irrelevant. These findings are roughly consistent with those in Tkac (1999).[23]

Both systematic and idiosyncratic risk, $\widehat{\beta}_{r,j}$ and $\widehat{\sigma}_{\epsilon,r,j}$, have positive and significant impact on turnover in all subperiods. However, the impact of excess expected returns $\widehat{\alpha}_{r,j}$ on turnover is erratic: negative and significant in the 1977–1981 and 1992–1996 subperiods, and positive and significant in the others.

The dividend-yield regressor is insignificant in all subperiods but two: 1982–1986 and 1992–1996. In these two subperiods, the coefficient is negative, which contradicts the notion that dividend-capture trading affects turnover.

In summary, the cross-sectional variation of turnover does seem related to several stock-specific characteristics such as risk, size, price, trading costs, and S&P 500 membership. The explanatory power of these cross-sectional regressions, as measured by R^2, range from 29.6 (1992–1996) to 44.7% (1967–1971), rivaling the R^2s of typical cross-sectional return regressions. With sample sizes ranging from 2073 (1962–1966) to 2644 (1982–1986) stocks, these R^2s provide some measure of confidence that cross-sectional variations in median turnover are not purely random, but do bear some relation to economic factors. To further analyze the cross-section of turnover, additional economic structure is needed. This is the task for the following two sections.

---

[23] In particular, she finds that S&P 500 membership becomes much less significant after controlling for the effects of size and institutional ownership. Of course, her analysis is not directly comparable to ours because she uses a different dependent variable (monthly relative dollar volume divided by relative market capitalization) in her cross-sectional regressions and considers only a small sample of the very largest NYSE/AMEX stocks (809) over the four-year period (1988–1991).

5. VOLUME IMPLICATIONS OF PORTFOLIO THEORY

The diversity in the portfolio holdings of individuals and institutions and in their motives for trade suggests that the time-series and cross-sectional patterns of trading activity can be quite complex. However, standard portfolio theory provides an enormous simplification: under certain conditions, *mutual fund separation* holds, i.e., investors are indifferent between choosing among the entire universe of securities and a small number of mutual funds (see, e.g., Cass and Stiglitz, 1970; Markowitz, 1952; Merton, 1973; Ross, 1978; Tobin, 1958). In this case, all investors trade only in these *separating funds* and simpler cross-sectional patterns in trading activity emerge. We derive such cross-sectional implications in this section.

While several models can deliver mutual fund separation, e.g., the CAPM and ICAPM, we do not specify any such model here, but simply assert that mutual-fund separation holds. In particular, in this section, we focus primarily on the cross-sectional properties of volume and assume nothing about the behavior of asset prices, e.g., a factor structure for asset returns may or may not exist. As long as mutual fund separation holds, the results in this section (in particular, Sections 5.1 and 5.2) must apply. However, in Section 6, we provide a specific ICAPM, in which mutual fund separation holds and the separating funds are linked with the underlying risk structure of the stocks.

The strong implications of mutual fund separation for volume that we derive in this section suggest that the assumptions underlying the theory may be quite restrictive and therefore implausible (see, e.g., Cass and Stiglitz, 1970; Markowitz, 1952; Ross, 1978; Tobin, 1958). For example, mutual fund separation is often derived in static settings in which the motives for trade are not explicitly modeled. Also, most models of mutual fund separation use a partial equilibrium framework with exogenously specified return distributions and strong restrictions on preferences. Furthermore, these models tend to focus on a rather narrow set of trading motives – changes in portfolio holdings due to changes in return distributions or preferences – ignoring other factors that may motivate individuals and institutions to adjust their portfolios, e.g., asymmetric information, idiosyncratic risk, transaction costs, taxes, and other market imperfections. Finally, it has sometimes been argued that recent levels of trading activity in financial markets are simply too high to be attributable to the portfolio-rebalancing needs of rational economic agents.

A detailed discussion of these concerns is beyond the scope of this chapter. Moreover, we are not advocating any particular structural model of mutual fund separation here but merely investigating the implications for trading volume when mutual fund separation holds. Nevertheless, before deriving these implications, it is important to consider how some of the limitations of mutual fund separation may affect the interpretation of our analysis.

First, many limitations of mutual fund separation theorems can be overcome to some degree. For example, extending mutual fund separation results to dynamic settings is possible. As in the static case, restrictive assumptions on preferences and/or return processes are often required to obtain mutual fund separation in a discrete-time setting. However, in a continuous-time setting, which has its own set of restrictive assumptions, Merton (1973) shows that mutual fund separation holds for quite general preferences and return processes.

Also, it is possible to embed mutual fund separation in a general equilibrium framework in which asset returns are determined endogenously. The CAPM is a well-known example of mutual fund separation in a static equilibrium setting. To obtain mutual fund separation in a dynamic equilibrium setting, stronger assumptions are required – Section 6 provides such an example.[24]

Of course, from a theoretical standpoint, no existing model is rich enough to capture the full spectrum of portfolio-rebalancing needs of all market participants, e.g., risk-sharing, hedging, liquidity, and speculation. Therefore, it is difficult to argue that current levels of trading activity are too high to be justified by rational portfolio rebalancing. Indeed, under the standard assumption of a diffusion information structure, volume is unbounded in absence of transaction costs. Moreover, from an empirical standpoint, little effort has been devoted to calibrating the level of trading volume within the context of a realistic asset market model (see Lo et al., 2004 for more discussions).

Despite the simplistic nature of mutual fund separation, we study its volume implications for several reasons. One compelling reason is the fact that mutual fund separation has become the workhorse of modern investment management. Although the assumptions of models such as the CAPM and ICAPM are known to be violated in practice, these models are viewed by many as a useful approximation for quantifying the trade-off between risk and expected return in financial markets. Thus, it seems natural to begin with such models in an investigation of trading activity in asset markets. Mutual fund separation may seem inadequate – indeed, some might say irrelevant – for modeling trading activity; nevertheless, it may yield an adequate approximation for quantifying the cross-sectional properties of trading volume. If it does not, then this suggests the possibility of important weaknesses in the theory, weaknesses that may have implications that extend beyond trading activity, e.g., preference restrictions, risk-sharing characteristics, asymmetric information, and liquidity. Of course, the virtue of such an approximation can only be judged by its empirical performance, which we examine in this chapter.

---

[24] Tkac (1999) also attempts to develop a dynamic equilibrium model, a multiasset extension of Dumas (1989), in which two-fund separation holds. However, her specification of the model is incomplete. Moreover, if it is in the spirit of Dumas (1989) in which risky assets take the form of investments in linear production technologies (as in Cox et al., 1985), the model has no volume implications for the risky assets since changes in investors' asset holdings involve changes in their own investment in production technologies, not in the trading of risky assets.

Another reason for focusing on mutual fund separation is that it can be an important benchmark in developing a more complete model of trading volume. The trading motives that mutual fund separation captures (such as portfolio rebalancing) may be simple and incomplete, but they are important, at least in the context of models such as the CAPM and ICAPM. Using mutual fund separation as a benchmark allows us to gauge how important other trading motives may be in understanding the different aspects of trading volume. For example, in studying the market reaction to corporate announcements and dividends, the factor model implied by mutual fund separation can be used as a "market model" in defining the abnormal trading activity that is associated with these events (Tkac, 1999 discusses this in the special case of two-fund separation).

Factors such as asymmetric information, idiosyncratic risks, transaction costs, and other forms of market imperfections are also likely to be relevant for determining the level and variability of trading activity. Each of these issues has been the focus of recent research, but only in the context of specialized models. To examine their importance in explaining volume, we need a more general and unified framework that can capture these factors. Unfortunately, such a model has not yet been developed.

For all these reasons, we examine the implications of mutual fund separation for trading activity in this section. The theoretical implications serve as valuable guides for our data construction and empirical analysis, but it is useful to keep their limitations in mind. We view this as the first step in developing a more complete understanding of trading and pricing in asset markets, and we hope to explore these other issues in future research (see also Section 6).

In Section 5.1, we consider the case of two-fund separation in which one fund is the riskless asset and the second fund is a portfolio of risky assets. In Section 5.2, we investigate the general case of $(K + 1)$-fund separation, one riskless fund, and K risky funds. Mutual fund separation with a riskless asset is often called *monetary separation* to distinguish it from the case without a riskless asset. We assume the existence of a riskless asset mainly to simplify the exposition, but for our purposes, this assumption entails no loss of generality.[25] Thus, in what follows, we consider only cases of monetary separation without further qualification. The analysis is mainly based on Lo and Wang (2000).

5.1. Two-Fund Separation

Without loss of generality, we normalize the total number of shares outstanding for each stock to one in this section, i.e., $N_j = 1, j = 1, \ldots, J$, and we begin by assuming two-fund separation, i.e., all investors invest in the same two mutual funds: the riskless asset and a stock fund. Market clearing requires that the stock fund is the "market" portfolio. Given

---

[25] For example, if two-fund separation holds, but both funds contain risky assets [as in Black et al. (1972) zero-beta CAPM], this is covered by our analysis of $(K + 1)$-fund separation in Section 5.2 for $K = 2$ (since two of the three funds are assumed to contain risky assets).

our normalization, the market portfolio S^M, measured in shares outstanding, is simply a vector of 1s: $S^M = [1 \cdots 1]^\top$. Two-fund separation implies that the stock holdings of any investor i at time t is given by

$$S_t^i = h_t^i S^M = h_t^i \begin{pmatrix} 1 \\ \vdots \\ 1 \end{pmatrix}, \quad i = 1, \ldots, I, \tag{5.1}$$

where h_t^i is the share of the market portfolio held by investor i (and $\sum_i h_t^i = 1$ for all t). His holding in stock j is then $S_{jt}^i = h_t^i, j = 1, \ldots, J$. Over time, investor i may wish to adjust his portfolio. If he does, he does so by trading only in the two funds (by the assumption of two-fund separation); hence he purchases or sells stocks in very specific proportions, as fractions of the market portfolio. His trading in stock j, normalized by shares outstanding, is: $S_{jt}^i - S_{jt-1}^i = h_t^i - h_{t-1}^i$, $i = 1, \ldots, I$. But this, in turn, implies $S_{jt}^i - S_{jt-1}^i = S_{j't}^i - S_{j't-1}^i, j, j' = 1, \ldots, J$. Thus, if two-fund separation holds, investor i's trading activity in each stock, normalized by shares outstanding, is identical across all stocks. This has an important implication for the turnover of stock j:

$$\tau_{jt} = \frac{1}{2} \sum_{i=1}^{I} \left| S_{jt}^i - S_{jt-1}^i \right| = \frac{1}{2} \sum_{i=1}^{I} \left| h_t^i - h_{t-1}^i \right|, \quad j = 1, \ldots, J, \tag{5.2}$$

which is given by the following proposition.

Proposition 1 *When two-fund separation holds, the turnover measures of all individual stocks are identical.*

Proposition 1 has strong implications for the turnover of the market portfolio. From the definition of Section 2.3, the turnover of the market portfolio is

$$\tau_t^{VW} \equiv \sum_{j=1}^{J} w_{jt}^{VW} \tau_{jt} = \tau_{jt}, \quad j = 1, \ldots, J.$$

The turnover of individual stocks is identical to the turnover of the market portfolio. This is not surprising given that individual stocks have identical values for turnover. Indeed, *all* portfolios of risky assets have the same turnover as individual stocks. For reasons that become apparent in Section 5.2, we can express the turnover of individual stocks as an exact linear one-factor model:

$$\tau_{jt} = b_j \tilde{F}_t, \quad j = 1, \ldots, J, \tag{5.3}$$

where $\tilde{F}_t = \tau_t^{VW}$ and $b_j = 1$.

Proposition 1 also implies that under two-fund separation, the share volume of individual stocks is proportional to the total number of shares outstanding, and dollar volume is proportional to market capitalization. Another implication is that each security's relative dollar volume is identical to its relative market capitalization for all t: $P_{jt}V_{jt}/(\sum_j P_{jt}V_{jt}) = P_{jt}N_j/(\sum_j P_{jt}N_j)$. This relation is tested in Tkac (1999). Tkac (1999) derives this result in the context of a continuous–time dynamic equilibrium model with a special form of heterogeneity in preferences, but it holds more generally for any model that implies two-fund separation.[26]

5.2. $(K + 1)$-Fund Separation

We now consider the more general case where $(K+1)$-fund separation holds. Let $S_{kt} = (S_{1t}^k, \ldots, S_{Jt}^k)^\top, k = 1, \ldots, K$, denote the K-separating stock funds, where the separating funds are expressed in terms of the number of shares of their component stocks. The stock holdings of any investor i are given by

$$
\begin{pmatrix} S_{1t}^i \\ \vdots \\ S_{Jt}^i \end{pmatrix} = \sum_{k=1}^K h_{kt}^i S_t^k, \quad i = 1, \ldots, I. \tag{5.4}
$$

In particular, his holding in stock j is $S_{jt}^i = \sum_{k=1}^K h_{kt}^i S_{jt}^k$. Therefore, the turnover of stock j at time t is

$$
\tau_{jt} = \frac{1}{2}\sum_{i=1}^I \left| S_{jt}^i - S_{jt-1}^i \right| = \frac{1}{2}\sum_{i=1}^I \left| \sum_{k=1}^K \left(h_{kt}^i S_{jt}^k - h_{kt-1}^i S_{jt}^k \right) \right|, \quad j = 1, \ldots, J. \tag{5.5}
$$

We now impose the following assumption on the separating stock funds:

Assumption 1 *The separating stock funds, S_t^k, $k = 1, \ldots, K$, are constant over time.*

Given that, in equilibrium, $\sum_{i=1}^I S_{i,t} = S_M$ for all t, we have

$$
\sum_{k=1}^K \left(\sum_{i=1}^I h_{kt}^i \right) S^k = S^M.
$$

---

[26]To see this, substitute $\tau_t N_j$ for V_{jt} in the numerator and denominator of the left side of the equation and observe that τ_t is constant over j, hence it can be factored out of the summation and cancelled.

Therefore, without loss of generality, we can assume that the market portfolio S_M is one of the separating stock funds, which we label as the first fund. Following Merton (1973), we call the remaining stock funds *hedging* portfolios.[27]

To simplify notation, we define $\Delta h_{kt}^i \equiv h_{kt}^i - h_{kt-1}^i$ as the change in investor i's holding of fund k from $t-1$ to t. In addition, we assume that the amount of trading in the hedging portfolios is small for all investors.

Assumption 2 *For $k = 1, \ldots, K$, and $i = 1, \ldots, I$, $\Delta h_{1t}^1 \equiv \tilde{h}_{1t}^1$ and $\Delta h_{kt}^i \equiv \lambda \tilde{h}_{kt}^i$ $(k \neq 1)$, where $|\tilde{h}_{kt}^i| \leq H < \infty$, $0 < \lambda \ll 1$ and $\tilde{h}_{1t}^i, \tilde{h}_{2t}^i, \ldots, \tilde{h}_{Jt}^i$ have a continuous joint probability density.*

We then have the following result (see the Appendix in Lo and Wang, 2000, for the proof):

Lemma 1 *Under Assumptions 1 and 2, the turnover of stock j at time t can be approximated by*

$$\tau_{jt} \approx \frac{1}{2} \sum_{i=1}^{I} |\Delta h_{1t}^i| + \frac{1}{2} \sum_{k=2}^{K} \left[\sum_{i=1}^{I} \text{sgn}(\Delta h_{1t}^i) \Delta h_{kt}^i \right] S_j^k, \quad j = 1, \ldots, J \qquad (5.6)$$

and the nth absolute moment of the approximation error is $o(\lambda^n)$.

Now define the following "factors":

$$\tilde{F}_{1t} \equiv \frac{1}{2} \sum_{i=1}^{I} |\Delta h_{1t}^i|$$

$$\tilde{F}_{kt} \equiv \frac{1}{2} \sum_{i=1}^{I} \text{sgn}(\Delta h_{1t}^i) \Delta h_{kt}^i, \quad k = 2, \ldots, K.$$

Then the turnover of each stock j can be represented by an approximate K-factor model

$$\tau_{jt} = \tilde{F}_{1t} + \sum_{k=2}^{K} S_j^k \tilde{F}_{kt} + o(\lambda), \quad j = 1, \ldots, J. \qquad (5.7)$$

In summary, we have

---

[27] In addition, we can assume that all the separating stock funds are mutually orthogonal, i.e., $S^{k\top} S^{k'} = 0, k = 1, \ldots, K, k' = 1, \ldots, K$, $k \neq k'$. In particular, $S^{M\top} S^k = \sum_{j=1}^{J} S_j^k = 0, k = 2, \ldots, K$, hence the total number of shares in each of the hedging portfolios sum to zero under our normalization. For this particular choice of the separating funds, h_{kt}^i has the simple interpretation that it is the projection coefficient of S_t^i on S^k. Moreover, $\sum_{i=1}^{I} h_{1t}^i = 1$ and $\sum_{i=1}^{I} h_{kt}^i = 0, k = 2, \ldots, K$.

Proposition 2 *Suppose that the riskless security, the market portfolio, and $K-1$ constant hedging portfolios are separating funds, and the amount of trading in the hedging portfolios is small. Then the turnover of each stock has an approximate K-factor structure. Moreover, the loading of each stock on the kth factor gives its share weight in the kth separating fund.*

5.3. Empirical Tests of $(K+1)$-Fund Separation

Since two-fund and $(K+1)$-fund separation imply an approximately linear factor structure for turnover, we can investigate these two possibilities by using principal components analysis to decompose the covariance matrix of turnover (see Muirhead, 1982, for an exposition of principal components analysis). If turnover is driven by a linear K-factor model, the first K principal components should explain most of the time-series variation in turnover. More formally, if

$$\tau_{jt} = \alpha_j + \delta_1 F_{1t} + \cdots + \delta_K F_{Kt} + \varepsilon_{jt}, \tag{5.8}$$

where $E[\varepsilon_{jt}\varepsilon_{j't}] = 0$ for any $j \neq j'$, then the covariance matrix Σ of the vector $\tau_t \equiv [\tau_{1t} \ldots \tau_{Jt}]^\top$ can be expressed as

$$\text{Var}[\tau_t] \equiv \Sigma = \eta\Theta\eta^\top \tag{5.9}$$

$$\Theta = \begin{pmatrix} \theta_1 & 0 & \cdots & 0 \\ 0 & \theta_2 & & 0 \\ \vdots & & \ddots & \vdots \\ 0 & \cdots & 0 & \theta_N \end{pmatrix}, \tag{5.10}$$

where Θ contains the eigenvalues of Σ along its diagonal and η is the matrix of corresponding eigenvectors. Since Σ is a covariance matrix, it is positive semidefinite, hence all the eigenvalues are nonnegative. When normalized to sum to one, each eigenvalue can be interpreted as the fraction of the total variance of turnover attributable to the corresponding principal component. If (5.8) holds, it can be shown that as the size N of the cross section increases without bound, exactly K normalized eigenvalues of Σ approach positive finite limits, and the remaining $N-K$ eigenvalues approach 0 (see, e.g., Chamberlain, 1983; Chamberlain and Rothschild, 1983). Therefore, the plausibility of (5.8) and the value of K can be gauged by examining the magnitudes of the eigenvalues of Σ.

The only obstacle is the fact that the covariance matrix Σ must be estimated; hence, we encounter the well-known problem that the standard estimator

$$\widehat{\Sigma} \equiv \frac{1}{T}\sum_{t=1}^{T}(\tau_t - \bar{\tau})(\tau_t - \bar{\tau})^\top$$

is singular if the number of securities J in the cross section is larger than the number of time-series observations T.[28] Since J is typically much larger than T, for a five-year subperiod T is generally 261 weeks and J is typically well over 2000, we must limit our attention to a smaller subset of stocks. We do this by following the common practice of forming a small number of portfolios (see Campbell et al., 1997, chapter 5), sorted by turnover beta to maximize the dispersion of turnover beta among the portfolios.[29] In particular, within each five-year subperiod, we form 10 turnover-beta-sorted portfolios using betas estimated from the previous five-year subperiod, estimate the covariance matrix $\widehat{\Sigma}$ using 261 time-series observations, and perform a principal-components decomposition on $\widehat{\Sigma}$. For purposes of comparison and interpretation, we perform a parallel analysis for returns using 10 return-beta-sorted portfolios. The results are reported in Table 17.13.

Table 17.13 contains the principal components decomposition for portfolios sorted on out-of-sample betas, where the betas are estimated in two ways: relative to value-weighted indexes (τ^{VW} and R^{VW}) and equal-weighted indexes (τ^{EW} and R^{EW}).[30] The first principal component typically explains between 70 and 85% of the variation in turnover, and the first two principal components explain almost all the variations. For example, the upper-left subpanel of Table 17.13 shows that in the second five-year subperiod (1967–1971), 85.1% of the variation in the turnover of turnover-beta-sorted portfolios (using turnover betas relative to the value-weighted turnover index) is captured by the first principal component and 93.6% is captured by the first two principal components. Although using betas computed with value-weighted instead of equal-weighted indexes generally yields smaller eigenvalues for the first principal component (and therefore larger values for the remaining principal components) for both turnover and returns, the differences are typically not large.

The importance of the second principal component grows steadily through time for the value-weighted case, reaching a peak of 15.6% in the last subperiod, and the first two principal components account for 87.3% of the variation in turnover in the last subperiod. This is roughly comparable with the return portfolios sorted on value-weighted return betas – the first principal component is by far the most important, and

---

[28] Singularity by itself does not pose any problems for the computation of eigenvalues – this follows from the singular-value decomposition theorem – but it does have implications for the statistical properties of estimated eigenvalues. In some preliminary Monte Carlo experiments, we have found that the eigenvalues of a singular estimator of a positive-definite covariance matrix can be severely biased. We thank Bob Korajczyk and Bruce Lehmann for bringing some of these issues to our attention and plan to investigate them more thoroughly in ongoing research.

[29] Our desire to maximize the dispersion of turnover beta is motivated by the same logic used in Black et al. (1972): a more dispersed sample provides a more powerful test of a cross-sectional relationship driven by the sorting characteristic. This motivation should not be taken literally in our context because the theoretical implications of Section 5.1 need not imply a prominent role for turnover beta (indeed, in the case of two-fund separation, there is no cross-sectional variation in turnover betas!). However, given the factor structure implied by $(K+1)$-fund separation (see Section 5.2), sorting by turnover betas seems appropriate.

[30] In particular, the portfolios in a given period are formed by ranking on betas estimated in the immediately preceding subperiod, e.g., the 1992–1996 portfolios were created by sorting on betas estimated in the 1987–1991 subperiod, hence the first subperiod in Table 17.13 begins in 1967, not in 1962.

Table 17.13 Eigenvalues $\widehat{\theta}_i$, $i = 1, \ldots, 10$ of the covariance matrix of 10 out-of-sample-beta-sorted portfolios of weekly turnover and returns of NYSE and AMEX ordinary common shares (CRSP share codes 10 and 11, excluding 37 stocks containing Z-errors in reported volume), in percentages (where the eigenvalues are normalized to sum to 100%), for subperiods of the sample period from July 1962 to December 1996

Top panel (VW)

	Turnover-beta-sorted turnover portfolios (τ^{VW})										Period	Return-beta-sorted return portfolios (R^{VW})									
	θ_1	θ_2	θ_3	θ_4	θ_5	θ_6	θ_7	θ_8	θ_9	θ_{10}		θ_1	θ_2	θ_3	θ_4	θ_5	θ_6	θ_7	θ_8	θ_9	θ_{10}
	85.1	8.5	3.6	1.4	0.8	0.3	0.2	0.1	0.0	0.0	1967–1971	85.7	5.9	2.0	1.4	1.4	1.1	0.8	0.7	0.5	0.4
	(7.5)	(0.7)	(0.3)	(0.1)	(0.1)	(0.0)	(0.0)	(0.0)	(0.0)	(0.0)		(7.5)	(0.5)	(0.2)	(0.1)	(0.1)	(0.1)	(0.1)	(0.1)	(0.0)	(0.0)
	82.8	7.3	4.9	2.0	1.4	0.8	0.5	0.2	0.1	0.1	1972–1976	90.0	3.8	1.8	1.0	0.9	0.7	0.6	0.6	0.4	0.3
	(7.3)	(0.6)	(0.4)	(0.2)	(0.1)	(0.1)	(0.0)	(0.0)	(0.0)	(0.0)		(7.9)	(0.3)	(0.2)	(0.1)	(0.1)	(0.1)	(0.1)	(0.0)	(0.0)	(0.0)
	83.6	8.6	2.3	2.0	1.2	0.8	0.6	0.4	0.4	0.1	1977–1981	85.4	4.8	4.3	1.4	1.3	0.9	0.6	0.5	0.4	0.3
	(7.3)	(0.8)	(0.2)	(0.2)	(0.1)	(0.1)	(0.1)	(0.0)	(0.0)	(0.0)		(7.5)	(0.4)	(0.4)	(0.1)	(0.1)	(0.1)	(0.1)	(0.0)	(0.0)	(0.0)
	78.9	7.9	3.6	2.9	2.4	1.4	1.3	0.8	0.5	0.4	1982–1986	86.6	6.1	2.4	1.6	1.0	0.6	0.5	0.5	0.4	0.3
	(6.9)	(0.7)	(0.3)	(0.3)	(0.2)	(0.1)	(0.1)	(0.1)	(0.0)	(0.0)		(7.6)	(0.5)	(0.2)	(0.1)	(0.1)	(0.1)	(0.0)	(0.0)	(0.0)	(0.0)
	80.1	6.2	5.2	2.4	1.6	1.3	1.0	1.0	0.8	0.5	1987–1991	91.6	2.9	1.7	1.1	0.7	0.6	0.6	0.4	0.3	0.2
	(7.0)	(0.5)	(0.5)	(0.2)	(0.1)	(0.1)	(0.1)	(0.1)	(0.1)	(0.0)		(8.0)	(0.3)	(0.1)	(0.1)	(0.1)	(0.1)	(0.0)	(0.0)	(0.0)	(0.0)
	71.7	15.6	4.5	2.9	1.8	1.2	0.9	0.8	0.5	0.3	1992–1996	72.4	11.6	4.4	3.5	2.2	1.8	1.5	1.1	0.8	0.6
	(6.3)	(1.4)	(0.4)	(0.3)	(0.2)	(0.1)	(0.1)	(0.1)	(0.0)	(0.0)		(6.3)	(1.0)	(0.4)	(0.3)	(0.2)	(0.2)	(0.1)	(0.1)	(0.1)	(0.1)

Bottom panel (EW)

	Turnover-beta-sorted turnover portfolios (τ^{EW})										Period	Return-beta-sorted return portfolios (R^{EW})									
	θ_1	θ_2	θ_3	θ_4	θ_5	θ_6	θ_7	θ_8	θ_9	θ_{10}		θ_1	θ_2	θ_3	θ_4	θ_5	θ_6	θ_7	θ_8	θ_9	θ_{10}
	86.8	7.5	3.0	1.3	0.6	0.5	0.2	0.1	0.1	0.0	1967–1971	87.8	4.3	2.2	1.5	1.0	0.9	0.8	0.5	0.5	0.5
	(7.6)	(0.7)	(0.3)	(0.1)	(0.0)	(0.0)	(0.0)	(0.0)	(0.0)	(0.0)		(7.7)	(0.4)	(0.2)	(0.1)	(0.1)	(0.1)	(0.1)	(0.0)	(0.0)	(0.0)
	82.8	6.0	5.4	2.9	1.2	1.0	0.4	0.2	0.1	0.0	1972–1976	91.6	4.1	0.9	0.8	0.6	0.5	0.4	0.4	0.3	0.3
	(7.3)	(0.5)	(0.5)	(0.3)	(0.1)	(0.1)	(0.0)	(0.0)	(0.0)	(0.0)		(8.0)	(0.4)	(0.1)	(0.1)	(0.0)	(0.0)	(0.0)	(0.0)	(0.0)	(0.0)
	79.1	8.5	5.4	2.8	1.4	1.0	0.7	0.6	0.3	0.1	1977–1981	91.5	3.9	1.4	0.8	0.6	0.5	0.4	0.3	0.3	0.3
	(6.9)	(0.7)	(0.5)	(0.2)	(0.1)	(0.1)	(0.1)	(0.0)	(0.0)	(0.0)		(8.0)	(0.3)	(0.1)	(0.1)	(0.1)	(0.0)	(0.0)	(0.0)	(0.0)	(0.0)
	78.0	10.4	3.1	2.3	2.0	1.3	1.3	0.8	0.6	0.4	1982–1986	88.9	4.4	2.3	1.3	0.7	0.7	0.6	0.5	0.4	0.4
	(6.8)	(0.9)	(0.3)	(0.2)	(0.2)	(0.1)	(0.1)	(0.1)	(0.1)	(0.0)		(7.8)	(0.4)	(0.2)	(0.1)	(0.1)	(0.1)	(0.1)	(0.0)	(0.0)	(0.0)
	82.5	4.8	3.2	2.4	2.0	1.4	1.3	0.9	0.9	0.6	1987–1991	92.7	3.0	1.2	0.7	0.7	0.4	0.4	0.4	0.3	0.2
	(7.2)	(0.4)	(0.3)	(0.2)	(0.2)	(0.1)	(0.1)	(0.1)	(0.1)	(0.1)		(8.1)	(0.3)	(0.1)	(0.1)	(0.1)	(0.0)	(0.0)	(0.0)	(0.0)	(0.0)
	79.0	8.5	4.9	2.6	1.5	1.1	0.9	0.6	0.5	0.4	1992–1996	76.8	10.4	3.9	2.7	1.9	1.1	1.0	0.9	0.7	0.6
	(6.9)	(0.7)	(0.4)	(0.2)	(0.1)	(0.1)	(0.1)	(0.1)	(0.0)	(0.0)		(6.7)	(0.9)	(0.3)	(0.2)	(0.2)	(0.1)	(0.1)	(0.1)	(0.1)	(0.1)

Turnover portfolios are sorted by out-of-sample turnover betas and return portfolios are sorted by out-of-sample return betas, where the symbols "τ^{VW}" and "R^{VW}" indicate that the betas are computed relative to value-weighted indexes, and "τ^{EW}" and "R^{EW}" indicate that they are computed relative to equal-weighted indexes. Standard errors for the normalized eigenvalues are given in parentheses and are calculated under the assumption of i.i.d. normality.

the importance of the of the second principal component is most pronounced in the last subperiod. However, the lower left subpanel of Table 17.13 shows that for turnover portfolios sorted by betas computed against equal-weighted indexes, the second principal component explains approximately the same variation in turnover, varying between 6.0 and 10.4% across the six subperiods.

Of course, one possible explanation for the dominance of the first principal component is the existence of a time trend in turnover. Despite the fact that we have limited our analysis to five-year subperiods, within each subperiod there is a certain drift in turnover; might this account for the first principal component? To investigate this conjecture, we perform eigenvalue decompositions for the covariance matrices of the *first differences* of turnover for the 10 turnover portfolios.

These results are reported in Table 17.14 and are consistent with those in Table 17.13: the first principal component is still the most important, explaining between 60 and 88% of the variation in the first differences of turnover. The second principal component is typically responsible for another 5–20%. In one case, in-sample sorting on betas relative to the equal-weighted index during 1987–1991, the third principal component accounts for an additional 10%. These figures suggest that the trend in turnover is unlikely to be the source of the dominant first principal component.

In summary, the results of Tables 17.13 and 17.14 indicate that a one-factor model for turnover is a reasonable approximation, at least in the case of turnover-beta-sorted portfolios, and that a two-factor model captures well over 90% of the time-series variation in turnover. This lends some support to the practice of estimating "abnormal" volume by using an event-study style "market model," e.g., Bamber (1986), Jain and Joh (1988), Lakonishok and Smidt (1986), Morse (1980), Richardson et al. (1986), Stickel and Verrecchia (1994), and Tkac (1999).

As compelling as these empirical results are, several qualifications should be kept in mind. First, we have provided little statistical inference for our principal components decomposition. In particular, the asymptotic standard errors reported in Tables 17.13 and 17.14 were computed under the assumption of IID Gaussian data, hardly appropriate for weekly U.S. stock returns and even less convincing for turnover (see Muirhead, 1982, Chapter 9, for further details). Perhaps nonparametric methods such as the moving-block bootstrap can provide better indications of the statistical significance of our estimated eigenvalues. Monte Carlo simulations should also be conducted to check the finite-sample properties of our estimators.

More importantly, the economic interpretation of the first two principal components or, alternatively, identifying the specific factors is a challenging issue that principal components cannot resolve. More structure must be imposed on the data – in particular, an intertemporal model of trading – to obtain a better understanding for the sources of turnover variation, and we present such structure in the next section.

Table 17.14   Eigenvalues $\widehat{\theta}_i$, $i = 1, \ldots, 10$ of the covariance matrix of the first-differences of the weekly turnover of 10 out-of-sample-beta-sorted portfolios of NYSE and AMEX ordinary common shares (CRSP share codes 10 and 11, excluding 37 stocks containing Z-errors in reported volume), in percentages (where the eigenvalues are normalized to sum to 100%), for subperiods of the sample period from July 1962 to December 1996. Turnover betas are calculated in two ways: with respect to a value-weighted turnover index (τ^{VW}) and an equal-weighted turnover index (τ^{EW}). Standard errors for the normalized eigenvalues are given in parentheses and are calculated under the assumption of i.i.d. normality

Period	$\widehat{\theta}_1$	$\widehat{\theta}_2$	$\widehat{\theta}_3$	$\widehat{\theta}_4$	$\widehat{\theta}_5$	$\widehat{\theta}_6$	$\widehat{\theta}_7$	$\widehat{\theta}_8$	$\widehat{\theta}_9$	$\widehat{\theta}_{10}$
Out-of-sample turnover-beta-sorted turnover-differences portfolios (τ^{VW})										
1967–1971	82.6	7.1	5.1	2.0	1.6	0.8	0.5	0.1	0.1	0.1
	(7.2)	(0.6)	(0.5)	(0.2)	(0.1)	(0.1)	(0.0)	(0.0)	(0.0)	(0.0)
1972–1976	81.2	6.8	4.7	2.8	2.0	1.0	0.9	0.4	0.2	0.1
	(7.1)	(0.6)	(0.4)	(0.2)	(0.2)	(0.1)	(0.1)	(0.0)	(0.0)	(0.0)
1977–1981	85.2	4.5	2.9	2.6	1.6	1.2	0.8	0.5	0.5	0.2
	(7.5)	(0.4)	(0.3)	(0.2)	(0.1)	(0.1)	(0.1)	(0.0)	(0.0)	(0.0)
1982–1986	81.3	5.1	3.5	2.7	2.2	1.7	1.3	0.9	0.7	0.6
	(7.1)	(0.4)	(0.3)	(0.2)	(0.2)	(0.2)	(0.1)	(0.1)	(0.1)	(0.1)
1987–1991	73.1	10.9	4.1	3.0	2.2	1.7	1.6	1.4	1.1	0.9
	(6.4)	(1.0)	(0.4)	(0.3)	(0.2)	(0.2)	(0.1)	(0.1)	(0.1)	(0.1)
1992–1996	78.4	8.6	4.0	2.8	2.1	1.2	1.0	0.9	0.6	0.4
	(6.9)	(0.8)	(0.4)	(0.2)	(0.2)	(0.1)	(0.1)	(0.1)	(0.0)	(0.0)
Out-of-sample turnover-beta-sorted turnover-differences portfolios (τ^{EW})										
1967–1971	82.2	8.0	4.5	2.3	1.4	0.7	0.4	0.3	0.1	0.0
	(7.2)	(0.7)	(0.4)	(0.2)	(0.1)	(0.1)	(0.0)	(0.0)	(0.0)	(0.0)
1972–1976	79.3	7.5	4.8	4.0	1.9	1.3	0.6	0.4	0.2	0.1
	(7.0)	(0.7)	(0.4)	(0.4)	(0.2)	(0.1)	(0.1)	(0.0)	(0.0)	(0.0)
1977–1981	80.3	5.3	4.8	3.8	2.0	1.4	1.2	0.7	0.5	0.2
	(7.0)	(0.5)	(0.4)	(0.3)	(0.2)	(0.1)	(0.1)	(0.1)	(0.0)	(0.0)
1982–1986	82.6	5.0	3.0	2.6	2.0	1.7	1.1	0.9	0.7	0.4
	(7.3)	(0.4)	(0.3)	(0.2)	(0.2)	(0.1)	(0.1)	(0.1)	(0.1)	(0.0)
1987–1991	77.2	5.5	4.3	2.7	2.5	2.3	1.8	1.6	1.2	1.0
	(6.8)	(0.5)	(0.4)	(0.2)	(0.2)	(0.2)	(0.2)	(0.1)	(0.1)	(0.1)
1992–1996	80.4	6.4	4.6	2.6	1.7	1.4	1.1	0.7	0.5	0.4
	(7.1)	(0.6)	(0.4)	(0.2)	(0.1)	(0.1)	(0.1)	(0.1)	(0.0)	(0.0)

6. VOLUME IMPLICATIONS OF INTERTEMPORAL ASSET PRICING MODELS

In this section, we analyze the volume implications of intertemporal asset pricing models and how volume is related to returns. We first develop an intertemporal equilibrium model of stock trading and pricing with multiple assets and heterogeneous investors. We then derive the behavior of volume and returns. We show that both volume and returns are driven by the underlying risks of the economy. The results presented here are from Lo and Wang (2006).

6.1. An ICAPM

Since our purpose is to draw qualitative implications on the joint behavior of return and volume, the model is kept as parsimonious as possible. Several generalizations of the model are discussed in Lo and Wang (2006).

6.1.1. The Economy

We consider an economy defined on a set of discrete dates: $t = 0, 1, 2, \ldots$. There are J risky stocks, each paying a stream of dividends over time. As before, D_{jt} denote the dividend of stock j at date $t, j = 1, \ldots, J$, and $D_t \equiv [D_{1t} \ldots D_{Jt}]$ denote the column vector of dividends. Without loss of generality, in this section, we assume that the total number of shares outstanding is one for each stock.

A stock portfolio can be expressed in terms of its shares of each stock, denoted by $S \equiv [S_1 \ldots S_J]$, where S_j is the number of stock j shares in the portfolio ($j = 1, \ldots, J$). A portfolio of particular importance is the market portfolio, denoted by S^M, which is given by

$$S^M = \iota \qquad (6.1)$$

where ι is a vector of 1s with rank J. $D_{Mt} \equiv \iota^\top D_t$ gives the dividend of the market portfolio, which is the aggregate dividend.

In addition to the stocks, there is also a risk-free bond that yields a constant, positive interest r per time period.

There are I investors in the economy. Each investor is endowed with equal shares of the stocks and no bond. Every period, investor $i, i = 1, \ldots, I$, maximizes his expected utility of the following form

$$\mathrm{E}_t\left[-\mathrm{e}^{-W^i_{t+1}-(\lambda_X X_t+\lambda_Y Y^i_t)D_{Mt+1}-\lambda_Z(1+Z^i_t)X_{t+1}}\right], \qquad (6.2)$$

where W^i_{t+1} is investor is wealth next period, X_t, Y^i_t, Z^i_t are three one-dimensional state variables, and $\lambda_X, \lambda_Y, \lambda_Z$ are nonnegative constants. Apparently, the utility function in (6.2) is state-dependent. We further assume

$$\sum_{i=1}^{I} Y^i_t = \sum_{i=1}^{I} Z^i_t = 0, \qquad (6.3)$$

where $t = 0, 1, \ldots$.

For simplicity, we assume that all the exogenous shocks, $D_t, X_t, \{Y_t^i, Z_t^i, i = 1, \ldots, I\}$, are i.i.d. over time with zero means. For tractability, we further assume that D_{t+1} and X_{t+1} are jointly normally distributed:

$$u_{t+1} \equiv \begin{pmatrix} D_{t+1} \\ X_{t+1} \end{pmatrix} \overset{d}{\sim} N(\cdot, \sigma), \quad \text{where} \quad \sigma = \begin{pmatrix} \sigma_{DD} & \sigma_{DX} \\ \sigma_{XD} & \sigma_{XX} \end{pmatrix}. \tag{6.4}$$

Without loss of generality, σ_{DD} is assumed to be positive definite.

Our model has several features that might seem unusual. One feature of the model is that investors are assumed to have a myopic, but state-dependent utility function in (6.2). The purpose for using this utility function is to capture the dynamic nature of the investment problem without explicitly solving a dynamic optimization problem. The state dependence of the utility function is assumed to have the following properties. The marginal utility of wealth depends on the dividend of the market portfolio (the aggregate dividend), as reflected in the second term in the exponential of the utility function. When the aggregate dividend goes up, the marginal utility of wealth goes down. The marginal utility of wealth also depends on future state variables, in particular X_{t+1}, as reflected in the third term in the exponential of the utility function. This utility function can be interpreted as the equivalent of a value function from an appropriately specified dynamic optimization problem (see, e.g., Wang, 1994; Lo and Wang, 2003). More discussion is given in Lo and Wang (2006) on this point.

Another feature of the model is the i.i.d. assumption for the state variables. This might leave the impression that the model is effectively static. This impression, however, is false since the state-dependence of investors' utility function introduces important dynamics over time. We can allow richer dynamics for the state variables without changing the main properties of the model.

The particular form of the utility function and the normality of distribution for the state variables are assumed for tractability. These assumptions are restrictive, but we hope with some confidence that the qualitative predictions of the model that we explore in this chapter are not sensitive to these assumptions.

In the model, we also assumed an exogenous interest rate for the bond without requiring the bond market to clear. This is a modeling choice we have made to simplify our analysis and to focus on the stock market. As will become clear later, changes in the interest rate are not important for the issues we examine in this chapter.

6.1.2. Equilibrium

Let $P_t \equiv [P_{1t} \ldots P_{Jt}]$ and $S_t^i \equiv [S_{1t}^i; \ldots; S_{Jt}^i]$ be the (column) vectors of (ex-dividend) stock prices and investor i's stock holdings, respectively. We now derive the equilibrium of the economy.

Definition 4 *An equilibrium is given by a price process* $\{P_t : t = 0, 1, \ldots\}$ *and the investors' stock positions* $\{S_t^i : i = 1, \ldots, I; t = 0, 1, \ldots\}$ *such that*

1. S_t^i *solves investor i's optimization problem:*

$$S_t^i = \arg \quad \max \quad \mathrm{E}\left[-e^{-W_{t+1}^i - (\lambda_X X_t + \lambda_Y Y_t^i) D M_{t+1} - \lambda_Z (1 + Z_t^i) X_{t+1}}\right]$$

$$\text{s. t.} \quad W_{t+1}^i = W_t^i + S_t^{i\prime}[D_{t+1} + P_{t+1} - (1+r)P_t]$$

(6.5)

2. *stock market clears:*

$$\sum_{i=1}^{i} S_t^i = \iota.$$

(6.6)

The above definition of equilibrium is standard, except that the bond market does not clear here. As discussed earlier, the interest rate is given exogenously and there is an elastic supply of bonds at that rate.

For $t = 0, 1, \ldots$, let Q_{t+1} denote the vector of excess dollar returns on the stocks:

$$Q_{t+1} \equiv D_{t+1} + P_{t+1} - (1+r)P_t.$$

(6.7)

Thus, $Q_{jt+1} = D_{jt+1} + P_{jt+1} - (1+r)P_{jt}$ gives the dollar return on one share of stock j in excess of its financing cost for period $t + 1$. For the remainder of the chapter, we simply refer to Q_{jt+1} as the dollar return of stock j, omitting the qualifier "excess." Dollar return Q_{jt+1} differs from the conventional (excess) return measure R_{jt+1}, which is the dollar return normalized by the share price: $R_{jt+1} \equiv Q_{jt+1}/P_{jt}$. We refer to R_{jt+1} simply as the return on stock j in period $t + 1$.

We can now state the solution to the equilibrium in the following theorem:

Theorem 1 *The economy defined above has a unique linear equilibrium in which*

$$P_t = -a - bX_t$$

(6.8)

and

$$S_t^i = \left(I^{-1} - \lambda_Y Y_t^i\right)\iota - \left(\lambda_Z Z_t^i + \lambda_Y (b'\iota) Y_t^i\right)\left(\sigma_{QQ}\right)^{-1}\sigma_{QX},$$

(6.9)

where

$$\sigma_{QQ} = \sigma_{DD} - b\sigma_{XD} - \sigma_{DX}b' + \sigma_X^2 b b'$$

$$\sigma_{QX} = \sigma_{DX} - \sigma_X^2 b$$

$$a = \frac{1}{r}(\bar{\alpha}\sigma_{QQ}\iota + \lambda_Z\sigma_{QX}$$

$$b = \lambda_X[(1+r) + \lambda_Z\sigma_{XD}\iota)]^{-1}\sigma_{DD}\iota$$

and $\bar{a} = 1/I$.

The nature of the equilibrium is intuitive. In our model, an investor's utility function depends not only on his wealth, but also on the stock payoffs directly. In other words, even though he holds no stocks, his utility fluctuates with the payoff of the stocks. Such a "market spirit" affects his demand for the stocks, in addition to the usual factors such as the stocks' expected returns. The market spirit of investor i is measured by $(\lambda_X X_t + \lambda_Y Y_t^i)$. When $(\lambda_X X_t + \lambda_Z Y_t^i)$ is positive, investor i extracts positive utility when the aggregate stock payoff is high. Such a positive "attachment" to the market makes holding stocks less attractive to him. When $(\lambda_X X_t + \lambda_Y Y_t^i)$ is negative, he has a negative "attachment" to the market, which makes holding stocks more attractive. Such a market spirit at the aggregate level, which is captured by X_t, affects the aggregate stock demand, which in turn affects their equilibrium prices. Given the particular form of the utility function, X_t affects the equilibrium stock prices linearly. The idiosyncratic differences among investors in their market spirit, which are captured by Y_t^i, offset each other at the aggregate level, thus do not affect the equilibrium stock prices. However, they do affect individual investors' stock holdings. As the first term of (6.9) shows, investors with positive Y_t^is hold less stocks (they are already happy by just "watching" the stocks pay off).

Since the aggregate utility variable X_t is driving the stock prices, it is also driving the stock returns. In fact, the expected returns on the stocks are changing with X_t (see the discussion in the next section). The form of the utility function further states that the investors' utility function directly depends on X_t, which fully characterizes the investment opportunities investors face. Such a dependence endogenously arises when investors optimize dynamically. In our setting, however, we assume that investors optimize myopically, but insert such a dependence directly into the utility function. This dependence induces investors to care about future investment opportunities when they choose their portfolios. In particular, they prefer those portfolios whose returns can help them to smooth fluctuations in their utility due to changes in investment opportunities. Such a preference gives rise to the hedging component in their asset demand, which is captured by the second term in (6.9).

6.2. The Behavior of Returns and Volume

Given the intertemporal CAPM defined above, we can derive its implications on the behavior of return and volume. For the stocks, their dollar return vector can be reexpressed as follows:

$$Q_{t+1} = ra + (1+r)bX_t + \tilde{Q}_{t+1}, \tag{6.10}$$

where $\tilde{Q}_{t+1} \equiv D_{t+1} - bZ_{t+1}$ denotes the vector of unexpected dollar returns on the stocks, which are i.i.d. over time with zero mean. Equation (6.10) shows that the expected returns on the stocks change over time. In particular, they are driven by a single-state variable X_t.

The investors' stock holdings can be expressed in the following form:

$$S_t^i = h_{Mt}^i \iota + h_{Ht}^i S^H \quad \forall \, i = 1, 2, \ldots, I, \tag{6.11}$$

where $h_{Mt}^i \equiv I^{-1} - \lambda_Y Y_t^i, h_{Ht}^i \equiv \lambda_Z(b'\iota) Y_t^i - \lambda_Y Z_t^i$, and

$$S^H \equiv \left(\sigma_{QQ}\right)^{-1} \sigma_{QX}. \tag{6.12}$$

Equation (6.11) simply states that three-fund separation holds for the investors' stock portfolios. That is, all investors' portfolios can be viewed as investments in three common funds: the risk-free asset and two stock funds. The two stock funds are the market portfolio, ι, and the hedging portfolio, S_H. Moreover, in our current model, these two portfolios, expressed in terms of stock shares, are constant over time.

The particular structure of the returns and the investors' portfolios lead to several interesting predictions about the behavior of volume and returns. We present these predictions through a set of propositions.

6.2.1. The Cross Section of Volume

Given that investors only hold and trade in two stock funds, the results obtained in Section 5 apply here. The turnover of stock j is given by

$$\tau_{jt} \equiv \frac{1}{2} \sum_{i=1}^{I} \left| \left(h_{Mt}^i - h_{Mt-1}^i\right) + \left(h_{Ht}^i - h_{Ht-1}^i\right) S_j^H \right| \quad \forall \, j = 1, \ldots, J. \tag{6.13}$$

Let τ_t denote the vector of turnover for all stocks. We have the following proposition on the cross section of volume, which follows from Proposition 2:

Proposition 3 *When investors' trading in the hedging portfolio is small relative to their trading in the market portfolio, the two-fund separation in their stock holdings leads to an approximate two-factor structure for stock turnover:*

$$\tau_t \approx \iota F_{Mt} + S^H F_{Ht}, \tag{6.14}$$

where

$$F_{Mt} = \frac{1}{2} \sum_{i=1}^{I} \left| h_{Mt}^i - h_{Mt-1}^i \right| \quad and \quad F_{Ht} = \frac{1}{2} \sum_{i=1}^{I} \mathrm{sgn}\left(h_{Mt}^i - h_{Mt-1}^i\right) \left(h_{Ht}^i - h_{Ht-1}^i\right).$$

In the special case when two-fund separation holds (when $X_t = 0 \; \forall \, t$), turnover would have an exact one-factor structure, $\tau_t = \iota F_{Mt}$.

In the general case when three–fund separation holds, turnover has an approximate two–factor structure as given in (6.14). It is important to note that the loading of stock j's turnover on the second factor is proportional to its share weight in the hedging portfolio. Thus, empirically if we can identify the two common factors, F_{Mt} and F_{Ht}, the stocks' loadings on the second factor allow us to identify the hedging portfolio. In our empirical analysis, we explore this information that the cross section of volume conveys. As we discuss below, the hedging portfolio has important properties that allow us to better understand the behavior of returns. Merton (1971) has discussed the properties of hedging portfolios in a continuous-time framework as a characterization of equilibrium. Our discussion here follows Merton in spirit but is in a discrete-time, equilibrium environment.

6.2.2. Time-Series Implications for the Hedging Portfolio

By the definition of the hedging portfolio in (6.12), it is easy to show that its current return gives the best forecast of future market return.

Let Q_{Mt+1} denote the dollar return on the market portfolio in period $t+1$ and Q_{Ht+1} denote the dollar return on the hedging portfolio. Then,

$$Q_{Mt+1} = \iota^\top Q_{t+1} \quad \text{and} \quad Q_{Ht+1} = S^{H\top} Q_{t+1}. \tag{6.15}$$

For an arbitrary portfolio S, its dollar return in period t, which is $Q_t \equiv S' Q_t$, can serve as a predictor for the dollar of the market next period:

$$Q_{Mt+1} = \gamma_0 + \gamma_1 Q_t + \varepsilon_{Mt+1}.$$

The predictive power of S is measured by the R^2 of the above regression. We can solve for the portfolio that maximizes the R^2. The solution, up to a scaling constant, is the hedging portfolio. Thus, we have the following result:

Proposition 4 *Among the returns of all portfolios, the dollar return of the hedging portfolio, S_H, provides the best forecast for the future dollar return of the market.*

In other words, if we regress the market dollar return on the lagged dollar return of any portfolios, the hedging portfolio gives the highest R^2.

6.2.3. Cross-Sectional Implications for the Hedging Portfolio

We now turn to examine the predictions of our model on the cross section of returns. For expositional simplicity, we introduce some additional notation. Let Q_{pt+1} be the dollar return of a stock or a portfolio (of stocks). $\tilde{Q}_{pt+1} \equiv Q_{pt+1} - E_t[Q_{pt+1}]$ then denotes its unexpected dollar return and $\bar{Q}_p$ its unconditional mean. Thus, $\tilde{Q}_{Mt+1}$ and $\tilde{Q}_{Ht+1}$ denote, respectively, the unexpected dollar returns on the market portfolio and the hedging portfolio, and

$$\sigma_M^2 \equiv \mathrm{Var}\big[\tilde{Q}_{Mt+1}\big], \quad \sigma_H^2 \equiv \mathrm{Var}\big[\tilde{Q}_{Ht+1}\big], \quad \sigma_{MH} \equiv \mathrm{Cov}\big[\tilde{Q}_{Mt+1}, \tilde{Q}_{Ht+1}\big]$$

denote their conditional variances and covariance. It is easy to show that

$$\sigma_M^2 = \iota' \sigma_{QQ} \iota, \quad \sigma_H^2 = \sigma_{XQ} \sigma_{QQ}^{-1} \sigma_{QX}, \quad \sigma_{MH} = \iota' \sigma_{QX},$$

where σ_{QQ} and σ_{QZ} are given in Theorem 1. From Theorem 1, we have

$$\bar{Q} = \bar{\alpha} \sigma_{QQ} \iota + \lambda_Y \sigma_{QX} \tag{6.16a}$$

$$\bar{Q}_M = \bar{\alpha} \sigma_M^2 + \lambda_Y \sigma_{MH} \tag{6.16b}$$

$$\bar{Q}_H = \bar{\alpha} \sigma_{MH} + \lambda_Y \sigma_H^2. \tag{6.16c}$$

Equation (6.16) characterizes the cross-sectional variation in the stocks' expected dollar returns.

To develop more intuition about (6.16), we first consider the special case when $X_t = 0 \; \forall \; t$. In this case, returns are i.i.d. over time. The risk of a stock is measured by its covariability with the market portfolio. We have the following result:

Proposition 5 *When $X_t = 0 \; \forall \; t$, we have*

$$\mathrm{E}\big[\tilde{Q}_{t+1} | \tilde{Q}_{Mt+1}\big] = \beta_M \tilde{Q}_{Mt+1}, \tag{6.17}$$

where

$$\beta_M \equiv \mathrm{Cov}\big[\tilde{Q}_{t+1}, \tilde{Q}_{Mt+1}\big] / \mathrm{Var}\big[\tilde{Q}_{Mt+1}\big] = \sigma_{DD} \iota / (\iota' \sigma_{DD} \iota)$$

is the vector of the stocks' market betas. Moreover,

$$\bar{Q} = \beta_M \bar{Q}_M, \tag{6.18}$$

where $\bar{Q}_M = \bar{\lambda} \sigma_M^2$.

Obviously in this case, the CAPM holds for the dollar returns. It can be shown that it also holds for the returns.

In the general case when X_t changes over time, there is an additional risk due to changing market conditions (dynamic risk). Moreover, this risk is represented by the dollar return of the hedging portfolio Q_{Ht}. In this case, the risk of a stock is measured by its risk with respect to the market portfolio *and* its risk with respect to the hedging portfolio. In other words, there are two risk factors, the (contemporaneous) market risk and the (dynamic) risk of changing market conditions. The expected returns of the stocks are then determined by their exposures to these two risks and the associated risk premia. The result is summarized in the following proposition:

Proposition 6 *When Z_t changes over time, we have*

$$\mathrm{E}\big[\tilde{Q}_{t+1}|\tilde{Q}_{Mt+1}, \tilde{Q}_{Ht+1}\big] = \beta_M \tilde{Q}_{Mt+1} + \beta_H \tilde{Q}_{Ht+1}, \tag{6.19}$$

where

$$(\beta_M, \beta_H) = \mathrm{Cov}\big[\tilde{Q}_{t+1}, (\tilde{Q}_{Mt+1}, \tilde{Q}_{Ht+1})\big]\big\{\mathrm{Var}\big[(\tilde{Q}_{Mt+1}, \tilde{Q}_{Ht+1})\big]\big\}^{-1}$$

$$= (\sigma_{QM}, \sigma_{QH})\begin{pmatrix} \sigma_M^2 & \sigma_{MH} \\ \sigma_{MH} & \sigma_H^2 \end{pmatrix}^{-1}$$

is the vector of the stocks' market betas and hedging betas. Moreover, The stocks' expected dollar returns satisfy

$$\bar{Q} = \beta_M \bar{Q}_M + \beta_H \bar{Q}_H, \tag{6.20}$$

where $\bar{Q}_M = \bar{\alpha}\sigma_M^2 + \lambda_Y \sigma_{MH}$ and $\bar{Q}_H = \bar{\alpha}\sigma_{MH} + \lambda_Y \sigma_H^2$.

Thus, a stock's market risk is measured by its beta with respect to the market portfolio, and its risk to a changing environment is measured by its beta with respect to the hedging portfolio. The expected dollar return on the market portfolio gives the premium of the market risk and the expected dollar return on the hedging portfolio gives the premium of the dynamic risk. Equation (6.20) simply states that the premium on a stock is then given by the sum of the product of its exposure to each risk and the associated premium.

The pricing relation we obtain in Proposition 6 is in the spirit of Merton's Intertemporal CAPM in a continuous-time framework (Merton, 1971). However, it is important to note that Merton's result is a characterization of the pricing relation under a (class of) proposed price processes and no equilibrium is provided to support these price processes. In contrast, our pricing relation is derived from a dynamic equilibrium model. In this sense, our model provides a particular equilibrium model for which Merton's characterization holds.

If we can identify the hedging portfolio empirically, its return provides the second risk factor. Differences in the stocks' expected returns can then be fully explained by their exposures to the two risks (market risk and dynamic risk), as measured by their market betas and hedging betas.

6.3. Empirical Construction of the Hedging Portfolio

In the rest of this section, we present some empirical evidence on the theoretical predictions. Our first step is to empirically identify the hedging portfolio using the turnover data. From (6.14), we know that in the two-factor model for turnover in Proposition 3, stock j's loading on the second factor, F_{Ht}, yields the number of shares (as a fraction of its total number of shares outstanding) of stock j in the hedging portfolio. In principle, this specifies the hedging portfolio. However, we face two challenges in practice. First, the exact two-factor specification (6.14) is, at best, an approximation for the true data-generating process of turnover. Second, the two common factors are generally not observable. We address both of these problems in turn.

A more realistic starting point for modeling turnover is an approximate two-factor model:

$$\tau_{jt} = F_{Mt} + \theta_{Hj} F_{Ht} + \varepsilon_{jt}, \quad j = 1, \ldots, J, \tag{6.21}$$

where F_{Mt} and F_{Ht} are the two factors that generate trading in the market portfolio and the hedging portfolio, respectively, θ_{Hj} is the percentage of shares of stock j in the hedging portfolio (as a percentage of its total number of shares outstanding), and ε_{jt} is the error term, which is assumed to be independent across stocks.[31]

Since we do not have any sufficient theoretical foundation to identify the two common factors, F_{Mt} and F_{Ht}, we use two turnover indexes as their proxies: the equally-weighted and share-weighted turnover of the market. Specifically, let N_j denote the total number of shares outstanding for stock j and $N \equiv \sum_j N_j$ the total number of shares outstanding of all stocks. The two turnover indexes are

$$\tau_t^{EW} \equiv \frac{1}{J} \sum_{j=1}^{J} \tau_{jt} = F_{Mt} + n^{EW} F_{Ht} + \varepsilon_t^{EW} \tag{6.22a}$$

$$\tau_t^{SW} \equiv \sum_{j=1}^{J} \frac{N_j}{N} \tau_{jt} = F_{Mt} + n^{SW} F_{Ht} + \varepsilon_t^{SW}, \tag{6.22b}$$

where

$$n^{EW} = \frac{1}{J} \sum_{j=1}^{J} \theta_{Hj} \quad \text{and} \quad n^{SW} = \sum_{j=1}^{J} \frac{N_j}{N} \theta_{Hj}$$

are the average percentage of shares of each stock in the hedging portfolio and the percentage of all shares (of all stocks) in the hedging portfolio, respectively, and ε_t^{EW} and ε_t^{SW} are the error terms for the two indexes.[32] Since the error terms in (6.21) are assumed to be independent across stocks, the error terms of the two indexes, which are

---

[31] Cross-sectional independence of the errors is a restrictive assumption. If, for example, there are other common factors in addition to F_{Mt} and F_{Ht}, then ε_{jt} is likely to be correlated across stocks. However, the evidence presented in Section 5 seems to support the two-factor structure, which provides limited justification for our assumption here.

[32] To avoid degeneracy, we need $N_j \neq N_k$ for some $j \neq k$, which is surely valid empirically.

weighted averages of the error terms of individual stocks, become negligible when the number of stocks is large. For the remainder of our analysis, we shall ignore them.

Simple algebra then yields the following relation between individual turnover and the two indexes (see Lo and Wang, 2006, for more details):

$$\tau_{jt} = \beta_{\tau j}^{SW} \tau_t^{SW} + \beta_{\tau j}^{EW} \tau_t^{EW} + \varepsilon_{jt}, \qquad j = 1, \ldots, J \tag{6.23a}$$

$$\text{s.t.} \quad \beta_{\tau j}^{EW} + \beta_{\tau j}^{SW} = 1 \tag{6.23b}$$

$$\sum_{j=1}^{J} \beta_{\tau j}^{EW} = J, \tag{6.23c}$$

where

$$\beta_{\tau j}^{EW} = \frac{n^{EW} - \theta_{Hj}}{n^{EW} - n^{SW}} \quad \text{and} \quad \beta_{\tau j}^{SW} = \frac{\theta_{Hj} - n^{SW}}{n^{EW} - n^{SW}}.$$

Using the MiniCRSP volume database, we can empirically estimate $\{\beta_{\tau j}^{EW}\}$ and $\{\beta_{\tau j}^{SW}\}$ by estimating (6.23). From the estimates $\{\widehat{\beta}_{\tau j}^{EW}\}$, we can construct estimates of the portfolio weights of the hedging portfolio in the following manner

$$\widehat{\theta}_{Hj} = \left(n^{EW} - n^{SW}\right) \widehat{\beta}_{\tau j}^{EW} + n^{SW}. \tag{6.24}$$

However, there are two remaining parameters, n^{EW} and n^{SW}, that need to be estimated. It should be emphasized that these two remaining degrees of freedom are inherent in the model (6.21). When the two common factors are not observed, the parameters $\{\theta_{Hj}\}$ are only identified up to a scaling constant and a rotation. Clearly, (6.21) is invariant when F_{Ht} is rescaled as long as $\{\theta_{Hj}\}$ is also rescaled appropriately. In addition, when the two factors are replaced by their linear combinations, (6.21) remains formally the same as long as $\{\theta_{Hj}\}$ is also adjusted with an additive constant.[33] Since the hedging portfolio $\{\theta_{Hj}\}$ is defined only up to a scaling constant, we let

$$n^{SW} = 1 \tag{6.25a}$$

$$n^{EW} - n^{SW} = \phi, \tag{6.25b}$$

where ϕ is a parameter that we calibrate to the data (see Section 6.4). This yields the final expression for the J components of the hedging portfolio:

$$\widehat{\theta}_{Hj} = \phi \, \widehat{\beta}_{\tau j}^{EW} + 1. \tag{6.26}$$

---

[33] For example, for any a, we have $\forall j$:

$$\tau_{jt} = F_{Mt} + \theta_{Hj} F_{Ht} + \varepsilon_{jt} = (F_{Mt} + aF_{Ht}) + (\theta_{Hj} - a)F_{Ht} + \varepsilon_{jt} = \tilde{F}_{Mt} + \tilde{\theta}_{Hj} F_{Ht} + \varepsilon_{jt},$$

where $\tilde{F}_{Mt} = F_{Mt} + aF_{Ht}$ and $\tilde{\theta}_{Hj} = \theta_{Hj} - a$.

The normalization $n^{\text{SW}} = 1$ sets the total number of shares in the portfolio to a positive value. If $\phi = 0$, the portfolio has equal percentage of all the shares of each company, implying that it is the market portfolio. Nonzero values of ϕ represent deviations from the market portfolio.

To estimate $\{\beta_{\tau j}^{\text{EW}}\}$ and $\{\beta_{\tau j}^{\text{SW}}\}$, we first construct the two turnover indexes. We estimate (6.23a)–(6.23b) for each of the seven five-year subperiods, ignoring the global constraint (6.23c).[34] Therefore, we estimate constrained linear regressions of the weekly turnover for each stock on equal- and share-weighted turnover indexes in each of the seven five-year subperiods of our sample.

Table 17.15 contains summary statistics for these constrained regressions. To provide a clearer sense of the dispersion of these regressions, we first sort them into deciles based on $\{\widehat{\beta}_{\tau j}^{\text{EW}}\}$, and then compute the means and standard deviations of the estimated coefficients $\{\widehat{\beta}_{\tau j}^{\text{EW}}\}$ and $\{\widehat{\beta}_{\tau j}^{\text{SW}}\}$, their t-statistics, and the R^2s within each decile. The t-statistics indicate that the estimated coefficients are generally significant – even in the fifth and sixth deciles, the average t-statistic for $\{\widehat{\beta}_{\tau j}^{\text{EW}}\}$ is 4.585 and 6.749, respectively (we would, of course, expect significant t-statistics in the extreme deciles even if the true coefficients were zero, purely from sampling variation). The $\bar{R}^2$s also look impressive; however, they must be interpreted with some caution because of the imposition of the constraint (6.23b), which can yield $\bar{R}^2$ greater than unity and less than zero.[35] Table 17.15 shows that negative $\bar{R}^2$s appear mainly in the two extreme deciles, except in the last subperiod when they are negative for all the deciles, presumably an indication that the constraint is not consistent with the data in this last subperiod.

For comparison, we estimate the unconstrained version of (6.23a) and compute the same summary statistics, reported in Table 17.16, along with the mean and standard deviation within each decile of p values corresponding to the statistic that (6.23b) holds. Except for the last subperiod, the constraint seems to be reasonably consistent with the data, with average p values well above 5% for all but the extreme deciles in most subperiods. For example, in the first subperiod, the average p values range from a minimum of 4.0% in decile 1 to a maximum of 32.4% in decile 6, and with a value of 19.4% in decile 10. However, in the last subperiod, the average p value is less than 5% in deciles 2–6 and close to significance for most of the other deciles, which explains the negative $\bar{R}^2$s in Table 17.15.

Without the constraint, the $\bar{R}^2$s in Table 17.16 are well-behaved, and of similar magnitude to those in Table 17.15 that are between 0 and 100%, ranging from 40 to 60%, even in the last subperiod. Clearly the two-factor model of turnover accounts for a significant amount of variation in the weekly turnover of individual stocks.

---

[34] We ignore this constraint for two reasons. First, given the large number of stocks in our sample, imposing a global constraint like (6.23c) requires a large amount of computer memory, which was unavailable to us. Second, because of the large number of individual regressions involved, neglecting the reduction of one dimension should not significantly affect any of the final results.

[35] For example, a negative $\bar{R}^2$ arises when the variance of $\widehat{\beta}_{\tau j}^{\text{EW}} \tau_t^{\text{EW}} + \widehat{\beta}_{\tau j}^{\text{SW}} \tau_t^{\text{SW}}$ exceeds the variance of the dependent variable τ_{jt}, which can happen when the constraint (6.23b) is imposed.

Table 17.15 Summary statistics for the restricted volume betas using weekly returns and volume data for NYSE and AMEX stocks from 1962 to 1996 in five-year subperiods

Decile	Sample size	$\widehat{\beta}_\tau^{EW}$ Mean	$\widehat{\beta}_\tau^{EW}$ S.D.	$t(\widehat{\beta}_\tau^{EW})$ Mean	$t(\widehat{\beta}_\tau^{EW})$ S.D.	$\widehat{\beta}_\tau^{SW}$ Mean	$\widehat{\beta}_\tau^{SW}$ S.D.	$t(\widehat{\beta}_\tau^{SW})$ Mean	$t(\widehat{\beta}_\tau^{SW})$ S.D.	$\bar{R}^2$ (%) Mean	$\bar{R}^2$ (%) S.D.
					July 1962–December 1966 (234 weeks)						
1	218	−0.906	0.119	−49.394	19.023	1.906	0.119	103.944	38.755	−2520.4	27817.4
2	219	−0.657	0.069	−26.187	12.805	1.657	0.069	65.488	30.083	56.5	19.5
3	219	−0.432	0.064	−10.917	5.956	1.432	0.064	35.879	17.907	55.0	20.4
4	218	−0.188	0.082	−3.812	2.732	1.188	0.082	22.907	10.555	57.1	17.8
5	219	0.107	0.097	1.273	1.243	0.893	0.097	11.365	4.570	51.5	16.0
6	219	0.494	0.119	4.585	1.943	0.506	0.119	4.847	2.401	50.6	16.5
7	218	0.927	0.145	6.749	2.258	0.073	0.145	0.639	1.190	50.7	15.5
8	219	1.520	0.229	8.229	2.893	−0.520	0.229	−2.714	1.348	49.2	15.4
9	219	2.568	0.434	10.410	3.491	−1.568	0.434	−6.292	2.401	49.4	15.2
10	218	6.563	4.100	11.682	3.880	−5.563	4.100	−9.500	3.332	47.1	15.3
					January 1967–December 1971 (261 weeks)						
1	242	−0.783	0.134	−36.725	17.343	1.783	0.134	84.302	38.946	−175.3	976.2
2	243	−0.529	0.056	−18.772	8.459	1.529	0.056	53.969	22.871	58.2	16.1
3	242	−0.315	0.068	−7.905	4.099	1.315	0.068	32.431	13.771	56.4	16.3
4	243	−0.054	0.089	−1.139	1.845	1.054	0.089	18.479	7.855	55.2	14.3
5	242	0.264	0.087	3.269	1.482	0.736	0.087	9.228	3.260	54.1	13.2
6	243	0.623	0.126	6.035	2.217	0.377	0.126	3.723	1.871	53.5	13.4
7	243	1.110	0.154	8.367	2.719	−0.110	0.154	−0.735	1.178	54.4	13.0
8	242	1.782	0.205	10.314	3.151	−0.782	0.205	−4.477	1.630	53.2	13.2
9	243	2.661	0.330	12.249	3.120	−1.661	0.330	−7.609	2.149	54.6	11.0
10	242	5.410	2.540	13.019	4.172	−4.410	2.540	−10.260	3.383	52.6	14.2

January 1972–December 1977 (261 weeks)

1	262	−2.013	0.845	−13.276	4.901	3.013	0.845	20.755	8.319	−1147.6	5034.9
2	263	−1.069	0.129	−10.986	3.890	2.069	0.129	21.239	7.045	25.4	44.6
3	263	−0.697	0.096	−6.014	2.466	1.697	0.096	14.600	5.619	44.3	27.1
4	263	−0.359	0.105	−2.825	1.444	1.359	0.105	10.608	4.044	50.3	22.8
5	263	0.015	0.114	0.062	0.765	0.985	0.114	6.620	2.466	53.0	19.2
6	263	0.485	0.156	2.577	1.159	0.515	0.156	2.792	1.354	52.8	15.4
7	263	1.084	0.187	4.684	1.801	−0.084	0.187	−0.322	0.870	51.4	14.5
8	263	1.888	0.289	6.827	2.426	−0.888	0.289	−3.180	1.421	52.8	14.2
9	263	3.161	0.501	8.894	3.311	−2.161	0.501	−6.060	2.431	52.5	14.0
10	262	7.770	4.940	11.202	4.447	−6.770	4.940	−9.480	3.965	52.3	13.8

January 1977–December 1981 (261 weeks)

1	242	−3.096	0.347	−22.164	4.591	4.096	0.347	29.341	5.815	−872.7	6958.8
2	243	−2.284	0.192	−15.799	4.883	3.284	0.192	22.701	6.846	32.7	23.6
3	243	−1.654	0.208	−10.524	4.628	2.654	0.208	16.861	7.167	48.9	20.8
4	243	−1.021	0.156	−5.505	2.335	2.021	0.156	10.884	4.304	54.1	18.4
5	243	−0.394	0.189	−1.833	1.180	1.394	0.189	6.387	2.655	55.6	17.1
6	243	0.355	0.250	1.277	1.045	0.645	0.250	2.472	1.438	55.5	16.5
7	243	1.330	0.308	3.864	1.519	−0.330	0.308	−0.894	0.971	53.6	15.7
8	243	2.599	0.457	6.198	2.242	−1.599	0.457	−3.782	1.560	54.5	15.7
9	243	4.913	0.809	8.860	2.983	−3.913	0.809	−7.038	2.487	55.3	14.5
10	242	10.090	4.231	11.202	3.618	−9.090	4.231	−9.980	3.311	55.2	13.4

January 1982–December 1986 (261 weeks)

1	227	−6.968	3.038	−5.636	2.328	7.968	3.038	6.525	2.577	46.6	15.9
2	228	−2.257	0.624	−3.249	1.604	3.257	0.624	4.724	2.199	52.7	20.2
3	228	−0.640	0.380	−1.223	0.967	1.640	0.380	3.180	1.667	45.5	136.9
4	227	0.501	0.283	1.166	0.841	0.499	0.283	1.177	0.903	55.4	22.4
5	228	1.357	0.231	3.540	1.655	−0.357	0.231	−0.954	0.786	41.3	90.7
6	228	2.077	0.201	5.319	2.159	−1.077	0.201	−2.758	1.216	−19.5	686.3
7	227	2.754	0.196	7.402	2.342	−1.754	0.196	−4.710	1.531	28.3	52.8

(Continued)

Table 17.15 (Continued)

Decile	Sample size	$\hat{\beta}_\tau^{\text{EW}}$ Mean	S.D.	$t\left(\hat{\beta}_\tau^{\text{EW}}\right)$ Mean	S.D.	$\hat{\beta}_\tau^{\text{SW}}$ Mean	S.D.	$t\left(\hat{\beta}_\tau^{\text{SW}}\right)$ Mean	S.D.	$\bar{R}^2$ (%) Mean	S.D.
						January 1982–December 1986 (261 weeks)					
8	228	3.431	0.201	9.244	2.667	−2.431	0.201	−6.548	1.922	3.2	101.8
9	228	4.168	0.237	11.354	2.905	−3.168	0.237	−8.630	2.248	−163.1	1678.6
10	227	5.399	1.170	14.045	5.229	−4.399	1.170	−11.392	4.405	−348.1	1027.1
						January 1987–December 1991 (261 weeks)					
1	216	−8.487	7.040	−7.093	3.763	9.487	7.040	8.082	4.137	50.2	16.8
2	217	−2.866	0.725	−4.616	2.439	3.866	0.725	6.263	3.224	54.8	18.8
3	217	−0.843	0.494	−1.832	1.512	1.843	0.494	4.097	2.537	56.8	21.0
4	217	0.441	0.330	1.196	1.277	0.559	0.330	1.423	1.268	57.0	19.9
5	217	1.502	0.317	4.887	3.062	−0.502	0.317	−1.693	1.583	57.8	18.8
6	217	2.510	0.280	8.434	4.070	−1.510	0.280	−5.074	2.582	51.2	18.7
7	217	3.389	0.234	12.139	4.615	−2.389	0.234	−8.567	3.325	42.2	15.6
8	217	4.157	0.196	15.329	4.607	−3.157	0.196	−11.637	3.513	23.8	19.8
9	217	4.836	0.212	18.370	4.580	−3.836	0.212	−14.572	3.673	−27.0	66.1
10	217	5.743	0.402	21.430	5.101	−4.743	0.402	−17.682	4.229	−921.9	4682.1
						January 1992–December 1996 (261 weeks)					
1	241	−4.275	2.858	−2.409	1.092	5.275	2.858	3.097	1.342	−423.6	3336.7
2	241	−1.074	0.384	−1.277	0.741	2.074	0.384	2.538	1.369	−147.7	2631.2
3	242	−0.245	0.155	−0.371	0.301	1.245	0.155	1.944	0.899	−14.7	508.2
4	241	0.189	0.100	0.298	0.203	0.811	0.100	1.296	0.534	−135.1	899.3
5	241	0.520	0.098	0.779	0.313	0.480	0.098	0.729	0.330	−1353.9	5755.2
6	242	0.865	0.106	1.226	0.414	0.135	0.106	0.196	0.177	−197.6	669.1
7	241	1.303	0.159	1.725	0.641	−0.303	0.159	−0.400	0.260	−130.3	931.7
8	242	2.022	0.254	2.391	0.824	−1.022	0.254	−1.202	0.480	−58.9	684.5
9	241	3.271	0.498	3.061	1.027	−2.271	0.498	−2.117	0.769	−24.9	225.8
10	241	8.234	9.836	3.844	1.360	−7.234	9.836	−3.237	1.190	−219.9	1145.7

Turnover over individual stocks is regressed on the equally-weighted and share-weighted turnover indices, subject to the restriction that the two regression coefficients, $\hat{\beta}_\tau^{\text{EW}}$ and $\hat{\beta}_\tau^{\text{SW}}$, must add up to one. The stocks are then sorted into 10 deciles by $\hat{\beta}_\tau^{\text{EW}}$. The summary statistics are then reported for each decile.

Table 17.16 Summary statistics for the unrestricted volume betas using weekly returns and volume data for NYSE and AMEX stocks from 1962 to 1996 in five-year subperiods

Decile	Sample size	$\widehat{\beta}_\tau^{\text{EW}}$ Mean	S.D.	$t(\widehat{\beta}_\tau^{\text{EW}})$ Mean	S.D.	$\widehat{\beta}_\tau^{\text{SW}}$ Mean	S.D.	$t(\widehat{\beta}_\tau^{\text{SW}})$ Mean	S.D.	$\bar{R}^2(\%)$ Mean	S.D.	p value (%) Mean	S.D.
					July 1962–December 1966 (234 weeks)								
1	218	−4.749	6.337	−4.121	2.174	11.761	14.451	5.608	2.556	51.4	18.7	0.7	4.0
2	219	−1.321	0.249	−3.622	2.152	3.891	1.043	5.351	2.670	57.3	16.7	2.3	8.5
3	219	−0.730	0.110	−3.500	2.466	2.398	0.786	5.394	3.054	59.5	17.5	16.7	23.8
4	218	−0.406	0.071	−2.756	1.971	1.548	0.664	4.706	2.593	61.0	17.0	23.3	29.2
5	219	−0.195	0.055	−2.603	2.262	0.967	0.644	4.810	3.103	63.0	20.2	13.2	24.8
6	219	0.034	0.090	−0.012	0.960	0.790	0.806	1.723	1.250	54.6	19.1	19.0	28.6
7	218	0.508	0.206	1.554	1.080	0.337	1.058	−0.015	1.111	52.0	16.4	26.0	32.4
8	219	1.470	0.336	2.675	1.481	−0.768	1.834	−1.218	1.375	51.7	14.3	26.9	31.5
9	219	3.400	0.875	3.685	1.817	−3.639	2.059	−2.392	1.670	46.7	14.2	22.0	30.1
10	218	11.334	8.125	5.387	2.376	−15.963	12.976	−4.137	2.147	46.3	14.7	9.6	19.4
					January 1967–December 1971 (261 weeks)								
1	242	−5.109	17.101	−4.306	2.689	12.966	35.908	6.280	3.303	52.1	16.3	1.0	4.3
2	243	−0.770	0.141	−4.458	3.052	2.694	1.188	7.022	3.776	59.3	14.3	10.3	20.3
3	242	−0.409	0.078	−4.600	3.229	1.534	0.634	7.725	4.170	64.3	14.8	19.8	27.7
4	243	−0.176	0.071	−2.299	2.609	1.128	0.729	5.222	3.639	60.6	15.5	16.3	27.9
5	242	0.086	0.087	0.628	1.123	0.851	0.968	2.003	1.537	57.5	15.6	15.5	27.2
6	243	0.492	0.152	2.139	1.441	0.447	0.924	0.260	1.289	56.9	13.0	20.5	29.4
7	243	1.096	0.201	3.379	1.886	−0.383	0.931	−1.096	1.617	56.0	12.0	20.6	28.1
8	242	1.906	0.307	4.567	2.143	−1.583	1.057	−2.328	1.825	56.4	12.2	18.3	28.5
9	243	3.275	0.556	5.533	2.246	−3.417	1.223	−3.202	1.760	56.5	12.3	16.8	24.9
10	242	7.499	3.595	6.827	2.626	−9.674	5.563	−4.641	2.050	55.6	11.7	10.1	21.8

(Continued)

Table 17.16 (Continued)

Decile	Sample size	$\widehat{\beta}_\tau^{EW}$		$t\left(\widehat{\beta}_\tau^{EW}\right)$		$\widehat{\beta}_\tau^{SW}$		$t\left(\widehat{\beta}_\tau^{SW}\right)$		$\bar{R}^2$ (%)		p value (%)	
		Mean	S.D.	Mean	S.D.	Mean	S.D.	Mean	S.D.	Mean	S.D.	Mean	S.D.
					January 1972–December 1976 (261 weeks)								
1	262	−1.908	1.364	−4.116	2.584	4.371	2.731	7.313	3.930	57.0	17.7	3.2	11.7
2	263	−0.603	0.131	−3.849	3.151	1.874	0.665	8.135	4.806	66.3	17.2	11.0	24.0
3	263	−0.237	0.094	−1.949	1.632	1.120	0.481	6.085	3.129	64.7	16.6	8.4	20.6
4	263	0.032	0.071	0.316	0.872	0.714	0.570	3.258	1.805	58.0	17.2	5.3	16.8
5	263	0.308	0.091	2.249	1.733	0.480	0.659	1.076	1.942	56.1	15.5	6.1	16.7
6	263	0.645	0.114	3.586	2.285	0.120	0.807	−0.517	2.197	54.3	14.8	7.1	18.9
7	263	1.107	0.141	4.929	2.814	−0.361	0.611	−1.996	2.475	55.5	14.3	7.7	20.9
8	263	1.700	0.218	6.180	3.237	−0.910	0.736	−3.229	2.838	56.8	13.7	9.9	23.6
9	263	2.846	0.497	7.823	3.678	−2.054	0.894	−4.950	3.194	57.0	13.8	9.6	22.2
10	262	6.609	3.411	10.196	4.149	−5.892	3.463	−7.409	3.566	59.3	11.8	13.1	25.6
					January 1977–December 1981 (261 weeks)								
1	242	−2.622	1.777	−2.975	1.647	4.749	2.675	4.516	2.251	54.0	20.0	6.4	16.0
2	243	−0.805	0.175	−2.356	1.508	1.920	0.662	4.251	2.176	61.6	17.5	13.2	23.9
3	243	−0.364	0.101	−1.559	1.160	1.186	0.539	3.553	1.876	62.0	18.7	7.7	19.3
4	243	−0.072	0.076	−0.337	0.564	0.733	0.481	2.061	0.999	56.3	19.0	8.8	21.7
5	243	0.218	0.093	0.780	0.585	0.504	0.673	0.781	0.823	53.5	15.9	7.0	18.3
6	243	0.575	0.119	1.604	0.998	0.238	0.643	0.002	1.053	56.1	14.5	11.0	21.7
7	243	1.081	0.184	2.241	1.194	−0.209	0.641	−0.727	1.161	54.5	13.9	12.1	24.8
8	243	1.900	0.284	3.108	1.530	−0.917	0.758	−1.610	1.446	54.7	13.1	13.3	24.4
9	243	2.993	0.398	3.819	1.593	−1.995	0.784	−2.326	1.482	54.6	14.8	15.9	27.8
10	242	7.240	4.979	4.819	1.899	−6.163	5.374	−3.419	1.788	54.5	13.8	20.8	29.3

January 1982–December 1986 (261 weeks)

1	−3.038	1.819	−2.588	1.102	4.377	2.097	4.014	1.497	49.6	18.2	14.6	26.1
2	−0.939	0.245	−1.940	1.284	1.821	0.593	3.799	2.206	57.6	19.9	7.7	19.0
3	−0.342	0.123	−1.021	0.686	1.045	0.477	2.945	1.427	58.7	18.5	4.9	17.0
4	0.028	0.087	0.116	0.513	0.631	0.459	1.704	0.933	57.6	16.7	5.0	15.9
5	0.349	0.101	1.247	0.917	0.340	0.465	0.548	1.118	55.9	19.0	4.0	14.4
6	0.732	0.117	2.306	1.561	0.073	0.587	−0.507	1.641	57.9	16.4	4.6	16.0
7	1.204	0.178	3.278	1.885	−0.396	0.486	−1.647	1.842	55.3	13.8	7.7	19.7
8	1.908	0.249	3.840	1.907	−0.907	0.525	−2.252	1.856	54.8	14.6	11.2	24.1
9	3.020	0.459	5.012	2.350	−1.754	0.663	−3.369	2.197	57.8	12.7	11.0	23.4
10	6.772	3.345	6.400	2.616	−4.903	2.873	−4.976	2.415	54.9	13.1	4.9	15.2

January 1987–December 1991 (261 weeks)

1	−3.153	3.353	−1.997	1.036	4.278	3.325	3.224	1.656	47.5	23.3	20.7	30.0
2	−0.620	0.236	−1.246	0.866	1.367	0.546	2.872	1.734	57.4	21.7	10.2	22.9
3	−0.098	0.093	−0.307	0.417	0.673	0.440	1.899	1.156	56.2	21.5	5.0	16.5
4	0.194	0.077	0.795	0.781	0.332	0.417	0.739	1.123	55.9	20.3	4.6	16.0
5	0.479	0.086	1.443	0.873	0.150	0.438	−0.013	1.000	55.5	17.8	5.1	18.0
6	0.764	0.084	2.059	1.074	−0.082	0.433	−0.623	1.185	56.0	17.9	6.7	19.5
7	1.177	0.146	2.344	1.068	−0.338	0.474	−1.053	1.105	52.9	16.8	07.8	19.8
8	1.806	0.246	2.756	1.259	−0.719	0.508	−1.436	1.170	53.9	16.3	14.0	26.3
9	2.972	0.452	3.104	1.371	−1.531	0.610	−1.921	1.231	51.3	15.3	11.5	22.3
10	6.485	3.351	3.830	1.656	−4.209	2.654	−2.823	1.538	47.5	15.8	4.1	12.6

(Continued)

Table 17.16 (Continued)

Decile	Sample size	$\widehat{\beta}_\tau^{EW}$		$t\left(\widehat{\beta}_\tau^{EW}\right)$		$\widehat{\beta}_\tau^{SW}$		$t\left(\widehat{\beta}_\tau^{SW}\right)$		$\bar{R}^2$ (%)		p value (%)	
		Mean	S.D.	Mean	S.D.	Mean	S.D.	Mean	S.D.	Mean	S.D.	Mean	S.D.
						January 1992–December 1996 (261 weeks)							
1	241	−2.894	2.074	−2.174	1.107	4.563	2.659	3.498	1.595	57.4	19.6	5.5	16.3
2	241	−0.681	0.206	−1.335	0.822	1.613	0.622	2.886	1.450	61.3	21.0	4.8	16.3
3	242	−0.197	0.093	−0.623	0.612	0.924	0.534	2.192	1.396	59.8	22.6	2.3	9.7
4	241	0.072	0.072	0.308	0.485	0.526	0.488	1.057	0.905	56.0	20.7	2.8	13.4
5	241	0.344	0.085	1.064	0.731	0.261	0.441	0.281	0.951	55.6	20.0	3.5	12.8
6	242	0.624	0.093	1.430	0.778	0.124	0.659	−0.176	0.909	55.1	18.2	2.7	10.3
7	241	1.018	0.130	2.028	1.151	−0.224	0.578	−0.836	1.176	53.3	17.0	6.4	18.8
8	242	1.618	0.230	2.357	1.122	−0.694	0.647	−1.248	1.110	51.4	17.2	6.1	18.1
9	241	2.720	0.454	2.624	1.170	−1.477	0.830	−1.616	1.088	49.4	15.1	10.7	23.7
10	241	7.977	9.529	3.706	1.411	−6.205	9.055	−2.823	1.339	45.3	14.5	6.2	17.4

Turnover over individual stocks are regressed on the equally-weighted and share-weighted turnover indices, giving two regression coefficients, β_τ^{EW} and β_τ^{SW}. The stocks are then sorted into 10 deciles by the estimates of their $\widehat{\beta}_\tau^{EW}$. The summary statistics are reported for each decile. The last two columns report the test statistic for the condition that β_τ^{EW} and β_τ^{SW} add up to one.

6.4. The Forecast Power of the Hedging Portfolio

Having constructed the hedging portfolio up to a parameter ϕ to be determined, we can examine its time-series properties as predicted by the model. In particular, in this section, we focus on the degree to which the hedging portfolio can predict future stock returns, especially the return on the market portfolio. We first construct the returns of the hedging portfolio in Section 6.4.1 by calibrating ϕ and then comparing its forecast power with other factors in Sections 6.4.2 and 6.4.3.

6.4.1. Hedging-Portfolio Returns

To construct the return on the hedging portfolio, we begin by calculating its dollar value and dollar returns. Let k denote subperiod k, $k = 2, \ldots, 7$, $V_{jt}(k)$ denote the total market capitalization of stock j at time period t (the end of week t) in subperiod k, $Q_{jt}(k)$ denote its dividend-adjusted excess dollar return for the same period, and $R_{jt}(k)$ denote the dividend-adjusted excess return, and $\theta_j(k)$ the estimated share (as fraction of its total shares outstanding) in the hedging portfolio in subperiod k.

For stock j to be included in the hedging portfolio in subperiod k, which we shall refer to as the "testing period," we require it to have volume data for at least one-third of the sample in the previous subperiod $(k-1)$, which we call the "estimation period." Among the stocks satisfying this criteria, we eliminate those ranked in the top and bottom 0.5% according to their volume betas (or their share weights in the hedging portfolio) to limit the potential impact of outliers.[36] We let $J_t(k)$ denote the set of stocks that survive these two filters and that have price and return data for week t of subperiod k. The hedging portfolio in week t of subperiod k is then given by

$$\theta_{Hjt}(k) = \begin{cases} \widehat{\theta}_{Hj}, & j \in J_t(k) \\ 0, & j \notin J_t(k). \end{cases} \tag{6.27}$$

The dollar return of the hedging portfolio for week t follows naturally:

$$Q_{Ht}(k) \equiv \sum_j \theta_{Hjt}(k) V_{jt} R_{jt}. \tag{6.28}$$

and the (rate of) return of the hedging portfolio is given by

$$R_{Ht}(k) \equiv \frac{Q_{Hjt}(k)}{V_{Ht}(k)}, \tag{6.29}$$

---

[36] See Lo and Wang (2000) for the importance of outliers in volume data.

where

$$V_{Ht}(k) \equiv \sum_j \theta_{Hjt}(k) V_{jt-1} \qquad (6.30)$$

is the value of the hedging portfolio at the beginning of the week.

The procedure outlined above yields the return and the dollar return of the hedging portfolio up to the parameter ϕ, which must be calibrated. To do so, we exploit a key property of the hedging portfolio: its return is the best forecaster of future market returns (see Section 6.2). Therefore, for a given value of ϕ, we can estimate the following regression

$$R_{Mt+1} = \delta_0 + \delta_1 \{R_{Ht} \text{ or } Q_{Ht}\} + \varepsilon_{Mt+1}, \qquad (6.31)$$

where the single regressor is either the return of the hedging portfolio R_{Ht} or its dollar return for a given choice of ϕ, and then vary ϕ to maximize the $\bar{R}^2$.[37]

In all cases, there is a unique global maximum, from which we obtain ϕ. However, for some values of ϕ, the value of the hedging portfolio changes sign, and in these cases, defining the return on the portfolio becomes problematic. Therefore, we eliminate these values from consideration, and for all subperiods except subperiods 4 and 7 (i.e., subperiods 2, 3, 5, 6), the omitted values of ϕ do not seem to affect the choice of ϕ for the maximum R^2 (see Lo and Wang, 2006, for more discussions on the choice of ϕ).

For subperiods 2–7, the values for ϕ that give the maximum R^2 are 1.25, 4.75, 1.75, 47, 38, and 0.25, respectively, using R_{Ht} as the predictor. Using Q_{Ht}, the values of ϕ are 1.5, 4.25, 2, 20, 27, and 0.75, respectively. With these values of ϕ in hand, we have fully specified the hedging portfolio, its return, and dollar return. Table 17.17 reports the summary statistics for the return and dollar return on the hedging portfolio.

6.4.2. Optimal Forecasting Portfolios
Having constructed the return of the hedging portfolio in Section 6.4.1, we wish to compare its forecast power to those of other forecastors. According to Proposition 4, the returns of the hedging portfolio should outperform the returns of any other portfolios in predicting future market returns. Specifically, if we regress R_{Mt} on the lagged return of any arbitrary portfolio p, the $\bar{R}^2$ should be less than that of (6.31).

It is impractical to compare (6.31) to all possible portfolios and is uninformative to compare it to random portfolios. Instead, we need only make comparisons to "optimal forecast portfolios," portfolios that are optimal forecasters of R_{Mt}; since by construction, no other portfolios can have higher levels of predictability than these. The following proposition shows how to construct optimal forecasting portfolios (OFPs) (see Lo and Wang, 2006, for details):

---

[37] This approach ignores the impact of statistical variation on the "optimal" ϕ, which is beyond the scope of this chapter but is explored further in related contexts by Foster et al. (1997) and Lo and MacKinlay (1997).

Table 17.17   Summary statistics for the returns and dollar returns of the hedging portfolio constructed from individual stocks' volume data using weekly returns and volume data for NYSE and AMEX stocks from 1962 to 1996

Statistic	Entire	67–71	72–76	77–81	82–86	87–91	92–96
				Sample period			

Hedging-portfolio return R_{Ht}

Statistic	Entire	67–71	72–76	77–81	82–86	87–91	92–96
Mean	0.013	0.001	0.005	0.007	0.011	0.052	0.003
S.D.	0.198	0.029	0.039	0.045	0.046	0.477	0.013
Skewness	24.092	0.557	0.542	−0.330	0.270	10.200	−0.214
Kurtosis	747.809	1.479	7.597	0.727	1.347	130.476	0.945
ρ_1	0.017	0.199	0.141	0.196	0.125	0.004	−0.165
ρ_2	−0.058	0.018	0.006	0.071	0.036	−0.070	−0.028
ρ_3	0.104	−0.028	−0.036	−0.010	0.073	0.099	−0.003
ρ_4	0.184	0.070	0.043	0.045	−0.113	0.182	−0.010
ρ_5	−0.086	0.114	0.144	−0.026	−0.103	−0.099	−0.025
ρ_6	0.079	−0.003	0.258	−0.089	−0.093	0.072	0.020
ρ_7	0.217	0.037	0.083	−0.031	−0.173	0.218	0.098
ρ_8	−0.098	0.002	−0.124	−0.008	0.006	−0.111	−0.130
ρ_9	0.048	−0.002	−0.008	−0.060	0.011	0.041	0.006
ρ_{10}	−0.044	−0.017	0.174	−0.037	−0.117	−0.055	0.035

Hedging-portfolio dollar-return Q_{Ht}

Statistic	Entire	67–71	72–76	77–81	82–86	87–91	92–96
Mean	2.113	0.072	1.236	2.258	5.589	3.244	0.281
S.D.	16.836	3.639	11.059	21.495	25.423	20.906	1.845
Skewness	0.717	0.210	−0.144	−0.495	−0.080	2.086	0.215
Kurtosis	14.082	−0.085	0.500	2.286	6.537	13.286	2.048
ρ_1	0.164	0.219	0.251	0.200	0.098	0.157	−0.122
ρ_2	0.082	0.014	0.148	0.052	0.125	−0.015	−0.095
ρ_3	0.039	0.003	0.077	0.010	0.071	−0.041	0.037
ρ_4	0.021	0.061	0.084	0.127	−0.037	−0.066	0.014
ρ_5	0.036	0.116	0.102	−0.002	0.051	−0.016	−0.027
ρ_6	−0.010	−0.044	0.127	−0.094	−0.053	0.057	−0.014
ρ_7	−0.006	0.034	0.013	−0.060	−0.014	0.010	0.107
ρ_8	−0.046	0.005	−0.055	−0.028	−0.127	0.016	−0.075
ρ_9	0.027	−0.016	0.045	−0.006	0.047	0.005	−0.006
ρ_{10}	−0.001	−0.030	0.042	0.026	0.014	−0.082	0.031

Proposition 7 *Let Γ_0 and Γ_1 denote the contemporaneous and first-order autocovariance matrix of the vector of all returns. For any arbitrary target portfolio q with weights $w_q = (w_{q1}; \ldots; w_{qN})$, define $A \equiv \Gamma_0^{-1}\Gamma_1 w_q w_q' \Gamma_1'$. The optimal forecast portfolio of w_q is given by the normalized eigenvector of A corresponding to its largest eigenvalue.*

Since Γ_0 and Γ_1 are unobservable, they must be estimated using historical data. Given the large number of stocks in our sample (over 2000 in each subperiod) and the relatively short time series in each subperiod (261 weekly observations), the standard estimators for Γ_0 and Γ_1 are not viable. However, it is possible to construct OFPs from a much smaller number of "basis portfolios," and then compare the predictive power of these OFPs to the hedging portfolio. As long as the basis portfolios are not too specialized, the $\bar{R}^2$s are likely to be similar to those obtained from the entire universe of all stocks.

We form several sets of basis portfolios by sorting all the J stocks into K groups of equal numbers ($K \leq J$) according to market capitalization, market beta, and SIC codes, and then construct value-weighted portfolios within each group.[38] This procedure yields K basis portfolios for which the corresponding Γ_0 and Γ_1 can be estimated using the portfolios' weekly returns within each subperiod. Based on the estimated autocovariance matrices, the OFP can be computed easily according to Proposition 7.

In selecting the number of basis portfolios K, we face the following trade-off: fewer portfolios yield better sampling properties for the covariance matrix estimators, but less desirable properties for the OFP since the predictive power of the OFP is obviously maximized when $K=J$. As a compromise, for the OFP-based market capitalization and market betas, we choose K to be 10, 15, 20, and 25. For the OFP based on SIC codes, we choose 13 industry groupings, described in more detail below.

Specifically, for each five-year subperiod in which we wish to evaluate the forecast power of the hedging portfolio (the testing period), we use the previous five-year subperiod (the estimation period) to estimate the OFPs. For the OFP based on 10 market-capitalization-sorted portfolios, which we call "CAP10," we construct 10 value-weighted portfolios each week, one for each market-capitalization decile. Market-capitalization deciles are recomputed each week, and the time series of decile returns form the 10 basis portfolio returns of CAP10, with which we can estimate Γ_0 and Γ_1. To compute the OFP, we also require the weights, ω_q, of the target portfolio, in this case the market portfolio. Since the testing period follows the estimation period, we use the market capitalization of each group in the last week of the estimation period to map the weights of the market portfolio into a 10×1-vector of weights for the 10 basis portfolios. The weights of the OFP for the basis portfolios CAP10 follow immediately from Proposition 7. The same procedure is used to form OFPs for CAP15, CAP20, and CAP25 basis portfolios.

The OFPs of market-beta-sorted basis portfolios are constructed in a similar manner. We first estimate the market betas of individual stocks in the estimation period, sort them according to their estimated betas, and then form small groups of basis portfolios,

---

[38] It is important that we use value-weighted portfolios here so that the market portfolio, whose return we wish to predict, is a portfolio of these basis portfolios (recall that the target portfolio ω_q that we wish to forecast is a linear combination of the vector of returns for which Γ_k is the kth order autocovariance matrix).

calculating value-weighted returns for each group. We consider 10, 15, 20, and 25 groups denoted by "Beta10," "Beta15," and so forth. The same procedure is then followed to construct the OFPs for each of these sets of basis portfolios.

Finally, the industry portfolios are based on SIC-code groupings. The first two digits of the SIC code yield 60–80 industry categories, depending on the sample period, and some of categories contain only one or two stocks. On the other hand, the first digit yields only eight broad industry categories. As a compromise, we use a slightly more disaggregated grouping of 13 industries, given by the following correspondence[39]:

No.	SIC Codes	Description
1	1–14	Agriculture, forest, fishing, mining
2	15–19, 30, 32–34	Construction, basic materials (steel, glass, concrete, etc.)
3	20–21	Food and tobacco
4	22, 23, 25, 31, 39	Textiles, clothing, consumer products
5	24, 26–27	Logging, paper, printing, publishing
6	28	Chemicals
7	29	Petroleum
8	35–36, 38	Machinery and equipment supply, including computers
9	37, 40–47	Transportation-related
10	48–49	Utilities and telecommunications
11	50–59	Wholesale distributors, retail
12	60–69	Financial
13	70–89, 98–99	Recreation, entertainment, services, conglomerates, etc.

Each week, stocks are sorted according to their SIC codes into the 13 categories defined above, and value-weighted returns are computed for each group, yielding the 13 basis portfolios, which we denote by "SIC13." The autocovariance matrices are then estimated and the OFP are constructed according to Proposition 7.

6.4.3. Hedging-Portfolio Return as a Predictor of Market Returns

Table 17.18 reports the results of the regressions of R_{Mt} on various lagged OFP returns and on the hedging portfolios R_{Ht} and Q_{Ht}. For completeness, we have also included four additional regressions, with lagged value- and equal-weighted CRSP index returns, the logarithm of the reciprocal of lagged market capitalization, and the lagged three-month constant-maturity Treasury bill return as predictors.[40] Table 17.18 shows that the

---

[39]We are grateful to Jonathan Lewellen for sharing his industry classification scheme.

[40]We also considered nine other interest-rate predictors [six-month and one-year Treasury bill rates, three-month, six-month, and one-year off-the-run Treasury bill rates, one-month and three-month CD and Eurodollar rates, and the Fed Funds rate (all obtained from the Federal Reserve Bank of St. Louis, http://www.stls.frb.org/fred/data/wkly.html)]. Each of these variables produced results similar to those for the three-month constant-maturity Treasury bill return; hence, we omit those regressions from Table 17.18.

Table 17.18 Forecast of weekly market-portfolio returns by lagged weekly returns of the beta-sorted optimal forecast portfolios (OFPs), the market-capitalization-sorted OFPs, the SIC-sorted OFPs, the return and dollar return on the hedging portfolio, minus log-market-capitalization, the lagged returns on the CRSP value- and equal-weighted portfolios, and lagged constant-maturity (three-month) Treasury bill rates from 1962 to 1996 in five-year subperiods

Parameter	Beta10	Beta15	Beta20	Beta25	Cap10	Cap15	Cap20	Cap25	SIC13	R_H	Q_H	log(Cap^{-1})	VW	EW	TBill
									January 1967–December 1971 (261 weeks)						
Intercept	0.002	0.002	0.001	0.002	0.001	0.002	0.002	0.002	0.001	0.001	0.172	0.746	0.001	0.001	—
t-stat	1.330	1.360	1.150	1.430	1.240	1.520	1.400	1.380	0.920	1.270	1.200	2.330	1.240	1.250	—
Slope	0.103	−0.034	−0.153	0.171	−0.262	0.173	−0.039	−0.176	−0.208	0.138	0.154	0.027	0.191	0.092	—
t-stat	1.810	−0.550	−1.890	1.780	−1.900	1.079	−0.240	−1.070	−2.860	3.460	3.900	2.330	3.130	2.080	—
$\bar{R}^2$	0.013	0.001	0.014	0.012	0.014	0.005	0.000	0.005	0.031	0.045	0.056	0.021	0.037	0.016	—
									January 1972–December 1976 (261 weeks)						
Intercept	0.001	0.001	0.001	0.001	0.001	0.001	0.001	0.001	0.001	0.001	0.103	0.389	0.001	0.001	—
t-stat	0.650	0.640	0.560	0.670	0.830	0.640	0.730	0.630	0.630	0.820	0.760	1.410	0.700	0.640	—
Slope	0.023	0.204	−0.315	0.079	0.235	0.098	−0.169	0.069	0.040	−0.054	−0.023	0.014	−0.003	0.048	—
t-stat	0.120	1.150	−2.630	0.580	1.660	0.660	−1.180	0.430	0.430	−1.430	−1.900	1.410	−0.060	0.910	—
$\bar{R}^2$	0.000	0.005	0.026	0.001	0.011	0.002	0.005	0.001	0.001	0.008	0.014	0.008	0.000	0.003	—
									January 1977–December 1981 (261 weeks)						
Intercept	0.002	0.002	0.002	0.002	0.002	0.002	0.002	0.002	0.002	0.002	0.223	0.151	0.002	0.002	—
t-stat	1.750	1.600	1.800	1.640	1.770	1.760	1.800	1.530	1.749	1.500	1.370	0.720	1.570	1.380	—
Slope	0.007	0.071	0.065	0.033	0.075	0.003	−0.204	−0.186	0.150	0.049	0.013	0.005	0.069	0.080	—
t-stat	0.040	0.870	0.460	0.510	0.230	0.010	−0.850	−0.990	1.130	1.810	1.760	0.710	1.110	1.370	—
$\bar{R}^2$	0.000	0.003	0.001	0.001	0.000	0.000	0.003	0.004	0.005	0.013	0.012	0.002	0.005	0.007	—

January 1982–December 1986 (261 weeks)

Intercept	0.004	0.004	0.004	0.004	0.004	0.004	0.003	0.004	0.672	0.179	0.003	0.003	0.010
t-stat	3.150	3.130	3.180	3.160	3.150	3.150	2.640	3.500	3.190	1.130	2.690	2.710	1.860
Slope	-0.006	-0.309	0.154	-0.054	-0.105	0.099	-0.203	-0.047	-0.012	0.006	0.068	0.053	-4.053
t-stat	-0.030	-1.990	1.180	-0.220	-0.470	0.530	-1.890	-1.760	-1.490	1.110	1.100	0.820	-1.212
$\bar{R}^2$	0.000	0.015	0.005	0.000	0.001	0.001	0.014	0.012	0.009	0.005	0.005	0.003	0.006

January 1987–December 1991 (261 weeks)

Intercept	0.003	0.002	0.003	0.003	0.003	0.003	0.003	0.003	0.392	0.559	0.003	0.003	0.10
t-stat	1.700	1.650	1.770	1.730	1.680	1.800	1.720	2.280	2.050	1.460	1.820	1.880	1.098
Slope	0.294	-0.353	0.120	-0.062	-0.540	0.210	-0.033	-0.014	-0.023	0.020	0.058	0.032	-5.598
t-stat	1.580	-2.000	0.680	-0.320	-2.320	2.320	-0.190	-4.500	-2.490	1.460	0.930	0.550	-0.810
$\bar{R}^2$	0.010	0.015	0.002	0.000	0.021	0.021	0.000	0.073	0.024	0.008	0.003	0.001	0.003

January 1992–December 1996 (261 weeks)

Intercept	0.003	0.003	0.003	0.003	0.003	0.003	0.003	0.003	0.416	-0.107	0.003	0.003	-0.003
t-stat	3.170	3.120	3.110	3.130	3.060	3.120	3.130	3.700	3.510	-0.780	3.710	4.000	-0.881
Slope	0.118	-0.009	0.090	-0.040	-0.191	0.033	-0.047	-0.194	-0.153	-0.004	-0.163	-0.192	7.280
t-stat	1.060	-0.080	0.930	-0.270	-1.090	0.240	-0.700	-2.910	-2.410	-0.800	-2.710	-3.320	1.661
$\bar{R}^2$	0.004	0.000	0.003	0.005	0.005	0.000	0.002	0.032	0.022	0.003	0.028	0.041	0.011

The value of ϕ is 1.25 for the return R_H and 1.5 for the dollar return Q_H on the hedging portfolio, respectively.

hedging portfolios outperform all the other competing portfolios in forecasting future market returns in three of the six subperiods (subperiods 2, 4, and 6). In subperiod 3, only one OFP (Beta20) outperforms the hedging portfolio, and in subperiod 5, Beta20 and SIC13's OFPs outperform the hedging portfolio, but only marginally. In subperiod 7, the equal-weighted CRSP index return outperforms the hedging portfolio.

Several caveats should be kept in mind with regard to the three subperiods in which the hedging portfolios were surpassed by one or two competing portfolios. First, in these three subperiods, the hedging portfolio still outperforms most of the other competing portfolios. Second, there is no consistent winner in these subperiods. Third, the performance of the hedging portfolios is often close to the best performer. Moreover, the best performers in these subperiods performed poorly in the other subperiods, raising the possibility that their performance might be due to sampling variation. In contrast, the hedging portfolios forecasted R_{Mt} consistently in every subperiod. Indeed, among all the regressors, the hedging portfolios were the most consistent across all six subperiods, a remarkable confirmation of the properties of the model of Sections 6.1 and 6.2.[41]

6.5. The Hedging-Portfolio Return as a Risk Factor

To evaluate the success of the hedging-portfolio return as a risk factor in the cross section of expected returns, we implement a slightly modified version of the well-known regression tests outlined in Fama and MacBeth (1973). The basic approach is the same: form portfolios sorted by an estimated parameter such as market-beta coefficients in one time period (the "portfolio-formation period"), estimate betas for those same portfolios in a second nonoverlapping time period (the "estimation period"), and perform a cross-sectional regression test for the explanatory power of those betas using the returns of a third nonoverlapping time period (the "testing period"). However, in contrast to Fama and MacBeth (1973), we use weekly instead of monthly returns, and our portfolio-formation, estimation, and testing periods are five years each.[42]

Specifically, we run the following bivariate regression for each security in the portfolio-formation period, using only those securities that exist in all three periods[43]:

$$R_{jt} = \alpha_j + \beta_j^M R_{Mt} + \beta_j^H R_{Ht} + \varepsilon_{it}, \tag{6.32}$$

[41] On the other hand, the results in Table 17.18 must be tempered by the fact that the OFPs are only as good as the basis portfolios from which they are constructed. Increasing the number of basis portfolios should, in principle, increase the predictive power of the OFP. However, as the number of basis portfolios increases, the estimation errors in the autocovariance estimators $\widehat{\gamma}_0$ and $\widehat{\gamma}_1$ also increase for a fixed set of time-series observations; hence, the impact on the predictive power of the OFP is not clear.

[42] Our first portfolio-formation period, from 1962 to 1966, is only 4.5 years because the CRSP Daily Master file begins in July 1962. Fama and MacBeth (1973) original procedure used a seven-year portfolio-formation period, a five-year estimation period, and a four-year testing period.

[43] This induces a certain degree of survivorship bias, but the effects may not be as severe given that we apply the selection criterion three periods at a time. Moreover, while survivorship bias has a clear impact on expected returns and on the size effect, its implications for the cross-sectional explanatory power of the hedging portfolio is less obvious, hence we proceed cautiously with this selection criterion.

where R_{Mt} is the return on the CRSP value-weighted index and R_{Ht} is the return on the hedging portfolio. Using the estimated coefficients $\{\widehat{\beta}_i^M\}$ and $\{\widehat{\beta}_i^H\}$, we perform a double sort among the individual securities in the estimation period, creating 100 portfolios corresponding to the deciles of the estimated market and hedging-portfolio betas. We reestimate the two betas for each of these 100 portfolios in the estimation period and use these estimated betas as regressors in the testing period, for which we estimate the following cross-sectional regression:

$$R_{pt} = \gamma_{0t} + \gamma_{1t}\widehat{\beta}_p^M + \gamma_{2t}\widehat{\beta}_p^H + \eta_{pt}, \tag{6.33}$$

where R_{pt} is the equal-weighted portfolio return for securities in portfolio p, $p = 1, \ldots, 100$, constructed from the double-sorted rankings of the portfolio-estimation period, and $\widehat{\beta}_{pt}^M$ and $\widehat{\beta}_{pt}^H$ are the market and hedging-portfolio returns, respectively, of portfolio p obtained from the estimation period. This cross-sectional regression is estimated for each of the 261 weeks in the five-year testing period, yielding a time series of coefficients $\{\widehat{\gamma}_{0t}\}$, $\{\widehat{\gamma}_{1t}\}$, and $\{\widehat{\gamma}_{2t}\}$. Summary statistics for these coefficients and their diagnostics are then reported, and this entire procedure is repeated by incrementing the portfolio-formation, estimation, and testing periods by five years. We then perform the same analysis for the hedge-portfolio dollar-return series $\{Q_{Ht}\}$.

Because we use weekly instead of monthly data, it may be difficult to compare our results to other cross-sectional tests in the extant literature, e.g., Fama and French (1992). Therefore, we apply our procedure to three other benchmark models: the standard CAPM in which R_{Mt} is the only regressor in (6.32) and 100 market-beta-sorted portfolios constructed, a two-factor model in which the hedging-portfolio return factor is replaced by a "small-minus-big capitalization" or "SMB" portfolio return factor as in Fama and French (1993), and a two-factor model in which the hedging-portfolio return factor is replaced by the OFP return factor described in Section 6.4.2.[44] Table 17.19 reports the correlations between the different portfolio return factors, returns on CRSP value- and equal-weighted portfolios, return and dollar return on the hedging portfolio, returns on the SMB portfolio and, OFP, Beta20, and the two turnover indices.

Table 17.20 summarizes the results of all these cross-sectional regression tests for each of the five testing periods from 1972 to 1996. In the first subpanel, corresponding to the first testing period from 1972 to 1976, there is little evidence in support of the CAPM or any of the two-factor models estimated.[45] For example, the first three rows show that the time-series average of the market-beta coefficients, $\{\widehat{\gamma}_{1t}\}$, is 0.000, with a t-statistic

---

[44]Specifically, the SMB portfolio return is constructed by taking the difference of the value-weighted returns of securities with market capitalization below and above the median market capitalization at the start of the five-year subperiod.

[45]The two-factor model with OFP as the second factor is not estimated until the second testing period because we use the 1962–1966 period to estimate the covariances from which the OFP returns in the 1967–1971 period are constructed. Therefore, the OFP returns are not available in the first portfolio-formation period.

Table 17.19 Correlation matrix for weekly returns on the CRSP value-weighted index (R_{VWt}), the CRSP equal-weighted index (R_{EWt}), the hedging-portfolio return (R_{Ht}), the hedging-portfolio dollar-return (Q_{Ht}), the return of the SMB capitalization stocks portfolio (R_{SMBt}), the return R_{OFPt} of the OFP for the set of 25 market-beta-sorted basis portfolios, and the equal-weighted and share-weighted turnover indices (τ_t^{EW} and τ_t^{SW}), using CRSP weekly returns and volume data for NYSE and AMEX stocks from 1962 to 1996 and in five-year subperiods

	R_{VWt}	R_{EWt}	R_{Ht}	Q_{Ht}	R_{SMBt}	R_{OFPt}	τ_t^{EW}	τ_t^{SW}
	July 1962–December 1996 (1800 weeks)							
R_{VWt}	100.0	88.7	−13.2	15.6	14.0	−26.9	10.6	8.1
R_{EWt}	88.7	100.0	−15.8	4.6	53.5	−25.3	12.6	5.5
R_{Ht}	−13.2	−15.8	100.0	40.3	−10.7	−11.0	14.9	16.8
Q_{Ht}	15.6	4.6	40.3	100.0	−13.3	−6.7	7.5	9.9
R_{SMBt}	14.0	53.5	−10.7	−13.3	100.0	−4.8	4.6	−5.8
R_{OFPt}	−26.9	−25.3	−11.0	−6.7	−4.8	100.0	−4.9	−2.4
τ_t^{EW}	10.6	12.6	14.9	7.5	4.6	−4.9	100.0	86.2
τ_t^{SW}	8.1	5.5	16.8	9.9	−5.8	−2.4	86.2	100.0
	January 1967–December 1971 (261 weeks)							
R_{VWt}	100.0	92.6	95.6	91.5	62.7	−76.2	19.1	26.3
R_{EWt}	92.6	100.0	92.3	88.4	84.5	−71.9	32.8	36.9
R_{Ht}	95.6	92.3	100.0	97.4	70.7	−65.0	22.0	29.6
Q_{Ht}	91.5	88.4	97.4	100.0	69.8	−60.1	22.9	29.8
R_{SMBt}	62.7	84.5	70.7	69.8	100.0	−46.6	39.7	38.2
R_{OFPt}	−76.2	−71.9	−65.0	−60.1	−46.6	100.0	−7.5	−10.4
τ_t^{EW}	19.1	32.8	22.0	22.9	39.7	−7.5	100.0	93.1
τ_t^{SW}	26.3	36.9	29.6	29.8	38.2	−10.4	93.1	100.0
	January 1972–December 1977 (261 weeks)							
R_{VWt}	100.0	84.5	13.3	14.2	−6.9	−59.5	19.0	27.6
R_{EWt}	84.5	100.0	−11.5	−18.2	44.1	−45.4	24.3	35.4
R_{Ht}	13.3	−11.5	100.0	86.6	−55.2	−8.3	−2.8	−1.9
Q_{Ht}	14.2	−18.2	86.6	100.0	−70.4	−11.6	−4.1	−4.2
R_{SMBt}	−6.9	44.1	−55.2	−70.4	100.0	15.0	11.3	16.3
R_{OFPt}	−59.5	−45.4	−8.3	−11.6	15.0	100.0	−6.7	−12.4
τ_t^{EW}	19.0	24.3	−2.8	−4.1	11.3	−6.7	100.0	87.3
τ_t^{SW}	27.6	35.4	−1.9	−4.2	16.3	−12.4	87.3	100.0
	January 1977–December 1981 (261 weeks)							
R_{VWt}	100.0	90.2	85.4	82.3	23.8	22.6	12.6	15.7
R_{EWt}	90.2	100.0	88.5	82.0	59.3	12.7	7.6	8.1
R_{Ht}	85.4	88.5	100.0	87.1	51.2	9.3	7.6	8.6

Table 17.19 (*Continued*)

	$R_{\mathrm{VW}t}$	$R_{\mathrm{EW}t}$	R_{Ht}	Q_{Ht}	$R_{\mathrm{SMB}t}$	$R_{\mathrm{OFP}t}$	τ_t^{EW}	τ_t^{SW}
			January 1977–December 1981 (261 weeks)					
Q_{Ht}	82.3	82.0	87.1	100.0	49.0	10.4	11.0	12.3
$R_{\mathrm{SMB}t}$	23.8	59.3	51.2	49.0	100.0	−16.7	−8.3	−12.7
$R_{\mathrm{OFP}t}$	22.6	12.7	9.3	10.4	−16.7	100.0	10.7	10.4
τ_t^{EW}	12.6	7.6	7.6	11.0	−8.3	10.7	100.0	94.9
τ_t^{SW}	15.7	8.1	8.6	12.3	−12.7	10.4	94.9	100.0
			January 1982–December 1986 (261 weeks)					
$R_{\mathrm{VW}t}$	100.0	92.1	−17.0	6.1	−2.8	−23.5	27.1	28.6
$R_{\mathrm{EW}t}$	92.1	100.0	−34.1	−10.2	30.6	−30.6	36.0	31.6
R_{Ht}	−17.0	−34.1	100.0	73.3	−54.5	13.5	−12.2	−7.8
Q_{Ht}	6.1	−10.2	73.3	100.0	−41.1	8.0	1.3	4.2
$R_{\mathrm{SMB}t}$	−2.8	30.6	−54.5	−41.1	100.0	−15.9	19.9	6.5
$R_{\mathrm{OFP}t}$	−23.5	−30.6	13.5	8.0	−15.9	100.0	−20.7	−17.9
τ_t^{EW}	27.1	36.0	−12.2	1.3	19.9	−20.7	100.0	93.2
τ_t^{SW}	28.6	31.6	−7.8	4.2	6.5	−17.9	93.2	100.0
			January 1987–December 1991 (261 weeks)					
$R_{\mathrm{VW}t}$	100.0	91.2	−40.4	−36.0	8.1	18.9	−15.0	−17.0
$R_{\mathrm{EW}t}$	91.2	100.0	−44.3	−46.5	44.6	36.3	−16.7	−20.9
R_{Ht}	−40.4	−44.3	100.0	58.1	−23.8	−26.2	43.2	43.7
Q_{Ht}	−36.0	−46.5	58.1	100.0	−37.1	−32.8	25.3	24.0
$R_{\mathrm{SMB}t}$	8.1	44.6	−23.8	−37.1	100.0	45.1	−11.4	−16.9
$R_{\mathrm{OFP}t}$	18.9	36.3	−26.2	−32.8	45.1	100.0	−18.5	−19.7
τ_t^{EW}	−15.0	−16.7	43.2	25.3	−11.4	−18.5	100.0	94.7
τ_t^{SW}	−17.0	−20.9	43.7	24.0	−16.9	−19.7	94.7	100.0
			January 1992–December 1996 (261 weeks)					
$R_{\mathrm{VW}t}$	100.0	84.3	95.5	66.5	−1.2	−13.1	15.5	10.4
$R_{\mathrm{EW}t}$	84.3	100.0	73.2	40.5	46.1	−5.2	18.2	5.4
R_{Ht}	95.5	73.2	100.0	84.8	−19.7	−8.7	15.3	11.2
Q_{Ht}	66.5	40.5	84.8	100.0	−41.6	0.2	12.0	9.2
$R_{\mathrm{SMB}t}$	−1.2	46.1	−19.7	−41.6	100.0	11.3	3.0	−10.1
$R_{\mathrm{OFP}t}$	−13.1	−5.2	−8.7	0.2	11.3	100.0	−3.0	−3.3
τ_t^{EW}	15.5	18.2	15.3	12.0	3.0	−3.0	100.0	92.7
τ_t^{SW}	10.4	5.4	11.2	9.2	−10.1	−3.3	92.7	100.0

Table 17.20   Cross-sectional regression tests of various linear factor models along the lines of Fama and MacBeth (1973) using weekly returns for NYSE and AMEX stocks from 1962 to 1996, five-year subperiods for the portfolio formation, estimation, and testing periods, and 100 portfolios in the cross-sectional regressions each week

Model	Statistic	$\widehat{\gamma}_{0t}$	$\widehat{\gamma}_{1t}$	$\widehat{\gamma}_{2t}$	$\bar{R}^2(\%)$
January 1972–December 1976 (261 weeks)					
$R_{pt} = \gamma_{0t} + \gamma_{1t}\widehat{\beta}_p^M + \epsilon_{pt}$	Mean:	0.002	0.000		10.0
	S.D.:	0.015	0.021		10.9
	t-stat:	1.639	0.348		
$R_{pt} = \gamma_{0t} + \gamma_{1t}\widehat{\beta}_p^M + \gamma_{2t}\widehat{\beta}_p^{HR} + \epsilon_{pt}$ ($\phi = 1.25$)	Mean:	0.004	−0.002	−0.002	14.3
	S.D.:	0.035	0.035	0.037	10.9
	t-stat:	2.040	−1.047	−0.820	
$R_{pt} = \gamma_{0t} + \gamma_{1t}\widehat{\beta}_p^M + \gamma_{2t}\widehat{\beta}_p^{HQ} + \epsilon_{pt}$ ($\phi = 1.50$)	Mean:	0.004	−0.002	−0.104	15.5
	S.D.:	0.032	0.034	3.797	10.9
	t-stat:	2.162	−1.081	−0.442	
$R_{pt} = \gamma_{0t} + \gamma_{1t}\widehat{\beta}_p^M + \gamma_{2t}\widehat{\beta}_p^{SMB} + \epsilon_{pt}$	Mean:	0.001	0.000	0.063	12.1
	S.D.:	0.014	0.024	1.142	10.8
	t-stat:	1.424	0.217	0.898	
January 1977–December 1981 (261 weeks)					
$R_{pt} = \gamma_{0t} + \gamma_{1t}\widehat{\beta}_p^M + \epsilon_{pt}$	Mean:	0.001	0.003		11.7
	S.D.:	0.011	0.022		12.8
	t-stat:	1.166	2.566		
$R_{pt} = \gamma_{0t} + \gamma_{1t}\widehat{\beta}_p^M + \gamma_{2t}\widehat{\beta}_p^{HR} + \epsilon_{pt}$ ($\phi = 4.75$)	Mean:	0.003	−0.001	−0.012	13.1
	S.D.:	0.014	0.020	0.051	12.4
	t-stat:	3.748	−0.902	−3.712	
$R_{pt} = \gamma_{0t} + \gamma_{1t}\widehat{\beta}_p^M + \gamma_{2t}\widehat{\beta}_p^{HQ} + \epsilon_{pt}$ ($\phi = 4.25$)	Mean:	0.003	−0.001	−1.564	12.5
	S.D.:	0.013	0.020	6.104	12.2
	t-stat:	3.910	−0.754	−4.140	
$R_{pt} = \gamma_{0t} + \gamma_{1t}\widehat{\beta}_p^M + \gamma_{2t}\widehat{\beta}_p^{SMB} + \epsilon_{pt}$	Mean:	0.001	0.000	0.299	14.9
	S.D.:	0.011	0.017	1.088	13.4
	t-stat:	2.251	−0.164	4.433	
$R_{pt} = \gamma_{0t} + \gamma_{1t}\widehat{\beta}_p^M + \gamma_{2t}\widehat{\beta}_p^{OFP} + \epsilon_{pt}$	Mean:	0.003	0.001	0.001	14.1
	S.D.:	0.018	0.023	0.036	11.6
	t-stat:	2.735	0.843	0.632	

Table 17.20 (*Continued*)

Model	Statistic	$\widehat{\gamma}_{0t}$	$\widehat{\gamma}_{1t}$	$\widehat{\gamma}_{2t}$	$\bar{R}^2(\%)$
January 1982–December 1986 (261 weeks)					
$R_{pt} = \gamma_{0t} + \gamma_{1t}\widehat{\beta}_p^M + \epsilon_{pt}$	Mean:	0.006	−0.001		9.4
	S.D.:	0.011	0.019		11.1
	t-stat:	8.169	−1.044		
$R_{pt} = \gamma_{0t} + \gamma_{1t}\widehat{\beta}_p^M + \gamma_{2t}\widehat{\beta}_p^{HR} + \epsilon_{pt}$	Mean:	0.006	−0.001	−0.006	9.6
$(\phi = 1.75)$	S.D.:	0.011	0.020	0.055	9.4
	t-stat:	8.390	−0.780	−1.732	
$R_{pt} = \gamma_{0t} + \gamma_{1t}\widehat{\beta}_p^M + \gamma_{2t}\widehat{\beta}_p^{HQ} + \epsilon_{pt}$	Mean:	0.006	−0.002	−0.740	10.4
$(\phi = 2.00)$	S.D.:	0.011	0.019	19.874	9.5
	t-stat:	8.360	−1.297	−0.602	
$R_{pt} = \gamma_{0t} + \gamma_{1t}\widehat{\beta}_p^M + \gamma_{2t}\widehat{\beta}_p^{SMB} + \epsilon_{pt}$	Mean:	0.005	−0.002	0.038	10.0
	S.D.:	0.012	0.019	1.154	8.4
	t-stat:	7.451	−1.264	0.531	
$R_{pt} = \gamma_{0t} + \gamma_{1t}\widehat{\beta}_p^M + \gamma_{2t}\widehat{\beta}_p^{OFP} + \epsilon_{pt}$	Mean:	0.005	−0.001	0.000	11.7
	S.D.:	0.011	0.020	0.021	10.8
	t-stat:	7.545	−0.818	0.199	
January 1987–December 1991 (261 weeks)					
$R_{pt} = \gamma_{0t} + \gamma_{1t}\widehat{\beta}_p^M + \epsilon_{pt}$	Mean:	0.002	0.000		5.9
	S.D.:	0.013	0.023		8.7
	t-stat:	2.649	0.204		
$R_{pt} = \gamma_{0t} + \gamma_{1t}\widehat{\beta}_p^M + \gamma_{2t}\widehat{\beta}_p^{HR} + \epsilon_{pt}$	Mean:	0.002	0.000	0.000	5.4
$(\phi = 47)$	S.D.:	0.016	0.019	0.060	6.1
	t-stat:	2.254	0.105	0.132	
$R_{pt} = \gamma_{0t} + \gamma_{1t}\widehat{\beta}_p^M + \gamma_{2t}\widehat{\beta}_p^{HQ} + \epsilon_{pt}$	Mean:	0.002	0.000	0.189	6.0
$(\phi = 20)$	S.D.:	0.016	0.019	18.194	6.7
	t-stat:	2.434	−0.147	0.168	
$R_{pt} = \gamma_{0t} + \gamma_{1t}\widehat{\beta}_p^M + \gamma_{2t}\widehat{\beta}_p^{SMB} + \epsilon_{pt}$	Mean:	0.003	0.000	−0.075	7.8
	S.D.:	0.014	0.020	1.235	8.2
	t-stat:	3.101	0.158	−0.979	
$R_{pt} = \gamma_{0t} + \gamma_{1t}\widehat{\beta}_p^M + \gamma_{2t}\widehat{\beta}_p^{OFP} + \epsilon_{pt}$	Mean:	0.003	−0.001	0.000	6.4
	S.D.:	0.015	0.021	0.021	7.3
	t-stat:	2.731	−0.385	−0.234	

(*Continued*)

Table 17.20 (*Continued*)

Model	Statistic	$\widehat{\gamma}_{0t}$	$\widehat{\gamma}_{1t}$	$\widehat{\gamma}_{2t}$	$\bar{R}^2$ (%)
		January 1992–December 1996 (261 weeks)			
$R_{pt} = \gamma_{0t} + \gamma_{1t}\widehat{\beta}_p^M + \epsilon_{pt}$	Mean:	0.002	0.001		5.7
	S.D.:	0.013	0.020		7.7
	t-stat:	2.679	1.178		
$R_{pt} = \gamma_{0t} + \gamma_{1t}\widehat{\beta}_p^M + \gamma_{2t}\widehat{\beta}_p^{HR} + \epsilon_{pt}$	Mean:	0.002	0.001	−0.004	6.9
($\phi = 38$)	S.D.:	0.013	0.020	0.091	6.8
	t-stat:	2.785	1.164	−0.650	
$R_{pt} = \gamma_{0t} + \gamma_{1t}\widehat{\beta}_p^M + \gamma_{2t}\widehat{\beta}_p^{HQ} + \epsilon_{pt}$	Mean:	0.003	0.000	−1.584	6.2
($\phi = 27$)	S.D.:	0.015	0.022	12.992	6.6
	t-stat:	3.279	−0.178	−1.970	
$R_{pt} = \gamma_{0t} + \gamma_{1t}\widehat{\beta}_p^M + \gamma_{2t}\widehat{\beta}_p^{SMB} + \epsilon_{pt}$	Mean:	0.002	0.001	0.154	6.7
	S.D.:	0.015	0.019	1.157	7.0
	t-stat:	1.653	0.861	2.147	
$R_{pt} = \gamma_{0t} + \gamma_{1t}\widehat{\beta}_p^M + \gamma_{2t}\widehat{\beta}_p^{OFP} + \epsilon_{pt}$	Mean:	0.001	0.002	0.002	7.9
	S.D.:	0.016	0.020	0.015	7.4
	t-stat:	0.895	1.236	2.407	

The five linear-factor models are: the standard CAPM $(\widehat{\beta}_p^M)$, and four two-factor models in which the first factor is the market beta and the second factors are, respectively, the hedging-portfolio return-beta $(\widehat{\beta}_p^{HR})$, the hedging-portfolio dollar-return beta $(\widehat{\beta}_p^{HQ})$, the beta of a SMB cap portfolio return $(\widehat{\beta}_p^{SMB})$, and the beta of the optimal forecast portfolio based on a set of 25 market-beta-sorted basis portfolios $(\widehat{\beta}_p^{OFP})$.

of 0.348 and an average $\bar{R}^2$ of 10.0%.[46] When the hedging-portfolio beta $\widehat{\beta}_t^H$ is added to the regression, the $\bar{R}^2$ does increase to 14.3%, but the average of the coefficients $\{\widehat{\gamma}_{2t}\}$ is −0.002 with a t-statistic of −0.820. The average market-beta coefficient is still insignificant, but it has now switched sign. The results for the two-factor model with the hedging-portfolio dollar-return factor and the two-factor model with the SMB factor are similar.

In the second testing period, both specifications with the hedging-portfolio factor exhibit statistically significant means for the hedging-portfolio betas, with average coefficients and t-statistics of −0.012 and −3.712 for the hedging-portfolio return factor and −1.564 and −4.140 for the hedging-portfolio dollar-return factor. In contrast, the market-beta coefficients are not significant in either of these specifications and are also

---

[46]The t-statistic is computed under the assumption of i.i.d. coefficients $\{\gamma_{1t}\}$, which may not be appropriate. However, since this has become the standard method for reporting the results of these cross-sectional regression tests, we follow this convention to make our results comparable to those in the literature.

of the wrong sign. The only other specification with a significant mean coefficient is the two-factor model with SMB as the second factor, with an average coefficient of 0.299 for the SMB factor and a *t*-statistic of 4.433.

For the three remaining test periods, the only specifications with any statistically significant factors are the SMB and MPP two-factor models in the 1992–1996 testing period. However, the $\bar{R}^2$s in the last two testing periods are substantially lower than in the earlier periods, perhaps reflecting the greater volatility of equity returns in recent years.

Overall, the results do not provide overwhelming support for any factor in explaining the cross-sectional variation of expected returns. There is, of course, the ubiquitous problem of lack of power in these cross-sectional regression tests; hence, we should not be surprised that no single factor stands out.[47] However, the point estimates of the cross-sectional regressions show that the hedging-portfolio factor is comparable in magnitude and in performance to other commonly proposed factors.

6.6. Updated Empirical Results

Since writing the initial draft of this chapter, we have updated the empirical results of Sections 6.4 and 6.5 with data from 1997 to 2004, yielding true out-of-sample tests of our intertemporal asset pricing model in Tables 17.21–17.23. Table 17.21 shows that the hedging portfolios continue to outperform the OFPs in the new subperiods, confirming the predictive power of the hedging portfolios as specified by Proposition 4.

Table 17.22 is an update of Table 17.19, containing correlation matrices of the factors used in Table 17.23's updated cross-sectional tests of the explanatory power of the hedging portfolios (only three subperiods are included to conserve space). The cross-sectional regressions in Table 17.23 contain one additional factor beyond those of Table 17.20: the Fama and French (1992) high-minus-low (HML) book-to-market factor.

The results in Table 17.23 for the original subperiods in Table 17.20 are not much different from the results without the HML factor – in the first subpanel, which corresponds to the first testing period from 1972 to 1976, there is little evidence in support of either the CAPM or any of the other linear models estimated. When the hedging portfolio beta $\widehat{\beta}_t^H$ is added to the regression, the $\bar{R}^2$ increases to 14.3%, but the average of the coefficients $\{\widehat{\gamma}_{2t}\}$ is −0.2% with a *t*-statistic of −0.82. The average market-beta coefficient is still insignificant, but it has now switched sign. The results for the two-factor model with the hedging-portfolio dollar-return factor and the two-factor model with the SMB factor are similar. The three-factor model is even less successful, with statistically insignificant coefficients close to 0.0% and an average R^2 of 8.8%.

---

[47]See, e.g., MacKinlay (1987, 1994).

Table 17.21 Forecast of weekly market-portfolio returns by lagged weekly returns of the beta-sorted optimal forecast portfolios (OFPs), the market-capitalization-sorted OFPs, the SIC-sorted OFP, the return and dollar return on the hedging portfolio, minus log-market-capitalization, the lagged returns on the CRSP value- and equal-weighted portfolios, and lagged constant-maturity (three-month) Treasury bill rates from 1997 to 2004 in two subperiods

Parameter	Beta10	Beta15	Beta20	Beta25	Cap10	Cap15	Cap20	Cap25	SIC13	R_H	Q_H	−Cap	VW	EW	TBill
								January 1997–December 2001 (261 weeks)							
Intercept	0.006	0.005	0.005	0.006	0.006	0.005	0.005	0.005	0.006	0.006	0.894	0.648	0.006	0.006	0.008
t-stat	3.844	3.639	3.660	3.844	3.778	3.680	3.703	3.619	3.826	3.941	2.718	2.246	3.873	3.863	1.006
Slope	0.095	0.093	0.034	0.095	−0.045	0.087	0.018	−0.152	−0.039	−0.057	−0.029	0.022	−0.078	−0.094	−2.414
t-stat	1.033	1.003	0.360	1.033	−0.434	0.936	0.205	−1.772	−0.721	−3.199	−3.204	2.227	−1.247	−1.363	−0.303
$\bar{R}^2$	0.004	0.004	0.001	0.004	0.001	0.003	0.000	0.012	0.002	0.039	0.041	0.019	0.006	0.007	0.000
								January 2002–December 2004 (156 weeks)							
Intercept	0.003	0.003	0.003	0.003	0.003	0.002	0.003	0.003	0.003	0.003	0.342	0.620	0.003	0.004	0.008
t-stat	1.536	1.365	1.516	1.355	1.552	1.196	1.708	1.698	1.670	1.787	1.852	1.203	1.765	2.107	1.116
Slope	−0.334	0.205	−0.314	−0.275	−0.283	−0.198	0.404	−0.295	−0.202	−0.056	0.028	0.021	−0.146	−0.216	−19.368
t-stat	−1.847	1.219	−2.006	−1.561	−1.005	−0.679	1.949	−1.185	−2.301	−2.853	1.600	1.197	−1.834	−2.738	−0.728
$\bar{R}^2$	0.022	0.010	0.026	0.016	0.007	0.003	0.025	0.009	0.034	0.051	0.017	0.009	0.021	0.046	0.004

The value of ϕ is 1.25 for the return R_H and 1.5 for the dollar return Q_H on the hedging portfolio.

Table 17.22   Correlation matrix for weekly returns on the CRSP value-weighted index (R_{VWt}), the CRSP equal-weighted index (R_{EWt}), the hedging-portfolio return (R_{Ht}), the hedging-portfolio dollar-return (Q_{Ht}), the return of the SMB capitalization stocks portfolio (R_{SMBt}), the return R_{OFPt} of the OFP for the set of 20 market-beta-sorted basis portfolios, and the equal-weighted and share-weighted turnover indices (τ_t^{EW} and τ_t^{SW}), using CRSP weekly returns and volume data for NYSE and AMEX stocks for three subperiods: January 1967–December 1971, January 1997–December 2001, and January 2002–December 2004

	R_{VWt}	R_{EWt}	R_{Ht}	Q_{Ht}	R_{SMBt}	R_{HMLt}	R_{OFPt}	τ_t^{EW}	τ_t^{SW}
	January 1967–December 1971 (261 weeks)								
R_{VWt}	100.0	92.6	95.6	91.5	62.7	−44.1	−76.2	19.1	26.3
R_{EWt}	92.6	100.0	92.3	88.4	84.5	−40.8	−71.9	32.8	36.9
R_{Ht}	95.6	92.3	100.0	97.4	70.7	−52.4	−65.0	22.0	29.6
Q_{Ht}	91.5	88.4	97.4	100.0	69.8	−49.4	−60.1	22.9	29.8
R_{SMBt}	62.7	84.5	70.7	69.8	100.0	−40.6	−46.6	39.7	38.2
R_{HMLt}	−44.1	−40.8	−52.4	−49.4	−40.6	100.0	14.5	−9.0	−15.0
R_{OFPt}	−76.2	−71.9	−65.0	−60.1	−46.6	14.5	100.0	−7.5	−10.4
τ_t^{EW}	19.1	32.8	22.0	22.9	39.7	−9.0	−7.5	100.0	93.1
τ_t^{SW}	26.3	36.9	29.6	29.8	38.2	−15.0	−10.4	93.1	100.0
	January 1997–December 2001 (261 weeks)								
R_{VWt}	100.0	80.4	57.9	43.4	−20.7	−48.7	−45.7	3.3	−0.9
R_{EWt}	80.4	100.0	54.8	42.6	24.9	−46.7	−33.1	7.9	−1.4
R_{Ht}	57.9	54.8	100.0	89.2	17.0	−71.0	−15.5	0.0	−2.2
Q_{Ht}	43.4	42.6	89.2	100.0	25.3	−70.0	−1.2	3.8	0.4
R_{SMBt}	−20.7	24.9	17.0	25.3	100.0	−41.8	25.8	7.0	0.1
R_{HMLt}	−48.7	−46.7	−71.0	−70.0	−41.8	100.0	2.5	−0.1	4.4
R_{OFPt}	−45.7	−33.1	−15.5	−1.2	25.8	2.5	100.0	−0.9	1.8
τ_t^{EW}	3.3	7.9	0.0	3.8	7.0	−0.1	−0.9	100.0	92.4
τ_t^{SW}	−0.9	−1.4	−2.2	0.4	0.1	4.4	1.8	92.4	100.0
	January 2002–December 2004 (156 weeks)								
R_{VWt}	100.0	91.8	68.6	−11.5	−17.1	−6.6	55.0	9.3	4.1
R_{EWt}	91.8	100.0	76.3	−32.7	15.8	10.2	50.3	5.5	−3.1
R_{Ht}	68.6	76.3	100.0	−60.4	14.1	−2.0	31.5	5.4	−0.4
Q_{Ht}	−11.5	−32.7	−60.4	100.0	−56.5	−2.4	−2.5	−3.9	3.3
R_{SMBt}	−17.1	15.8	14.1	−56.5	100.0	9.4	−7.2	−5.6	−9.1
R_{HMLt}	−6.6	10.2	−2.0	−2.4	9.4	100.0	−17.2	−18.3	−27.9
R_{OFPt}	55.0	50.3	31.5	−2.5	−7.2	−17.2	100.0	12.1	3.7
τ_t^{EW}	9.3	5.5	5.4	−3.9	−5.6	−18.3	12.1	100.0	77.8
τ_t^{SW}	4.1	−3.1	−0.4	3.3	−9.1	−27.9	3.7	77.8	100.0

Table 17.23   Cross-sectional regression tests of six linear factor models along the lines of Fama and MacBeth (1973), using weekly returns for NYSE and AMEX stocks from 1962 to 2004 in five-year subperiods for the portfolio formation, estimation, and testing periods, and 100 portfolios in the cross-sectional regressions each week. The six linear factor models are the standard CAPM ($\widehat{\beta}_p^M$); four two-factor models in which the first factor is the market beta and the second factors are, respectively, the hedging-portfolio return-beta ($\widehat{\beta}_p^{HR}$), the hedging-portfolio dollar-return beta ($\widehat{\beta}_p^{HQ}$), the beta of a SMB cap portfolio return ($\widehat{\beta}_p^{SMB}$), the beta of the Fama and French (1992) HML book-to-market portfolio return ($\widehat{\beta}_p^{HML}$), and the beta of the optimal forecast portfolio based on a set of 25 market-beta-sorted basis portfolios ($\widehat{\beta}_p^{OFP}$); and a three-factor model with $\widehat{\beta}_p^M$, $\widehat{\beta}_p^{SMB}$, and $\widehat{\beta}_p^{HML}$ as the three factors

Model	Statistic	$\widehat{\gamma}_{0t}$	$\widehat{\gamma}_{1t}$	$\widehat{\gamma}_{2t}$	$\widehat{\gamma}_{3t}$	$\bar{R}^2$ (%)
	January 1972–December 1976 (261 weeks)					
$R_{pt} = \gamma_{0t} + \gamma_{1t}\widehat{\beta}_p^M + \varepsilon_{pt}$	Mean (%):	0.2	0.0			10.0
	S.D. (%):	1.5	2.1			10.9
	t-stat:	1.64	0.35			
$R_{pt} = \gamma_{0t} + \gamma_{1t}\widehat{\beta}_p^M + \gamma_{2t}\widehat{\beta}_p^{HR} + \varepsilon_{pt}$	Mean (%):	0.4	−0.2	−0.2		14.3
($\phi = 1.25$)	S.D. (%):	3.5	3.5	3.7		10.9
	t-stat:	2.04	−1.05	−0.82		
$R_{pt} = \gamma_{0t} + \gamma_{1t}\widehat{\beta}_p^M + \gamma_{2t}\widehat{\beta}_p^{HQ} + \varepsilon_{pt}$	Mean (%):	0.4	−0.2	−10.4		15.5
($\phi = 1.50$)	S.D. (%):	3.2	3.4	379.7		10.9
	t-stat:	2.16	−1.08	−0.44		
$R_{pt} = \gamma_{0t} + \gamma_{1t}\widehat{\beta}_p^M + \gamma_{2t}\widehat{\beta}_p^{SMB} + \varepsilon_{pt}$	Mean (%):	0.1	0.0	6.3		12.1
	S.D. (%):	1.4	2.4	114.2		10.8
	t-stat:	1.42	0.22	0.90		
$R_{pt} = \gamma_{0t} + \gamma_{1t}\widehat{\beta}_p^M + \gamma_{2t}\widehat{\beta}_p^{HML} + \varepsilon_{pt}$	Mean (%):	0.0	0.1	0.2		7.8
	S.D. (%):	1.8	1.9	1.5		7.8
	t-stat:	0.40	1.08	1.66		
$R_{pt} = \gamma_{0t} + \gamma_{1t}\widehat{\beta}_p^M + \gamma_{2t}\widehat{\beta}_p^{SMB}$ $+\gamma_{3t}\widehat{\beta}_p^{HML} + \varepsilon_{pt}$	Mean (%):	0.0	0.1	0.0	0.1	8.8
	S.D. (%):	1.8	2.1	1.2	1.5	7.6
	t-stat:	0.28	0.80	0.50	1.27	
	January 1977–December 1981 (261 weeks)					
$R_{pt} = \gamma_{0t} + \gamma_{1t}\widehat{\beta}_p^M + \varepsilon_{pt}$	Mean (%):	0.1	0.3			11.7
	S.D. (%):	1.1	2.2			12.8
	t-stat:	1.17	2.57			
$R_{pt} = \gamma_{0t} + \gamma_{1t}\widehat{\beta}_p^M + \gamma_{2t}\widehat{\beta}_p^{HR} + \varepsilon_{pt}$	Mean (%):	0.3	−0.1	−1.2		13.1
($\phi = 4.75$)	S.D. (%):	1.4	2.0	5.1		12.4
	t-stat:	3.75	−0.90	−3.71		

Table 17.23 (*Continued*)

Model	Statistic	$\widehat{\gamma}_{0t}$	$\widehat{\gamma}_{1t}$	$\widehat{\gamma}_{2t}$	$\widehat{\gamma}_{3t}$	$\bar{R}^2$ (%)
	January 1977–December 1981 (261 weeks)					
$R_{pt} = \gamma_{0t} + \gamma_{1t}\widehat{\beta}_p^M + \gamma_{2t}\widehat{\beta}_p^{HQ} + \varepsilon_{pt}$	Mean (%):	0.3	−0.1	−156.4		12.5
($\phi = 4.25$)	S.D. (%):	1.3	2.0	610.4		12.2
	t-stat:	3.91	−0.75	−4.14		
$R_{pt} = \gamma_{0t} + \gamma_{1t}\widehat{\beta}_p^M + \gamma_{2t}\widehat{\beta}_p^{SMB} + \varepsilon_{pt}$	Mean (%):	0.1	0.0	29.9		14.9
	S.D. (%):	1.1	1.7	108.8		13.4
	t-stat:	2.25	−0.16	4.43		
$R_{pt} = \gamma_{0t} + \gamma_{1t}\widehat{\beta}_p^M + \gamma_{2t}\widehat{\beta}_p^{HML} + \varepsilon_{pt}$	Mean (%):	0.2	0.2	0.1		9.3
	S.D. (%):	1.3	1.9	0.9		9.2
	t-stat:	2.15	1.52	1.58		
$R_{pt} = \gamma_{0t} + \gamma_{1t}\widehat{\beta}_p^M + \gamma_{2t}\widehat{\beta}_p^{OFP} + \varepsilon_{pt}$	Mean (%):	0.3	0.1	0.1		14.1
	S.D. (%):	1.8	2.3	3.6		11.6
	t-stat:	2.74	0.84	0.63		
$R_{pt} = \gamma_{0t} + \gamma_{1t}\widehat{\beta}_p^M + \gamma_{2t}\widehat{\beta}_p^{SMB}$	Mean (%):	0.2	−0.0	0.3	−0.1	11.5
$\quad + \gamma_{3t}\widehat{\beta}_p^{HML} + \varepsilon_{pt}$	S.D. (%):	1.2	1.7	1.0	1.0	10.0
	t-stat:	2.72	−0.07	4.61	−0.85	
	January 1982–December 1986 (261 weeks)					
$R_{pt} = \gamma_{0t} + \gamma_{1t}\widehat{\beta}_p^M + \varepsilon_{pt}$	Mean (%):	0.6	−0.1			9.4
	S.D. (%):	1.1	1.9			11.1
	t-stat:	8.17	−1.04			
$R_{pt} = \gamma_{0t} + \gamma_{1t}\widehat{\beta}_p^M + \gamma_{2t}\widehat{\beta}_p^{HR} + \varepsilon_{pt}$	Mean (%):	0.6	−0.1	−0.6		9.6
($\phi = 1.75$)	S.D. (%):	1.1	2.0	5.5		9.4
	t-stat:	8.39	−0.78	−1.73		
$R_{pt} = \gamma_{0t} + \gamma_{1t}\widehat{\beta}_p^M + \gamma_{2t}\widehat{\beta}_p^{HQ} + \varepsilon_{pt}$	Mean (%):	0.6	−0.2	−74.0		10.4
($\phi = 2.00$)	S.D. (%):	1.1	1.9	1987.4		9.5
	t-stat:	8.36	−1.30	−0.60		
$R_{pt} = \gamma_{0t} + \gamma_{1t}\widehat{\beta}_p^M + \gamma_{2t}\widehat{\beta}_p^{SMB} + \varepsilon_{pt}$	Mean (%):	0.5	−0.2	3.8		10.0
	S.D. (%):	1.2	1.9	115.4		8.4
	t-stat:	7.45	−1.26	0.53		
$R_{pt} = \gamma_{0t} + \gamma_{1t}\widehat{\beta}_p^M + \gamma_{2t}\widehat{\beta}_p^{HML} + \varepsilon_{pt}$	Mean (%):	0.5	−0.1	0.2		9.2
	S.D. (%):	1.4	1.9	1.5		8.5
	t-stat:	5.57	−0.83	1.81		

(*Continued*)

Table 17.23 (*Continued*)

Model	Statistic	$\hat{\gamma}_{0t}$	$\hat{\gamma}_{1t}$	$\hat{\gamma}_{2t}$	$\hat{\gamma}_{3t}$	$\bar{R}^2$ (%)
January 1982–December 1986 (261 weeks)						
$R_{pt} = \gamma_{0t} + \gamma_{1t}\widehat{\beta}_p^M + \gamma_{2t}\widehat{\beta}_p^{OFP} + \varepsilon_{pt}$	Mean (%):	0.5	−0.1	0.0		11.7
	S.D. (%):	1.1	2.0	2.1		10.8
	t-stat:	7.55	−0.82	0.20		
$R_{pt} = \gamma_{0t} + \gamma_{1t}\widehat{\beta}_p^M + \gamma_{2t}\widehat{\beta}_p^{SMB}$ $+ \gamma_{3t}\widehat{\beta}_p^{HML} + \varepsilon_{pt}$	Mean (%):	0.4	−0.0	0.0	0.1	10.0
	S.D. (%):	1.4	2.2	1.0	1.1	8.5
	t-stat:	4.49	−0.24	0.55	1.97	
January 1987–December 1991 (261 weeks)						
$R_{pt} = \gamma_{0t} + \gamma_{1t}\widehat{\beta}_p^M + \varepsilon_{pt}$	Mean (%):	0.2	0.0			5.9
	S.D. (%) :	1.3	2.3			8.7
	t-stat:	2.65	0.20			
$R_{pt} = \gamma_{0t} + \gamma_{1t}\widehat{\beta}_p^M + \gamma_{2t}\widehat{\beta}_p^{HR} + \varepsilon_{pt}$ ($\phi = 47$)	Mean (%):	0.2	0.0	0.0		5.4
	S.D. (%):	1.6	1.9	6.0		6.1
	t-stat:	2.25	0.11	0.13		
$R_{pt} = \gamma_{0t} + \gamma_{1t}\widehat{\beta}_p^M + \gamma_{2t}\widehat{\beta}_p^{HQ} + \varepsilon_{pt}$ ($\phi = 20$)	Mean (%):	0.2	0.0	18.9		6.0
	S.D. (%):	1.6	1.9	1819.4		6.7
	t-stat:	2.43	−0.15	0.17		
$R_{pt} = \gamma_{0t} + \gamma_{1t}\widehat{\beta}_p^M + \gamma_{2t}\widehat{\beta}_p^{SMB} + \varepsilon_{pt}$	Mean (%):	0.3	0.0	−7.5		7.8
	S.D. (%):	1.4	2.0	123.5		8.2
	t-stat:	3.10	0.16	−0.98		
$R_{pt} = \gamma_{0t} + \gamma_{1t}\widehat{\beta}_p^M + \gamma_{2t}\widehat{\beta}_p^{HML} + \varepsilon_{pt}$	Mean (%):	0.2	0.0	0.0		6.3
	S.D. (%):	1.6	2.0	1.8		7.6
	t-stat:	2.11	0.03	−0.38		
$R_{pt} = \gamma_{0t} + \gamma_{1t}\widehat{\beta}_p^M + \gamma_{2t}\widehat{\beta}_p^{OFP} + \varepsilon_{pt}$	Mean (%):	0.3	−0.1	0.0		6.4
	S.D. (%):	1.5	2.1	2.1		7.3
	t-stat:	2.73	−0.39	−0.23		
$R_{pt} = \gamma_{0t} + \gamma_{1t}\widehat{\beta}_p^M + \gamma_{2t}\widehat{\beta}_p^{SMB}$ $+ \gamma_{3t}\widehat{\beta}_p^{HML} + \varepsilon_{pt}$	Mean (%):	0.3	0.0	−0.1	−0.1	7.8
	S.D. (%):	1.9	2.1	1.2	1.5	6.8
	t-stat:	2.21	0.16	−0.97	−1.10	
January 1992–December 1996 (261 weeks)						
$R_{pt} = \gamma_{0t} + \gamma_{1t}\widehat{\beta}_p^M + \varepsilon_{pt}$	Mean (%):	0.2	0.1			5.7
	S.D. (%):	1.3	2.0			7.7
	t-stat:	2.68	1.18			

Table 17.23 (*Continued*)

Model	Statistic	$\widehat{\gamma}_{0t}$	$\widehat{\gamma}_{1t}$	$\widehat{\gamma}_{2t}$	$\widehat{\gamma}_{3t}$	$\bar{R}^2$ (%)
	January 1992–December 1996 (261 weeks)					
$R_{pt} = \gamma_{0t} + \gamma_{1t}\widehat{\beta}_p^M + \gamma_{2t}\widehat{\beta}_p^{HR} + \varepsilon_{pt}$ ($\phi = 38$)	Mean (%):	0.2	0.1	−0.4		6.9
	S.D. (%):	1.3	2.0	9.1		6.8
	t-stat:	2.79	1.16	−0.65		
$R_{pt} = \gamma_{0t} + \gamma_{1t}\widehat{\beta}_p^M + \gamma_{2t}\widehat{\beta}_p^{HQ} + \varepsilon_{pt}$ ($\phi = 27$)	Mean (%):	0.3	0.0	−158.4		6.2
	S.D. (%):	1.5	2.2	1299.2		6.6
	t-stat:	3.28	−0.18	−1.97		
$R_{pt} = \gamma_{0t} + \gamma_{1t}\widehat{\beta}_p^M + \gamma_{2t}\widehat{\beta}_p^{SMB} + \varepsilon_{pt}$	Mean (%):	0.2	0.1	15.4		6.7
	S.D. (%):	1.5	1.9	115.7		7.0
	t-stat:	1.65	0.86	2.15		
$R_{pt} = \gamma_{0t} + \gamma_{1t}\widehat{\beta}_p^M + \gamma_{2t}\widehat{\beta}_p^{HML} + \varepsilon_{pt}$	Mean (%):	0.3	0.1	0.0		7.7
	S.D. (%):	1.4	1.9	1.0		7.9
	t-stat:	3.19	0.78	−0.43		
$R_{pt} = \gamma_{0t} + \gamma_{1t}\widehat{\beta}_p^M + \gamma_{2t}\widehat{\beta}_p^{OFP} + \varepsilon_{pt}$	Mean (%):	0.1	0.2	0.2		7.9
	S.D. (%):	1.6	2.0	1.5		7.4
	t-stat:	0.90	1.24	2.41		
$R_{pt} = \gamma_{0t} + \gamma_{1t}\widehat{\beta}_p^M + \gamma_{2t}\widehat{\beta}_p^{SMB}$ $+ \gamma_{3t}\widehat{\beta}_p^{HML} + \varepsilon_{pt}$	Mean (%):	0.3	0.0	0.2	−0.0	6.6
	S.D. (%):	1.5	2.0	1.1	1.1	5.8
	t-stat:	2.76	0.08	2.21	−0.27	
	January 1997–December 2001 (261 weeks)					
$R_{pt} = \gamma_{0t} + \gamma_{1t}\widehat{\beta}_p^M + \varepsilon_{pt}$	Mean (%):	0.3	0.0			8.1
	S.D. (%):	1.4	2.5			9.9
	t-stat:	2.98	0.27			
$R_{pt} = \gamma_{0t} + \gamma_{1t}\widehat{\beta}_p^M + \gamma_{2t}\widehat{\beta}_p^{HR} + \varepsilon_{pt}$ ($\phi = 1.75$)	Mean (%):	0.3	0.0	0.0		10.3
	S.D. (%):	1.4	2.2	2.0		10.4
	t-stat:	3.35	−0.05	−0.21		
$R_{pt} = \gamma_{0t} + \gamma_{1t}\widehat{\beta}_p^M + \gamma_{2t}\widehat{\beta}_p^{HQ} + \varepsilon_{pt}$ ($\phi = 2.00$)	Mean (%):	0.3	0.0	−17.9		9.4
	S.D. (%):	1.7	2.3	307.4		8.5
	t-stat:	2.86	−0.23	−0.94		
$R_{pt} = \gamma_{0t} + \gamma_{1t}\widehat{\beta}_p^M + \gamma_{2t}\widehat{\beta}_p^{SMB} + \varepsilon_{pt}$	Mean (%):	0.3	−0.1	0.1		9.3
	S.D. (%):	1.6	2.4	1.3		8.3
	t-stat:	3.58	−0.97	1.76		

(*Continued*)

Table 17.23 (*Continued*)

Model	Statistic	$\widehat{\gamma}_{0t}$	$\widehat{\gamma}_{1t}$	$\widehat{\gamma}_{2t}$	$\widehat{\gamma}_{3t}$	$\bar{R}^2$ (%)
January 1997–December 2001 (261 weeks)						
$R_{pt} = \gamma_{0t} + \gamma_{1t}\widehat{\beta}_p^M + \gamma_{2t}\widehat{\beta}_p^{HML} + \varepsilon_{pt}$	Mean (%):	0.3	0.0	−0.1		8.8
	S.D. (%):	1.5	2.5	1.8		8.4
	t-stat:	3.35	−0.05	−0.78		
$R_{pt} = \gamma_{0t} + \gamma_{1t}\widehat{\beta}_p^M + \gamma_{2t}\widehat{\beta}_p^{OFP} + \varepsilon_{pt}$	Mean (%):	0.3	0.0	0.1		6.4
	S.D. (%):	1.5	2.2	1.6		7.5
	t-stat:	2.91	0.26	0.71		
$R_{pt} = \gamma_{0t} + \gamma_{1t}\widehat{\beta}_p^M + \gamma_{2t}\widehat{\beta}_p^{SMB} + \gamma_{3t}\widehat{\beta}_p^{HML} + \varepsilon_{pt}$	Mean (%):	0.4	−0.2	0.2	−0.0	9.3
	S.D. (%):	1.7	2.8	1.5	1.8	7.3
	t-stat:	4.31	−1.39	1.8	−0.37	
January 2002–December 2004 (156 weeks)						
$R_{pt} = \gamma_{0t} + \gamma_{1t}\widehat{\beta}_p^M + \varepsilon_{pt}$	Mean (%):	0.4	0.0			3.9
	S.D. (%):	1.7	1.3			4.2
	t-stat:	3.26	−0.27			
$R_{pt} = \gamma_{0t} + \gamma_{1t}\widehat{\beta}_p^M + \gamma_{2t}\widehat{\beta}_p^{HR} + \varepsilon_{pt}$ ($\phi = 1.75$)	Mean (%):	0.6	−0.2	0.6		9.3
	S.D. (%):	1.7	2.5	8.0		9.6
	t-stat:	4.54	−0.94	0.94		
$R_{pt} = \gamma_{0t} + \gamma_{1t}\widehat{\beta}_p^M + \gamma_{2t}\widehat{\beta}_p^{HQ} + \varepsilon_{pt}$ ($\phi = 2.00$)	Mean (%):	0.7	−0.3	−106.5		5.8
	S.D. (%):	2.2	2.2	699.7		6.2
	t-stat:	4.29	−1.71	−1.90		
$R_{pt} = \gamma_{0t} + \gamma_{1t}\widehat{\beta}_p^M + \gamma_{2t}\widehat{\beta}_p^{SMB} + \varepsilon_{pt}$	Mean (%):	0.5	−0.1	0.1		4.2
	S.D. (%):	2.2	0.7	0.6		4.9
	t-stat:	2.71	−1.43	1.59		
$R_{pt} = \gamma_{0t} + \gamma_{1t}\widehat{\beta}_p^M + \gamma_{2t}\widehat{\beta}_p^{HML} + \varepsilon_{pt}$	Mean (%):	0.5	−0.1	0.0		6.1
	S.D. (%):	2.0	1.4	1.0		5.4
	t-stat:	3.17	−0.86	−0.55		
$R_{pt} = \gamma_{0t} + \gamma_{1t}\widehat{\beta}_p^M + \gamma_{2t}\widehat{\beta}_p^{OFP} + \varepsilon_{pt}$	Mean (%):	0.4	0.0	0.0		4.1
	S.D. (%):	1.7	1.3	0.4		4.0
	t-stat:	3.15	0.01	−0.19		
$R_{pt} = \gamma_{0t} + \gamma_{1t}\widehat{\beta}_p^M + \gamma_{2t}\widehat{\beta}_p^{SMB} + \gamma_{3t}\widehat{\beta}_p^{HML} + \varepsilon_{pt}$	Mean (%):	0.4	0.0	0.0	0.1	5.8
	S.D. (%):	2.4	0.5	0.4	1.1	5.3
	t-stat:	2.03	0.03	1.57	0.75	

In the second testing period, both specifications with the hedging-portfolio factor exhibit statistically significant means for the hedging-portfolio betas, with average coefficients and t-statistics of -1.2% and -3.71 for the hedging-portfolio return factor and -1.56 and -4.14 for the hedging-portfolio dollar-return factor, respectively. The market-beta coefficients are not significant in either of these specifications, and are also of the wrong sign. The only other specifications with a significant mean coefficient are the two-factor model with SMB as the second factor (with an average coefficient of 29.9% for the SMB factor and a t-statistic of 4.43), and the three-factor model in which the SMB factor is also significant (an average coefficient of 0.3% and a t-statistic of 4.61).

For the five remaining test periods, the only specifications with any statistically significant factors are the SMB and OFP two-factor models in the 1992–1996 testing period (though the hedging-portfolio dollar-return factor is close to significant in the 1997–2001 subperiod). However, the $\bar{R}^2$s in the last four testing periods are substantially lower than in the earlier periods perhaps reflecting the greater volatility of equity returns in recent years.

As before, no single factor is particularly compelling in explaining the cross-sectional variation of expected returns, but the point estimates of the cross-sectional regressions show that the hedging-portfolio factor is comparable both in magnitude and in performance to other commonly proposed factors, and we continue to be optimistic regarding its relevance for intertemporal asset pricing models.

7. CONCLUSION

Trading volume is an important aspect of the economic interactions in financial markets among different investors. Both volume and prices are driven by underlying economic forces, and thus convey important information about the workings of the market. Although the literature on financial markets has focused on analyzing the behavior of returns based on simplifying assumptions about the market such as allocational and informational efficiency, we wish to develop a more realistic framework to understand the empirical characteristics of prices and volume.

In this chapter, we hope to have made a contribution towards this goal. By deriving an explicit link between economic fundamentals and the dynamic properties of asset returns and volume, we have shown that interactions between prices and quantities in equilibrium yield a rich set of implications for any asset pricing model. Indeed, by exploiting the relation between prices and volume in our dynamic equilibrium model, we are able to identify and construct the hedging portfolio that all investors use to hedge against changes in market conditions. Moreover, our empirical analysis shows that this hedging portfolio has considerable forecast power in predicting future returns of the market portfolio, a property of the true hedging portfolio, and its abilities to explain cross-sectional variation in expected returns is comparable to other popular risk factors such as market betas, the Fama and French (1993) SMB factor, and optimal forecast portfolios.

Although our model is purposefully parsimonious so as to focus attention on the essential features of risk-sharing and trading activity, it underscores the general point that quantities, together with prices, should be an integral part of any analysis of asset markets, both theoretically and empirically. Our results provide compelling motivation for determining risk factors from economic fundamentals rather than through statistical means. Although this is an old theme that has its origins in Black (1972), Mayers (1973), and Merton (1973), it has become somewhat less fashionable in recent years than the statistical approach of Roll and Ross (1980) and Chamberlain and Rothschild (1983), and the empirical approach of Fama and French (1992). We hope to revive interest in the more ambitious goal of identifying risk factors through the logic of equilibrium analysis and by exploiting the information contained in trading volume in particular.

An important direction for future research is to incorporate more specific aspects of the market microstructure in the analysis of trading volume. In particular, the two standard assumptions of perfect competition and symmetric information – assumptions that we have also adopted in our theoretical framework – do not hold in practice. For example, for most individual investors, financial markets have traditionally been considered close to perfectly competitive so that the size of a typical investment has little impact on prices. For such scale-free investment opportunities, quantities are largely irrelevant and returns become the basic objects of study, not prices. But as institutional investors have grown in size and sophistication over the past several decades, and as frictions in the trading process have become more important because of the sheer volume of trade, it has become clear that securities markets are not perfectly competitive, at least not in the short run.

Moreover, when investors possess private information about price movements, their own trading intentions, and other market factors, perfect competition is even less likely to hold. For example, if a large pension fund were to liquidate a substantial position in one security, that security's price would drop precipitously if the liquidation was attempted through a single sell order, yielding a significant loss in the value of the security to be sold. Instead, such a liquidation would typically be accomplished over several days, with a professional trading desk managing the liquidation process by breaking up the entire order into smaller pieces, each executed at opportune moments so as to minimize trading costs and the overall price impact of the sale.[48] This suggests that there is information to be garnered from quantities as well as prices; a 50,000-share trade has different implications than a 5000-share trade, and the *sequence* of trading volume contains information as well. The fact that the demand curves of even the most liquid financial securities are downward-sloping for large institutional investors and that information is often revealed

---

[48] See Chan and Lakonishok (1995) for further discussion of the price impact of institutional trades.

through the price-discovery process, implies that quantities are as fundamental as prices, and equally worthy of investigation.

Finally, the presence of market frictions, such as transactions costs, can influence the level of trading volume and serve as a bridge between the market microstructure literature and the broader equilibrium asset pricing literature. In particular, despite the many market microstructure studies that relate trading behavior to market-making activities and the price-discovery mechanism,[49] the seemingly high level of volume in financial markets has often been considered puzzling from a rational asset pricing perspective (see, e.g., Ross, 1989). Some have even argued that additional trading frictions or "sand in the gears" ought to be introduced in the form of a transactions tax to discourage high-frequency trading.[50] Yet in the absence of transaction costs, most dynamic equilibrium models will show that it is quite rational and efficient for trading volume to be *infinite* when the information flow to the market is continuous, i.e., a diffusion. An equilibrium model with fixed transactions costs, e.g., Lo et al. (2004), may reconcile these two disparate views of trading volume.

ACKNOWLEDGMENTS

We are grateful to the following excellent research assistants who contributed to various aspects of our volume project over the years: Petr Adamek, Joon Chae, Lewis Chan, Jayna Cummings, Mila Getmansky, Li Jin, Terence Lim, Harry Mamaysky, Jannette Papastaikoudi, Antti Petajisto, and Jean-Paul Sursock. Financial support from the MIT Laboratory for Financial Engineering and the National Science Foundation (Grant No. SBR–9709976) is gratefully acknowledged.

REFERENCES

Admati, A.R. and P. Pfleiderer, 1988, A Theory of Intraday Patterns: Volume and Price Variability, *Review of Financial Studies* 1, 3–40.

Amihud, Y. and H. Mendelson, 1986a, Asset Pricing and the Bid-Ask Spread, *Journal of Financial Economics* 17, 223–249.

Amihud, Y. and H. Mendelson, 1986b, Liquidity and Stock Returns, *Financial Analysts Journal* 42, 43–48.

Andersen, T., 1996, Return Volatility and Trading Volume: An Information Flow Interpretation, *Journal of Finance* 51, 169–204.

Atkins, A. and E. Dyl, 1997, Market Structure and Reported Trading Volume: NASDAQ versus the NYSE, *Journal of Financial Research* 20, 291–304.

---

[49] See, e.g., Admati and Pfleiderer (1988), Bagehot (1971), Easley and O'Hara (1987), Foster and Viswanathan (1993), Kyle (1985), Wang (1994), and Llorente et al. (2002).

[50] See, e.g., Stiglitz (1989), Summers and Summers (1990a,b), and Tobin (1984).

Bagehot, W. (a.k.a. J. Treynor), 1971, The Only Game in Town, *Financial Analysts Journal* 22, 12–14.

Bamber, L., 1986, The Information Content of Annual Earnings Releases: A Trading Volume Approach, *Journal of Accounting Research* 24, 40–56.

Bamber, L., 1987, Unexpected Earnings, Firm Size, and Trading Volume Around Quarterly Earnings Announcements, *Accounting Review* 62, 510–532.

Banz, R., 1981, The Relation between Return and Market Value of Common Stocks, *Journal of Financial Economics* 9, 3–18.

Black, F., 1972, Capital Market Equilibrium with Restricted Borrowing, *Journal of Business* 45, 444–454.

Black, F., 1976, Studies of Stock Price Volatility Changes, in *Proceedings of the 1976 Meetings of the Business and Economic Statistics Section, American Statistical Association*, 177–181.

Black, F., M. Jensen and M. Scholes, 1972, The Capital Asset Pricing Model: Some Empirical Tests, In Jensen, M., ed. *Studies in the Theory of Capital Markets.* New York: Praeger Publishers, 79–121.

Brown, K., W. Van Harlow and S. Tinic, 1993, The Risk and Required Return of Common Stock Following Major Price Innovations, *Journal of Financial and Quantitative Analysis* 28, 101–116.

Campbell, J., A. Lo and C. MacKinlay, 1997, *The Econometrics of Financial Markets.* Princeton, NJ: Princeton University Press.

Campbell, J., S. Grossman and J. Wang, 1993, Trading Volume and Serial Correlation in Stock Returns, *Quarterly Journal of Economics* 108, 905–939.

Cass, D. and J. Stiglitz, 1970, The Structure of Investor Preferences and Asset Returns, and Separability in Portfolio Allocation: A Contribution to the Pure Theory of Mutual Funds, *Journal of Economic Theory* 2, 122–160.

Chamberlain, G. and M. Rothschild, 1983, Arbitrage, Factor Structure, and Mean-Variance Analysis on Large Asset Markets, *Econometrica* 51, 1281–1304.

Chamberlain, G., 1983, Funds, Factors, and Diversification in Arbitrage Pricing Models, *Econometrica* 51, 1305–1323.

Chan, L. and J. Lakonishok, 1995, The Behavior of Stock Prices Around Institutional Trades, *Journal of Finance* 50, 1147–1174.

Chopra, N., J. Lakonishok and J. Ritter, 1992, Measuring Abnormal Performance: Do Stocks Overreact? *Journal of Financial Economics* 31, 235–286.

Conrad, J., A. Hameed and C. Niden, 1994, Volume and Autocovariances in Short-Horizon Individual Security Returns, *Journal of Finance* 49, 1305–1329.

Cox, J., J. Ingersoll and S. Ross, 1985, An Intertemporal General Equilibrium Model of Asset Prices, *Econometrica* 53, 363–384.

Cross, F., 1973, The Behavior of Stock Prices on Fridays and Mondays, *Financial Analysts Journal* 29, 67–69.

DeBondt, W. and R. Thaler, 1985, Does the Stock Market Overreact? *Journal of Finance* 40, 793–805.

Dhillon, U. and H. Johnson, 1991, Changes in the Standard and Poor's 500 List, *Journal of Business* 64, 75–85.

Dumas, B., 1989, Two Person Dynamic Equilibrium in the Capital Market, *Review of Financial Studies* 2, 157–188.

Easley, D. and M. O'Hara, 1987, Price, Trade Size, and Information In Securities Markets, *Journal of Financial Economics* 18, 69–90.

Epps, T. and M. Epps, 1976, The Stochastic Dependence of Security Price Changes and Transaction Volumes: Implications for the Mixture of Distribution Hypothesis, *Econometrica* 44, 305–321.

Fama, E. and J. MacBeth, 1973, Risk, Return, and Equilibrium: Empirical Tests, *Journal of Political Economy* 81, 607–636.

Fama, E. and K. French, 1992, The Cross-Section of Expected Stock Returns, *Journal of Finance* 47, 427–465.

Fama, E. and K. French, 1993, Common Risk Factors in the Returns on Stock and Bonds, *Journal of Financial Economics* 33, 3–56.

Foster, D., T. Smith and R. Whaley, 1997, Assessing Goodness-of-Fit of Asset-Pricing Models: The Distribution of the Maximal R-Squared, *Journal of Finance* 52, 591–607.

Foster, F.D. and S. Viswanathan, 1993, Variations in Trading Volume, Return Volatility, and Trading Costs: Evidence on Recent Price Formation Models, *Journal of Finance* 48, 187–211.

French, K., 1980, Stock Returns and the Weekend Effect, *Journal of Financial Economics* 8, 55–69.

Gallant, R., P. Rossi and G. Tauchen, 1992, Stock Prices and Volume, *Review of Financial Studies* 5, 199–242.

Gibbons, M. and P. Hess, 1981, Day of the Week Effects and Asset Returns, *Journal of Business* 54, 579–596.

Goetzmann, W. and M. Garry, 1986, Does Delisting From the S&P 500 Affect Stock Prices? *Financial Analysts Journal* 42, 64–69.

Hamilton, J., 1994, *Times Series Analysis*. Princeton, NJ: Princeton University Press.

Harris, L., 1986, A Transaction Data Study of Weekly and Intradaily Patterns in Stock Returns, *Journal of Financial Economics* 16, 99–117.

Harris, L. and E. Gurel, 1986, Price and Volume Effects Associated with Changes in the S&P 500 List: New Evidence for the Existence of Price Pressures, *Journal of Finance* 46, 815–829.

He, H. and J. Wang, 1995, Differential Information and Dynamic Behavior of Stock Trading Volume, *Review of Financial Studies* 8, 919–972.

Hiemstra, C. and J. Jones, 1994, Testing for Linear and Nonlinear Granger Causality in the Stock Price-Volume Relation, *Journal of Finance* 49, 1639–1664.

Hu, S., 1997, Trading Turnover and Expected Stock Returns: Does It Matter and Why? Working Paper, National Taiwan University.

Jacques, W., 1988, The S&P 500 Membership Anomaly, or Would You Join This Club? *Financial Analysts Journal* 44, 73–75.

Jaffe, J. and R. Westerfield, 1985, The Week-End Effect in Common Stock Returns: The International Evidence, *Journal of Finance* 40, 433–454.

Jain, P., 1987, The Effect on Stock Price of Inclusion in or Exclusion from the S&P 500, *Financial Analysts Journal* 43, 58–65.

Jain, P. and G. Joh, 1988, The Dependence between Hourly Prices and Trading Volume, *Journal of Financial and Quantitative Analysis* 23, 269–282.

James, C. and R. Edmister, 1983, The Relation between Common Stock Returns, Trading Activity and Market Value, *Journal of Finance* 38, 1075–1086.

Karpoff, J., 1987, The Relation between Price Changes and Trading Volume: A Survey, *Journal of Financial and Quantitative Analysis* 22, 109–126.

Karpoff, J. and R. Walkling, 1988, Short-Term Trading Around Ex-Dividend Days: Additional Evidence, *Journal of Financial Economics* 21, 291–298.

Karpoff, J. and R. Walkling, 1990, Dividend Capture in NASDAQ Stocks, *Journal of Financial Economics* 28, 39–65.

Keim, D. and R. Stambaugh, 1984, A Further Investigation of the Weekend Effect in Stock Returns, *Journal of Finance* 39, 819–840.

Kwiatkowski, D., P. Phillips, P. Schmidt and Y. Shin, 1992, Testing the Null Hypothesis of Stationarity Against the Alternative of a Unit Root: How Sure are We that Economic Time Series Have a Unit Root? *Journal of Econometrics* 54, 159–178.

Kyle, A., 1985, Continuous Auctions and Insider Trading, *Econometrica* 53, 1315–1335.

Lakonishok, J. and M. Levi, 1982, Weekend Effects on Stock Returns, *Journal of Finance* 37, 883–889.

Lakonishok, J. and S. Smidt, 1986, Volume for Winners and Losers: Taxation and Other Motives for Stock Trading, *Journal of Finance* 41, 951–974.

Lakonishok, J. and S. Smidt, 1988, Are Seasonal Anomalies Real? A Ninety-Year Perspective, *Review of Financial Studies* 1, 403–425.

Lakonishok, J. and T. Vermaelen, 1986, Tax-Induced Trading Around Ex-Dividend Days, *Journal of Financial Economics* 16, 287–319.

Lamoureux, C. and J. Wansley, 1987, Market Effects of Changes in the Standard & Poor's 500 Index, *Financial Review* 22, 53–69.

Lamoureux, C. and W. Lastrapes, 1990, Heteroskedasticity in Stock Return Data: Volume vs. GARCH Effects, *Journal of Finance* 45, 487–498.

Lamoureux, C. and W. Lastrapes, 1994, Endogenous Trading Volume and Momentum in Stock-Return Volatility, *Journal of Business and Economic Statistics* 12, 253–160.

LeBaron, B., 1992, Persistence of the Dow Jones Index on Rising Volume, Working Paper, University of Wisconsin.

Lehmann, B., 1990, Fads, Martingales, and Market Efficiency, *Quarterly Journal of Economics* 105, 1–28.

Lim, T., A. Lo, J. Wang and P. Adamek, 1998, Trading Volume and the MiniCRSP Database: An Introduction and User's Guide, MIT Laboratory for Financial Engineering Working Paper No. LFE–1038–98.

Llorente, G., R. Michaely, G. Saar and J. Wang, 2002, Dynamic Volume-Return Relations for Individual Stocks, *Review of Financial Studies* 15, 1005–1047.

Lo, A. and C. MacKinlay, 1997, Maximizing Predictability in the Stock and Bond Markets, *Macroeconomic Dynamics* 1, 102–134.

Lo, A. and J. Wang, 2000, Trading Volume: Definitions, Data Analysis, and Implications of Portfolio Theory, *Review of Financial Studies* 13, 257–300.

Lo, A. and J. Wang, 2003, Trading Volume, In Dewatripont, M., Hansen, L. and Turnovsky, S., eds., *Advances in Economics and Econometrics: Theory and Applications*, Eighth World Congress, Volume II, Econometric Society Monograph. Cambridge: Cambridge University Press, 206–277.

Lo, A. and J. Wang, 2006, Trading Volume: Implications of an Intertemporal Capital Asset-Pricing Model, *Journal of Finance* 61, 2805–2840.

Lo, A., H. Mamaysky and J. Wang, 2004, Asset Prices and Trading Volume under Fixed Transaction Costs, *Journal of Political Economy* 112, 1054–1090.

Lynch-Koski, J., 1996, A Microstructure Analysis of Ex-Dividend Stock Price Behavior Before and After the 1984 and 1986 Tax Reform Acts, *Journal of Business* 69, 313–338.

MacKinlay, C., 1987, On Multivariate Tests of the CAPM, *Journal of Financial Economics* 18, 341–371.

MacKinlay, C., 1994, Multi-Factor Models Do Not Explain Deviations from the CAPM, *Journal of Financial Economics* 38, 3–28.

Markowitz, H., 1952, Portfolio Selection, *Journal of Finance* 7, 77–91.

Marsh, T. and R. Merton, 1987, Dividend Behavior for the Aggregate Stock Market, *Journal of Business* 60, 1–40.

Mayers, D., 1973, Nonmarketable Assets and the Determination of Capital Asset Prices in the Absence of a Riskless Asset, *Journal of Business* 46, 258–267.

Merton, R., 1971, Optimal Consumption and Portfolio Rules in a Continuous-Time Model, *Journal of Economic Theory* 3, 373–413.

Merton, R., 1973, An Intertemporal Capital Asset Pricing Model, *Econometrica* 41, 867–887.

Merton, R., 1987, A Simple Model of Capital Market Equilibrium with Incomplete Information, *Journal of Finance* 42, 483–510.

Michaely, R., 1991, Ex-Dividend Day Stock Price Behavior: The Case of the 1986 Tax Reform Act, *Journal of Finance* 46, 845–860.

Michaely, R. and J. Vila, 1995, Investors' Heterogeneity, Prices and Volume around the Ex-Dividend Day, *Journal of Financial and Quantitative Analysis* 30, 171–198.

Michaely, R. and J. Vila, 1996, Trading Volume with Private Valuation: Evidence from the Ex-Dividend Day, *Review of Financial Studies* 9, 471–509.

Morse, D., 1980, Asymmetric Information in Securities Markets and Trading Volume, *Journal of Financial and Quantitative Analysis* 15, 1129–1148.

Muirhead, R., 1982, *Aspects of Multivariate Statistical Theory*. New York: John Wiley and Sons.

Pruitt, S. and J. Wei, 1989, Institutional Ownership and Changes in the S&P 500, *Journal of Finance* 44, 509–513.

Reinganum, M., 1992, A Revival of the Small-Firm Effect, *Journal of Portfolio Management* 18, 55–62.

Richardson, G., S. Sefcik and R. Thompson, 1986, A Test of Dividend Irrelevance Using Volume Reaction to a Change in Dividend Policy, *Journal of Financial Economics* 17, 313–333.

Roll, R., 1984, A Simple Implicit Measure of the Effective Bid-Ask Spread in an Efficient Market, *Journal of Finance* 39, 1127–1140.

Roll, R. and S. Ross, 1980, An Empirical Investigation of the Arbitrage Pricing Theory, *Journal of Finance* 35, 1073–1103.

Ross, S., 1978, Mutual Fund Separation in Financial Theory—The Separating Distributions, *Journal of Economic Theory* 17, 254–286.

Ross, S., 1989, Discussion: Intertemporal Asset Pricing, Bhattacharya, S. and Constantinides, G., eds., *Theory of Valuation*. New Jersey: Rowman & Littlefield Publishers, Inc., 85–96.

Shleifer, A., 1986, Do Demand Curves for Stocks Slope Down? *Journal of Finance* 41, 579–590.

Smidt, S., 1990, Long-Run Trends in Equity Turnover, *Journal of Portfolio Management* 17, 66–73.

Stickel, S., 1991, The Ex-Dividend Day Behavior of Nonconvertible Preferred Stock Returns and Trading Volume, *Journal of Financial and Quantitative Analysis* 26, 45–61.

Stickel, S. and R. Verrecchia, 1994, Evidence that Trading Volume Sustains Stock Price Changes, *Financial Analysts Journal* 50, 57–67.

Stiglitz, J., 1989, Using Tax Policy to Curb Speculative Short-term Trading, *Journal of Financial Services Research* 3, 101–115.

Summers, L. and V. Summers, 1990a, The Case for a Securities Transactions Excise Tax, *Tax Notes* 13, 879–884.

Summers, L. and V. Summers, 1990b, When Financial Markets Work Too Well: A Cautious Case for a Securities Transactions Tax, *Journal of Financial Services Research* 3, 261–286.

Tauchen, G. and M. Pitts, 1983, The Price Variability-Volume Relationship on Speculative Markets, *Econometrica* 51, 485–506.

Tkac, P., 1999, A Trading Volume Benchmark: Theory and Evidence, *Journal of Financial and Quantitative Analysis* 34, 89–114.

Tobin, J., 1984, On the Efficiency of the Financial Market System, *Lloyds Bank Review* 153, 1–15.

Tobin, J., 1958, Liquidity Preference as Behavior Towards Risk, *Review of Economic Studies* 25, 68–85.

Wang, J., 1994, A Model of Competitive Stock Trading Volume, *Journal of Political Economy* 102, 127–168.

Woolridge, J. and C. Ghosh, 1986, Institutional Trading and Security Prices: The Case of Changes in the Composition of the S&P 500 Market Index, *Journal of Financial Research* 9, 13–24.

Ying, C.C., 1966, Stock Market Prices and Volume of Sales, *Econometrica* 34, 676–686.

INDEX

Printed and bound by CPI Group (UK) Ltd, Croydon, CR0 4YY

08/05/2025

01864815-0004